Modern Arm Assembly Language Programming

Covers Armv8-A 32-bit, 64-bit, and SIMD

Daniel Kusswurm

Apress®

Modern Arm Assembly Language Programming: Covers Armv8-A 32-bit, 64-bit, and SIMD

Daniel Kusswurm
Geneva, IL, USA

ISBN-13 (pbk): 978-1-4842-6266-5   ISBN-13 (electronic): 978-1-4842-6267-2
https://doi.org/10.1007/978-1-4842-6267-2

Managing Director, Apress Media LLC: Welmoed Spahr
Acquisitions Editor: Steve Anglin
Development Editor: Matthew Moodie
Coordinating Editor: Mark Powers

Cover designed by eStudioCalamar

Cover image by Veeterzy on Unsplash (www.unsplash.com)

Distributed to the book trade worldwide by Apress Media, LLC, 1 New York Plaza, New York, NY 10004, U.S.A. Phone 1-800-SPRINGER, fax (201) 348-4505, e-mail orders-ny@springer-sbm.com, or visit www.springeronline.com. Apress Media, LLC is a California LLC and the sole member (owner) is Springer Science + Business Media Finance Inc (SSBM Finance Inc). SSBM Finance Inc is a **Delaware** corporation.

For information on translations, please e-mail booktranslations@springernature.com; for reprint, paperback, or audio rights, please e-mail bookpermissions@springernature.com.

Apress titles may be purchased in bulk for academic, corporate, or promotional use. eBook versions and licenses are also available for most titles. For more information, reference our Print and eBook Bulk Sales web page at http://www.apress.com/bulk-sales.

Any source code or other supplementary material referenced by the author in this book is available to readers on GitHub via the book's product page, located at www.apress.com/9781484262665. For more detailed information, please visit http://www.apress.com/source-code.

Printed on acid-free paper

Table of Contents

About the Author

Daniel Kusswurm has over 35 years of professional experience as a software developer and computer scientist. During his career, he has developed innovative software for medical devices, scientific instruments, and image-processing applications. On many of these projects, he successfully employed assembly language to significantly improve the performance of computationally intensive algorithms or solve unique programming challenges. His educational background includes a BS in electrical engineering technology from Northern Illinois University along with an MS and PhD in computer science from DePaul University.

Daniel Kusswurm is also the author of *Modern X86 Assembly Language Programming* (ISBN: 978-1484200650) and *Modern X86 Assembly Language Programming, Second Edition* (ISBN: 978-1484240625), both published by Apress.

About the Technical Reviewer

Paul Cohen joined Intel Corporation during the very early days of the x86 architecture, starting with the 8086, and retired from Intel after 26 years in sales/marketing/management. He is currently partnered with Douglas Technology Group, focusing on the creation of technology books on behalf of Intel and other corporations. Paul also teaches a class that transforms middle- and high-school students into real, confident entrepreneurs, in conjunction with the Young Entrepreneurs Academy (YEA), and is a Traffic Commissioner for the City of Beaverton, Oregon, and on the Board of Directors of multiple nonprofit organizations.

Acknowledgments

The production of a motion picture and the publication of a book are somewhat analogous. Movie trailers extol the performances of the lead actors. The front cover of a book trumpets the authors' names. Actors and authors ultimately receive public acclamation for their efforts. It is, however, impossible to produce a movie or publish a book without the dedication, expertise, and creativity of a professional behind-the-scenes team. This book is no exception.

I would like to thank the talented editorial team at Apress including Steve Anglin, Mark Powers, and Matthew Moodie for their efforts and contributions. Paul Cohen deserves kudos for his meticulous technical review and practical suggestions. Ed Kusswurm merits recognition for reviewing each chapter and providing constructive feedback. I accept full responsibility for any remaining imperfections.

I would also like to thank my professional colleagues for their support and encouragement. Finally, I would like to recognize parental nodes Armin (RIP) and Mary along with sibling nodes Mary, Tom, Ed, and John for their inspiration during the writing of this book.

Introduction

Since the invention of the microprocessor, software developers have used assembly language to create innovative solutions for a wide variety of algorithmic challenges. During the early days of the microprocessor era, it was common practice to code large portions of a program or entire applications using assembly language. Given the twenty-first-century prevalence of high-level languages such as C++, C#, Java, and Python, it may be surprising to learn that many software developers still employ assembly language to code performance-critical sections of their programs. And while compilers have improved remarkably over the years in terms of generating machine code that is both spatially and temporally efficient, situations still exist where it makes sense for a software developer to exploit (or at least consider) the benefits of assembly language programming.

The single-instruction multiple-data (SIMD) architectures of modern microprocessors provide another explanation for the continued interest in assembly language programming. A SIMD-capable processor contains computational resources that facilitate simultaneous calculations using multiple data values, which can significantly improve the performance of applications that must deliver real-time responsiveness. SIMD architectures are also well suited for computationally intensive application domains such as machine learning, image processing, audio and video encoding, computer-aided design, computer graphics, and data mining. Unfortunately, many high-level languages and development tools are still unable to fully exploit the SIMD capabilities of a modern processor. Assembly language, on the other hand, enables the software developer to take full advantage of a processor's SIMD resources.

Modern Arm Assembly Language Programming

Modern Arm Assembly Language Programming is an instructional text focusing on Armv8-A 32-bit and 64-bit assembly language programming. The book's content and organization are designed to help you quickly understand Armv8-A assembly language programming and the computational resources of the Armv8-A Advanced SIMD platform. It also contains an abundance of source code that is structured to accelerate learning and comprehension of essential Armv8-A assembly language constructs and SIMD programming concepts. After reading this book, you will be able to code performance-enhancing functions and algorithms using Armv8-A 32-bit and 64-bit assembly language.

While it is still theoretically possible to write an entire application program using assembly language, the demanding requirements of contemporary software development make such an approach impractical and ill advised. Instead, this book concentrates on coding Armv8-A 32-bit and 64-bit assembly language functions that are callable from C++. Each source code example was developed using the GNU toolchain (g++, gas, and make) and tested on a Raspberry Pi 4 Model B running Raspberry Pi OS (32-bit) or Raspberry Pi OS (64-bit).

Before proceeding, it should be noted that this book focuses exclusively on Armv8-A assembly language programming independent of any specific hardware platform. It does not discuss how to write code that exploits the unique hardware features of the Raspberry Pi 4 such as the GPIO port. It also does not examine architectural features or privileged instructions that are used by operating systems and hypervisors. However, if your goal is to develop Armv8-A assembly language code for use in these environments, you will need to thoroughly understand the material that is presented in this book.

Target Audience

The target audience for this book is software developers including:

- Software developers who are creating programs for Armv8-A platforms and want to learn how to code performance-enhancing algorithms and functions using the Armv8-A 32-bit and 64-bit instruction sets

- Software developers who need to learn how to write SIMD functions or accelerate the performance of existing code using the Armv8-A 32-bit and 64-bit SIMD instruction sets

- Computer science/engineering students and hobbyists who want or need to gain a better understanding of the Armv8-A platform and its SIMD architecture

Readers of this book should have previous high-level language programming experience and a basic understanding of C++. Should you desire to run or modify any of the source code examples published in this book, a smidgen of familiarity with Linux and the GNU toolchain will be helpful. However, previous experience with Linux and the GNU toolchain is not necessary to benefit from this book.

Content Overview

The primary objective of this book is to help you learn Armv8-A 32-bit and 64-bit assembly language programming. The book's chapters and content are structured to achieve this goal. Here is a brief overview of what you can expect to learn.

Armv8-32 Architecture Chapter 1 introduces Armv8-A and the AArch32 execution state. It includes a discussion of fundamental data types, internal architecture, register sets, instruction operands, and memory addressing modes. Chapters 2, 3, and 4 explain the fundamentals of Armv8-32 assembly language programming using the A32 instruction set and common programming constructs including arrays and structures. The source code examples presented in these (and subsequent) chapters are packaged as working programs, which means that you can run, modify, or otherwise experiment with the code to enhance your learning experience.

Armv8-32 Floating-Point Programming Chapter 5 examines the floating-point resources of the AArch32 execution state. It also covers important floating-point programming concepts. Chapter 6 explains how to perform scalar floating-point arithmetic using single-precision and double-precision values.

Armv8-32 SIMD Programming Chapter 7 describes Armv8-32 SIMD resources including register sets, data types, and the instruction set. It also includes a short primer on SIMD programming techniques. Chapters 8 and 9 cover Armv8-32 SIMD programming using packed integer and packed floating-point operands.

Armv8-64 Architecture Chapter 10 introduces the AArch64 execution state. This chapter expounds relevant data types, architectural features, general-purpose and SIMD register sets, and memory addressing modes. Chapters 11 and 12 describe the fundamentals of Armv8-64 assembly language programming using the A64 instruction set.

Armv8-64 Floating-Point Programming Chapter 13 demonstrates how to perform scalar floating-point arithmetic using the A64 instruction set.

Armv8-64 SIMD Programming Chapters 14 and 15 delve into the details of the Armv8-64 SIMD architecture. These chapters contain a variety of programming examples that illustrate how to use the A64 instruction set to carry out calculations using packed integer and packed floating-point operands.

Armv8-64 Advanced Programming Chapter 16 includes source code examples that illustrate how to perform sophisticated arithmetic calculations using the A64 SIMD instruction set. Chapter 17 outlines specific coding strategies and techniques that you can use to boost the performance of your Armv8 assembly language code.

Appendices Appendix A describes how to build and execute the source code examples using a Raspberry Pi 4 Model B and the GNU toolchain. Appendix B contains a list of this book's references and additional resources that you can consult for more information about Arm assembly language programming.

Source Code

Download information for this book's source code is available on the Apress website at www.apress.com/us/book/978-1484262665. You can also access the source code on GitHub at www.github.com/apress/modern-arm-assembly-language-programming.

■ **Caution** The sole purpose of the source code is to elucidate programming examples that are directly related to the topics discussed in this book. Minimal attention is given to essential software engineering concerns such as robust error handling, security risks, numerical stability, rounding errors, or ill-conditioned functions. You are responsible for addressing these concerns should you decide to use any of the source code in your own programs.

Some of the source code examples presented in this book are adaptations of the source code examples first published in *Modern X86 Assembly Language Programming* and *Modern X86 Assembly Language Programming, Second Edition*. If you have read one of these books or have previous X86 assembly language programming experience, perusing this book will strengthen your overall programming proficiency and versatility since it explains assembly language programming for a processor architecture with a RISC heritage.

Terminology

The Arm technical documentation uses its own nomenclature to elucidate different aspects of Arm's technology including Armv8, Armv8-A, AArch32, AArch64, A32, and A64. These terms have precise meanings that you will learn about in Chapter 1. When explaining or referencing general features of Armv8 32-bit and 64-bit technology, this book uses the terms Armv8-32 and Armv8-64, respectively.

Additional Resources

An extensive set of programming documentation is available from Arm. Appendix B lists several important resources that both aspiring and experienced Arm assembly language programmers will find useful. Of all the resources listed in Appendix B, the most valuable reference is the *Arm Architecture Reference Manual (Armv8, for Armv8-A architecture profile)*, which can be downloaded from the Arm website using the URL that is shown in the aforementioned appendix. This 8000+ page tome contains comprehensive programming information for every A32 and A64 instruction including detailed operational descriptions, lists of valid operands, affected condition flags, and potential exceptions. You are strongly encouraged to consult this indispensable resource when developing your own Armv8-A assembly language code to verify correct instruction usage.

CHAPTER 1

■ ■ ■

Armv8-32 Architecture

Chapter 1 introduces the Armv8 computing architecture and the AArch32 execution state as viewed from the perspective of an application program. It begins with a brief overview of the Armv8 computing architecture, which provides a frame of reference for subsequent content. This is followed by a review of fundamental, numerical, and single-instruction multiple-data (SIMD) data types. Programming details of the AArch32 execution state are examined next and include descriptions of the general-purpose registers, condition flags, instruction operands, and memory addressing modes.

Unlike high-level languages such as C and C++, assembly language programming requires the software developer to comprehend specific architectural features of the target processor before attempting to write any code. The topics discussed in this chapter fulfill this requirement and provide a foundation for understanding the source code that is presented later in this book. This chapter also provides the base material that is necessary to understand the SIMD capabilities of the AArch32 execution state.

Armv8 Overview

Arm Limited ("Arm") designs and licenses computing architectures to third parties who incorporate their intellectual property into physical processors or products for sale to consumers. Arm computing architectures are embedded in a myriad of industrial control systems, IoT devices, and consumer products with the most notable being the ubiquitous smartphone. Since its inception, Arm has released eight major versions of its computing architecture. The latest major version is called Armv8 and supports both 32-bit and 64-bit execution states. Armv8-compliant processors are required (except in rare instances) to include hardware support for floating-point arithmetic and SIMD operations. Since the release of Armv8 in 2013, Arm has announced several architecture extensions. These extensions, which are denoted by a .x suffix, supplement the base architecture with additional computing features and resources. For example, the Armv8.2-FP16 extension adds instructions that perform half-precision floating-point arithmetic.

The Armv8 computing architecture is a reduced instruction set computing (RISC) platform. Like many RISC platforms, Armv8 supports a versatile set of elementary fixed-length instructions. It also implements a load/store memory architecture. In a load/store memory architecture, program code uses dedicated instructions to load data from memory into the processor's internal registers. A function then performs any required arithmetic or processing operations using only the values in these registers as operands. Results are then saved to memory using corresponding store instructions.

Arm defines distinct Armv8 architecture profiles for specific use cases. The Armv8-A profile targets mainstream computing applications and includes two discrete execution states. The AArch32 execution state uses 32-bit wide registers and 32-bit memory addressing. It also supports two similar but slightly different instruction sets: A32 and T32. In the A32 instruction set, all instruction encodings are 32 bits in length. Programs can use A32 assembly language instructions to fully exploit the processing capabilities of

© Daniel Kusswurm 2020
D. Kusswurm, *Modern Arm Assembly Language Programming*,
https://doi.org/10.1007/978-1-4842-6267-2_1

the AArch32 execution state. The T32 instruction set is an older instruction set that employs both 16- and 32-bit wide instruction encodings. The AArch32 execution state allows runtime switching between the A32 and T32 instruction sets, which facilitates execution of legacy T32 code on newer processors. The content of this and subsequent AArch32 chapters will focus exclusively on the A32 instruction set.

The AArch64 execution state is a modern computing environment that resembles the AArch32 execution state. It uses 64-bit wide registers and 64-bit memory addresses. It also includes a larger register file than the AArch32 execution state. The AArch64 execution state supports the A64 instruction set, which also employs fixed-length 32-bit wide instruction encodings. Compared to the A32 instruction set, the A64 instruction set uses different register operands and some different assembly language mnemonics. This means that assembly language source code written for the AArch64 execution state is not compatible with the AArch32 execution state and vice versa.

As mentioned earlier, Armv8-A-compliant processors are generally required to implement floating-point and SIMD capabilities in hardware. This means that both AArch32 and AArch64 include floating-point and SIMD register files. It also means that the A32 and A64 instruction sets incorporate instructions for performing scalar floating-point arithmetic and vector (or packed) SIMD operations. Many Armv8-A software development tools and application programming interfaces (APIs) also expect these hardware floating-point and SIMD resources to be available. Arm's SIMD technology is commonly called NEON.

Before proceeding, a couple of words about terminology are warranted. In all ensuing discussions, I will use the terms Armv8, AArch32, AArch64, A32, and A64 as defined in the preceding paragraphs to explain identifiable capabilities of the Armv8-A architecture profile. If you are interested in writing assembly language code for other Armv8 profiles such as Armv8-M (microcontroller optimized) or Armv8-R (real-time enhanced), the content of this book will help you achieve that goal. However, you should also consult the documentation resources listed in Appendix B for important programming information about these profiles. I will also use the terms Armv8-32 and Armv8-64 as umbrella expressions for A32/AArch32 and A64/AArch64 when explaining or referencing general characteristics of Arm's 32-bit and 64-bit technology.

The remainder of this chapter explains the core architecture of the AArch32 execution state. Chapter 10 discusses the core architecture of the AArch64 execution state.

Data Types

Programs written using the A32 instruction set can use a wide variety of data types. Most program data types originate from a small set of fundamental data types that are intrinsic to the AArch32 execution state. These data types enable the processor to perform numerical and logical operations using signed and unsigned integers; half-precision (16-bit), single-precision (32-bit), and double-precision (64-bit) floating-point numbers; and SIMD values. In this section, you will learn about these data types.

Fundamental Data Types

A fundamental data type is an elementary unit of data that is manipulated by the processor during program execution. The AArch32 and AArch64 execution states support fundamental data types ranging in size from 8 bits (1 byte) to 128 bits (16 bytes). Table 1-1 shows these types along with typical use patterns.

Table 1-1. *AArch32 and AArch64 fundamental data types*

Data Type	Size (bits)	Typical Use
Byte	8	Characters Byte integers
Halfword	16	Halfword integers Half-precision floating-point
Word	32	Wide characters Word integers Single-precision floating-point
Doubleword	64	Doubleword integers Double-precision floating-point Packed integers Packed half-precision floating-point Packed single-precision floating-point
Quadword	128	Quadword integers (AArch64 only) Packed integers Packed half-precision floating-point Packed single-precision floating-point Packed double-precision floating-point (AArch64 only)

Unsurprisingly, the fundamental data types are sized using integer powers of two. The bits of a fundamental data type are numbered from right to left with zero and size - 1 used to identify the least- and most-significant bits as shown in Figure 1-1.

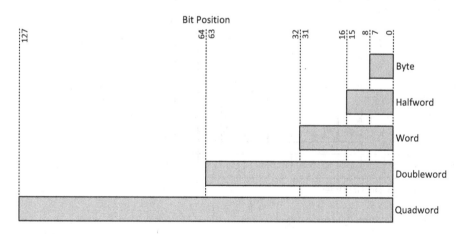

Figure 1-1. *Bit position numbering for fundamental data types*

A properly aligned fundamental data type is one whose address is evenly divisible by its size in bytes. For example, a word is properly aligned when it is stored at a memory location with an address that is evenly divisible by four. Similarly, doublewords are properly aligned at addresses evenly divisible by eight. An Armv8-A processor does not require proper alignment of multibyte fundamental data types in memory unless misaligned access trapping is enabled by the host operating system. However, it is a standard (and strongly recommended) practice to properly align all multibyte fundamental data types whenever possible to avoid potential performance penalties that can occur if the processor is required to access misaligned data in memory. All A32 instruction encodings must be aligned on a word boundary and this requisite is handled automatically by the compiler or assembler.

Fundamental data types larger than a single byte are stored in memory using one of two different ordering schemes: little-endian and big-endian. In little-endian, the bytes of a fundamental data type are stored in consecutive memory locations starting with the least-significant byte at the lowest memory address. Big-endian byte ordering uses the opposite ordering scheme and stores the most-significant byte at the lowest memory address. Figure 1-2 illustrates these ordering schemes.

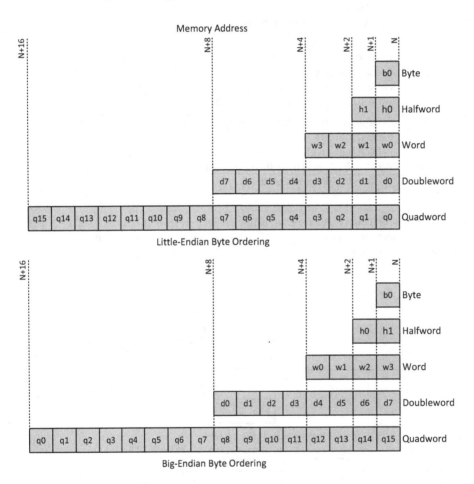

Figure 1-2. *Little-endian and big-endian byte ordering*

A32 instruction encodings always used little-endian byte ordering. For multibyte data values, the AArch32 memory model can be configured by the host operating system to support either little-endian or big-endian byte ordering. An Armv8-32 application program or individual function/subroutine can also select either little-endian or big-endian ordering for its own multibyte data values provided the appropriate A32 instruction is enabled by the host operating system. It is important to note, however, that this functionality is deprecated and should not be used in new code. Programs should instead use the designated A32 instructions that perform little-endian to big-endian and vice versa conversions. The remaining Armv8-32 discussions in this book and all source code examples assume the that processor and host operating system are configured for little-endian byte ordering.

Numerical Data Types

A numerical data type is an elementary scalar value such as an integer or floating-point number. All numerical data types recognized by an Armv8-A processor are represented using one of the fundamental data types discussed in the previous section. Table 1-2 lists the numerical data types for the AArch32 execution state along with the corresponding C++ types. This table also includes the fixed-size types that are defined in the C++ header file <cstdint> for comparison purposes. The A32 instruction set intrinsically supports arithmetic, bitwise logical, load, and store operations using 8-, 16-, and 32-bit wide integers, both signed and unsigned. Only a few A32 instructions support direct calculations using 64-bit integers. Signed integers are encoded using two's complement representation. The A32 instruction set also supports arithmetic calculations and data manipulation operations using single-precision and double-precision floating-point values. Half-precision floating-point arithmetic instructions are available on processors that support the Armv8.2-FP16 extension.

Table 1-2. *AArch32 numerical data types*

Type	Size (bits)	C++ Type	<cstdint>
Signed integers	8	char	int8_t
	16	short	int16_t
	32	int, long	int32_t
	64	long long	int64_t
Unsigned integers	8	unsigned char	uint8_t
	16	unsigned short	uint16_t
	32	unsigned int, unsigned long	uint32_t
	64	unsigned long long	uint64_t
Floating-point	16	n/a	n/a
	32	float	n/a
	64	double	n/a

SIMD Data Types

A SIMD data type is contiguous collection of bytes that is used by the processor to perform a single operation or calculation using multiple values. A SIMD data type can be regarded as a container object that holds several instances of the same numerical data type. The bits of a SIMD data types are numbered from right to left with zero and size - 1 denoting the least- and most-significant bits, respectively. When stored in memory, the bytes of a SIMD data type are ordered using the same endianness as other multibyte values.

Programmers can use SIMD data types to perform simultaneous calculations using either integers or floating-point values. For example, a 128-bit wide packed data type can hold sixteen 8-bit integers, eight 16-bit integers, four 32-bit integers, or two 64-bit integers. The same packed data type can also hold eight half-precision or four single-precision floating-point values. Armv8-32 does not support SIMD operations using packed double-precision floating-point values. Chapter 7 discusses the SIMD capabilities of Armv8-32 in greater detail.

Internal Architecture

From the perspective of an executing application program, the internal architecture of an AArch32-compliant processor (or processing element in Arm parlance) can be logically partitioned into several distinct units. These include the general-purpose register file, application program status register (APSR), floating-point and SIMD registers, and floating-point status and control register (FPSCR). An executing program, by definition, uses the general-purpose register file and the APSR register. Program utilization of the floating-point registers, SIMD registers, and FPSCR is optional. Figure 1-3 illustrates the internal architecture of an AArch32 processor.

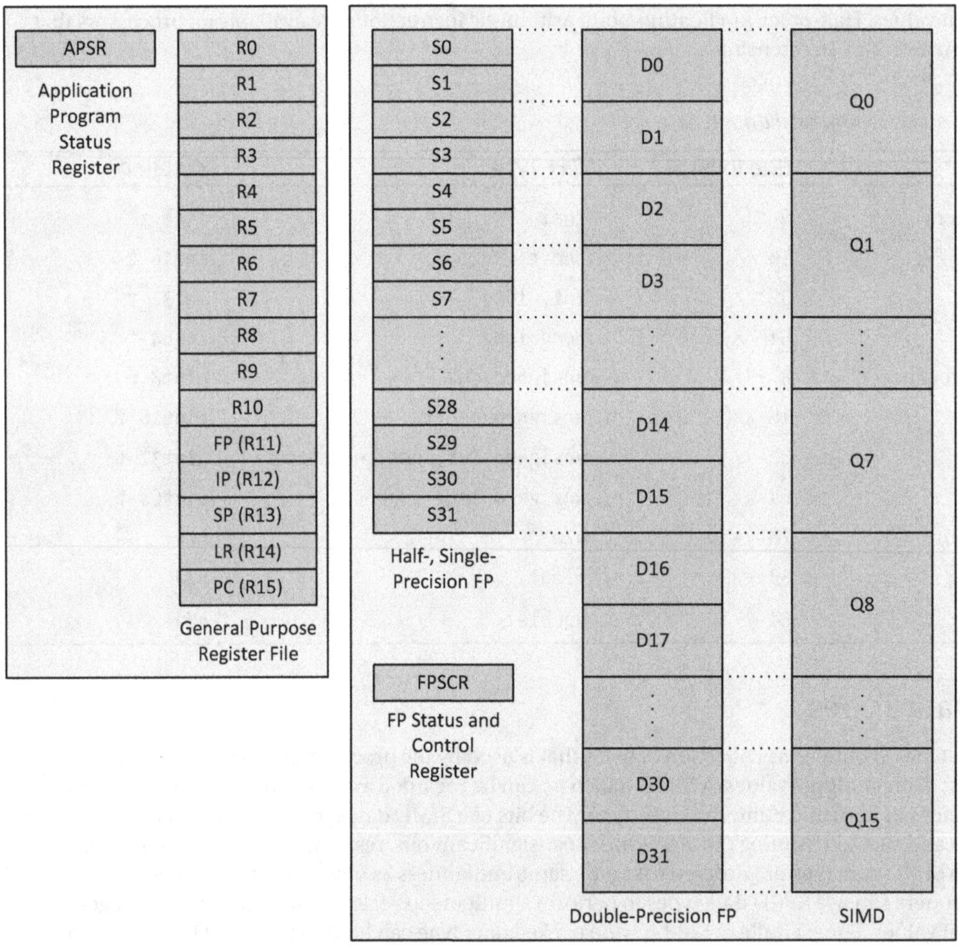

Figure 1-3. *AArch32 internal processor architecture*

General-Purpose Registers

The AArch32 general-purpose register file contains sixteen 32-bit wide registers. Registers R0–R10 are used to perform arithmetic, logical, compare, data transfer, and address calculation operations. They can also be used as temporary storage locations for constant values, intermediate results, and pointers to data values stored in memory.

Register FP (R11) is the frame pointer. This register supports function stack frames. A stack frame is a block of stack memory that contains function-related data including argument values, local variables, and (sometimes) links to other stack frames. You will learn more about stack frames in Chapter 3. When not used as a frame pointer, FP can be used as a general-purpose register.

Register IP (R12) is the intra-procedure-call scratch register. The linker uses this register to support veneers. A veneer is a small code patch that allows a branch instruction to access the full 32-bit address space of the AArch32 execution state. On most systems, the IP register can also be used as a general-purpose register.

Register SP (R13) is the stack pointer. The stack itself is simply a contiguous block of memory that is assigned to a process or thread by the operating system. Programs use the stack to preserve register values, pass function arguments, and store temporary data.

The AArch32 execution state supports multiple implementations of a stack. When used with the A32 push instruction, the stack grows down in memory toward lower addresses. Execution of an A32 pop instruction has the opposite effect. The SP register always points to the stack's topmost item. Stack push and pop operations are performed using 32-bit wide operands. This means that the location of the stack in memory must always be aligned on a word boundary. Some runtime environments align stack memory and the SP register on a doubleword boundary, especially across function interfaces, to avoid improperly aligned doubleword memory transfers (e.g., 64-bit integer or double-precision floating-point) values. While it is technically possible to use the SP register as a general-purpose register, such use is strongly discouraged since many operating systems and API libraries do not support this type of usage.

Register LR (R14) is the link register. This register facilitates function (subroutine) calls and returns. A function can also use the LR register as a general-purpose register provided it preserves the original contents on the stack or in another register.

Register PC (R15) is the program counter. The PC register contains the address of the next instruction that the processor will fetch from memory. Some instructions (e.g., branch instructions and the pop {pc} instruction) update the contents of the PC register during program execution. The PC register also can be employed as base register to load values from memory. The use of the PC register as a destination operand general-purpose register is deprecated.

You may have noticed that registers R11–R15 have dual names that reflect their specific roles. Either name can be used in assembly language code; however, the nonparenthetical name should always be used whenever the register is employed in its specific role.

Application Program Status Register

The application program status register (APSR) is a 32-bit wide register that contains state information for executing instructions. Table 1-3 describes this information in greater detail.

Table 1-3. *APSR status bit fields*

Bit Position	Symbol	Name
31	N	Negative condition flag
30	Z	Zero condition flag
29	C	Carry condition flag
28	V	Overflow condition flag
27	Q	Overflow or saturation flag
26:24		Reserved 0
23:20		Reserved for system features or future expansion
19:16	GE[3:0]	Parallel add/sub greater than or equal flags
15:0		Reserved for system features or future expansion

The APSR is a subset of the current program status register (CPSR), which contains additional status and control flags that are used by operating systems and T32 code. Most Armv8-32 application programs interact only with the nonreserved bits shown in Table 1-3.

For application programs, the most important bits in the APSR register are the negative (N) condition flag, zero (Z) condition flag, carry (C) condition flag, and overflow (V) condition flag. Collectively, these are called the NZCV condition flags. The N condition flag signifies if the result of an operation yields a negative (two's complement representation) value. The Z condition flag denotes a zero result. The C condition flag reports occurrences of carries or not borrows (i.e., no borrow occurred) when performing unsigned addition or subtraction, respectively. It is also used by some shift and rotate instructions. Finally, the V flag signifies an overflow condition (i.e., result too small or large) when performing signed integer arithmetic.

The Q and GE[3:0] flags are used by A32 instructions that perform simple SIMD operations using the general-purpose registers. Programs can still these instructions, but new code should be written to fully exploit the Advanced SIMD register file for better performance.

Floating-Point and SIMD Registers

AArch32 processors include 32 registers named S0–S31. Programs can use these registers to perform single-precision floating-point calculations. They also can be used to perform half-precision floating-point arithmetic on processors that support the Armv8.2-FP16 extension. The D0–D31 registers carry out calculations using double-precision floating-point values. The Q0–Q15 registers support SIMD operations using either packed integer or packed single-precision floating-point operands. The floating-point and SIMD registers are organized using an overlapping arrangement. Chapter 5 explains this arrangement in greater detail. The FPSCR contains status flags and control bits for floating-point operations. You will learn more about the floating-point capabilities of the AArch32 execution state in Chapters 5 and 6. Chapters 7, 8, and 9 provide additional details regarding AArch32 SIMD concepts and programming.

Instruction Set Overview

The A32 instruction set encompasses a versatile collection of arithmetic, bitwise logical, and data manipulation operations. As previously mentioned, all A32 instruction encodings are 32 bits wide and must be aligned on a word boundary. An instruction encoding is a unique bit pattern that directs the processor to perform a precise operation. Nearly all A32 instructions use operands, which designate the specific registers, values, or memory locations that an instruction uses. Most instructions require one or more source operands along with a single destination operand. A few instructions utilize two destination operands.

Instruction Operands

There are three basic types of instruction operands: immediate, register, and memory. An immediate operand is a constant value that is encoded as part of the instruction. Only source operands can specify an immediate value. Register operands are contained in a general-purpose or SIMD register. A memory operand specifies a value located in memory, which can contain any of the data types described earlier in this chapter. Table 1-4 contains several examples of instructions that employ various operand types.

Table 1-4. *Examples of A32 instruction operands*

Type	Example Instruction	Analogous C++ Statement
Immediate	mov r0,#42	r0 = 42
	add r1,r0,#8	r1 = r0 + 8
	add r0,#17	r0 += 17
	lsl r2,r1,#2	r2 = r1 << 2
Register	mov r1,r0	r1 = r0
	and r2,r1,r0	r2 = r1 & r0
	mul r2,r1,r0	r2 = r1 * r0
	smull r4,r5,r0,r1	r4:r5 = r0 * r1
Memory	ldr r0,[sp]	r0 = *sp
	str r7,[r4]	*r4 = r7

A few comments about the examples in Table 1-4. The mov r0,#42 (move immediate) instruction loads register R0 with the value 42. In this example, mov is the A32 instruction mnemonic, R0 is the destination operand, and the constant 42 is an immediate operand. Note that the constant 42 is prefixed with the # symbol. This symbol is normally used in A32 code, but some assemblers will accept an immediate operand without the # prefix character.

The add r1,r0,#8 (add immediate) instruction adds the contents of register R0 and the constant 8. It then saves the result in register R1. The add r0,#17 instruction is a concise form of the official instruction add r0,r0,#17; both styles can be used in A32 code.

The mul r2,r1,r0 (multiply) instruction multiplies the 32-bit wide (signed or unsigned) integers in registers R1 and R0. It then saves the low-order 32 bits of the calculated product in register R2 (recall that the product of two 32-bit integers is always a 64-bit integer). The smull r4,r5,r0,r1 (signed multiply long) multiplies the 32-bit wide signed integers in registers R0 and R1 and saves the entire 64-bit wide product in registers R4 (low-order 32 bits) and R5 (high-order 32 bits).

The ldr r0,[sp] (load register) instruction copies the word value pointed to by register SP into register R0. Finally, the str r7,[r4] (store register) instruction saves the word value in R7 to the memory location pointed to by R4. In this instruction, the positions of the source and destination operands are reversed. You will learn more about A32 operands and instruction use in the programming chapters of this book.

Memory Addressing Modes

The A32 instruction set supports four distinct addressing modes for memory load and store operations: offset addressing, pre-indexed addressing, post-indexed addressing, and PC relative addressing. In offset addressing, memory addresses are derived by summing a base register with a positive or negative offset value. Pre-indexed addressing is similar to offset addressing except that the base register is updated with the calculated memory address. This facilitates faster processing of array elements. Post-indexed addressing employs a single base register for the target memory address. Following the memory access, the contents of the base register are updated using the offset value. Post-indexed addressing can also be used to accelerate array operations. In all three of these address modes, the offset value can be an immediate constant, an index register, or a shifted index register.

PC relative addressing is used to load a value from a memory location that is designated by a label. The target label must be located within ±4 kilobytes of the ldr instruction. Table 1-5 contains examples of instructions that use these memory addressing modes along with analogous C++ statements.

Table 1-5. *Examples of A32 memory addressing modes*

Mode	Example	Analogous C++ Statements
Offset	ldr r2,[r1]	r2 = *r1
	ldr r2,[r1,#8]	r2 = *(r1 + 8)
	ldr r2,[r1,r0]	r2 = *(r1 + r0)
	ldr r2,[r1,r0,lsl #2]	r2 = *(r1 + (r0 << 2))
Pre-indexed	ldr r2,[r1,#8]!	r2 = *(r1 + 8); r1 += 8
	ldr r2,[r1,r0]!	r2 = *(r1 + r0); r1 += r0
	ldr r2,[r1,r0,lsl #2]!	r2 = *(r1 + (r0 << 2)); r1 += r0 << 2
Post-indexed	ldr r2,[r1],#8	r2 = *r1; r1 += 8
	ldr r2,[r1],r0	r2 = *r1; r1 += r0
	ldr r2,[r1],r0,lsl #2	r2 = *r1; r1 += r0 << 2
PC relative	ldr r2,label	r2 = *(pc + label_offset)

The ! symbol that is used in the pre-indexed examples is called a writeback operator. It instructs the processor to update the base register following the load operation. The label_offset that is shown in the PC relative instruction ldr r2,label is automatically calculated by the assembler. The addressing modes listed in Table 1-5, except for PC relative, can also be used with the str instruction. Do not worry if some of the examples in Table 1-5 seem a little abstruse. You will encounter a plethora of memory addressing mode examples in the programming chapters of this book.

Summary

Here are the key learning points for Chapter 1:

- The Armv8-A profile supports two discrete execution states: AArch32 and AArch64.

- The AArch32 execution state employs 32-bit wide registers and 32-bit memory addresses. Similarly, the AArch64 execution state uses 64-bit wide registers and memory addresses.

- Assembly language functions written for the AArch32 and AArch64 execution states use the A32 and A64 instructions sets, respectively. These instruction sets are not source code compatible.

- The AArch32 execution state intrinsically supports the standard integer and floating-point data types that are used by high-level languages such as C and C++.

- The AArch32 execution state includes 16 general-purpose registers named R0–R10, FP, IP, SP, LR, and PC. It also encompasses 32 registers (S0–S31) for half- and single-precision floating-point arithmetic, 32 registers (D0–D31) for double-precision floating-point arithmetic, and 16 registers (Q0–Q15) for SIMD operations.

- The AArch32 execution state also includes the APSR register, which contains status flags that reflect results of common arithmetic and logical instructions.

- The A32 instruction set supports multiple operand types including immediate, register, and memory operands.

- The A32 instruction set supports multiple addressing modes including offset, PC relative, pre-indexed, and post-indexed. The latter two modes facilitate faster processing of array elements.

CHAPTER 2

■ ■ ■

Armv8-32 Core Programming – Part 1

In the previous chapter, you learned about the fundamentals of the AArch32 execution state including its data types, register sets, and memory addressing modes. In this chapter, you will learn how to code basic A32 assembly language functions that are callable from C++. You will also learn about the semantics and syntax of an A32 assembly language source code file. The source code examples and accompanying remarks of this chapter are intended to complement the informative material presented in Chapter 1.

The content of Chapter 2 is partitioned into two sections. The first section describes how to code functions that perform simple integer arithmetic such as addition, subtraction, multiplication, and division. You will also learn the basics of passing arguments and return values between functions written in C++ and A32 assembly language. The second section highlights how to use essential A32 assembly language instructions including data loads, stores, moves, and bitwise logical operations. If you have previous assembly language programming experience using other processor architectures, this section is especially important given the distinctive nature of the A32 instruction set.

It should be noted that the primary purpose of the sample code presented in this chapter (and the next two) is to elucidate proper use of the A32 instruction set and basic assembly language programming techniques. The assembly language code is straightforward, but not necessarily optimal since understanding optimized assembly language code can be challenging especially for beginners. The source code that is presented in later chapters places more emphasis on efficient coding techniques. Chapter 17 also discusses strategies that you can use to improve the efficiency of your assembly language code.

As mentioned in this book's "Introduction," the source code examples were created using the GNU toolchain. Appendix A contains additional information on how to build and run the A32 source code examples. Depending on your personal preference, you may want to peruse Appendix A first and set up a test system before proceeding with the discussions in this chapter.

Integer Arithmetic

In this section, you will learn the basics of A32 assembly language programming. It begins with a simple program that demonstrates how to perform integer addition and subtraction. This is followed by a source code example that illustrates integer multiplication and division. Besides common arithmetic operations, the source code examples in this section elucidate passing argument and return values between a C++ and assembly language function. They also show how to employ commonly used assembler directives.

© Daniel Kusswurm 2020
D. Kusswurm, *Modern Arm Assembly Language Programming*,
https://doi.org/10.1007/978-1-4842-6267-2_2

■ **Note** Each source code example in this book includes one or more functions written in Armv8 assembly language plus some C++ code that demonstrates how to execute the assembly language code. The C++ code also contains ancillary functions that perform test case initialization and display results. For each source code example, a single listing that includes both the C++ and assembly language source code is used to minimize the number of listing references in the main text. The actual source code uses separate files for the C++ (.cpp) and assembly language (.s) code.

Addition and Subtraction

The first source code example of this chapter is called Ch02_01. This example demonstrates how to use the A32 assembly language instructions add (integer add) and sub (integer subtract). It also illustrates some basic assembly language programming concepts including argument passing, returning values, and directive usage. Listing 2-1 shows the source code for example Ch02_01.

Listing 2-1. Example Ch02_01

```
//----------------------------------------------------
//                  Ch02_01.cpp
//----------------------------------------------------

#include <iostream>

using namespace std;

extern "C" int IntegerAddSub_(int a, int b, int c, int d);

void PrintResult(const char* msg, int a, int b, int c, int d, int result)
{
    const char nl = '\n';

    cout << msg << nl;
    cout << "a = " << a << nl;
    cout << "b = " << b << nl;
    cout << "c = " << c << nl;
    cout << "d = " << d << nl;
    cout << "result = " << result << nl;
    cout << nl;
}

int main(int argc, char** argv)
{
    int a, b, c, d, result;

    a = 10; b = 20; c = 30; d = 18;
    result = IntegerAddSub_(a, b, c, d);
    PrintResult("Test case #1", a, b, c, d, result);
```

```
    a = 101; b = 34; c = -190; d = 25;
    result = IntegerAddSub_(a, b, c, d);
    PrintResult("Test case #2", a, b, c, d, result);
}

//--------------------------------------------------
//                Ch02_01_.s
//--------------------------------------------------

// extern "C" int IntegerAddSub_(int a, int b int c, int d);

            .text
            .global IntegerAddSub_
IntegerAddSub_:

// Calculate a + b + c - d
            add  r0,r0,r1                   // r0 = a + b
            add  r0,r0,r2                   // r0 = a + b + c
            sub  r0,r0,r3                   // r0 = a + b + c - d

            bx lr                          // return to caller
```

The C++ code in Listing 2-1 is mostly straightforward but includes a few lines that warrant some explanatory comments. The line extern "C" int IntegerAddSub_(int a, int b, int c, int d) is a declaration statement that defines the parameters and return value for the assembly language function IntegerAddSub_. All assembly language function names used in this book include a trailing underscore for easier recognition. The declaration statement's "C" modifier instructs the C++ compiler to use C-style naming for function IntegerAddSub_ instead of a C++ decorated name (a C++ decorated name includes extra suffix and prefix characters that facilitate function overloading).

The C++ function main contains the code that calls the assembly language function IntegerAddSub_. This function requires four arguments of type int and returns a single int value. Like many programming languages, C++ uses a combination of processor registers and the stack to pass argument values to a function. In the current example, the GNU C++ compiler generates code that loads argument values a, b, c, and d into registers R0, R1, R2, and R3, respectively, prior to calling the function IntegerAddSub_. The use of these specific registers is mandated by the GNU C++ calling convention. You will learn more about the GNU C++ calling convention later in this and subsequent chapters. The A32 instruction emitted by the GNU C++ compiler to call IntegerAddSub_ also loads the return address into the LR register.

In Listing 2-1, the A32 assembly language code for example Ch02_01 is shown immediately after the C++ function main. The first thing to notice is the // symbol. Like C++, the GNU assembler treats any text that follows a // as comment text. The @ symbol can also be used for appended comments in A32 assembly language source files. The source code in this book uses the // symbol for appended comments since the same symbol is also valid in A64 source code files whereas the @ symbol is not. Block comments are also supported in A32 assembly language source code files using the /* and */ symbols.

The .text statement is an assembler directive that defines the start of an assembly language code section. An assembler directive is a command that instructs the assembler to perform a specific action during assembly of the source code. The next statement, .global IntegerAddSub_, is another directive that tells the assembler to treat the function IntegerAddSub_ as a global function. This allows functions that are defined in other source code files to call IntegerAddSub_. You will learn how to use additional assembler directives throughout this book. The statement IntegerAddSub_: defines the entry point (or start address) for function IntegerAddSub_. This statement is called a label. Besides designating entry points, labels are also used to define assembly language variable names and targets for branch instructions.

15

The assembly language function IntegerAddSub_ calculates a + b + c - d and returns this value to the calling C++ function. It begins with an add r0,r0,r1 instruction that adds the values in registers R0 and R1 (argument values a and b) and saves this sum in register R0. The next instruction, add r0,r0,r2, adds the contents of R2 (argument value c) to R0, which now contains a + b + c. This is followed by a sub r0,r0,r3 instruction that subtracts R3 (argument value d) from the value in R0 and yields the final result of a + b + c - d.

An A32 assembly language function must use register R0 to return a single 32-bit wide integer (or C++ int) value to its calling function. In the current example, no additional instructions are necessary to achieve this requirement since R0 already contains the correct return value. The final bx lr (branch and exchange) instruction transfers control back to the calling function main. This instruction copies the contents of the LR register, which contains the return address, into the PC register. You will learn more about how the LR register facilitates function calls and returns in later source code examples. Following the execution of IntegerAddSub_, the function main displays the results on the console. Here is the output for example Ch02_01:

```
Test case #1
a = 10
b = 20
c = 30
d = 18
result = 42

Test case #2
a = 101
b = 34
c = -190
d = 25
result = -80
```

Multiplication

Listing 2-2 shows the source code for example Ch02_02, which illustrates how to perform integer multiplication. Toward the top of the C++ file are three declaration statements for the assembly language functions that demonstrate integer multiplication. The function IntegerMulA_ accepts two int arguments and returns an int value. Function IntegerMulB_ is similar except that it returns a value of type long long, which is a 64-bit wide signed integer. Finally, function IntegerMulC_ accepts two arguments of type unsigned int and returns a value of type unsigned long long. The remaining C++ code is akin to what you saw in the first example. It initializes some test cases, calls the corresponding assembly language functions, and prints the results.

Listing 2-2. Example Ch02_02

```
//----------------------------------------------------
//              Ch02_02.cpp
//----------------------------------------------------

#include <iostream>

using namespace std;

extern "C" int IntegerMulA_(int a, int b);
```

```cpp
extern "C" long long IntegerMulB_(int a, int b);
extern "C" unsigned long long IntegerMulC_(unsigned int a, unsigned int b);

template <typename T1, typename T2>
void PrintResult(const char* msg, T1 a, T1 b, T2 result)
{
    const char nl = '\n';

    cout << msg << nl;
    cout << "a = " << a << ", b = " << b;
    cout << " result = " << result << nl << nl;
}

int main(int argc, char** argv)
{
    int a1 = 50;
    int b1 = 25;
    int result1 = IntegerMulA_(a1, b1);
    PrintResult("Test case #1", a1, b1, result1);

    int a2 = -300;
    int b2 = 7;
    int result2 = IntegerMulA_(a2, b2);
    PrintResult("Test case #2", a2, b2, result2);

    int a3 = 4000;
    int b3 = 1000000;;
    long long result3 = IntegerMulB_(a3, b3);
    PrintResult("Test case #3", a3, b3, result3);

    int a4 = 100000;
    int b4 = -20000000;
    long long result4 = IntegerMulB_(a4, b4);
    PrintResult("Test case #4", a4, b4, result4);

    unsigned int a5 = 0x80000000;
    unsigned int b5 = 0x80000000;
    unsigned long long result5 = IntegerMulC_(a5, b5);
    PrintResult("Test case #5", a5, b5, result5);

    return 0;
}

//-------------------------------------------------
//                  Ch02_02_.s
//-------------------------------------------------

// extern "C" int IntegerMulA_(int a, int b);

            .text
            .global IntegerMulA_
```

```
IntegerMulA_:

// Calculate a * b and save result
            mul r0,r0,r1                    // calc a * b (32-bit)
            bx lr


// extern "C" long long IntegerMulB_(int a, int b);

            .global IntegerMulB_
IntegerMulB_:

// Calculate a * b and save result
            smull r0,r1,r0,r1               // calc a * b (signed 64-bit)
            bx lr


// extern "C" unsigned long long IntegerMulC_(unsigned int a, unsigned int b);

            .global IntegerMulC_
IntegerMulC_:

// Calculate a * b and save result
            umull r0,r1,r0,r1               // calc a * b (unsigned 64-bit)
            bx lr
```

The function IntegerMulA_ calculates the product of two 32-bit integer values. The first instruction of this function, mul r0,r0,r1, multiplies the contents of R0 (argument value a) by R1 (argument value b) and saves the multiplicative product in register R0. The mul (multiply) instruction can be used whenever a function needs to calculate the product of two 32-bit wide integers and only requires the low-order 32 bits of the 64-bit product (recall that the product of two 32-bit integers is always a 64-bit result). The mul instruction can be used with either signed or unsigned integers.

The function IntegerMulB_ uses a smull r0,r1,r0,r1 (signed multiply long) instruction to calculate the product of two signed 32-bit wide integers (r0 * r1) and saves the complete 64-bit product in registers R0 (low-order 32 bits) and R1 (high-order 32 bits). When returning a 64-bit value from an A32 assembly language function, the low-order 32 bits must be placed in register R0 and the high-order 32 bits in R1. The smull instruction is an example of an A32 instruction that requires two destination operands.

Function IntegerMulC_ is similar to IntegerMulB_ except that it calculates the product of two 32-bit wide unsigned integers using the umull r0,r1,r0,r1 (unsigned multiply long) instruction. This instruction produces a 64-bit wide unsigned integer result that is returned to the caller in registers R0 and R1. Note that all three assembly language functions in this example use the same assembly language directives that you saw in the first example of this chapter. They also use the bx lr instruction to return program control back to the calling function main. Here are the results for source code example Ch02_02:

```
Test case #1
a = 50, b = 25 result = 1250

Test case #2
a = -300, b = 7 result = -2100

Test case #3
a = 4000, b = 1000000 result = 4000000000
```

```
Test case #4
a = 100000, b = -20000000 result = -2000000000000

Test case #5
a = 2147483648, b = 2147483648 result = 4611686018427387904
```

Division

Listing 2-3 shows the source code for example Ch02_03, which demonstrates how to perform signed 32-bit integer division. This example also illustrates how to load 32-bit integers from memory, save 32-bit integers to memory, and preserve registers on the stack.

Listing 2-3. Example Ch02_03

```cpp
//--------------------------------------------------
//                  Ch02_03.cpp
//--------------------------------------------------

#include <iostream>

using namespace std;

extern "C" void CalcQuoRem_(const int* a, const int* b, int* quo, int* rem);

void PrintResult(const char* msg, int a, int b, int quo, int rem)
{
    const char nl = '\n';

    cout << msg << nl;
    cout << "a = " << a << nl;
    cout << "b = " << b << nl;
    cout << "quotient = " << quo << nl;
    cout << "remainder = " << rem << nl;
    cout << nl;
}

int main(int argc, char** argv)
{
    int a, b, quo, rem;

    a = 100; b = 7;
    CalcQuoRem_(&a, &b, &quo, &rem);
    PrintResult("Test case #1", a, b, quo, rem);

    a = 200; b = 10;
    CalcQuoRem_(&a, &b, &quo, &rem);
    PrintResult("Test case #2", a, b, quo, rem);

    a = 300; b = -17;
    CalcQuoRem_(&a, &b, &quo, &rem);
    PrintResult("Test case #3", a, b, quo, rem);
}
```

19

```
//----------------------------------------------------
//                  Ch02_03_.s
//----------------------------------------------------

// extern "C" void CalcQuoRem_(const int* a, const int* b, int* quo, int* rem);

            .text
            .global CalcQuoRem_
CalcQuoRem_:

// Save non-volatile registers
            push {r4,r5}                    // save r4 and r5 on stack

// Load a and b
            ldr r4,[r0]                     // r4 = a (dividend)
            ldr r5,[r1]                     // r5 = b (divisor)

// Calculate quotient and remainder
            sdiv r0,r4,r5                   // r0 = quotient
            str r0,[r2]                     // save quotient

            mul r1,r0,r5                    // r1 = quotient * b
            sub r2,r4,r1                    // r2 = a - quotient * b
            str r2,[r3]                     // save remainder

// Restore non-volatile registers and return
            pop {r4,r5}                     // restore r4 & r5
            bx lr                           // return to caller
```

The C++ code in Listing 2-3 begins with the declaration of the assembly language function CalcQuoRem_. Unlike the first two examples, this function uses pointer instead of value arguments. Pointer arguments are employed in this example since the function CalcQuoRem_ needs to return two distinct values to its caller: the quotient and remainder of a signed division operation. The C++ function main includes code that initializes a few test cases for CalcQuoRem_. Note that the C++ address operator (&) is applied to each CalcQuoRem_ argument as required by the function declaration.

Before looking at the assembly language code for example Ch02_03, I need to explain a few more particulars about the GNU C++ calling convention. A calling convention is a protocol that describes how argument and return values are exchanged between two functions. As you have already seen, the GNU C++ calling convention for the AArch32 execution state requires a calling function to pass the first four integer (or pointer) arguments using registers R0, R1, R2, and R3. Any additional arguments are passed using the stack. You will learn how to pass arguments via the stack in Chapter 3.

The GNU C++ calling convention also designates each general-purpose register as volatile or non-volatile. A called function can alter the contents of a volatile register, but it must preserve the contents of a non-volatile register prior to modifying it. Non-volatile registers are typically preserved on the stack as you will soon see. The GNU C++ calling convention designates registers R0–R3 and R12 as volatile and registers R4–R10, FP, SP, and LR as non-volatile. Table 2-1 summarizes the GNU C++ calling convention requirements for the general-purpose registers.

Table 2-1. *Calling convention requirements for general-purpose registers*

Register	Type	Use
R0	Volatile	First integer argument value, scratch register 32-bit integer return value 64-bit integer return value (low-order 32 bits)
R1	Volatile	Second integer argument value, scratch register 64-bit integer return value (high-order 32 bits)
R2	Volatile	Third integer argument value, scratch register
R3	Volatile	Fourth integer argument value, scratch register
R4 – R10	Non-volatile	Scratch registers
FP (R11)	Non-volatile	Frame pointer, scratch register
IP (R12)	Volatile	Intra-procedure-call register, scratch register
SP (R13)	Non-volatile	Stack pointer
LR (R14)	Non-volatile	Link register, scratch register

As mentioned in Chapter 1, the use of register SP as a general-purpose scratch register is discouraged. The GNU C++ calling convention also defines additional requirements including rules for passing floating-point values, allocating space for local variables, and stack frames. You will learn about these requirements in Chapters 3 and 6.

▪ **Note** The GNU C++ calling convention requirements that are described in this section and in subsequent chapters may be different for other C++ compilers, high-level programming languages, or host operating systems. If you are reading this book to learn Armv8-32 assembly language and plan on using it with a different C++ compiler, high-level programming language, or host operating system, you should consult the appropriate documentation for more information regarding the target platform's calling convention requirements.

The first instruction in function CalcQuoRem_, push {r4, r5}, saves non-volatile registers R4 and R5 on the stack. It accomplishes this by subtracting 8 from the value in register SP and then storing the values in R4 and R5 to the memory locations pointed to by register SP as illustrated in Figure 2-1. The push (push registers) instruction allows registers to be listed individually between the curly braces or in a condensed list format (e.g., push {r4-r7}). It should be noted that the push instruction is an alias for the A32 stmdb (store multiple decrement before) instruction. The A32 instruction set defines numerous alias instructions that provide more meaningful descriptions of the operation that is being performed. This is normally not a concern when writing A32 code, but something that you need to be aware of when using a debugger or viewing a listing of disassembled code.

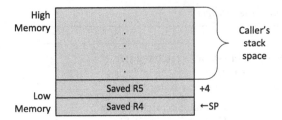

Figure 2-1. Stack following execution of push {r4,r5} instruction

Following the push operation is the instruction ldr r4,[r0]. The ldr (load register) instruction copies a word value from the memory location pointed to by the source operand into the destination operand. In the current example, R0 contains a pointer to argument value a, which means that the ldr r4,[r0] instruction loads argument value a into register R4. The next instruction, ldr r5,[r1], loads argument value b into register R5.

The sdiv r0,r4,r5 instruction divides the contents of R4 (argument value a) by R5 (argument value b) and saves the resultant quotient in register R0. The A32 instruction set also includes a udiv instruction for unsigned integer division. Following execution of the sdiv instruction, the str r0,[r2] instruction saves the quotient to the memory location pointed to by R2, which contains a pointer to quo. The sdiv and udiv instructions do not provide remainders for their respective integer division operations. The remainder of an integer division operation such as a / b can be calculated using the formula rem = a - quo * b. The mul r1,r0,r5 instruction calculates quo * b. This is followed by a sub r2,r4,r1 instruction that calculates the final remainder. The ensuing str r2,[r3] instruction saves the remainder to the memory location specified by the pointer argument rem.

Before program control is returned to the calling function, CalcQuoRem_ needs to restore the contents of the non-volatile registers that were preserved on the stack. The pop {r4,r5} (pop registers) instruction restores the contents of R4 and R5 from the stack. This instruction also adds 8 to the SP register. The pop instruction is an alias of the A32 ldmia (load multiple increment after) instruction. Following non-volatile register restoration, the bx lr instruction returns program control back to the calling function.

One final note about example Ch02_03. Recall that the first two pointer arguments of CalcQuoRem_ were declared using the C++ const qualifier. Unlike the GNU C++ compiler, the GNU assembler will not issue a warning if an assembly language function uses a str instruction to modify a value in memory pointed to by a const pointer. On some systems, execution of a str instruction using a const pointer may cause the processor to raise an exception if the processor has been configured to trap invalid writes to read-only memory. Here are the results for source code example Ch02_03:

```
Test case #1
a = 100
b = 7
quotient = 14
remainder = 2

Test case #2
a = 200
b = 10
quotient = 20
remainder = 0

Test case #3
a = 300
```

```
b = -17
quotient = -17
remainder = 11
```

Integer Operations

In this section, you will learn how to use common integer load, store, and move instructions. Mastery of these instructions is critical given their frequency of use. The A32 instruction set uses 32-bit wide fixed-length encodings for all instructions. This means that it is impossible for an instruction encoding to contain a complete 32-bit address, constant value, or base register offset since most of the bits in an encoding are used to specify the operation to perform and its register operands. When coding an A32 assembly language function, it is sometimes necessary to use multiple instructions or pseudo instructions to complete an integer load or move operation as you will soon see.

Load Instructions

Listing 2-4 shows the source code for example Ch02_04. This example demonstrates additional forms of the ldr instruction. It also shows how to use assembler directives to define and initialize data variables in an assembly language file.

Listing 2-4. Example Ch02_04

```
//--------------------------------------------------
//                 Ch02_04.cpp
//--------------------------------------------------

#include <iostream>

using namespace std;

extern "C" int TestLDR_(void);

int main(int argc, char** argv)
{
    int result = TestLDR_();
    cout << "result = " << result << '\n';
    return 0;
}

//--------------------------------------------------
//                 Ch02_04_.s
//--------------------------------------------------

        .data
Foo:    .word 100, 200, 300, 400

// extern "C" void TestLDR_(void);

        .text
```

```
            .global TestLDR_

TestLDR_:   ldr r1,=Foo                 // r1 = address of Foo

            ldr r2,[r1]                 // r2 = Foo[0]
            ldr r3,[r1,#4]              // r3 = Foo[1]

            add r0,r2,r3                // r0 = Foo[0] + Foo[1]

            ldr r2,[r1,#8]             // r2 = Foo[2]
            add r0,r0,r2                // r0 += Foo[2]

            ldr r2,[r1,#12]           // r2 = Foo[3]
            add r0,r0,r2                // r0 += Foo[3]

            bx lr                       // return to caller
```

The C++ code for example Ch02_04 is straightforward. It simply calls the assembly language function TestLDR_ and displays its return value. Toward the top of file Ch02_04_.s is a line that contains a .data directive. This directive designates the start of a memory block that contains modifiable data. The .word directive that follows allocates and initializes four word (32-bit wide integer) values in memory. These values will be referenced later in function TestLDR_ using the label Foo that is located to the left of the .word directive. This entire statement is equivalent to the C++ expression int32_t Foo[4] = {100, 200, 300, 400};. Table 2-2 summarizes the GNU assembler directives that you can use to allocate storage space and initialize data values. The integer directives in this table can be used for either signed or unsigned values. Each numerical directive that emits a multibyte value uses the endianness of the host system. You will learn how to use the other directives in Table 2-2 later in this book.

Table 2-2. *GNU assembler directives for numerical data values*

Directive	Data Type
.byte	8-bit integer
.hword, .short	16-bit integer
.word, .int	32-bit integer
.quad	64-bit integer
.octa	128-bit integer
.single	single-precision (32-bit) floating-point
.double	double-precision (64-bit) floating-point
.ascii	ASCII text string
.asciz	ASCII text string (null-terminated)

The first assembly language statement in function TestLDR_, ldr r1,=Foo, loads register R1 with the address of Foo. This variant of the ldr instruction is called a pseudo instruction and will be examined more closely later in this section. The next instruction, ldr r2,[r1], loads the word value in memory pointed to by R1 (Foo[0]) into R2. This is followed by an ldr r3,[r1,#4] instruction that loads Foo[1] into R3. The second ldr instruction is an example of offset addressing (see Table 1-5) where the processor calculates the target memory address by summing the value in base register R1 and the constant value 4. Recall that with offset addressing, the value in the base register is not modified during execution of the instruction. The ensuing add r0,r2,r3 instruction sums R2 and R3; the result is then saved in R0.

The next two instructions, ldr r2,[r1,#8] and add r0,r0,r2, load Foo[2] into R2 and add it to the intermediate sum in R0. Another ldr and add instruction pair is then employed to complete the array element summing operation. It is important to recognize that each element of array Foo was first loaded into a register using a ldr instruction before each add instruction. As discussed in Chapter 1, RISC processors typically implement a load/store memory architecture, which means that there is no form of the add instruction that can directly reference an operand in memory (e.g., add r0,r0,[r1] is invalid).

Figure 2-2 shows a GNU debugger log file (with minor edits to improve readability) of the executable machine code for function TestLDR_. Note that the pseudo instruction ldr r1,=Foo, which was used in the original source code, has been replaced with the instruction ldr r1,[pc,#28]. During AArch32 program execution, the PC register contains the address of the currently executing instruction plus 8 bytes. This means that the ldr r1,[pc,#28] instruction loads R1 with the word value that is located at memory address PC + 8 + 28. If you look closely at Figure 2-2, you will notice that the address of the ldr r1,[pc,#28] instruction is 0x00010730. Adding 36 (0x24) to this value yields 0x00010754. Referring again to Figure 2-2, the word value located at address 0x00010754 (immediately after the bx lr instruction) is 0x00021038, which is the address of Foo. Beginning at this memory location, Figure 2-2 shows the four values in array Foo. Note that the values in array Foo are stored using little-endian byte ordering.

```
Dump of assembler code for function TestLDR_:
   0x00010730 <+0>:    1c 10 9f e5  ldr r1, [pc, #28]  ;0x10754 <TestLDR_+36>
   0x00010734 <+4>:    00 20 91 e5  ldr r2, [r1]
   0x00010738 <+8>:    04 30 91 e5  ldr r3, [r1, #4]
   0x0001073c <+12>:   03 00 82 e0  add r0, r2, r3
   0x00010740 <+16>:   08 20 91 e5  ldr r2, [r1, #8]
   0x00010744 <+20>:   02 00 80 e0  add r0, r0, r2
   0x00010748 <+24>:   0c 20 91 e5  ldr r2, [r1, #12]
   0x0001074c <+28>:   02 00 80 e0  add r0, r0, r2
   0x00010750 <+32>:   1e ff 2f e1  bx  lr
   0x00010754 <+36>:   38 10 02 00 ◄──  Literal pool value
End of assembler dump.

Dump of Foo
   0x00021038          64 00 00 00        ;100
   0x0002103c          c8 00 00 00        ;200
   0x00021040          2c 01 00 00        ;300
   0x00021044          90 01 00 00        ;400
```

Figure 2-2. *GNU debugger log for function* TestLDR_

The section of memory where the assembler stored the address of Foo is called a literal pool. Whenever an A32 function uses the pseudo instruction ldr rx,=label (where RX is any general-purpose), the GNU assembler automatically creates a literal pool entry that contains the address of label. It then generates a substitute ldr rx,[pc,#offset] instruction that loads the address of label into RX. Note that the value of offset must be less than 4KB.

The GNU assembler automatically allocates space for a literal pool at the end of a .text section when one is needed. In large sections of code where the 4KB limit is problematic, the assembler directive .ltorg can be used to manually generate a literal pool. Extreme care must be employed when using the .ltorg directive to avoid intermixing literal pool data with executable code. The assembler also uses literal pools to support the loading of 32-bit constants using the ldr instruction (e.g., ldr r0,=0x12345678). You will see an example of this in the next section. Here is the output for source code example Ch02_04:

```
result = 1000
```

Move Instructions

Listing 2-5 shows the source code for example Ch02_05. This is the first of two examples that demonstrate various A32 move instructions. Like the previous example, the C++ source code for example Ch02_05 is not complicated. It simply exercises the test functions MoveImmA_, MoveImmB_, and MoveImmC_ and displays results.

Listing 2-5. Example Ch02_05

```cpp
//-------------------------------------------------
//                  Ch02_05.cpp
//-------------------------------------------------

#include <iostream>

using namespace std;

extern "C" int MoveImmA_(void);
extern "C" int MoveImmB_(void);
extern "C" int MoveImmC_(void);

int main(int argc, char** argv)
{
    int a = MoveImmA_();
    int b = MoveImmB_();
    int c = MoveImmC_();

    cout << "a = " << a << '\n';
    cout << "b = " << b << '\n';
    cout << "c = " << c << '\n';

    return 0;
}
```

```
//-------------------------------------------------
//                  Ch02_05_.s
//-------------------------------------------------

// extern "C" int MoveImmA_(void);

            .text
            .global MoveImmA_
MoveImmA_:

// Move immediate examples using unsigned integers
            mov r0,#25                  // r0 = 25
            mov r1,#1000                // r1 = 1000

            mov r2,#1001                // movw r2,#1001
            mov r3,#50000               // movw r3,#50000
            bx lr

// extern "C" int MoveImmB_(void);
```

```
          .global MoveImmB_
MoveImmB_:

// Move immediate example - 32-bit unsigned integers
          mov r0,#260096                      // r0 = 260096

// Move immediate example - invalid constant after fixup error

//        mov r1,#260097                      // invalid constant

// Alternative move immediate examples
          movw r1,#0xf801
          movt r1,#0x0003                     // r1 = 260097

          movw r2,#(260097 & 0xffff)
          movt r2,#(260097 >> 16)             // r2 = 260097

          ldr r3,=#260097                     // r3 = 260097
          bx lr


// extern "C" int MoveImmC_(void);

          .global MoveImmC_
MoveImmC_:

// Move immediate examples - negative numbers
          mov r0,#-57                         // mvn r0,#56
          mov r1,#-6401                       // mvn r1,#6400

// Move immediate example - invalid constant after fixup error

//        mov r1,#-1000                       // invalid constant

// Alternative move immediate examples
          movw r0,#0xfc18
          movt r0,#0xffff                     // r0 = -1000

          movw r1,#(-1000 & 0xffff)
          movt r1,#(-1000 >> 16)              // r1 = -1000

          ldr r2,=#-1000                      // r2 = -1000

          mvn r3,#1000
          add r3,#1                           // r3 = -1000
          bx lr
```

The first two instructions of function MoveImmA_, mov r0,#25 and mov r1,#1000, load constant values 25 and 1000 into registers R0 and R1, respectively. The next two instructions, mov r2,#1001 and mov r3,#50000, load 1001 and 50000 into their respective destination operands. The assembler translates these two mov instructions, which appear to be the same as the first two mov instructions, into movw instructions. The reason for this is that the A32 instruction set uses different mov instruction encodings that vary depending on the constant value. The movw instruction performs a straightforward copy of a 16-bit unsigned constant into the specified destination operand (the 16-bit constant is zero-extended to 32 bits during the move operation). The mov r0,#25 and mov r1,#1000 instructions use modified immediate constants. A modified immediate constant is a 32-bit wide integer value that is encoded in the instruction using only 12 bits.

Figure 2-3 illustrates the encoding scheme that is used to express a 32-bit wide constant using 12 bits. The top portion of this figure shows the hexadecimal instruction encoding for the mov r1,#1000 instruction, which is 0xE3A01FFA. The middle portion of Figure 2-3 displays this hexadecimal value in binary format. Toward the right are two boxed values, one labeled Rot and the other labeled RotValue. The processor generates the constant value 1000 by taking RotValue and performing a right rotate using a bit count that is equal to Rot * 2. This is illustrated in the bottom portion of Figure 2-3.

Instruction	Encoding		Rot	RotValue
mov r1,#1000	E3 A0 1F FA			
Binary encoding	1110 0011 1010 0000 0001		1111	1111 1010
Before rotate right 30	0000 0000 0000 0000 0000 0000 1111 1010			
After rotate right 30	0000 0000 0000 0000 0000 0011 1110 1000			

Figure 2-3. *Encoding of modified immediate constant 1000*

The advantage of the modified immediate constant scheme is that it permits frequently used 32-bit wide constants to be encoded using only 12 bits. When writing code, a single mov instruction is often the only instruction that is needed to load a 32-bit wide constant into a register, and the assembler will automatically generate any necessary modified immediate constant encodings or movw instruction substitutions. The drawback of this technique is that it does not support the loading of all possible 32-bit wide constants. A different approach is necessary to load constants that cannot be encoded in a single mov or movw instruction.

Returning to Listing 2-5, the first instruction of MoveImmB_ is a mov r0,#260096, which is another example of a mov instruction that uses a modified immediate constant as illustrated in Figure 2-4. Note that the next instruction, mov r1,#260097, is commented out. If you remove the comment and run make, the assembler will generate an "invalid constant (3f801) after fixup" error. The value 260097 is an example of a constant that cannot be loaded into a register using a single mov or movw instruction.

Instruction	Encoding			
mov r0,#260096	E3 A0 0B FE			
			Rot	RotValue
Binary encoding	1110 0011 1010 0000 0000			1011	1111 1110
Before rotate right 30	0000 0000 0000 0000 0000 0000 1111 1110			
After rotate right 30	0000 0000 0000 0011 1111 1000 0000 0000			

Figure 2-4. *Encoding of modified immediate constant 260096*

There are a few alternatives that can be used to load 260097 (0x0003F801) into R1. The first alternative uses a movw r1,#0xf801 instruction followed by a movt r1,#0x0003. The first movw instruction loads 0xF801 into R1 (recall that the movw instruction zero-extends the specified constant to 32 bits). The ensuing movt instruction loads 0x0003 into the upper 16 bits of R1 *without* modifying the lower 16 bits. This alternative achieves the required objective; however, using hexadecimal constants makes the code harder to understand in many cases.

The second alternative, movw r2,#(260097 & 0xffff) and movt r2,#(260097 >> 16), exploits the assembler's expression evaluator to load the required constant. With this method, the specified constant value is plainly visible, but the instruction sequence requires some extra expression text. Note that in these instructions, the # symbol is located before the parenthetical expression. The final alternative uses an ldr r3,=#260097 instruction, which generates a literal pool entry for the constant 260097 as described earlier in this chapter. This is clearly the easiest to type and read, but it is also the slowest since it requires the processor to perform an extra memory read operation (with the possibility of a cache miss) during execution. The ldr r3,=#260097 technique is convenient for a one-time initialization but should be avoided inside for-loops. For best performance, a sequential movw/movt instruction pair is the preferred method since Armv8 processors have been optimized to support this type of register load.

The final function in Listing 2-5 is MoveImmC_. This function demonstrates using various move instructions with negative numbers. The first instruction of MoveImmC_, mov r0,#-57, loads -57 into R0. In this statement, the assembler substitutes a mvn r0,#56 (move bitwise not) instruction, which loads the bitwise inverse of 56 (i.e., -57) into register R0. The next statement, mov r1,#-6401, loads -6401 into R1. The assembler also substitutes a mvn r1,#6400 instruction for this statement. Both substitute mvn instructions use the modified immediate constant encoding scheme that was described earlier. The commented out mov r1,#-1000 instruction contains a negative value that cannot be encoded using a modified immediate constant. If you remove the comment and run make, you will get an "invalid constant (fffffc18) after fixup" error.

The code block that follows demonstrates several alternatives that load -1000 into register R0. The first alternative uses the instruction sequence movw r0,#0xfc18 and movt r0,#0xffff to load 0xFFFFFC18 (or -1000) into register R0. The next instruction sequence, movw r1,#(-1000 & 0xffff) and movt r1,#(-1000 >> 16), exploits the assembler's expression evaluator that makes the code easier to read. The third alternative uses a ldr r2,=#-1000 instruction. The previously described advantages and disadvantages of using a sequential movw/movt pair vs. a ldr instruction also apply here. The fourth alternative uses an mvn r3,#1000 instruction followed by add r3,#1 instruction to load -1000 into R3. This instruction sequence calculates the two's complement representation for -1000. Here is the output for source code example Ch02_05:

```
a = 25
b = 260096
c = -1000
```

Many A32 arithmetic and logical instructions also use modified immediate constants. For example, the instruction add r1,r0,#260096 uses such an encoding. If a function needs to add a constant that cannot be encoded using a modified immediate constant, a separate movw instruction or a movw/movt instruction pair will be needed to load the constant into a register prior to the arithmetic operation. Source code example Ch02_07 demonstrates this type of usage, which appears later in this chapter.

Listing 2-6 show the source code for example Ch02_06. This example explains how to use the mov instruction to perform shift and rotate operations. Toward the top of the C++ file are the declarations for the assembly language functions MoveRegA_ and MoveRegB_. Note that these functions include an argument of type unsigned int* that points to a small results array. The declarations for the C++ functions that print results are next. The source code for these functions is not shown in Listing 2-6 but is included with the downloadable source code package (see Appendix A for more information). The C++ function main contains code that exercises the functions MoveRegA_ and MoveRegB_ using test data.

Listing 2-6. Example Ch02_06

```cpp
//-----------------------------------------------
//                 Ch02_06.cpp
//-----------------------------------------------

#include <iostream>

using namespace std;

// Ch02_06_.s
extern "C" void MoveRegA_(unsigned int a, unsigned int* b);
extern "C" void MoveRegB_(unsigned int a, unsigned int* b, unsigned int count);

// Ch02_06_Misc.cpp
extern void PrintResultA(const char* msg, unsigned int a, const unsigned int* b, size_t n);
extern void PrintResultB(const char* msg, unsigned int a, const unsigned int* b, size_t n,
size_t count);

int main(int argc, char** argv)
{
    // Exercise function MoveRegA_
    const size_t n = 5;

    unsigned int a1 = 0x12345678;
    unsigned int b1[5];
    MoveRegA_(a1, b1);
    PrintResultA("MoveRegA_ Test Case #1", a1, b1, n);

    unsigned int a2 = 0xfedcba91;
    unsigned int b2[n];
    MoveRegA_(a2, b2);
    PrintResultA("MoveRegA_ Test Case #2", a2, b2, n);
    cout << "\n";
```

```
          // Exercise function MoveRegB_
          const size_t nn = 4;
          const size_t count = 8;

          unsigned int a3 = 0x12345678;
          unsigned int b3[nn];
          MoveRegB_(a3, b3, count);
          PrintResultB("MoveRegB_ Test Case #1", a3, b3, nn, count);

          unsigned int a4 = 0xfedcba91;
          unsigned int b4[nn];
          MoveRegB_(a4, b4, count);
          PrintResultB("MoveRegB_ Test Case #2", a4, b4, nn, count);

          return 0;
      }

//-------------------------------------------------
//                    Ch02_06_.s
//-------------------------------------------------

// extern "C" void MoveRegA_(void a, unsigned int* b);

              .text
              .global MoveRegA_
MoveRegA_:
              push {r4-r7}

// Register to register move
              mov r7,r1                       // copy value in r1 to r7

// Register moves with shift/rotate operator
              mov r2,r0,asr #2                 // arithmetic shift right
              mov r3,r0,lsl #4                 // logical shift left
              mov r4,r0,lsr #5                 // logical shift right
              mov r5,r0,ror #3                 // rotate right
              mov r6,r0,rrx                    // rotate right extended

              str r2,[r7]                      // save asr result to b[0]
              str r3,[r7,#4]                   // save lsl result to b[1]
              str r4,[r7,#8]                   // save lsr result to b[2]
              str r5,[r7,#12]                  // save ror result to b[3]
              str r6,[r7,#16]                  // save rrx result to b[4]

              pop {r4-r7}
              bx lr

// extern "C" void MoveRegB_(unsigned int a, unsigned int* b, unsigned int count);

              .global MoveRegB_
MoveRegB_:
```

```
          push {r4-r6}

// Register moves with shift/rotate operator
          mov r3,r0,asr r2              // arithmetic shift right
          mov r4,r0,lsl r2              // logical shift left
          mov r5,r0,lsr r2             // logical shift right
          mov r6,r0,ror r2              // rotate right

          str r3,[r1]                  // save asr result to b[0]
          str r4,[r1,#4]               // save lsl result to b[1]
          str r5,[r1,#8]               // save lsr result to b[2]
          str r6,[r1,#12]              // save ror result to b[3]

          pop {r4-r6}
          bx lr
```

The function MoveRegA_ begins with a push {r4-r7} instruction that saves non-volatile registers R4, R5, R6, and R7 on the stack. Recall from the discussions earlier in this chapter that a function must preserve the contents of any non-volatile register it uses. Subsequent to the mov r7,r1 instruction, which copies the value in R1 (argument b) into R7, is the instruction mov r2,r0,asr #2. This instruction performs an arithmetic shift right of the contents in R0 (argument value a) by two bits and saves the result in R2. Execution of this instruction does not alter the value in R0.

The next instruction, mov r3,r0,lsl #4, shifts left R0 by four bits and saves the result to R3. The next three instructions, mov r4,r0,lsr #5, mov r5,r0,ror #3, and mov r6,r0,rrx, carry out logical shift right (lsr), rotate right (ror), and rotate right extended (rrx) operations. The rrx operator differs from the ror instruction in that it includes the carry condition flag as part of the rotation. The rrx operator also does not support a bit count operand; it always performs a single bit rotation. Function MoveRegA_ then uses a series of str instructions that save the results of each shift/rotate operation. Note that each str instruction employs offset addressing. A pop {r4-r7} instruction restores the previously saved non-volatile registers from the stack before program control is returned to the caller.

The assembly language function MoveRegB_ also uses various forms of the mov instruction to carry out shift and rotate operations. This function differs slightly from MoveRegA_ in that the bit count is included as one of the arguments. Following the push {r4-r7} operation, the instruction mov r3,r0,asr r2 performs an arithmetic shift right of R0 that uses the value in R2 for the bit count. Execution of this instruction does not alter the value in either R0 or R2. The next three instructions illustrate logical shift left, logical shift right, and rotate right operations using the value in R2 as the bit count. The A32 instruction set does not support rotate right extended operations using a register shift count. Here is the output for source code example Ch02_06:

```
MoveRegA_ Test Case #1
a:      0x12345678 | 0001 0010 0011 0100 0101 0110 0111 1000 |
b[0]: 0x048d159e | 0000 0100 1000 1101 0001 0101 1001 1110 | asr #2
b[1]: 0x23456780 | 0010 0011 0100 0101 0110 0111 1000 0000 | lsl #4
b[2]: 0x0091a2b3 | 0000 0000 1001 0001 1010 0010 1011 0011 | lsr #5
b[3]: 0x02468acf | 0000 0010 0100 0110 1000 1010 1100 1111 | ror #3
b[4]: 0x891a2b3c | 1000 1001 0001 1010 0010 1011 0011 1100 | rrx

MoveRegA_ Test Case #2
a:      0xfedcba91 | 1111 1110 1101 1100 1011 1010 1001 0001 |
b[0]: 0xffb72ea4 | 1111 1111 1011 0111 0010 1110 1010 0100 | asr #2
b[1]: 0xedcba910 | 1110 1101 1100 1011 1010 1001 0001 0000 | lsl #4
b[2]: 0x07f6e5d4 | 0000 0111 1111 0110 1110 0101 1101 0100 | lsr #5
b[3]: 0x3fdb9752 | 0011 1111 1101 1011 1001 0111 0101 0010 | ror #3
b[4]: 0xff6e5d48 | 1111 1111 0110 1110 0101 1101 0100 1000 | rrx

MoveRegB_ Test Case #1 - count = 8
a:      0x12345678 | 0001 0010 0011 0100 0101 0110 0111 1000 |
b[0]: 0x00123456 | 0000 0000 0001 0010 0011 0100 0101 0110 | asr
b[1]: 0x34567800 | 0011 0100 0101 0110 0111 1000 0000 0000 | lsl
b[2]: 0x00123456 | 0000 0000 0001 0010 0011 0100 0101 0110 | lsr
b[3]: 0x78123456 | 0111 1000 0001 0010 0011 0100 0101 0110 | ror

MoveRegB_ Test Case #2 - count = 8
a:      0xfedcba91 | 1111 1110 1101 1100 1011 1010 1001 0001 |
b[0]: 0xfffedcba | 1111 1111 1111 1110 1101 1100 1011 1010 | asr
b[1]: 0xdcba9100 | 1101 1100 1011 1010 1001 0001 0000 0000 | lsl
b[2]: 0x00fedcba | 0000 0000 1111 1110 1101 1100 1011 1010 | lsr
b[3]: 0x91fedcba | 1001 0001 1111 1110 1101 1100 1011 1010 | ror
```

The A32 instruction set defines several alias instructions that can be used to perform shift/rotate operations. The alias instructions use the mov instruction shift/rotate operators as instruction mnemonics, which makes source code easier to read. Table 2-3 lists these alias instructions. Finally, source operand shift/rotate operators can also be used with many A32 arithmetic instructions such as add and sub. You will see examples of this usage type in Chapter 4.

Table 2-3. *A32 shift and rotate alias instructions*

Alias Instruction	Move Instruction	Operation
asr r2,r1,#imm	mov r2,r1,asr #imm	Arithmetic shift right
asr r2,r1,r0	mov r2,r1,asr r0	Arithmetic shift right
lsl r2,r1,#imm	mov r2,r1,lsl #imm	Logical shift left
lsl r2,r1,r0	mov r2,r1,lsl r0	Logical shift left
lsr r2,r1,#imm	mov r2,r1,lsr #imm	Logical shift right
lsr r2,r1,r0	mov r2,r1,lsr r0	Logical shift right
ror r2,r1,#imm	mov r2,r1,ror #imm	Rotate right
ror r2,r1,r0	mov r2,r1,ror r0	Rotate right
rrx r2,r1	mov r2,r2,rrx	Rotate right extended

Bitwise Logical Operations

The final source code example in this chapter shows how to perform bitwise logical operations such as AND, OR, and exclusive OR. Listing 2-7 shows the source code for example Ch02_07.

Listing 2-7. Example Ch02_07

```cpp
//--------------------------------------------------
//                 Ch02_07.cpp
//--------------------------------------------------

#include <iostream>

using namespace std;

// Ch02_07_.s
extern "C" void TestBitOpsA_(unsigned int a, unsigned int b, unsigned int* c);
extern "C" void TestBitOpsB_(unsigned int a, unsigned int* b);

// Ch02_07_Misc.cpp
extern void PrintResultA(const char* msg, unsigned int a, unsigned int b, const unsigned
int* c, size_t n);
extern void PrintResultB(const char* msg, unsigned int a, const unsigned int* b, size_t n);

int main(int argc, char** argv)
{
    // Exercise function TestBitOpsA_
    const size_t n = 3;
    unsigned int a1 = 0x12345678;
    unsigned int b1 = 0xaa55aa55;
    unsigned int c1[n];
    TestBitOpsA_(a1, b1, c1);
    PrintResultA("TestBitOpsA_ Test Case #1", a1, b1, c1, n);

    unsigned int a2 = 0x12345678;
    unsigned int b2 = 0x00ffc384;
    unsigned int c2[n];
    TestBitOpsA_(a2, b2, c2);
    PrintResultA("TestBitOpsA_ Test Case #2", a2, b2, c2, n);

    cout << "\n";

    // Exercise function TestBitOpsB_
    const size_t nn = 4;
    unsigned int a3 = 0x12345678;
    unsigned int b3[nn];
    TestBitOpsB_(a3, b3);
    PrintResultB("TestBitOpsB_ Test Case #1", a3, b3, nn);

    unsigned int a4 = 0xaa55aa55;
    unsigned int b4[nn];
    TestBitOpsB_(a4, b4);
```

```
    PrintResultB("TestBitOpsB_ Test Case #2", a4, b4, nn);

    return 0;
}
```

The C++ code in Listing 2-7 includes code that initializes a few test cases and exercises the assembly language functions TestBitOpsA_ and TestBitOpsB_. Note that Listing 2-7 does not show the C++ code for the print functions, but this code is included with the downloadable software package. The first assembly function in Listing 2-7, TestBitOpsA_, illustrates the use of the and (bitwise AND), orr (bitwise OR), and eor (bitwise exclusive OR) instructions. The and r3,r0,r1 instruction performs a bitwise AND of argument values a and b. The ensuing str r3,[r2] instruction saves the result to c[0]. The function TestBitOpsA_ then uses similar instruction sequences to carry out bitwise OR and bitwise exclusive OR operations.

The function TestBitOpsB_ also illustrates the use of the and, orr, and eor instructions, but uses a constant value instead of a register for the second operand. The and r2,r0,#0x0000ff00 instruction performs a bitwise AND of argument a and the constant value 0x0000FF00. The machine language encoding for this instruction uses a modified immediate constant as described earlier in this chapter. The same is true for the subsequent orr r3,r0,#0x00ff0000 and eor r4,r0,#0xff000000 instructions. If you remove the comment from the and r5,r0,#0x00ffff00 instruction and run make, you will get an "invalid constant (ffff00) after fixup" error message. Like the earlier examples of this chapter, the modified immediate constant scheme is unable to encode 0x00FFFF00. Instead, TestBitOpsA_ uses two instructions, movw r5,#0xff00 and movt r5,#0x00ff, to load the required constant into R5. The ensuing and r6,r0,r5 instruction then performs the bitwise AND. Here are the results for source code example Ch02_07:

```
TestBitOpsA_ Test Case #1
a:     0x12345678 | 0001 0010 0011 0100 0101 0110 0111 1000
b:     0xaa55aa55 | 1010 1010 0101 0101 1010 1010 0101 0101
c[0]: 0x02140250 | 0000 0010 0001 0100 0000 0010 0101 0000 a & b
c[1]: 0xba75fe7d | 1011 1010 0111 0101 1111 1110 0111 1101 a | b
c[2]: 0xb861fc2d | 1011 1000 0110 0001 1111 1100 0010 1101 a ^ b

TestBitOpsA_ Test Case #2
a:     0x12345678 | 0001 0010 0011 0100 0101 0110 0111 1000
b:     0x00ffc384 | 0000 0000 1111 1111 1100 0011 1000 0100
c[0]: 0x00344200 | 0000 0000 0011 0100 0100 0010 0000 0000 a & b
c[1]: 0x12ffd7fc | 0001 0010 1111 1111 1101 0111 1111 1100 a | b
c[2]: 0x12cb95fc | 0001 0010 1100 1011 1001 0101 1111 1100 a ^ b

TestBitOpsB_ Test Case #1
a:     0x12345678 | 0001 0010 0011 0100 0101 0110 0111 1000
b[0]: 0x00005600 | 0000 0000 0000 0000 0101 0110 0000 0000 a & 0x0000ff00
b[1]: 0x12ff5678 | 0001 0010 1111 1111 0101 0110 0111 1000 a | 0x00ff0000
b[2]: 0xed345678 | 1110 1101 0011 0100 0101 0110 0111 1000 a ^ 0xff000000
b[3]: 0x00345600 | 0000 0000 0011 0100 0101 0110 0000 0000 a & 0x00ffff00

TestBitOpsB_ Test Case #2
a:     0xaa55aa55 | 1010 1010 0101 0101 1010 1010 0101 0101
b[0]: 0x0000aa00 | 0000 0000 0000 0000 1010 1010 0000 0000 a & 0x0000ff00
b[1]: 0xaaffaa55 | 1010 1010 1111 1111 1010 1010 0101 0101 a | 0x00ff0000
b[2]: 0x5555aa55 | 0101 0101 0101 0101 1010 1010 0101 0101 a ^ 0xff000000
b[3]: 0x0055aa00 | 0000 0000 0101 0101 1010 1010 0000 0000 a & 0x00ffff00
```

Summary

Here are the key learning points for Chapter 2:

- The add and sub instructions perform integer addition and subtraction.

- The mul instruction multiplies two 32-bit wide integers and saves low-order 32 bits of the multiplicative product.

- The smull and umull instructions multiply 32-bit wide signed and unsigned integers, respectively, and save the entire 64-bit multiplicative product.

- The sdiv and udiv instructions perform 32-bit signed and unsigned integer division.

- The ldr rx,=label is a pseudo instruction that loads the address of label into RX. It also generates a literal pool entry for label.

- A function can use the mov, movw, movt, and mvn instructions to load a constant value into a register. A two-instruction sequence may be required depending on the specific constant.

- The asr, lsl, and lsr alias instructions perform arithmetic and logical shift operations. The ror and rrx alias instructions carry out rotate right operations.

- The asr, lsl, lsr, and ror operators can be applied to the second operand of many A32 instructions.

- The GNU assembler uses the .text and .data directives to designate code and data sections in an assembly language file. A function must use the .global directive to designate a function or variable as public. The .word directive allocates and initializes a 32-bit integer value.

- The GNU C++ calling convention requires a function caller to pass its first four integer (or pointer) arguments in registers R0, R1, R2, and R3. Any remaining arguments are passed via the stack. A called function must use R0 for a 32-bit return value and register pair R0:R1 for a 64-bit return value.

- The GNU C++ calling convention designates registers R0–R3 and R12 as volatile and need not be preserved by a called function. Registers R4–R10, FP, SP, and LR are volatile and must be preserved.

- Assembly language functions must be declared using the extern "C" modifier to disable generation of decorated C++ function names.

CHAPTER 3

■ ■ ■

Armv8-32 Core Programming – Part 2

In the previous chapter, you learned how to perform simple integer arithmetic including addition, subtraction, multiplication, and division in an assembly language function. You also learned how to use common assembler directives and basic details of the GNU C++ calling convention. Finally, you studied important particulars of various data load, move, and store instructions.

In this chapter, you will continue learning about the fundamentals of Armv8-32 assembly language programming. The first section explains how to access function arguments that are passed via the stack. The second section covers advanced stack use including allocating space for local variables and using frame pointers. The third and final section examines using the APSR condition flags to perform branching operations and implement for-loops.

Stack Arguments

The source code examples that you have seen thus far used a maximum of four argument values. These arguments are always passed in registers R0, R1, R2, and R3. The source examples of this section demonstrate how to access and use additional arguments that are passed via the stack. The first example illustrates passing 32-bit integers via the stack. The second source example extends this to include a mix of different integer sizes.

Basic Stack Arguments

Listing 3-1 shows the source code for example Ch03_01. This example illustrates basic stack usage using 32-bit wide integers. It also explains how to use the .equ (equate) directive.

Listing 3-1. Example Ch03_01

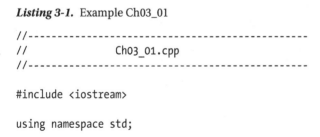

```
//------------------------------------------------
//              Ch03_01.cpp
//------------------------------------------------

#include <iostream>

using namespace std;
```

D. Kusswurm, *Modern Arm Assembly Language Programming*,
https://doi.org/10.1007/978-1-4842-6267-2_3

```cpp
extern "C" int SumSquares_(int a, int b, int c, int d, int e, int f, int g);

void PrintResult(const char* msg, int a, int b, int c, int d, int e, int f, int g, int sum)
{
    const char nl = '\n';
    const char* sep = " | ";

    cout << msg << nl;
    cout << "a = " << a << sep;
    cout << "b = " << b << sep;
    cout << "c = " << c << sep;
    cout << "d = " << d << nl;
    cout << "e = " << e << sep;
    cout << "f = " << f << sep;
    cout << "g = " << g << sep;
    cout << "sum= " << sum << nl;
    cout << nl;
}

int main(int argc, char** argv)
{
    int a, b, c, d, e, f, g, sum;

    a = 10; b = 20; c = 30; d = 40;
    e = 50; f = 60; g = 70;
    sum = SumSquares_(a, b, c, d, e, f, g);
    PrintResult("SumSquares - Test Case #1", a, b, c, d, e, f, g, sum);

    a = 10; b = -200; c = 30; d = 40;
    e = -500; f = 60; g = -700;
    sum = SumSquares_(a, b, c, d, e, f, g);
    PrintResult("SumSquares - Test Case #2", a, b, c, d, e, f, g, sum);

}

//--------------------------------------------------
//              Ch03_01_.s
//--------------------------------------------------

// extern "C" int SumSquares_(int a, int b, int c, int d, int e,
//       int f, int g);

            .equ ARG_E,0                    // stack offset for e
            .equ ARG_F,4                    // stack offset for f
            .equ ARG_G,8                    // stack offset for g

            .text
            .global SumSquares_
SumSquares_:
```

```
mul r0,r0,r0            // r0 = a * a
mul r1,r1,r1            // r1 = b * b
add r0,r0,r1            // r0 = a * a + b * b

mul r2,r2,r2            // r2 = c * c
mul r3,r3,r3            // r3 = d * d
add r2,r2,r3            // r2 = c * c + d * d

add r0,r0,r2            // r0 = intermediate sum

ldr r1,[sp,#ARG_E]      // r1 = e
mul r1,r1,r1            // r1 = e * e
add r0,r0,r1            // r0 = intermediate sum

ldr r1,[sp,#ARG_F]      // r1 = f
mul r1,r1,r1            // r1 = f * f
add r0,r0,r1            // r0 = intermediate sum

ldr r1,[sp,#ARG_G]      // r1 = g
mul r1,r1,r1            // r1 = g * g
add r0,r0,r1            // r0 = final sum

bx lr
```

Toward the top of Listing 3-1 is the declaration for the assembly language function SumSquares_. Note that this function requires seven argument values of type int. The remaining C++ code in Listing 3-1 initializes a test case, calls SumSquares_, and prints the result.

The assembly language code begins with a series of statements that contain .equ directives. This directive assigns the value of a constant expression to a symbolic name. For example, the statement .equ ARG_E,0 assigns the value 0 to the symbolic name ARG_E. Whenever ARG_E appears in a subsequent instruction, the assembler will substitute the value 0. The .equ directive that is used here is analogous to the C++ preprocessor statement #define ARG_E 0. The subsequent .equ directives assign 4 to ARG_F and 8 to ARG_G. All of these .equ directive constants represent offsets for the argument values that are passed via the stack.

Figure 3-1 shows the argument values that are passed to SumSquares_. Like the examples you saw in Chapter 2, the first four argument values a, b, c, and d are passed in registers R0, R1, R2, and R3, respectively. The remaining three argument values, e, f, and g, are passed via the stack. Note that upon entry to function SumSquares_, the SP register points to the first argument value passed via the stack. The remaining stack arguments are located at fixed offsets from the SP register.

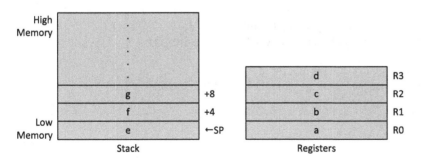

Figure 3-1. *Argument registers and stack content at entry to function SumSquares_*

The function SumSquares_ sums the squares of its argument values. The first instruction, mul r0,r0,r0, calculates a * a. This is followed by a mul r1,r1,r1 instruction that calculates b * b. Execution of the ensuing add r0,r0,r1 instruction yields a * a + b * b. SumSquares_ then uses similar sequences of mul and add instructions to calculate c * c + d * d. This is followed by an add r0,r0,r2 instruction that updates the intermediate sum in R0.

The ldr r1,[sp,#ARG_E] instruction loads argument value e into register R1. This instruction uses offset addressing with SP as the base register. Like the examples you saw in Chapter 2, the processor calculates the memory address for the load by summing the contents SP and the constant value ARG_E. Note that this instruction uses the constant prefix operator # before the symbolic name ARG_E. Following the load operation, the instructions mul r1,r1,r1 and add r0,r0,r1 calculate e * e and add it to the intermediate sum in R0. A similar chain of instructions is then used to calculate f * f, g * g, and the final sum. Here is the output for example Ch03_01:

```
SumSquares - Test Case #1
a = 10 | b = 20 | c = 30 | d = 40
e = 50 | f = 60 | g = 70 | sum= 14000

SumSquares - Test Case #2
a = 10 | b = -200 | c = 30 | d = 40
e = -500 | f = 60 | g = -700 | sum= 786200
```

Stack Arguments Using Mixed Integers

The next source code example is named Ch03_02. This example explains how to load stack arguments for a function that uses an assorted mix of integer types. It also demonstrates the use of additional load instructions and the mla (multiply accumulate) instruction. Listing 3-2 shows the C++ and assembly language source code for example Ch03_02.

Listing 3-2. Example Ch03_02

```
//----------------------------------------------------
//                  Ch03_02.cpp
//----------------------------------------------------

#include <iostream>
#include <iomanip>

using namespace std;

extern "C" int SumCubes_(unsigned char a, short b, int c, int d,
    signed char e, short f, unsigned char g, unsigned short h, int i);

int SumCubes(unsigned char a, short b, int c, int d,
    signed char e, short f, unsigned char g, unsigned short h, int i)
{
    int aa = (int)a * a * a;
    int bb = (int)b * b * b;
    int cc = c * c * c;
    int dd = d * d * d;
    int ee = (int)e * e * e;
```

```
    int ff = (int)f * f * f;
    int gg = (int)g * g * g;
    int hh = (int)h * h * h;
    int ii = i * i * i;

    return aa + bb + cc + dd + ee + ff + gg + hh + ii;
}

void PrintResult(const char* msg, int a, int b, int c, int d, int e,
    int f, int g, int h, int i, int sum1, int sum2)
{
    const char nl = '\n';
    const char* sep = " | ";
    const size_t w = 6;

    cout << msg << nl;
    cout << "a = " << setw(w) << a << sep;
    cout << "b = " << setw(w) << b << sep;
    cout << "c = " << setw(w) << c << sep;
    cout << "d = " << setw(w) << d << sep;
    cout << "e = " << setw(w) << e << nl;
    cout << "f = " << setw(w) << f << sep;
    cout << "g = " << setw(w) << g << sep;
    cout << "h = " << setw(w) << h << sep;
    cout << "i = " << setw(w) << i << nl;
    cout << "sum1 = " << setw(w) << sum1 << nl;
    cout << "sum2 = " << setw(w) << sum2 << nl;

    if (sum1 != sum2)
        cout << "Compare error!\n";

    cout << nl;
}

int main(int argc, char** argv)
{
    unsigned char a;
    short b, f;
    int c, d, i, sum1, sum2;
    signed char e;
    unsigned char g;
    unsigned short h;

    a = 10; b = -20; c = 30; d = -40;
    e = -50; f = -60; g = 70, h = 80, i = 90;
    sum1 = SumCubes(a, b, c, d, e, f, g, h, i);
    sum2 = SumCubes_(a, b, c, d, e, f, g, h, i);
    PrintResult("SumCubes - Test Case #1", a, b, c, d, e, f, g, h, i, sum1, sum2);

    a = 10; b = -20; c = -30; d = 40;
    e = -50; f = 60; g = 70, h = 80, i = -90;
```

```
    sum1 = SumCubes(a, b, c, d, e, f, g, h, i);
    sum2 = SumCubes_(a, b, c, d, e, f, g, h, i);
    PrintResult("SumCubes - Test Case #2", a, b, c, d, e, f, g, h, i, sum1, sum2);

    a = -100; b = 200; c = 300; d = 400;
    e = 50; f = -600; g = 70, h = 800, i = -900;
    sum1 = SumCubes(a, b, c, d, e, f, g, h, i);
    sum2 = SumCubes_(a, b, c, d, e, f, g, h, i);
    PrintResult("SumCubes - Test Case #3", a, b, c, d, e, f, g, h, i, sum1, sum2);
}


//-------------------------------------------------
//              Ch03_02_.s
//-------------------------------------------------

// extern "C" int SumCubes_(unsigned char a, short b, int c, int d,
//     signed char e, short f, unsigned char g, unsigned short h, int i);

            .equ ARG_E, 8               // stack offset for e
            .equ ARG_F, 12              // stack offset for f
            .equ ARG_G, 16              // stack offset for g
            .equ ARG_H, 20              // stack offset for h
            .equ ARG_I, 24              // stack offset for i

            .text
            .global SumCubes_
SumCubes_:  push {r4,r5}

            mul r4,r0,r0                // r4 = a * a
            mul r0,r4,r0                // r0 = a * a * a

            mul r4,r1,r1                // r4 = b * b
            mla r0,r4,r1,r0             // r0 += b * b * b

            mul r4,r2,r2                // r4 = c * c
            mla r0,r4,r2,r0             // r0 += c * c * c

            mul r4,r3,r3                // r4 = d * d
            mla r0,r4,r3,r0             // r0 += d * d * d

            ldrsb r1,[sp,#ARG_E]        // r1 = e (sign-extended)
            mul r4,r1,r1                // r4 = e * e
            mla r0,r4,r1,r0             // r0 += e * e * e

            ldrsh r1,[sp,#ARG_F]        // r1 = f (sign-extended)
            mul r4,r1,r1                // r4 = f * f
            mla r0,r4,r1,r0             // r0 += f * f * f

            ldrb r1,[sp,#ARG_G]         // r1 = g (zero-extended)
            mul r4,r1,r1                // r4 = g * g
            mla r0,r4,r1,r0             // r0 += g * g * g
```

```
ldrh r1,[sp,#ARG_H]          // r1 = h (zero-extended)
mul r4,r1,r1                 // r4 = h * h
mla r0,r4,r1,r0              // r0 += h * h * h

ldr r1,[sp,#ARG_I]           // r1 = i
mul r4,r1,r1                 // r4 = i * i
mla r0,r4,r1,r0              // r0 += i * i * i

pop {r4,r5}
bx lr
```

The C++ code begins with the declaration of assembly language function SumCubes_. Note that this function requires a mix of assorted integer arguments, both signed and unsigned. The C++ counterpart of this function, SumCubes, is next. This function is included to verify the accuracy of SumCubes_. The remaining C++ code performs test case initialization and displays the results.

Like the previous example, the assembly language code begins with a series of .equ directives that define offsets for the arguments that are passed via the stack. Unlike the previous example, the offset for the first argument e is 8 instead of 0. The reason for this is that the function SumCubes_ preserves non-volatile registers R4 and R5 on the stack per the requirements of the GNU C++ calling convention. This affects the offsets for the argument values on the stack. Figure 3-2 illustrates the stack in greater detail. Note that in this figure, each stack argument value is aligned on a word boundary.

The GNU C++ calling convention applies two distinct rules when passing 8-bit and 16-bit integer arguments to a function. Argument values that are passed in a register are always sign- or zero-extended to 32 bits. In the current example, this means that registers R0 and R1 contain 32-bit values for arguments unsigned char a and short b. Argument values passed via the stack are *not* sign- or zero-extended. Figure 3-2 illustrates this using a darker shading pattern. These darker areas of the stack contain undefined values.

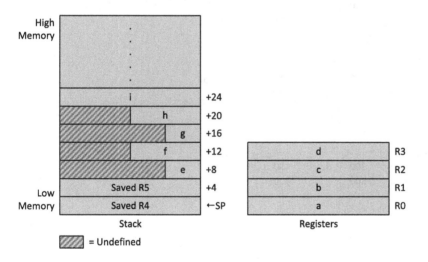

Figure 3-2. *Argument registers and stack content following execution of the push {r4,r5} instruction in function SumCubes_*

The function SubCubes_ sums the cubes of its argument values. Following preservation of non-volatile registers R4 and R5 on the stack using a push {r4,r5} instruction, the instructions mul r4,r0,r0 and mul r0,r4,r0 calculate a * a * a. The next instruction, mul r4,r1,r1, calculates b * b. This is followed by a mla r0,r4,r1,r0 instruction. The mla instruction is a four-operand instruction that multiplies the first source operand R4 (b * b) by the second source operand R1 (b). It then sums this product with the third source operand R0 (a * a * a). The result of the summation is then copied to the destination operand, which also happens to be R0. Following execution of this mul/mla instruction sequence, R0 contains a * a * a + b * b * b. SubCubes_ then uses two more mul/mla instruction pairs to calculate c * c * c and d * d * d; it then updates the intermediate cube sum that is maintained in R0.

SubCubes_ cannot use the ldr instruction to load argument values e, f, g, and h from the stack since this instruction loads only word values. These argument values must be loaded from the stack and either sign- or zero-extended to carry out the required calculations. The ldrsb r1,[sp,#ARG_E] (load register signed byte) instruction loads signed char e from the stack, sign-extends it to 32 bits, and saves the result in R1. The ensuing mul/mla instruction sequence then calculates e * e * e and adds it to the intermediate cube sum in R0. The ldrsh r1,[sp,#ARG_F] instruction (load register signed halfword) loads short f from the stack, sign-extends it to 32 bits, and saves the result in R1. And you would be correct if you guessed that another mul/mla instruction sequence calculates f * f * f and adds it to the intermediate cube sum in R0.

Argument values unsigned char g and unsigned short h are processed in a similar manner using the instructions ldrb (load register byte) and ldrh (load register halfword), respectively. The ldrb r1,[sp,#ARG_G] instruction loads g from the stack, zero-extends it to 32 bits, and saves the result in R1. The ldrh r1,[sp,#ARG_H] instruction loads h and zero-extends it to 32 bits before saving it in R1. The final argument value i is loaded using a ldr r1,[sp,#ARG_I] instruction since it is an int. Three more mul/mla instruction pairs calculate and sum the cubes for argument values g, h, and i. Here is the output for source code example Ch03_02:

```
SumCubes - Test Case #1
a =      10 | b =     -20 | c =      30 | d =     -40 | e =     -50
f =     -60 | g =      70 | h =      80 | i =      90
sum1 = 1199000
sum2 = 1199000

SumCubes - Test Case #2
a =      10 | b =     -20 | c =     -30 | d =      40 | e =     -50
f =      60 | g =      70 | h =      80 | i =     -90
sum1 = 247000
sum2 = 247000

SumCubes - Test Case #3
a =     156 | b =     200 | c =     300 | d =     400 | e =      50
f =    -600 | g =      70 | h =     800 | i =    -900
sum1 = -329735584
sum2 = -329735584
```

Advance Stack Use

In the previous section, you learned how to access and use argument values passed via the stack. A function can also use the stack to store intermediate results. In this section, you will learn how to do this. You will also learn how to use a stack frame pointer.

Stack Use with Local Storage

Listing 3-3 shows the source code for example Ch03_03. This example demonstrates how to allocate and use local variables on the stack.

Listing 3-3. Example Ch03_03

```cpp
//-------------------------------------------------
//                  Ch03_03.cpp
//-------------------------------------------------

#include <iostream>
#include <iomanip>

using namespace std;

extern "C" void LocalVarsA_(int a, int b, int c, int d, int e, int f,
    int* g, int* h);

void LocalVarsA(int a, int b, int c, int d, int e, int f, int* g, int* h)
{
    int temp0 = a + b + c;
    int temp1 = d + e + f;
    int temp2 = a + c + e;
    int temp3 = b + d + f;

    *g = temp0 * temp1;
    *h = temp2 * temp3;
}

void PrintResult(const char* msg, int a, int b, int c, int d, int e,
    int f, int g1, int g2, int h1, int h2)
{
    const char nl = '\n';
    const char* sep = " | ";
    const size_t w = 8;

    cout << msg << nl;
    cout << "a =  " << setw(w) << a << sep;
    cout << "b =  " << setw(w) << b << sep;
    cout << "c =  " << setw(w) << c << nl;
    cout << "d =  " << setw(w) << d << sep;
    cout << "e =  " << setw(w) << e << sep;
    cout << "f =  " << setw(w) << f << nl;
    cout << "g1 = " << setw(w) << g1 << sep;
    cout << "g2 = " << setw(w) << g2 << nl;
    cout << "h1 = " << setw(w) << h1 << sep;
    cout << "h2 = " << setw(w) << h2 << nl;

    if (g1 != g2 || h1 != h2)
        cout << "Compare Error!\n";
    cout << nl;
}
```

```c
int main(int argc, char** argv)
{
    int a, b, c, d, e, f, g1, g2, h1, h2;

    // Test Case #1
    a = 10; b = -20; c = 30; d = -40; e = -50; f = -60;
    LocalVarsA(a, b, c, d, e, f, &g1, &h1);
    LocalVarsA_(a, b, c, d, e, f, &g2, &h2);

    PrintResult("Test Case #1", a, b, c, d, e, f,
        g1, g2, h1, h2);

    // Test Case #2
    a = 100; b = -200; c = 300; d = -400; e = -500; f = -600;
    LocalVarsA(a, b, c, d, e, f, &g1, &h1);
    LocalVarsA_(a, b, c, d, e, f, &g2, &h2);

    PrintResult("Test Case #2", a, b, c, d, e, f,
        g1, g2, h1, h2);

    return 0;
}
```

```asm
//---------------------------------------------------
//                  Ch03_03_.s
//---------------------------------------------------

// extern "C" void LocalVarsA_(int a, int b, int c, int d, int e, int f, int* g, int* h)

            .equ ARG_E,32                       // sp offset for e
            .equ ARG_F,36                       // sp offset for f
            .equ ARG_G,40                       // sp offset for g
            .equ ARG_H,44                       // sp offset for h

            .equ TEMP0,0                        // sp offset for temp0
            .equ TEMP1,4                        // sp offset for temp1
            .equ TEMP2,8                        // sp offset for temp2
            .equ TEMP3,12                       // sp offset for temp3

            .text
            .global LocalVarsA_
LocalVarsA_:

// Function prologue
            push {r4-r7}                        // save non-volatile regs
            sub sp,#16                          // allocate local var space

// Load e, f, g, and h from stack
            ldr r4,[sp,#ARG_E]                  // r4 = e
            ldr r5,[sp,#ARG_F]                  // r5 = f
            ldr r6,[sp,#ARG_G]                  // r6 = g (pointer)
```

```
        ldr r7,[sp,#ARG_H]              // r7 = h (pointer)

// Calculate and save temp0, temp1, temp2, and temp3
        add r12,r0,r1
        add r12,r12,r2                  // r12 = a + b + c
        str r12,[sp,#TEMP0]             // save temp0 on stack

        add r12,r3,r4
        add r12,r12,r5                  // r12 = d + e + f
        str r12,[sp,#TEMP1]             // save temp1 on stack

        add r12,r0,r2
        add r12,r12,r4                  // r12 = a + c + e
        str r12,[sp,#TEMP2]             // save temp2 on stack

        add r12,r1,r3
        add r12,r12,r5                  // r12 = b + d + f
        str r12,[sp,#TEMP3]             // save temp3 on stack

// Calculate and save g and h
        ldr r0,[sp,#TEMP0]
        ldr r1,[sp,#TEMP1]
        mul r0,r0,r1                    // calculate temp0 * temp1
        str r0,[r6]                     // save g

        ldr r0,[sp,#TEMP2]
        ldr r1,[sp,#TEMP3]
        mul r0,r0,r1                    // calculate temp2 * temp3
        str r0,[r7]                     // save h

// Function epilogue
        add sp,#16                      // release local var space
        pop {r4-r7}                     // restore non-volatile regs
        bx lr
```

Toward the top of the C++ code is a function named LocalVarsA. Note that this function manipulates four local variables: temp0, temp1, temp2, and temp3. When defining a function in C++, the compiler allocates space for local variables on the stack. Doing this facilitates function reentrancy. It also reduces overall memory requirements since the local variable stack space is only consumed during function execution. (It should be noted that in this trivial example, a modern C++ compiler would likely generate code that forgoes the use of the stack for the local variables and use registers instead.) The function LocalVarsA calculates four intermediate results using integer arguments a, b, c, d, e, and f. It then performs two final calculations that generate values for g and h.

The assembly language function LocalVarsA_ carries out the same calculations as its C++ counterpart. It also allocates and uses stack space for the four intermediate values. In Listing 3-3, the assembly language code begins with a series of .equ directives that define stack offsets for all argument and local variables. The first instruction of LocalVarsA_, push {r4-r7}, saves non-volatile register R4-R7 on the stack. This is followed by a sub sp,#16 instruction which allocates stack space for local variables temp0, temp1, temp2, and temp3. Figure 3-3 illustrates the contents of the stack following execution of the sub sp,#16 instruction. The block of code at the beginning of a function that preserves non-volatile registers and allocates stack space for local use is called a function prologue.

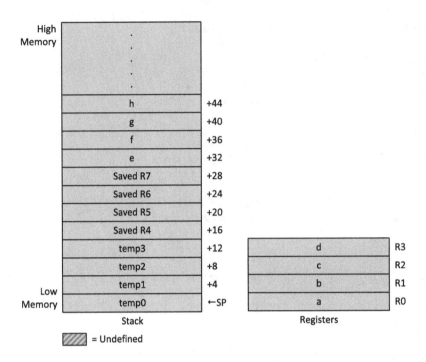

Figure 3-3. *Argument registers and stack content following execution of the sub* sp,#16 *instruction in function* LocalVarsA_

Following its prologue, function LocalVarsA_ employs four consecutive ldr instructions to load argument values e, f, g, and h into registers R4, R5, R6, and R7, respectively. The ensuing add r12,r0,r1 and add r12,r12,r2 instructions calculate temp0 = a + b + c. The instruction str r12,[sp,#TEMP0] saves temp0 on the stack for later use. Function LocalVarsA_ then calculates and saves temp1, temp2, and temp3 using similar sequences of instructions.

Calculation of g begins with a ldr r0,[sp,#TEMP0] instruction that loads temp0 from its location on the stack into R0. The ensuing ldr r1,[sp,#TEMP1] loads temp1 into R1. This is followed by the instructions mul r0,r0,r1 and str r0,[r6], which calculate temp0 * temp1 and save the result. The function LocalVarsA_ calculates and saves temp2 * temp3 using a similar sequence of instructions. The next instruction, add sp,#16, releases the stack storage space that was allocated in the prologue. Note that this *must* be done before the pop {r4-r7} instruction, which restores the non-volatile registers that were used in LocalVarsA_. The block of code at the end of a function that releases prologue-allocated stack space and restores non-volatile registers is called a function epilogue. Here is the output for source code example Ch03_03:

```
Test Case #1
a =          10 | b =       -20 | c =        30
d =         -40 | e =       -50 | f =       -60
g1 =      -3000 | g2 =    -3000
h1 =       1200 | h2 =     1200


Test Case #2
a =         100 | b =      -200 | c =       300
d =        -400 | e =      -500 | f =      -600
g1 =    -300000 | g2 =  -300000
h1 =      120000 | h2 =   120000
```

Stack Use with Frame Pointer

Listing 3-4 shows the source code for example Ch03_04, which demonstrates how to reference argument values and local variables on the stack using a frame pointer. A frame pointer points to a block of stack memory that contains function-related data including argument values, local variables, and (sometimes) links to other stack frames. The assembly language code in this example performs the same calculations as the previous example to facilitate easy comparisons between the frame pointer and nonframe pointer methods. The C++ that is shown in Listing 3-4 is identical to what you saw in the previous example except for some function name changes.

Listing 3-4. Example Ch03_04

```
//-------------------------------------------------
//                  Ch03_04.cpp
//-------------------------------------------------

#include <iostream>
#include <iomanip>

using namespace std;

extern "C" void LocalVarsB_(int a, int b, int c, int d, int e, int f,
    int* g, int* h);

void LocalVarsB(int a, int b, int c, int d, int e, int f, int* g, int* h)
{
    int temp0 = a + b + c;
    int temp1 = d + e + f;
    int temp2 = a + c + e;
    int temp3 = b + d + f;

    *g = temp0 * temp1;
    *h = temp2 * temp3;
}

void PrintResult(const char* msg, int a, int b, int c, int d, int e,
    int f, int g1, int g2, int h1, int h2)
{
    const char nl = '\n';
    const char* sep = " | ";
    const size_t w = 8;

    cout << msg << nl;
    cout << "a =  " << setw(w) << a << sep;
    cout << "b =  " << setw(w) << b << sep;
    cout << "c =  " << setw(w) << c << nl;
    cout << "d =  " << setw(w) << d << sep;
    cout << "e =  " << setw(w) << e << sep;
    cout << "f =  " << setw(w) << f << nl;
    cout << "g1 = " << setw(w) << g1 << sep;
    cout << "g2 = " << setw(w) << g2 << nl;
    cout << "h1 = " << setw(w) << h1 << sep;
```

49

```
    cout << "h2 = " << setw(w) << h2 << nl;

    if (g1 != g2 || h1 != h2)
        cout << "Compare Error!\n";
    cout << nl;
}

int main(int argc, char** argv)
{
    int a, b, c, d, e, f, g1, g2, h1, h2;

    // Test Case #1
    a = 10; b = -20; c = 30; d = -40; e = -50; f = -60;
    LocalVarsB(a, b, c, d, e, f, &g1, &h1);
    LocalVarsB_(a, b, c, d, e, f, &g2, &h2);

    PrintResult("Test Case #1", a, b, c, d, e, f,
        g1, g2, h1, h2);

    // Test Case #2
    a = 100; b = -200; c = 300; d = -400; e = -500; f = -600;
    LocalVarsB(a, b, c, d, e, f, &g1, &h1);
    LocalVarsB_(a, b, c, d, e, f, &g2, &h2);

    PrintResult("Test Case #2", a, b, c, d, e, f,
        g1, g2, h1, h2);

    return 0;
}
```

```
//----------------------------------------------------
//                  Ch03_04_.s
//----------------------------------------------------

// extern "C" void LocalVarsB_(int a, int b, int c, int d, int e, int f, int* g, int* h)

                .equ ARG_E,24               // fp offset for e
                .equ ARG_F,28               // fp offset for f
                .equ ARG_G,32               // fp offset for g
                .equ ARG_H,36               // fp offset for h

                .equ TEMP0,-16              // fp offset for temp0
                .equ TEMP1,-12              // fp offset for temp1
                .equ TEMP2,-8               // fp offset for temp2
                .equ TEMP3,-4               // fp offset for temp3

                .text
                .global LocalVarsB_
LocalVarsB_:
```

```
// Function prologue
          push {r4-r7,fp,lr}               // save NV regs, fp, lr
          mov fp,sp                        // initialize fp
          sub sp,#16                       // allocate local var space

// Load e, f, g, and h from stack
          ldr r4,[fp,#ARG_E]               // r4 = e
          ldr r5,[fp,#ARG_F]               // r5 = f
          ldr r6,[fp,#ARG_G]               // r6 = g (pointer)
          ldr r7,[fp,#ARG_H]               // r7 = h (pointer)

// Calculate and save temp0, temp1, temp2, and temp3
          add lr,r0,r1
          add lr,lr,r2                     // lr = a + b + c
          str lr,[fp,#TEMP0]               // save temp0 on stack

          add lr,r3,r4
          add lr,lr,r5                     // lr = d + e + f
          str lr,[fp,#TEMP1]               // save temp1 on stack

          add lr,r0,r2
          add lr,lr,r4                     // lr = a + c + e
          str lr,[fp,#TEMP2]               // save temp2 on stack

          add lr,r1,r3
          add lr,lr,r5                     // lr = b + d + f
          str lr,[fp,#TEMP3]               // save temp3 on stack

// Calculate and save g and h
          ldr r0,[fp,#TEMP0]
          ldr r1,[fp,#TEMP1]
          mul r0,r0,r1                     // calculate temp0 * temp1
          str r0,[r6]                      // save g

          ldr r0,[fp,#TEMP2]
          ldr r1,[fp,#TEMP3]
          mul r0,r0,r1                     // calculate temp2 * temp3
          str r0,[r7]                      // save h

// Function epilogue
          add sp,#16                       // release local var space
          pop {r4-r7,fp,pc}                // restore NV regs and return
```

The assembly language code in Listing 3-4 starts with the requisite .equ directives. Note that the constants used for local variables temp0, temp1, temp2, and temp3 are negative values. When a function uses a frame pointer, local variables typically have negative offsets, whereas argument variables have positive offsets. The first executable instruction in the prologue of LocalVarsB_ is push {r4-r7,fp,lr}. Note that both the FP and LR registers are saved on the stack. The next instruction, mov fp,sp, initializes the frame pointer for LocalVarsB_. The final prologue instruction, sub sp,#16, allocates space on the stack for the local variables. Figure 3-4 shows the stack following execution of this instruction.

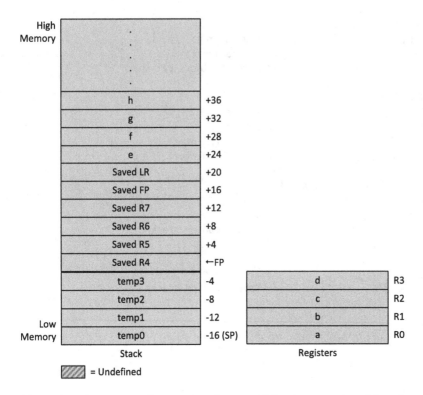

Figure 3-4. *Argument registers and stack content following execution of the* sub sp,#16 *instruction in function* LocalVarsB_

Like the previous example, LocalVarsB_ uses four consecutive ldr instructions to load argument values e, f, g, and h into registers R4, R5, R6, and R7, respectively. Note that these instructions use FP as the base register. It then carries out the same calculations as LocalVarsA_ with the only difference being that LR is used as the scratch register instead of R12. The epilogue for function LocalVarsB_ uses an add sp,#16 to release the previously allocated stack space. This is followed by a pop {r4-r7,fp,pc} instruction, which restores the contents of non-volatile register R4–R7 and FP. It also removes from the stack the original value of LR (i.e., the return address) that was saved in the prologue and copies it to the PC register. Loading the PC register in this manner returns program control to the calling function. Note that there is no bx lr instruction following the pop {r4-r7,fp,pc} instruction. Here is the output for source code example Ch03_04:

```
Test Case #1
a =         10 | b =        -20 | c =         30
d =        -40 | e =        -50 | f =        -60
g1 =     -3000 | g2 =     -3000
h1 =      1200 | h2 =      1200


Test Case #2
a =        100 | b =       -200 | c =        300
d =       -400 | e =       -500 | f =       -600
g1 =   -300000 | g2 =   -300000
h1 =    120000 | h2 =    120000
```

Frame pointers are most useful when a function requires a large amount of stack space for local variables or needs to dynamically allocate a variable-length local array on the stack. Some execution environments (e.g., Windows on ARM) also use frame pointers to facilitate stack walking for function tracing and profiling.

Using the APSR Condition Flags

In this section you will learn how to use instructions that set the negative (N), zero (Z), carry (C), and overflow (V) condition flags in the APSR (see Table 1-3). You will also discover how to use these flags to perform branching operations and conditionally execute A32 instructions.

Comparisons

Listing 3-5 shows the source code for example Ch03_05. This example demonstrates the use of the cmp (compare) instruction. It also illustrates how to perform program branches (or jumps) and conditionally execute A32 instructions.

Listing 3-5. Example Ch03_05

```
//-------------------------------------------------
//                  Ch03_05.cpp
//-------------------------------------------------

#include <iostream>

using namespace std;

extern "C" bool CompareSumA_(int a, int b, int c, int* sum);
extern "C" bool CompareSumB_(int a, int b, int c, int* sum);
extern "C" bool CompareSumC_(int a, int b, int c, int* sum);

void PrintResult(const char* msg, int a, int b, int c, int sum, bool result)
{
    const char nl = '\n';
    const char* sep = " | ";

    cout << msg << nl;
    cout << "a = " << a << sep;
    cout << "b = " << b << sep;
    cout << "c = " << c << sep;
    cout << "sum = " << sum << sep;
    cout << "result = " << boolalpha << result << nl << nl;
}

void CompareSumA(void)
{
    bool result;
    int a, b, c, sum;

    a = 10; b = 20; c = 30;
```

```
    result = CompareSumA_(a, b, c, &sum);
    PrintResult("CompareSumA - Test Case #1", a, b, c, sum, result);

    a = 100; b = -200; c = 400;
    result = CompareSumA_(a, b, c, &sum);
    PrintResult("CompareSumA - Test Case #2", a, b, c, sum, result);

    a = 100; b = -200; c = 200;
    result = CompareSumA_(a, b, c, &sum);
    PrintResult("CompareSumA - Test Case #3", a, b, c, sum, result);
}

void CompareSumB(void)
{
    bool result;
    int a, b, c, sum;

    a = 10; b = 20; c = 30;
    result = CompareSumB_(a, b, c, &sum);
    PrintResult("CompareSumB - Test Case #1", a, b, c, sum, result);

    a = 100; b = -200; c = 50;
    result = CompareSumB_(a, b, c, &sum);
    PrintResult("CompareSumB - Test Case #2", a, b, c, sum, result);

    a = 100; b = -200; c = 100;
    result = CompareSumB_(a, b, c, &sum);
    PrintResult("CompareSumB - Test Case #3", a, b, c, sum, result);
}

void CompareSumC(void)
{
    bool result;
    int a, b, c, sum;

    a = 0x7ffffff0; b = 5; c = 10;
    result = CompareSumC_(a, b, c, &sum);
    PrintResult("CompareSumC - Test Case #1", a, b, c, sum, result);

    a = 0x7ffffff0; b = 5; c = 11;
    result = CompareSumC_(a, b, c, &sum);
    PrintResult("CompareSumC - Test Case #2", a, b, c, sum, result);

    a = 0x7ffffff0; b = 100; c = 200;
    result = CompareSumC_(a, b, c, &sum);
    PrintResult("CompareSumC - Test Case #3", a, b, c, sum, result);

    a = 0x8000000f; b = -5; c = -10;
    result = CompareSumC_(a, b, c, &sum);
    PrintResult("CompareSumC - Test Case #4", a, b, c, sum, result);
```

```
    a = 0x8000000f; b = 100; c = -200;
    result = CompareSumC_(a, b, c, &sum);
    PrintResult("CompareSumC - Test Case #5", a, b, c, sum, result);
}

int main(int argc, char** argv)
{
    const char nl = '\n';
    string sep(75, '-');

    CompareSumA();
    cout << sep << nl << nl;
    CompareSumB();
    cout << sep << nl << nl;
    CompareSumC();
}

//----------------------------------------------------
//                  Ch03_05_.s
//----------------------------------------------------

// extern "C" bool CompareSumA_(int a, int b, int c, int* sum);

            .text
            .global CompareSumA_
CompareSumA_:

// Calculate a + b + c and save sum
            add r0,r0,r1                 // r0 = a + b
            add r0,r0,r2                 // r0 = a + b + c
            str r0,[r3]                  // save sum

// Is sum >= 100?
            cmp r0,#100                  // Compare sum and 100
            bge SumGE100                 // jump if sum >= 100

            mov r0,#0                    // set return code to false
            bx lr

SumGE100:   mov r0,#1                    // set return code to true
            bx lr

// extern "C" bool CompareSumB_(int a, int b, int c, int* sum);

            .global CompareSumB_
CompareSumB_:

// Calculate a + b + c and save sum
            add r0,r0,r1                 // r0 = a + b
            adds r0,r0,r2                // r0 = a + b + c
            str r0,[r3]                  // save sum
```

55

```
            bgt SumGT0                          // jump if sum > 0

            mov r0,#0                           // set return code to false
            bx lr

SumGT0:     mov r0,#1                           // set return code to true
            bx lr

// extern "C" bool CompareSumC_(int a, int b, int c, int* sum);

            .global CompareSumC_
CompareSumC_:

            push {r4,r5}

            mov r4,r0                           // r4 = a
            mov r0,#0                           // r0 = 0 (no overflow)

            adds r4,r4,r1                       // r4 = a + b
            orrvs r0,#1                         // r0 = 1 if overflow

            adds r5,r4,r2                       // r5 = a + b + c
            orrvs r0,#1                         // r0 = 1 if overflow

            str r5,[r3]                         // save sum

            pop {r4,r5}
            bx lr
```

Toward the top of Listing 3-5 you will find the declarations for the assembly language functions CompareSumA_, CompareSumB_, and CompareSumC_. These functions demonstrate the use of various assembly language instructions that set the NZCV condition flags. The remaining C++ code performs test case initialization and displays results.

The first assembly language function is named CompareSumA_. This function returns a value of type bool that signifies whether the sum of argument values a, b, and c is greater than or equal to 100. The first two instructions of this function, add r0,r0,r1 and add r0,r0,r2, calculate a + b + c. This is followed by a str r0,[r3] instruction that saves the resultant sum. The next instruction, cmp r0,#100, compares the contents of R0 (a + b + c) to the constant value 100. It does this by calculating r0 - 100 and updating the condition flags based on the result. The actual result of the subtraction is discarded (i.e., R0 is *not* updated). If R0 is greater than or equal to 100, the bge SumGE100 instruction (conditional branch to target address) that follows will transfer program control to the first assembly language instruction that follows the label SumGE100. If not, execution continues with the instruction immediately following the bge SumGE100 instruction. The remaining code in CompareSumA_ loads R0 with a return code that signifies the result of the compare operation.

The conditional branch to target instruction can be employed to conditionally alter the execution sequence of a function based on the state of the condition flags. The general form of this instruction is b<c>, where <c> denotes one of the mnemonic extensions shown in Table 3-1. These mnemonic extensions can also be used to conditionally execute most A32 instructions as you will soon see. Note that different mnemonic extensions are used for signed and unsigned integer values. A b<c> instruction without a mnemonic extension performs an unconditional branch.

Table 3-1. *Condition code mnemonic extensions and meanings*

Mnemonic Extension	Meaning	Condition Flags
EQ	Equal	Z == 1
NE	Not equal	Z == 0
HI	Unsigned greater than	C == 1 && Z == 0
HS or CS	Unsigned greater than or equal	C == 1
LO or CC	Unsigned less than	C == 0
LS	Unsigned less than or equal	C == 0 || Z == 1
GT	Signed greater than	Z == 0 && N == V
GE	Signed greater than or equal	N == V
LT	Signed less than	N != V
LE	Signed less than or equal	Z == 1 || N != V
MI	Negative value	N == 1
PL	Positive value or zero	N == 0
VS	Overflow	V == 1
VC	No overflow	V == 0

The assembly language function CompareSumB_ tests the sum of a, b, and c for a value greater than zero. This function begins with an add r0,r0,r1 that sums a and b. The next instruction, adds r0,r0,r2, adds R2 (c) to the sum in R0. Unlike the add instruction, the adds instruction also updates the NZCV condition flags based on the result. Following the str r0,[r3] instruction, which saves sum, is a bgt SumGT0 instruction that branches to the label SumGT0 if the value in R0 is greater than zero. Note that in function CompareSumB_, a separate cmp instruction is not required since the adds instruction has already set the NZCV condition flags.

Like add and adds, many other A32 arithmetic and logical operations also support two distinct instruction forms: one that simply carries out the stated operation and one that carries out the stated operation and updates the NZCV condition flags. The latter form requires an "s" suffix as the last character of the instruction mnemonic. Arm recommends that the non-condition-flag setting instruction forms be used except when condition flag results are "explicitly required for subsequent branches or conditional instructions."

The final assembly language function in Listing 3-5 is named CompareSumC_. This function returns a result that signifies whether or not an arithmetic overflow occurs when summing argument values a, b, and c. Following preservation of R4 and R5 on the stack, a mov r4,r0 instruction copies argument value a into R4. This is followed by a mov r0,#0 instruction, which initializes the function return code to 0 (no overflow). The adds r4,r4,r1 instruction calculates a + b, saves the result in R4, and updates the NZCV condition flags. The next instruction, orrvs r0,#1, is a conditional form of the orr instruction. The orrvs instruction performs a bitwise OR of R0 and the constant 1 only if the overflow condition flag V is set to 1; otherwise, no operation is performed. Note that the "vs" suffix in the orrvs instruction is one of the mnemonic extensions shown in Table 3-1. The next two instructions, adds r5,r4,r2 and orrvs r0,#1, generate the final sum of a + b + c and update the return code in R0. The final sum result is then saved using an str r5,[r3] instruction.

It is important to recognize that no branch instructions were used in CompareSumC_. All logical decisions were made using conditionally executed instructions. Doing this often results in better performance since branch instructions can sometimes disrupt the processor's front-end and execution pipelines, which affects overall performance. You will learn more about this in Chapter 17. Most A32 instructions support conditional execution. This is accomplished by appending one of the mnemonic extensions shown in Table 3-1 to the standard instruction mnemonic. Here is the output for source code example Ch03_05:

```
CompareSumA - Test Case #1
a = 10 | b = 20 | c = 30 | sum = 60 | result = false

CompareSumA - Test Case #2
a = 100 | b = -200 | c = 400 | sum = 300 | result = true

CompareSumA - Test Case #3
a = 100 | b = -200 | c = 200 | sum = 100 | result = true
-------------------------------------------------------------------------
CompareSumB - Test Case #1
a = 10 | b = 20 | c = 30 | sum = 60 | result = true

CompareSumB - Test Case #2
a = 100 | b = -200 | c = 50 | sum = -50 | result = false

CompareSumB - Test Case #3
a = 100 | b = -200 | c = 100 | sum = 0 | result = false
-------------------------------------------------------------------------
CompareSumC - Test Case #1
a = 2147483632 | b = 5 | c = 10 | sum = 2147483647 | result = false

CompareSumC - Test Case #2
a = 2147483632 | b = 5 | c = 11 | sum = -2147483648 | result = true

CompareSumC - Test Case #3
a = 2147483632 | b = 100 | c = 200 | sum = -2147483364 | result = true

CompareSumC - Test Case #4
a = -2147483633 | b = -5 | c = -10 | sum = -2147483648 | result = false

CompareSumC - Test Case #5
a = -2147483633 | b = 100 | c = -200 | sum = 2147483563 | result = true
```

Looping

The final source code example of this chapter, Ch03_06, explains how to code a for-loop using assembly language. It also demonstrates how to perform argument validity checks and call functions. Listing 3-6 shows the source code for this example Ch03_06.

Listing 3-6. Example Ch03_06

```
//--------------------------------------------------
//              Ch03_06.cpp
//--------------------------------------------------

#include <iostream>
```

```cpp
using namespace std;

const int c_ArgnMin = 1;
const int c_ArgnMax = 1023;

// Ch03_06_.s
extern "C" void CalcSum_(int n, int* sum1, int* sum2);

// Ch03_06_Misc.cpp
extern void PrintResult(const char* msg, int n, int sum1_cpp,
    int sum1_asm, int sum2_cpp, int sum2_asm);

static int CalcSum1(int n)
{
    int sum = 0;

    for (int i = 1; i <= n; i++)
        sum += i * i;
    return sum;
}

static int CalcSum2(int n)
{
    int sum = (n * (n + 1) * (2 * n + 1)) / 6;
    return sum;
}

void CalcSum(int n, int* sum1, int* sum2)
{
    *sum1 = *sum2 = 0;

    if (n < c_ArgnMin || n > c_ArgnMax)
        return;

    *sum1 = CalcSum1(n);
    *sum2 = CalcSum2(n);
    return;
}

int main(int argc, char** argv)
{
    int n;
    int sum1_cpp, sum1_asm;
    int sum2_cpp, sum2_asm;

    n = 3;
    CalcSum(n, &sum1_cpp, &sum2_cpp);
    CalcSum_(n, &sum1_asm, &sum2_asm);
    PrintResult("CalcSum - Test Case #1",
        n, sum1_cpp, sum1_asm, sum2_cpp, sum2_asm);
```

```
    n = 7;
    CalcSum(n, &sum1_cpp, &sum2_cpp);
    CalcSum_(n, &sum1_asm, &sum2_asm);
    PrintResult("CalcSum - Test Case #2",
        n, sum1_cpp, sum1_asm, sum2_cpp, sum2_asm);

    n = 17;
    CalcSum(n, &sum1_cpp, &sum2_cpp);
    CalcSum_(n, &sum1_asm, &sum2_asm);
    PrintResult("CalcSum - Test Case #3",
        n, sum1_cpp, sum1_asm, sum2_cpp, sum2_asm);

    n = 40;
    CalcSum(n, &sum1_cpp, &sum2_cpp);
    CalcSum_(n, &sum1_asm, &sum2_asm);
    PrintResult("CalcSum - Test Case #4",
        n, sum1_cpp, sum1_asm, sum2_cpp, sum2_asm);

    return 0;
}

//----------------------------------------------------
//                  Ch03_06_.s
//----------------------------------------------------

// extern "C" void CalcSum_(int n, int* sum1, int* sum2);

            .equ SAVE_N,0                       // offset for save of n
            .equ SAVE_SUM1,4                    // offset for save of sum1
            .equ SAVE_SUM2,8                    // offset for save of sum2

            .equ ARG_N_MIN,1                    // argument n minimum value
            .equ ARG_N_MAX,1023                 // argument n maximum value

            .text
            .global CalcSum_
CalcSum_:

// Function prologue
            push {lr}                           // save lr
            sub sp,#12                          // allocate local var space

// Save arguments to stack
            str r0,[sp,#SAVE_N]                 // save arg n
            str r1,[sp,#SAVE_SUM1]              // save arg sum1
            str r2,[sp,#SAVE_SUM2]              // save arg sum2

// Set sum1 and sum2 to zero
            mov r3,#0
            str r3,[r1]                         // sum1 = 0
            str r3,[r2]                         // sum2 = 0
```

```
// Verify n >= ARG_N_MIN && n <= ARG_N_MAX
            cmp r0,#ARG_N_MIN
            blt Done                            // jump if n < ARG_N_MIN
            mov r3,#ARG_N_MAX
            cmp r0,r3
            bgt Done                            // jump if n > ARG_N_MAX

// Calculate sum1
            bl CalcSum1_
            ldr r1,[sp,#SAVE_SUM1]
            str r0,[r1]                         // save sum1

// Calculate sum2
            ldr r0,[sp,#SAVE_N]
            bl CalcSum2_
            ldr r1,[sp,#SAVE_SUM2]
            str r0,[r1]                         // save sum2

// Function epilogue
Done:       add sp,#12                          // release local var space
            pop {pc}                            // return

// int static CalcSum1_(int n);

CalcSum1_:

// Calculate sum1 using for-loop
            mov r1,#1                           // i = 1
            mov r2,#0                           // sum = 0

Loop1:      mla r2,r1,r1,r2                     // sum += i * i
            add r1,#1                           // i += 1

            cmp r1,r0
            ble Loop1                           // jump if i <= n

            mov r0,r2                           // r0 = final sum1
            bx lr

// int CalcSum2_(int n);

CalcSum2_:

// Calculate sum2 = (n * (n + 1) * (2 * n + 1)) / 6
            add r1,r0,#1                        // r1 = n + 1
            mul r2,r0,r1                        // r2 = n * (n + 1)

            lsl r3,r0,#1                        // r3 = 2 * n
            add r3,#1                           // r3 = 2 * n + 1
            mul r3,r3,r2                        // r3 = dividend
```

```
            mov r1,#6                           // r1 = divisor
            sdiv r0,r3,r1                        // r0 = final sum2
            bx lr
```

Listing 3-6 includes both C++ and assembly language functions that calculate sum values using the following equations:

$$sum_1 = \sum_{i=1}^{n} i^2$$

$$sum_2 = \frac{n(n+1)(2n+1)}{6}$$

The C++ code in Listing 3-6 contains two functions named CalcSum1 and CalcSum2, which calculate sum1 and sum2, respectively. The assembly language functions CalcSum1_ and CalcSum2_ also calculate sum1 and sum2 using the same methods as the corresponding C++ functions. The C++ function main initializes several test cases, exercises the base functions CalcSum and CalcSum_, and displays the results on the console.

The assembly language function CalcSum_ begins its execution with a push {lr} instruction that saves register LR on the stack. Saving LR on the stack is mandatory in this example since CalcSum_ calls other functions. The next instruction sub sp,#12 allocates storage on the stack that will be used to temporarily save argument values n, sum1, and sum2 on the stack. It is important to note that following the execution of prologue instructions push {lr} and sub sp,#12, SP is aligned on a doubleword boundary. This is required by the GNU C++ calling convention for any non-leaf function. A leaf function is a function that does not call other functions.

Following it prologue, CalcSum_ saves argument values n (R0), sum1 (R1), and sum2 (R2) on the stack as shown in Figure 3-5. The reason for doing this is that CalcSum_ is going to call other functions, and these functions are not obligated to preserve the contents of registers R0, R1, and R2, which are volatile per the GNU C++ calling convention (see Table 2-1). Following argument value preservation, CalcSum_ sets the memory locations pointed to by sum1 and sum2 equal to zero using instruction sequence mov r3,#0, str r3,[r1], and str r3,[r2].

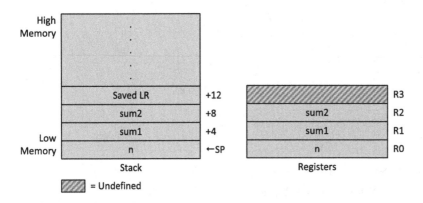

Figure 3-5. *Argument registers and stack content following execution of the* str r2,[sp,#SAVE_SUM2] *instruction in function* CalcSum_

In high-level languages such as C++, it is considered good programming practice to validate most if not all argument values before performing any calculations. Assembly language functions should do the same whenever possible. In the current function, minimum and maximum values for argument n have been (arbitrarily) defined using a two .equ directives. The cmp r0,#ARG_N_MIN instruction compares the contents of R0 (n) to the immediate constant ARG_N_MIN. The ensuing blt Done instruction transfers program control to the label Done if n is less than ARG_N_MIN. The next three instructions, mov r3,#ARG_N_MAX, cmp r0,r3, and bgt Done, perform the same action if n is greater than ARG_N_MAX. The reason for loading R3 with the constant ARG_N_MAX is that a cmp r0,#ARG_N_MAX instruction is invalid here since ARG_N_MAX cannot be encoded using a modified immediate constant as explained in Chapter 2.

Following argument validation, CalcSum_ uses a bl CalcSum1_ to call the assembly language function CalcSum1_. The bl (branch with link) instruction copies the address of the instruction immediately following it into register LR. It then transfers program control to the instruction that is located at the address designated by the label operand. The reason why CalcSum_ employed a push {lr} instruction in its prologue should now be obvious. Without this instruction, CalcSum_ would be unable to return program control back to its calling function.

Following execution of CalcSum1_, whose instructions will be explained shortly, a ldr r1,[sp,#SAVE_SUM1] instruction loads R1 with argument value sum1. It then uses a str r0,[r1] to save sum1. It should be noted that the technique used in this example to call CalcSum1_ observes the GNU C++ calling convention. CalcSum_ passed argument value n to CalcSum1_ in register R0, and CalcSum1_ passed back its return value in R0 as required by the calling convention. The same method is then used to call CalcSum2_. Note that a ldr r0,[sp,#SAVE_N] instruction is used before the bl CalcSum2_ instruction, which reloads R0 with argument n. Function CalcSum_ concludes with an epilogue that uses an add sp,#12 instruction to release the previously allocated stack space and a pop {pc} instruction that returns program control back to main.

Function CalcSum1_ calculates sum1 using an assembly language implementation of a for-loop. The first two instructions, mov r1,#1 and mov r2,#0, initialize i = 1 and sum = 0, respectively. The next instruction, mla r2,r1,r1,r2, calculates sum += i * i. Note that this statement is tagged with the label Loop1. The ensuing add r1,#1 calculates i += 1. This is followed by a cmp r1,r0 instruction that compares i to n. If i <= n is true, the ble Loop1 instruction transfers program control back to Loop1 and another iteration of the for-loop is executed. Once i becomes greater than n, the final sum is copied from R2 to R0 and program control is transferred back to CalcSum_.

The function CalcSum2_ starts its computation of sum2 = (n * (n + 1) * (2 * n + 1)) / 6 with an add r1,r0,#1 instruction that calculates n + 1. Execution of the ensuing mul r2,r0,r1 instruction yields n * (n + 1). The next three instructions, lsl r3,r0,#1, add r3,#1, and mul r3,r3,r2 complete the calculation of the dividend. This value is then divided by 6 using the instructions mov r1,#6 and sdiv r0,r3,r1. Here is the output for source code example Ch03_06:

```
CalcSum - Test Case #1
n =             3
sum1_cpp =     14 | sum1_asm =     14
sum2_cpp =     14 | sum2_asm =     14

CalcSum - Test Case #2
n =             7
sum1_cpp =    140 | sum1_asm =    140
sum2_cpp =    140 | sum2_asm =    140

CalcSum - Test Case #3
n =            17
sum1_cpp =   1785 | sum1_asm =   1785
sum2_cpp =   1785 | sum2_asm =   1785

CalcSum - Test Case #4
n =            40
sum1_cpp = 22140 | sum1_asm =  22140
sum2_cpp = 22140 | sum2_asm =  22140
```

Summary

Here are the key learning points for Chapter 3:

- The .equ directive is used to define symbolic names for constant expressions.

- Integer arguments passed via a register are either sign- or zero-extended to 32 bits; stack arguments are not size- or zero-extended. The ldrb, ldrh, ldrsb, and ldrsh instructions can be used to load byte and halfword values from the stack.

- A function prologue uses the push instruction to preserve non-volatile registers on the stack. It also can allocate space on the stack for local variables and optionally establish a frame pointer. A function epilogue releases local variable stack space and restores non-volatile registers using the pop instruction.

- Functions can use the cmp instruction to set the NZCV condition flags in the APSR. A function also can use a b<c> instruction, where <c> is one of the mnemonic extensions shown in Table 3-1 to alter execution flow based on the status of the NZCV condition flags.

- Most arithmetic and logical instructions have two forms: a base form that carries out a specific operation and an "s" form that also sets the NZCV condition flags. Functions should use the condition-flag setting forms only when condition flag results are required for subsequent branches or conditional instruction executions.

- A function can conditionally execute most A32 instructions by appending a mnemonic extension (Table 3-1) to the instruction mnemonic.

- An assembly language function can call another function using the bl,label instruction provided it observes all calling convention requirements.

CHAPTER 4

■ ■ ■

Armv8-32 Core Programming – Part 3

The content of this and the previous two chapters can be regarded as a trilogy of Arm8-32 assembly language fundamentals. In Chapters 2 and 3, you learned how to perform integer arithmetic, carry out data load and store operations, manipulate the stack, and programmatically exploit the NZCV condition flags. You also acquired useful knowledge about the GNU C++ calling convention and the GNU assembler.

This chapter you are about to read imparts additional Armv8-32 assembly language programming concepts that complete the trilogy. It begins with section that elucidates array use in an assembly language function. This is followed by a section that covers matrices and the programming techniques necessary to properly access the elements of a matrix. The final section of Chapter 4 explicates additional load and store instructions. It also explains how to reference the members of a C++ structure in an assembly language function.

Integer Arrays

Arrays are an indispensable data construct in virtually all programming languages. In C++, there is an inherent connection between arrays and pointers since the name of an array is essentially a pointer to its first element. Moreover, whenever an array variable name is used as a C++ function parameter, a pointer is passed instead of duplicating the array on the stack. In C++, one-dimensional arrays are stored in a contiguous block of memory that can be statically allocated at compile time or dynamically allocated during program execution. The elements of a C++ array are accessed using zero-based indexing, which means that valid indices for an array of size N range from 0 to N - 1.

The source code in this section discusses assembly language code that processes arrays. The first source code example explains how to perform simple arithmetic using the elements of an integer array. The second source code example demonstrates arithmetic using elements from multiple arrays.

Array Arithmetic

Listing 4-1 shows the source code for example Ch04_01. This example illustrates how to access the elements of an integer array. It also explains additional forms of the ldr instruction.

© Daniel Kusswurm 2020
D. Kusswurm, *Modern Arm Assembly Language Programming*,
https://doi.org/10.1007/978-1-4842-6267-2_4

Listing 4-1. Example Ch04_01

```
//---------------------------------------------------
//                   Ch04_01.cpp
//---------------------------------------------------

#include <iostream>
#include <iomanip>
#include <cstdint>

using namespace std;

extern "C" int CalcSumA_(const int* x, int n);
extern "C" uint64_t CalcSumB_(const uint32_t* x, uint32_t n);

int CalcSumA(const int* x, int n)
{
    int sum = 0;

    for (int i = 0; i < n; i++)
        sum += *x++;

    return sum;
}

uint64_t CalcSumB(const uint32_t* y, uint32_t n)
{
    uint64_t sum = 0;

    for (uint32_t i = 0; i < n; i++)
        sum += y[i];

    return sum;
}

int main()
{
    const char nl = '\n';

    int x[] {3, 17, -13, 25, -2, 9, -6, 12, 88, -19};
    int nx = sizeof(x) / sizeof(int);

    uint32_t y[] = {0x10000000, 0x20000000, 0x40000000, 0x80000000,
                    0x50000000, 0x70000000, 0x90000000, 0xC0000000};
    uint32_t ny = sizeof(y) / sizeof(uint32_t);

    // Calculate sum of elements in array x
    cout << "Results for CalcSumA" << nl;

    for (int i = 0; i < nx; i++)
        cout << "x[" << i << "] = " << x[i] << nl;
```

```cpp
    int sum_x1 = CalcSumA(x, nx);
    int sum_x2 = CalcSumA_(x, nx);

    cout << "sum_x1 = " << sum_x1 << nl;
    cout << "sum_x2 = " << sum_x2 << nl << nl;

    // Calculate sum of elements in array y
    cout << "Results for CalcSumB" << nl;

    for (uint32_t i = 0; i < ny; i++)
        cout << "y[" << i << "] = " << y[i] << nl;

    uint64_t sum_y1 = CalcSumB(y, ny);
    uint64_t sum_y2 = CalcSumB_(y, ny);

    cout << "sum_y1 = " << sum_y1 << nl;
    cout << "sum_y2 = " << sum_y2 << nl << nl;

    return 0;
}

//----------------------------------------------------
//                  Ch04_01_.s
//----------------------------------------------------

// extern "C" int CalcSumA_(const int* x, int n);

            .text
            .global CalcSumA_
CalcSumA_:
            mov r2,#0                       // sum = 0

            cmp r1,#0                       // is n <= 0?
            ble DoneA                       // jump if n <= 0

LoopA:      ldr r3,[r0],#4                  // r3 = *r0; r0 += 4
            add r2,r2,r3                    // add current x to sum
            subs r1,r1,#1                   // n -= 1
            bne LoopA                       // jump if more data

DoneA:      mov r0,r2                       // r0 = final sum
            bx lr

// extern "C" uint64_t CalcSumB_(const uint32_t* x, uint32_t n);

            .global CalcSumB_
CalcSumB_:
            push {r4,r5}

            mov r2,#0
            mov r3,#0                       // sum (r2:r3) = 0
```

```
                cmp  r1,#0                      // is n == 0?
                beq  DoneB                      // jump if n == 0

                mov  r4,#0                       // i = 0

LoopB:          ldr  r5,[r0,r4,lsl #2]          // r5 = x[i]

                adds r2,r2,r5
                adc  r3,r3,#0                    // sum += x[i]

                add  r4,#1                       // i += 1
                cmp  r4,r1                       // is i == n?
                bne  LoopB.                      // jump if more data

DoneB:          mov  r0,r2
                mov  r1,r3                       // r0:r1 = final 64-bit sum

                pop  {r4,r5}
                bx   lr
```

Near the top of the C++ code are the now-familiar declarations for the assembly language functions CalcSumA_ and CalcSumB_. Both functions sum the elements of an array. Note that the declaration of CalcSumB_ uses the fixed-sized unsigned integer types uint64_t and uint32_t that are declared in the header file <cstdint> instead of the normal unsigned long long and unsigned int. Some assembly language programmers (including me) prefer to use fixed-sized integer types for assembly language function declarations since it accentuates the exact size of the argument.

The function CalcSumA_ begins with a mov r2,#0 instruction that initializes sum to zero. The cmp r1,#0 and ble DoneA instructions prevent execution of for-loop LoopA if n <= 0 is true. Sweeping through the array to sum the elements requires only four instructions. The ldr r3,[r0],#4 instruction loads the array element pointed to by R0 into R3. It then adds 4 to R0, which points it to the next array element. This is an example of post-indexed addressing (see Table 1-5). The next instruction, add r2,r2,r3, adds the current array element to sum in R2. The subs r1,r1,#1 instruction subtracts one from n and also sets the NZCV condition flags, which allows the ensuing bne LoopA instruction to terminate LoopA when n equals zero.

The function CalcSumB_ sums the elements of a uint32_t array and returns a result of type uint64_t. This function starts by setting registers R2 and R3 to zero. Function CalcSumB_ uses this register pair to hold an intermediate 64-bit sum. The number of array elements n is then tested to make sure it is not equal to zero. The mov r4,#0 instruction then sets the array index variable i to zero.

CalcSumB_ uses a different technique than CalcSumA_ to sum the elements of the target array. The first instruction of for-loop LoopB, ldr r5,[r0,r4,lsl #2], loads array element x[i] into R5. In this instruction, the address of source operand x[i] is R0 + (R4 << 2) (R0 contains the address of array x and R4 contains index variable i). Register R4 is left shifted by 2 bits since the size of each element of array x is 4 bytes. Note that this form of the ldr instruction does not modify the values in both R0 and R4.

The next instruction, adds r2,r2,r5, adds x[i] to the low-order 32 bits of the intermediate sum that is maintained in register pair R2:R3. The adds instruction also sets the C condition flag to one if an unsigned overflow occurs when adding x[i] to the running sum; otherwise, C is set to zero. The ensuing adc r3,r3,#0 (add with carry) instruction adds the value of the C condition flag to the high-order 32 bits of the 64-bit running sum. The adds/adc instruction pair is often used to perform 64-bit integer addition as demonstrated in this function.

Following the 64-bit addition, CalcSumB_ uses an add r4,#1 instruction, which adds one to the array index i that is maintained in R4. The next two instructions, cmp r4,r1 and bne LoopB, test i and repeat LoopB if i != n is true. Following the summing loop, the final 64-bit sum in register pair R2:R3 is copied to R0:R1 so that it can be passed back to the calling function. Here is the output for source code example Ch04_01:

```
Results for CalcSumA
x[0] = 3
x[1] = 17
x[2] = -13
x[3] = 25
x[4] = -2
x[5] = 9
x[6] = -6
x[7] = 12
x[8] = 88
x[9] = -19
sum_x1 = 114
sum_x2 = 114

Results for CalcSumB
y[0] = 268435456
y[1] = 536870912
y[2] = 1073741824
y[3] = 2147483648
y[4] = 1342177280
y[5] = 1879048192
y[6] = 2415919104
y[7] = 3221225472
sum_y1 = 12884901888
sum_y2 = 12884901888
```

Array Arithmetic Using Multiple Arrays

Listing 4-2 shows the source code for example Ch04_02. This example demonstrates how to carry out calculations using elements from multiple arrays. It also illustrates how to reference and use a C++ global variable in an assembly language function.

Listing 4-2. Example Ch04_02

```
//--------------------------------------------------
//                 Ch04_02.cpp
//--------------------------------------------------

#include <iostream>
#include <iomanip>
#include <random>

using namespace std;

int32_t g_Val1 = 2;
int32_t g_Val2 = 100;
```

```cpp
extern "C" int32_t CalcZ_(int32_t* z, const int8_t* x, const int16_t* y, int32_t n);

void Init(int8_t* x, int16_t* y, int32_t n)
{
    unsigned int seed = 7;
    uniform_int_distribution<> dist {-128, 127};
    mt19937 rng {seed};

    for (int32_t i = 0; i < n; i++)
    {
        x[i] = (int8_t)dist(rng);
        y[i] = (int16_t)dist(rng);
    }
}

int32_t CalcZ(int32_t* z, const int8_t* x, const int16_t* y, int32_t n)
{
    int32_t sum = 0;

    for (int32_t i = 0; i < n; i++)
    {
        int32_t temp;

        if (x[i] < 0)
            temp = y[i] * g_Val1;
        else
            temp = y[i] * g_Val2;

        sum += temp;
        z[i] = temp;
    }

    return sum;
}

int main()
{
    const int32_t n = 12;
    int8_t x[n];
    int16_t y[n];
    int32_t z1[n], z2[n];

    Init(x, y, n);

    int32_t sum_z1 = CalcZ(z1, x, y, n);
    int32_t sum_z2 = CalcZ_(z2, x, y, n);

    const char nl = '\n';
    const char* sep = "   ";

    for (int32_t i = 0; i < n; i++)
```

```
        {
            cout << "i: " << setw(2) << i << sep;
            cout << "x: " << setw(5) << (int)x[i] << sep;
            cout << "y: " << setw(5) << y[i] << sep;
            cout << "z1: " << setw(7) << z1[i] << sep;
            cout << "z2: " << setw(7) << z2[i] << nl;
        }

        cout << nl;
        cout << "sum_z1 = " << sum_z1 << nl;
        cout << "sum_z2 = " << sum_z2 << nl;
        return 0;
    }

//----------------------------------------------------
//                   Ch04_02_.s
//----------------------------------------------------

// extern "C" int32_t CalcZ_(int32_t* z const int8_t* x, const int16_t* y, int32_t n);

            .text
            .global CalcZ_
CalcZ_:     push {r4-r9}

            mov r4,#0                   // sum = 0
            cmp r3,#0
            ble Done                    // jump if n <= 0

            ldr r5,=g_Val1
            ldr r5,[r5]                 // r5 = g_Val1

            ldr r6,=g_Val2
            ldr r6,[r6]                 // r6 = g_Val2

// Main processing loop
Loop1:      ldrsb r7,[r1],#1            // r7 = x[i]
            ldrsh r8,[r2],#2            // r8 = y[i]

            cmp r7,#0                   // is x[i] < 0?

            mullt r9,r8,r5              // temp = y[i] * g_Val1
                                        // (if x[i] < 0)

            mulge r9,r8,r6              // temp = y[i] * g_Val2
                                        // (if x[i] >= 0)

            add r4,r4,r9                // sum += temp
            str r9,[r0],#4              // save result z[i]

            subs r3,#1                  // n -= 1
            bne Loop1                   // repeat until done
```

```
Done:       mov r0,r4                          // r0 = final sum
            pop {r4-r9}
            bx lr
```

The C++ code in Listing 4-2 starts with the definition of global variables g_Val1 and g_Val2. These values are used in functions CalcZ and CalcZ_. Following the declaration of CalcZ_ is a function named Init, which initializes the test arrays for this example using random numbers. This function uses the C++ Standard Template Library (STL) classes uniform_int_distribution and mt19937 to generate random values for the array. Appendix B contains a list of references that you can consult if you are interested in learning more about these classes. The definition of function CalcZ is next. This function performs some admittedly contrived arithmetic for demonstration purposes. Note that different integer types are used for the arrays x, y, and z. The remaining C++ code performs test case initialization, exercises the functions CalcZ and CalcZ_, and displays the results.

The first nonprologue instruction of CalcZ_ is a mov r4,#0, which initializes sum to zero. The value of n is then tested to make sure it is greater than zero. The next instruction, ldr r5,=g_Val1, loads the address of g_Val1 into R5. This is followed by a ldr r5,[r5] instruction that loads g_Val1 into R5. Function CalcZ_ uses a similar sequence of instructions to load g_Val2 into R6.

Each iteration of for-loop Loop1 begins with a ldrsb r7,[r1],#1 instruction that loads x[i] into R7. Note that a post-indexed offset value of one is used since array x is of type int8_t. The ldrsh r8,[r2],#2 instruction loads y[i] into R8. This instruction uses a post-indexed offset value of two since array y is of type int16_t. The ensuing cmp r7,#0 sets the NZCV condition flags. The next instruction, mullt r9,r8,r5, calculates temp = y[i] * g_Val1 only if x[i] < 0 is true. Otherwise, no operation is performed. The mullt instruction is an example of an A32 conditional instruction that was discussed in Chapter 3. Following the mullt instruction is another conditionally executed instruction mulge r9,r8,r6, which calculates temp y[i] * g_Val2 only if x[i] >= 0 is true.

The add r4,r4,r9 instruction updates the sum that is maintained in R4. This is followed by a str r9,[r0],#4 instruction that saves temp to z[i]. This instruction uses a post-indexed offset value of four since array z is of type int32_t. The processing for-loop Loop1 repeats until all elements have been examined. Here is the output for source code example Ch04_02:

```
i:  0  x:  -109  y:   -70  z1:    -140  z2:    -140
i:  1  x:    71  y:   -47  z1:   -4700  z2:   -4700
i:  2  x:   -16  y:   122  z1:     244  z2:     244
i:  3  x:    57  y:   -12  z1:   -1200  z2:   -1200
i:  4  x:   122  y:   -50  z1:   -5000  z2:   -5000
i:  5  x:     9  y:   -61  z1:   -6100  z2:   -6100
i:  6  x:     0  y:  -106  z1:  -10600  z2:  -10600
i:  7  x:  -110  y:   -21  z1:     -42  z2:     -42
i:  8  x:   -60  y:  -124  z1:    -248  z2:    -248
i:  9  x:    -1  y:     7  z1:      14  z2:      14
i: 10  x:    45  y:    94  z1:    9400  z2:    9400
i: 11  x:    77  y:   -44  z1:   -4400  z2:   -4400

sum_z1 = -22772
sum_z2 = -22772
```

Integer Matrices

C++ also uses a contiguous block of memory to implement a two-dimensional array or matrix. The elements of a C++ matrix in memory are organized using row-major ordering. Row-major ordering arranges the elements of a matrix first by row and then by column. For example, elements of the matrix int x[3][2] are stored in consecutive memory locations as follows: x[0][0], x[0][1], x[1][0], x[1][1], x[2][0], and x[2][1]. Figure 4-1 illustrates this memory ordering scheme. In order to access a specific element in the matrix, a function (or a compiler) must know the starting address of the matrix (i.e., the address of its first element), the row and column indices, the total number of columns, and the size in bytes of each element. Using this information, a function can use simple addition and multiplication to access a specific element in a matrix as exemplified by the source codes examples in this section.

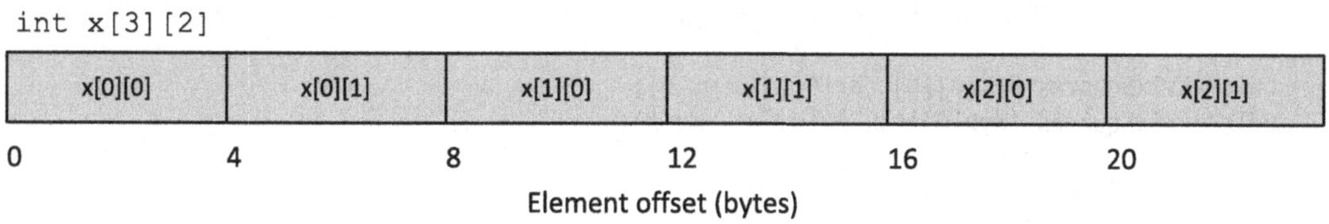

```
int x[3][2]
```

x[0][0]	x[0][1]	x[1][0]	x[1][1]	x[2][0]	x[2][1]

0   4   8   12   16   20

Element offset (bytes)

Figure 4-1. *Row-major ordering for matrix int x[3][2]*

Accessing Matrix Elements

Listing 4-3 shows the source code for example Ch04_03, which demonstrates how to use assembly language to access the elements of a matrix. In this example, the functions CalcMatrixSquares and CalcMatrixSquares_ perform the following matrix calculation: y[i][j] = x[j][i] * x[j][i]. Note that in this expression, the indices i and j for matrix x are intentionally reversed to make the code in this example a little more interesting.

Listing 4-3. Example Ch04_03

```cpp
//----------------------------------------------------
//                  Ch04_03.cpp
//----------------------------------------------------

#include <iostream>
#include <iomanip>

using namespace std;

extern "C" void CalcMatrixSquares_(int* y, const int* x, int m, int n);

void CalcMatrixSquares(int* y, const int* x, int m, int n)
{
    for (int i = 0; i < m; i++)
    {
        for (int j = 0; j < n; j++)
        {
            int kx = j * m + i;
            int ky = i * n + j;
            y[ky] = x[kx] * x[kx];
```

```cpp
        }
    }
}

int main()
{
    const int m = 6;
    const int n = 3;
    int y1[m][n], y2[m][n];

    int x[n][m] {{ 1, 2, 3, 4, 5, 6 },
                 { 7, 8, 9, 10, 11, 12 },
                 { 13, 14, 15, 16, 17, 18 }};

    CalcMatrixSquares(&y1[0][0], &x[0][0], m, n);
    CalcMatrixSquares_(&y2[0][0], &x[0][0], m, n);

    for (int i = 0; i < m; i++)
    {
        for (int j = 0; j < n; j++)
        {
            cout << "y1[" << setw(2) << i << "][" << setw(2) << j << "] = ";
            cout << setw(6) << y1[i][j] << ' ' ;

            cout << "y2[" << setw(2) << i << "][" << setw(2) << j << "] = ";
            cout << setw(6) << y2[i][j] << ' ';

            cout << "x[" << setw(2) << j << "][" << setw(2) << i << "] = ";
            cout << setw(6) << x[j][i] << '\n';

            if (y1[i][j] != y2[i][j])
                cout << "Compare failed\n";
        }
    }

    return 0;
}

//----------------------------------------------------
//                  Ch04_03_.s
//----------------------------------------------------

// extern "C" void CalcMatrixSquares_(int* y, const int* x, int m, int n);

            .text
            .global CalcMatrixSquares_
CalcMatrixSquares_:
            push {r4-r8}
```

```
                cmp  r2,#0
                ble  Done                    // jump if m <= 0
                cmp  r3,#0
                ble  Done                    // jump if n <= 0

                mov  r4,#0                    // i = 0

Loop1:          mov  r5,#0                    // j = 0

Loop2:          mov  r6,r5                    // r6 = j
                mul  r6,r6,r2                 // r6 = j * m
                add  r6,r6,r4                 // kx = j * m + i
                ldr  r7,[r1,r6,lsl #2]        // r7 = x[kx] (x[j][i])

                mul  r7,r7,r7                 // r7 = x[j][i] * x[j][i]

                mov  r8,r4                    // r8 = i
                mul  r8,r8,r3                 // r8 = i * n
                add  r8,r8,r5                 // ky = i * n + j
                str  r7,[r0,r8,lsl #2]        // save y[ky] (y[i][j])

                add  r5,#1                    // j += 1
                cmp  r5,r3
                blt  Loop2                    // jump if j < n

                add  r4,#1                    // i += 1
                cmp  r4,r2
                blt  Loop1                    // jump if i < m

Done:           pop  {r4-r8}
                bx   lr
```

The function CalcMatrixSquares illustrates how to access an element in a C++ matrix using explicit arithmetic. At entry to this function, arguments x and y point to the memory blocks that contain their respective matrices. Inside the second for-loop, the expression kx = j * m + i calculates the offset necessary to access element x[j][i]. Similarly, the expression ky = i * n + j calculates the offset for element y[i][j]. Note that the code employed in CalcMatrixSquares to calculate kx and ky requires x to be a matrix of size n × m and y to be a matrix of size m × n.

The assembly language function CalcMatrixSquares_ uses the same technique as the C++ code to access elements in matrices x and y. This function begins its execution by checking argument values m and n to make sure they are greater than zero. A mov r4,#0 instruction is then used to initialize index i to zero. Each iteration of for-loop Loop1 starts with a mov r5,#0 instruction that sets index j to zero. The ensuing mov r6,r5, mul r6,r6,r2, and add r6,r6,r4 instructions calculate kx = j * m + i. This is followed by a ldr r7,[r1,r6,lsl #2] instruction that loads x[j][i] into R7. The mul r7,r7,r7 instruction calculates x[j][i] * x[j][i].

Function CalcMatrixSquares_ employs a similar sequence of instructions to calculate the address of y[i][j]. Variable ky is calculated using the instruction pair mul r8,r8,r3 and add r8,r8,r5. The str r7,[r0,r8,lsl #2] instruction then saves the previously calculated squared result to y[i][j]. Like the corresponding C++ code, the nested for-loops in CalcMatrixSquares_ continue to execute until the index counters j and i (registers R4 and R5) reach their respective termination values. Here is the output for source code example Ch04_03:

```
y1[ 0][ 0] =      1 y2[ 0][ 0] =      1 x[ 0][ 0] =      1
y1[ 0][ 1] =     49 y2[ 0][ 1] =     49 x[ 1][ 0] =      7
y1[ 0][ 2] =    169 y2[ 0][ 2] =    169 x[ 2][ 0] =     13
y1[ 1][ 0] =      4 y2[ 1][ 0] =      4 x[ 0][ 1] =      2
y1[ 1][ 1] =     64 y2[ 1][ 1] =     64 x[ 1][ 1] =      8
y1[ 1][ 2] =    196 y2[ 1][ 2] =    196 x[ 2][ 1] =     14
y1[ 2][ 0] =      9 y2[ 2][ 0] =      9 x[ 0][ 2] =      3
y1[ 2][ 1] =     81 y2[ 2][ 1] =     81 x[ 1][ 2] =      9
y1[ 2][ 2] =    225 y2[ 2][ 2] =    225 x[ 2][ 2] =     15
y1[ 3][ 0] =     16 y2[ 3][ 0] =     16 x[ 0][ 3] =      4
y1[ 3][ 1] =    100 y2[ 3][ 1] =    100 x[ 1][ 3] =     10
y1[ 3][ 2] =    256 y2[ 3][ 2] =    256 x[ 2][ 3] =     16
y1[ 4][ 0] =     25 y2[ 4][ 0] =     25 x[ 0][ 4] =      5
y1[ 4][ 1] =    121 y2[ 4][ 1] =    121 x[ 1][ 4] =     11
y1[ 4][ 2] =    289 y2[ 4][ 2] =    289 x[ 2][ 4] =     17
y1[ 5][ 0] =     36 y2[ 5][ 0] =     36 x[ 0][ 5] =      6
y1[ 5][ 1] =    144 y2[ 5][ 1] =    144 x[ 1][ 5] =     12
y1[ 5][ 2] =    324 y2[ 5][ 2] =    324 x[ 2][ 5] =     18
```

Row-Column Sums

Listing 4-4 shows the source code for example Ch04_04, which demonstrates how to sum the rows and columns of an integer matrix. The C++ code for this example begins with a function named Init that initializes a test matrix with random values. The function CalcMatrixRowColSums is a C++ implementation of the row-column summing algorithm. This function sweeps through matrix x using a set of nested for-loops. During each inner loop iteration, CalcMatrixRowColsSums adds matrix element x[i][j] to col_sums[j]. The outer for-loop updates row_sums[i]. Function CalcMatrixRowColSums also uses the same matrix element offset arithmetic that you saw in the previous example.

Listing 4-4. Example Ch04_04

```cpp
//---------------------------------------------------
//              Ch04_04.cpp
//---------------------------------------------------

#include <iostream>
#include <random>

using namespace std;

// Ch04_04_.s
extern "C" bool CalcMatrixRowColSums_(int* row_sums, int* col_sums, const int* x, int nrows,
int ncols);

// Ch04_04_Misc.cpp
extern void PrintResult(const char* msg, const int* row_sums, const int* col_sums, const
int* x, int nrows, int ncols);
```

```
void Init(int* x, int nrows, int ncols)
{
    unsigned int seed = 13;
    uniform_int_distribution<> d {1, 200};
    mt19937 rng {seed};

    for (int i = 0; i < nrows * ncols; i++)
        x[i] = d(rng);
}

bool CalcMatrixRowColSums(int* row_sums, int* col_sums, const int* x, int nrows, int ncols)
{
    if (nrows <= 0 || ncols <= 0)
        return false;

    for (int j = 0; j < ncols; j++)
        col_sums[j] = 0;

    for (int i = 0; i < nrows; i++)
    {
        int row_sums_temp = 0;
        int k = i * ncols;

        for (int j = 0; j < ncols; j++)
        {
            int temp = x[k + j];
            row_sums_temp += temp;
            col_sums[j] += temp;
        }

        row_sums[i] = row_sums_temp;
    }

    return true;
}

int main()
{
    const int nrows = 8;
    const int ncols = 6;
    int x[nrows][ncols];

    Init((int*)x, nrows, ncols);

    int row_sums1[nrows], col_sums1[ncols];
    int row_sums2[nrows], col_sums2[ncols];

    const char* msg1 = "Results for CalcMatrixRowColSums";
    const char* msg2 = "Results for CalcMatrixRowColSums_";

    bool rc1 = CalcMatrixRowColSums(row_sums1, col_sums1, (int*)x, nrows, ncols);
```

```
        bool rc2 = CalcMatrixRowColSums_(row_sums2, col_sums2, (int*)x, nrows, ncols);

        if (!rc1)
            cout << "\nCalcMatrixRowSums failed\n";
        else
            PrintResult(msg1, row_sums1, col_sums1, (int*)x, nrows, ncols);

        if (!rc2)
            cout << "\nCalcMatrixRowSums_ failed\n";
        else
            PrintResult(msg2, row_sums2, col_sums2, (int*)x, nrows, ncols);

        return 0;
}

//--------------------------------------------------
//               Ch04_04_.s
//--------------------------------------------------

// extern "C" bool CalcMatrixRowColSums_(int* row_sums, int* col_sums, const int* x, int
nrows, int ncols);

                .text
                .global CalcMatrixRowColSums_

                .equ ARG_NCOLS,32

CalcMatrixRowColSums_:
                push {r4-r11}

                cmp r3,#0
                movle r0,#0                     // set error return code
                ble Done                        // jump if nrows <= 0

                ldr r4,[sp,#ARG_NCOLS]
                cmp r4,#0
                movle r0,#0                     // set error return code
                ble Done                        // jump if ncols <= 0

// Set elements of col_sums to zero
                mov r5,r1                       // r5 = col_sums
                mov r6,r4                       // r6 = ncols
                mov r7,#0

Loop0:          str r7,[r5],#4                  // col_sums[j] = 0
                subs r6,#1                      // j -= 1
                bne Loop0                       // jump if j != 0

// Main processing loops
                mov r5,#0                       // i = 0
```

```
Loop1:      mov r6,#0                      // j = 0
            mov r12,#0                     // row_sums_temp = 0
            mul r7,r5,r4                   // r7 = i * ncols

Loop2:      add r8,r7,r6                   // r8 = i * ncols + j
            ldr r9,[r2,r8,lsl #2]          // r9 = x[i][j]

// Update row_sums and col_sums using current x[i][j]
            add r12,r12,r9                 // row_sums_temp += x[i][j]

            add r10,r1,r6,lsl #2           // r10 = ptr to col_sums[j]
            ldr r11,[r10]                  // r11 = col_sums[j]
            add r11,r11,r9                 // col_sums[j] += x[i][j]
            str r11,[r10]                  // save col_sums[j]

            add r6,r6,#1                   // j += 1
            cmp r6,r4
            blt Loop2                      // jump if j < ncols

            str r12,[r0],#4                // save row_sums[i]

            add r5,r5,#1                   // i += 1
            cmp r5,r3
            blt Loop1                      // jump if i < nrows

            mov r0,#1                      // set success return code

Done:       pop {r4-r11}
            bx lr
```

The assembly language function CalcMatrixRowColSums_ implements the same algorithm as its C++ counterpart. Following preservation of non-volatile registers R4–R11 on the stack, arguments nrows and ncols are tested for validity. Note that ncols was passed via the stack. Also note the two uses of the movle r0,#0 instruction, which load R0 with the correct return code if either ncols or nrows is invalid. For-loop Loop0 then initializes each element in col_sums to zero.

Prior to the start of for-loop Loop1, a mov r5,#0 instruction sets index i equal to zero. Each Loop1 iteration begins with the instruction pair mov r6,#0 and mov r12,#0. These instructions initialize both index j (R6) and row_sums_temp (R12) to zero. The next instruction, mul r7,r5,r4, calculates i * ncols. At the start of for-loop Loop2, an add r8,r7,r6 instruction calculates the offset i * ncols + j for matrix element x[i][j]. The ensuing ldr r9,[r2,r8,lsl #2] instruction loads x[i][j] into R9 as illustrated in Figure 4-2. This is followed by an add r12,r12,r9 instruction that calculates row_sums_temp += x[i][j].

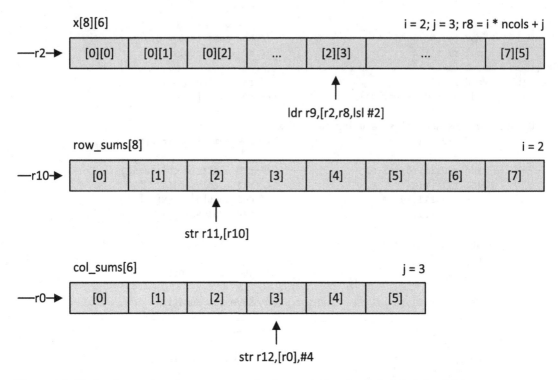

Figure 4-2. *Update instructions for* row_sums *and* col_sums *in function* CalcMatrixRowColSums_

The add r10,r1,r6,lsl #2 instruction computes the address of cols_sums[j]. In this instruction, which calculates R10 = R1 + (R6 << 2), R1 contains a pointer to the array cols_sums and R6 contains index j. The ensuing instruction triplet, ldr r11,[r10], add r11,r11,r9, and str r11,[r10], adds x[i] [j] to col_sums[j]. For-loop Loop2 continues to repeat so long as j < ncols is true. Following each Loop2 execution cycle, the str r12,[r0],#4 instruction saves row_sums_temp (R12) to row_sums[i]. Index i is then updated and Loop1 repeats while i < nrows is true. Here is the output for source code example Ch04_04:

```
Results for CalcMatrixRowColSums
-------------------------------------------------
    156    122     48    172    165    179    842
    194     36    195    152     91    151    819
    122    122    156    159    129     78    766
    145     69      8    133     60    182    597
     12    145    172     95     75    100    599
    136     90     52    107     70    199    654
      2    123     72     37    190    145    569
     44    188     64    108    184     95    683

    811    895    767    963    964   1129
```

Results for CalcMatrixRowColSums_

```
    156    122     48    172    165    179     842
    194     36    195    152     91    151     819
    122    122    156    159    129     78     766
    145     69      8    133     60    182     597
     12    145    172     95     75    100     599
    136     90     52    107     70    199     654
      2    123     72     37    190    145     569
     44    188     64    108    184     95     683

    811    895    767    963    964   1129
```

Advanced Programming

The source code examples in this section highlight a few advanced programming techniques. The first example introduces additional load and store instructions that you can use to access the elements of an array. The second example explains how to reference the members of a C++ structure in an assembly language function.

Array Reversal

Source code example Ch04_05 demonstrates a couple of array reversal techniques that use the ldmda (load multiple decrement after), ldmia (load multiple increment after), stmda (store multiple decrement after), and stmia (store multiple increment after) instructions. These instructions load or store multiple registers. Listing 4-5 shows the C++ and assembly language source code for example Ch04_05.

Listing 4-5. Example Ch04_05

```
//--------------------------------------------------
//                  Ch04_05.cpp
//--------------------------------------------------

#include <iostream>
#include <iomanip>
#include <random>

using namespace std;

extern "C" void ReverseArrayA_(int* y, const int* x, int n);
extern "C" void ReverseArrayB_(int* x, int n);

void Init(int* x, int n, unsigned int seed)
{
    uniform_int_distribution<> d {1, 1000};
    mt19937 rng {seed};

    for (int i = 0; i < n; i++)
        x[i] = d(rng);
}
```

```cpp
void PrintArray(const char* msg, const int* x, int n)
{
    const char nl = '\n';s

    cout << nl << msg << nl;

    for (int i = 0; i < n; i++)
    {
        cout << setw(5) << x[i];

        if ((i + 1) % 10 == 0)
            cout << nl;
    }
    cout << nl;
}

void ReverseArrayA(void)
{
    const int n = 25;
    int x[n], y[n];

    Init(x, n, 32);
    PrintArray("ReverseArrayA - original array x", x, n);
    ReverseArrayA_(y, x, n);
    PrintArray("ReverseArrayA - reversed array y", y, n);
}

void ReverseArrayB(void)
{
    const int n = 25;
    int x[n];

    Init(x, n, 32);
    PrintArray("ReverseArrayB - array x before reversal", x, n);
    ReverseArrayB_(x, n);
    PrintArray("ReverseArrayB - array x after reversal", x, n);
}

int main()
{
    ReverseArrayA();
    ReverseArrayB();
    return 0;
}

//-------------------------------------------------
//                 Ch04_05_.s
//-------------------------------------------------

// extern "C" void ReverseArrayA_(int* y, const int* x, int n);
```

```
            .text
            .global ReverseArrayA_
ReverseArrayA_:
              push {r4-r11}

// Initialize
            add r1,r1,r2,lsl #2
            sub r1,#4                       // r1 points to x[n - 1]
            cmp r2,#4
            blt SkipLoopA                   // jump if n < 4

// Main loop
LoopA:      ldmda r1!,{r4-r7}               // r4 = *r1
                                            // r5 = *(r1 - 4)
                                            // r6 = *(r1 - 8)
                                            // r7 = *(r1 - 12)
                                            // r1 -= 16

            mov r8,r7                        // reorder elements in
            mov r9,r6                        // r4 - r7 for use with
            mov r10,r5                       // stmia instruction
            mov r11,r4

            stmia r0!,{r8-r11}               // *r0 = r8
                                            // *(r0 + 4) = r9
                                            // *(r0 + 8) = r10
                                            // *(r0 + 12) = r11
                                            // r0 += 16

            sub r2,#4                        // n -= 4
            cmp r2,#4
            bge LoopA                        // jump if n >= 4

// Process remaining (0 - 3) array elements
SkipLoopA:  cmp r2,#0
            ble DoneA                        // jump if no more elements

            ldr r4,[r1],#-4                  // load single element from x
            str r4,[r0],#4                   // save element to y
            subs r2,#1                       // n -= 1
            beq DoneA                        // jump if n == 0

            ldr r4,[r1],#-4                  // load single element from x
            str r4,[r0],#4                   // save element to y
            subs r2,#1                       // n -= 1
            beq DoneA                        // jump if n == 0

            ldr r4,[r1]                      // load final element from x
            str r4,[r0]                      // save final element to y

DoneA:      pop {r4-r11}
```

```
            bx lr

// extern "C" void ReverseArrayB_(int* x, int n);

            .global ReverseArrayB_
ReverseArrayB_:
            push {r4-r11}

// Initialize
            mov r2,r1                        // r2 = n
            add r1,r0,r2,lsl #2
            sub r1,#4                        // r1 points to x[n - 1]
            cmp r2,#4
            blt SkipLoopB                    // jump if n < 4

LoopB:      ldmia r0,{r4,r5}                 // r4 = *r0, r5 = *(r0 + 4)
            ldmda r1,{r6,r7}                 // r6 = *r1, r7 = *(r1 - 4)

            mov r8,r7                        // reorder elements
            mov r9,r6                        // for use with stmia and
            mov r10,r5                       // stmda instructions
            mov r11,r4

            stmia r0!,{r8,r9}                // *r0 = r8, *(r0 + 4) = r9, r0 += 8
            stmda r1!,{r10,r11}              // *r1 = r10, *(r1 - 4) = r11, r1 -= 8

            sub r2,#4                        // n -= 4
            cmp r2,#4
            bge LoopB                        // jump if n >= 4

// Process remaining (0 - 3) array elements
SkipLoopB:  cmp r2,#1
            ble DoneB                        // jump if done

            ldr r4,[r0]                      // load final element
            ldr r5,[r1]                      // pair into r4:r5

            str r4,[r1]                      // save elements
            str r5,[r0]

DoneB:      pop {r4-r11}
            bx lr
```

The function ReverseArrayA_ copies elements from a source array to a destination array in reverse order. This function requires three parameters: a pointer to destination array y, a pointer to source array x, and the number of elements n. During its initialization phase, ReverseArrayA_ uses the instructions add r1,r1,r2,lsl #2 and sub r1,#4 to calculate the address of the last element in array x. It then checks the value of n to see if it is less than four. If n < 4 is true, ReverseArrayA_ skips over for-loop LoopA. The reason for this is that for-loop LoopA processes four elements during each iteration.

Figure 4-3 illustrates the ldmda/stmia instruction sequence that is used in for-loop LoopA. The first instruction of LoopA, ldmda r1!,{r4-r7}, loads four array elements into registers R4, R5, R6, and R7. This instruction also updates R1 so that it points to the preceding group of four elements. Next is a series of mov instructions that rearrange the elements in registers R4-R7 for use with the stmia instruction. Following the four mov instructions, R8, R9, R10, and R11 contain y[i], y[i+1], y[i+2], and y[i+3], respectively. The ensuing stmia r0!,{r8-r11} saves R8, R9, R10, and R11 to y[i:i+3]. This instruction also updates R0 so that it points to element y[i+4].

Array pointers before execution of ldmda r1!,{r4-r7} and stmia r0!,{r8-r11}

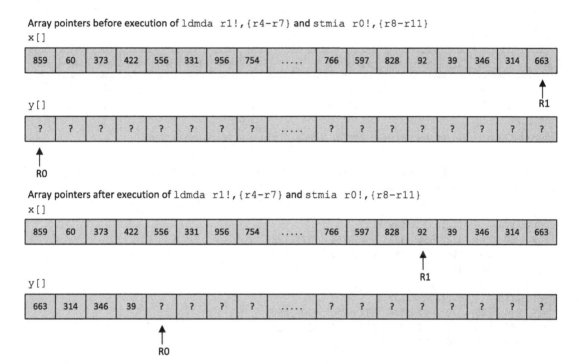

Figure 4-3. First execution of ldmda r1!,{r4-r7} *and* stmia r0!,{r8-r11} *instructions in function* ReverseArrayA_

Following execution of the stmia instruction, n is decremented by four and Loop1 repeats until n < 4 is true. The block of code that follows Loop1 reverses the final few elements of array x using ldr and str instructions. Note that after an element is reversed, n is decremented by one and tested to see if it is equal to zero.

Function ReverseArrayB_ performs an in-place reversal of an integer array. This function begins its execution by initializing R0 and R1 as pointers to the first and last elements of the input array x, respectively. The first instruction of for-loop LoopB, ldmia r0,{r4,r5}, loads two elements from the beginning of array x. The ldmda r1,{r6,r7} instruction that follows loads two elements from the end of array x. Following a series of mov instructions that rearrange these elements, ReverseArrayB_ uses the instructions stmia r0!,{r8,r9} and stmda r1!,{r10,r11} to finalize a four-element reversal as shown in Figure 4-4.

Array pointers before execution of `ldmia r0,{r4,r5}` and `ldmda r1,{r6,r7}`

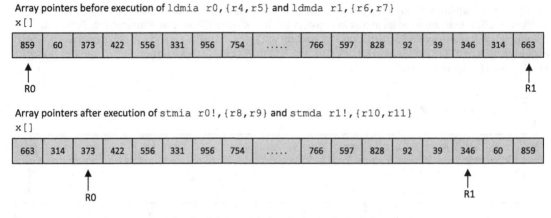

Figure 4-4. *Four-element reversal using* `ldmia, ldmda, stmia, and stmda` *instructions*

The block of code that follows LoopB performs a final two-element reversal if one is required. Here is the output for source code example Ch04_05:

```
ReverseArrayA - original array x
  859   60  373  422  556  331  956  754  737  732
  817  354  102  456  929  286  610  766  597  828
   92   39  346  314  663

ReverseArrayA - reversed array y
  663  314  346   39   92  828  597  766  610  286
  929  456  102  354  817  732  737  754  956  331
  556  422  373   60  859

ReverseArrayB - array x before reversal
  859   60  373  422  556  331  956  754  737  732
  817  354  102  456  929  286  610  766  597  828
   92   39  346  314  663

ReverseArrayB - array x after reversal
  663  314  346   39   92  828  597  766  610  286
  929  456  102  354  817  732  737  754  956  331
  556  422  373   60  859
```

Structures

A structure is a programming language construct that facilitates the definition of new data types using one or more existing data types. In C++, a structure is essentially the same as a class. When a data type is defined using the keyword struct instead of class, all members are public by default. A C++ struct that is declared sans any member functions or operators is analogous to a C-style structure such as typedef struct { ... } MyStruct;. C++ structure declarations are usually placed in a header (.h) file so they can be easily referenced by multiple C++ files.

The address of a structure member is simply the starting address of the structure in memory plus the member's offset in bytes. During compilation, most C++ compilers align structure members to their natural boundary, which means that structures frequently contain extra padding bytes. It is not possible to define a structure in a header file and include this file in both C++ and assembly language source code files. However, a simple solution to this dilemma is to use the C++ offsetof macro to determine the offset for each structure member and then use .equ directives in the assembly language file. You will learn how to do this shortly.

Listing 4-6 shows the C++ and assembly language source code for example Ch04_06. In the C++ code, a simple structure named TestStruct is defined. This structure uses sized integer types instead of the more common C++ types to highlight the exact size of each member.

Listing 4-6. Example Ch04_06

```
//---------------------------------------------------
//                 Ch04_06.cpp
//---------------------------------------------------

#include <iostream>
#include <iomanip>
#include <cstdint>
#include <cstddef>

using namespace std;

struct TestStruct
{
    int8_t ValA;
    int8_t ValB;
    int32_t ValC;
    int16_t ValD;
    int32_t ValE;
    uint8_t ValF;
    uint16_t ValG;
};

extern "C" int32_t CalcTestStructSum_(const TestStruct* ts);

void PrintTestStructOffsets(void)
{
    const char nl = '\n';

    cout << "offsetof(ts.ValA) = " << offsetof(TestStruct, ValA) << nl;
    cout << "offsetof(ts.ValB) = " << offsetof(TestStruct, ValB) << nl;
    cout << "offsetof(ts.ValC) = " << offsetof(TestStruct, ValC) << nl;
    cout << "offsetof(ts.ValD) = " << offsetof(TestStruct, ValD) << nl;
    cout << "offsetof(ts.ValE) = " << offsetof(TestStruct, ValE) << nl;
    cout << "offsetof(ts.ValF) = " << offsetof(TestStruct, ValF) << nl;
    cout << "offsetof(ts.ValG) = " << offsetof(TestStruct, ValG) << nl;
}
```

```
int32_t CalcTestStructSum(const TestStruct* ts)
{
    int32_t temp1 = ts->ValA + ts->ValB + ts->ValC + ts->ValD;
    int32_t temp2 = ts->ValE + ts->ValF + ts->ValG;

    return temp1 + temp2;
}

int main()
{
    const char nl = '\n';
    PrintTestStructOffsets();

    TestStruct ts;
    ts.ValA = -100;
    ts.ValB = 75;
    ts.ValC = 1000000;
    ts.ValD = -3000;
    ts.ValE = 400000;
    ts.ValF = 200;
    ts.ValG = 50000;

    int32_t sum1 = CalcTestStructSum(&ts);
    int32_t sum2 = CalcTestStructSum_(&ts);

    cout << nl << "Results for CalcTestStructSum" << nl;
    cout << "ts1.ValA = " << (int)ts.ValA << nl;
    cout << "ts1.ValB = " << (int)ts.ValB << nl;
    cout << "ts1.ValC = " << ts.ValC << nl;
    cout << "ts1.ValD = " << ts.ValD << nl;
    cout << "ts1.ValE = " << ts.ValE << nl;
    cout << "ts1.ValF = " << (int)ts.ValF << nl;
    cout << "ts1.ValG = " << ts.ValG << nl;
    cout << "sum1 =      " << sum1 << nl;
    cout << "sum2 =      " << sum2 << nl;

    if (sum1 != sum2)
        cout << "Compare error!" << nl;

    return 0;
}

//---------------------------------------------------
//                  Ch04_06_.s
//---------------------------------------------------

// extern "C" int32_t CalcTestStructSum_(const TestStruct* ts);

// Offsets for TestStruct
            .equ S_ValA,0                       // int8_t
            .equ S_ValB,1                       // int8_t
```

```
            .equ S_ValC,4                   // int32_t
            .equ S_ValD,8                   // int16_t
            .equ S_ValE,12                  // int32_t
            .equ S_ValF,16                  // uint8_t
            .equ S_ValG,18                  // uint16_t

            .text
            .global CalcTestStructSum_
CalcTestStructSum_:

// Sum the elements of TestStruct
            ldrsb r1,[r0,#S_ValA]           // r1 = ValA (sign-extended)
            ldrsb r2,[r0,#S_ValB]           // r2 = ValB (sign-extended)
            add r1,r1,r2

            ldr r2,[r0,#S_ValC]             // r2 = ValC
            add r1,r1,r2

            ldrsh r2,[r0,#S_ValD]           // r2 = ValD (sign-extended)
            add r1,r1,r2

            ldr r2,[r0,#S_ValE]             // r2 = ValE
            add r1,r1,r2

            ldrb r2,[r0,#S_ValF]            // r2 = ValF (zero-extended)
            add r1,r1,r2

            ldrh r2,[r0,#S_ValG]            // r2 = ValG (zero-extended)
            add r1,r1,r2

            mov r0,r1
            bx lr
```

Following the definition of TestStruct is a function named PrintTestStructOffsets. The function main calls this function, which prints the offset in bytes of each member in TestStruct. These results were then used to define .equ directives in the assembly language file for the members in TestStruct. The remaining code in main initializes an instance of TestStruct, calls CalcTestStructSum and CalcTestStructSum_, and displays results. The functions CalcTestStructSum and CalcTestStructSum_ both sum the members in TestStruct.

The assembly language code in Listing 4-6 begins with the aforementioned .equ directives that define offsets for each structure member. The sole argument value for CalcTestStructSum_ is a pointer to the caller's TestStruct. The calculating code in CalcTestStructSum_ uses various forms of the ldr instruction, which you have already seen, to load each structure member into a register. Note that each ldr instruction uses simple offset addressing. Here is the output for source code example Ch04_06:

```
offsetof(ts.ValA) = 0
offsetof(ts.ValB) = 1
offsetof(ts.ValC) = 4
offsetof(ts.ValD) = 8
offsetof(ts.ValE) = 12
offsetof(ts.ValF) = 16
```

```
offsetof(ts.ValG) = 18

Results for CalcTestStructSum
ts1.ValA = -100
ts1.ValB = 75
ts1.ValC = 1000000
ts1.ValD = -3000
ts1.ValE = 400000
ts1.ValF = 200
ts1.ValG = 50000
sum1 =      1447175
sum2 =      1447175
```

You will see other examples of assembly language structure use later in this book.

Summary

Here are the key learning points for Chapter 4:

- The address of an element in a one-dimensional array can be calculated using the base address (i.e., the address of the first element) of the array, the index of the element, and the size in bytes of each element. The address of an element in a two-dimensional array can be calculated using the base address of the array, the row and column indices, the number of columns, and the size in bytes of each element.

- Post-indexed addressing (e.g., ldr r1,[r0],#4) is often used to implement a for-loop that processes the elements of an array that contains 32-bit wide integers. Post-indexed addressing can also be used for arrays containing 8- and 16-bit wide integers.

- A function can use the lsl operator in a ldr instruction (e.g., ldr r2,[r0,r1,lsl #2]) to load array element x[i] into a register. In this example, R0 contains the address of array x and R1 contains the index i.

- A function can use the instruction pair ldr r0,=VarName and ldr r0,[r0] to load the value of C++ global variable VarName into register R0.

- Functions can use the ldmdb, ldmia, stmdb, and stmia instructions to load multiple elements from or store multiple elements to an array.

- Assembly language load and store instructions can reference members of a structure in memory using .equ directives and the output of the C++ offsetof operator.

CHAPTER 5

■ ■ ■

Armv8-32 Floating-Point Architecture

Chapter 5 examines the scalar floating-point capabilities of Armv8-32. It begins with a section that explains important floating-point concepts including data types, bit encodings, and special values. Software developers who understand these concepts are often able to improve the performance of algorithms that make heavy use of floating-point arithmetic and minimize potential floating-point errors. The next section describes the Armv8-32 floating-point architecture. It begins with an overview of the Armv8-32 floating-point register file and its overlapping register scheme. This is followed by a detailed description of the floating-point status and control register (FPSCR).

While the primary focus of this chapter is Armv8-32 scalar floating-point, most of the content also applies to Armv8-64 scalar floating-point. You will also need to thoroughly understand the discussions presented in this chapter to comprehend Armv8-32 and Armv8-64 floating-point SIMD resources, which are described in later chapters.

Floating-Point Programming Concepts

In mathematics, a real-number system depicts an infinite continuum of all possible positive and negative numbers including integers, rational numbers, and irrational numbers. Given their finite resources, modern computing architectures typically employ a floating-point system to approximate a real-number system. Like many other computing platforms, the Armv8-A floating-point system is based on the IEEE 754 standard for binary floating-point arithmetic. This standard includes specifications that define bit encodings, range limits, and precisions for scalar floating-point values. The IEEE 754 standard also specifies important details related to floating-point arithmetic operations, rounding rules, and numerical exceptions.

The Armv8-A profile supports common floating-point operations using single-precision (32-bit) and double-precision (64-bit) values. Many compilers including GNU C++ use the Armv8-A intrinsic single-precision and double-precision types to implement the C++ types float and double. Figure 5-1 illustrates the memory organization of half-, single-, and double-precision floating-point values. This figure also includes common integer types for comparison purposes.

© Daniel Kusswurm 2020
D. Kusswurm, *Modern Arm Assembly Language Programming*,
https://doi.org/10.1007/978-1-4842-6267-2_5

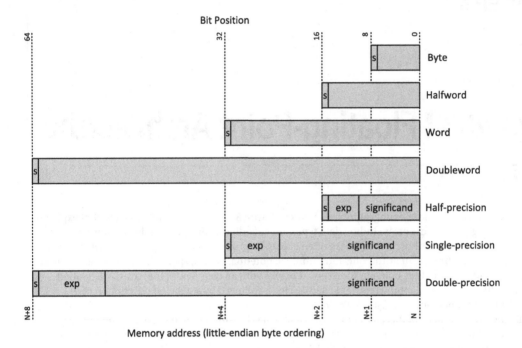

Figure 5-1. *Memory organization of floating-point values*

The binary encoding of a floating-point value requires three distinct fields: a significand, an exponent, and a sign bit. The significand field represents a number's significant digits (or fractional part). The exponent specifies the location of the binary "decimal" point in the significand, which determines the magnitude. The sign bit indicates whether the number is positive (s = 0) or negative (s = 1). Table 5-1 lists the various size parameters that are used to encode half-, single-, and double-precision floating-point values.

Table 5-1. *Floating-point size parameters*

Parameter	Half-Precision	Single-Precision	Double-Precision
Total width	16 bits	32 bits	64 bits
Significand width	10 bits	23 bits	52 bits
Exponent width	5 bits	8 bits	11 bits
Sign width	1 bit	1 bit	1 bit
Exponent bias	+15	+127	+1023

Figure 5-2 illustrates how to convert a decimal number into an IEEE 754–compatible floating-point encoded value. In this example, the number 237.8125 is transformed from a decimal number to its single-precision floating-point encoding. The process starts by converting the number from base 10 to base 2. Next, the base 2 value is transformed to a binary scientific value. The value to the right of the E_2 symbol is the binary exponent. A properly encoded floating-point value uses a biased exponent instead of the true exponent since this expedites floating-point compare operations. For a single-precision floating-point number, the bias value is +127. Adding the exponent bias value to the true exponent generates a binary scientific number with a biased exponent value. In the example that is shown in Figure 5-2, adding 111b (+7) to 1111111b (+127) yields a binary scientific with a biased exponent value of 10000110b (+134).

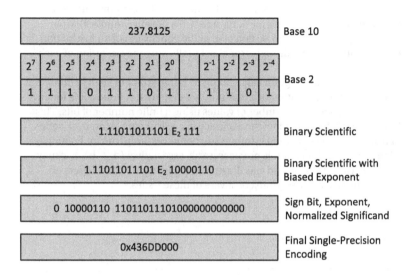

Figure 5-2. *Single-precision floating-point encoding process*

When encoding a floating-point value, the leading 1 digit of the significand is implied and not included in the final binary representation. Dropping the leading 1 digit forms a normalized significand. The three fields required for an IEEE 754–compliant encoding are now available, as shown in Figure 5-2. A reading of these bit fields from left to right yields the 32-bit value 0x436DD000, which is the final single-precision floating-point encoding of 237.8125.

The IEEE 754 floating-point encoding scheme reserves a small set of bit patterns for special values that are used to handle specific processing conditions. The first group of special values includes denormalized numbers (also called subnormal numbers). The IEEE 754 standard uses denormalized numbers to mitigate the effects of arithmetic underflows. As explained in the earlier encoding example, the standard encoding of a floating-point number assumes that the leading digit of the significand is always a 1. One limitation of IEEE 754 floating-point encoding scheme is its inability to accurately represent numbers very close to zero. In these cases, values are encoded using a nonstandard encoding, which enables tiny numbers (both positive and negative) close to zero to be encoded using less precision. This nonstandard encoding is a denormalized number. In algorithms where the use of denormalized numbers is problematic (e.g., when precision is critical), the processor can be configured to generate an exception. The processor can also be configured automatically flush (or round) a denormalized number to zero.

Another application of special values involves the encodings that are used for floating-point zero. The IEEE 754 standard supports two different representations of floating-point zero: positive zero (+0.0) and negative zero (-0.0). A negative zero can be generated either algorithmically or as a side effect of the floating-point rounding mode. Computationally, the processor treats positive and negative zero the same and the programmer typically does not need to be concerned.

The IEEE 754 encoding scheme also supports positive and negative representations of infinity. Infinities are produced by certain numerical algorithms, overflow conditions, or division by zero. As discussed later in this chapter, the processor can be configured to generate an exception whenever a floating-point overflow occurs or if a program attempts to divide a number by zero.

The final special value is called Not a Number (NaN). NaNs are floating-point encodings that represent invalid numbers. The IEEE 754 standard defines two types of NaNs: signaling NaN (SNaN) and quiet NaN (QNaN). SNaNs are created by software. An Armv8-A processor will not generate a SNaN during execution of an arithmetic operation. Any attempt by an instruction to use a SNaN operand will cause the processor to raise an invalid operation exception unless the exception is disabled. SNaNs are sometimes employed to debug floating-point code. They can also be used to test floating-point exception handlers. QNaNs are used to signify an invalid result (e.g., calculating the square root of a negative number) when exceptions are masked. This allows floating-point errors to be detected at the conclusion of an instruction sequence instead of performing explicit and time-consuming error checks following the execution of each floating-point instruction.

When developing software that performs floating-point calculations, it is important to keep in mind that the IEEE 754 encoding scheme is simply an approximation of a real-number system. It is impossible for any floating-point encoding system to represent an infinite number of values using a finite number of bits. This leads to floating-point rounding imprecisions that can affect the accuracy of a calculation. Moreover, some mathematical properties that hold true for integers and real numbers are not necessarily true for floating-point numbers. For example, floating-point multiplication is not necessarily associative; (a * b) * c may not equal a * (b * c) depending on the values of a, b, and c as illustrated in Listing 5-1. Developers of algorithms that require high levels of numerical accuracy must be aware of these issues.

Listing 5-1. Example Ch05_01

```
//--------------------------------------------------
//                  Ch05_01.cpp
//--------------------------------------------------

#include <iostream>
#include <iomanip>

using namespace std;

union Val
{
    float f;
    unsigned int u;
};

void PrintResult(const char* msg, float a, float b, float c, float d)
{
    const char nl = '\n';
    const size_t w = 8;

    Val v;
    v.f = d;

    cout << fixed << setprecision(8);
    cout << nl << msg << nl;
    cout << "a:          " << setw(w) << a << nl;
    cout << "b:          " << setw(w) << b << nl;
    cout << "c:          " << setw(w) << c << nl;
    cout << scientific << setprecision(8);
    cout << "d (float):  " << setw(w) << d << nl;
    cout << "d (binary):  0x" << hex << setw(8) << v.u << nl;
}
```

```
int main(int argc, char** argv)
{
    float a = 0.01;
    float b = 0.001;
    float c = 0.0001;
    float d1 = (a * b) * c;
    float d2 = a * (b * c);

    PrintResult("Results for (a * b) * c", a, b, c, d1);
    PrintResult("Results for a * (b * c)", a, b, c, d2);
}
```

Here are the results for source code example Ch05_01:

```
Results for (a * b) * c
a:            0.01000000
b:            0.00100000
c:            0.00010000
d (float):    1.00000008e-09
d (binary):   0x30897060

Results for a * (b * c)
a:            0.01000000
b:            0.00100000
c:            0.00010000
d (float):    9.99999972e-10
d (binary):   0x3089705f
```

Armv8-32 Floating-Point Architecture

In this section, you will learn about the Armv8-32 floating-point architecture. The architecture includes an independent floating-point register file that programs can use to perform scalar floating-point arithmetic and other floating-point operations. It also incorporates a 32-bit wide status and control register that reports floating-point status information and enables floating-point option configuration.

Floating-Point Registers

The AArch32 execution state encompasses a register file that supports floating-point calculations using single-precision and double-precision floating-point values. It also supports half-precision floating-point arithmetic on processors that include the Armv8.2-FP16 extension. The floating-point register file includes 32 registers named S0–S31. These 32-bit wide registers hold single-precision floating-point operands. The S registers (low-order 16 bits) also support half-precision floating-point operands. The floating-point register file also includes 32 registers named D0–D31. These 64-bit wide registers facilitate calculations using double-precision floating-point operands. Figure 5-3 illustrates the floating-point register file in greater detail.

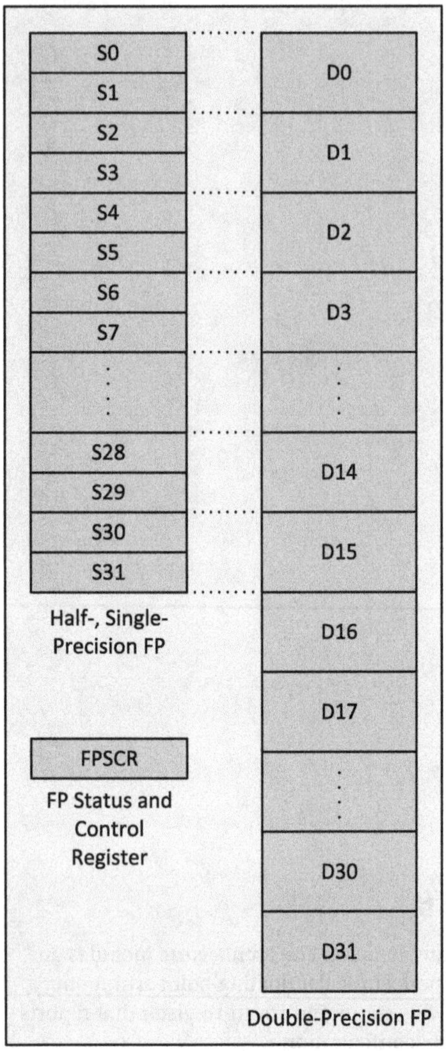

Figure 5-3. *AArch32 floating-point register file*

Registers S0–S31 and D0–D15 are organized using an overlapping arrangement. Register S<2n> maps to the low-order 32 bits of register D<n>, and register S<2n+1> maps to the high-order 32 bits of register D<n>. This means that when register S<2n> or S<2n+1> contains a single-precision floating-point value, the corresponding mapped D<n> register cannot hold a double-precision value. Similarly, when register D<n> contains a double-precision value, registers S<2n> and S<2n+1> cannot store single-precision values. This register overlapping arrangement also extends to the SIMD registers. You will learn more about this in Chapter 7.

Floating-Point Status and Control Register

The floating-point status and control register (FPSCR) contains status bits that provide information about floating-point operations. It also includes control bits that specify floating-point processing options including rounding mode, default NaN mode, flush-to-zero mode, and exception trapping. Figure 5-4 shows the organization of the status and control bits in the FPSCR. Table 5-2 describes the function of each bit field.

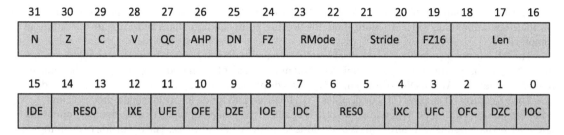

31	30	29	28	27	26	25	24	23	22	21	20	19	18	17	16
N	Z	C	V	QC	AHP	DN	FZ	RMode		Stride		FZ16	Len		

15	14	13	12	11	10	9	8	7	6	5	4	3	2	1	0
IDE	RES0		IXE	UFE	OFE	DZE	IOE	IDC	RES0		IXC	UFC	OFC	DZC	IOC

Figure 5-4. *FPSCR status and control bits*

Table 5-2. *Description of FPSCR bit fields*

Bit Field	Description
N	Negative condition flag. Updated during floating-point compare operations.
Z	Zero condition flag. Updated during floating-point compare operations.
C	Carry condition flag. Updated during floating-point compare operations.
V	Overflow condition flag. Updated during floating-point compare operations.
QC	Cumulative saturation bit. Integer SIMD saturation status bit (1 = saturation occurred).
AHP	Alternate half-precision control bit. Specifies format for half-precision conversions.
DN	Default NaN mode control bit. Instructs processor to use a default NaN for some operations.
FZ	Flush-to-zero control. Enables flush-to-zero mode for scalar floating-point arithmetic.
RMode	Rounding mode control bits. Selects rounding mode for scalar floating-point operations.
Stride	Stride field. This field is obsolete in Armv8.
FZ16	Flush-to-zero control F16. Enables flush-to-zero mode for half-precision arithmetic.
Len	Length field. This field is obsolete in Armv8.
IDE	Input denormal exception trap enable bit.
RES0	Reserved bits.
IXE	Inexact floating-point exception trap enable control bit.
UFE	Underflow floating-point exception trap enable control bit.
OFE	Overflow floating-point exception trap enable control bit.
DZE	Divide by zero floating-point exception trap control bit.
IOE	Invalid operation floating-point exception trap control bit.
IDC	Invalid denormal cumulative floating-point exception status bit.
RES0	Reserved bits.
IXC	Inexact cumulative floating-point exception status bit.
UFC	Underflow cumulative floating-point exception status bit.
OFC	Overflow cumulative floating-point exception status bit.
DZC	Divide by zero cumulative floating-point exception status bit.
IOC	Invalid operation cumulative floating-point exception status bit.

The floating-point compare instructions use the FPSCR's NZCV condition flags to report results of compare operations. You will learn more about the floating-point condition flags and compare operations in Chapter 6.

The DN control bit enables ("1") or disables ("0") the use of default NaNs. When DN is enabled, the processor returns an Armv8-defined default NaN whenever a scalar floating-point operation involves one or more NaN operands. When DN is disabled, NaN operands propagate through to the destination operand.

The FZ control bit enables ("1") or disables ("0") flush-to-zero mode for scalar single-precision and double-precision arithmetic. When flush-to-zero is enabled, the processor replaces denormalized operands and intermediate results with zero. This is often done to improve performance. The downside of enabling flush-to-zero mode is noncompliance with the IEEE 754 floating-point standard.

The RMode field specifies the rounding mode for scalar floating-point operations. Options include round to nearest (0b00), round toward plus infinity (0b01), round toward minus infinity (0b10), and round toward zero (0b11). You will learn more about floating-point rounding modes in Chapter 6.

The FZ16 control bit enables ("1") or disables ("0") flush-to-zero mode for scalar half-precision floating-point arithmetic.

The IDE, IXE, UFE, OFE, DZE, and IOE control bits enable processor exceptions for the floating-point error conditions. Table 5-3 summarizes these control bits and the corresponding error conditions. On many systems, application programs are not allowed to modify the control bits that enable floating-point exceptions. However, most C++ runtime environments provide a library function that allows an application program to designate a callback function that gets invoked whenever a floating-point exception occurs.

Table 5-3. *Floating-point exceptions and error conditions*

Bit Field	Exception	Error Condition
IDE	Input denormal	Operation replaced a denormalized input operand with zero.
IXE	Inexact operation	Operation generated a result that is not equivalent to a corresponding unbounded precision and exponent range value.
UFE	Underflow	Operation produced (before rounding) a result whose absolute value is less than the minimum positive normalized number for the destination precision.
OFE	Overflow	Operation produced (before rounding) a result whose absolute value is greater than the maximum positive normalized number for the destination precision.
DZE	Division by zero	Operation used a zero divisor with a dividend that is not zero, infinity, or NaN.
IOE	Invalid operation	Operation has no mathematical value or is unrepresentable.

The IDC, IXC, UFC, OFC, DZC, and IOC status bits report a floating-point error condition when the corresponding floating-point exception is disabled. An application program can read and write these bits using the vmrs (move special register to general-purpose register) and vmsr (move general-purpose register to special register) instructions, respectively. The floating-point error condition status bits are not automatically cleared by the processor after an error is detected; they must be manually reset. Some of the FPSCR's status and control bits are also used for SIMD operations. You will learn more about this in Chapter 7.

Summary

Here are the key learning points for Chapter 5:

- Armv8 floating-point operations are based on the IEEE 754 standard for floating-point arithmetic.

- Armv8 supports scalar floating-point operations using single-precision and double-precision values. Half-precision values are supported on processors that include the Armv8.2-FP16 extension.

- The AArch32 execution state includes registers S0–S31 for half- and single-precision operands and registers D0–D31 for double-precision operands. Registers S0–S31 overlap registers D0–D15.

- The FPSCR contains status bits that provide information about floating-point operations. It also includes control bits that specify floating-point processing options including rounding mode, default NaN mode, flush-to-zero mode, and exception trapping.

CHAPTER 6

■ ■ ■

Armv8-32 Floating-Point Programming

This chapter covers scalar floating-point programming. The first set of source code examples teaches the basics of floating-point arithmetic using single-precision and double-precision floating-point values. The next set of examples explains how to perform floating-point comparisons and conversions. This is followed by a couple of source code examples that illustrate the use of floating-point arrays and matrices. The final source code example describes how to call a C++ library function from an assembly language function. Besides these topics, Chapter 6 also discusses important details about the GNU C++ calling convention and its requirements for floating-point argument and return values.

■ **Note** Developing software that employs floating-point arithmetic always entails some noteworthy caveats. The floating-point source code examples presented in this and subsequent chapters are designed to illustrate the use of various Armv8-A floating-point instructions. The examples do not address important floating-point concerns such as rounding errors, numerical stability, or ill-conditioned functions. Software developers must always be cognizant of these issues during the design and implementation of any algorithm that employs floating-point arithmetic. Appendix B contains a list of references that you can consult if you are interested in learning more about the potential pitfalls of floating-point arithmetic.

Floating-Point Arithmetic

In this section, you will learn how to code functions that perform scalar floating-point arithmetic using the A32 instruction set. The source code examples demonstrate fundamental operations using both single-precision and double-precision values. You will also learn important details about passing floating-point argument and return values between a C++ and assembly function.

Single-Precision Arithmetic

Listing 6-1 shows the C++ and assembly language source code for a simple program that performs temperature conversions between Fahrenheit and Celsius using single-precision floating-point arithmetic. The C++ code begins with a declaration for the assembly language function ConvertFtoC_. Note that this function requires one argument of type float and returns a value of type float. A similar declaration is also used for the assembly language function ConvertCtoF_. The remaining C++ code exercises the two temperature conversion functions using several test values and displays the results.

Listing 6-1. Example Ch06_01

```
//---------------------------------------------------
//                  Ch06_01.cpp
//---------------------------------------------------

#include <iostream>
#include <iomanip>

using namespace std;

extern "C" float ConvertFtoC_(float deg_f);
extern "C" float ConvertCtoF_(float deg_c);

int main(int argc, char** argv)
{
    const char nl = '\n';
    const int w = 10;
    float deg_fvals[] = {-459.67f, -40.0f, 0.0f, 32.0f,
                         72.0f, 98.6f, 212.0f};
    size_t nf = sizeof(deg_fvals) / sizeof(float);

    cout << setprecision(6);

    cout << "\n-------- ConvertFtoC Results --------\n";

    for (size_t i = 0; i < nf; i++)
    {
        float deg_c = ConvertFtoC_(deg_fvals[i]);

        cout << "  i: " << i << "  ";
        cout << "f: " << setw(w) << deg_fvals[i] << "  ";
        cout << "c: " << setw(w) << deg_c << nl;
    }

    cout << "\n-------- ConvertCtoF Results --------\n";

    float deg_cvals[] = {-273.15f, -40.0f, -17.777778f, 0.0f,
                         25.0f, 37.0f, 100.0f};
    size_t nc = sizeof(deg_cvals) / sizeof(float);

    for (size_t i = 0; i < nc; i++)
    {
        float deg_f = ConvertCtoF_(deg_cvals[i]);

        cout << "  i: " << i << "  ";
        cout << "c: " << setw(w) << deg_cvals[i] << "  ";
        cout << "f: " << setw(w) << deg_f << nl;
    }
```

```
        return 0;
}

//----------------------------------------------------
//                  Ch06_01_.s
//----------------------------------------------------

// Constants for temperature conversion functions
                .text
r4_ScaleFtoC:   .single 0.55555556          // 5 / 9
r4_ScaleCtoF:   .single 1.8                 // 9 / 5
r4_32p0:        .single 32.0

// extern "C" float ConvertFtoC_(float deg_f);

                .global ConvertFtoC_
ConvertFtoC_:
                vldr.f32 s1,r4_32p0          // s1 = 32
                vldr.f32 s2,r4_ScaleFtoC     // s2 = 5 / 9
                vsub.f32 s3,s0,s1            // s3 = deg_f - 32
                vmul.f32 s0,s3,s2            // s0 = (deg_f - 32) * 5 / 9
                bx lr

// extern "C" float ConvertCtoF_(float deg_c);

                .global ConvertCtoF_
ConvertCtoF_:
                vldr.f32 s1,r4_32p0          // s1 = 32
                vldr.f32 s2,r4_ScaleCtoF     // s2 = 9 / 5
                vmul.f32 s3,s0,s2            // s3 = deg_c * 9 / 5
                vadd.f32 s0,s3,s1            // s3 = deg_c * 9 / 5 + 32
                bx lr
```

Assembly language functions ConvertFtoC_ and ConvertCtoF_ use the following equations to carry out their respective conversions:

$$C = (F - 32) \times 5 / 9$$
$$F = C \times 9 / 5 + 32$$

The assembly language code in Listing 6-1 begins with a series of .single directives that define the floating-point constants needed to convert a temperature value from Fahrenheit to Celsius and vice versa. Note that these constants are defined in the same .text section as the assembly language functions ConvertFtoC_ and ConvertCtoF_. The first instruction of ConvertFtoC_, vldr.f32 s1,r4_32p0 (load SIMD/FP register), loads the single-precision floating-point value that is specified by the label r4_32p0 (32.0) into register S1. The form of the vldr instruction that is used here requires the source operand r4_32p0 to be stored in memory on a word boundary at an offset ±1020 bytes from the address of the vldr instruction + 8 bytes, which explains the positioning of the constants in the .text section. Note that the use of the .f32 size suffix on the vldr instruction mnemonic is optional in this instance but required in others. The source code examples in this book use size suffixes on all A32 floating-point instructions for consistency and improved readability. The next instruction, vldr.f32 s2,r4_ScaleFtoC, loads the Fahrenheit to Celsius scale factor 0.55555556 into register S2.

Before examining the remaining assembly language code, a few additional words about the GNU C++ calling convention are warranted. According to the calling convention, floating-point argument values are passed to a called function using registers S0–S15 (single-precision) or registers D0–D7 (double-precision). Any remaining arguments are passed via the stack. The GNU C++ calling convention also designates floating-point registers S0–S15 (D0–D7) and D16–D31 as volatile registers, which means that they need not be preserved by a called function. Registers S16–S32 (D8–D15) are designated as non-volatile. A called function must preserve the values in these registers on the stack before first use. Functions that return a single-precision or double-precision floating-point value must use S0 or D0, respectively. Table 6-1 summarizes these GNU C++ calling convention requirements. You will see examples of the GNU C++ calling convention requirements for SIMD registers Q0–Q15 in Chapters 8 and 9.

Table 6-1. *GNU C++ calling convention requirements for floating-point and SIMD registers*

Single-Precision	Double-Precision	SIMD	Type	Role
S0–S1	D0	Q0 (low 64 bits)	Volatile	Argument values, return value, scratch registers
S2–S3	D1	Q0 (upper 64 bits)	Volatile	Argument values, scratch registers
S4–S7	D2–D3	Q1	Volatile	Argument values, scratch registers
S8–S11	D4–D5	Q2	Volatile	Argument values, scratch registers
S12–S15	D6–D7	Q3	Volatile	Argument values, scratch registers
S16–S31	D8–D15	Q4–Q7	Non-volatile	Scratch registers
None	D16–D31	Q8–Q15	Volatile	Scratch registers

Following the two vldr instructions that load r4_32p0 and r4_ScaleFtoC into registers S1 and S2, ConvertFtoC_ uses a vsub.f32 s3,s0,s1 (floating-point subtract) instruction that calculates deg_f - 32.0. Note that argument value deg_f was passed to ConvertFtoC_ in register S0. The next instruction, vmul.f32 s0,s3,s2 (floating-point multiply), calculates (deg_f - 32) * 5 / 9. No additional instructions are necessary since the required return value is already in register S0.

Assembly language function ConvertCtoF_ uses similar instructions to perform a Celsius to Fahrenheit conversion. The vldr.f32 s1,r4_32p0 and vldr.f32 s2,r4_ScaleCtoF instructions load the requisite constants into registers S1 and S2. The ensuing vmul.f32 s3,s0,s2 instruction calculates deg_c * 9 / 5. This is followed by a vadd.f32 s0,s3,s1 (floating-point add) instruction that computes the final result. At this point, it would be scientifically remiss for me not to mention that neither ConvertFtoC_ nor ConvertCtoF_ perform any validity checks for argument values that are physically impossible (e.g., -1000 degrees Fahrenheit). Such checks require floating-point compare instructions, and you will learn how to use these instructions later in this chapter. Here are the results for source code example Ch06_01:

```
-------- ConvertFtoC Results --------
 i: 0  f:   -459.67  c:   -273.15
 i: 1  f:       -40  c:       -40
 i: 2  f:         0  c:  -17.7778
 i: 3  f:        32  c:         0
 i: 4  f:        72  c:   22.2222
 i: 5  f:      98.6  c:        37
 i: 6  f:       212  c:       100
```

```
-------- ConvertCtoF Results --------
  i: 0  c:    -273.15  f:   -459.67
  i: 1  c:        -40  f:       -40
  i: 2  c:   -17.7778  f:         0
  i: 3  c:          0  f:        32
  i: 4  c:         25  f:        77
  i: 5  c:         37  f:      98.6
  i: 6  c:        100  f:       212
```

Double-Precision Arithmetic

The two source code examples presented in this section illustrate simple floating-point arithmetic using double-precision values. Listing 6-2 shows the source code for example Ch06_02. In this example, the assembly language function CalcSphereAreaVolume_ calculates the surface area and volume of a sphere using the supplied radius value.

Listing 6-2. Example Ch06_02

```cpp
//---------------------------------------------------
//                  Ch06_02.cpp
//---------------------------------------------------

#include <iostream>
#include <iomanip>

using namespace std;

extern "C" void CalcSphereAreaVolume_(double r, double* sa, double* vol);

int main(int argc, char** argv)
{
    double r[] = { 0.0, 1.0, 2.0, 3.0, 5.0, 10.0, 20.0, 32.0 };
    size_t num_r = sizeof(r) / sizeof(double);

    cout << setprecision(8);
    cout << "\n------ Results for CalcSphereAreaVolume ------\n";

    for (size_t i = 0; i < num_r; i++)
    {
        double sa = -1, vol = -1;

        CalcSphereAreaVolume_(r[i], &sa, &vol);

        cout << "r: " << setw(6) << r[i] << "   ";
        cout << "sa: " << setw(11) << sa << "   ";
        cout << "vol: " << setw(11) << vol << '\n';
    }

    return 0;
}
```

```
//---------------------------------------------------
//                 Ch06_02_.s
//---------------------------------------------------

            .text
r8_PI:      .double 3.14159265358979323846

// extern "C" void CalcSphereAreaVolume_(double r, double* sa, double* vol);

            .global CalcSphereAreaVolume_
CalcSphereAreaVolume_:

// Calculate sphere surface area and volume
            vldr.f64 d5,r8_PI               // d5 = PI
            vmov.f64 d6,#4.0                // d6 = 4.0
            vmov.f64 d7,#3.0               // d7 = 3.0

            vmul.f64 d1,d0,d0              // d1 = r * r
            vmul.f64 d1,d1,d5             // d1 = r * r * PI
            vmul.f64 d1,d1,d6            // d1 = r * r * PI * 4
            vstr.f64 d1,[r0]              // save surface area

            vmul.f64 d2,d1,d0            // d2 = sa * r
            vdiv.f64 d3,d2,d7            // d3 = sa * r / 3
            vstr.f64 d3,[r1]             // save volume
            bx lr
```

The declaration of function CalcSphereAreaVolume_ includes an argument value of type double for the radius and two pointers of type double* for the computed surface area and volume. The surface area and volume of a sphere can be calculated using the following formulas:

$$a = 4\pi r^2$$

$$v = \frac{4\pi r^3}{3} = \frac{ar}{3}$$

The assembly language code in Listing 6-2 begins with a .double directive that allocates storage space for the floating-point constant π. The first instruction of CalcSphereAreaVolume_, vldr.f64 d5,r8_PI, loads the constant π from memory into register D5. Note that this instruction uses the .f64 size suffix to designate a double-precision value. The next two instructions, vmov.f64 d6,#4.0 (floating-point move) and vmov.f64 d7,#3.0, load floating-point constants 4.0 and 3.0 into registers D6 and D7, respectively. A function can use the vmov instruction to load any of the floating-point modified immediate constants, both single-precision and double-precision, that are shown in Table 6-2. The vmov instruction can also be used with the corresponding negative values from this table. The GNU assembler will generate an "immediate out of range" error message if a vmov instruction attempts to use an invalid modified immediate constant. In these cases, the vldr instruction can be employed to load the required constant.

Table 6-2. *Floating-point modified immediate constants*

0.125	0.1328125	0.140625	0.1484375	0.15625	0.1640625	0.171875	0.1796875
0.1875	0.1953125	0.203125	0.2109375	0.21875	0.2265625	0.234375	0.2421875
0.25	0.265625	0.28125	0.296875	0.3125	0.328125	0.34375	0.359375
0.375	0.390625	0.40625	0.421875	0.4375	0.453125	0.46875	0.484375
0.5	0.53125	0.5625	0.59375	0.625	0.65625	0.6875	0.71875
0.75	0.78125	0.8125	0.84375	0.875	0.90625	0.9375	0.96875
1.0	1.0625	1.125	1.1875	1.25	1.3125	1.375	1.4375
1.5	1.5625	1.625	1.6875	1.75	1.8125	1.875	1.9375
2.0	2.125	2.25	2.375	2.5	2.625	2.75	2.875
3.0	3.125	3.25	3.375	3.5	3.625	3.75	3.875
4.0	4.25	4.5	4.75	5.0	5.25	5.5	5.75
6.0	6.25	6.5	6.75	7.0	7.25	7.5	7.75
8.0	8.5	9.0	9.5	10.0	10.5	11.0	11.5
12.0	12.5	13.0	13.5	14.0	14.5	15.0	15.5
16.0	17.0	18.0	19.0	20.0	21.0	22.0	23.0
24.0	25.0	26.0	27.0	28.0	29.0	30.0	31.0

Following constant loading, the vmul.f64 d1,d0,d0 instruction calculates r * r. Note that argument value r was passed to CalcSphereAreaVolume_ in register D0. The next two instructions, vmul.f64 d1,d1,d5 and vmul.f64 d1,d1,d6, calculate r * r * PI * 4, which is the surface area. The ensuing vstr.f64 d1,[r0] (floating-point store) instruction then saves the surface area to the specified buffer. The pointer for the surface area result was passed in R0. When a function requires a mix of integer and floating-point argument values, arguments are always passed in the lowest-numbered unallocated register for the specific data type.

Subsequent to the surface area calculation, CalcSphereAreaVolume_ uses the instruction pair vmul.f64 d2,d1,d0 and vdiv.f64 d3,d2,d7 (floating-point divide) to calculate sphere's volume. This is followed by a vstr.f64 d3,[r1] instruction that saves the calculated volume. Note that the volume pointer vol was passed in R1. Here are the results for source code example Ch06_02:

```
------ Results for CalcSphereAreaVolume ------
r:    0  sa:          0  vol:          0
r:    1  sa:  12.566371  vol:  4.1887902
r:    2  sa:  50.265482  vol:  33.510322
r:    3  sa:  113.09734  vol:  113.09734
r:    5  sa:  314.15927  vol:  523.59878
r:   10  sa:  1256.6371  vol:  4188.7902
r:   20  sa:  5026.5482  vol:  33510.322
r:   32  sa:  12867.964  vol:  137258.28
```

Listing 6-3 contains the source code for example Ch06_03, which also illustrates how to carry out calculations using double-precision floating-point arithmetic.

Listing 6-3. Example Ch06_03

```cpp
//----------------------------------------------------
//                    Ch06_03.cpp
//----------------------------------------------------

#include <iostream>
#include <iomanip>
#include <random>
#include <cmath>

using namespace std;

extern "C" double CalcDist_(double x1, double y1, double z1, double x2, double y2, double z2);

void Init(double* x, double* y, double* z, size_t n, unsigned int seed)
{
    uniform_int_distribution<> ui_dist {1, 100};
    mt19937 rng {seed};

    for (size_t i = 0; i < n; i++)
    {
        x[i] = ui_dist(rng);
        y[i] = ui_dist(rng);
        z[i] = ui_dist(rng);
    }
}

double CalcDist(double x1, double y1, double z1, double x2, double y2, double z2)
{
    double tx = (x2 - x1) * (x2 - x1);
    double ty = (y2 - y1) * (y2 - y1);
    double tz = (z2 - z1) * (z2 - z1);
    double dist = sqrt(tx + ty + tz);

    return dist;
}

int main()
{
    const size_t n = 20;
    double x1[n], y1[n], z1[n];
    double x2[n], y2[n], z2[n];
    double dist1[n];
    double dist2[n];

    Init(x1, y1, z1, n, 29);
    Init(x2, y2, z2, n, 37);
```

```cpp
    for (size_t i = 0; i < n; i++)
    {
        dist1[i] = CalcDist(x1[i], y1[i], z1[i], x2[i], y2[i], z2[i]);
        dist2[i] = CalcDist_(x1[i], y1[i], z1[i], x2[i], y2[i], z2[i]);
    }

    cout << fixed;

    for (size_t i = 0; i < n; i++)
    {
        cout << setw(2) << i << "  ";

        cout << setprecision(0);

        cout << "p1(";
        cout << setw(3) << x1[i] << ",";
        cout << setw(3) << y1[i] << ",";
        cout << setw(3) << z1[i] << ") | ";

        cout << "p2(";
        cout << setw(3) << x2[i] << ",";
        cout << setw(3) << y2[i] << ",";
        cout << setw(3) << z2[i] << ") | ";

        cout << setprecision(4);
        cout << "dist1: " << setw(8) << dist1[i] << " | ";
        cout << "dist2: " << setw(8) << dist2[i] << '\n';
    }

    return 0;
}

//--------------------------------------------------
//                Ch06_03_.s
//--------------------------------------------------

// extern "C" double CalcDist_(double x1, double y1, double z1, double x2, double y2,
//              double z2);

            .text
            .global CalcDist_

CalcDist_:  vsub.f64 d0,d3,d0                   // d0 = x2 - x1
            vmul.f64 d0,d0,d0                   // d0 = (x2 - x1) ** 2

            vsub.f64 d1,d4,d1                   // d1 = y2 - y1
            vfma.f64 d0,d1,d1                   // d0 += (y2 - y1) ** 2

            vsub.f64 d2,d5,d2                   // d2 = z2 - z1
            vfma.f64 d0,d2,d2                   // d0 += (z2 - z1) ** 2
```

```
            vsqrt.f64 d0,d0                    // d0 = final distance
            bx lr
```

In Listing 6-3, the assembly language function CalcDist_ calculates the Euclidean distance between two points in 3D space using the following equation:

$$dist = \sqrt{\left(x_2 - x_1\right)^2 + \left(y_2 - y_1\right)^2 + \left(z_2 - z_1\right)^2}$$

If you examine the declaration of function CalcDist_, you will notice that it requires six double-precision floating-point argument values. These values are passed in registers D0–D5. The first instruction of CalcDist_, vsub.f64 d0,d3,d0, calculates x2 - x1. This is followed by a vmul.f64 d0,d0,d0 instruction that completes the calculation of (x2 - x1) ** 2. The ensuing vsub.f64 d1,d4,d1 instruction calculates y2 - y1. The next instruction, vfma.f64 d0,d1,d1 (fused multiply accumulate), computes (y2 - y1) ** 2; it then adds this product to D0. Note that the vfma instruction performs only a single rounding operation following the addition; the intermediate multiplicative product is *not* rounded. This is different than the vmla (multiply accumulate) instruction, which carries out a separate rounding operation following both the multiplication and addition operations.

CalcDist_ then uses another vsub/vfma instruction sequence to compute (z2 - z1) ** 2 and the final sum of squares. The vsqrt.f64 d0,d0 (floating-point square root) instruction calculates the 3D distance. No other instructions are necessary since the return value is already in register D0. Here are the results for source code example Ch06_03:

```
 0  p1( 87, 81, 29) | p2( 95, 14, 47) | dist1:   69.8355 | dist2:   69.8355
 1  p1( 35,  8, 98) | p2( 53, 20, 76) | dist1:   30.8545 | dist2:   30.8545
 2  p1( 77, 50, 46) | p2( 59, 31, 63) | dist1:   31.2090 | dist2:   31.2090
 3  p1( 34, 55, 34) | p2( 86, 69,  7) | dist1:   60.2412 | dist2:   60.2412
 4  p1( 73, 86, 85) | p2( 11, 63, 75) | dist1:   66.8805 | dist2:   66.8805
 5  p1( 84, 77, 68) | p2( 63, 29, 13) | dist1:   75.9605 | dist2:   75.9605
 6  p1( 74, 85, 25) | p2( 76, 31, 80) | dist1:   77.1038 | dist2:   77.1038
 7  p1( 14, 73, 18) | p2( 58, 63, 58) | dist1:   60.2993 | dist2:   60.2993
 8  p1(  6, 36, 41) | p2( 45,  1, 97) | dist1:   76.6942 | dist2:   76.6942
 9  p1( 51, 62, 15) | p2( 61, 90, 71) | dist1:   63.4035 | dist2:   63.4035
10  p1( 26,  3, 29) | p2( 20, 41, 60) | dist1:   49.4065 | dist2:   49.4065
11  p1(  7, 69,100) | p2( 10, 58, 92) | dist1:   13.9284 | dist2:   13.9284
12  p1( 85, 32, 81) | p2( 71, 68, 93) | dist1:   40.4475 | dist2:   40.4475
13  p1( 65,  1, 26) | p2( 83,  6, 24) | dist1:   18.7883 | dist2:   18.7883
14  p1( 93, 48, 81) | p2( 14, 86, 12) | dist1:  111.5616 | dist2:  111.5616
15  p1( 78, 96, 40) | p2( 21, 37, 73) | dist1:   88.4251 | dist2:   88.4251
16  p1( 49, 73, 67) | p2( 81, 37, 98) | dist1:   57.2800 | dist2:   57.2800
17  p1( 40, 74, 38) | p2( 61, 34, 61) | dist1:   50.6952 | dist2:   50.6952
18  p1( 47, 68, 81) | p2( 48, 54, 18) | dist1:   64.5446 | dist2:   64.5446
19  p1( 25, 44,  2) | p2( 66, 91, 47) | dist1:   76.9090 | dist2:   76.9090
```

Floating-Point Comparisons and Conversions

Any function that carries out basic floating-point arithmetic is also likely to perform floating-point comparisons and conversions. The source code examples of this section illustrate scalar floating-point comparisons and conversions. It begins with an example that demonstrates methods for comparing two floating-point values and making a logical decision based on the result. This is followed by an example that illustrates floating-point conversion operations using different numerical data types.

Floating-Point Comparisons

Listing 6-4 shows the source code for example Ch06_04, which demonstrates how to perform comparisons using single-precision floating-point values.

Listing 6-4. Example Ch06_04

```cpp
//----------------------------------------------------
//                  Ch06_04.cpp
//----------------------------------------------------

#include <iostream>
#include <iomanip>
#include <string>
#include <limits>

using namespace std;

extern "C" void CompareF32_(bool* results, float a, float b);

const char* c_OpStrings[] = {"UO", "LT", "LE", "EQ", "NE", "GT", "GE"};
const size_t c_NumOpStrings = sizeof(c_OpStrings) / sizeof(char*);

template <typename T> void PrintResults(const bool* cmp_results, T a, T b)
{
    cout << "a = " << a << ", ";
    cout << "b = " << b << '\n';

    for (size_t i = 0; i < c_NumOpStrings; i++)
    {
        cout << c_OpStrings[i] << '=';
        cout << boolalpha << left << setw(6) << cmp_results[i] << ' ';
    }

    cout << "\n\n";
}

void CompareF32(void)
{
    const size_t n = 7;
    float a[n] {120.0, 250.0, 300.0, -18.0, -81.0, -250.0, 42.0};
    float b[n] {130.0, 240.0, 300.0, 32.0, -100.0, -75.0, 0.0};

    // Set NAN test value
    b[n - 1] = numeric_limits<float>::quiet_NaN();

    const string dashes(72, '-');
    cout << "\nResults for CompareF32\n";
```

```
    cout << dashes << '\n';

    for (size_t i = 0; i < n; i++)
    {
        bool cmp_results[c_NumOpStrings];

        CompareF32_(cmp_results, a[i], b[i]);
        PrintResults(cmp_results, a[i], b[i]);
    }
}

int main()
{
    CompareF32();
    return 0;
}

//----------------------------------------------------
//                   Ch06_04_.s
//----------------------------------------------------

// extern "C" void CompareF32_(bool* results, float a, float b);
            .text
            .global CompareF32_

CompareF32_:
            vcmpe.f32 s0,s1                 // compare F32 values a and b
            vmrs APSR_nzcv,fpscr            // move compare results

            mov r1,#0
            movvs r1,#1                     // r1 = 1 if unordered
            strb r1,[r0,#0]                 // save result

            mov r1,#0
            movlo r1,#1                     // r1 = 1 if a < b
            strb r1,[r0,#1]                 // save result

            mov r1,#0
            movls r1,#1                     // r1 = 1 if a <= b
            strb r1,[r0,#2]                 // save result

            mov r1,#0
            moveq r1,#1                     // r1 = 1 if a == b
            strb r1,[r0,#3]                 // save result

            mov r1,#0
            movne r1,#1                     // r1 = 1 if a != b
            strb r1,[r0,#4]                 // save result

            mov r1,#0
            movgt r1,#1                     // r1 = 1 if a > b
```

```
    strb r1,[r0,#5]                 // save result

    mov r1,#0
    movge r1,#1                     // r1 = 1 if a >= b
    strb r1,[r0,#6]                 // save result

    bx lr
```

Before examining the code in Listing 6-4, some preliminary elucidations are necessary. When two numbers are compared mathematically, the result can one of the following three outcomes: less than, equal, or greater than. When two floating-point numbers are compared per the IEEE 754 standard, a fourth outcome of unordered is possible, and this outcome occurs if one or both operands are NaNs.

The A32 instruction set includes two instructions that perform scalar floating-point compares: vcmp (vector compare) and vcmpe (vector compare raising invalid operation on NaN). These instructions report their results using the FPSCR's NZCV condition flags. The primary difference between the vcmp and vcmpe instructions is that the former generates an invalid operation (IXE) exception only when a SNaN operand is used; the latter generates an IXE exception for any NaN type. If the IXE exception is disabled, both instructions will set the IXC status bit in the FPSCR.

To make logical decisions based on a floating-point compare, a function must copy the FPSCR's NZCV condition flags to the APSR's NZCV condition flags. A function can then make any logical decisions using conditionally executed branch or other instructions. You will learn how to do this shortly. Table 6-3 lists the mnemonic extensions and condition flag states for floating-point comparisons. In this table, the term unordered means at least one compare operand is a NaN.

Table 6-3. *Condition code mnemonic extensions for floating-point comparisons*

Mnemonic Extension	Meaning	Condition Flags
EQ	Equal	Z == 1
NE	Not equal or unordered	Z == 0
HS or CS	Greater than, equal, or unordered	C == 1
LO or CC	Less than	C == 0
MI	Less than	N == 1
PL	Greater than, equal, or unordered	N == 0
VS	Unordered	V == 1
VC	Ordered	V == 0
HI	Greater than, or unordered	C == 1 && Z == 0
LS	Less than or equal	C == 0 || Z == 1
GE	Greater than or equal	N == V
LT	Less than, or unordered	N != V
GT	Greater than	Z == 0 && N == V
LE	Less than, equal, or unordered	Z == 1 || N != V

The C++ code in Listing 6-4 performs test case setup and exercises the assembly language function CompareF32_. Note that one of the test values in array b is a QNaN. The first instruction in CompareF32_, vcmpe.f32 s0,s1, compares the values in registers S0 and S1, which contain argument values a and b, respectively. This is followed by a vmrs APSR_nzcv,fpscr (move SIMD/FP special register to general-purpose register) instruction that transfers the FPSCR's NZCV condition flags into the corresponding APSR condition flags. The remaining code in CompareF32_ consists of conditional mov instructions that decode and save the floating-point compare results. A function can also use conditional branch instructions to make logical decisions following execution of a vcmp/vcmpe and vmrs instruction sequence. You will see an example of this in Chapter 9. The vcmp/vcmpe instructions can also perform double-precision floating-point comparisons when used with the .f64 size suffix and D register operands. Here is the output for source code example Ch06_04:

```
Results for CompareF32
----------------------------------------------------------------------
a = 120, b = 130
UO=false  LT=true   LE=true   EQ=false  NE=true   GT=false  GE=false

a = 250, b = 240
UO=false  LT=false  LE=false  EQ=false  NE=true   GT=true   GE=true

a = 300, b = 300
UO=false  LT=false  LE=true   EQ=true   NE=false  GT=false  GE=true

a = -18, b = 32
UO=false  LT=true   LE=true   EQ=false  NE=true   GT=false  GE=false

a = -81, b = -100
UO=false  LT=false  LE=false  EQ=false  NE=true   GT=true   GE=true

a = -250, b = -75
UO=false  LT=true   LE=true   EQ=false  NE=true   GT=false  GE=false

a = 42, b = nan
UO=true   LT=false  LE=false  EQ=false  NE=true   GT=false  GE=false
```

Floating-Point Conversions

A common operation in many C++ programs is to cast a single-precision or double-precision floating-point value to an integer or vice versa. Other frequent operations include the promotion of a floating-point value from single-precision to double-precision and the narrowing of a double-precision value to single-precision. Listing 6-5 shows the code for a sample program that demonstrates the use of several A32 floating-point conversion instructions. It also illustrates how to modify the RMode control field in the FPSCR.

Listing 6-5. Example Ch06_05

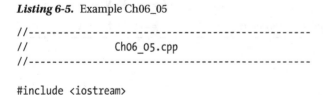

```
//--------------------------------------------------
//              Ch06_05.cpp
//--------------------------------------------------

#include <iostream>
```

```cpp
#include <iomanip>
#include <string>
#include <cmath>

using namespace std;

enum RmOp
{
    // Values below correspond to RMode field in FPSCR
    Nearest = 0, PlusInf = 1, MinusInf = 2, Zero = 3
};

// Miscellaneous values
const string c_RmOpStrings[] = {"Nearest", "PlusInf", "MinusInf", "Zero"};
const RmOp c_RmOpVals[] = {RmOp::Nearest, RmOp::PlusInf, RmOp::MinusInf, RmOp::Zero};
const size_t c_NumRmOps = sizeof(c_RmOpVals) / sizeof (RmOp);

// Assembly language functions defined in Ch06_05_.s
extern "C" RmOp GetRm_(void);
extern "C" void SetRm_(RmOp rm_op);
extern "C" int ConvertA_(double a);
extern "C" double ConvertB_(int a, unsigned int b);
extern "C" float ConvertC_(double a, float b, double c, float d);

void TestConvertA(void)
{
    const char nl = '\n';
    const size_t n = 4;
    double a[n] = {M_PI, M_SQRT2 + 0.5, -M_E, -M_SQRT2};

    cout << fixed << setprecision(8);
    cout << "\n----------Results for TestConvertA ----------\n";

    for (size_t i = 0; i < n; i++)
    {
        cout << "Test case #" << i << " using value " << a[i] << nl;

        for (size_t j = 0; j < c_NumRmOps; j++)
        {
            RmOp rm_old = GetRm_();
            RmOp rm_new = c_RmOpVals[j];

            SetRm_(rm_new);
            int b = ConvertA_(a[i]);
            SetRm_(rm_old);

            cout << left << setw(10) << c_RmOpStrings[j];
            cout << b << nl;
        }
```

```cpp
        cout << nl;
    }
}

void TestConvertB(void)
{
    const char nl = '\n';
    const size_t n = 4;
    int a[n] = {1, -2, 3, -4};
    unsigned int b[n] = {100, 200, 300, 400};

    cout << fixed << setprecision(2);
    cout << "\n----------Results for TestConvertB ----------\n";

    for (size_t i = 0; i < n; i++)
    {
        double c = ConvertB_(a[i], b[i]);

        cout << "a: " << setw(6) << a[i] << " ";
        cout << "b: " << setw(6) << b[i] << " ";
        cout << "c: " << setw(6) << c << nl;
    }
}

void TestConvertC(void)
{
    const char nl = '\n';
    double a = 2.5, c = 4.0;
    float b = 1.5f, d = 20.0f;

    float e = ConvertC_(a, b, c, d);

    cout << fixed << setprecision(4);
    cout << "\n----------Results for TestConvertC ----------\n";
    cout << "a: " << a << nl << "b: " << b << nl << "c: " << c << nl;
    cout << "d: " << d << nl << "e: " << e << nl;
}

int main(void)
{
    TestConvertA();
    TestConvertB();
    TestConvertC();
    return 0;
}

//-------------------------------------------------
//                  Ch06_05_.s
//-------------------------------------------------

// extern "C" Rm GetRm_(void);
```

```
            .text
            .global GetRm_
GetRm_:     vmrs r1,fpscr                   // r1 = fpscr
            lsr r2,r1,#22
            and r0,r2,#3                    // RMode in bits 1:0
            bx lr


// extern "C" void SetRm_(Rm rm);

            .global SetRm_
SetRm_:     vmrs r1,fpscr                   // r1 = fpscr
            bfi r1,r0,#22,#2                // insert new RMode bits
            vmsr fpscr,r1                   // save updated fpscr
            bx lr


// extern "C" int ConvertA_(double a);

            .global ConvertA_
ConvertA_:  vcvtr.s32.f64 s0,d0             // convert a to signed int
            vmov r0,s0                      // copy result to r0
            bx lr


// extern "C" double ConvertB_(int a, unsigned int b);

            .global ConvertB_
ConvertB_:  vmov s0,r0                      // s0 = a
            vcvt.f64.s32 d1,s0              // convert a to double

            vmov s1,r1                      // s1 = b
            vcvt.f64.u32 d2,s1             // convert b to double

            vadd.f64 d0,d1,d2               // d0 = a + b
            bx lr


// extern "C" float ConvertC_(double a, float b, double c, float d);

            .global ConvertC_
ConvertC_:  vcvt.f64.f32 d3,s2             // convert b to double
            vcvt.f64.f32 d4,s3             // convert d to double

            vadd.f64 d5,d0,d3               // Perform arithmetic
            vsub.f64 d6,d2,d4               // using doubles
            vdiv.f64 d7,d5,d6

            vcvt.f32.f64 s0,d7             // Convert result to float
            bx lr
```

Near the top of the C++ code is an enumeration named RmOp. This enumeration defines the constants that are used to specify a rounding mode for the RMode field in the FPSCR (see Figure 5-4). The RmOp enumeration is used in the C++ function TestConvertA, which exercises the assembly language function ConvertA_. The function ConvertA_ converts a double-precision floating-point value to a signed 32-bit integer using the current FPSCR rounding mode. The C++ function TestConvertB employs the assembly language function ConvertB_. This function illustrates integer to double-precision floating-point conversions. The final C++ function, TestConvertC, invokes the assembly language function ConvertC_. This function implements single-precision to double-precision conversions and vice versa.

The first assembly language function in Listing 6-5 is named GetRm_. This function reads the current FPSCR rounding mode and returns it to the caller. Function GetRm_ begins its execution with a vmrs r1,fpscr instruction that copies the contents of the FPSCR to R1. The ensuing lsr r2,r1,#22 and and r0,r2,#3 instructions mask out unneeded FPSCR bits and save the current rounding mode in the two low-order bits of R0. The function SetRm_ modifies the RMode field in the FPSCR. This function also begins with a vmrs r1,fpscr that copies FPSCR to R1. The bfi r1,r0,#22,#2 (bit field insert) instruction copies the two low-order bits of R0 to bit positions 22 and 23 of R1. The other bits in R1 are not altered. Function SetRm_ then uses a vmsr fpscr,r1 (move general-purpose register to SIMD/FP special register) instruction to save the updated FPSCR.

The assembly language function ConvertA_ begins its execution with a vcvtr.s32.f64 s0,d0 (convert floating-point to integer) instruction. This instruction converts the double-precision floating-point value in D0 to a signed 32-bit integer and saves the signed integer result in S0. Note the use of the .s32 and .f64 size suffixes. The conversion is performed using the current FPSCR rounding mode. The next instruction, vmov r0,s0 (move floating-point to general-purpose register), copies the value in S0 to general-purpose register R0.

The function ConvertB_ uses a vmov s0,r0 (move general-purpose register to SIMD/FP register) instruction that copies the value in R0 (argument value a) to register S0. Note that this instruction only performs a value copy; it *does not* carry out any conversion operations. The ensuing vcvt.f64.s32 d1,s0 (convert integer to floating-point) instruction converts the signed integer in S0 to a double-precision floating-point value and saves the result in D1. The next two instructions, vmov s1,r1 and vcvt.f64.u32 d2,s1, convert argument value b from an unsigned 32-bit integer to a double-precision floating-point value. The vadd.f64 d0,d1,d2 instruction sums the double-precision floating-point values in D1 and D2. It should be noted that unlike the vcvtr instruction, the vcvt instructions used in ConvertB_ use round-toward-zero rounding instead of the rounding mode that is specified in the FPSCR.

Function ConvertC_ illustrates single-precision floating-point to double-precision floating-point conversions. This function uses a mix of double and float argument values. Argument value a is passed in register D0. Note that argument value b is passed in S2. Register S1 is not employed here since it overlaps the high-order 32 bits of register D0. Argument values c and d are passed in registers D2 and S3, respectively. The GNU C++ calling convention dictates that floating-point values are always passed using the lowest-numbered unallocated register.

The first two instructions of ConvertC_, vcvt.f64.f32 d3,s2 and vcvt.f64.f32 d4,s3, convert single-precision argument values b and d into double-precision values. Following some double-precision arithmetic, the vcvt.f32.f64 s0,d7 instruction converts the double-precision floating-point value in D7 to single-precision floating-point and saves the result in S0. The vcvt instructions used in function ConvertC_ also carry out their conversions using the current FPSCR rounding mode.

A couple of final comments. All FPSCR control bits including the RMode field are considered non-volatile. Any function that modifies the RMode field must always restore its original value. Note that function TestConvertA saved the RMode prior to calling ConvertA_ and then immediately restored the original value. If the original RMode value is not restored, some C++ library functions may fail to work properly or generate inconsistent results. Here are the results for source code example Ch06_05:

```
----------Results for TestConvertA ----------
Test case #0 using value 3.14159265
Nearest    3
PlusInf    4
MinusInf   3
Zero       3
```

```
Test case #1 using value 1.91421356
Nearest   2
PlusInf   2
MinusInf  1
Zero      1

Test case #2 using value -2.71828183
Nearest   -3
PlusInf   -2
MinusInf  -3
Zero      -2

Test case #3 using value -1.41421356
Nearest   -1
PlusInf   -1
MinusInf  -2
Zero      -1

----------Results for TestConvertB ----------
a: 1      b: 100    c: 101.00
a: -2     b: 200    c: 198.00
a: 3      b: 300    c: 303.00
a: -4     b: 400    c: 396.00

----------Results for TestConvertC ----------
a: 2.5000
b: 1.5000
c: 4.0000
d: 20.0000
e: -0.2500
```

The conversion examples in this section illustrated the use of the most common A32 floating-point conversion instructions. The A32 instruction set also includes additional floating-point conversion instructions that are useful for specific calculations. For more information regarding these instructions, consult the Arm programming reference manuals listed in Appendix B.

Floating-Point Arrays and Matrices

In Chapter 4, you learned how to access individual elements and carry out calculations using integer arrays and matrices. In this section, you will learn how to perform similar operations using floating-point arrays and matrices. As you will soon see, the same assembly language coding techniques are often used for both integer and floating-point arrays and matrices.

Floating-Point Arrays

Listing 6-6 shows the source code for example Ch06_06. This example illustrates how to calculate the sample mean and sample standard deviation of an array of double-precision floating-point values.

Listing 6-6. Example Ch06_06

```cpp
//-------------------------------------------------
//                  Ch06_06.cpp
//-------------------------------------------------

#include <iostream>
#include <iomanip>
#include <cmath>

using namespace std;

extern "C" bool CalcMeanStdev_(double* mean, double* stdev, const double* x, int n);

bool CalcMeanStdev(double* mean, double* stdev, const double* x, int n)
{
    if (n < 2)
        return false;

    double sum = 0.0;
    double sum2 = 0.0;

    for (int i = 0; i < n; i++)
        sum += x[i];

    *mean = sum / n;

    for (int i = 0; i < n; i++)
    {
        double temp = x[i] - *mean;
        sum2 += temp * temp;
    }

    *stdev = sqrt(sum2 / (n - 1));
    return true;
}

int main()
{
    const char nl = '\n';
    double x[] = { 10, 2, 33, 19, 41, 24, 75, 37, 18, 97, 14, 71, 88, 92, 7};
    const int n = sizeof(x) / sizeof(double);

    double mean1 = 0.0, stdev1 = 0.0;
    double mean2 = 0.0, stdev2 = 0.0;

    bool rc1 = CalcMeanStdev(&mean1, &stdev1, x, n);
    bool rc2 = CalcMeanStdev_(&mean2, &stdev2, x, n);

    cout << fixed << setprecision(2);

    for (int i = 0; i < n; i++)
```

```
    {
        cout << "x[" << setw(2) << i << "] = ";
        cout << setw(6) << x[i] << nl;
    }

    cout << setprecision(6);

    cout << nl;
    cout << "rc1 = " << boolalpha << rc1;
    cout << "  mean1 = " << mean1 << "  stdev1 = " << stdev1 << nl;
    cout << "rc2 = " << boolalpha << rc2;
    cout << "  mean2 = " << mean2 << "  stdev2 = " << stdev2 << nl;
}
```

```
//-------------------------------------------------
//                Ch06_06_.s
//-------------------------------------------------


            .text
r8_zero:    .double 0.0

// extern "C" bool CalcMeanStdev_(double* mean, double* stdev, const double* x, int n);

            .global CalcMeanStdev_
CalcMeanStdev_:
            push {r4,r5}

            cmp r3,#2                   // is n < 2?
            blt InvalidArg              // jump if n < 2

// Calculate mean
            vldr.f64 d0,r8_zero         // sum1 = 0.0
            vmov d4,d0                  // sum2 = 0.0

            mov r4,#0                   // i = 0
            mov r5,r2                   // r5 = ptr to x

Loop1:      vldmia r5!,{d1}            // d1 = x[i]
            vadd.f64 d0,d0,d1           // sum1 += x[i]

            add r4,#1                   // i += 1
            cmp r4,r3
            blt Loop1                   // jump if i < n

            vmov s4,r3                  // s4 = n
            vcvt.f64.s32 d1,s4          // d1 = n as double
            vdiv.f64 d2,d0,d1           // d2 = sum1 / n (mean)
            vstr.f64 d2,[r0]            // save mean

// Calculate standard deviation
            mov r4,#0                   // i = 0
```

```
            mov  r5,r2                      // r5 = ptr to x

Loop2:      vldmia r5!,{d1}                 // d1 = x[i]
            vsub.f64 d3,d1,d2               // d3 = x[i] - mean
            vfma.f64 d4,d3,d3               // sum2 += (x[i] - mean) ** 2

            add  r4,#1                      // i += 1
            cmp  r4,r3
            blt  Loop2                      // jump if i < n

            sub  r3,#1                      // r3 = n - 1
            vmov s2,r3
            vcvt.f64.s32 d1,s2              // d1 = n - 1 as double

            vdiv.f64 d2,d4,d1               // d2 = sum2 / (n - 1)
            vsqrt.f64 d3,d2                 // d3 = stdev
            vstr.f64 d3,[r1]                // save stdev

            mov  r0,#1                      // set success return code

Done:       pop  {r4,r5}
            bx   lr

InvalidArg: mov  r0,#0                      // set error return code
            b    Done
```

Here are the formulas that example Ch06_06 uses to calculate the sample mean and sample standard deviation:

$$\bar{x} = \frac{1}{n}\sum_i x_i$$

$$s = \sqrt{\frac{1}{n-1}\sum_i (x_i - \bar{x})^2}$$

The C++ code in Listing 6-6 is straightforward. It includes a function named CalcMeanStdev that calculates the sample mean and sample standard deviation of an array of double-precision floating-point values. Note that this function and its assembly language equivalent return the calculated mean and standard deviation using pointers. The remaining C++ code initializes a test array and exercises both calculating functions.

Upon entry to the assembly language function CalcMeanStdev_, the number of array elements n is checked for validity. When calculating a sample standard deviation, the number of array elements must be greater than one. Calculation of the mean begins with a vldr.f64 d0,r8_zero instruction that initializes sum1 to 0.0. The vmov d4,d0 instruction that follows sets sum2 to 0.0. The next two instructions, mov r4,#0 and mov r5,r2, set i to 0 and R5 as a pointer to the input array x.

The for-loop Loop1 sums the elements in array x. Each iteration begins with a vldmia r5!,{d1} (load multiple SIMD/FP registers) instruction that loads element x[i] into register D0. Note that this instruction also updates the array pointer that is maintained in R5. The vldmia instruction is used here instead of vldr since the latter cannot be used with the writeback (!) operator. The next instruction, vadd.f64 d0,d0,d1, adds element x[i] to sum1. Following completion of Loop1, CalcMeanStdev_ uses the instructions vmov s4,r3 and vcvt.f64.s32 d1,s4 to convert n into a double-precision floating-point value. This is followed by a vdiv.f64 d2,d0,d1 instruction that calculates the mean. The ensuing vstr.f64 d2,[r0] instruction then saves the calculated mean.

For-loop Loop2 calculates sum2 = (x[i] - mean) ** 2. Like Loop1, each iteration of Loop2 begins with a vldmia r5!,{d1} instruction that loads x[i] into register D1. The next instruction, vsub.f64 d3,d1,d2, calculates x[i] - mean. This is followed by a vfma.f64 d4,d3,d3 instruction that calculates sum2 += (x[i] - mean) ** 2. Following completion of Loop2, another vcvt.f64.s32 instruction is used to convert n - 1 into a double-precision floating-point value. The final sample standard deviation is then calculated using the instructions vdiv.f64 d2,d4,d1 and vsqrt.f64 d3,d2. Here is the output for source code example Ch06_06:

```
x[ 0] =   10.00
x[ 1] =    2.00
x[ 2] =   33.00
x[ 3] =   19.00
x[ 4] =   41.00
x[ 5] =   24.00
x[ 6] =   75.00
x[ 7] =   37.00
x[ 8] =   18.00
x[ 9] =   97.00
x[10] =   14.00
x[11] =   71.00
x[12] =   88.00
x[13] =   92.00
x[14] =    7.00

rc1 = true  mean1 = 41.866667  stdev1 = 33.530086
rc2 = true  mean2 = 41.866667  stdev2 = 33.530086
```

Floating-Point Matrices

Listing 6-7 shows the source code for example Ch06_07. This example contains an assembly language function that calculates the trace of a square matrix.

Listing 6-7. Example Ch06_07

```
//----------------------------------------------------
//              Ch06_07.cpp
//----------------------------------------------------

#include <iostream>
#include <iomanip>
#include <string>
#include <random>

using namespace std;

extern "C" bool CalcTrace_(double* trace, const double* x, int nrows, int ncols);

void Init(double* x, int nrows, int ncols)
```

```
{
    unsigned int seed = 47;
    uniform_int_distribution<> d {1, 1000};
    mt19937 rng {seed};

    for (int i = 0; i < nrows; i++)
    {
        for (int j = 0; j < ncols; j++)
            x[i * ncols + j] = (double)d(rng);
    }
}

bool CalcTrace(double* trace, const double* x, int nrows, int ncols)
{
    if (nrows != ncols || nrows <= 0)
        return false;

    double sum = 0.0;

    for (int i = 0; i < nrows; i++)
        sum += x[i * ncols + i];

    *trace = sum;
    return true;
}

int main()
{
    const char nl = '\n';
    const int nrows = 11;
    const int ncols = 11;
    double x[nrows][ncols];
    double trace1, trace2;
    string dashes(72, '-');

    Init(&x[0][0], nrows, ncols);

    CalcTrace(&trace1, &x[0][0], nrows, ncols);
    CalcTrace_(&trace2, &x[0][0], nrows, ncols);

    cout << "\nTest Matrix\n";
    cout << dashes << nl;

    for (int i = 0; i < nrows; i++)
    {
        for (int j = 0; j < ncols; j++)
            cout << setw(5) << x[i][j] << ' ';

        cout << nl;
    }
```

```
    cout << "\ntrace1 = " << trace1 << nl;
    cout << "trace2 = " << trace2 << nl;

    return 0;
}

//----------------------------------------------------
//                  Ch06_07_.s
//----------------------------------------------------

            .text
r8_zero:    .double 0.0

// extern "C" bool CalcTrace_(double* trace, const double* x, int nrows, int ncols);

            .global CalcTrace_
CalcTrace_: push {r4,r5}
            cmp r2,r3
            bne InvalidArg              // jump if nrows != ncols
            cmp r2,#0
            ble InvalidArg              // jump if nrows <= 0

// Calculate trace
            vldr.f64 d0,r8_zero         // sum = 0.0
            mov r4,#0                   // i = 0

Loop1:      mul r5,r4,r3                // r5 = i * ncols
            add r5,r5,r4                // r5 = i * ncols + i
            add r5,r1,r5,lsl #3         // r5 = ptr to x[i][i]

            vldr.f64 d1,[r5]            // d1 = x[i][i]
            vadd.f64 d0,d0,d1           // sum += x[i][i]

            add r4,#1                   // i += 1
            cmp r4,r2
            blt Loop1                   // jump if not done

            vstr.f64 d0,[r0]            // save trace value

            mov r0,#1                   // set success return code
Done:       pop {r4,r5}
            bx lr

InvalidArg: mov r0,#0                   // set error return code
            b Done
```

The trace of a square matrix is simply the sum of its diagonal elements:

$$tr = \sum_i x_{ii}$$

The C++ code in Listing 6-7 includes a function named CalcTrace, which calculates the trace of a square matrix containing double-precision floating-point values. This function is used to verify the result that is calculated by the assembly language function CalcTrace_.

Function CalcTrace_ begins its execution by testing argument values ncols and nrows to make sure the input matrix is square. It then uses a vldr.f64 d0,r8_zero instruction to set sum = 0.0. This is followed by a mov r4,#0 instruction that sets index variable i equal to 0. The first two instructions of Loop1, mul r5,r4,r3 and add r5,r5,r4, calculate i * ncols + i. This is followed by an add r5,r1,r5,lsl #3 instruction that calculates the address of x[i][i]. The lsl #3 shift operator is used here since the matrix contains double-precision floating-point values (lsl #2 can be used for single-precision floating-point matrices). Following the address calculation, a vldr.f64 d1,[r5] loads x[i][i] into register D1. The ensuing vadd.f64 d0,d0,d1 instruction updates the trace value that is maintained in D0. Following completion of Loop1, a vstr.f64 d0,[r0] instruction saves the final trace value. Here is the output for source code example Ch06_07:

```
Test Matrix
----------------------------------------------------------------------
   114   852   975   910   729   824   352   373   708   979   800
   934   646   396   415   307   707   231   247   635   256   515
    25   400    99   355   301   763   641    52   323   734   186
   770   918   289   271   697   274   510   955   806   128   924
   748   366     6   514   857   760   696   129   554   548   936
   878   513   482   178   910   537   906   294    29    11   453
   884   347   657   827   943   844   745   351   268   928   362
   310   527   532   547   294   259   187   175   755   361   229
   141   152   390   108   472    79   969   434   146   348   515
   369   528   797   306   998   160   990   597   828   104   303
   568   983   387   742    85   750   562   690   649   277   662

trace1 = 4356
trace2 = 4356
```

Using C++ Floating-Point Library Functions

Listing 6-8 shows the source code for example Ch06_08. This example demonstrates how to convert rectangular coordinates to polar coordinates and vice versa. It also illustrates how to call C++ library functions from an assembly language function.

Listing 6-8. Example Ch06_08

```cpp
//---------------------------------------------------
//                  Ch06_08.cpp
//---------------------------------------------------

#include <iostream>
#include <iomanip>

using namespace std;

extern "C" void RectToPolar_(double* r, double* theta, double x, double y);
extern "C" void PolarToRect_(double* x, double* y, double r, double theta);

int main()
{
```

```cpp
//?? Add a few more test cases?
const int n = 7;
const double x1[n] = { 3.0, -4.0, 1.0,  1.0, 1.5, -5.0, -8.0 };
const double y1[n] = { 4.0,  3.0, 1.0, -1.0, 6.0, -4.0,  9.0 };

cout << fixed << setprecision(4);

for (int i = 0; i < n; i++)
{
    const int w = 9;
    const char nl = '\n';

    double r, theta, x2, y2;

    RectToPolar_(&r, &theta, x1[i], y1[i]);
    PolarToRect_(&x2, &y2, r, theta);

    cout << setw(w) << x1[i] << ", " << setw(w) << y1[i] << " | ";
    cout << setw(w) << r << ", " << setw(w) << theta << " | ";
    cout << setw(w) << x2 << ", " << setw(w) << y2 << nl;
}

return 0;
}


//---------------------------------------------------
//                  Ch06_08_.s
//---------------------------------------------------

// extern "C" void RectToPolar_(double* r, double* theta, double x, double y);

                .text
r8_RadToDeg:    .double 57.2957795131
r8_DegToRad:    .double 0.0174532925


            .global RectToPolar_
RectToPolar_:
// Prologue
            push {r4,lr}

            mov r4,r1                    // save theta for later

// Calculate r
            vmul.f64 d2,d0,d0            // d2 = x * x
            vfma.f64 d2,d1,d1            // d2 = x * x + y * y
            vsqrt.f64 d3,d2             // d3 = r
            vstr.f64 d3,[r0]            // save r

// Calculate theta
            vmov d2,d1
            vmov d1,d0                   // d1 = x
```

```
            vmov d0,d2                        // d0 = y
            bl atan2                          // calc arctan(y / x)
            vldr d1,r8_RadToDeg
            vmul.f64 d2,d0,d1                 // d2 = theta in degrees
            vstr.f64 d2,[r4]                  // save theta

// Epilogue
            pop {r4,pc}

// extern "C" void PolarToRect_(double* x, double* y, double r, double theta);

            .global PolarToRect_
PolarToRect_:
// Prologue
            push {r4-r6,lr}
            vpush {d8,d9}

// Save r, x, and y for later use
            vmov d8,d0                        // d8 = r
            mov r4,r0                         // r4 = x
            mov r5,r1                         // r5 = y

// Calculate x
            vldr d2,r8_DegToRad
            vmul.f64 d0,d1,d2                 // d0 = theta in radians
            vmov.f64 d9,d0                    // save theta for later
            bl cos                            // calc cos(theta)
            vmul.f64 d1,d8,d0                 // d1 = r * cos(theta)
            vstr.f64 d1,[r4]                  // save x

// Calculate y
            vmov.f64 d0,d9                    // d0 = theta in radians
            bl sin                            // calc sin(theta)
            vmul.f64 d1,d8,d0                 // d1 = r * sin(theta)
            vstr.f64 d1,[r5]                  // save y

// Epilogue
            vpop {d8,d9}
            pop {r4-r6,pc}
```

Before examining the source code in Listing 6-8, a quick review of two-dimensional coordinate systems is warranted. A point on a two-dimensional plane can be uniquely specified using an (x, y) ordered pair. The values for x and y represent signed distances from an origin point, which is located at the intersection of two perpendicular axes. An ordered (x, y) pair is called a rectangular or Cartesian coordinate. A point on a two-dimensional plane also can be uniquely specified using a radius vector r and angle θ as illustrated in Figure 6-1. An ordered (r, θ) pair is called a polar coordinate.

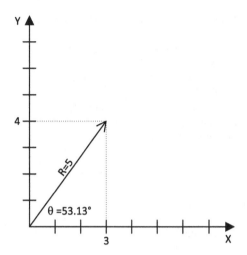

Figure 6-1. *Specification of a point using rectangular and polar coordinates*

A rectangular coordinate is converted to a polar coordinate using the following equations:

$$r = \sqrt{x^2 + y^2}$$

$$\theta = atan2\left(\frac{y}{x}\right) \text{ where } \theta = [-\pi, +\pi]$$

A polar coordinate is converted to a rectangular coordinate using the following equations:

$$x = r \cos \theta$$

$$y = r \sin \theta$$

The C++ code in Listing 6-8 begins with the declarations for assembly language functions `RectToPolar_` and `PolarToRect_`. Note that these functions require double-precision floating-point argument values. The remaining C++ code performs test data initialization, exercises the coordinate conversion functions, and displays results.

The first instruction of `RectToPolar_`, push `{r4,lr}`, saves non-volatile registers R4 and LR on the stack. The `mov r4,r1` instruction that follows saves argument value `theta` in register R4 for later use. The saving of `theta` in a non-volatile register is required since `RectToPolar_` calls other functions. The next three instructions, `vmul.f64 d2,d0,d0`, `vfma.f64 d2,d1,d1`, and `vsqrt.f64 d3,d2`, calculate r = sqrt(x * x + y * y). The ensuing `vstr.f64 d3,[r0]` instruction then saves the calculated result to the memory location pointed to by argument value r.

The calculation of `theta` starts with a few `vmov` instructions that load registers D0 and D1 with argument values y and x, respectively. The `bl  atan2` instruction calls the C++ library function `atan2`. Following this call, the `vldr d1,r8_RadToDeg` instruction loads the radian to degree conversion factor into register D1. The `vmul.f64 d2,d0,d1` instruction converts `theta` from radians to degrees. This result is then saved using a `vstr.f64 d2,[r4]` instruction.

The function `PolarToRect_` begins its execution with a push `{r4-r6,lr}` instruction that saves registers R4, R5, R6, and LR on the stack. It should be noted that R6 is not used in this function but included in the push instruction register list to maintain doubleword alignment of SP. According to the GNU C++ calling convention, register SP must always be aligned on a doubleword boundary in a non-leaf function. The `vpush {d8,d9}` (push SIMD/FP register to stack) instruction saves non-volatile floating-point registers D8 and D9

129

on the stack. The next three instructions, vmov d8,d0, mov r4,r0, and mov r5,r1, save argument values r, x, and y in non-volatile registers for later use.

Calculation of the x coordinate begins with the conversion of argument value theta from degrees to radians. The instruction vmov.f64 d9,d0 saves a copy of the converted theta in D9 for later use. The ensuing bl cos and vmul.f64 d1,d8,d0 instructions calculate x = r * cos(theta), and the vstr.f64 d1,[r4] instruction then saves the calculated x value. The calculation of y = r * sin(theta) is next. Note that theta is loaded into D0 using the instruction vmov.f64 d0,d9 before execution of the bl sin instruction. The final two instructions of PolarToRect_, vpop {d8,d9} and pop {r4-r6,pc}, restore the non-volatile floating-point and general-purpose registers that were saved on the stack in the function prologue. Here is the output for source code example Ch06_08:

```
  3.0000,    4.0000 |    5.0000,    53.1301 |    3.0000,    4.0000
 -4.0000,    3.0000 |    5.0000,   143.1301 |   -4.0000,    3.0000
  1.0000,    1.0000 |    1.4142,    45.0000 |    1.0000,    1.0000
  1.0000,   -1.0000 |    1.4142,   -45.0000 |    1.0000,   -1.0000
  1.5000,    6.0000 |    6.1847,    75.9638 |    1.5000,    6.0000
 -5.0000,   -4.0000 |    6.4031,  -141.3402 |   -5.0000,   -4.0000
 -8.0000,    9.0000 |   12.0416,   131.6335 |   -8.0000,    9.0000
```

Summary

Here are the key learning points for Chapter 6:

- A function can use the vadd, vsub, vmul, vdiv, and vsqrt instructions to carry out basic single-precision and double-precision floating-point arithmetic.

- The vldr rx,label instruction loads a value from memory into a floating-point register. The source operand label must be located within ±1020 bytes of the vldr instruction's address + 8 bytes and aligned on a word boundary.

- A function can use the vmov instruction to load select floating-point immediate constants into a floating-point register.

- The vcmp and vcmpe instructions perform floating-point comparisons. A function must use the vmrs instruction to transfer the FPSCR's NZCV condition flags into the APSCR to make logical decisions based on a floating-point compare result.

- A function can use the vcvt and vcvtr instructions to carry out floating-point conversions.

- The vldmia instruction loads multiple floating-point registers from an address that is specified by a general-purpose register.

- The vpush instruction saves floating-point registers on the stack. The vpop instruction removes floating-point registers from the stack.

- A function can use the vmsr instruction to change the RMode or other control bits (if allowed by the operating system) in the FPSCR. The GNU C++ calling convention treats all FPSCR control bits as non-volatile.

- The GNU C++ calling convention designates S0–S15 (or D0–D7) and D16–D31 as volatile registers. Registers D8–D15 are classified as non-volatile. Floating-point argument values are passed in registers S0–S15 or D0–D7 or via the stack if there are not enough registers for all argument values. A function returns a single-precision or double-precision floating-point value in register S0 or D0, respectively.

CHAPTER 7

■ ■ ■

Armv8-32 SIMD Architecture

The first six chapters of this book examined the core aspects of the Armv8-32 architecture. You learned about data types, general-purpose registers, memory addressing modes, and the core A32 instruction set. You also studied a cornucopia of sample code that illustrated the nuts and bolts of Armv8-32 assembly language programming including operands, integer arithmetic, compare operations, conditional jumps, and manipulation of data structures. This was followed by an explanation of Armv8-32 floating-point resources and how to write assembly language code that performs scalar floating-point arithmetic.

The next three chapters highlight the SIMD (single-instruction multiple data) resources of Armv8-32. In this chapter, you will learn about basic SIMD programming concepts. You will also learn about SIMD wraparound and saturated arithmetic and when it is appropriate to use the latter. The Armv8-32 SIMD architecture is presented next and includes descriptions of the register set and data types. It should be noted that most of the material presented in this chapter also applies to the Armv8-64 SIMD architecture, which is examined more closely in Chapter 10.

Arm uses the expression "Advanced SIMD" in programming reference manuals and other documentation to differentiate its current SIMD technology from an earlier (and very limited) SIMD architecture that employed the Armv8-32 general-purpose registers as operands. The content of this and subsequent chapters focuses exclusively on Arm's Advanced SIMD technology, frequently called NEON, that leverages the 128-bit wide SIMD registers.

Armv8-32 SIMD Architecture Overview

A packed operand (also called a vector operand) is an operand that contains multiple values of the same data type. It is often viewed as a numerical container object. You will learn more about packed operands later in this chapter. Armv8-32 supports SIMD operations using packed 8-, 16-, 32-, or 64-bit wide integer operands. It also supports SIMD operations using packed half-precision (on processors that include the ARMv8.2-FP16 extension) and single-precision floating-point values.

Armv8-32 SIMD extends the floating-point register set to support 128-bit wide operands. It also includes a distinct set of instructions that perform SIMD arithmetic calculations, load and store operations, and data processing operations. The remainder of this chapter introduces SIMD programming concepts and the Armv8-32 SIMD architecture. You will learn about the Armv8-32 SIMD instruction set in Chapters 8 and 9.

SIMD Programming Concepts

As implied by the words of the acronym, a SIMD computing element executes the same operation on multiple data items simultaneously. Universal SIMD operations include basic arithmetic such as addition, subtraction, multiplication, and division. SIMD processing techniques can also be applied to a variety of other computational tasks including data comparisons, conversions, bitwise Boolean operations, element

© Daniel Kusswurm 2020
D. Kusswurm, *Modern Arm Assembly Language Programming*,
https://doi.org/10.1007/978-1-4842-6267-2_7

rearrangements, and shifts. Processors facilitate SIMD operations by reinterpreting the bits of an operand in a register or memory location. For example, a 128-bit wide operand can hold two independent 64-bit integers. It is also capable of accommodating four 32-bit integers, eight 16-bit integers, or sixteen 8-bit integers as illustrated in Figure 7-1.

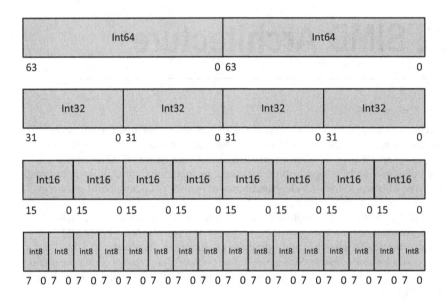

Figure 7-1. *128-bit wide SIMD operand using distinct integer types*

Figure 7-2 exemplifies a few SIMD arithmetic operations in greater detail. In this figure, integer addition is illustrated using two 64-bit integers, four 32-bit integers, and eight 16-bit integers. Faster algorithmic processing takes place when multiple data items are exercised since the processor can carry out the operations in parallel. For example, when 16-bit integer operands are specified by an instruction, the processor performs all eight 16-bit integer additions simultaneously.

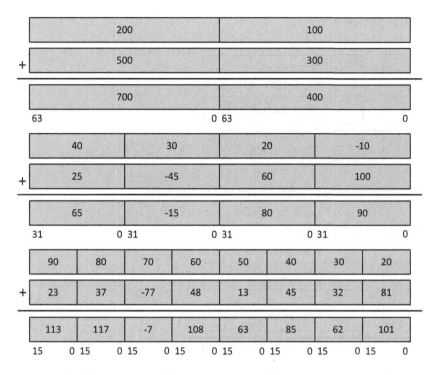

Figure 7-2. *SIMD integer addition*

Wraparound and Saturated Arithmetic

One extremely useful feature of Armv8-32 SIMD technology is its support for saturated integer arithmetic. In saturated integer arithmetic, computational results are automatically clipped by the processor to prevent overflow and underflow conditions. This differs from normal wraparound integer arithmetic where an overflow or underflow result is retained. Saturated arithmetic is handy when working with pixel values since it eliminates the need to explicitly check the result of each pixel calculation for an overflow or underflow condition. Armv8-32 includes instructions that perform saturated arithmetic using 8-bit and 16-bit integers, both signed and unsigned.

Figure 7-3 shows an example of 16-bit signed integer addition using wraparound and saturated arithmetic. An overflow condition occurs if the two 16-bit signed integers are added using wraparound arithmetic. With saturated arithmetic, however, the result is clipped to the largest possible 16-bit signed integer value. Figure 7-4 illustrates a similar example using 8-bit unsigned integers. Besides addition, Armv8-32 also supports saturated integer subtraction as shown in Figure 7-5.

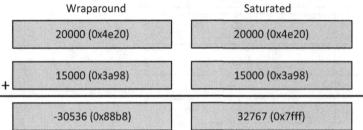

Figure 7-3. *16-bit signed integer addition using wraparound and saturated arithmetic*

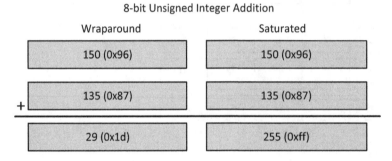

Figure 7-4. *8-bit unsigned integer addition and subtraction using wraparound and saturated arithmetic*

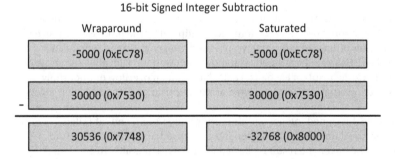

Figure 7-5. *16-bit signed integer subtraction using wraparound and saturated arithmetic*

Table 7-1 summarizes the saturated arithmetic range limits for all supported integer sizes and sign types.

Table 7-1. *Range limits for saturated arithmetic*

Integer Type	Lower Limit	Upper Limit
8-bit signed	-128 (0x80)	+127 (0x7F)
8-bit unsigned	0	+255 (0xFF)
16-bit signed	-32768 (0x8000)	+32767 (0x7FFF)
16-bit unsigned	0	+65535 (0xFFFF)

Armv8-32 SIMD Architecture

In this section, you will learn about the Armv8-32 SIMD register set. You will also learn about Armv8-32 data types and important details regarding the processing of these data types.

Register Set

Armv8-32 SIMD extends the scalar floating-point register set to support SIMD operands. Figure 7-6 shows this extension in greater detail. Each Q register is 128 bits wide and overlaps four S and two D registers. More specifically, registers S<4n>, S<4n+1>, S<4n+2>, and S<4n+3> map to bits 31:0, 63:32, 95:64, and 127:96 of register Q<n>, respectively. Registers D<2n> and D<2n+1> map to bits 63:0 and 127:64 of register Q<n>. This overlapping scheme is sometimes useful when writing Armv8-32 SIMD assembly language code, but extreme care must be taken to avoid inadvertently altering data values in a register.

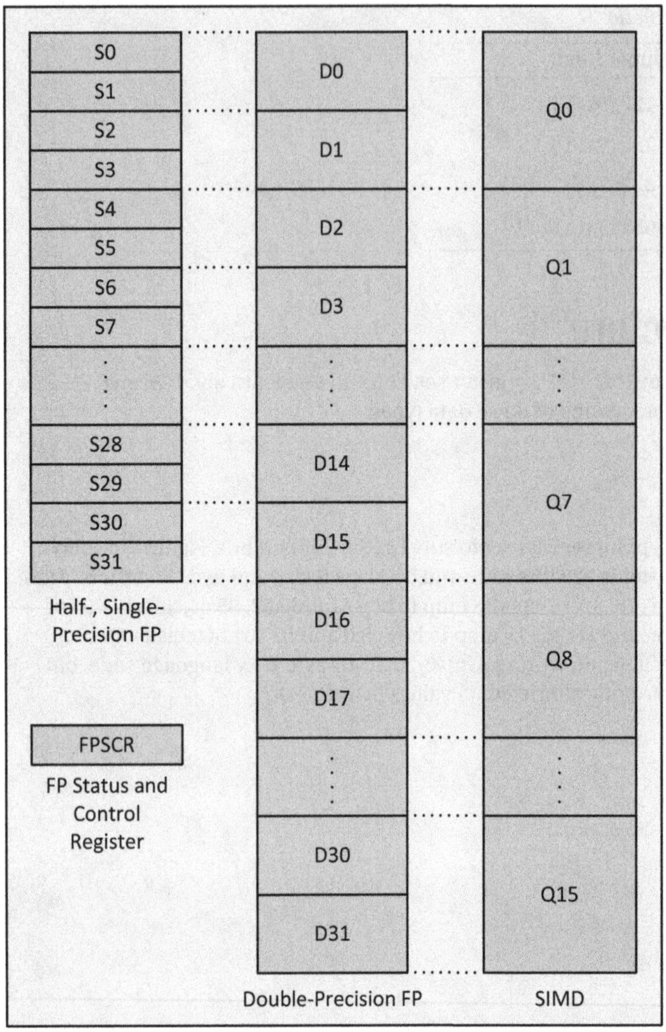

Figure 7-6. *Armv8-32 SIMD register file*

Most Armv8-32 SIMD instructions support both D (64-bit wide) and Q (128-bit wide) register variants. For example, the vadd.i8 d2,d0,d1 instruction performs packed integer addition using eight 8-bit values, while the vadd.i8 q2,q0,q1 instruction carries out the same arithmetic operation using sixteen 8-bit values.

Data Types

Armv8-32 SIMD instructions can be used with a variety of packed operand data types. A 128-bit wide Q register can hold sixteen 8-bit integers, eight 16-bit integers, four 32-bit integers, or two 64-bit integers. A Q register can also hold eight half-precision or four single-precision floating-point values. Figure 7-7 illustrates these data types. Armv8-32 SIMD does not support packed double-precision floating-point operands.

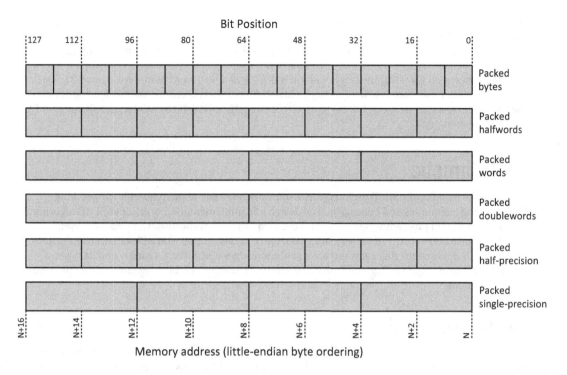

Figure 7-7. *Armv8-32 SIMD data types*

Like scalar floating-point, Armv8-32 SIMD performs floating-point operations per the IEEE 754 standard with the following exceptions:

- Floating-point arithmetic operations always use round-to-nearest rounding.

- Denormalized numbers are always flushed to zero. The FPSCR.FZ flag is ignored.

- The Arm defined default NaN is the only supported NaN type.

- All floating-point exceptions use untrapped floating-point exception handling.

Table 7-2. *Data type size specifiers for Armv8-32 SIMD instructions*

	8-bit	16-bit	32-bit	64-bit
Signed integer	s8	s16	s32	s64
Unsigned integer	u8	u16	u32	u64
Signed or unsigned integer	i8	i16	i32	i64
Floating-point	---	f16	f32	---

Table 7-2 shows the data type size specifiers that are used with most Armv8-32 SIMD instructions. You will learn more about these specifiers in Chapters 8 and 9.

It is always a good idea properly align 64- and 128-bit wide SIMD operands in memory. Common Armv8-32 SIMD load and store instructions (e.g., vldm, vldr, vpop, vpush, vstm, and vstr) will generate an alignment fault exception if a SIMD memory operand is not aligned on a word boundary. Armv8-32 SIMD element-structure load and store instructions (e.g., vld1–vld4, vst1–vst4) can be used with an optional alignment modifier to either weaken (128-bit to 64-bit) or strengthen (128-bit to 256-bit) the alignment of a SIMD operand in memory.

SIMD Arithmetic

To fully exploit the benefits of a SIMD architecture, a software developer must frequently "forget" long-established coding techniques and constructs. The design and implementation of effective SIMD algorithms usually requires a shift in programming mindset for even experienced software developers. However, Armv8-32 SIMD instruction use is often very straightforward. In this section, you will see several examples of Armv8-32 SIMD instructions that carry out basic arithmetic operations using a variety of data types. The purpose of these examples is to gently introduce Armv8-32 SIMD assembly language instructions and arithmetic operations.

Packed Integer Arithmetic

As mentioned earlier, Armv8-32 SIMD supports packed integer operations using 64-bit and 128-bit wide operands. When used with a 128-bit wide operand, most Armv8-32 SIMD instructions support arithmetic operations using sixteen bytes, eight halfword, four words, or two doublewords as shown in Figure 7-8. In this figure, vadd.i8 q2,q0,q1 instruction illustrates packed integer addition using byte values. The vmax.s16 q2,q0,q1 instruction saves the maximum value of each halfword pair. The next instruction, vand.u32 q2,q0,q1, performs a bitwise AND using the two operands. In this example, the instruction mnemonic size suffix is optional, but it is often included as a reminder of the data types being manipulated. Finally, the vshl.i64 q2,q1,#2 left shifts each doubleword element by two bits.

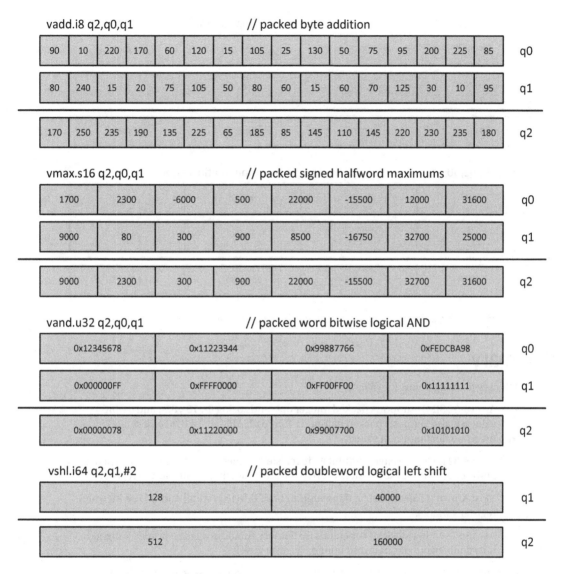

Figure 7-8. *Packed integer example instructions.*

Packed Floating-Point Arithmetic

Figure 7-9 illustrates two packed single-precision floating-point operations using 128-bit wide operands. The first example shows packed subtraction using the instruction vsub.f32 q2,q0,q1. The second example employs a vmul.f32 q2,q0,q1 instruction to carry out packed single-precision floating-point multiplication.

vsub.f32 q2,q0,q1   // packed single-precision subtraction

4.125	96.75	255.5	450.0	q0
0.5	-8.0	0.625	-9.5	q1

3.625	104.75	254.875	459.5	q2

vmul.f32 q2,q0,q1   // packed single-precision multiplication

4.125	96.75	255.5	450.0	q0
0.5	-8.0	0.625	-9.375	q1

2.0625	-774.0	159.6875	4218.75	q2

Figure 7-9. Packed single-precision floating-point example instructions

Summary

Here are the key learning points for Chapter 7:

- Armv8-32 SIMD supports packed integer operands using 8-, 16-, 32-, and 64-bit values. It also supports packed half-precision (with ARMv8.2-FP16) and single-precision floating-point values.

- Armv8-32 includes sixteen 128-bit wide registers named Q0–Q15 that can be used for SIMD operands. These registers overlap the scalar floating-point S and D registers.

- Most Armv8-32 SIMD instructions support both D (64-bit wide) and Q (128-bit wide) register variants.

- 64- and 128-bit wide SIMD operands in memory should always be properly aligned on a doubleword or quadword boundary, respectively.

- Functions that process arrays of 8- and 16-bit integers can use Armv8-32 SIMD instructions to perform saturated arithmetic, which eliminates the need to explicitly check for underflow and overflow conditions.

- Armv8-32 floating-point SIMD instructions always use round-to-nearest rounding. Denormalized numbers are always flushed to zero.

CHAPTER 8

Armv8-32 SIMD Integer Programming

This chapter covers Armv8-32 SIMD programming using packed integer operands. The content is partitioned into two major sections. The first section focuses on SIMD arithmetic including addition, subtraction, multiplication, and shift operations. The purpose of this section is to illustrate basic Armv8-32 SIMD instruction usage. The second section presents SIMD functions that are useful for image-processing applications. This section also introduces a simple method of benchmarking the performance of an assembly language function. The discussions in this chapter assume that you are familiar with the material introduced in Chapter 7.

Packed Integer Arithmetic

This section contains examples that explain how to perform fundamental SIMD arithmetic using packed integer operands. The first source code example involves packed addition and subtraction using both wraparound and saturated arithmetic. The second source code example shows how to perform packed shift operations. The third and final source code example illustrates packed integer multiplication.

Addition and Subtraction

Listing 8-1 shows the C++ and assembly language source code for example Ch08_01. This example demonstrates how to perform packed integer addition and subtraction using signed and unsigned 16-bit integers. It also illustrates both wraparound and saturated arithmetic.

Listing 8-1. Example Ch08_01

```
//-------------------------------------------------
//              Vec128.h
//-------------------------------------------------

#pragma once
#include <string>
#include <cstdint>
#include <sstream>
#include <iomanip>
```

© Daniel Kusswurm 2020
D. Kusswurm, *Modern Arm Assembly Language Programming*,
https://doi.org/10.1007/978-1-4842-6267-2_8

```cpp
struct alignas(16) Vec128
{
public:
    union
    {
        int8_t m_I8[16];
        int16_t m_I16[8];
        int32_t m_I32[4];
        int64_t m_I64[2];
        uint8_t m_U8[16];
        uint16_t m_U16[8];
        uint32_t m_U32[4];
        uint64_t m_U64[2];
        float m_F32[4];
        double m_F64[2];
    };
};

//---------------------------------------------------
//                  Ch08_01.cpp
//---------------------------------------------------
#include <iostream>
#include <string>
#include "Vec128.h"

using namespace std;

extern "C" void PackedAddI16_(Vec128 x[2], const Vec128& a, const Vec128& b);
extern "C" void PackedSubI16_(Vec128 x[2], const Vec128& a, const Vec128& b);
extern "C" void PackedAddU16_(Vec128 x[2], const Vec128& a, const Vec128& b);
extern "C" void PackedSubU16_(Vec128 x[2], const Vec128& a, const Vec128& b);

void PackedAddI16(void)
{
    Vec128 x[2], a, b;
    const char nl = '\n';

    a.m_I16[0] = 10;        b.m_I16[0] = 100;
    a.m_I16[1] = 200;       b.m_I16[1] = -200;
    a.m_I16[2] = 30;        b.m_I16[2] = 32760;
    a.m_I16[3] = -32766;    b.m_I16[3] = -400;
    a.m_I16[4] = 50;        b.m_I16[4] = 500;
    a.m_I16[5] = 60;        b.m_I16[5] = -600;
    a.m_I16[6] = 32000;     b.m_I16[6] = 1200;
    a.m_I16[7] = -32000;    b.m_I16[7] = -950;

    PackedAddI16_(x, a, b);

    cout << "\nResults for PackedAddI16 - Wraparound Addition\n";
    cout << "a:      " << a.ToStringI16() << nl;
    cout << "b:      " << b.ToStringI16() << nl;
    cout << "x[0]:   " << x[0].ToStringI16() << nl;
```

```
    cout << "\nResults for PackedAddI16 - Saturated Addition\n";
    cout << "a:      " << a.ToStringI16() << nl;
    cout << "b:      " << b.ToStringI16() << nl;
    cout << "x[1]:   " << x[1].ToStringI16() << nl;
}

void PackedSubI16(void)
{
    Vec128 x[2], a, b;
    const char nl = '\n';

    a.m_I16[0] = 10;           b.m_I16[0] = 100;
    a.m_I16[1] = 200;          b.m_I16[1] = -200;
    a.m_I16[2] = -30;          b.m_I16[2] = 32760;
    a.m_I16[3] = -32766;       b.m_I16[3] = 400;
    a.m_I16[4] = 50;           b.m_I16[4] = 500;
    a.m_I16[5] = 60;           b.m_I16[5] = -600;
    a.m_I16[6] = 32000;        b.m_I16[6] = 1200;
    a.m_I16[7] = -32000;       b.m_I16[7] = 950;

    PackedSubI16_(x, a, b);

    cout << "\nResults for PackedSubI16 - Wraparound Subtraction\n";
    cout << "a:      " << a.ToStringI16() << nl;
    cout << "b:      " << b.ToStringI16() << nl;
    cout << "x[0]:   " << x[0].ToStringI16() << nl;
    cout << "\nResults for PackedSubI16 - Saturated Subtraction\n";
    cout << "a:      " << a.ToStringI16() << nl;
    cout << "b:      " << b.ToStringI16() << nl;
    cout << "x[1]:   " << x[1].ToStringI16() << nl;
}

void PackedAddU16(void)
{
    const char nl = '\n';
    Vec128 x[2], a, b;

    a.m_U16[0] = 10;           b.m_U16[0] = 100;
    a.m_U16[1] = 200;          b.m_U16[1] = 200;
    a.m_U16[2] = 300;          b.m_U16[2] = 65530;
    a.m_U16[3] = 32766;        b.m_U16[3] = 40000;
    a.m_U16[4] = 50;           b.m_U16[4] = 500;
    a.m_U16[5] = 20000;        b.m_U16[5] = 25000;
    a.m_U16[6] = 32000;        b.m_U16[6] = 1200;
    a.m_U16[7] = 32000;        b.m_U16[7] = 50000;

    PackedAddU16_(x, a, b);

    cout << "\nResults for PackedAddU16 - Wraparound Addition\n";
    cout << "a:      " << a.ToStringU16() << nl;
    cout << "b:      " << b.ToStringU16() << nl;
```

```
        cout << "x[0]:   " << x[0].ToStringU16() << nl;
        cout << "\nResults for PackedAddU16 - Saturated Addition\n";
        cout << "a:      " << a.ToStringU16() << nl;
        cout << "b:      " << b.ToStringU16() << nl;
        cout << "x[1]:   " << x[1].ToStringU16() << nl;
}

void PackedSubU16(void)
{
        const char nl = '\n';
        Vec128 x[2], a, b;

        a.m_U16[0] = 10;            b.m_U16[0] = 100;
        a.m_U16[1] = 200;           b.m_U16[1] = 200;
        a.m_U16[2] = 30;            b.m_U16[2] = 7;
        a.m_U16[3] = 65000;         b.m_U16[3] = 5000;
        a.m_U16[4] = 60;            b.m_U16[4] = 500;
        a.m_U16[5] = 25000;         b.m_U16[5] = 28000;
        a.m_U16[6] = 32000;         b.m_U16[6] = 1200;
        a.m_U16[7] = 1200;          b.m_U16[7] = 950;

        PackedSubU16_(x, a, b);

        cout << "\nResults for PackedSubU16 - Wraparound Subtraction\n";
        cout << "a:      " << a.ToStringU16() << nl;
        cout << "b:      " << b.ToStringU16() << nl;
        cout << "x[0]:   " << x[0].ToStringU16() << nl;
        cout << "\nResults for PackedSubI16 - Saturated Subtraction\n";
        cout << "a:      " << a.ToStringU16() << nl;
        cout << "b:      " << b.ToStringU16() << nl;
        cout << "x[1]:   " << x[1].ToStringU16() << nl;
}

int main()
{
        const char nl = '\n';
        string sep(75, '-');

        PackedAddI16();
        PackedSubI16();
        cout << nl << sep << nl;
        PackedAddU16();
        PackedSubU16();
        return 0;
}
```

```
//---------------------------------------------------
//                Ch08_01_.s
//---------------------------------------------------

// extern "C" void PackedAddI16_(Vec128 x[2], const Vec128& a, const Vec128& b);

            .text
            .global PackedAddI16_
PackedAddI16_:

            vldm r1,{q0}                    // q0 = a
            vldm r2,{q1}                    // q1 = b

            vadd.i16 q2,q0,q1               // q2 = a + b (wraparound)
            vqadd.s16 q3,q0,q1              // q3 = a + b (saturated)

            vstm r0,{q2,q3}                 // save result to x
            bx lr

// extern "C" void PackedSubI16_(Vec128 x[2], const Vec128& b, const Vec128& c);

            .global PackedSubI16_
PackedSubI16_:

            vldm r1,{q0}                    // q0 = a
            vldm r2,{q1}                    // q1 = b

            vsub.i16 q2,q0,q1               // q2 = a - b (wraparound)
            vqsub.s16 q3,q0,q1              // q3 = a - b (saturated)

            vstm r0,{q2,q3}                 // save result to x
            bx lr

// extern "C" void PackedAddU16_(Vec128 x[2], const Vec128& a, const Vec128& b);

            .global PackedAddU16_
PackedAddU16_:

            vldm r1,{q0}                    // q0 = a
            vldm r2,{q1}                    // q1 = b

            vadd.i16 q2,q0,q1               // q2 = a + b (wraparound)
            vqadd.u16 q3,q0,q1              // q3 = a + b (saturated)

            vstm r0,{q2,q3}                 // save result to x
            bx lr

// extern "C" void PackedSubU16_(Vec128 x[2], const Vec128& a, const Vec128& b);

            .global PackedSubU16_
PackedSubU16_:
```

```
vldm r1,{q0}                          // q0 = a
vldm r2,{q1}                          // q1 = b

vsub.i16 q2,q0,q1                     // q2 = a - b (wraparound)
vqsub.u16 q3,q0,q1                    // q3 = a - b (saturated)

vstm r0,{q2,q3}                       // save result to x
bx lr
```

Listing 8-1 begins with the declaration of a C++ structure named Vec128 that is declared in the header file Vec128.h. This structure contains a publicly accessible anonymous union that facilitates packed operand data exchange between functions written in C++ and Armv8 assembly language. The members of this union correspond to the packed data types that can be used with a Q register. Note that the declaration of Vec128 uses the alignas specifier. This specifier instructs the C++ compiler to align each Vec128 instance on a 16-byte boundary. The structure Vec128 also includes several member functions that format and display the contents of a Vec128 variable. The source code for these member functions is not shown in Listing 8-1 but is included in the downloadable software package.

Toward the top of the file Ch08_01.cpp are the declarations for the assembly language functions that perform packed integer addition and subtraction. Each function takes two Vec128 arguments and saves its results to a Vec128 array. Note that argument values a and b are passed by reference to avoid the overhead of a Vec128 copy operation. Using pointers for these argument values would also work since pointers and references are the same from the perspective of the assembly language functions.

The C++ function PackedAddI16 contains test code that exercises the assembly language function PackedAddI16_. This function performs packed signed 16-bit integer (halfword) addition using both wraparound and saturated arithmetic. Following the execution of function PackedaddI16_, results are displayed using a series of stream writes to cout. The C++ function PackedSubI16, which resembles PackedAddI16, exercises the assembly language function PackedSubI16_. A parallel set of C++ functions named PackedAddU16 and PackedSubU16 contain code that exercise the assembly language functions PackedAddU16_ and PackedSubU16_. These functions perform packed unsigned 16-bit integer addition and subtraction, respectively.

The assembly language function PackedAddI16_ begins its execution with a vldm r1,{q0} (load multiple SIMD/FP registers) instruction that loads argument value a into register Q0. The ensuing vldm r2,{q1} instruction loads argument value b into Q1. This is followed by a vadd.i16 q2,q0,q1 (vector add) instruction that performs packed addition using 16-bit integer elements. The .i16 mnemonic size specifier is used with instructions that operate on both signed and unsigned integer elements. The next instruction, vqadd.s16 q3,q0,q1 (vector saturating add), performs packed saturated addition using 16-bit signed integers. In this instruction, the .s16 size specifier suffix signifies signed 16-bit integer elements. The results of these operations are then saved to array x using a vstm r0,{q2,q3} (store multiple SIMD/FP registers) instruction.

The assembly language function PackedSubI16_ is next. The organization of this function mimics PackedAddI16_ except that it performs packed integer subtraction using 16-bit integers. This function uses the instructions vsub.i16 q2,q0,q1 (vector subtract) and vqsub.s16 q3,q0,q1 (vector saturating subtract). For saturating arithmetic instructions like vqsub and vqadd, it is essential to use the correct size specifier. Otherwise, the results will be invalid.

The final two assembly language functions in Listing 8-1, PackedAddU16_ and PackedSubU16_, are the unsigned counterparts of PackedAddI16_ and PackedSubI16_. These functions use the instructions vadd.i16 q2,q0,q1, vqadd.u16 q3,q0,q1, vsub.i16 q2,q0,q1, and vqsub.u16 q3,q0,q1 to carry out their respective operations. Note the use of the .u16 size specifier suffixes on the vqadd and vqsub instructions. The output for source code example Ch08_01 follows this paragraph. Note that each column in the output shows corresponding elements from the source SIMD operands along with the calculated result.

```
Results for PackedAddI16 - Wraparound Addition
a:         10      200       30  -32766  |    50       60    32000  -32000
b:        100     -200    32760    -400  |   500     -600     1200    -950
x[0]:     110        0   -32746   32370  |   550     -540   -32336   32586

Results for PackedAddI16 - Saturated Addition
a:         10      200       30  -32766  |    50       60    32000  -32000
b:        100     -200    32760    -400  |   500     -600     1200    -950
x[1]:     110        0    32767  -32768  |   550     -540    32767  -32768

Results for PackedSubI16 - Wraparound Subtraction
a:         10      200      -30  -32766  |    50       60    32000  -32000
b:        100     -200    32760     400  |   500     -600     1200     950
x[0]:     -90      400    32746   32370  |  -450      660    30800   32586

Results for PackedSubI16 - Saturated Subtraction
a:         10      200      -30  -32766  |    50       60    32000  -32000
b:        100     -200    32760     400  |   500     -600     1200     950
x[1]:     -90      400   -32768  -32768  |  -450      660    30800  -32768


----------------------------------------------------------------------

Results for PackedAddU16 - Wraparound Addition
a:         10      200      300   32766  |    50    20000    32000    32000
b:        100      200    65530   40000  |   500    25000     1200    50000
x[0]:     110      400      294    7230  |   550    45000    33200    16464

Results for PackedAddU16 - Saturated Addition
a:         10      200      300   32766  |    50    20000    32000    32000
b:        100      200    65530   40000  |   500    25000     1200    50000
x[1]:     110      400    65535   65535  |   550    45000    33200    65535

Results for PackedSubU16 - Wraparound Subtraction
a:         10      200       30   65000  |    60    25000    32000     1200
b:        100      200        7    5000  |   500    28000     1200      950
x[0]:   65446        0       23   60000  | 65096    62536    30800      250

Results for PackedSubI16 - Saturated Subtraction
a:         10      200       30   65000  |    60    25000    32000     1200
b:        100      200        7    5000  |   500    28000     1200      950
x[1]:       0        0       23   60000  |     0        0    30800      250
```

Shift Operations

Listing 8-2 shows the source code for example Ch08_02. This example demonstrates how to perform packed shift operations. The C++ code in Listing 8-2 contains three functions named PackedShiftA, PackedShiftB, and PackedShiftC. These functions perform test case initialization for the assembly language functions PackedShiftA_, PackedShiftB_, and PackedShiftC_. They also display results on the console.

Listing 8-2. Example Ch08_02

```
//--------------------------------------------------
//                  Ch08_02.cpp
//--------------------------------------------------

#include <iostream>
#include "Vec128.h"

using namespace std;

extern "C" bool PackedShiftA_(Vec128* x, const Vec128& a);
extern "C" bool PackedShiftB_(Vec128* x, const Vec128& a, const Vec128& b);
extern "C" bool PackedShiftC_(Vec128* x, const Vec128& a, const Vec128& b);

void PackedShiftA(void)
{
    const char nl = '\n';
    Vec128 x[2], a;

    a.m_U16[0] = 0x1234;
    a.m_U16[1] = 0xFF9B;
    a.m_U16[2] = 0x00CC;
    a.m_U16[3] = 0xBD98;
    a.m_U16[4] = 0x00FF;
    a.m_U16[5] = 0xAAAA;
    a.m_U16[6] = 0x0F0F;
    a.m_U16[7] = 0x0065;

    PackedShiftA_(x, a);
    cout << "\nPackedShiftA_ (vshl.u16, vshr.u16, immediate)\n";
    cout << "a:    " << a.ToStringX16() << nl;
    cout << "x[0]: " << x[0].ToStringX16() << nl;
    cout << "x[1]: " << x[1].ToStringX16() << nl;
}

void PackedShiftB(void)
{
    const char nl = '\n';
    Vec128 x, a, b;

    a.m_U16[0] = 0x1234;     b.m_I16[0] = 3;
    a.m_U16[1] = 0xFF9B;     b.m_I16[1] = -4;
    a.m_U16[2] = 0x00CC;     b.m_I16[2] = 2;
    a.m_U16[3] = 0xBD98;     b.m_I16[3] = -6;
    a.m_U16[4] = 0x00FF;     b.m_I16[4] = 7;
    a.m_U16[5] = 0xAAAA;     b.m_I16[5] = 1;
    a.m_U16[6] = 0x0F0F;     b.m_I16[6] = -2;
    a.m_U16[7] = 0x0065;     b.m_I16[7] = 5;
```

```
    PackedShiftB_(&x, a, b);
    cout << "\nPackedShiftB_ (vshl.u16, register)\n";
    cout << "a:    " << a.ToStringX16() << nl;
    cout << "b:    " << b.ToStringI16() << nl;
    cout << "x:    " << x.ToStringX16() << nl;
}

void PackedShiftC(void)
{
    const char nl = '\n';
    Vec128 x[3], a, b;

    a.m_I16[0] = 4660;      b.m_I16[0] = 4;
    a.m_I16[1] = -105;      b.m_I16[1] = -2;
    a.m_I16[2] = 204;       b.m_I16[2] = 3;
    a.m_I16[3] = -17000;    b.m_I16[3] = 2;
    a.m_I16[4] = 255;       b.m_I16[4] = 4;
    a.m_I16[5] = -21846;    b.m_I16[5] = -1;
    a.m_I16[6] = 3855;      b.m_I16[6] = 8;
    a.m_I16[7] = 101;       b.m_I16[7] = -3;

    PackedShiftC_(x, a, b);
    cout << "\nPackedShiftC_ (vshl.s16, vqshl.s16, vrshl.s16)\n";
    cout << "a:    " << a.ToStringI16() << nl;
    cout << "b:    " << b.ToStringI16() << nl;
    cout << "x[0]: " << x[0].ToStringI16() << nl;
    cout << "x[1]: " << x[1].ToStringI16() << nl;
    cout << "x[2]: " << x[2].ToStringI16() << nl;
}

int main(void)
{
    const char nl = '\n';
    string sep(75, '-');

    PackedShiftA();
    cout << '\n' << sep << nl;
    PackedShiftB();
    cout << '\n' << sep << nl;
    PackedShiftC();
    return 0;
}

//--------------------------------------------------
//                 Ch08_02_.s
//--------------------------------------------------

// extern "C" bool PackedShiftA_(Vec128* x, const Vec128& a);

            .text
            .global PackedShiftA_
```

```
PackedShiftA_:

            vldm r1,{q0}                        // q0 = a

            vshl.u16 q1,q0,#4                   // vector left shift by 4
            vshr.u16 q2,q0,#2                   // vector right shift by 2

            vstm r0,{q1,q2}                     // save results to x
            bx lr


// extern "C" bool PackedShiftB_(Vec128* x, const Vec128& a, const Vec128& b);

        .global PackedShiftB_
PackedShiftB_:
            vldm r1,{q0}                        // q0 = a
            vldm r2,{q1}                        // q1 = b (shift counts)

            vshl.u16 q2,q0,q1                   // vector shift using counts

            vstm r0,{q2}                        // save result to x
            bx lr


// extern "C" bool PackedShiftC_(Vec128* x, const Vec128& a, const Vec128& b);

        .global PackedShiftC_
PackedShiftC_:
            vpush {q4}

            vldm r1,{q0}                        // q0 = a
            vldm r2,{q1}                        // q1 = b (shift counts)

            vshl.s16 q2,q0,q1                   // vector left shift
            vqshl.s16 q3,q0,q1                  // vector left shift - sat
            vrshl.s16 q4,q0,q1                  // vector left shift - round

            vstm r0,{q2-q4}                     // save result to x

            vpop {q4}
            bx lr
```

The assembly language function PackedShiftA_ illustrates the use of the vshl (vector shift left) and vshr (vector shift right) using immediate shift counts. The first instruction of PackedShiftA_, vldm r1,{q0}, loads argument value a into register Q0. The next instruction, vshl.u16 q1,q0,#4, left shifts each 16-bit element in Q0 by four bits. The ensuing vshr.u16 q2,q0,#2 instruction right shifts each 16-bit element in Q0 by two bits. This is followed by a vstm r0,{q1,q2} that saves the results to array x.

Function PackedShiftB_ also performs shifts. In this function, the vshl.u16 q2,q0,q1 instruction uses the low-order byte of each 16-bit element in Q1 for the shift count. If the shift count is positive, the corresponding 16-bit element in Q0 is shifted left. If the shift count is negative, the 16-bit element is shifted right.

The final assembly language shift function, PackedShiftC_, begins its execution with a vpush {q4} instruction. Recall from discussions in Chapter 6 that the GNU C++ calling convention designates registers

D8–D15 as non-volatile, which means they must be preserved on the stack before any use. This designation also applies to the overlapping registers Q4–Q7. (Registers Q8–Q15 are volatile and one of these could have been used, but I want to demonstrate the use of the vpush and vpop instructions in this example.) Following the vpush instruction, PackedShiftC_ uses two vldm instructions to load argument values a (test vector) and b (shift counts) into registers Q0 and Q1. This is followed by a vshl.s16 q2,q0,q1 that left or right shifts each 16-bit element. The ensuing vqshl.s16 q3,q0,q1 (vector saturating left shift) performs a saturating left or right shift of each 16-bit integer element in Q0. The use of the .s16 size specifier instructs the processor to use signed 16-bit integer saturation [-32768, +32767] when shifting each element. The final shift instruction, vrshl.s16 q4,q0,q1 (vector rounding left shift), performs a rounding left or right shift of each 16-bit signed integer element. Unlike a normal shift, which performs truncations, a rounding shift rounds the shift result to the nearest integer value. Here is the output for example Ch08_02:

```
PackedShiftA_ (vshl.u16, vshr.u16, immediate)
a:      1234    FF9B    00CC    BD98  |   00FF    AAAA    0F0F    0065
x[0]:   2340    F9B0    0CC0    D980  |   0FF0    AAA0    F0F0    0650
x[1]:   048D    3FE6    0033    2F66  |   003F    2AAA    03C3    0019


------------------------------------------------------------------------


PackedShiftB_ (vshl.u16, register)
a:      1234    FF9B    00CC    BD98  |   00FF    AAAA    0F0F    0065
b:         3      -4       2      -6  |      7       1      -2       5
x:      91A0    0FF9    0330    02F6  |   7F80    5554    03C3    0CA0


------------------------------------------------------------------------


PackedShiftC_ (vshl.s16, s.s16, vrshl.s16)
a:      4660    -105     204  -17000  |    255  -21846    3855     101
b:         4      -2       3       2  |      4      -1       8      -3
x[0]:   9024     -27    1632   -2464  |   4080  -10923    3840      12
x[1]:  32767     -27    1632  -32768  |   4080  -10923   32767      12
x[2]:   9024     -26    1632   -2464  |   4080  -10923    3840      13
```

Multiplication

Armv8-32 SIMD includes several instructions that carry out packed integer multiplication. Listing 8-3 shows the source code for example Ch08_03, which demonstrates packed integer multiplication. The C++ code that is shown in Listing 8-3 performs test case initialization for the assembly language function PackedMulA_. The function requires two values (a and b) of type Vec128 that have been initialized with signed 16-bit signed integer values, a single 16-bit signed integer scalar (c), and a results array of type Vec128 (x).

Listing 8-3. Example Ch08_03

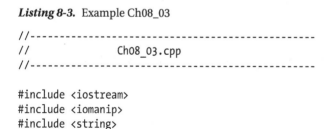

```cpp
//------------------------------------------------------
//              Ch08_03.cpp
//------------------------------------------------------

#include <iostream>
#include <iomanip>
#include <string>
```

```cpp
#include "Vec128.h"

using namespace std;

extern "C" bool PackedMulA_(Vec128* x, const Vec128& a, const Vec128& b, int16_t c);

void PackedMulA(void)
{
    Vec128 x[4], a, b;
    const int c = 5;
    const char nl = '\n';
    string sep(75, '-');

    a.m_I16[0] = 10;          b.m_I16[0] = 6;
    a.m_I16[1] = 7;           b.m_I16[1] = 13;
    a.m_I16[2] = -23;         b.m_I16[2] = -75;
    a.m_I16[3] = 41;          b.m_I16[3] = 9;
    a.m_I16[4] = 6;           b.m_I16[4] = 37;
    a.m_I16[5] = -33;         b.m_I16[5] = 28;
    a.m_I16[6] = 19;          b.m_I16[6] = 56;
    a.m_I16[7] = 16;          b.m_I16[7] = -18;

    PackedMulA_(x, a, b, c);

    cout << "\nResults for PackedMulA_\n";
    cout << sep << nl;

    cout << "a:    " << a.ToStringI16() << nl;
    cout << "b:    " << b.ToStringI16() << nl;
    cout << "c:    " << setw(8) << c << nl << nl;
    cout << "x[0]: " << x[0].ToStringI16() << nl << nl;
    cout << "x[1]: " << x[1].ToStringI16() << nl << nl;
    cout << "x[2]: " << x[2].ToStringI32() << nl;
    cout << "x[3]: " << x[3].ToStringI32() << nl;
}

int main(void)
{
    PackedMulA();
    return 0;
}

//-------------------------------------------------
//                Ch08_03_.s
//-------------------------------------------------

// extern "C" bool PackedMulA_(Vec128 x[4], const Vec128& a, const Vec128& b, int16_t c);

            .text
            .global PackedMulA_
PackedMulA_:
```

```
vldm r1,{q0}                    // q0 = a
vldm r2,{q1}                    // q1 = b

vmov s14,r3                     // s14 = c
vmul.i16 q2,q0,d7[0]            // q2 = a * c (scalar mul)
vstm r0!,{q2}                   // save result to x[0]

vmul.i16 q2,q0,q1               // q2 = a * b (vector 16-bit)
vstm r0!,{q2}                   // save result to x[1]

vmull.s16 q2,d0,d2              // q2 = a[0:3] * b[0:3] (32-bit)
vstm r0!,{q2}                   // save result to x[2]
vmull.s16 q2,d1,d3              // q2 = a[4:7] * b[4:7] (32-bit)
vstm r0,{q2}                    // save result to x[3]

bx lr
```

PackedMulA_ begins its execution with a couple of vldm instructions that load argument values a and b into register Q0 and Q1, respectively. It then uses a vmov s14,r3 instruction to copy argument value c into register S14. Note that this instruction does not perform any conversions. Also keep in mind that argument value c, which is a value of type int16_t, is already sign-extended to 32 bits in R3 per the GNU C++ calling convention. The ensuing vmul.i16 q2,q0,d7[0] (vector multiply by scalar) instruction multiples each signed 16-bit integer element in Q0 by D7[0]. In this instruction, the notation D7[0] designates the low-order 16 bits of register D7 as the scalar value, which overlaps register S14. The result is then saved to x[0] using a vstm r0!,{q2} instruction.

The next instruction in PackedMulA_, vmul.i16 q2,q0,q1 (vector multiply), carries out packed multiplication using signed or unsigned 16-bit integers. Note that this instruction truncates each product to 16 bits. Another vstm r0!,{q2} instruction then saves the result to x[1].

The final code block in PackedMulA_ illustrates the use of the vmull (vector multiply long) instruction. The first instance of this instruction, vmull.s16 q2,d0,d2, performs signed 16-bit integer multiplication using the four low-order elements of argument values a and b. The complete 32-bit products are saved in Q2. Note that registers D0 and D2 overlap the low-order 64 bits of registers Q0 and Q1, respectively. The vstm r0!,{q2} instruction saves this result to x[2]. The ensuing vmull.s16 q2,d1,d3 instruction performs signed 16-bit integer multiplication using the four high-order elements of a and b. In this instruction, D1 and D3 overlap the high-order 64 bits of Q0 and Q1, respectively. The instruction vstm r0,{q2} then saves the result to x[3].

```
Here are the results for source code example Ch08_03:Results for PackedMulA_
-------------------------------------------------------------------------
a:        10        7      -23       41  |      6     -33       19       16
b:         6       13      -75        9  |     37      28       56      -18
c:         5

x[0]:     50       35     -115      205  |     30    -165       95       80

x[1]:     60       91     1725      369  |    222    -924     1064     -288

x[2]:            60                91  |           1725              369
x[3]:           222              -924  |           1064             -288
```

Packed Integer Image Processing

The source code examples presented in the previous section were designed to familiarize you with Armv8-32 SIMD packed integer programming. Each example included a simple assembly language function that demonstrated the operation of several Armv8-32 SIMD instructions using instances of the structure Vec128. For some real-world application programs, it may be appropriate to create a small set of functions like the ones you have seen thus far. However, to fully exploit the benefits of SIMD processing, you need to code functions that implement complete algorithms using common data structures.

The source code examples in this section describe algorithms that process arrays of unsigned 8-bit integers using the Armv8-32 SIMD instruction set. In the first example, you will learn how to determine the minimum and maximum values of an array. This example program has a certain practicality to it since digital images often use arrays of unsigned 8-bit integers to represent images in memory, and many image-processing algorithms (e.g., contrast enhancement) often need to determine the minimum (darkest) and maximum (lightest) pixels in an image. The second sample program illustrates how to calculate the mean value of an array of unsigned 8-bit integers. This is another example of a realistic algorithm that is directly relevant to the province of image processing (mean values are sometimes used in algorithms that adjust image intensity). The final source code example demonstrates image thresholding.

Pixel Minimum and Maximum

Source code example Ch08_04, shown in Listing 8-4, calculates the minimum and maximum values in an array of unsigned 8-bit integers. It also contains code that shows how to perform benchmark timing measurements of an assembly language function.

Listing 8-4. Example Ch08_04

```
//-------------------------------------------------
//                  Ch08_04.h
//-------------------------------------------------

#pragma once
#include <cstdint>

// Ch08_04.cpp
extern void Init(uint8_t* x, uint32_t n, unsigned int seed);
extern bool CalcMinMaxU8(uint8_t* x_min, uint8_t* x_max, const uint8_t* x, uint32_t n);

// Ch08_04_BM.cpp
extern void MinMaxU8_BM(void);

// Ch08_04_.s
extern "C" bool CalcMinMaxU8_(uint8_t* x_min, uint8_t* x_max, const uint8_t* x, uint32_t n);

// Common constants
const uint32_t c_NumElements = 16 * 1024 * 1024 + 7;
const unsigned int c_RngSeedVal = 23;

//-------------------------------------------------
//                  Ch08_04.cpp
//-------------------------------------------------
```

```cpp
#include <iostream>
#include <cstdint>
#include <random>
#include "Ch08_04.h"
#include "AlignedMem.h"

using namespace std;

void Init(uint8_t* x, uint32_t n, unsigned int seed)
{
    uniform_int_distribution<> ui_dist {5, 250};
    mt19937 rng {seed};

    for (uint32_t i = 0; i < n; i++)
        x[i] = (uint8_t)ui_dist(rng);

    // Use known values for min & max (for test purposes)
    x[(n / 4) * 3 + 1] = 2;
    x[n / 4 + 11] = 3;
    x[n / 2] = 252;
    x[n / 2 + 13] = 253;
    x[n / 8 + 5] = 4;
    x[n / 8 + 7] = 254;
}

bool CalcMinMaxU8(uint8_t* x_min, uint8_t* x_max, const uint8_t* x, uint32_t n)
{
    if (n == 0)
        return false;

    if (!AlignedMem::IsAligned(x, 16))
        return false;

    uint8_t x_min_temp = 255;
    uint8_t x_max_temp = 0;

    for (uint32_t i = 0; i < n; i++)
    {
        uint8_t val = *x++;

        if (val < x_min_temp)
            x_min_temp = val;
        else if (val > x_max_temp)
            x_max_temp = val;
    }

    *x_min = x_min_temp;
    *x_max = x_max_temp;
    return true;
}
```

155

```
void MinMaxU8()
{
    uint32_t n = c_NumElements;
    AlignedArray<uint8_t> x_aa(n, 16);
    uint8_t* x = x_aa.Data();

    Init(x, n, c_RngSeedVal);

    uint8_t x_min1 = 0, x_max1 = 0;
    uint8_t x_min2 = 0, x_max2 = 0;
    bool rc1 = CalcMinMaxU8(&x_min1, &x_max1, x, n);
    bool rc2 = CalcMinMaxU8_(&x_min2, &x_max2, x, n);

    cout << "\nResults for MinMaxU8\n";
    cout << "rc1: " << rc1 << "  x_min1: " << (int)x_min1;
    cout << "  x_max1: " << (int)x_max1 << '\n';
    cout << "rc2: " << rc2 << "  x_min2: " << (int)x_min2;
    cout << "  x_max2: " << (int)x_max2 << '\n';
}

int main()
{
    MinMaxU8();
    MinMaxU8_BM();
    return 0;
}

//---------------------------------------------------
//                  Ch08_04_.s
//---------------------------------------------------

// extern "C" bool CalcMinMaxU8_(uint8_t* x_min, uint8_t* x_max, const uint8_t* x, size_t n);

            .text
            .global CalcMinMaxU8_
CalcMinMaxU8_:
// Prologue
            push {r4-r6,lr}

// Validate arguments
            cmp r3,#0
            beq InvalidArg                      // jump if n == 0

            tst r2,#0x0f
            bne InvalidArg                      // jump if x not 16b aligned

// Initialize
            vmov q2.i8,#255
            vmov q3.i8,#255                     // q2:q3 = packed minimums
```

```
                vmov q8.i8,#0
                vmov q9.i8,#0                    // q8:q9 = packed maximums

// Main processing loop
                cmp r3,#32
                blo SkipLoop1                    // jump if n < 32

Loop1:          vldm r2!,{q0,q1}                 // load block of 32 pixels

                vmin.u8 q2,q2,q0
                vmin.u8 q3,q3,q1                 // update pixel minimums

                vmax.u8 q8,q8,q0
                vmax.u8 q9,q9,q1                 // update pixel maximums

                sub r3,#32                       // n -= 32
                cmp r3,#32
                bhs Loop1                        // jump if n >= 32

// Reduce packed minimums and maximums to scalar values
SkipLoop1:      vmin.u8 q2,q2,q3                 // q2 = pixel minimums (16)
                vmin.u8 d6,d4,d5                 // d6 = pixel minimums (8)
                vpmin.u8 d7,d6,d6                // d7 = pixel minimums (4)
                vpmin.u8 d20,d7,d7               // d20 = pixel minimums (2)
                vpmin.u8 d21,d20,d20             // d21[0] = pixel minimum
                vmov.u8 r4,d21[0]

                vmax.u8 q2,q8,q9                 // q2 = pixel maximums (16)
                vmax.u8 d6,d4,d5                 // d6 = pixel maximums (8)
                vpmax.u8 d7,d6,d6                // d7 = pixel maximums (4)
                vpmax.u8 d20,d7,d7               // d20 = pixel maximums (2)
                vpmax.u8 d21,d20,d20             // d21[0] = pixel maximum
                vmov.u8 r5,d21[0]

// Process final pixels
                cmp r3,#0
                beq SaveMinMax                   // jump if n == 0

Loop2:          ldrb r6,[r2],#1                  // r6 = pixel value
                cmp r6,r4
                movlo r4,r6                      // update pixel minimum
                cmp r6,r5
                movhi r5,r6                      // update pixel maximum
                subs r3,#1
                bne Loop2                        // repeat until done

// Save results
SaveMinMax:     strb r4,[r0]                     // save minimum to x_min
                strb r5,[r1]                     // save maximum to x_max
                mov r0,#1                        // set success return code
```

```
// Epilogue
Done:          pop {r4-r6,pc}

InvalidArg: mov r0,#0                           // set error return code
            b Done
```

The C++ code in Listing 8-4 begins with a function named Init. This function initializes an array of type uint8_t using random values. The next function, CalcMinMaxU8, is a C++ implementation of the min-max algorithm. Note that this function checks argument value n to make sure that it is not equal to zero. It also checks array x for alignment to a 16-byte boundary using AlignedMem::IsAligned. Class AlignedMem is a simple wrapper class that performs aligned memory allocations. This class is defined in the header file AlignedMem.h, which is not shown in Listing 8-4 but is included in the downloadable software package. The remaining code in CalcMinMaxU8 computes the minimum and maximum values in array x using a simple for-loop.

The assembly language function MinMaxU8_ uses the instruction pair cmp r3,#0 and beq InvalidArg to verify that argument value n is not equal to zero. The next instruction, tst r2,#0x0f (test), performs a bitwise AND of R2 (argument value x) and 0x0F. It then updates the NZCV condition flags based on the result, which is discarded. A nonzero result means that array x is not aligned on a 16-byte boundary. The tst instruction is often used as an alternative to the cmp instruction when performing argument validation or other types of comparisons. Following argument validation, the vmov q2.i8,#255 (vector copy immediate value) and vmov q3.i8,#255 instructions initialize each 8-bit element in registers Q2 and Q3 to 255. These registers are used in for-loop Loop1 to maintain packed pixel minimum values. The vmov q8.i8,#0 and vmov q9.i8,#0 instructions initialize registers Q4 and Q5 as packed pixel maximum values.

The min-max processing loop is next. Note that just before the start of for-loop Loop1 is the instruction pair cmp r3,#32 and blo SkipLoop1. This sequence tests argument value n to see if it is less than 32. If it is, the branch instruction skips over Loop1. The reason for this test is that Loop1 processes 32 pixels during each iteration; execution of this for-loop with less than 32 available pixels would generate an invalid result.

Each iteration of Loop1 begins with a vldm r2!,{q0,q1} instruction that loads a block of 32 pixels into registers Q0 and Q1. The next two instructions, vmin.u8 q2,q2,q0 and vmin.u8 q3,q3,q1 (vector minimum), update the pixel minimums that are maintained in registers Q2 and Q3. The vmin instruction compares corresponding elements in the two source operands and saves the smaller value in the corresponding element of the destination operand. The pixel maximum values in registers Q8 and Q9 are updated next using the instruction pair vmax.u8 q8,q8,q0 and vmax.u8 q9,q9,q1 (vector maximum). The ensuing sub r3,#32 instruction calculates n -= 32 and Loop1 repeats until the number of remaining pixels is less than 32.

After execution of for-loop Loop1, register pairs Q2:Q3 and Q8:Q9 contain packed pixel minimums and maximums, respectively. The next step of the algorithm is to reduce the packed pixel minimums and maximums to scalar values. The vmin.u8 q2,q2,q3 instruction reduces the number of pixel minimums from 32 to 16. This is followed by a vmin.u8 d6,d4,d5 instruction that yields eight pixel minimums. Next is a series of vpmin (vector pairwise minimum) instructions that reduce the pixel minimum values in register Q2 to a scalar value. Unlike the vmin instruction, vpmin performs minimum compares using adjacent elements of the two source operands. Figure 8-1 illustrates this in greater detail. Following the vpmin instruction sequence, CalcMinMaxU8_ uses a vmov.u8 r4,d21[0] to copy the scalar minimum value into register R4. A similar series of vmax and vpmax (vector pairwise maximum) instructions then calculates the scalar maximum. It should be noted that vpmin and vpmax do not support Q register operands.

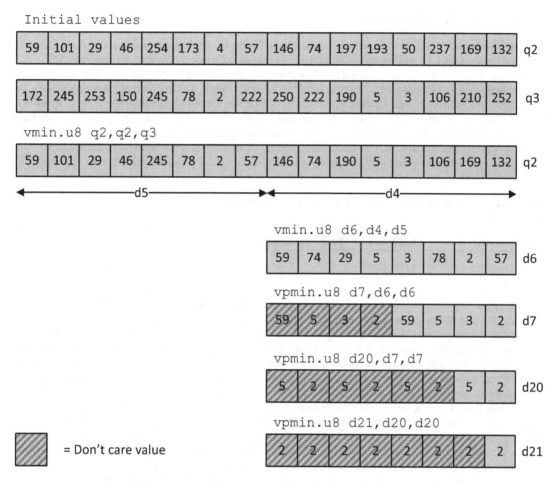

Figure 8-1. Reduction of packed pixel minimums using the instructions vmin *and* vpmin

The for-loop Loop2 processes the final few pixels (if any remain) in the array using scalar instructions and the general-purpose registers. Note that Loop2 is skipped if n (R3) is equal to zero. CalcMinMaxU8_ saves the final pixel minimum and maximum values using the instructions strb r4,[r0] and strb r5,[r1]. Here are the results for source code example Ch08_04:

```
Results for MinMaxU8
rc1: 1  x_min1: 2  x_max1: 254
rc2: 1  x_min2: 2  x_max2: 254

Running benchmark function MinMaxU8_BM - please wait
Benchmark times save to file Ch08_04_MinMaxU8_BM_RpiBeta.csv
```

Performance Benchmarking

Source code example Ch08_04 includes a function named MinMaxU8_BM that contains code for measuring execution times of the C++ and assembly language pixel min-max functions. Most of the benchmark timing measurement code is encapsulated in a C++ class named BmThreadTimer. This class includes two member functions, BmThreadTimer::Start and BmThreadTimer::Stop, that implement a simple software stopwatch. Class BmThreadTimer also includes a member function named BmThreadTimer::SaveElapsedTimes, which saves the timing measurements to a comma-separated-value (CSV) text file. The source code for class BmThreadTimer is not shown in Listing 8-4 but included as part of the source code download package. Table 8-1 contains benchmark timing measurements for the functions CalcMinMaxU8 and CalcMinMaxU8_. These measurements were made using the hardware and software configurations described in Appendix A.

Table 8-1. *Mean execution times (microseconds) for pixel min-max functions (16777223 elements)*

C++ (MinMaxU8)	Assembly Language (MinMaxU8_)
35116	4345

The values shown in Table 8-1 were computed using the Excel spreadsheet function TRIMMEAN (array, 0.10) and the execution times in the CSV file. In source code example Ch08_04, the assembly language implementation of the min-max algorithm clearly outperforms the C++ version by a wide margin. I should mention that the performance gains observed in this example are somewhat atypical. Nevertheless, it is not uncommon to achieve significant speed improvements using Armv8-32 assembly language, especially by algorithms that can exploit the SIMD parallelism of an Armv8 processor. You will see additional examples of accelerated algorithmic performance throughout the remainder of this book.

The benchmark timing measurements included in this book are intended to provide an estimate of potential assembly language performance improvements. Like automobile fuel economy estimates and smartphone battery runtime approximations, software performance benchmarking is not an exact science. Measurements must be made and results construed in a context that is appropriate for the specific benchmark and target execution environment. The methods used here to benchmark execution times are generally worthwhile, but results can vary between runs depending on the hardware and software configuration of the target platform.

Mean Intensity

The next source code example, Ch08_05, contains code that calculates the arithmetic mean of an array of 8-bit unsigned integers. This example also illustrates how to size-promote packed unsigned integers. Listing 8-5 shows the source code for example Ch08_05.

Listing 8-5. Example Ch08_05

```
//-------------------------------------------------
//              Ch08_05.h
//-------------------------------------------------

#pragma once
#include <cstdint>

// Ch08_05.cpp
```

```
extern void Init(uint8_t* x, size_t n, unsigned int seed);
extern bool CalcMeanU8(uint32_t* sum_x, double* mean, const uint8_t* x, uint32_t n);

// Ch08_05_BM.cpp
extern void MeanU8_BM(void);

// Ch08_05_.s
extern "C" bool CalcMeanU8_(uint32_t* sum_x, double* mean, const uint8_t* x, uint32_t n);

// Common constants
const uint32_t c_NumElements = 8 * 1024 * 1024 + 19;
const uint32_t c_NumElementsMax = 16 * 1024 * 1024;
const unsigned int c_RngSeedVal = 29;

//--------------------------------------------------
//                  Ch08_05.cpp
//--------------------------------------------------

#include <iostream>
#include <iomanip>
#include <random>
#include "Ch08_05.h"
#include "AlignedMem.h"

using namespace std;

uint32_t g_NumElementsMax = c_NumElementsMax;

void Init(uint8_t* x, size_t n, unsigned int seed)
{
    uniform_int_distribution<> ui_dist {0, 255};
    mt19937 rng {seed};

    for (size_t i = 0; i < n; i++)
        x[i] = (uint8_t)ui_dist(rng);
}

bool CalcMeanU8(uint32_t* sum_x, double* mean_x, const uint8_t* x, uint32_t n)
{
    if (n == 0 || n > g_NumElementsMax)
        return false;

    if (!AlignedMem::IsAligned(x, 16))
        return false;

    uint32_t sum_x_temp = 0;

    for (uint32_t i = 0; i < n; i++)
        sum_x_temp += x[i];

    *sum_x = sum_x_temp;
```

```
    *mean_x = (double)sum_x_temp / n;
    return true;
}

void MeanU8()
{
    const char nl = '\n';
    const uint32_t n = c_NumElements;
    AlignedArray<uint8_t> x_aa(n, 16);
    uint8_t* x = x_aa.Data();

    Init(x, n, c_RngSeedVal);

    bool rc1, rc2;
    uint32_t sum_x1, sum_x2;
    double mean_x1, mean_x2;

    rc1 = CalcMeanU8(&sum_x1, &mean_x1, x, n);
    rc2 = CalcMeanU8_(&sum_x2, &mean_x2, x, n);

    cout << "\nResults for MeanU8\n";
    cout << fixed << setprecision(4);
    cout << "rc1: " << boolalpha << rc1 << "   ";
    cout << "sum_x1:   " << sum_x1 << "   ";
    cout << "mean_x1: " << mean_x1 << nl;;
    cout << "rc2: " << boolalpha << rc2 << "   ";
    cout << "sum_x2:   " << sum_x2 << "   ";
    cout << "mean_x2: " << mean_x2 << nl;
}

int main()
{
    MeanU8();
    MeanU8_BM();
    return 0;
}

//--------------------------------------------------
//                 Ch08_05_.s
//--------------------------------------------------

// extern "C" bool CalcMeanU8_(uint32_t* sum_x, double* mean, const uint8_t* x, uint32_t n);

            .text
            .global CalcMeanU8_

CalcMeanU8_:
// Prologue
            push {r4-r6,lr}
            vpush {q4-q6}
```

```
// Validate arguments
          cmp r3,#0
          beq InvalidArg                  // jump if n == 0

          ldr r4,=g_NumElementsMax
          ldr r5,[r4]
          cmp r3,r5                       // n > g_NumElementsMax?
          bhi InvalidArg                  // jump if yes

          tst r2,#0x0f
          bne InvalidArg                  // jump if x not 16b aligned

// Initialize
          mov r6,r3                       // save n for later
          veor q6,q6,q6                   // set packed sums to zero

// Main processing loop
          cmp r3,#32
          blo SkipLoop1                   // jump if n < 32

Loop1:    vldm r2!,{q0,q1}                // q0:q1 = 32 pixels

          vaddl.u8 q2,d0,d1               // zero-extend to h-words
          vaddl.u8 q3,d2,d3               // and sum

          vaddl.u16 q4,d4,d5              // zero-extend to words
          vaddl.u16 q5,d6,d7             // and sum

          vadd.u32 q6,q6,q4               // update packed sums
          vadd.u32 q6,q6,q5

          sub r3,#32
          cmp r3,#32
          bhs Loop1                       // jump if n >= 32

SkipLoop1: vpadd.u32 d0,d12,d13           // reduce packed uint32
          vpadd.u32 d1,d0,d0              // sums to scalar
          vmov r4,d1[0]                   // r4 = current sum

// Process final array elements
          cmp r3,#0                       // more pixels to process?
          beq CalcMean                    // jump if no

Loop2:    ldrb r5,[r2],#1                 // r5 = pixel value
          add r4,r4,r5                    // sum += pixel value
          subs r3,#1
          bne Loop2                       // jump if n > 0

CalcMean: str r4,[r0]                     // save sum

          vmov s0,r4
```

```
            vcvt.f64.u32 d1,s0              // d1 = sum as double
            vmov s0,r6
            vcvt.f64.u32 d2,s0              // d2 = n as double

            vdiv.f64 d3,d1,d2               // calculate mean
            vstr.f64 d3,[r1]               // save mean

            mov r0,#1                      // set success return code

// Epilogue
Done:       vpop {q4-q6}
            pop {r4-r6,pc}

InvalidArg: mov r0,#0                      // set error return code
            b Done
```

The organization of the C++ code in example Ch08_05 resembles the previous example. The function CalcMeanU8 uses a simple summing loop and scalar arithmetic to calculate the mean of an array of 8-bit unsigned integers. Like the previous example, the source array must be aligned to a 16-byte boundary. Note that the function CalcMeanU8 also verifies that the number of array elements is not greater than g_NumElementsMax. This size restriction is also used in the assembly language function CalcMeanU8_ so that it can carry out its calculations using packed unsigned words sans any safeguards for arithmetic overflows. The remaining C++ code that is shown in Listing 8-5 performs test array initialization and streams results to cout.

The assembly language function CalcMeanU8_ begins with a prologue that uses the instructions push {r4-r6,lr} and vpush {q4-q6} to preserve non-volatile registers on the stack. Note that when vpush and vpop are used with multiple registers, the registers must be consecutively numbered (e.g., vpush {q4,q7} is invalid). CalcMeanU8_ then performs the same validations of the array size as its C++ counterpart. The address of the array x is also checked for alignment on a 16-byte boundary. Following argument validation, CalcMeanU8_ carries out its required initializations. Note that register Q6 is initialized to all zeros using a veor q6,q6,q6 instruction; this register maintains a packed pixel sum. Prior to execution of for-loop Loop1, argument value n is tested to make sure that it is not less than 32. If it is, the code in Loop1 is not executed since it processes blocks of 32 pixels.

The first instruction of Loop1, vldm r2!,{q0,q1}, loads 32 pixels into registers Q0 and Q1. This is followed by a vaddl.u8 q2,d0,d1 (vector add long) instruction. The vaddl.u8 instruction zero-extends the 8-bit elements of source operands D0 and D1 (Q0) to 16 bits; it then sums the 16-bit elements and saves the result to Q2. The ensuing vaddl.u8 q3,d2,d3 instruction performs the same operation using the pixel values in D2 and D3 (Q1). The next two instructions, vaddl.u16 q4,d4,d5 and vaddl.u16 q5,d6,d7, zero-extend the intermediate pixel sums in their source operands to 32 bits; the 32-bit elements are then summed. The two vadd.u32 instructions update the packed 32-bit sum that is maintained in Q6. Figure 8-2 illustrates this process in greater detail.

Following execution of for-loop Loop1, CalcMeanU8_ uses the instruction pair vpadd.u32 d0,d12,d13 and vpadd.u32 d1,d0,d0 (vector pairwise add) to reduce the packed word sums in Q6 to a scalar value. It then uses for-loop Loop2 to process any remaining pixel values. Following execution of Loop2, the variables sum and n are converted to double-precision floating-point values using two vcvt.f64.u32 instructions. The mean is then calculated using a vdiv.f64 d3,d1,d2 instruction. Here is the output for source code example Ch08_05:

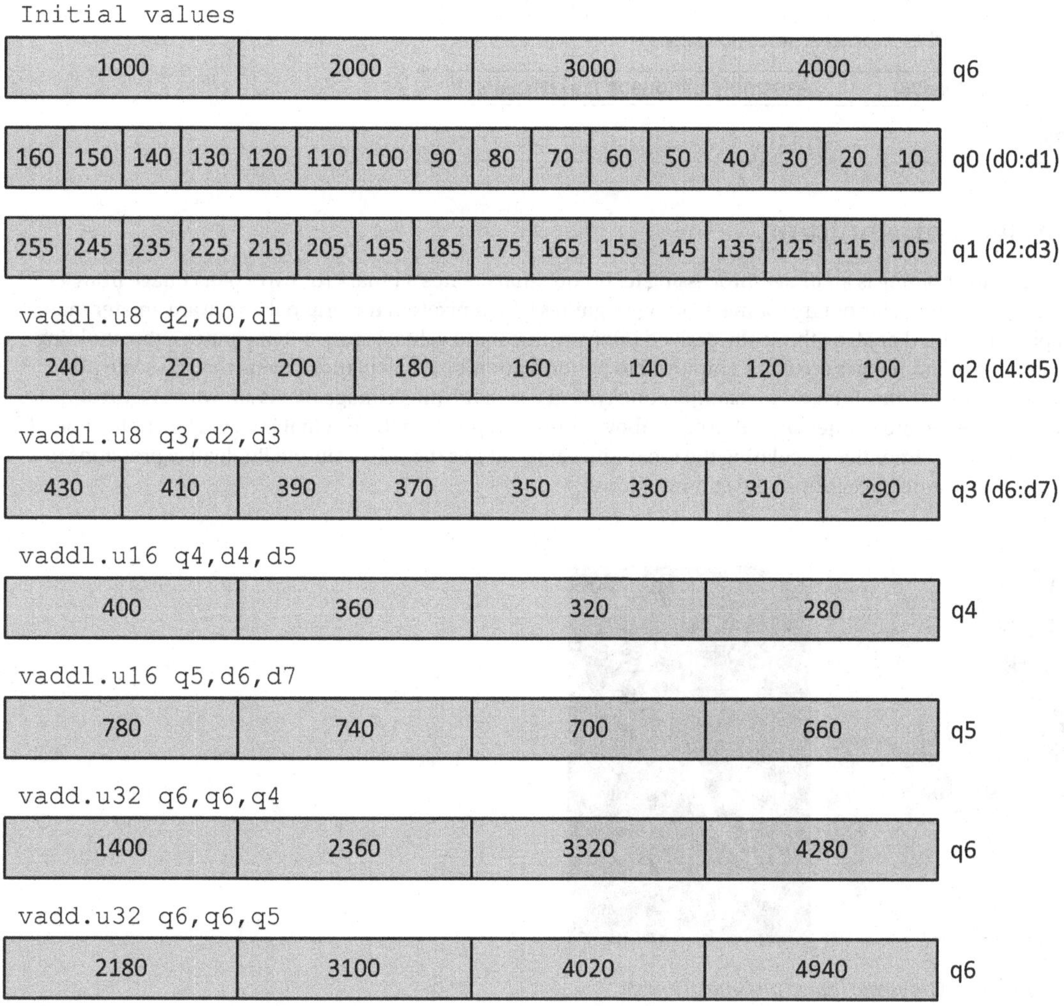

Initial values

| 1000 | 2000 | 3000 | 4000 | q6 |

| 160 | 150 | 140 | 130 | 120 | 110 | 100 | 90 | 80 | 70 | 60 | 50 | 40 | 30 | 20 | 10 | q0 (d0:d1) |

| 255 | 245 | 235 | 225 | 215 | 205 | 195 | 185 | 175 | 165 | 155 | 145 | 135 | 125 | 115 | 105 | q1 (d2:d3) |

`vaddl.u8 q2,d0,d1`

| 240 | 220 | 200 | 180 | 160 | 140 | 120 | 100 | q2 (d4:d5) |

`vaddl.u8 q3,d2,d3`

| 430 | 410 | 390 | 370 | 350 | 330 | 310 | 290 | q3 (d6:d7) |

`vaddl.u16 q4,d4,d5`

| 400 | 360 | 320 | 280 | q4 |

`vaddl.u16 q5,d6,d7`

| 780 | 740 | 700 | 660 | q5 |

`vadd.u32 q6,q6,q4`

| 1400 | 2360 | 3320 | 4280 | q6 |

`vadd.u32 q6,q6,q5`

| 2180 | 3100 | 4020 | 4940 | q6 |

Figure 8-2. *Pixel summing in* Loop1 *of CalcMeanU8_*

```
Results for MeanU8
rc1: true  sum_x1:  1069497485  mean_x1: 127.4937
rc2: true  sum_x2:  1069497485  mean_x2: 127.4937

Running benchmark function MeanU8_BM - please wait
Benchmark times save to file Ch08_05_MeanU8_BM_RpiBeta.csv
```

Table 8-2 shows some benchmark timing measurements for source code example Ch08_05.

Table 8-2. *Mean execution times (microseconds) for* CalcMeanU8
and CalcMeanU8_ *functions (8388627 pixels)*

C++ (CalcMeanU8)	Assembly Language (CalcMeanU8_)
9339	2147

Image Thresholding

Image thresholding is an image-processing technique that creates a binary (or two-color) image from a grayscale image. This binary (or mask) image signifies which pixels in the original image are greater than a predetermined or algorithmically derived intensity threshold value. Figure 8-3 illustrates a thresholding operation. Mask images are often employed to perform additional calculations using the grayscale pixel values of the original image. For example, one typical use of the mask image that is shown in Figure 8-3 is to compute the mean intensity value of all above-threshold pixels in the original image. The application of a mask image simplifies calculating the mean since it facilitates the use of simple Boolean expressions to exclude unwanted pixels from the computations.

Figure 8-3. *Grayscale image and mask image*

Source code example Ch08_06 demonstrates how to calculate the mean intensity of image pixels above a specified threshold. Listing 8-6 shows the source code for example Ch08_06.

Listing 8-6. Example Ch08_06

```
//--------------------------------------------------
//              Ch08_06.h
//--------------------------------------------------

#pragma once
#include <cstdint>

struct ITD
{
    uint8_t* PbSrc;              // Source image pixel buffer
```

```
    uint8_t* PbMask;                // Mask image pixel buffer
    uint32_t NumPixels;             // Number of source image pixels
    uint32_t NumMaskedPixels;       // Number of masked pixels
    uint32_t SumMaskedPixels;       // Sum of masked pixels
    uint8_t Threshold;              // Image threshold value
    double MeanMaskedPixels;        // Mean of masked pixels
};

// Ch08_06.cpp
extern bool ThresholdImage(ITD* itd);
extern void CalcMeanMaskedPixels(ITD* itd);

// Ch08_06_BM.cpp
extern void Threshold_BM(void);

// Ch08_06_.s
extern "C" bool CheckArgs_(const uint8_t* pb_src, const uint8_t* pb_mask, uint32_t num_
pixels);
extern "C" bool ThresholdImage_(ITD* itd);
extern "C" void CalcMeanMaskedPixels_(ITD* itd);

// Ch08_06_Misc.cpp
extern void SaveItdEquates(void);

// Miscellaneous constants
const uint8_t c_TestThreshold = 226;

//--------------------------------------------------
//                  Ch08_06_Misc.cpp
//--------------------------------------------------

#include <iostream>
#include <fstream>
#include "Ch08_06.h"

using namespace std;

void SaveItdEquates(void)
{
    const char nl = '\n';
    const char* fn = "Ch08_06_ITD_Equates.txt";

    ofstream ofs(fn);

    if (ofs.bad())
        ofs << "File create error - " << fn << nl;
    else
    {
        string s(12, ' ');

        ofs << s << ".equ S_PbSrc," << offsetof(ITD, PbSrc) << nl;
```

167

```
        ofs << s << ".equ S_PbMask," << offsetof(ITD, PbMask) << nl;
        ofs << s << ".equ S_NumPixels," << offsetof(ITD, NumPixels) << nl;
        ofs << s << ".equ S_NumMaskedPixels," << offsetof(ITD, NumMaskedPixels) << nl;
        ofs << s << ".equ S_SumMaskedPixels," << offsetof(ITD, SumMaskedPixels) << nl;
        ofs << s << ".equ S_Threshold," << offsetof(ITD, Threshold) << nl;
        ofs << s << ".equ S_MeanMaskedPixels," << offsetof(ITD, MeanMaskedPixels) << nl;

        ofs.close();
    }
}

//-------------------------------------------------
//                  Ch08_06.cpp
//-------------------------------------------------

#include <iostream>
#include <iomanip>
#include <cstdint>
#include "Ch08_06.h"
#include "AlignedMem.h"
#include "ImageMatrix.h"

using namespace std;

bool ThresholdImage(ITD* itd)
{
    uint8_t* pb_src = itd->PbSrc;
    uint8_t* pb_mask = itd->PbMask;
    uint8_t threshold = itd->Threshold;
    uint32_t num_pixels = itd->NumPixels;

    // Verify pixel count and buffer alignment
    if (!CheckArgs_(pb_src, pb_mask, num_pixels))
        return false;

    // Threshold the image
    for (uint32_t i = 0; i < num_pixels; i++)
        *pb_mask++ = (*pb_src++ > threshold) ? 0xff : 0x00;

    return true;
}

void CalcMeanMaskedPixels(ITD* itd)
{
    uint8_t* pb_src = itd->PbSrc;
    uint8_t* pb_mask = itd->PbMask;
    uint32_t num_pixels = itd->NumPixels;

    // Calculate mean of masked pixels
    uint32_t sum_masked_pixels = 0;
    uint32_t num_masked_pixels = 0;
```

```
    for (uint32_t i = 0; i < num_pixels; i++)
    {
        uint8_t mask_val = *pb_mask++;
        num_masked_pixels += mask_val & 1;
        sum_masked_pixels += (*pb_src++ & mask_val);
    }

    itd->NumMaskedPixels = num_masked_pixels;
    itd->SumMaskedPixels = sum_masked_pixels;

    if (num_masked_pixels == 0)
        itd->MeanMaskedPixels = -1.0;
    else
        itd->MeanMaskedPixels = (double)sum_masked_pixels / num_masked_pixels;
}

void Threshold(void)
{
    const char nl = '\n';
    const char* fn_src = "../../Data/ImageA.png";
    const char* fn_mask1 = "Ch08_06_ImageA_Mask1.png";
    const char* fn_mask2 = "Ch08_06_ImageA_Mask2.png";

    ImageMatrix im_src(fn_src, PixelType::Gray8, Channel::G);
    int im_h = im_src.GetHeight();
    int im_w = im_src.GetWidth();

    ITD itd1;
    ImageMatrix im_mask1(im_h, im_w, PixelType::Gray8);
    itd1.PbSrc = im_src.GetPixelBuffer<uint8_t>();
    itd1.PbMask = im_mask1.GetPixelBuffer<uint8_t>();
    itd1.NumPixels = im_src.GetNumPixels();
    itd1.Threshold = c_TestThreshold;

    ITD itd2;
    ImageMatrix im_mask2(im_h, im_w, PixelType::Gray8);
    itd2.PbSrc = im_src.GetPixelBuffer<uint8_t>();
    itd2.PbMask = im_mask2.GetPixelBuffer<uint8_t>();
    itd2.NumPixels = im_src.GetNumPixels();
    itd2.Threshold = c_TestThreshold;

    // Threshold image
    bool rc1 = ThresholdImage(&itd1);
    bool rc2 = ThresholdImage_(&itd2);

    if (!rc1 || !rc2)
    {
        cout << "\nInvalid return code: ";
        cout << "rc1 = " << rc1 << ", rc2 = " << rc2 << nl;
        return;
    }
```

```
    im_mask1.SaveToPngFile(fn_mask1);
    im_mask2.SaveToPngFile(fn_mask2);

    // Calculate mean of masked pixels
    CalcMeanMaskedPixels(&itd1);
    CalcMeanMaskedPixels_(&itd2);

    // Print results
    const int w = 12;
    cout << fixed << setprecision(4);

    cout << "\nResults for Threshold\n\n";
    cout << "                                  C++          Armv8-32\n";
    cout << "-------------------------------------------------\n";
    cout << "SumMaskedPixels:    ";
    cout << setw(w) << itd1.SumMaskedPixels << "  ";
    cout << setw(w) << itd2.SumMaskedPixels << nl;
    cout << "NumMaskedPixels:    ";
    cout << setw(w) << itd1.NumMaskedPixels << "  ";
    cout << setw(w) << itd2.NumMaskedPixels << nl;
    cout << "MeanMaskedPixels:   ";
    cout << setw(w) << itd1.MeanMaskedPixels << "  ";
    cout << setw(w) << itd2.MeanMaskedPixels << nl;
}

int main()
{
    const char nl = '\n';

    try
    {
        SaveItdEquates();
        Threshold();
        Threshold_BM();
    }

    catch (exception const& ex)
    {
        cout << "Unexpected exception has occurred - " << ex.what() << nl;
    }

    return 0;
}
//-------------------------------------------------
//                Ch08_06_.s
//-------------------------------------------------

// struct ITD offset equates
            .equ S_PbSrc,0
            .equ S_PbMask,4
            .equ S_NumPixels,8
```

```
                .equ S_NumMaskedPixels,12
                .equ S_SumMaskedPixels,16
                .equ S_Threshold,20
                .equ S_MeanMaskedPixels,24

// Miscellaneous equates
                .equ NumPixelMax,16777216

// extern "C" bool CheckArgs_(const uint8_t* pb_src, const uint8_t* pb_mask, uint32_t num_
pixels);

                .text
                .global CheckArgs_
CheckArgs_:

// Check pb_mask and pb_src for proper alignment
                tst r0,#0x0f
                bne InvalidArgA                 // pb_src not 16b aligned
                tst r1,#0x0f
                bne InvalidArgA                 // pb_mask not 16b aligned

// Check num_pixels for valid size
                cmp r2,#0
                beq InvalidArgA                 // jump if num_pixels == 0
                mov r3,#NumPixelMax
                cmp r2,r3
                bhi InvalidArgA                 // jump if num_pixels too big

                tst r2,#0x3f                    // make sure num_pixels is
                bne InvalidArgA                 // integral multiple of 64

                mov r0,#1                       // set success return code
                bx lr

InvalidArgA:
                mov r0,#0                       // set error return code
                bx lr

// extern "C" bool ThresholdImage_(ITD* itd);

                .global ThresholdImage_
ThresholdImage_:
                push {r4,lr}

// Validate args
                mov r4,r0                       // r4 points to ITD struct
                ldr r0,[r4,#S_PbSrc]            // r0 = PbSrc
                ldr r1,[r4,#S_PbMask]           // r1 = PbMask
                ldr r2,[r4,#S_NumPixels]        // r2 = NumPixels
                bl CheckArgs_
                cmp r0,#0
```

```
            beq InvalidArgB                      // jump if arg check failed

// Initialize
            ldr r0,[r4,#S_PbSrc]                 // r0 = PbSrc
            ldr r1,[r4,#S_PbMask]                // r1 = PbMask
            ldr r2,[r4,#S_NumPixels]             // r2 = NumPixels
            ldrb r3,[r4,#S_Threshold]            // r3 = threshold value
            vdup.u8 q8,r3                        // q8 = packed threshold

// Threshold image
Loop1B:     vldm r0!,{q0-q3}                      // q0:q3 = 64 pixels

            vcgt.u8 q12,q0,q8                     // compare pixels
            vcgt.u8 q13,q1,q8                     // to specified threshold
            vcgt.u8 q14,q2,q8
            vcgt.u8 q15,q3,q8

            vstm r1!,{q12-q15}                   // save mask result

            subs r2,#64                          // n -= 64
            bne Loop1B                           // jump if more pixels

            mov r0,#1                            // set success return code
DoneB:
            pop {r4,pc}

InvalidArgB:
            mov r0,#0                            // set error return code
            b DoneB

// extern "C" void CalcMeanMaskedPixels_(ITD* itd);

            .global CalcMeanMaskedPixels_
CalcMeanMaskedPixels_:
            push {r4,lr}

// Initialize
            mov r4,r0                            // r4 points to IDT struct
            ldr r0,[r4,#S_PbSrc]                 // r0 = PbSrc
            ldr r1,[r4,#S_PbMask]                // r1 = PbMask
            ldr r2,[r4,#S_NumPixels]             // r2 = NumPixels

            veor.u32 q8,q8,q8                    // q8 = num_masked_pixels
            veor.u32 q9,q9,q9                    // q9 = sum_mask_pixels
            vmov.u8 q10,#0x01                    // q10 = packed 0x01

// Calculate packed num_mask_pixels and sum_masked_pixels
Loop1C:     vldm r0!,{q0}                         // q0 = 16 pixels
            vldm r1!,{q1}                         // q1 = 16 mask pixels

            vand.u8 q2,q1,q10                    // q2 = 0x00 or 0x01
```

```
        vaddl.u8 q3,d4,d5                    // sum pixel counts
        vaddl.u16 q11,d6,d7                  // sum pixel counts
        vadd.u32 q8,q8,q11                   // update num_masked_pixels

        vand.u8 q2,q1,q0                     // q2 = 0x00 or pixel val
        vaddl.u8 q3,d4,d5                    // sum pixel intensities
        vaddl.u16 q11,d6,d7                  // sum pixel intensities
        vadd.u32 q9,q9,q11                   // update sum_masked_pixels

        subs r2,#16
        bne Loop1C

// Calculate final NumMaskedPixels and SumMaskedPixels
        vpadd.u32 d0,d16,d17
        vpadd.u32 d1,d0,d0
        vmov r0,d1[0]
        str r0,[r4,#S_NumMaskedPixels]

        vpadd.u32 d0,d18,d19
        vpadd.u32 d1,d0,d0
        vmov r1,d1[0]
        str r1,[r4,#S_SumMaskedPixels]

// Calculate MeanMaskedPixels
        cmp r0,#0                            // NumMaskedPixels == 0?
        vmov s0,r1                           // s0 = SumMaskedPixels
        vmov s1,r0                           // s1 = NumMaskedPixels
        vcvt.f64.u32 d1,s0
        vcvt.f64.u32 d2,s1

        vmoveq.f64 d0,#-1.0                  // if NumMaskedPixels == 0
        vdivne.f64 d0,d1,d2                  // calc mean or use -1.0

        vstr.f64 d0,[r4,#S_MeanMaskedPixels]  // save MeanMaskedPixels
        pop {r4,pc}
```

The algorithm used in example Ch08_06 consists of two phases. Phase 1 constructs the mask image that is shown in Figure 8-3. Phase 2 computes the mean intensity of all pixels in the grayscale image whose corresponding mask image pixel is white (i.e., above the specified threshold). The file Ch08_06.h shown in Listing 8-6 defines a structure named ITD that maintains algorithm data. Note that this structure contains two count values: NumPixels and NumMaskedPixels. The former value is the total number of image pixels, while the latter value represents the number of image pixels greater than Threshold.

The C++ code in Listing 8-6 contains separate thresholding and mean calculating functions. The function ThresholdImage constructs the mask image by comparing each pixel in the grayscale image to the threshold value that is specified by itd->Threshold. If a grayscale image pixel is greater than this value, its corresponding pixel in the mask image is set to 0xff; otherwise, the mask image pixel is set to 0x00. The function CalcMeanMaskedPixels uses this mask image to calculate the mean intensity value of all grayscale image pixels greater than the threshold value. Note that the for-loop used in this function computes num_mask_pixels and sum_mask_pixels using simple Boolean expressions instead of logical compare operations. The former technique is often faster and easy to implement using SIMD arithmetic as you will soon see.

The C++ function Threshold performs test case setup. This function uses a C++ class called ImageMatrix to load a PNG image file for test purposes. The source code for class ImageMatrix is not shown in Listing 8-6 but is included with the downloadable software package. The remaining code in function Threshold exercises the thresholding and mean calculating functions. It also saves the calculated mask images.

The assembly language code in Listing 8-6 begins with a series of .equ directives that define offsets for members of the ITD structure. These equates were generated automatically by the C++ function SaveItdEquates, which appears in Listing 8-6 immediately after the header file. Note that this function uses the C++ offsetof macro that you learned how to use in Chapter 4 (see example Ch04_06). The assembly language code also includes an .equ NumPixelMax,16777216 directive that defines the maximum number of image pixels. The function CheckArgs_ is called by both ThresholdImage and ThresholdImage_ to validate argument values. This function verifies that the pixel buffers pb_src and pb_mask are aligned to a 16-byte boundary. It also checks num_pixels for validity. Note that in this example, num_pixels must be an integral multiple of 64. Restricting the algorithm to images that contain an integral multiple of 64 pixels is not as inflexible as it might appear. Most digital cameras generate images that are integral multiples of 64 pixels due to the processing requirements of the JPEG compression algorithms.

Function ThresholdImage_ implements the same algorithm as its C++ counterpart. Following argument validation, a series of ldr instructions load PbSrc, PbMask, and NumPixels from the input ITD structure into registers R0, R1, and R2. The next two instructions, ldrb r3,[r4,#S_Threshold] and vdup.u8 q8,r3 (duplicate general-purpose register to vector), load Threshold into each byte element of Q8. Each iteration of for-loop Loop1B begins with a vldm r0!,{q0-q3} instruction that loads 64 pixels into registers Q0–Q3. Function ThresholdImage_ then uses four consecutive vcgt.u8 (vector compare greater than) instructions to compare the just loaded pixel values against the specified threshold. If a pixel value is greater than the specified threshold, the vcgt.u8 instruction sets the corresponding destination operand element to 0xff; otherwise, it is set to 0x00 as shown in Figure 8-4. Following the compare operations, ThresholdImage_ uses a vstm r1!,{q12-q15} to save the results to the mask image buffer. The right image in Figure 8-3 is the final mask image.

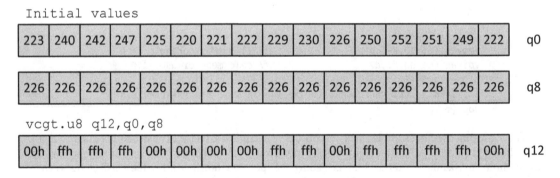

Figure 8-4. *Execution of* vcgt.u8 *instruction*

During its initialization phase, CalcMeanMaskedPixels_ loads PbSrc, PbMask, and NumPixels from the ITD structure into registers R0, R1, and R2. It also initializes packed num_masked_pixels (Q8) and packed sum_masked_pixels (Q9) to zero. The final initialization phase instruction, vmov.u8 q10,#0x01, loads 0x01 into each byte element of Q10. This value will be used to count the number of masked pixels.

The for-loop Loop1C in CalcMeanMaskedPixels_ begins each iteration with a vldm r0!,{q0} instruction that loads 16 image pixels into Q0. This is followed by a vldm r1!,{q1} instruction that loads 16 mask pixels into Q1. The ensuing vand.u8 q2,q1,q10 instruction performs a bitwise logical AND using the mask pixels in Q1 (which are either 0x00 or 0xff) and the packed 0x01 constants in Q10. Following execution of this instruction, each byte element in Q2 contains 0x00 (nonmask image pixel) or 0x01 (mask image pixel).

The vaddl.u8 q3,d4,d5 instruction zero-extends the unsigned byte values in D4 and D5 to halfwords and then adds the corresponding source operand elements; the halfword result elements are saved in Q3. The ensuing vaddl.u16 q11,d6,d7 instruction performs unsigned halfword to word promotions followed by an addition. CalcMeanMaskedPixels_ then uses a vadd.u32 q8,q8,q11 instruction to update num_masked_pixels that is maintained in Q8. Figure 8-5 illustrates this operation in greater detail.

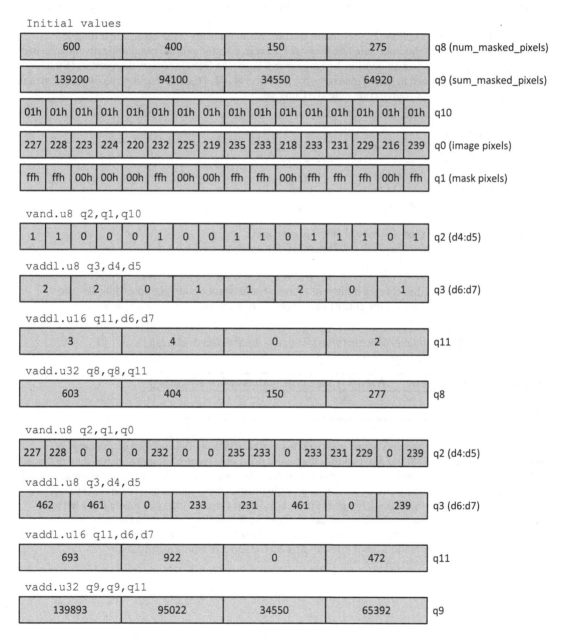

Figure 8-5. *Instruction sequence used to update* num_masked_pixels *and* sum_masked_pixels *in* Loop1C *of function* CalcMeanMaskedPixels_

The next code block updates sum_masked_pixels, which is also illustrated in Figure 8-5. This step uses a similar sequence of instructions that were employed to update num_masked_pixels. The only differences in this sequence are the first (vand.u8 q2,q1,q0) and last (vadd.u32 q9,q9,q11) instructions. Execution of the vand instruction yields 0x00 or the image pixel value in each element of Q2, while the vadd instruction updates sum_masked_pixels in Q9. Following completion of Loop1C, the vpadd.u32 d0,d16,d17 and vpadd.u32 d1,d0,d0 instructions reduce num_masked_pixels to a scalar value; this result is then saved to NumMaskedPixels in the ITD structure. A similar sequence of vpadd instructions is then employed to reduce and save SumMaskedPixels.

Function CalcMeanMaskedPixels_ calculates the final mean intensity value using scalar double-precision floating-point arithmetic. Note that NumMaskedPixels is tested prior to calculating the mean using a cmp r0,#0 instruction to avoid a division-by-zero error. If NumMaskedPixels is zero, the vmoveq.f64 d0,#-1.0 instruction sets the mean to -1.0. Otherwise, the vdivne.f64 d0,d1,d2 instruction calculates the actual mean. Here is the output for source code example Ch08_06:

```
Results for Threshold
                        C++         Armv8-32
-------------------------------------------------
SumMaskedPixels:        786993         786993
NumMaskedPixels:          3172           3172
MeanMaskedPixels:     248.1062       248.1062

Running benchmark function Threshold_BM - please wait
Benchmark times save to file Ch08_06_Threshold_BM_RpiBeta.csv
```

Table 8-3 shows some benchmark timing measurements for source code example Ch08_06. The measurements in this table are for the entire image thresholding and mean calculation sequence.

Table 8-3. *Mean execution times (microseconds) for image thresholding and mean calculation using test image ImageA.png*

C++ (CalcMeanMaskedPixels)	Assembly Language (CalcMeanMaskedPixels_)
895	121

A couple of closing comments about source code example Ch08_06. Besides the vector compare instruction vcgt, Armv8-32 SIMD also includes the instructions vcge (vector compare greater than or equal), vclt (vector compare less than), vcle (vector compare less than or equal), and vceq (vector compare equal). These instructions can be used with 8-, 16-, or 32-bit wide integers, both signed and unsigned. Finally, you may have noticed the gap in the mask image of Figure 8-3. This is caused by the shadow that the left tusk casts over the right tusk. Real-world image processing frequently requires some pixel cleanup following a thresholding operation to address artifacts like this. Appendix B contains some references that you can consult for additional information about thresholding and image-processing algorithms.

Summary

Here are the key learning points for Chapter 8:

- The `vadd` and `vsub` instructions perform wraparound packed integer addition and subtraction. These instructions can be used with 8-, 16-, 32-, and 64-bit signed or unsigned integers.

- The `vqadd` and `vqsub` instructions perform saturated packed integer addition and subtraction. These instructions can be used with 8-, 16-, 32- and 64-bit signed or unsigned integers.

- The `vmul` and `vmull` instructions perform packed integer multiplication. Both instructions can be used with 8-, 16-, and 32-bit signed or unsigned integers

- The `vshl` instruction performs left shifts when used with an immediate operand. When used with a register operand, the elements are shifted left (positive shift count) or right (negative shift count).

- The `vmin` and `vmax` instructions select minimum and maximum values using corresponding elements in the source operands. The `vpmin` and `vpmax` instructions select minimum and maximum values using adjacent elements in the source operands.

- The `vceq`, `vcgt`, `vcge`, `vclt`, and `vcle` instructions perform packed comparisons. These instructions set a destination operand element to all ones if the predicate condition is true; otherwise, the destination operand element is set to all zeros.

- The `vldm` and `vstm` instructions carry out vector load and store operations using one or more registers.

- The `tst` instruction can be used as an alternative to the `cmp` and `and` instructions to set the NZCV condition flags.

- The `vpush` and `vpop` instructions must use consecutively numbered registers when pushing or popping more than a single register.

- 128-bit wide SIMD operands in memory should be aligned to a 16-byte boundary whenever possible.

CHAPTER 9

■ ■ ■

Armv8-32 SIMD Floating-Point Programming

In the previous chapter, you learned basic Armv8-32 SIMD programming using packed integer operands. In this chapter, you will learn how to carry out SIMD operations using packed single-precision floating-point operands. The first section includes three source code examples that demonstrate common packed floating-point operations including essential arithmetic, data comparisons, and data conversions. The next section contains source code examples that illustrate SIMD computations using floating-point arrays. The final section explains how to use SIMD arithmetic to perform common operations using 4 × 4 floating-point matrices. The content of this chapter assumes that you are familiar with the Armv8-32 SIMD material presented in Chapter 7.

Packed Floating-Point Arithmetic

The source code examples of this section explicate fundamental SIMD arithmetic using packed single-precision floating-point operands. The first source code example encompasses essential packed floating-point arithmetic. The second source code example explains how to perform packed floating-point comparisons. The third and final source code example covers packed floating-point conversions. The purpose of these source code examples is to illustrate the use of Armv8-32 SIMD instructions with single-precision floating-point operands. You will learn how to code SIMD floating-point calculating functions later in this chapter.

Basic Arithmetic

Listing 9-1 shows the source code for example Ch09_01, which demonstrates common arithmetic operations using packed single-precision floating-point operands.

Listing 9-1. Example Ch09_01

```
//--------------------------------------------------
//              Ch09_01.cpp
//--------------------------------------------------

#include <iostream>
#include "Vec128.h"

using namespace std;
```

© Daniel Kusswurm 2020
D. Kusswurm, *Modern Arm Assembly Language Programming*,
https://doi.org/10.1007/978-1-4842-6267-2_9

```cpp
extern "C" void PackedMathF32_(Vec128 x[7], const Vec128& a, const Vec128& b);

void PackedMathF32(void)
{
    Vec128 x[7], a, b;
    const char nl = '\n';

    a.m_F32[0] = 36.0;              b.m_F32[0] = -0.125;
    a.m_F32[1] = 0.03125;           b.m_F32[1] = 64.0;
    a.m_F32[2] = 2.0;               b.m_F32[2] = -0.0625;
    a.m_F32[3] = -42.0;             b.m_F32[3] = 13.75;

    PackedMathF32_(x, a, b);

    cout << ("\nResults for PackedMathF32_\n");
    cout << "a:       " << a.ToStringF32() << nl;
    cout << "b:       " << b.ToStringF32() << nl;
    cout << nl;
    cout << "vadd:    " << x[0].ToStringF32() << nl;
    cout << "vsub:    " << x[1].ToStringF32() << nl;
    cout << "vmul:    " << x[2].ToStringF32() << nl;
    cout << "vabs(a): " << x[3].ToStringF32() << nl;
    cout << "vneg(b): " << x[4].ToStringF32() << nl;
    cout << "vminnm:  " << x[5].ToStringF32() << nl;
    cout << "vmaxnm:  " << x[6].ToStringF32() << nl;
}

int main()
{
    PackedMathF32();
    return 0;
}

//----------------------------------------------------
//              Ch09_01_.s
//----------------------------------------------------

// extern "C" void PackedMathF32_(Vec128 x[7], const Vec128& a, const Vec128& b);

            .text
            .global PackedMathF32_
PackedMathF32_:

// Simple packed floating-point (F32) arithmetic
            vldm.f32 r1,{q0}                    // q0 = a
            vldm.f32 r2,{q1}                    // q1 = b

            vadd.f32 q2,q0,q1                   // q2 = a + b
            vstm r0!,{q2}

            vsub.f32 q2,q0,q1                   // q2 = a - b
            vstm r0!,{q2}
```

```
vmul.f32 q2,q0,q1                    // q2 = a * b
vstm r0!,{q2}


vabs.f32 q2,q0                       // q2 = abs(a)
vstm r0!,{q2}


vneg.f32 q2,q1                       // q2 = -b
vstm r0!,{q2}


vminnm.f32 q2,q0,q1                  // q2 = min(a, b)
vstm r0!,{q2}


vmaxnm.f32 q2,q0,q1                  // q2 = max(a, b)
vstm r0,{q2}
bx lr
```

Source code example Ch09_01 uses the Vec128 structure that was introduced in Chapter 8 (see Listing 8-1). This structure facilitates packed operand data exchange between functions written in C++ and Armv8-32 assembly language. Members of the anonymous union in Vec128 correspond to the packed data types that can be used with an Armv8-32 SIMD register. Near the top of the C++ code in Listing 9-1 is a declaration for the assembly language function PackedMath32_. This function carries out ordinary packed arithmetic operations using the supplied Vec128 argument values. Note that the input arguments for PackedMath32_ are passed by reference to avoid a C++ Vec128 copy operation. The remaining C++ code in Listing 9-1 initializes test case data and displays results.

The assembly language function PackedMathF32_ starts its execution with loads of argument values a and b into registers Q0 and Q1 using the instructions vldm.f32 r1,{q0} and vldm.f32 r2,{q1}, respectively. The ensuing vadd.f32 q2,q0,q1 instruction performs packed single-precision floating-point addition. Note that the only difference between this instruction mnemonic and the vadd instructions used in Chapter 8 is the data type size specifier. The vstm r0! ,{q2} that follows saves the packed sum to x[0]. The next two arithmetic instructions, vsub.f32 q2,q0,q1 and vmul.f32 q2,q0,q1, carry out packed subtraction and multiplication, respectively. The Armv8-32 SIMD instruction set does not support division or square roots using packed single-precision floating-point operands.

The vabs.f32 q2,q0 instruction calculates packed absolute values, while the vneg.f32 q2,q1 instruction performs packed negation. The final two calculating instructions, vminnm.f32 q2,q0,q1 (vector floating-point minimum) and vmaxnm.f32 q2,q0,q1 (vector floating-point maximum), compute packed minimums and maximums. Unlike the vmin.f32 and vmax.f32 instructions, the vminnm.f32 and vmaxnm.f32 instructions handle NaN operands in accordance with the IEEE 754-2008 specification. Here are the results for source code example Ch09_01:

```
Results for PackedMathF32_
a:            36.000000      0.031250  |     2.000000     -42.000000
b:            -0.125000     64.000000  |    -0.062500      13.750000

vadd:         35.875000     64.031250  |     1.937500     -28.250000
vsub:         36.125000    -63.968750  |     2.062500     -55.750000
vmul:         -4.500000      2.000000  |    -0.125000    -577.500000
vabs(a):      36.000000      0.031250  |     2.000000      42.000000
vneg(b):       0.125000    -64.000000  |     0.062500     -13.750000
vminnm:       -0.125000      0.031250  |    -0.062500     -42.000000
vmaxnm:       36.000000     64.000000  |     2.000000      13.750000
```

Comparisons

Listing 9-2 shows the source code for example Ch09_02. This example illustrates packed comparisons using packed single-precision floating-point operands. The organization of the C++ code in Listing 9-2 mimics the previous example. It contains a function named PackedCompareF32 that initializes two instances of Vec128 for test purposes. Function PackedCompareF32 then exercises the assembly language function PackedCompareF32_ and displays results.

Listing 9-2. Example Ch09_02

```
//----------------------------------------------------
//                   Ch09_02.cpp
//----------------------------------------------------

#include <iostream>
#include <iomanip>
#include <limits>
#include "Vec128.h"

using namespace std;

extern "C" void PackedCompareF32_(Vec128 x[8], const Vec128& a, const Vec128& b);

const char* c_CmpStr[8] =
{
    "EQ", "NE", "LT", "LE", "GT", "GE", "LTO", "GTO"
};

void PackedCompareF32(void)
{
    const char nl = '\n';
    Vec128 x[8], a, b;

    a.m_F32[0] = 2.0;          b.m_F32[0] = -4.0;
    a.m_F32[1] = 17.0;         b.m_F32[1] = 12.0;
    a.m_F32[2] = -6.0;         b.m_F32[2] = -6.0;
    a.m_F32[3] = 3.0;          b.m_F32[3] = 8.0;

    PackedCompareF32_(x, a, b);

    cout << "\nResults for PackedCompareF32\n";
    cout << "a:  " << a.ToStringF32() << nl;
    cout << "b:  " << b.ToStringF32() << nl;
    cout << nl;

    for (int j = 0; j < 8; j++)
    {
        string s = string(c_CmpStr[j]) + ":";
        cout << left << setw(4) << s << x[j].ToStringX32() << nl;
    }
}
```

```
int main()
{
    PackedCompareF32_();
    return 0;
}
```

```
//-------------------------------------------------------
//                  Ch09_02_.s
//-------------------------------------------------------

// extern "C" void PackedCompareF32_(Vec128 x[8], const Vec128& a, const Vec128& b);

            .text
            .global PackedCompareF32_
PackedCompareF32_:

// Simple packed floating-point (F32) compare operations
            vldm.f32 r1,{q0}                // q0 = a
            vldm.f32 r2,{q1}                // q1 = b

            vceq.f32 q2,q0,q1               // packed a == b
            vstm r0!,{q2}

            vmvn.u32 q2,q2                  // packed a != b
            vstm r0!,{q2}

            vclt.f32 q2,q0,q1              // packed a < b
            vstm r0!,{q2}

            vcle.f32 q2,q0,q1              // packed a <= b
            vstm r0!,{q2}

            vcgt.f32 q2,q0,q1              // packed a > b
            vstm r0!,{q2}

            vcge.f32 q2,q0,q1             // packed a >= b
            vstm r0!,{q2}

            vclt.f32 q2,q0,#0             // packed a < 0
            vstm r0!,{q2}

            vcgt.f32 q2,q0,#0            // packed a > 0
            vstm r0,{q2}
            bx lr
```

The assembly language function PackedCompareF32_ uses a vldm.f32 r1,{q0} to load argument value a into register Q0. This is followed by a vldm.f32 r2,{q1} instruction that loads argument value b into Q1. The ensuing vceq.f32 q2,q0,q1 (vector compare equal) instruction compares corresponding elements in Q0 and Q1 for equality. If the elements are equal, the corresponding destination operand element is set to all ones; otherwise, it is set to all zeros. The next instruction, vmvn.u32 q2,q2 (vector bitwise NOT), inverts the elements in Q2 to generate a not equal result. The vmvn.u32 instruction is used here since the Armv8-32 SIMD instruction set does not include a vcne.f32 instruction.

183

The next four-instruction blocks carry out packed compare operations using the vclt.f32, vcle.f32, vcgt.f32, and vcge.f32 instructions. It should be noted that vclt and vcle are pseudo instructions of vcgt and vcge, respectively. Each Armv8-32 SIMD floating-point compare instruction used in this example can also be used with an immediate operand of zero. Function PackedCompareF32_ uses the instructions vclt.f32 q2,q0,#0 and vcgt.f32 q2,q0,#0 to compare the elements in Q0 (argument value a) for less than or greater than zero. The vector compare instructions cannot be used with any other immediate constants. Here are the results for source code example Ch09_02:

```
Results for PackedCompareF32
a:          2.000000      17.000000    |    -6.000000      3.000000
b:         -4.000000      12.000000    |    -6.000000      8.000000

EQ:        00000000      00000000     |    FFFFFFFF      00000000
NE:        FFFFFFFF      FFFFFFFF     |    00000000      FFFFFFFF
LT:        00000000      00000000     |    00000000      FFFFFFFF
LE:        00000000      00000000     |    FFFFFFFF      FFFFFFFF
GT:        FFFFFFFF      FFFFFFFF     |    00000000      00000000
GE:        FFFFFFFF      FFFFFFFF     |    FFFFFFFF      00000000
LT0:       00000000      00000000     |    FFFFFFFF      00000000
GT0:       FFFFFFFF      FFFFFFFF     |    00000000      FFFFFFFF
```

Conversions

The next source code example, named Ch09_03, is shown in Listing 9-3. This example exemplifies conversions between packed single-precision floating-point and integer operands. It also demonstrates how to use an Armv8-32 assembly language jump table.

Listing 9-3. Example Ch09_03

```cpp
//--------------------------------------------------
//              Ch09_03.cpp
//--------------------------------------------------

#include <iostream>
#include <iomanip>
#include <cmath>
#include "Vec128.h"

using namespace std;

// The values enum CvtOp must match the jump table
// that's defined in Ch09_03_.s.
enum CvtOp : unsigned int
{
    F32_I32 = 0, I32_F32 = 1, F32_U32 = 2, U32_F32 = 3
};

extern "C" bool PackedConvertF32_(Vec128& x, const Vec128& a, CvtOp cvt_op);
```

```
void PackedConvertF32(void)
{
    const char nl = '\n';
    bool rc;
    Vec128 x, a;

    // F32_I32
    a.m_I32[0] = 10;
    a.m_I32[1] = -500;
    a.m_I32[2] = 600;
    a.m_I32[3] = -1024;
    rc = PackedConvertF32_(x, a, CvtOp::F32_I32);
    cout << "\nResults for CvtOp::F32_I32\n";
    cout << "rc: " << boolalpha << rc << nl;
    cout << "a:  " << a.ToStringI32() << nl;
    cout << "b:  " << x.ToStringF32() << nl;

    // I32_F32
    a.m_F32[0] = -1.25;
    a.m_F32[1] = 100.875;
    a.m_F32[2] = -200.0;
    a.m_F32[3] = (float)M_PI;
    rc = PackedConvertF32_(x, a, CvtOp::I32_F32);
    cout << "\nResults for CvtOp::I32_F32\n";
    cout << "rc: " << boolalpha << rc << nl;
    cout << "a:  " << a.ToStringF32() << nl;
    cout << "b:  " << x.ToStringI32() << nl;

    // F32_U32
    a.m_U32[0] = 10;
    a.m_U32[1] = 40000;
    a.m_U32[2] = 600;
    a.m_U32[3] = 200000;
    rc = PackedConvertF32_(x, a, CvtOp::F32_U32);
    cout << "\nResults for CvtOp::F32_U32\n";
    cout << "rc: " << boolalpha << rc << nl;
    cout << "a:  " << a.ToStringU32() << nl;
    cout << "b:  " << x.ToStringF32() << nl;

    // U32_F32
    a.m_F32[0] = 10.0f;
    a.m_F32[1] = 0.625;
    a.m_F32[2] = (float)M_SQRT2;
    a.m_F32[3] = 400.75;
    rc = PackedConvertF32_(x, a, CvtOp::U32_F32);
    cout << "\nResults for CvtOp::U32_F32\n";
    cout << "rc: " << boolalpha << rc << nl;
    cout << "a:  " << a.ToStringF32() << nl;
    cout << "b:  " << x.ToStringU32() << nl;
}
```

185

```
int main()
{
    PackedConvertF32();
    return 0;
}

//-------------------------------------------------
//                  Ch09_03_.s
//-------------------------------------------------

// The order of entries in CvtTab must match
// the enum CvtOp that's defined in Ch09_03.cpp.

            .text
CvtTab:     .word F32_I32
            .word I32_F32
            .word F32_U32
            .word U32_F32

            .equ NumCvtTab,(. - CvtTab) / 4      // num CvtTab entries

// extern "C" bool PackedConvertF32_(Vec128& x, const Vec128& a, CvtOp cvt_op);

            .global PackedConvertF32_
PackedConvertF32_:
            cmp r2,#NumCvtTab                    // cvt_op >= NumCvtOp?
            bhs InvalidArg                       // jump if yes

            vldm r1,{q0}                         // q0 = a

            adr r3,CvtTab                        // r3 = points to CvtTab
            ldr r3,[r3,r2,lsl #2]                // r3 = target jump address

            mov r2,r0                            // r2 = ptr to x
            mov r0,#1                            // valid cvt_op return code
            bx r3                                // jump to target

// Convert packed I32 to packed F32
F32_I32:    vcvt.f32.s32 q1,q0
            vstm r2,{q1}
            bx lr

// Convert packed F32 to packed I32
I32_F32:    vcvt.s32.f32 q1,q0
            vstm r2,{q1}
            bx lr

// Convert packed U32 to packed F32
F32_U32:    vcvt.f32.u32 q1,q0
            vstm r2,{q1}
            bx lr
```

```
// Convert packed F32 to packed U32
U32_F32:    vcvt.u32.f32 q1,q0
            vstm r2,{q1}
            bx lr

InvalidArg: mov r0,#0                           // Invalid cvt_op return code
            bx lr
```

The C++ code begins with an enum named CvtOp that defines the conversion operations supported by the assembly language function PackedConvertF32_. The actual numerical values used in enum CvtOp are critical since PackedConvertF32_ employs them as indices into a jump table. Note that the declaration of PackedConvertF32_ includes a parameter of type CvtOp. The C++ function PackedConvertF32 contains code that initializes test cases and displays results.

The assembly language code in Listing 9-3 begins with the definition of the previously mentioned jump table. CvtTab encompasses a series of .word directives that contain addresses of labels defined in the function PackedConvertF32_. The target of each label is a short code block that performs a specific conversion. The .equ directive that follows sets NumCvtTab equal to the number of entries in CvtTab. Within the parenthetical expression of this directive, the symbol . represents the current value of the location counter. Subtracting CvtTab from this value and dividing by four yields the number of table entries. Note that CvtTab is defined in a .text section, which is okay since the table contains read-only data.

Function PackedConvertF32_ uses the instruction pair cmp r2,#NumCvtTab and bhs InvalidArg to validate argument value cvt_op. If cvt_op is valid, the vldm r1,{q0} instruction loads argument value a into register Q0. The next instruction, adr r3,CvtTab (form PC relative address), loads the address of CvtTab into R3. The adr instruction is used here instead of a ldr r3,=CvtTab instruction since the target label is located within ±4095 bytes of the PC. Using an adr instruction is also slightly faster since it eliminates the extra memory read cycle that the ldr instruction needs to load the target address from a literal pool as explained in Chapter 2. Following the adr instruction is a ldr r3,[r3,r2,lsl #2] instruction that loads the correct label address from CvtTab. Figure 9-1 shows a portion of the assembler listing file for Ch09_03_.s with minor edits to improve readability. Note that the values in CvtTab match the location counter offsets for each label, which are highlighted using bold text. Also note that during program execution, CvtTab contains actual addresses instead of location counter offsets.

```
 8                                 .text
 9 0000 30000000   CvtTab:         .word F32_I32
10 0004 3C000000                   .word I32_F32
11 0008 48000000                   .word F32_U32
12 000c 54000000                   .word U32_F32
13
14                                 .equ NumCvtTab,(. - CvtTab) / 4      // num CvtTab entries
15
16                  // extern "C" bool PackedConvertF32_(Vec128& x, const Vec128& a, CvtOp cvt_op);
17
18                                 .global PackedConvertF32_
19                  PackedConvertF32_:
20 0010 040052E3                   cmp r2,#NumCvtTab                    // cvt_op >= NumCvtOp?
21 0014 1100002A                   bhs InvalidArg                      // jump if yes
22
23 0018 040B91EC                   vldm r1,{q0}                        // q0 = a
24
25 001c 24304FE2                   adr r3,CvtTab                       // r3 = points to CvtTab
26 0020 023193E7                   ldr r3,[r3,r2,lsl #2]               // r3 = target jump address
27
28 0024 0020A0E1                   mov r2,r0                           // r2 = ptr to x
29 0028 0100A0E3                   mov r0,#1                           // valid cvt_op return code
30 002c 13FF2FE1                   bx r3                               // jump to target
31
32                  // Convert packed I32 to packed F32
33 0030 4026BBF3   F32_I32:        vcvt.f32.s32 q1,q0
34 0034 042B82EC                   vstm r2,{q1}
35 0038 1EFF2FE1                   bx lr
36
37                  // Convert packed F32 to packed I32
38 003c 4027BBF3   I32_F32:        vcvt.s32.f32 q1,q0
39 0040 042B82EC                   vstm r2,{q1}
40 0044 1EFF2FE1                   bx lr
41
42                  // Convert packed U32 to packed F32
43 0048 C026BBF3   F32_U32:        vcvt.f32.u32 q1,q0
44 004c 042B82EC                   vstm r2,{q1}
45 0050 1EFF2FE1                   bx lr
46
47                  // Convert packed F32 to packed U32
48 0054 C027BBF3   U32_F32:        vcvt.u32.f32 q1,q0
49 0058 042B82EC                   vstm r2,{q1}
50 005c 1EFF2FE1                   bx lr
51
52 0060 0000A0E3   InvalidArg:     mov r0,#0                           // Invalid cvt_op return code
53 0064 1EFF2FE1                   bx lr
```

Figure 9-1. Jump table CvtTab *location counter label offsets for example Ch09_03*

Following the ldr r3,[r3,r2,lsl #2] instruction, a mov r2,r0 instruction copies argument value x into R2. This is followed by a mov r0,#1 instruction that loads the return code into R0. Program control is then transferred to the target label using a bx r3 instruction. Each conversion code block in PackedConvertF32_ uses a vcvt (vector convert) instruction with the appropriate data type size specifiers. For example, the vcvt.f32.s32 q1,q0 instruction converts the signed 32-bit integer elements in Q0 to single-precision floating-point. The vcvt instruction uses round to zero rounding when performing floating-point to integer conversions, and round to nearest for integer to floating-point conversions. Here are the results for source code example Ch09_03:

```
Results for CvtOp::F32_I32
rc: true
a:             10             -500   |              600             -1024
b:       10.000000      -500.000000  |        600.000000      -1024.000000

Results for CvtOp::I32_F32
rc: true
a:       -1.250000       100.875000  |       -200.000000         3.141593
b:             -1              100   |             -200                 3

Results for CvtOp::F32_U32
rc: true
a:             10            40000   |              600            200000
b:       10.000000     40000.000000  |        600.000000     200000.000000

Results for CvtOp::U32_F32
rc: true
a:       10.000000        0.625000   |         1.414214        400.750000
b:             10                0   |                1               400
```

Armv8-32 SIMD also includes floating-point to integer conversion instructions that specify an explicit rounding mode. These include vcvta (vector convert using round to nearest with ties away), vcvtm (vector convert using round to minus infinity), vcvtn (vector convert using round to nearest), and vcvtp (vector convert using round to plus infinity). Appendix B contains a list of programming reference manuals that you can consult for more information about these instructions.

Packed Floating-Point Arrays

The source code examples in this section demonstrate how to use Armv8-32 SIMD instructions to carry out operations using arrays of single-precision floating-point values. The first example includes a function that determines the minimum and maximum values in a floating-point array. The second example illustrates a least-squares line fitting calculation using SIMD arithmetic.

Minimum and Maximum

Listing 9-4 shows the source code for example Ch09_04. This example demonstrates how to find the minimum and maximum values in an array of single-precision floating-point values using Armv8-32 SIMD instructions.

Listing 9-4. Example Ch09_04

```
//----------------------------------------------------
//                 Ch09_04.cpp
//----------------------------------------------------

#include <iostream>
#include <iomanip>
#include <random>
#include <limits>
#include "AlignedMem.h"
```

```cpp
using namespace std;

float g_MinValInit = numeric_limits<float>::max();
float g_MaxValInit = -numeric_limits<float>::max();

extern "C" bool CalcArrayMinMaxF32_(float* min_val, float* max_val, const float* x, size_t n);

void Init(float* x, size_t n, unsigned int seed)
{
    uniform_int_distribution<> ui_dist {1, 10000};
    mt19937 rng {seed};

    for (size_t i = 0; i < n; i++)
        x[i] = (float)ui_dist(rng);
}

bool CalcArrayMinMaxF32(float* min_val, float* max_val, const float* x, size_t n)
{
    // Make sure x is properly aligned
    if (!AlignedMem::IsAligned(x, 16))
        return false;

    // Find array minimum and maximum values
    float min_val_temp = g_MinValInit;
    float max_val_temp = g_MaxValInit;

    if (n > 0)
    {
        for (size_t i = 0; i < n; i++)
        {
            if (x[i] < min_val_temp)
                min_val_temp = x[i];

            if (x[i] > max_val_temp)
                max_val_temp = x[i];
        }
    }

    *min_val = min_val_temp;
    *max_val = max_val_temp;
    return true;
}

int main()
{
    const char nl = '\n';
    const size_t n = 45;
    AlignedArray<float> x_aa(n, 16);
    float* x = x_aa.Data();

    Init(x, n, 37);
```

```
    float min_val1, max_val1;
    float min_val2, max_val2;

    CalcArrayMinMaxF32(&min_val1, &max_val1, x, n);
    CalcArrayMinMaxF32_(&min_val2, &max_val2, x, n);

    cout << fixed << setprecision(1);
    cout << "-------------- Array x --------------\n";

    for (size_t i = 0; i < n; i++)
    {
        cout << "x[" << setw(2) << i << "]: " << setw(9) << x[i];

        if (i & 1)
            cout << nl;
        else
            cout << "    ";
    }

    unsigned int w = 8;
    cout << nl;

    cout << "\nResults for CalcArrayMinMaxF32\n";
    cout << "min_val: " << setw(w) << min_val1 << "   ";
    cout << "max_val: " << setw(w) << max_val1 << nl;

    cout << "\nResults for CalcArrayMinMaxF32_\n";
    cout << "min_val: " << setw(w) << min_val2 << "   ";
    cout << "max_val: " << setw(w) << max_val2 << nl;

    return 0;
}

//-------------------------------------------------
//               Ch09_04_.s
//-------------------------------------------------

// extern "C" bool CalcArrayMinMaxF32__(float* min_val, float* max_val, const float* x,
size_t n);

          .global CalcArrayMinMaxF32_
CalcArrayMinMaxF32_:
          push {r4,lr}

// Verify arguments
          cmp r3,#0
          beq InvalidArg                // jump if n == 0
          tst r2,#0x0f
          bne InvalidArg                // jump if x not aligned
```

```
// Initialize
            ldr r4,=g_MinValInit
            vldr s0,[r4]
            vdup.f32 q11,d0[0]                  // q11 = packed minimums
            ldr r4,=g_MaxValInit
            vldr s0,[r4]
            vdup.f32 q12,d0[0]                  // q12 = packed maximums

// Main processing loop
            cmp r3,#16
            blo SkipLoop1                       // skip loop if n < 16

Loop1:      vldm.f32 r2!,{q0-q3}                // load next 16 x values

            vminnm.f32 q8,q0,q1                 // update packed minimums
            vminnm.f32 q9,q2,q3
            vminnm.f32 q11,q11,q8
            vminnm.f32 q11,q11,q9

            vmaxnm.f32 q8,q0,q1                 // update packed maximums
            vmaxnm.f32 q9,q2,q3
            vmaxnm.f32 q12,q12,q8
            vmaxnm.f32 q12,q12,q9

            sub r3,#16                          // n -= 16
            cmp r3,#16
            bhs Loop1                           // repeat if n >= 16

// Reduce packed minimums and maximums to scalar values
SkipLoop1:  vminnm.f32 d0,d22,d23               // q11 overlaps d22:d23
            vminnm.f32 s0,s0,s1                 // s0 = min value
            vmaxnm.f32 d1,d24,d25               // q12 overlaps d24:d25
            vmaxnm.f32 s1,s2,s3                 // s1 = max value

// Process final values
            cmp r3,#0
            beq SaveResults

Loop2:      vldm.f32 r2!,{s2}                   // load next v value
            vminnm.f32 s0,s0,s2                 // update min value
            vmaxnm.f32 s1,s1,s2                 // update max value

            subs r3,#1                          // n -= 1
            bne Loop2                           // repeat until done

// Save final min & max values
SaveResults:
            vstr.f32 s0,[r0]                    // save min value
            vstr.f32 s1,[r1]                    // save max value
            mov r0,#1                           // set success return code
```

```
Done:          pop {r4,pc}

InvalidArg: mov r0,#0                          // set invalid arg return code
            b Done
```

The C++ code in Listing 9-4 defines a function named CalcArrayMinMaxF32, which calculates the minimum and maximum values of a single-precision floating-point array. This function uses global variables g_MinValInit and g_MaxValInit for the initial minimum and maximum values. Global variables are employed here to ensure that the functions CalcArrayMinMaxF32 and CalcArrayMinMaxF32_ use the same initial values. The remaining code in CalcArrayMinMaxF32 uses a simple for-loop to sweep through the array to find the minimum and maximum values.

Function CalcArrayMinMaxF32_ begins its execution by validating argument values n for size and x for alignment on a 16-byte boundary. The next three instructions, ldr r4,=g_MinValInit, vldr s0,[r4], and vdup.f32 q11,d0[0] (duplicate vector element), initialize each element in Q11 to g_MinValInit. For-loop Loop1 uses Q11 as a packed minimum. A similar series of instructions initializes Q12 as a packed maximum. Before execution of Loop1 commences, argument value n is tested to see if it is less than 16. If it is, the code skips over Loop1 since this for-loop processes 16 floating-point values during each iteration.

Each Loop1 iteration begins with a vldm.f32 r2!,{q0-q3} instruction that loads 16 elements from array x into registers Q0-Q3. For-loop Loop1 then uses four consecutive vminnm.f32 instructions to update the packed minimum value that is maintained in Q11. The packed maximum value in Q12 is updated next using four consecutive vmaxnm.f32 instructions. Execution of for-loop Loop1 continues so long as the number of remaining elements in array x is greater than or equal to 16.

The vminnm.f32 d0,d22,d23 instruction that follows Loop1 reduces the number of minimum values from four to two. Execution of the ensuing vminnm.f32 s0,s0,s1 instruction produces a single minimum value in register S0. A similar sequence of vmaxnm.f32 instructions produces a single maximum value in register S1. For-loop Loop2 processes the final few elements of array x using scalar versions of the vminnm.f32 and vmaxnm.f32 instructions. CalcArrayMinMaxF32_ uses the vstr.f32 s0,[r0] and vstr.f32 s1,[r1] instructions to save the final minimum and maximum values to min_val and max_val. Here are the results for source code example Ch09_04:

```
-------------- Array x --------------
x[ 0]:     9445.0    x[ 1]:     1393.0
x[ 2]:     4641.0    x[ 3]:     5241.0
x[ 4]:     1928.0    x[ 5]:     7564.0
x[ 6]:     5819.0    x[ 7]:     3097.0
x[ 8]:     6201.0    x[ 9]:     8582.0
x[10]:     6843.0    x[11]:      670.0
x[12]:     1035.0    x[13]:     6247.0
x[14]:     7455.0    x[15]:     6298.0
x[16]:     2820.0    x[17]:     1290.0
x[18]:     7535.0    x[19]:     3059.0
x[20]:     7928.0    x[21]:     5738.0
x[22]:     6275.0    x[23]:     5785.0
x[24]:     4435.0    x[25]:       53.0
x[26]:     9635.0    x[27]:     6069.0
x[28]:     8971.0    x[29]:     7051.0
x[30]:     1969.0    x[31]:     4066.0
x[32]:     5960.0    x[33]:      955.0
x[34]:     5734.0    x[35]:     9101.0
x[36]:     7050.0    x[37]:     6729.0
x[38]:     9293.0    x[39]:     8265.0
```

```
x[40]:     513.0    x[41]:    2392.0
x[42]:    1349.0    x[43]:    8593.0
x[44]:    1171.0

Results for CalcArrayMinMaxF32
min_val:      53.0  max_val:   9635.0

Results for CalcArrayMinMaxF32_
min_val:      53.0  max_val:   9635.0
```

Least-Squares

Simple linear regression is a statistical technique that models a linear relationship between two variables. One popular method of simple linear regression is called least-squares fitting. This technique uses a set of sample data points to determine a best-fit or optimal curve between two variables. When used with a simple linear regression model, the curve is a straight line whose equation is $y = mx + b$. In this equation, x denotes the independent variable, y represents the dependent (or measured) variable, m is the line's slope, and b is the line's y axis intercept point. The slope and intercept point of a least-squares line are determined using a series of computations that minimize the sum of the squared deviations between the line and sample data points. Following calculation of its slope and intercept point, a least-squares line is frequently used to predict an unknown y value using a known x value. If you are interested in learning more about the theory of simple linear regression and least-squares fitting, consult the references listed in Appendix B.

The following equations can be used to calculate a least-squares slope and intercept point:

$$m = \frac{n\sum_i x_i y_i - \sum_i x_i \sum_i y_i}{n\sum_i x_i^2 - \left(\sum_i x_i\right)^2}$$

$$b = \frac{\sum_i x_i^2 \sum_i y_i - \sum_i x_i \sum_i x_i y_i}{n\sum_i x_i^2 - \left(\sum_i x_i\right)^2}$$

At first glance, the slope and intercept equations may appear a little daunting. However, upon closer examination, a couple of simplifications become apparent. First, the slope and intercept point denominators are the same, which means that this value only needs to be computed once. Second, it is only necessary to calculate four straightforward summations (or sum variables) as shown in the following equations:

$$sum_x = \sum_i x_i$$

$$sum_y = \sum_i y_i$$

$$sum_{xy} = \sum_i x_i y_i$$

$$sum_{xx} = \sum_i x_i^2$$

After calculating the sum variables, the least-squares slope and intercept point are easily derived using basic multiplication, subtraction, and division.

Listing 9-5 shows the source code for example Ch09_05, which implements the just described least-squares fitting algorithm.

Listing 9-5. Example Ch09_05

```cpp
//----------------------------------------------------
//                  Ch09_05.cpp
//----------------------------------------------------

#include <iostream>
#include <iomanip>
#include <random>
#include "AlignedMem.h"

using namespace std;

extern "C" bool CalcLeastSquares_(float* m, float* b, const float* x, const float* y, int n,
float sums[5]);

float g_LsEpsilon = 1.0e-7;

void Init(float* x, float* y, int n)
{
    normal_distribution<float> dist1 {10.0, 3.0};
    normal_distribution<float> dist2 {0.0, 5.0};
    mt19937 rng {107};

    for (int i = 0; i < n; i++)
    {
        x[i] = dist1(rng);
        y[i] = x[i] + dist2(rng);
    }
}

bool CalcLeastSquares(float* m, float* b, const float* x, const float* y, int n, float
sums[5])
{
    if (n < 2)
        return false;

    if (!AlignedMem::IsAligned(x, 16) || !AlignedMem::IsAligned(y, 16))
        return false;

    float sum_x = 0.0, sum_y = 0.0, sum_xx = 0, sum_xy = 0.0;

    for (int i = 0; i < n; i++)
    {
        sum_x += x[i];
        sum_y += y[i];
```

```
        sum_xx += x[i] * x[i];
        sum_xy += x[i] * y[i];
    }

    float denom = n * sum_xx - sum_x * sum_x;

    sums[0] = sum_x;
    sums[1] = sum_y;
    sums[2] = sum_xx;
    sums[3] = sum_xy;
    sums[4] = denom;

    if (fabs(denom) >= g_LsEpsilon)
    {
        *m = (n * sum_xy - sum_x * sum_y) / denom;
        *b = (sum_xx * sum_y - sum_x * sum_xy) / denom;
    }
    else
        *m = *b = 0.0;

    return true;
}

int main()
{
    const char nl = '\n';
    const int n = 50;
    AlignedArray<float> x_aa(n, 16);
    AlignedArray<float> y_aa(n, 16);
    float* x = x_aa.Data();
    float* y = y_aa.Data();

    Init(x, y, n);

    float m1 = 0.0, m2 = 0.0;
    float b1 = 0.0, b2 = 0.0;
    float sums1[5], sums2[5];

    bool rc1 = CalcLeastSquares(&m1, &b1, x, y, n, sums1);
    bool rc2 = CalcLeastSquares_(&m2, &b2, x, y, n, sums2);

    size_t w = 14;
    cout << fixed << setprecision(6);

    cout << "\nResults from CalcLeastSquares\n";
    cout << "rc:        " << setw(w) << boolalpha << rc1 << nl;
    cout << "sum_x:     " << setw(w) << sums1[0] << nl;
    cout << "sum_y:     " << setw(w) << sums1[1] << nl;
    cout << "sum_xx:    " << setw(w) << sums1[2] << nl;
    cout << "sum_xy:    " << setw(w) << sums1[3] << nl;
    cout << "denom:     " << setw(w) << sums1[4] << nl;
```

```
        cout << "slope:      " << setw(w) << m1 << nl;
        cout << "intercept:  " << setw(w) << b1 << nl;

        cout << "\nResults from CalcLeastSquares_\n";
        cout << "rc:         " << setw(w) << boolalpha << rc2 << nl;
        cout << "sum_x:      " << setw(w) << sums2[0] << nl;
        cout << "sum_y:      " << setw(w) << sums2[1] << nl;
        cout << "sum_xx:     " << setw(w) << sums2[2] << nl;
        cout << "sum_xy:     " << setw(w) << sums2[3] << nl;
        cout << "denom:      " << setw(w) << sums2[4] << nl;
        cout << "slope:      " << setw(w) << m2 << nl;
        cout << "intercept:  " << setw(w) << b2 << nl;

    return 0;
}

//----------------------------------------------------
//                 Ch09_05_.s
//----------------------------------------------------

// extern "C" bool CalcLeastSquares_(double* m, double* b, const double* x, const double* y,
int n, float sums[5]);

        .equ ARG_N,8                    // stack offset for n
        .equ ARG_SUMS,12                // stack offset for sums

        .text
        .global CalcLeastSquares_
CalcLeastSquares_:
        push {r4,lr}

// Validate arguments
        ldr r4,[sp,#ARG_N]              // r4 = n
        cmp r4,#2
        blt InvalidArg                  // jump if n < 2
        tst r2,#0x0f
        bne InvalidArg                  // jump if x not aligned
        tst r3,#0x0f
        bne InvalidArg                  // jump if y not aligned

// Initialize
        veor q12,q12,q12                // sum_x = 0
        veor q13,q13,q13                // sum_y = 0
        veor q14,q14,q14                // sum_xx = 0
        veor q15,q15,q15                // sum_xy = 0

// Main processing loop
        cmp r4,#8
        blt SkipLoop1                   // jump if n < 8

Loop1:  vldm r2!,{q0,q1}                // q0:q1 = 8 x values
        vldm r3!,{q2,q3}                // q2:q3 = 8 y values
```

```
                vadd.f32 q12,q12,q0              // update sum_x
                vadd.f32 q12,q12,q1

                vadd.f32 q13,q13,q2              // update sum_y
                vadd.f32 q13,q13,q3

                vfma.f32 q14,q0,q0               // update sum_xx
                vfma.f32 q14,q1,q1

                vfma.f32 q15,q0,q2               // update sum_xy
                vfma.f32 q15,q1,q3

                sub r4,#8                        // n -= 8
                cmp r4,#8
                bhs Loop1                        // repeat if n >= 8

// Reduce packed variables to scalar values
SkipLoop1:      vpadd.f32 d0,d24,d25
                vpadd.f32 d0,d0,d0               // s0 = sum_x

                vpadd.f32 d1,d26,d27
                vpadd.f32 d1,d1,d1               // s2 = sum_y

                vpadd.f32 d2,d28,d29
                vpadd.f32 d2,d2,d2               // s4 = sum_xx

                vpadd.f32 d3,d30,d31
                vpadd.f32 d3,d3,d3               // s6 = sum_xy

                cmp r4,#0
                beq SkipLoop2

// Process final values in x & y arrays
Loop2:          vldm r2!,{s8}                    // s8 = x[i]
                vldm r3!,{s9}                    // s9 = y[i]
                vadd.f32 s0,s0,s8                // sum_x += x[i]
                vadd.f32 s2,s2,s9                // sum_y += y[i]
                vfma.f32 s4,s8,s8                // sum_xx += x[i] * x[i]
                vfma.f32 s6,s8,s9                // sum_xy += x[i] * y[i]
                subs r4,#1                       // n -= 1
                bne Loop2

// Compute denominator and make sure it's valid
// denom = n * sum_xx - sum_x * sum_x
SkipLoop2:      ldr r4,[sp,#ARG_N]               // r4 = n
                vmov s8,r4
                vcvt.f32.s32 s8,s8               // s8 = n (F32)
                vmul.f32 s9,s8,s4                // s9 = n * sum_xx
                vfms.f32 s9,s0,s0                // s9 -= sum_x * sum_x
```

```
          vabs.f32 s10,s9               // s10 = abs(denom)
          ldr r4,=g_LsEpsilon
          vldr s11,[r4]                 // s11 = g_LsEpsilon
          vcmp.f32 s10,s11              // denom < g_LsEpsilon?
          vmrs APSR_nzcv,fpscr
          blo InvalidDen                // jump if true

// Save sum values
          ldr r4,[sp,#ARG_SUMS]
          vstr s0,[r4,#0]               // save sum_x
          vstr s2,[r4,#4]               // save sum_y
          vstr s4,[r4,#8]               // save sum_xx
          vstr s6,[r4,#12]              // save sum_xy
          vstr s9,[r4,#16]              // save denom

// Compute and save slope
// slope = (n * sum_xy - sum_x * sum_y) / denom
          vmul.f32 s10,s8,s6            // s10 = n * sum_xy
          vfms.f32 s10,s0,s2            // s10 -= sum_x * xum_y
          vdiv.f32 s11,s10,s9           // s11 = slope
          vstr s11,[r0]                 // save slope

// Compute and save intercept
// intercept = (sum_xx * sum_y - sum_x * sum_xy) / denom
          vmul.f32 s10,s4,s2            // s10 = sum_xx * sum_y
          vfms.f32 s10,s0,s6            // s10 -= sum_x * sum_xy
          vdiv.f32 s11,s10,s9           // s11 = intercept
          vstr s11,[r1]                 // save intercept

          mov r0,#1                     // set valid arg return code

Done:     pop {r4,pc}

InvalidArg: mov r0,#0                   // set invalid arg return code
          b Done

// Invalid denominator detected, set m and b to 0.0
InvalidDen: veor d0,d0                  // s0 = 0.0
          vstr s0,[r0]                  // slope = 0.0
          vstr s0,[r1]                  // intercept = 0.0
          mov r0,#1                     // set valid arg code
          b Done
```

The C++ source code in Listing 9-5 includes a function named CalcLeastSquares that calculates a least-squares slope and intercept point. This function uses AlignedMem::IsAligned() to validate proper alignment of the two data arrays. Note that the number of data points must be greater than or equal to two. The remaining code in CalcLeastSquares calculates the four sum variables using a simple for-loop. It then calculates slope and intercept point using the previously defined equations. The C++ function main defines a couple of test arrays named x and y using instances of AlignedArray<float>. The source code for template class AlignedArray is not shown in Listing 9-5 but is included in the downloadable software package. The remaining code in main exercises both the C++ and assembly language implementations of the least-squares fitting algorithm and streams the results to cout.

The function `CalcLeastSquares_` performs the same argument validation checks as its C++ counterpart. Note that argument values n and sums are passed to `CalcLeastSquares_` via the stack. Following argument validation, packed versions of sum_x, sum_y, sum_xx, and sum_xy (Q12–Q15) are initialized to zero using the veor instruction. Argument value n is then checked to make sure it is not less than eight since for-loop Loop1 processes eight x and y data points during each iteration.

In function `CalcLeastSquares_`, Loop1 begins each iteration with a vldm r2!,{q0,q1} instruction that loads eight values from array x into registers Q0 and Q1. This is followed by a vldm r3!,{q2,q3} instruction that loads eight values from array y into registers Q2 and Q3. The packed sum variables are then updated. Loop1 uses four consecutive vadd.f32 instructions to update sum_x (Q12) and sum_y (Q13). It also uses four consecutive vfma.f32 (fused multiply accumulate) instructions to update sum_xx (Q14) and sum_xy (Q15). The vfma.f32 instruction performs fused multiply-accumulate (FMA) calculations using corresponding elements in the specified operands. More specifically, the instruction vfma.f32 q14,q0,q0 calculates q14[i] += q0[i] * q0[i] for i = {0, 1, 2, 3} (all four calculations are performed simultaneously). Similar to its scalar variant (see source code example Ch06_03), the vector form of vfma.f32 performs a single rounding operation following the addition; the intermediate multiplicative product is not rounded. Following execution of the vfma.f32 instructions, counter variable n is decremented by eight, and Loop1 repeats until the number of remaining elements is less than eight.

Following completion of Loop1, `CalcLeastSquares_` reduces sum_x to a scalar value using the instructions vpadd.f32 d0,d24,d25 and vpadd.f32 d0,d0,d0. Recall that the vpadd instruction adds adjacent elements from the two source operands (e.g., d0[0] = d24[0] + d24[1], d0[1] = d25[0] + d25[1]). Execution of these two instructions yields a scalar sum_x in register S0. Additional vpadd instruction sequences are then employed to reduce sum_y (S2), sum_xx (S4), and sum_xy (S6) to scalar values. For-loop Loop2 processes any remaining data points using scalar floating-point arithmetic, which completes calculation of the sum variables.

The next code block in `CalcLeastSquares_` computes the common denominator for the slope and intercept point. The vcvt.f32.s32 s8,s8 instruction converts n from a signed integer to a floating-point value. The ensuing vmul.f32 s9,s8,s4 instruction calculates n * sum_xx. This is followed by a vfms.f32 s9,s0,s0 (fused multiply subtract) instruction that computes denom = n * sum_xx - sum_x * sum_x. The value denom is then tested to make sure its absolute value is greater than or equal to g_LsEpsilon; an absolute value less than g_LsEpsilon (whose value is arbitrary in this example) is considered too close to zero to be valid. Following validation of denom, the slope and intercept values are calculated using straightforward scalar single-precision floating-point arithmetic. Here are the results for source code example Ch09_05:

```
Results from CalcLeastSquares
rc:                   true
sum_x:           505.502716
sum_y:           491.640961
sum_xx:         5503.316895
sum_xy:         5250.967773
denom:         19632.843750
slope:             0.714238
intercept:         2.611822

Results from CalcLeastSquares_
rc:                   true
sum_x:           505.502747
sum_y:           491.641022
sum_xx:         5503.317383
sum_xy:         5250.967773
denom:         19632.847656
slope:             0.714236
intercept:         2.611840
```

You may have noticed that there are some minor value discrepancies between the C++ and assembly language versions of the least-squares algorithm. Minor value discrepancies between different implementations of a floating-point algorithm, even when using the same programming language, are not unusual given the non-associativity of floating-point arithmetic (see source code Example Ch05_01).

Packed Floating-Point Matrices

Software applications such as computer graphics and computer-aided design programs often make extensive use of matrices. For example, three-dimensional (3D) computer graphics software typically employs matrices to perform common transformations such as translation, scaling, and rotation. When using homogeneous coordinates, each of these operations can be efficiently represented using a single 4 × 4 matrix. Multiple transformations can also be applied by merging a series of distinct transformation matrices into a single transformation matrix using matrix multiplication. This combined matrix is typically applied to an array of object vertices that defines a 3D model. It is important for 3D computer graphics software to carry out operations such as matrix-matrix and matrix-vector multiplication as quickly as possible since a 3D model may contain thousands or even millions of object vertices.

In this section, you will learn how to perform matrix transposition and multiplication using 4 × 4 matrices and the Armv8-32 SIMD instruction set. You will also learn about assembly language macros and how to write macro code.

Matrix Transposition

The transpose of a matrix is calculated by interchanging its rows and columns. More formally, if A is an $m \times n$ matrix, the transpose of A (denoted here by B) is an $n \times m$ matrix, where $b(i,j) = a(j,i)$. Figure 9-2 illustrates the transposition of a 4 × 4 matrix.

Matrix A

$$A = \begin{bmatrix} 2 & 7 & 8 & 3 \\ 11 & 14 & 16 & 10 \\ 24 & 21 & 27 & 29 \\ 31 & 34 & 38 & 33 \end{bmatrix}$$

Transpose of Matrix A

$$B = \begin{bmatrix} 2 & 11 & 24 & 31 \\ 7 & 14 & 21 & 34 \\ 8 & 16 & 27 & 38 \\ 3 & 10 & 29 & 33 \end{bmatrix}$$

Figure 9-2. *Transposition of a 4 × 4 matrix*

Listing 9-6 shows the source code for example Ch09_06, which demonstrates a how to transpose a 4 × 4 matrix of single-precision floating-point values. This example also explains how to create and use an assembly language macro.

Listing 9-6. Example Ch09_06

```
//----------------------------------------------
//              Ch09_06.cpp
//----------------------------------------------

#include <iostream>
#include "MatrixF32.h"
```

```
using namespace std;

extern "C" void Mat4x4TransposeF32a_(float* m_des, const float* m_src);
extern "C" void Mat4x4TransposeF32b_(float* m_des, const float* m_src);

void Mat4x4TransposeF32(MatrixF32& m_src)
{
    const char nl = '\n';
    const size_t nr = 4;
    const size_t nc = 4;
    MatrixF32 m_des1(nr ,nc);
    MatrixF32 m_des2(nr ,nc);
    MatrixF32 m_des3(nr ,nc);

    MatrixF32::Transpose(m_des1, m_src);
    Mat4x4TransposeF32a_(m_des2.Data(), m_src.Data());
    Mat4x4TransposeF32b_(m_des3.Data(), m_src.Data());

    cout << fixed << setprecision(1);
    m_src.SetOstream(12, "  ");
    m_des1.SetOstream(12, "  ");
    m_des2.SetOstream(12, "  ");
    m_des3.SetOstream(12, "  ");

    cout << "Results for Mat4x4TransposeF32\n";
    cout << "Matrix m_src \n" << m_src << nl;
    cout << "Matrix m_des1\n" << m_des1 << nl;
    cout << "Matrix m_des2\n" << m_des2 << nl;
    cout << "Matrix m_des3\n" << m_des3 << nl;

    if (m_des1 != m_des2 || m_des1 != m_des3)
        cout << "\nMatrix compare failed - Mat4x4TransposeF32\n";
}

int main()
{
    const size_t nr = 4;
    const size_t nc = 4;
    MatrixF32 m_src(nr ,nc);

    const float src_row0[] = {  2,  5,  7,  8 };
    const float src_row1[] = { 11, 14, 16, 19 };
    const float src_row2[] = { 24, 21, 25, 28 };
    const float src_row3[] = { 31, 34, 36, 39 };

    m_src.SetRow(0, src_row0);
    m_src.SetRow(1, src_row1);
    m_src.SetRow(2, src_row2);
    m_src.SetRow(3, src_row3);
```

```
        Mat4x4TransposeF32(m_src);
        return 0;
}


//--------------------------------------------------
//                  Ch09_06_.s
//--------------------------------------------------


// Macro Mat4x4TrF32
//
// Description:  This macro transposes a 4x4 matrix of single-precision
//               floating-point values.
//
//   Input Matrix                    Output Matrix
//   --------------------------------------------------
//   q0     a3 a2 a1 a0              q0     d0 c0 b0 a0
//   q1     b3 b2 b1 b0              q1     d1 c1 b1 a1
//   q2     c3 c2 c1 c0              q2     d2 c2 b2 a2
//   q3     d3 d2 d1 d0              q3     d3 c3 b3 a3

                .macro Mat4x4TrF32

                vtrn.f32 q0,q1                  // q0 = b2 a2 b0 a0
                                                // q1 = b3 a3 b1 a1

                vtrn.f32 q2,q3                  // q2 = d2 c2 d0 c0
                                                // q3 = d3 c3 d1 c1

                vswp d4,d1                      // q0 = d0 c0 b0 a0
                                                // q2 = d2 c2 b2 a2

                vswp d3,d6                      // q1 = d1 c1 b1 a1
                                                // q3 = d3 c3 b3 a3
                .endm

// extern "C" void Mat4x4TransposeF32a_(float* m_des, const float* m_src)

                .text
                .global Mat4x4TransposeF32a_
Mat4x4TransposeF32a_:

                vldm r1,{q0-q3}                 // load m_src into q0-q3

                Mat4x4TrF32                     // transpose m_src

                vstm r0,{q0-q3}                 // save result to m_des
                bx lr
```

```
// extern "C" void Mat4x4TransposeF32b_(float* m_des, const float* m_src)

        .global Mat4x4TransposeF32b_
Mat4x4TransposeF32b_:

        vld4.f32 {d0,d2,d4,d6},[r1]!        // q0:q3 = transpose of m_src
        vld4.f32 {d1,d3,d5,d7},[r1]

        vstm r0,{q0-q3}                      // save result to m_des
        bx lr
```

The C++ function Mat4x4TransposeF32 exercises code that transposes a 4 × 4 matrix of single-precision floating-point values using a couple of different techniques. Note that this function requires an argument of type MatrixF32. Class MatrixF32 (source code not shown but included in the download package) is a simple C++ wrapper class for a single-precision floating-point matrix. It is used by several source code examples in this book for test and benchmarking purposes. The internal buffer allocated by MatrixF32 is aligned on a 16-byte boundary, which means that the elements of a MatrixF32 object are optimally aligned for SIMD instruction use. Function Mat4x4TransposeF32 exercises two assembly language matrix transposition functions named Mat4x4TransposeF32a_ and Mat4x4TransposeF32b_. It also performs matrix transposition using the member function MatrixF32::Transpose for comparison purposes. The remaining code in Mat4x4TransposeF32 streams results to cout.

A macro is an assembler text substitution mechanism that enables a programmer to represent a sequence of assembly language instructions, data definitions, or other source code statements using a single text string. Assembly language macros are typically employed to generate sequences of instructions that are used more than once. Macros are also frequently exploited to avoid the performance overhead of a function call.

The assembly language code in Listing 9-6 begins with the definition of a macro. The assembler directive .macro Mat4x4TrF32 designates the start of a macro named Mat4x4TrF32. Besides the macro name, a .macro directive also can include arguments. You will learn more about this in Chapters 14 and 15. Macro Mat4x4TrF32 uses the vtrn.f32 (vector transpose) and vswp (vector swap) instructions to transpose a 4 × 4 matrix of single-precision floating-point values. The exact operations carried out by these instructions will be explained shortly. The assembler directive .endm signifies the end of a macro.

Following the definition of macro Mat4x4TrF32 is the assembly language function Mat4x4TransposeF32a_. This function transposes a 4 × 4 matrix of single-precision floating-point values and saves the result. The first instruction of Mat4x4TransposeF32a_, vldm r1,{q0-q3}, loads all 16 elements of matrix m_src into registers Q0–Q3. The next statement uses the macro Mat4x4TrF32 to generate the code that performs the actual transposition. Figure 9-3 contains a portion of the GNU assembler listing file that shows the expansion of macro Mat4x4TrF32. Note that the assembler substituted the assembly language instructions defined within the body of Mat4x4TrF32. Following the matrix transposition, the vstm r0,{q0-q3} instruction saves the result to m_des.

```
44                                        .global Mat4x4TransposeF32a_
45                    Mat4x4TransposeF32a_:
46
47 0000 100B91EC                          vldm r1,{q0-q3}                // load m_src into q0-q3
48
49                                        Mat4x4TrF32                    // transpose m_src
49                          >
49 0004 C200BAF3          >   vtrn.f32 q0,q1
49                          >
49                          >
49 0008 C640BAF3          >   vtrn.f32 q2,q3
49                          >
49                          >
49 000c 0140B2F3          >   vswp d4,d1
49                          >
49                          >
49 0010 0630B2F3          >   vswp d3,d6
49                          >
50
51 0014 100B80EC                          vstm r0,{q0-q3}                // save result to m_des
52 0018 1EFF2FE1                          bx lr
```

Figure 9-3. Expansion of macro Mat4x4TrF32

Figure 9-4 illustrates execution of the vtrn.f32 and vswp instructions that perform the 4 × 4 matrix transposition. The sequence of instructions employed here performs an in-place transposition; no other registers are used. Following execution of the vswp d3,d6 instruction, the transposed matrix resides in registers Q0–Q3. It is important to note that there are no calling conventions or protocols that govern argument passing or register use in a macro. The programmer is responsible for managing these items. The absence of a macro register convention means that macros must be employed judiciously since it is very easy to create convoluted or difficult to maintain code, especially when using nested macros.

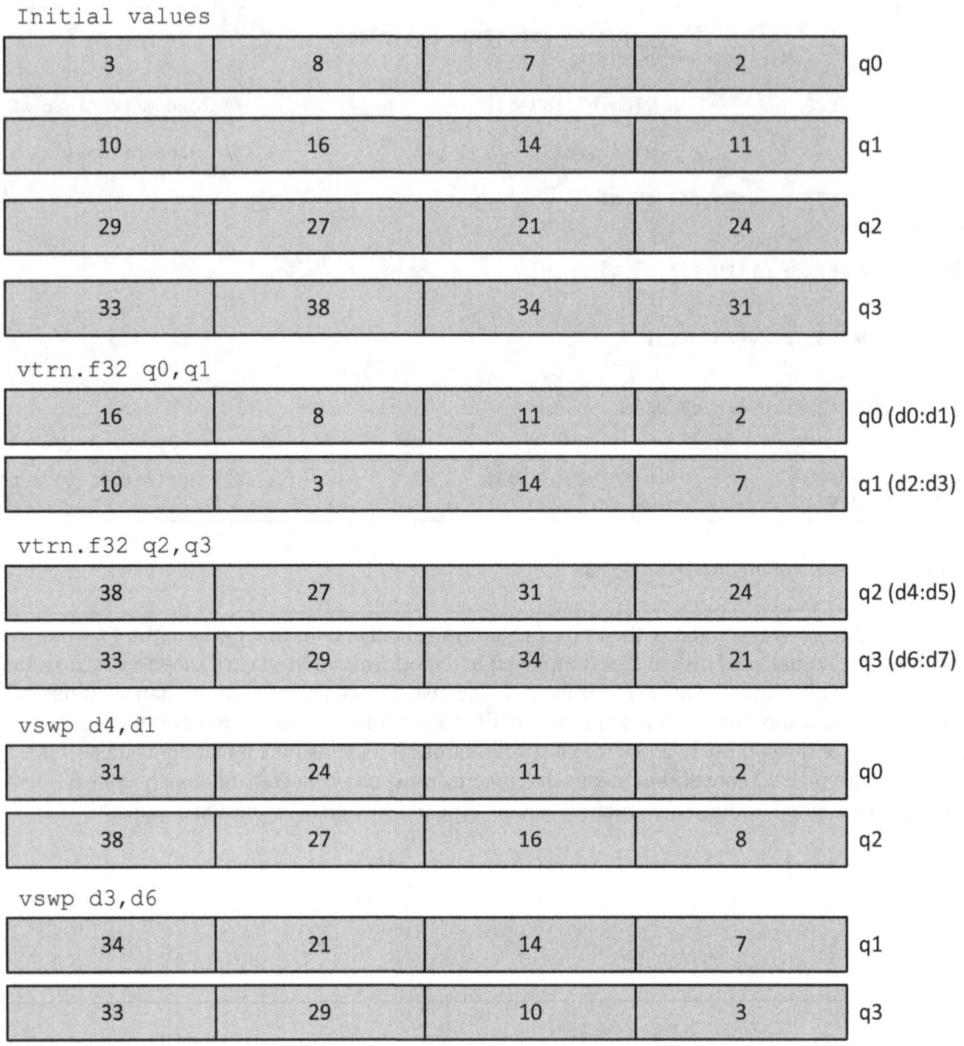

Initial values

3	8	7	2	q0

10	16	14	11	q1

29	27	21	24	q2

33	38	34	31	q3

vtrn.f32 q0,q1

16	8	11	2	q0 (d0:d1)

10	3	14	7	q1 (d2:d3)

vtrn.f32 q2,q3

38	27	31	24	q2 (d4:d5)

33	29	34	21	q3 (d6:d7)

vswp d4,d1

31	24	11	2	q0

38	27	16	8	q2

vswp d3,d6

34	21	14	7	q1

33	29	10	3	q3

Figure 9-4. Transposition of a 4 × 4 matrix using vtrn.f32 and vswp

The assembly language code in Listing 9-6 also includes a function named Mat4x4TransposeF32b_. This function uses the vld4.f32 (load multiple four-element structures) instruction to transpose a 4 × 4 matrix of single-precision floating-point elements as illustrated in Figure 9-5. Following execution of the second vld4.f32 instruction, registers Q0–Q3 contain the transposed matrix. The vstm r0,{q0-q3} instruction saves the transposed matrix to m_des.

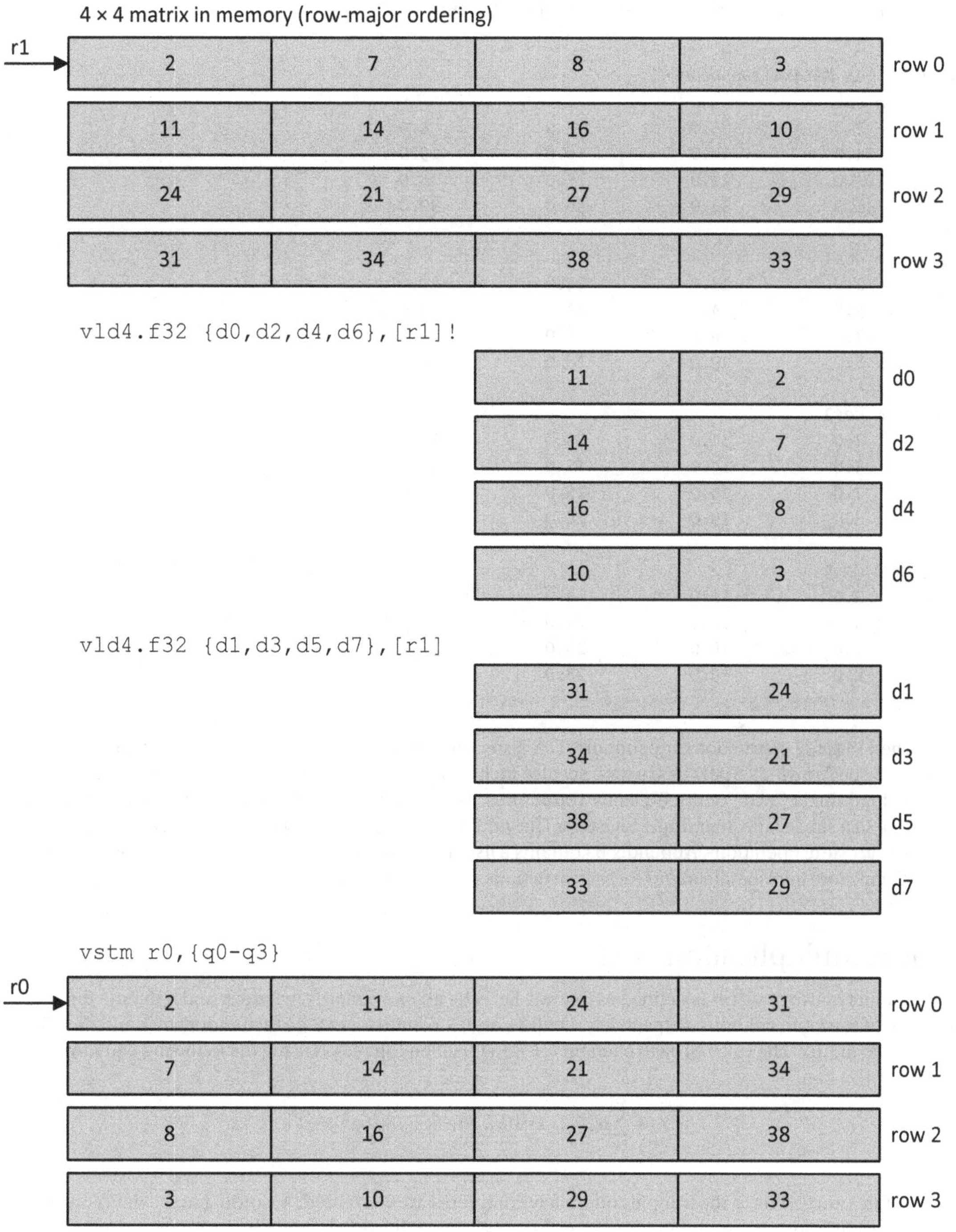

4 × 4 matrix in memory (row-major ordering)

r1 →					
2	7	8	3		row 0
11	14	16	10		row 1
24	21	27	29		row 2
31	34	38	33		row 3

```
vld4.f32 {d0,d2,d4,d6},[r1]!
```

11	2	d0
14	7	d2
16	8	d4
10	3	d6

```
vld4.f32 {d1,d3,d5,d7},[r1]
```

31	24	d1
34	21	d3
38	27	d5
33	29	d7

```
vstm r0,{q0-q3}
```

r0 →					
2	11	24	31		row 0
7	14	21	34		row 1
8	16	27	38		row 2
3	10	29	33		row 3

Figure 9-5 *Transposition of a 4 × 4 matrix using* vld4.f32 *instructions*

Here are the results for source code example Ch09_06:

```
Results for Mat4x4TransposeF32
Matrix m_src
       2.0            5.0            7.0            8.0
      11.0           14.0           16.0           19.0
      24.0           21.0           25.0           28.0
      31.0           34.0           36.0           39.0

Matrix m_des1
       2.0           11.0           24.0           31.0
       5.0           14.0           21.0           34.0
       7.0           16.0           25.0           36.0
       8.0           19.0           28.0           39.0

Matrix m_des2
       2.0           11.0           24.0           31.0
       5.0           14.0           21.0           34.0
       7.0           16.0           25.0           36.0
       8.0           19.0           28.0           39.0

Matrix m_des3
       2.0           11.0           24.0           31.0
       5.0           14.0           21.0           34.0
       7.0           16.0           25.0           36.0
       8.0           19.0           28.0           39.0
```

The vld4.f32 instruction only supports D register operands; it cannot be used with a Q register operand. The Armv8-32 SIMD instruction set also includes vld1, vld2, and vld3 instructions that can be used to load single-, two-, or three-element structures. These instructions can also load a multielement structure to a single lane in multiple registers. The vst1, vst2, vst3, and vst4 instructions carry out the counterpart store operations. Appendix B contains a list of programming reference manuals that you can consult for more information about these instructions.

Matrix Multiplication

The product of two matrices is defined as follows. Let **A** be an $m \times n$ matrix, where m and n denote the number of rows and columns, respectively. Let **B** be an $n \times p$ matrix. Let **C** be the product of **A** and **B**, which is an $m \times p$ matrix. The value of each element $c(i, j)$ in **C** can be calculated using the following equation:

$$c_{ij} = \sum_{k=0}^{n-1} a_{ik} b_{kj} \quad i = 0, \ldots, m-1; \quad j = 0, \ldots, p-1$$

Before proceeding to the sample code, a few comments are warranted. According to the definition of matrix multiplication, the number of columns in **A** must equal the number of rows in **B**. For example, if **A** is a 3×4 matrix and **B** is a 4×2 matrix, the product **AB** (a 3×2 matrix) can be calculated but the product **BA** is undefined. Note that the value of each $c(i, j)$ in **C** is simply the dot product of row i in matrix **A** and column j in matrix **B**. The assembly language code presented in the next example will exploit this fact to perform matrix multiplications using Armv8-32 SIMD instructions. Also note that unlike most mathematical textbooks, the subscripts in the matrix multiplication equation use zero-based indexing. This simplifies translating the equation into C++ and assembly language code.

Listing 9-7 shows the source code for example Ch09_07. This example demonstrates how to perform matrix multiplication using two 4 × 4 matrices of single-precision floating-point values. The C++ code in Listing 9-7 includes a function named Mat4x4MulF32. Like the previous example, this function uses the MatrixF32 class to carry out a matrix multiplication for comparison purposes. Function Mat4x4MulF32 also exercises the assembly language Mat4x4MulF32_ and displays results.

Listing 9-7. Source code example Ch09_07

```
//-------------------------------------------------
//                  Ch09_07.h
//-------------------------------------------------

#pragma once

// Ch09_07_.s
extern "C" void Mat4x4MulF32_(float* m_des, const float* m_src1, const float* m_src2);

// Ch09_07_BM.cpp
extern void Mat4x4MulF32_BM(void);


//-------------------------------------------------
//                  Ch09_07.cpp
//-------------------------------------------------

#include <iostream>
#include <iomanip>
#include "Ch09_07.h"
#include "MatrixF32.h"

using namespace std;

void Mat4x4MulF32(MatrixF32& m_src1, MatrixF32& m_src2)
{
    const size_t nr = 4;
    const size_t nc = 4;
    MatrixF32 m_des1(nr ,nc);
    MatrixF32 m_des2(nr ,nc);

    MatrixF32::Mul4x4(m_des1, m_src1, m_src2);
    Mat4x4MulF32_(m_des2.Data(), m_src1.Data(), m_src2.Data());

    cout << fixed << setprecision(1);

    m_src1.SetOstream(12, "  ");
    m_src2.SetOstream(12, "  ");
    m_des1.SetOstream(12, "  ");
    m_des2.SetOstream(12, "  ");
```

```
    cout << "\nResults for Mat4x4MulF32\n";
    cout << "Matrix m_src1\n" << m_src1 << '\n';
    cout << "Matrix m_src2\n" << m_src2 << '\n';
    cout << "Matrix m_des1\n" << m_des1 << '\n';
    cout << "Matrix m_des2\n" << m_des2 << '\n';

    if (m_des1 != m_des2)
        cout << "\nMatrix compare failed - Mat4x4MulF32\n";
}

int main()
{
    const size_t nr = 4;
    const size_t nc = 4;
    MatrixF32 m_src1(nr ,nc);
    MatrixF32 m_src2(nr ,nc);

    const float src1_row0[] = { 10, 11, 12, 13 };
    const float src1_row1[] = { 20, 21, 22, 23 };
    const float src1_row2[] = { 30, 31, 32, 33 };
    const float src1_row3[] = { 40, 41, 42, 43 };

    const float src2_row0[] = { 100, 101, 102, 103 };
    const float src2_row1[] = { 200, 201, 202, 203 };
    const float src2_row2[] = { 300, 301, 302, 303 };
    const float src2_row3[] = { 400, 401, 402, 403 };

    m_src1.SetRow(0, src1_row0);
    m_src1.SetRow(1, src1_row1);
    m_src1.SetRow(2, src1_row2);
    m_src1.SetRow(3, src1_row3);

    m_src2.SetRow(0, src2_row0);
    m_src2.SetRow(1, src2_row1);
    m_src2.SetRow(2, src2_row2);
    m_src2.SetRow(3, src2_row3);

    Mat4x4MulF32(m_src1, m_src2);
    Mat4x4MulF32_BM();
    return 0;
}


//--------------------------------------------------
//                 Ch09_07_.s
//--------------------------------------------------

// Macro Mat4x4MulF32
//
// Input:    q0:q3       matrix m_src1
//           q8:q11      matrix m_src2
//
```

```
// Output:   q12:q15     m_src1 * m_src2
//
// Note:      registers q0:q3 and q8:q11 are not modified.

            .macro Mat4x4MulF32

// Calc row 0
            vmul.f32 q12,q8,d0[0]
            vmla.f32 q12,q9,d0[1]
            vmla.f32 q12,q10,d1[0]
            vmla.f32 q12,q11,d1[1]

// Calc row 1
            vmul.f32 q13,q8,d2[0]
            vmla.f32 q13,q9,d2[1]
            vmla.f32 q13,q10,d3[0]
            vmla.f32 q13,q11,d3[1]

// Calc row 2
            vmul.f32 q14,q8,d4[0]
            vmla.f32 q14,q9,d4[1]
            vmla.f32 q14,q10,d5[0]
            vmla.f32 q14,q11,d5[1]

// Calc row 3
            vmul.f32 q15,q8,d6[0]
            vmla.f32 q15,q9,d6[1]
            vmla.f32 q15,q10,d7[0]
            vmla.f32 q15,q11,d7[1]
            .endm

// extern "C" void Mat4x4MulF32_(float* m_des, const float* m_src1, const float* m_src2);

            .global Mat4x4MulF32_
Mat4x4MulF32_:
            vldm r1,{q0-q3}                    // q0:q3 = m_src1
            vldm r2,{q8-q11}                   // q8:q11 = m_src2

            Mat4x4MulF32                       // calc m_src1 * m_src2

            vstm r0,{q12-q15}                  // save result to m_des
            bx lr
```

The standard method for performing matrix multiplication requires three nested for-loops that employ scalar floating-point multiplication and addition. Function MatrixF32::Mul4x4 uses this approach. The assembly language function MatMul4x4F32_ makes use of the equations that follow this paragraph to carry out a 4 × 4 matrix multiplication using SIMD arithmetic. Note that in each group of four equations, the rows of matrix **B** are multiplied by the same element from matrix **A**.

$$\begin{bmatrix} c_{00} & c_{01} & c_{02} & c_{03} \\ c_{10} & c_{11} & c_{12} & c_{13} \\ c_{20} & c_{21} & c_{22} & c_{23} \\ c_{30} & c_{31} & c_{32} & c_{33} \end{bmatrix} = \begin{bmatrix} a_{00} & a_{01} & a_{02} & a_{03} \\ a_{10} & a_{11} & a_{12} & a_{13} \\ a_{20} & a_{21} & a_{22} & a_{23} \\ a_{30} & a_{31} & a_{32} & a_{33} \end{bmatrix} \begin{bmatrix} b_{00} & b_{01} & b_{02} & b_{03} \\ b_{10} & b_{11} & b_{12} & b_{13} \\ b_{20} & b_{21} & b_{22} & b_{23} \\ b_{30} & b_{31} & b_{32} & b_{33} \end{bmatrix}$$

$$c_{00} = a_{00}b_{00} + a_{01}b_{10} + a_{02}b_{20} + a_{03}b_{30}$$

$$c_{01} = a_{00}b_{01} + a_{01}b_{11} + a_{02}b_{21} + a_{03}b_{31}$$

$$c_{02} = a_{00}b_{02} + a_{01}b_{12} + a_{02}b_{22} + a_{03}b_{32}$$

$$c_{03} = a_{00}b_{03} + a_{01}b_{13} + a_{02}b_{23} + a_{03}b_{33}$$

$$c_{10} = a_{10}b_{00} + a_{11}b_{10} + a_{12}b_{20} + a_{13}b_{30}$$

$$c_{11} = a_{10}b_{01} + a_{11}b_{11} + a_{12}b_{21} + a_{13}b_{31}$$

$$c_{12} = a_{10}b_{02} + a_{11}b_{12} + a_{12}b_{22} + a_{13}b_{32}$$

$$c_{13} = a_{10}b_{03} + a_{11}b_{13} + a_{12}b_{23} + a_{13}b_{33}$$

$$c_{20} = a_{20}b_{00} + a_{21}b_{10} + a_{22}b_{20} + a_{23}b_{30}$$

$$c_{21} = a_{20}b_{01} + a_{21}b_{11} + a_{22}b_{21} + a_{23}b_{31}$$

$$c_{22} = a_{20}b_{02} + a_{21}b_{12} + a_{22}b_{22} + a_{23}b_{32}$$

$$c_{23} = a_{20}b_{03} + a_{21}b_{13} + a_{22}b_{23} + a_{23}b_{33}$$

$$c_{30} = a_{30}b_{00} + a_{31}b_{10} + a_{32}b_{20} + a_{33}b_{30}$$

$$c_{31} = a_{30}b_{01} + a_{31}b_{11} + a_{32}b_{21} + a_{33}b_{31}$$

$$c_{32} = a_{30}b_{02} + a_{31}b_{12} + a_{32}b_{22} + a_{33}b_{32}$$

$$c_{33} = a_{30}b_{03} + a_{31}b_{13} + a_{32}b_{23} + a_{33}b_{33}$$

The assembly language code in Listing 9-7 begins with the definition of a macro named Mat4x4MulF32. This macro generates code that calculates the product of two 4 × 4 matrices of single-precision floating-point values. Prior to using this macro, the two matrices must be loaded into registers Q0–Q3 (m_src1) and Q8–Q11 (m_src2). The matrix product is returned in registers Q12–Q15. Macro Mat4x4MulF32 uses scalar variants of the vmul.f32 and vmla.f32 (vector multiply accumulate) instructions. The first vmul.f32 q12,q8,d0[0] instruction multiplies each single-precision floating-point element in register Q8 (matrix m_src2 row 0) by the scalar value (m_src1[0][0]) in D[0] (or S0); the resultant products are then saved in Q12. The first code block of vmul.f32 and vmla.f32 instructions calculate the result for row 0. The remaining code blocks carry out calculations for rows 1, 2, and 3.

Function Mat4x4MulF32_ employs macro Mat4x4MulF32 to multiply two 4 × 4 matrices. This function uses the instructions vldm r1,{q0-q3} and vldm r2,{q8-q11} to load the two source matrices m_src1 and m_src2. Following the matrix multiplication calculation, a vstm r0,{q12-q15} instruction saves the matrix product result to m_des. Here are the results for source code example Ch09_07:

```
Results for Mat4x4MulF32
Matrix m_src1
        10.0         11.0         12.0         13.0
        20.0         21.0         22.0         23.0
        30.0         31.0         32.0         33.0
        40.0         41.0         42.0         43.0

Matrix m_src2
       100.0        101.0        102.0        103.0
       200.0        201.0        202.0        203.0
       300.0        301.0        302.0        303.0
       400.0        401.0        402.0        403.0

Matrix m_des1
     12000.0      12046.0      12092.0      12138.0
     22000.0      22086.0      22172.0      22258.0
     32000.0      32126.0      32252.0      32378.0
     42000.0      42166.0      42332.0      42498.0

Matrix m_des2
     12000.0      12046.0      12092.0      12138.0
     22000.0      22086.0      22172.0      22258.0
     32000.0      32126.0      32252.0      32378.0
     42000.0      42166.0      42332.0      42498.0

Running benchmark function Mat4x4MulF32_BM - please wait
Benchmark times save to file Ch09_07_Mat4x4MulF32_BM_RpiBeta.csv
```

Source code example Ch09_07 also includes a function named Mat4x4MulF32_BM that performs benchmark timing measurements of the matrix multiplication functions. Table 9-1 shows the timing measurements.

Table 9-1. *Mean execution times (microseconds) for 4 × 4 matrix multiplication functions (500,000 multiplications)*

C++ (MatrixF32::Mul4x4)	Assembly Language (Mat4x4MulF32_)
42253	8061

Summary

Here are the key learning points for Chapter 9:

- The vadd.f32, vsub.f32, and vmul.f32 instructions perform packed single-precision floating-point addition, subtraction, and multiplication. Armv8-32 SIMD does not support packed single-precision floating-point division or square root operations.

- The vminnm.f32, vmaxnm.f32, vneg.f32, and vabs.f32 instructions carry out packed minimum, maximum, negation, absolute value operations.

- The vceq.f32, vcgt.f32, vcge.f32, vclt.f32, and vcle.f32 instructions perform packed single-precision floating-point compare operations.

- Functions can use variants of the vcvt instruction to perform conversions between single-precision floating-point and integer values.

- The vldm.f32 instruction loads multiple floating-point values into a D or Q register.

- The vtrn and vswp instructions are used to transpose or swap elements of packed operands.

- The vld1, vld2, vld3, and vld4 instructions can be used to load multiple element structures. A function can use the vst1, vst2, vst3, and vst4 instructions to store multiple element structures.

CHAPTER 10

■ ■ ■

Armv8-64 Architecture

In this chapter, you will learn about the AArch64 execution state as viewed from the perspective of an application program. It begins with a brief overview of the Armv8-64 computing architecture. This is followed by a review of Armv8-64 fundamental, numerical, and SIMD data types. Programming details of the AArch64 execution state are examined next and include descriptions of the general-purpose registers, condition flags, SIMD registers, instruction operands, and memory addressing modes.

The content of this chapter assumes that you have already read Chapters 1–9. If you have jumped ahead because you are eager to learn Armv8-64 assembly language programming, I recommend perusing Chapters 1, 5, and 7 before continuing. The information discussed in these chapters will help you understand the material presented in this chapter and the subsequent Armv8-64 programming chapters.

Armv8-64 Overview

The AArch64 execution state resembles the AArch32 execution state. It uses 64-bit wide registers and 64-bit memory addresses. It also provides a larger register file than the AArch32 execution state. The AArch64 execution state supports the A64 instruction set, which employs fixed-length 32-bit wide instruction encodings. Compared to the A32 instruction set, the A64 instruction set uses different register operands, some different assembly language mnemonics, and different instruction encodings. This means that assembly language source code written for the AArch64 execution state is not compatible with the AArch32 execution state and vice versa.

The A64 instruction set implements modern assembly language programming constructs while simultaneously embracing its RISC heritage. It supports a versatile set of elementary fixed-length instructions. It also implements a load/store memory architecture. As you saw in the Armv8-32 programming chapters, a load/store memory architecture uses dedicated instructions to load data from memory into the processor's internal registers. A function then performs any required arithmetic or processing operations using the values in these registers. Results are then saved to memory using corresponding store instructions.

The remainder of this chapter explains the core architecture of the AArch64 execution state. Like the first part of this book, I will use the expressions Armv8-32 and Armv8-64 when explaining or referencing general features of Armv8 32-bit and 64-bit technology, respectively. I will also use the terms Armv8, AArch32, AArch64, A32, and A64 as they apply to specific capabilities and resources of the Armv8-A architecture profile.

Data Types

The A64 instruction set supports a wide variety of data types. Most program data types originate from a small set of fundamental data types that are intrinsic to the AArch64 execution state. These data types enable the

© Daniel Kusswurm 2020
D. Kusswurm, *Modern Arm Assembly Language Programming*,
https://doi.org/10.1007/978-1-4842-6267-2_10

processor to perform numerical and logical operations using signed and unsigned integers; half-precision (16-bit), single-precision (32-bit), and double-precision (64-bit) floating-point numbers; and SIMD values. In this section, you will learn about these data types.

Fundamental Data Types

A fundamental data type is an elementary unit of data that is manipulated by the processor during program execution. The AArch64 execution state supports the same fundamental data types as AArch32 (see Table 1-1), which range in size from 8 bits to 128 bits. The bits of a fundamental data type are numbered from right to left with zero and size - 1 used to identify the least- and most-significant bits (see Figure 1-1).

A properly aligned fundamental data type is one whose address is evenly divisible by its size in bytes. The AArch64 execution state does not require proper alignment of multibyte fundamental data types in memory unless specifically enabled by the host operating system. However, fundamental data types should always be properly aligned whenever possible to avoid potential performance penalties that can occur if the processor is required to access improperly aligned data in memory.

Like AArch32, the AArch64 memory model can be configured by the host operating system to use either little-endian or big-endian byte ordering (see Figure 1-2). AArch64 application–level programs cannot change the endianness of their own data values; however, the A64 instruction set includes instructions that transform multibyte little-endian values to big-endian and vice versa. A64 instruction encodings always use little-endian byte ordering. The remaining Armv8-64 discussions in this book and all source code examples assume that the processor and host operating system are configured for little-endian byte ordering.

Numerical Data Types

A numerical data type is an elementary scalar value such as an integer or floating-point number. Table 10-2 lists the numerical data types for the AArch64 execution state along with the corresponding C++ types. This table also includes the fixed-size types that are defined in the C++ header file <cstdint>. The A64 instruction set intrinsically supports arithmetic, bitwise logical, load, and store operations using 8-, 16-, 32-, and 64-bit wide integers, both signed and unsigned. Signed integers are encoded using two's complement representation. The A64 instruction set also supports arithmetic calculations and data manipulation operations using single-precision and double-precision floating-point values. Half-precision floating-point arithmetic instructions are available on processors that support the Armv8.2-FP16 extension.

Table 10-1. *AArch64 numerical data types*

Type	Size (bits)	C++ Type	<cstdint>
Signed integer	8	char	int8_t
	16	short	int16_t
	32	int, long	int32_t
	64	long, long long	int64_t
Unsigned integer	8	unsigned char	uint8_t
	16	unsigned short	uint16_t
	32	unsigned int, unsigned long	uint32_t
	64	unsigned long, unsigned long long	uint64_t
Floating-point	32	float	n/a
	64	double	n/a

Note that in Table 10-1, the size of a C++ `long` and `unsigned long` varies. Linux uses 64-bit wide integers for both `long` and `unsigned long`; Windows on ARM uses 32-bit wide integers for `long` and `unsigned long`.

SIMD Data Types

In Chapter 7, you learned that a SIMD data type is contiguous collection of bytes that is used by the processor to perform an operation or calculation using multiple values. A SIMD data type can be regarded as a container object that holds several instances of the same numerical data type. When stored in memory, the bytes of a SIMD data type are ordered using the same endianness as other multibyte values.

AArch64 supports SIMD calculations using either packed integers or floating-point values. A 128-bit wide packed data type can hold sixteen 8-bit integers, eight 16-bit integers, four 32-bit integers, or two 64-bit integers. The same packed data types can also hold eight half-precision, four single-precision, or two double-precision floating-point values. Support for packed double-precision floating-point values is new in AArch64. Unlike Armv8-32, Armv8-64 also supports packed floating-point division and square root calculations.

Internal Architecture

From the perspective of an application program, the internal architecture of an AArch64-compliant processor (or processing element) can be partitioned into two distinct units. The core unit contains a general-purpose register file, a stack pointer, a program counter, and condition flags. Executing A64 code, by definition, uses the core unit. An AArch64 processing element also includes a SIMD and floating-point unit. This unit encompasses vector registers along with floating-point status flags and control bits. Program use of the SIMD and floating-point resources is optional. The remainder of this section describes each of these units in greater detail.

General-Purpose Registers

An AArch64 processing element includes 31 64-bit wide general-purpose registers. Each general-purpose register can be used as either a 64-bit or 32-bit wide operand. The 64-bit registers are named X0–X30 and the 32-bit registers are named W0–W30. Each W register overlaps the low-order 32 bits of the corresponding X register as shown in Figure 10-1.

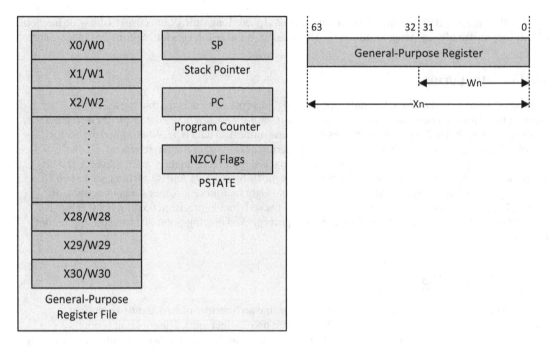

Figure 10-1. *Application-level view of AArch64 general-purpose registers*

Registers X0/W0–X28/W28 are used for common data processing operations including integer arithmetic, comparisons, bitwise logical manipulations, and load/store operations. Most programming environments define protocols that designate specific uses for the general-purpose registers. You will learn about general-purpose register use and the GNU C++ calling convention requirements in Chapters 11–15.

Register X29 is the frame pointer. This register supports function stack frames. A stack frame is a block of memory on the stack that contains function-related data including argument values, local variables, and (sometimes) links to other stack frames. When not used as a frame pointer, X29/W29 can be used as a general-purpose register.

Register X30 is the link register. A processing element uses this register for function (subroutine) return addresses. A function can also use X30/W30 as a general-purpose register provided it preserves the original contents on the stack or in another register.

There is no X31/W31 register. In A64 instruction encodings, the bit pattern for register X31/W31 is used to reference either the stack pointer or the zero register. The zero register is an abstract register that always contains a value of zero. Armv8-64 assembly instructions can use the register operands XZR and WZR to read the zero register; writes to these registers are always ignored.

Register SP is a 64-bit wide stack pointer. The stack itself is simply a contiguous block of memory that is assigned to a process or thread by the operating system. Programs use the stack to preserve register values, pass function arguments, and store temporary data. Unlike AArch32, the AArch64 SP is *not* a general-purpose register. The SP register can only be used as an operand in common arithmetic, bitwise logical, load, and store instructions; it cannot be used as an index or shifted register. The SP register is properly aligned when its value is evenly divisible by 16. Most host operating systems configure the processor to generate an exception if an application-level function attempts to access data on the stack using an improperly aligned SP register.

The PC (program counter) is a 64-bit wide register that contains the address of the currently executing instruction. AArch64 does not allow direct writes to the PC register. It can only be altered by a branch instruction, return instruction, or during exception processing.

The AArch64 execution state does not include a discrete application program status register (APSR) or current program status register (CPSR). Instead, it defines an abstract entity called PSTATE. For application programs, the most important PSTATE elements are the N (negative), Z (zero), C (carry), and V (overflow) condition flags. Programs can use arithmetic, bitwise logical, and compare instructions to update these condition flags. Programs can also exploit the PSTATE NZCV condition flags to carry out conditional branches.

Floating-Point and SIMD Registers

An AArch64 processing element includes 32 128-bit wide SIMD/FP registers that are used for scalar floating-point, packed integer, and packed floating-point operations. Each SIMD/FP register can be accessed as an 8-, 16-, 32-, 64-, or 128-bit wide register as illustrated in Figure 10-2. Note that the register mapping scheme used here differs from that used in AArch32. In AArch64 SIMD, higher-numbered registers do not encompass lower-numbered registers (e.g., register Q0 does not encompass registers D0 and D1; D0 does not encompass registers S0 and S1). The SIMD/FP registers also can be accessed as either 64- or 128-bit wide vectors of packed integer or floating-point elements.

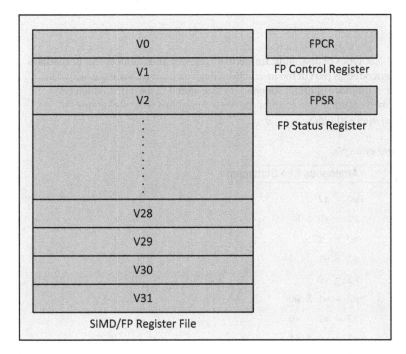

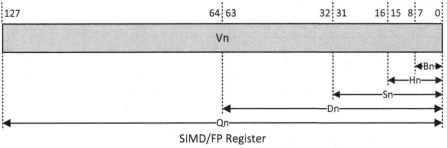

Figure 10-2. Application-level view of AArch64 SIMD registers

The FPCR is a 64-bit wide register that contains control bits for floating-point flush-to-zero mode, rounding control, and exception trap enabling. The bits in this register map to equivalent control bits in the AArch32 FPSCR register (see Figure 5-4 and Table 5-2). The FPSR is a 64-bit wide register that contains status information for floating-point arithmetic operations and floating-point comparisons. The bits in this register map to equivalent status bits in the AArch32 FPSCR register. The upper 32 bits of both the FPCR and FPSR are reserved. You will learn more about FPCR and FPSR usage in Chapter 13.

Instruction Set Overview

The A64 instruction set encompasses a versatile collection of arithmetic, logical, load, store, and data manipulation operations. As previously mentioned, all A64 instruction encodings are 32 bits wide and must be aligned on a word boundary. An A64 instruction encoding is the unique bit pattern that directs the processor to perform a specific operation. Nearly all A64 instructions use operands, which designate the specific values that an instruction will act upon. Most instructions require a single destination operand and one or more source operands.

Operands

The A64 instruction set uses three basic types of operands: immediate, register, and memory. An immediate operand is a constant value that is encoded as part of the instruction. Register operands are contained in a general-purpose or SIMD register. A memory operand specifies a value stored in memory, which can contain any of the data types described earlier in this chapter. Table 10-2 contains several examples of instructions that employ the various operand types.

Table 10-2. *A64 instruction operand examples*

Type	Example	Analogous C++ Statement
Immediate	mov w0,42	w0 = 42
	add x1,x0,8	x1 = x0 + 8
	add x0,x0,17	x0 += 17
	lsl w2,w1,2	w2 = w1 << 2
Register	mov x1,x0	x1 = x0
	and w2,w1,w0	w2 = w1 & w0
	mul x2,x1,x0	x2 = x1 * x0
	smull x2,w0,w1	x2 = w0 * w1
Memory	ldr x0,[sp]	r0 = *sp
	str w0,[x4]	*x4 = w0

A few comments about the examples in Table 10-2. The mov w0,42 (move immediate) instruction loads 42 into register W0. In this example, mov is the A64 instruction mnemonic, W0 is the destination operand, and the constant 42 is an immediate source operand. In A64 code, the prefix symbol # for an immediate constant is optional, which means that mov w0,#42 is also a valid instruction. The Armv8-64 source code examples that you will see in later chapters do not use the # prefix symbol for immediate constants.

The add x1,x0,8 (add immediate) instruction adds the contents of register X0 and the constant value eight. It then saves the result to register X1. The add x0,x0,17 adds 17 to the value in register X0. Unlike the A32 instruction set, the A64 instruction set does not support concise instruction forms (e.g., add x0,17 is invalid).

The smull x2,w0,w1 (signed multiply long) multiplies the two 32-bit wide signed integers in registers W0 and W1 and saves the 64-bit wide product in register X2. The ldr x0,[sp] (load register) instruction copies the doubleword value pointed to by register SP into register X0. Finally, the str w7,[x4] (store register) instruction saves the word value in W7 to the memory location pointed to by X4. In this instruction, the positions of the source and destination operands are reversed.

Whenever an A64 instruction uses a W register as a destination operand, the upper 32 bits of the corresponding X register are set to zero during execution. When an A64 instruction employs a W register a source operand, the upper 32 bits of the corresponding X register are ignored. You will learn more about A64 operands and instruction use in Chapters 11–16.

Memory Addressing Modes

The A64 instruction set supports several different addressing modes for memory load and store operations: base register, base register plus offset, pre-indexed addressing, post-indexed addressing, and PC relative. In base register addressing, values are loaded from or stored to a memory address using a single register. Base register plus offset addressing uses a base register with a positive or negative immediate offset value. Pre-indexed addressing is like base register plus offset addressing except that the base register is updated with the calculated memory address. This facilitates automatic indexing of arrays and other data structures. Post-indexed addressing employs a single base register for the target memory address. Following the memory access, the contents of the base register are updated using the offset value. Post-indexed addressing is also used to support automatic indexing of array operations.

PC relative addressing is used to access (load or store) a value in memory that is designated by a label. The target label must be located within ±1 megabyte of the ldr or str instruction. Table 10-3 contains several examples of instructions that use these memory addressing modes.

Table 10-3. *A64 memory addressing mode examples*

Addressing Mode	Example	Analogous C++ Statement
Base register	ldr w1,[x0]	w1 = *x0
	ldr x1,[x0]	x1 = *x0
Base register + offset	ldr w1,[x0,20]	w1 = *(x0 + 20)
	ldr x2,[x1,x0]	x2 = *(x1 + x0)
	ldr w2,[x1,x0,lsl 2]	w2 = *(x1 + (x0 << 2))
	ldr w2,[x0,w1,uxtw 2]	w2 = *(x0 + (w1 << 2))
Pre-indexed	ldr w1,[x0,4]!	w1 = *(x0 + 8); x0 += 4
	ldr x1,[x0,8]!	x1 = *(x0 + 8); x0 += 8
	ldr x2,[x1,x0]!	x2 = *(x1 + x0); x1 += x0
	ldr x2,[x1,x0,lsl 2]!	x2 = *(x1 + (x0 << 2)); x1 += x0 << 2
Post-indexed	ldr w2,[x1],4	w2 = *x1; x1 += 4
	ldr x2,[x1],8	x2 = *x1; x1 += 8
	ldr x2,[x1],x0	x2 = *x1; x1 += x0
	ldr x2,[x1],x0,lsl 2	x2 = *x1; x1 += x0 << 2
PC relative	ldr x2,label	x2 = *(pc + label_offset)

Most of the memory addressing mode examples in Table 10-3 are identical to the A32 memory addressing that you learned how to use in earlier chapters. Note that the base register in these example instructions is always 64-bit wide X register since AArch64 uses 64-bit memory addressing. The `ldr w2,[x0,w1,uxtw 2]` example illustrates a new AArch64 offset type called extended register. This instruction zero-extends the value in W1 to 64 bits, left shifts the result by two, and sums this value with X0 for the final address. Extended register offsets are often used to access the elements of an array using 32-bit wide integer indices. The `label_offset` that is shown in the PC relative instruction `ldr x2,label` is automatically calculated by the assembler. You will learn more about AArch64 addressing modes in the subsequent Armv8-64 programming chapters.

Summary

Here are the key learning points for Chapter 10:

- The AArch64 execution state supports 64-bit wide registers and uses 64-bit memory addressing.

- The AArch64 execution state includes 31 general-purpose registers that can be used with 64-bit (Xn) or 32-bit (Wn) wide operands. It also includes a separate stack pointer (SP), program counter (PC), and PSTATE.NZCV condition flags.

- The AArch64 SIMD unit contains 32 128-bit wide registers named V0–V31. Functions can use these registers to perform SIMD operations using packed 8-, 16-, 32-, and 64-bit integers. The V registers can also be employed to carry out packed half-, single-, and double-precision floating-point operations.

- Functions can use the low-order 16, 32, and 64 bits of a V register to perform scalar half-, single-, and double-precision floating-point arithmetic.

- The AArch32 execution state supports multiple memory addressing modes including base register, base register plus offset, pre-indexed, post-indexed, and PC relative.

CHAPTER 11

■ ■ ■

Armv8-64 Core Programming – Part 1

Chapter 11 introduces Armv8-64 core programming. It begins with a section that illustrates the use of basic integer arithmetic instructions including addition, subtraction, multiplication, and division. The section that follows covers data loads and stores, shift and rotate operations, and bitwise logical manipulations. This second section is especially important since it accentuates notable differences between A32 and A64 assembly language programming.

This chapter also covers details about the semantics and syntax of an A64 assembly language source code file. You will learn the basics of passing arguments and return values between functions written in C++ and A64 assembly language. The subsequent discussions and source code examples are intended to complement the material presented in Chapter 10.

Like the introductory A32 programming chapters, the primary purpose of the source code presented in this (and the next) chapter is to elucidate proper use of the A64 instruction set and basic assembly language programming techniques. The source code that is described in later A64 programming chapters places more emphasis on efficient coding techniques. Appendix A contains additional information on how to build and run the A64 source code examples. Depending on your personal preference, you may want to set up a test system before proceeding with the discussions in this chapter.

Integer Arithmetic

In this section, you will learn the basics of A64 assembly language programming. It begins with a simple program that demonstrates how to perform integer addition and subtraction. This is followed by a source code example that illustrates integer multiplication. The final example explains integer division. Besides common arithmetic operations, the source code examples in this section also explicate passing argument and return values between a C++ and assembly language function. They also show how to use common assembler directives.

Addition and Subtraction

Listing 11-1 shows the source code for example Ch11_01. This example demonstrates how to use the A64 assembly language instructions add (integer add) and sub (integer subtract). It also illustrates some basic A64 assembly language programming concepts including passing arguments, returning values, and using assembler directives.

© Daniel Kusswurm 2020
D. Kusswurm, *Modern Arm Assembly Language Programming*,
https://doi.org/10.1007/978-1-4842-6267-2_11

Listing 11-1. Example Ch11_01

```cpp
//---------------------------------------------------
//                    Ch11_01.cpp
//---------------------------------------------------

#include <iostream>

using namespace std;

extern "C" int IntegerAddSubA_(int a, int b, int c);
extern "C" long IntegerAddSubB_(long a, long b, long c);

template <typename T>
void PrintResult(const char* msg, T a, T b, T c, T result)
{
    const char nl = '\n';

    cout << msg << nl;
    cout << "a = " << a << nl;
    cout << "b = " << b << nl;
    cout << "c = " << c << nl;
    cout << "result (a + b - c) = " << result << nl;
    cout << nl;
}

int main(int argc, char** argv)
{
    int a1 = 100, b1 = 200, c1 = -50, result1;
    result1 = IntegerAddSubA_(a1, b1, c1);
    PrintResult("IntegerAddSubA_", a1, b1, c1, result1);

    long a2 = 1000, b2 = -2000, c2 = 500, result2;
    result2 = IntegerAddSubB_(a2, b2, c2);
    PrintResult("IntegerAddSubB_", a2, b2, c2, result2);
}

//---------------------------------------------------
//                 Ch11_01_.s
//---------------------------------------------------

// extern "C" int IntegerAddSubA_(int a, int b int c);

            .text
            .global IntegerAddSubA_
IntegerAddSubA_:

// Calculate a + b - c
            add w3,w0,w1                        // w3 = a + b
            sub w0,w3,w2                        // w0 = a + b - c
            ret                                 // return to caller
```

```
// extern "C" long IntegerAddSubB_(long a, long b long c);

        .global IntegerAddSubB_
IntegerAddSubB_:

// Calculate a + b - c
        add x3,x0,x1                  // x3 = a + b
        sub x0,x3,x2                  // x0 = a + b - c
        ret                           // return to caller
```

The C++ code in Listing 11-1 begins with the declarations of the assembly language functions IntegerAddSubA_ and IntegerAddSubB_. These functions carry out simple integer addition and subtraction operations using int (32-bit) and long (64-bit) argument values. The "C" modifier that is used in the function declarations instructs the C++ compiler to use a C-style function name instead of a C++ decorated name (recall that a C++ decorated name contains extra prefix and suffix characters to facilitate function overloading). Also included in the C++ code is a template function named PrintResult, which streams results to cout. The C++ function main includes code that exercises the assembly language functions IntegerAddSubA_ and IntegerAddSubB_.

The A64 assembly language code for example Ch11_01 is shown in Listing 11-1 immediately after the C++ code. The first thing to notice is the // symbol. Like the GNU C++ compiler, the GNU assembler treats any text on a line that follows a // as an appended comment. Unlike A32 code, the @ symbol cannot be used for appended comments in A64 assembly language source files. A64 assembly language source code files can also use block comments using the /* and */ symbols.

The .text statement is an assembler directive that defines the start of an assembly language code section. As explained in Chapter 2, an assembler directive is a statement that instructs the assembler to perform a specific action during assembly of the source code. The next statement, .global IntegerAddSubA_, is another directive that tells the assembler to treat the function IntegerAddSubA_ as a global function. A global function can be called by functions that are defined in other source code modules. The ensuing IntegerAddSubA_: statement defines the entry point (or start address) for function IntegerAddSubA_. The text that precedes the : symbol is called a label. Besides designating function entry points, labels are also employed to define assembly language variable names and targets for branch instructions.

The assembly language function IntegerAddSubA_ calculates a + b - c and returns this value to the calling function. It begins with an add w3,w0,w1 instruction that adds the values in registers W0 (argument value a) and W1 (argument value b); the result is then saved in register W3. The use of registers W0 and W1 for argument values a and b is mandated by the GNU C++ calling convention for Armv8-64. According to this convention, the first eight integer (or pointer) arguments are passed in registers W0/X0–W7/X7. Any remaining arguments are passed via the stack. You will learn more about the GNU C++ calling convention later in this chapter and in subsequent chapters.

The next instruction in IntegerAddSubA_, sub w0,w3,w2, subtracts W2 (c) from W3 (a + b) and saves the result in register W0. This completes the calculation of a + b - c. An A64 assembly language function must use register W0 to return a single 32-bit integer (or C++ int) value to its calling function. In the current example, no additional instructions are necessary to achieve this requirement since W0 already contains the correct return value. The final instruction of IntegerAddSubA_ is a ret (return from subroutine). This instruction returns program control back to the calling function. More specifically, the ret instruction performs an unconditional branch (or jump) to the address in register X30 (or link register). Unlike Armv8-32, Armv8-64 defines an explicit instruction mnemonic for function returns. This enables the processor to make better branch predictions since it can now differentiate between a function return and an ordinary branch operation. You will learn more about branch predictions in Chapter 17.

Listing 11-1 also includes the assembly language function IntegerAddSubB_. This function is the 64-bit counterpart of function IntegerAddSubA_. Function IntegerAddSubB_ begins with an add x3,x0,x1 instruction that calculates a + b. Function IntegerAddSubB_ uses X registers since argument values a, b, and c are long (64-bit) integers. The next instruction, sub x0,x3,x2, completes the calculation of a + b - c.

The GNU C++ calling convention for Armv8-64 specifies that a function must use register X0 for a 64-bit return value. The final instruction of IntegerAddSubB_, ret, returns program control back to the caller. Here is the output for source code example Ch11_01:

```
IntegerAddSubA_
a = 100
b = 200
c = -50
result (a + b - c) = 350

IntegerAddSubB_
a = 1000
b = -2000
c = 500
result (a + b - c) = -1500
```

Multiplication

The next source code example, Ch11_02, illustrates the use of common A64 multiplication instructions. Listing 11-2 shows the source code for this example. Like the previous example, the C++ code begins with the declarations of the assembly language functions IntegerMulA_, IntegerMulB_, IntegerMulC_, and IntegerMulD_. Note that these functions use assorted data types for parameters and return values. The template function PrintResult contains code that displays results. The function main contains code that initializes test case data and exercises the assembly language multiplication functions.

Listing 11-2. Example Ch11_02

```
//----------------------------------------------------
//                  Ch11_02.cpp
//----------------------------------------------------

#include <iostream>

using namespace std;

extern "C" int IntegerMulA_(int a, int b);
extern "C" long IntegerMulB_(long a, long b);
extern "C" long IntegerMulC_(int a, int b);
extern "C" unsigned long IntegerMulD_(unsigned int a, unsigned int b);

template <typename T1, typename T2>
void PrintResult(const char* msg, T1 a, T1 b, T2 result)
{
    const char nl = '\n';

    cout << msg << nl;
    cout << "a = " << a << ", b = " << b;
    cout << " result = " << result << nl << nl;
}
```

```
int main(int argc, char** argv)
{
    int a1 = 50;
    int b1 = 25;
    int result1 = IntegerMulA_(a1, b1);
    PrintResult("IntegerMulA_", a1, b1, result1);

    long a2 = -3000000000;
    long b2 = 7;
    long result2 = IntegerMulB_(a2, b2);
    PrintResult("IntegerMulB_", a2, b2, result2);

    int a3 = 4000;
    int b3 = 0x80000000;
    long result3 = IntegerMulC_(a3, b3);
    PrintResult("IntegerMulC_", a3, b3, result3);

    unsigned int a4 = 4000;
    unsigned int b4 = 0x80000000;
    unsigned long result4 = IntegerMulD_(a4, b4);
    PrintResult("IntegerMulD_", a4, b4, result4);

    return 0;
}

//----------------------------------------------------
//                    Ch11_02_.s
//----------------------------------------------------

// extern "C" int IntegerMulA_(int a, int b);

            .text
            .global IntegerMulA_
IntegerMulA_:

// Calculate a * b and save result
            mul w0,w0,w1                    // a * b (32-bit)
            ret

// extern "C" long IntegerMulB_(long a, long b);

            .global IntegerMulB_
IntegerMulB_:

// Calculate a * b and save result
            mul x0,x0,x1                    // a * b (64-bit)
            ret

// extern "C" long IntegerMulC_(int a, int b);

            .global IntegerMulC_
IntegerMulC_:
```

```
// Calculate a * b and save result
        smull x0,w0,w1                          // signed 64-bit
        ret


// extern "C" unsigned long IntegerMulD_(unsigned int a, unsigned int b);

        .global IntegerMulD_
IntegerMulD_:

// Calculate a * b and save result
        umull x0,w0,w1                          // unsigned signed 64-bit
        ret
```

The assembly language functions IntegerMulA_, IntegerMulB_, IntegerMulC_, and IntegerMulD_ illustrate the use of various A64 multiplication instructions. In function IntegerMulA_, the mul w0,w0,w1 (multiply) instruction multiplies registers W0 (argument value a) by W1 (argument value b). It then truncates the result to 32 bits and saves this value in register W0. The mul instruction is an alias instruction. Recall that an alias instruction is a distinct mnemonic that provides a more expressive description of the operation that is being performed. In the current example, the mul w0,w0,w1 instruction is an alias of madd w0,w0,w1,wzr (multiply-add). You will learn how to use the madd instruction in Chapter 12. Alias instructions are generally unimportant when writing A64 code. However, it is something that you need to be aware of when using a debugger or viewing a listing of disassembled code.

The assembly language function IntegerMulB_ uses a mul x0,x0,x1 instruction to multiply two 64-bit wide integers. It saves the low-order 64 bits of the 128-bit product in register X0. The mul instruction can be used with either signed or unsigned integer operands. Function IntegerMulC_ uses the smull x0,w0,w1 (signed multiply long) instruction. This instruction multiplies the 32-bit signed integer values in registers W0 and W1. It then saves the complete 64-bit signed integer product in register X0. The smull instruction is an alias instruction of smaddl (signed multiply-add long). The final integer multiplication function, IntegerMulD_, uses the umull (unsigned multiply long) instruction to perform unsigned integer multiplication. The umull instruction, which is an alias of umaddl (unsigned multiply-add long), calculates a 64-bit unsigned integer product using two unsigned 32-bit integer operands. Here are the results for source code example Ch11_02:

```
IntegerMulA_
a = 50, b = 25 result = 1250

IntegerMulB_
a = -3000000000, b = 7 result = -21000000000

IntegerMulC_
a = 4000, b = -2147483648 result = -8589934592000

IntegerMulD_
a = 4000, b = 2147483648 result = 8589934592000
```

Division

Listing 11-3 shows the source code for example Ch11_03. This source code example illustrates integer division. It also describes the use of the str (store) instruction. The C++ code in Listing 11-3 resembles the previous two examples in that it performs test case initialization and streams its results to cout. Note that the declarations for assembly language functions CalcQuoRemA_ and CalcQuoRemB_ include a mixture of integer and pointer arguments.

Listing 11-3. Example Ch11_03

```cpp
//---------------------------------------------------
//                  Ch11_03.cpp
//---------------------------------------------------

#include <iostream>

using namespace std;

extern "C" void CalcQuoRemA_(int a, int b, int* quo, int* rem);
extern "C" void CalcQuoRemB_(long a, long b, long* quo, long* rem);

template <typename T>
void PrintResult(const char* msg, T a, T b, T quo, T rem)
{
    const char nl = '\n';

    cout << msg << nl;
    cout << "a = " << a << nl;
    cout << "b = " << b << nl;
    cout << "quotient = " << quo << nl;
    cout << "remainder = " << rem << nl;
    cout << nl;
}

int main(int argc, char** argv)
{
    int a1 = 100, b1 = 7, quo1, rem1;
    CalcQuoRemA_(a1, b1, &quo1, &rem1);
    PrintResult("CalcQuoRemA_", a1, b1, quo1, rem1);

    long a2 = -2000000000, b2 = 11, quo2, rem2;
    CalcQuoRemB_(a2, b2, &quo2, &rem2);
    PrintResult("CalcQuoRemB_", a2, b2, quo2, rem2);
}

//---------------------------------------------------
//                  Ch11_03_.s
//---------------------------------------------------

// extern "C" void CalcQuoRemA_(int a, int b, int* quo, int* rem);

        .text
        .global CalcQuoRemA_
CalcQuoRemA_:

// Calculate quotient and remainder
        sdiv w4,w0,w1                   // a / b
        str w4,[x2]                     // save quotient
```

```
        mul w5,w4,w1                    // quotient * b
        sub w6,w0,w5                    // a - quotient * b
        str w6,[x3]                     // save remainder
        ret                             // return to caller


// extern "C" void CalcQuoRemB_(long a, long b, long* quo, long* rem);

        .global CalcQuoRemB_
CalcQuoRemB_:

// Calculate quotient and remainder
        sdiv x4,x0,x1                   // a / b
        str x4,[x2]                     // save quotient

        mul x5,x4,x1                    // quotient * b
        sub x6,x0,x5                    // a - quotient * b
        str x6,[x3]                     // save remainder
        ret                             // return to caller
```

The assembly language function CalcQuoRemA_ begins its execution with a sdiv w4,w0,w1 (signed divide) instruction. This instruction divides the value in register W0 (argument value a) by W1 (argument value b) and saves the quotient in register W4. The next instruction, str w4,[x2], saves the 32-bit signed integer quotient to the memory location pointed to by register X2 (argument value quo). The ensuing mul w5,w4,w1 and sub w6,w0,w5 instructions calculate the remainder (the sdiv instruction does not return a remainder). The final instruction of CalcQuoRemA_, str w6,[x3], saves the remainder to memory location pointed to by rem.

Function CalcQuoRemB_ is identical to function CalcQuoRemA_ except that it uses 64-bit signed integer values. The A64 instruction set also includes a udiv (unsigned divide) instruction, which performs division using 32- or 64-bit wide unsigned integers. Here are the results for source code example Ch11_03:

```
CalcQuoRemA_
a = 100
b = 7
quotient = 14
remainder = 2

CalcQuoRemB_
a = -2000000000
b = 11
quotient = -181818181
remainder = -9
```

Integer Operations

The source code examples of this section explain how to use common integer load, store, move, shift, and bitwise logical instructions. It is important to master these instructions given their frequency of use. Like A32 assembly language programming, it is sometimes necessary to use multiple instructions or pseudo instructions when writing A64 code especially for load and move operations as you will soon see.

Load and Store Instructions

Listing 11-4 shows the source code for example Ch11_04, which explains how to use the ldr (load register) instruction. It also illustrates the use of several Armv8-64 memory addressing modes.

Listing 11-4. Example Ch11_04

```
//----------------------------------------------------
//                  Ch11_04.cpp
//----------------------------------------------------

#include <iostream>

using namespace std;

extern "C" int TestLDR1_(unsigned int i, unsigned long j);
extern "C" long TestLDR2_(unsigned int i, unsigned long j);
extern "C" short TestLDR3_(unsigned int i, unsigned long j);

void TestLDR1(void)
{
    const char nl = '\n';
    unsigned int i = 3;
    unsigned long j = 6;

    int test_ldr1 = TestLDR1_(i, j);

    cout << "TestLDR1_(" << i << ", " << j << ") = " << test_ldr1 << nl;
}

void TestLDR2(void)
{
    const char nl = '\n';
    unsigned int i = 2;
    unsigned long j = 7;

    long test_ldr2 = TestLDR2_(i, j);

    cout << "TestLDR2_(" << i << ", " << j << ") = " << test_ldr2 << nl;
}

void TestLDR3(void)
{
    const char nl = '\n';
    unsigned int i = 5;
    unsigned long j = 1;

    short test_ldr3 = TestLDR3_(i, j);

    cout << "TestLDR3_(" << i << ", " << j << ") = " << test_ldr3 << nl;
}
```

```
int main(int argc, char** argv)
{
    TestLDR1();
    TestLDR2();
    TestLDR3();
}

//---------------------------------------------------
//                  Ch11_04_.s
//---------------------------------------------------

// Test arrays
            .data
A1:         .word 1, 2, 3, 4, 5, 6, 7, 8
A2:         .quad 10, -20, 30, -40, 50, -60, 70, -80

            .text
A3:         .short 100, 200, -300, 400, 500, -600, 700, 800

// extern "C" int TestLDR1_(unsigned int i, unsigned long j);

            .global TestLDR1_
TestLDR1_:  ldr x2,=A1                          // x2 = ptr to A1

            ldr w3,[x2,w0,uxtw 2]               // w3 = A1[i]
            ldr w4,[x2,x1,lsl 2]                // w4 = A1[j]

            add w0,w3,w4                        // w0 = A1[i] + A1[j]
            ret

// extern "C" long TestLDR2_(unsigned int i, unsigned long j);

            .global TestLDR2_
TestLDR2_:  ldr x2,=A2                          // x2 = ptr to A2

            ldr x3,[x2,w0,uxtw 3]               // x3 = A2[i]
            ldr x4,[x2,x1,lsl 3]                // x4 = A2[j]

            add x0,x3,x4                        // w0 = A2[i] + A2[j]
            ret

// extern "C" short TestLDR3_(unsigned int i, unsigned long j);

            .global TestLDR3_
TestLDR3_:  adr x2,A3                           // x2 = ptr to A3

            ldrsh w3,[x2,w0,uxtw 1]             // w3 = A3[i]
            ldrsh w4,[x2,x1,lsl 1]              // w4 = A3[j]

            add w0,w3,w4                        // w0 = A3[i] + A3[j]
            ret
```

The C++ code begins with the declarations of the assembly language functions TestLDR1_, TestLDR2_, and TestLDR3_. These functions require two integer arguments, which are used as indices to access elements in a small test array. They also return integer values of varying sizes. The C++ functions TestLDR1, TestLDR2, and TestLDR3 contain code that exercise the aforementioned assembly language functions and display results.

The assembly language code in Listing 11-4 starts with a .data directive. This directive signifies the beginning of section in memory that contains read-write data. The line that starts with the label A1: initializes an eight-element array of .word (32-bit) integers. This is followed by an eight-element array of .quad (64-bit) integers named A2. The final test array, A3, contains eight .short (16-bit) integer elements. Note that the definition of array A3 follows the .text directive, which means that it is a read-only array since the elements are allocated in a code section. Table 2-1 (see Chapter 2) summarizes the GNU assembler directives that are used to allocate storage space and initialize data values.

The assembly language function TestLDR1_ begins its execution with a ldr x2,=A1 that loads the address array A1 into register X2. Recall from the discussions in Chapter 2 that this form of the ldr instruction is a pseudo instruction. The assembler replaces the ldr x2,=A2 instruction with a ldr x2,offset instruction that loads the address of array A1 from a literal pool. Figure 11-1 illustrates this in greater detail. This figure contains output from the GNU debugger (with minor edits to improve readability) that shows the machine code for the TestLDRx_ functions. Note that the GNU debugger output displays runtime addresses for the ldr pseudo instructions instead of the offsets that are embedded in the instruction encodings.

```
Dump of .text section
  0x0000aaaaaaaaae80 <A3>:                 100 200 -300 400 500 -600 700 800

  0x0000aaaaaaaaae90 <TestLDR1_+0>:        02 02 00 58  ldr x2, 0xaaaaaaaaaed0
  0x0000aaaaaaaaae94 <TestLDR1_+4>:        43 58 60 b8  ldr w3, [x2, w0, uxtw #2]
  0x0000aaaaaaaaae98 <TestLDR1_+8>:        44 78 61 b8  ldr w4, [x2, x1, lsl #2]
  0x0000aaaaaaaaae9c <TestLDR1_+12>:       60 00 04 0b  add w0, w3, w4
  0x0000aaaaaaaaaea0 <TestLDR1_+16>:       c0 03 5f d6  ret
  0x0000aaaaaaaaaea4 <TestLDR2_+0>:        a2 01 00 58  ldr x2, 0xaaaaaaaaaed8
  0x0000aaaaaaaaaea8 <TestLDR2_+4>:        43 58 60 f8  ldr x3, [x2, w0, uxtw #3]
  0x0000aaaaaaaaaeac <TestLDR2_+8>:        44 78 61 f8  ldr x4, [x2, x1, lsl #3]
  0x0000aaaaaaaaaeb0 <TestLDR2_+12>:       60 00 04 8b  add x0, x3, x4
  0x0000aaaaaaaaaeb4 <TestLDR2_+16>:       c0 03 5f d6  ret
  0x0000aaaaaaaaaeb8 <TestLDR3_+0>:        42 fe ff 10  adr x2, 0xaaaaaaaaae80 ◄——— PC relative address (A3)
  0x0000aaaaaaaaaebc <TestLDR3_+4>:        43 58 e0 78  ldrsh w3, [x2, w0, uxtw #1]
  0x0000aaaaaaaaaec0 <TestLDR3_+8>:        44 78 e1 78  ldrsh w4, [x2, x1, lsl #1]
  0x0000aaaaaaaaaec4 <TestLDR3_+12>:       60 00 04 0b  add w0, w3, w4
  0x0000aaaaaaaaaec8 <TestLDR3_+16>:       c0 03 5f d6  ret
  0x0000aaaaaaaaaecc <TestLDR3_+20>:       00 00 00 00
  0x0000aaaaaaaaaed0 <TestLDR3_+24>:       10 c0 ab aa aa aa 00 00 ◄——— Literal pool address (A1)
  0x0000aaaaaaaaaed8 <TestLDR3_+32>:       30 c0 ab aa aa aa 00 00 ◄——— Literal pool address (A2)

Dump of .data section
  0x0000aaaaaaaabc010 <A1>:                1 2 3 4
  0x0000aaaaaaaabc020 <A1+16>:             5 6 7 8
  0x0000aaaaaaaabc030 <A2>:                10 -20
  0x0000aaaaaaaabc040 <A2+16>:             30 -40
  0x0000aaaaaaaabc050 <A2+32>:             50 -60
  0x0000aaaaaaaabc060 <A2+48>:             70 -80
```

Figure 11-1. Machine code for TestLDRx_ functions

The next instruction in TestLDR1_, ldr w3,[x2,w0,uxtw 2], uses extended register memory addressing (see Chapter 10, Table 10-3) to load element A1[i] into register W3. This instruction zero-extends (as specified by the extended operator uxtw) the word value in W0 (argument value i) to 64 bits, left shifts this 64-bit intermediate result by two, and adds X2 (address of array A1) to calculate the address of element A1[i]. Extended register addressing also supports other operators including sxtb, sxth, sxtw, uxtb, and uxth (the "s" versions sign-extend the index register operand). The ensuing ldr w4,[x2,x1,lsl 2] instruction loads A1[j] into register W4. This instruction employs a lsl operator to calculate the required address since X1 (argument value j) is already a 64-bit wide integer.

Function TestLDR2_ uses a similar sequence of instructions to load elements from array A2, which contains quadword instead of word values. Note that the uxtw and lsl operators shift the array indices in registers W0 and X1 by three instead of two bits since the target array contains quadword elements.

Function TestLDR3_ uses an adr x2,A3 (form PC relative address) instruction to load the address of array A3 into register X2. An adr instruction can be used here since array A3 is defined in the same .text section (just before function TestLDR1_) as the executable code. Note that in Figure 11-1, there is no literal pool entry for array A3 since the adr instruction uses PC relative offsets instead of literal pools. The next instruction, ldrsh w3,[x2,w0,uxtw 1] (load register signed halfword), loads A3[i] into register W3. The ensuing ldrsh w4,[x2,x1,lsl 1] instruction then loads A3[j] into register W4. Note that in these ldrsh instructions, the shift count is 1 since halfword values are being loaded. Here is the output for source code example Ch11_04:

```
TestLDR1_(3, 6) = 11
TestLDR2_(2, 7) = -50
TestLDR3_(5, 1) = -400
```

Move Instructions

Recall from the discussions in Chapter 10 that the A64 instruction set uses 32-bit wide fixed-length encodings for all instructions. This means that it is sometimes necessary to use multiple instructions or pseudo instructions to load an integer constant into a register. Listing 11-5 shows the source code for example Ch11_05. This example explains how to use various A64 move instructions to load integer constants.

Listing 11-5. Example Ch11_05

```cpp
//----------------------------------------------------
//              Ch11_05.cpp
//----------------------------------------------------

#include <iostream>
#include <cstdint>

using namespace std;

extern "C" void MoveA_(int32_t& a0, int32_t& a1, int32_t& a2, int32_t& a3);
extern "C" void MoveB_(int64_t& b0, int64_t& b1, int64_t& b2, int64_t& b3);
extern "C" void MoveC_(int32_t& c0, int32_t& c1);
extern "C" void MoveD_(int64_t& d0, int64_t& d1, int64_t& d2);

int main(int argc, char** argv)
{
    const char nl = '\n';
```

```
    int32_t a0, a1, a2, a3;
    MoveA_(a0, a1, a2, a3);
    cout << "\nResults for MoveA_" << nl;
    cout << "a0 = " << a0 << nl;
    cout << "a1 = " << a1 << nl;
    cout << "a2 = " << a2 << nl;
    cout << "a3 = " << a3 << nl;

    int64_t b0, b1, b2, b3;
    MoveB_(b0, b1, b2, b3);
    cout << "\nResults for MoveB_" << nl;
    cout << "b0 = " << b0 << nl;
    cout << "b1 = " << b1 << nl;
    cout << "b2 = " << b2 << nl;
    cout << "b3 = " << b3 << nl;

    int32_t c0, c1;
    MoveC_(c0, c1);
    cout << "\nResults for MoveC_" << nl;
    cout << "c0 = " << c0 << nl;
    cout << "c1 = " << c1 << nl;

    int64_t d0, d1, d2;
    MoveD_(d0, d1, d2);
    cout << "\nResults for MoveD_" << nl;
    cout << "d0 = " << d0 << nl;
    cout << "d1 = " << d1 << nl;
    cout << "d2 = " << d2 << nl;

    return 0;
}

//----------------------------------------------------
//                  Ch11_05_.s
//----------------------------------------------------

// extern "C" MoveA_(int32_t& a0, int32_t& a1, int32_t& a2, int32_t& a3);

            .text
            .global MoveA_
MoveA_:     mov w7,1000                         // w7 = 1000
            str w7,[x0]

            mov w7,65536000                     // w7 = 65536000
            str w7,[x1]

            movz w7,1000,lsl 16                 // w7 = 65536000
            str w7,[x2]

            mov w7,-131072                      // w7 = -131027
            str w7,[x3]
            ret
```

```
// extern "C" MoveB_(int64_t& b0, int64_t& b1, int64_t& b2, int64_t& b3);

            .global MoveB_
MoveB_:     mov x7,131072000              // x7 = 131072000
            str x7,[x0]

            movz x7,2000,lsl 16           // x7 = 131072000
            str x7,[x1]

            mov x7,429496729600           // x7 = 429496729600
            str x7,[x2]

            movz x7,100,lsl 32            // x7 = 429496729600
            str x7,[x3]
            ret

// extern "C" void MoveC_(int32_t& c0, int32_t& c1);

            .equ VAL1,2000000
            .equ VAL1_LO16,(VAL1 & 0xffff)
            .equ VAL1_HI16,((VAL1 & 0xffff0000) >> 16)

            .global MoveC_
MoveC_:
//          mov w7,VAL1                   // invalid value

            mov w7,VAL1_LO16              // w7 = 33920
            movk w7,VAL1_HI16,lsl 16      // w7 = 2000000
            str w7,[x0]

            ldr w7,=VAL1                  // w7 = 2000000
            str w7,[x1]
            ret

// extern "C" void MoveD_(int64_t& d0, int64_t& d1, int64_t& d2);

            .equ VAL2,-1000000000000000
            .equ VAL2_00,(VAL2 & 0xffff)
            .equ VAL2_16,(VAL2 & 0xffff0000) >> 16
            .equ VAL2_32,(VAL2 & 0xffff00000000) >> 32
            .equ VAL2_48,(VAL2 & 0xffff000000000000) >> 48

            .equ VAL3,0x100000064         // (2**32 + 100)
            .equ VAL3_00,(VAL3 & 0xffff)
            .equ VAL3_32,(VAL3 & 0xffff00000000) >> 32

            .global MoveD_
MoveD_:
//          mov x7,VAL2                   // invalid value
```

```
        mov x7,VAL2_00
        movk x7,VAL2_16,lsl 16
        movk x7,VAL2_32,lsl 32
        movk x7,VAL2_48,lsl 48              // x7 = VAL2
        str x7,[x0]

        ldr x7,=VAL2                        // x7 = VAL2
        str x7,[x1]

        mov x7,VAL3_00
        movk x7,VAL3_32,lsl 32              // x7 = 0x100000064
        str x7,[x2]
        ret
```

The C++ code in Listing 11-5 is straightforward. It begins with the declarations of the assembly language functions MoveA_, MoveB_, MoveC_, and MoveD_. These functions contain code that illustrate the loading of constant values using a variety of A64 move instructions. The remaining C++ code exercises the assembly language move functions and displays results.

Assembly language function MoveA_ begins with a mov w7,1000 (move wide immediate) that loads 1000 into register W7. This instruction (and all other A64 instructions that use a W register destination operand) also sets the upper 32 bits of X0 to zero. Like its A32 counterpart, the A64 mov instruction can be used to load a subset of all possible 32-bit wide integer constants into a W register. Following the str w7,[x0] instruction is a mov w7,65536000 instruction that loads 65536000 into register W7. The mov instruction is an alias of the movz (move wide with zero) instruction. This instruction moves an optionally shifted 16-bit constant value into a register.

The ensuing movz w7,1000,lsl 16 instruction also loads 65536000 into register W7. When loading a 32-bit constant into a W register, the alias instruction mov should be employed when possible instead of a movz instruction since the former is easier to read and type. The final move instruction example in MoveA_, mov w7,-131072, loads a negative value into W7.

Function MoveB_ illustrates the use of the mov and movz instructions using 64-bit constants and X register destination operands. Note than when a movz instruction uses an X register destination operand, the lsl operator can use a shift bit count of 0 (the default), 16, 32, or 48 bits.

Just prior to the start of function MoveC_ are three .equ directives. The .equ VAL1,2000000 defines VAL1 as a symbolic name for the constant 2000000. The next two directive statements, .equ VAL1_LO16,(VAL1 & 0xffff) and .equ VAL1_HI16,((VAL1 & 0xffff0000) >> 16), define symbolic names for the low- and high-order 16 bits of VAL1, respectively. The first instruction of MoveC_, mov w7,VAL1, is commented out. If you remove the comment and build the project using make, the GNU assembler will generate an "immediate cannot be moved by a single instruction" error message. The next two instructions, mov w7,VAL1_LO16 and movk w7,VAL1_HI16,lsl 16 (move wide with keep), illustrate an instruction sequence that loads 2000000 into register W7. The mov instruction loads VAL1_LO16 into register W7. The ensuing movk instruction loads VAL1_HI into bit positions 31:16 of register W7 and leaves bits 15:0 unchanged. Function MoveC_ also contains an ldr w7,=VAL1 instruction that loads VAL1 into W7. This instruction form is easier to read but is also slower since it requires an extra memory read cycle to load VAL1 from a literal pool.

The final move function is named MoveD_. This function illustrates how to use the movk instruction to load a 64-bit constant into an X register. The .equ directives that precede the start of MoveD_ include expressions that split the constant VAL2 into four 16-bit wide values. The constant VAL3 is also split into two 16-bit wide values. Removing the comment from the mov x7,VAL2 instruction and running make will generate another GNU assembler error message. To load VAL2 into register X7, a series of mov and movk instructions is required. The first instruction of the sequence, mov x7,VAL2_00, loads VAL2_00 into register X7. The ensuing movk x7,VAL2_16,lsl 16 instruction loads VAL2_16 into bit positions 31:16 of register X7 and leaves all other bits unchanged. The movk x7,VAL2_32,lsl 32 and movk x7,VAL2_48,lsl 48 instructions load bit positions 47:32 and 63:48, respectively. When necessary, this four-instruction sequence is the recommended method for loading a 64-bit wide constant since the AArch64 execution state is optimized for this type of sequence. It is often reasonable to use a ldr x7,=VAL2 instruction for a one-time initialization since it is easier to read and type, but this approach should be avoided inside a for-loop.

In many cases, it is not necessary to use a quartet of mov and movk instructions to load a 64-bit wide constant. Function MoveD_ employs the instruction sequence mov x7,VAL3_00 and movk x7,VAL3_32,lsl 32 to load VAL3 into register X7. The reason only two instructions are required here is that bit positions 63:48 and 31:16 of the 64-bit constant VAL3 are all zeros. Execution of the mov x7,VAL3_00 instruction has already set these bits in register X7 to zero. Here are the results for source code example Ch11_05:

```
Results for MoveA_
a0 = 1000
a1 = 65536000
a2 = 65536000
a3 = -131072

Results for MoveB_
b0 = 131072000
b1 = 131072000
b2 = 429496729600
b3 = 429496729600

Results for MoveC_
c0 = 2000000
c1 = 2000000

Results for MoveD_
d0 = -1000000000000000
d1 = -1000000000000000
d2 = 4294967396
```

Shift Instructions

Listing 11-6 contains the code for source code example Ch11_06. This example illuminates the use of the asr (arithmetic shift right), lsl (logical shift left), lsr (logical shift right), and ror (rotate right) instructions. The C++ code begins the requisite function declarations. Note that the source code for function PrintResult is not shown in Listing 11-6 but is included with the downloadable software package. The remaining C++ code performs test case initialization and exercises the assembly language functions ShiftA_ and ShiftB_.

Listing 11-6. Example Ch11_06

```
//----------------------------------------------------
//              Ch11_06.cpp
//----------------------------------------------------

#include <iostream>
#include <cstdint>

using namespace std;
```

```cpp
// Ch11_06_Misc.cpp
extern void PrintResult(const char* msg, const uint32_t* x, uint32_t a,
    size_t n, int count = -1);

// Ch11_06_.s
extern "C" void ShiftA_(uint32_t* x, uint32_t a);
extern "C" void ShiftB_(uint32_t* x, uint32_t a, uint32_t count);

void ShiftA(void)
{
    const size_t n = 4;

    uint32_t a = 0xC1234561;
    uint32_t x[4];
    ShiftA_(x, a);
    PrintResult("ShiftA_", x, a, n);
}

void ShiftB(void)
{
    const size_t n = 4;

    uint32_t a = 0xC1234561;
    uint32_t x[4];
    uint32_t count = 8;
    ShiftB_(x, a, count);
    PrintResult("ShiftB_", x, a, n, (int)count);
}

int main(int argc, char** argv)
{
    ShiftA();
    ShiftB();
    return 0;
}

//-------------------------------------------------
//              Ch11_06_.s
//-------------------------------------------------

// extern "C" void ShiftA_(uint32_t* x, uint32_t a);


        .text
        .global ShiftA_
ShiftA_:    asr w2,w1,2                     // arithmetic shift right - 2 bits
            lsl w3,w1,4                     // logical shift left - 4 bits
            lsr w4,w1,5                     // logical shift right - 5 bits
            ror w5,w1,3                     // rotate right - 3 bits
```

```
                    str w2,[x0]              // save asr result to x[0]
                    str w3,[x0,4]            // save lsl result to x[1]
                    str w4,[x0,8]            // save lsr result to x[2]
                    str w5,[x0,12]           // save ror result to x[3]
                    ret

// extern "C" void ShiftB_(uint32_t* x, uint32_t a, uint32_t count);

                    .global ShiftB_
ShiftB_ :           asr w3,w1,w2             // arithmetic shift right
                    lsl w4,w1,w2             // logical shift left
                    lsr w5,w1,w2             // logical shift right
                    ror w6,w1,w2             // rotate right

                    str w3,[x0]              // save asr result to x[0]
                    str w4,[x0,4]            // save lsl result to x[1]
                    str w5,[x0,8]            // save lsr result to x[2]
                    str w6,[x0,12]           // save ror result to x[3]
                    ret
```

Assembly language function ShiftA_ demonstrates the use of the asr, lsl, lsr, and ror instructions using immediate operand bit counts. Following execution of these instructions, ShiftA_ uses a series of str instructions that save the result of each shift/rotate operation to array x. It should be noted that the immediate bit count forms of the asr, lsl, lsr, and ror instructions are aliases for sbmf (signed bit field move), ubfm (unsigned bit field move), ubfm, and extr (extract register), respectively. This is something to keep in mind when using a debugger.

Function ShiftB_ resembles ShiftA_ in that it employs the same shift and rotate instructions. However, ShiftB_ uses the variable bit count forms of the asr, lsl, lsr, and ror instructions. Note that the second source operand of these instructions is a register that contains the shift/rotate bit count. The variable bit count forms of asr, lsl, lsr, and ror instructions are aliases for asrv (arithmetic shift right variable), lslv (logical shift left variable), lsrv (logical shift right variable, and rorv (rotate right variable), respectively.

In this source code example, functions ShiftA_ and ShiftB_ both used 32-bit W register operands. The asr, lsl, lsr, and ror instructions can also be used with 64-bit wide X register operands. Finally, unlike the A32 instruction set, the A64 instruction set does not include a rrx (rotate right with extend) instruction. Here is the output for source code example Ch11_06:

```
ShiftA_
a:     0xc1234561 | 1100 0001 0010 0011 0100 0101 0110 0001 |
x[0]: 0xf048d158 | 1111 0000 0100 1000 1101 0001 0101 1000 | asr #2
x[1]: 0x12345610 | 0001 0010 0011 0100 0101 0110 0001 0000 | lsl #4
x[2]: 0x06091a2b | 0000 0110 0000 1001 0001 1010 0010 1011 | lsr #5
x[3]: 0x382468ac | 0011 1000 0010 0100 0110 1000 1010 1100 | ror #3

ShiftB_  - count = 8
a:     0xc1234561 | 1100 0001 0010 0011 0100 0101 0110 0001 |
x[0]: 0xffc12345 | 1111 1111 1100 0001 0010 0011 0100 0101 | asr
x[1]: 0x23456100 | 0010 0011 0100 0101 0110 0001 0000 0000 | lsl
x[2]: 0x00c12345 | 0000 0000 1100 0001 0010 0011 0100 0101 | lsr
x[3]: 0x61c12345 | 0110 0001 1100 0001 0010 0011 0100 0101 | ror
```

Bitwise Logical Operations

The final source code example of this chapter is called Ch11_07. This example demonstrates how to carry out bitwise logical operations including AND, OR, and exclusive OR. Listing 11-7 shows the source code for example Ch11_07.

Listing 11-7. Example Ch11_07

```
//----------------------------------------------------
//                  Ch11_07.cpp
//----------------------------------------------------

#include <iostream>
#include <cstdint>

using namespace std;

// Ch11_07_Misc.cpp
extern void PrintResultA(const char* msg, const uint32_t* x, uint32_t a, uint32_t b,
size_t n);
extern void PrintResultB(const char* msg, const uint32_t* x, uint32_t a, size_t n);

// Ch11_07_.s
extern "C" void BitwiseOpsA_(uint32_t* x, uint32_t a, uint32_t b);
extern "C" void BitwiseOpsB_(uint32_t* x, uint32_t a);

void BitwiseOpsA(void)
{
    const size_t n = 3;
    uint32_t a, b, x[n];

    a = 0x12345678;
    b = 0xaa55aa55;
    BitwiseOpsA_(x, a, b);
    PrintResultA("BitwiseOpsA_ Test #1", x, a, b, n);

    a = 0x12345678;
    b = 0x00ffc384;
    BitwiseOpsA_(x, a, b);
    PrintResultA("BitwiseOpsA_ Test #2", x, a, b, n);
}

void BitwiseOpsB(void)
{
    const size_t n = 4;
    uint32_t a, x[n];

    a = 0x12345678;
    BitwiseOpsB_(x, a);
    PrintResultB("BitwiseOpsB_ Test #1", x, a, n);
```

```
    a = 0xaa55aa55;
    BitwiseOpsB_(x, a);
    PrintResultB("BitwiseOpsB_ Test #2", x, a, n);
}

int main(int argc, char** argv)
{
    BitwiseOpsA();
    cout << "\n";
    BitwiseOpsB();
    return 0;
}

//-------------------------------------------------
//                 Ch11_07_.s
//-------------------------------------------------

// extern "C" void BitwiseOpsA_(uint32_t* x, uint32_t a, uint32_t b);

            .text
            .global BitwiseOpsA_
BitwiseOpsA_:

// Perform various bitwise logical operations
            and w3,w1,w2                    // a AND b
            str w3,[x0]

            orr w3,w1,w2                    // a OR b
            str w3,[x0,4]

            eor w3,w1,w2                    // a EOR b
            str w3,[x0,8]
            ret

// extern "C" void BitwiseOpsB_(uint32_t* x, uint32_t a);

            .global BitwiseOpsB_
BitwiseOpsB_:

            and w2,w1,0x0000ff00            // a AND 0x0000ff00
            str w2,[x0]

            orr w2,w1,0x00ff0000            // a OR 0x00ff0000
            str w2,[x0,4]

            eor w2,w1,0xff000000            // a EOR 0xff000000
            str w2,[x0,8]
```

```
//              and w2,w1,0xcc00ff00          // invalid imm. operand
                mov w2,0xff00
                movk w2,0xcc00,lsl 16          // w2 = 0xcc00ff00
                and w2,w1,w2                   // a AND 0xcc00ff00
                str w2,[x0,12]
                ret
```

The C++ code in Listing 11-7 performs straightforward test case initialization and displays results. Function BitwiseOpsA_ illustrates the use of the and (bitwise AND), orr (bitwise OR), and eor (bitwise exclusive OR) instructions using W register operands. These instructions can also be used with X register operands.

Function BitwiseOpsB_ highlights the use of the and, or, and eor instructions with immediate operands. Note that the and w2,w1,0xcc00ff00 instruction is commented out. Removing this comment and running make will cause the GNU assembler to generate an "immediate out of range" error message. The reason for this is that the machine language bit pattern for the and instruction does not support encoding of the constant 0xCC00FF00. In cases like this, the required constant must be loaded into a register using one or more mov, movz, or movk instructions. BitwiseOpsB_ uses the instruction pair mov w2,0xff00 and movk w2,0xcc00,lsl 16 to load 0xCC00FF00 into register W2. The and instruction constant encoding limitation also applies to other calculating instructions that use immediate constants including add and sub. Here are the results for source code example Ch11_07:

```
BitwiseOpsA_ Test #1
a:    0x12345678 | 0001 0010 0011 0100 0101 0110 0111 1000
b:    0xaa55aa55 | 1010 1010 0101 0101 1010 1010 0101 0101
x[0]: 0x02140250 | 0000 0010 0001 0100 0000 0010 0101 0000 | a AND b
x[1]: 0xba75fe7d | 1011 1010 0111 0101 1111 1110 0111 1101 | a OR  b
x[2]: 0xb861fc2d | 1011 1000 0110 0001 1111 1100 0010 1101 | a EOR b

BitwiseOpsA_ Test #2
a:    0x12345678 | 0001 0010 0011 0100 0101 0110 0111 1000
b:    0x00ffc384 | 0000 0000 1111 1111 1100 0011 1000 0100
x[0]: 0x00344200 | 0000 0000 0011 0100 0100 0010 0000 0000 | a AND b
x[1]: 0x12ffd7fc | 0001 0010 1111 1111 1101 0111 1111 1100 | a OR  b
x[2]: 0x12cb95fc | 0001 0010 1100 1011 1001 0101 1111 1100 | a EOR b

BitwiseOpsB_ Test #1
a:    0x12345678 | 0001 0010 0011 0100 0101 0110 0111 1000
x[0]: 0x00005600 | 0000 0000 0000 0000 0101 0110 0000 0000 | a AND 0x0000ff00
x[1]: 0x12ff5678 | 0001 0010 1111 1111 0101 0110 0111 1000 | a OR  0x00ff0000
x[2]: 0xed345678 | 1110 1101 0011 0100 0101 0110 0111 1000 | a EOR 0xff000000
x[3]: 0x00005600 | 0000 0000 0000 0000 0101 0110 0000 0000 | a AND 0xcc00ff00

BitwiseOpsB_ Test #2
a:    0xaa55aa55 | 1010 1010 0101 0101 1010 1010 0101 0101
x[0]: 0x0000aa00 | 0000 0000 0000 0000 1010 1010 0000 0000 | a AND 0x0000ff00
x[1]: 0xaaffaa55 | 1010 1010 1111 1111 1010 1010 0101 0101 | a OR  0x00ff0000
x[2]: 0x5555aa55 | 0101 0101 0101 0101 1010 1010 0101 0101 | a EOR 0xff000000
x[3]: 0x8800aa00 | 1000 1000 0000 0000 1010 1010 0000 0000 | a AND 0xcc00ff00
```

Summary

Here are the key learning points for Chapter 11:

- The add and sub instructions perform signed and unsigned integer addition and subtraction using 32- or 64-bit wide operands.

- The mul instruction performs signed and unsigned integer multiplication; it saves the low-order 32/64 bits of the resultant 64-/128-bit product. The smull and umull instructions carry out multiplication using 32-bit signed or unsigned integers. The full 64-bit wide product is saved.

- The sdiv and udiv instructions perform signed and unsigned integer division, respectively. These instructions calculate only the quotient.

- Extended register addressing can be used to load elements from an array using byte, halfword, or word indices.

- The movz instruction loads a 16-bit immediate constant (with optional shift) into a W or X register. The mov instruction is an alias of movz and is often used instead of movz to improve code readability.

- The movk instruction loads a 16-bit immediate constant (with optional shift) into a register without altering other bits.

- The and, orr, and eor instructions carry out bitwise logical AND, OR, and exclusive OR operations.

- The GNU C++ calling convention for Armv8-64 uses registers X0/W0–X7/W7 to pass integer or pointer arguments to a function. A function must use register X0 or W0 to return a 64-bit or 32-bit wide integer value to its caller.

CHAPTER 12

■ ■ ■

Armv8-64 Core Programming – Part 2

This chapter examines source code examples that elucidate additional Armv8-64 core programming fundamentals. It begins with a section that explains how to access argument values that are passed via the stack. This section also discusses how to load and store local variables on the stack. The next section includes source code examples that make use of the PSTATE.NZCV condition flags. You will learn how to carry out compare operations, perform conditional branching, and code for-loops. The final section of Chapter 12 presents source code examples that perform calculations using the elements of an array or matrix.

Some of the source examples in this chapter are modified versions of the Armv8-32 source code examples that you saw in Chapters 3 and 4. This gives you an opportunity to compare the assembly language semantics of Armv8-64 vs. Armv8-32. It also highlights the similarities and differences between the A64 and A32 instruction sets.

Stack Arguments and Local Storage

The source examples presented in this section demonstrate how to access and use argument values that are passed via the stack. The first example illustrates passing mixed integer arguments using both the general-purpose registers and the stack. The second source example explains how to allocate stack space for local variables. You will also learn additional details regarding the GNU C++ calling convention for Armv8-64 functions.

Stack Arguments Using Mixed Integers

Listing 12-1 shows the source code for example Ch12_01. This example expounds on using mixed integer types in a function. It also illustrates how to access argument values that are passed via the stack.

Listing 12-1. Example Ch12_01

```
//--------------------------------------------------
//              Ch12_01.cpp
//--------------------------------------------------

#include <iostream>
#include <iomanip>
#include <cstdint>
```

© Daniel Kusswurm 2020
D. Kusswurm, *Modern Arm Assembly Language Programming*,
https://doi.org/10.1007/978-1-4842-6267-2_12

```
using namespace std;

extern "C" int64_t SumCubes_(uint8_t a, int16_t b, int32_t c, int64_t d,
        int8_t e, int16_t f, uint8_t g, uint16_t h, int32_t i, int8_t j);

void PrintResult(const char* msg, int a, int b, int c, int64_t d, int e,
        int f, int g, int h, int i, int j, int64_t sum1, int64_t sum2)
{
    const char nl = '\n';
    const char* sep = " | ";
    const size_t w = 6;

    cout << msg << nl;
    cout << "a = " << setw(w) << a << sep;
    cout << "b = " << setw(w) << b << sep;
    cout << "c = " << setw(w) << c << sep;
    cout << "d = " << setw(w) << d << sep;
    cout << "e = " << setw(w) << e << nl;
    cout << "f = " << setw(w) << f << sep;
    cout << "g = " << setw(w) << g << sep;
    cout << "h = " << setw(w) << h << sep;
    cout << "i = " << setw(w) << i << sep;
    cout << "j = " << setw(w) << j << nl;
    cout << "sum1 = " << setw(w) << sum1 << nl;
    cout << "sum2 = " << setw(w) << sum2 << nl;

    if (sum1 != sum2)
        cout << "Compare error!\n";

    cout << nl;
}

int64_t SumCubes(uint8_t a, int16_t b, int32_t c, int64_t d,
        int8_t e, int16_t f, uint8_t g, uint16_t h, int32_t i, int8_t j)
{
    int64_t aa = (int64_t)a * a * a;
    int64_t bb = (int64_t)b * b * b;
    int64_t cc = (int64_t)c * c * c;
    int64_t dd = d * d * d;
    int64_t ee = (int64_t)e * e * e;
    int64_t ff = (int64_t)f * f * f;
    int64_t gg = (int64_t)g * g * g;
    int64_t hh = (int64_t)h * h * h;
    int64_t ii = (int64_t)i * i * i;
    int64_t jj = (int64_t)j * j * j;

    return aa + bb + cc + dd + ee + ff + gg + hh + ii + jj;
}
```

```
int main(int argc, char** argv)
{
    uint8_t a, g;
    int16_t b, f;
    int32_t c, i;
    int64_t d, sum1, sum2;
    int8_t e, j;
    uint16_t short h;

    a = 10; b = -20; c = 30; d = -40;
    e = -50; f = -60; g = 70, h = 80, i = -90, j = 100;
    sum1 = SumCubes(a, b, c, d, e, f, g, h, i, j);
    sum2 = SumCubes_(a, b, c, d, e, f, g, h, i, j);
    PrintResult("SumCubes - Test #1", a, b, c, d, e, f, g, h, i, j, sum1, sum2);

    a = 10; b = -20; c = -30; d = 40;
    e = -50; f = 60; g = 70, h = 80, i = 90, j = -100;
    sum1 = SumCubes(a, b, c, d, e, f, g, h, i, j);
    sum2 = SumCubes_(a, b, c, d, e, f, g, h, i, j);
    PrintResult("SumCubes - Test #2", a, b, c, d, e, f, g, h, i, j, sum1, sum2);

    a = -100; b = 200; c = 300; d = 400;
    e = 50; f = -600; g = 70, h = 800, i = -900, j = -25;
    sum1 = SumCubes(a, b, c, d, e, f, g, h, i, j);
    sum2 = SumCubes_(a, b, c, d, e, f, g, h, i, j);
    PrintResult("SumCubes - Test #3", a, b, c, d, e, f, g, h, i, j, sum1, sum2);
}

//----------------------------------------------------
//                  Ch12_01_.s
//----------------------------------------------------

// extern "C" int64_t SumCubes_(uint8_t a, int16_t b, int32_t c, int64_t d,
//    int8_t e, int16_t f, uint8_t g, uint16_t h, int32_t i, int8_t j);

            .equ ARG_I,0                        // stack offset for arg i
            .equ ARG_J,8                        // stack offset for arg j

            .text
            .global SumCubes_
SumCubes_:
            ldrsw x8,[SP,ARG_I]                  // x8 = i (sign-extended)
            ldrsb x9,[SP,ARG_J]                  // x9 = j (sign-extended)

            and w0,w0,0xff                       // zero-extend a to 64 bits
            mul x10,x0,x0                        // x10 = a * a
            mul x10,x10,x0                       // x10 = a * a * a

            sxth x1,w1                           // sign-extend b to 64 bits
            mul x11,x1,x1                        // x11 = b * b
            madd x10,x11,x1,x10                  // x10 += b * b * b
```

```
        sxtw x2,w2                      // sign-extend c to 64 bits
        mul x11,x2,x2                   // x11 = c * c (64 bits)
        madd x10,x11,x2,x10             // x10 += c * c * c

        mul x11,x3,x3                   // x11 = d * d
        madd x10,x11,x3,x10             // x10 += d * d * d

        sxtb x4,w4                      // sign-extend e to 64 bits
        mul x11,x4,x4                   // x11 = e * e
        madd x10,x11,x4,x10             // x10 += e * e * e

        sxth x5,w5                      // sign-extend f to 64 bits
        mul x11,x5,x5                   // x11 = f * f
        madd x10,x11,x5,x10             // x10 += f * f * f

        and w6,w6,0xff                  // zero-extend g to 64 bits
        mul x11,x6,x6                   // x11 = g * g
        madd x10,x11,x6,x10             // x10 += g * g * g

        uxth x7,w7                      // zero-extend h to 64 bits
        mul x11,x7,x7                   // x11 = h * h
        madd x10,x11,x7,x10             // x10 += h * h * h

        mul x11,x8,x8                   // x11 = i * i
        madd x10,x11,x8,x10             // x10 += i * i * i

        mul x11,x9,x9                   // x11 = j * j
        madd x0,x11,x9,x10              // x0 = final result
        ret
```

The C++ code in Listing 12-1 begins with the declaration of the assembly language function CalcCubes_. This function sums the cubes of its argument values. Note that the function declaration for CalcCubes_ contains a mix of signed and unsigned integer types. Following the declaration of CalcCubes_ is the function PrintResult, which streams results to cout. The C++ function CalcCubes contains code that carries out the same calculations as its assembly language counterpart. Function main performs test case initialization and exercises the cube summing calculating functions.

In Chapter 11, you learned that the first eight integer type arguments are passed to an Armv8-64 function using registers X0/W0–X7/W7. Any remaining arguments are passed via the stack. Function CalcCubes_ requires ten argument values, which means that the final two are passed via the stack as illustrated in Figure 12-1. Note that in this figure, argument values i and j are *not* size-extended to 64 bits. Likewise, argument values a – h in registers X0–X7 are not size-extend to 64 bits. This means that function SumCubes_ must employ additional instructions to either zero- or sign-extend its argument values to 64 bits before using them in any calculations.

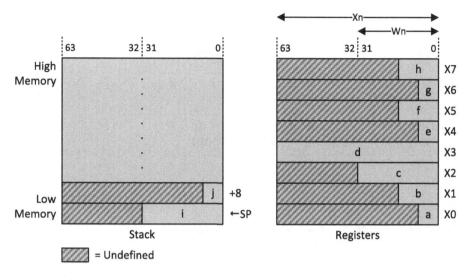

Figure 12-1. *Register and stack arguments for function* CalcCubes_

The assembly language source code in Listing 12-1 begins with the statements .equ ARG_I,0 and .equ ARG_J,8. These equates define stack offsets for argument values i and j. The first instruction of SumCubes_, ldrsw x8,[SP,ARG_I] (load register signed word), loads the word value on the stack pointed to by SP + ARG_I (argument value i), sign-extends it to 64 bits, and saves the result in register X8. The next instruction, ldrsb x9,[SP,ARG_J] (load register signed byte), loads and sign-extends argument value j to 64 bits and saves the result in register X9.

The and w0,w0,0xff instruction that follows the ldrsb instruction zero-extends argument value a to 64 bits. This instruction performs two distinct operations: it zeros out the undefined bits of register W0 (bitwise AND) and sets bits 63:32 of register X0 to zero. Recall from the discussions in Chapter 10 that whenever an A64 instruction uses a W register as a destination operand, the upper 32 bits of the corresponding X register are always set to zero. The next two instructions, mul x10,x0,x0 and mul x10,x10,x0, calculate a * a * a.

The next code block calculates b * b * b and updates the cube sum that is maintained in register X10. The first instruction of this block, sxth x1,w1 (sign-extend halfword), sign-extends the halfword value in the low-order 16 bits of register W1 to 64 bits and saves the result in register X1. This is followed by a mul x11,x1,x1 instruction that calculates b * b. The ensuing madd x10,x11,x1,x10 (multiply-add) instruction multiplies the contents of registers X11 and X1, which yields b * b * b. It then sums this value with X10 and saves the result in X10. The next instruction triplet, sxtw x2,w2 (sign-extend word), mul x11,x2,x2, and madd x10,x11,x2,x10, calculates c * c * c and updates the cube sum in register X10. Similarly, the mul x11,x3,x3 and madd x10,x11,x3,x10 instructions calculate d * d * d and update the cube sum in R10.

The remaining code blocks in SumCubes_ contain similar sequences of instructions that complete the cube summing operation. The sxtb x4,w4 (sign-extend byte) instruction sign-extends the low-order 8 bits of register W4 (argument value e) to 64 bits and saves the result in X4. Similarly, the sxth x5,w5 instruction sign-extends the low-order 16 bits of register W5 (argument value f) to 64 bits. The and w6,w6,0xff instruction zero-extends the low-order 8 bits of register W6 (argument value g) to 64 bits. The uxth x7,w7 (zero-extend halfword) instruction zero-extends the low-order 16 bits of register W7 (argument value h) to 64 bits and saves the result in register X7.

The penultimate instruction pair of SumCubes_, mul x11,x8,x8 and madd x10,x11,x8,x10, calculates i * i * i and adds this value to the intermediate cube sum in register X10. This is followed by another instruction pair, mul x11,x9,x9 and madd x0,x11,x9,x10, that calculates j * j * j and the final cube sum. Here are the results for source code example Ch12_01:

```
SumCubes - Test #1
a =       10 | b =      -20 | c =      30 | d =     -40 | e =     -50
f =      -60 | g =       70 | h =      80 | i =     -90 | j =     100
sum1 = 741000
sum2 = 741000

SumCubes - Test #2
a =       10 | b =      -20 | c =     -30 | d =      40 | e =     -50
f =       60 | g =       70 | h =      80 | i =      90 | j =    -100
sum1 = 705000
sum2 = 705000

SumCubes - Test #3
a =      156 | b =      200 | c =     300 | d =     400 | e =      50
f =     -600 | g =       70 | h =     800 | i =    -900 | j =     -25
sum1 = -329751209
sum2 = -329751209
```

Table 12-1 summarizes the GNU C++ calling convention requirements for the AArch64 general-purpose registers. Note that the calling convention designates each general-purpose register as volatile or non-volatile. A function can modify any volatile register but must preserve the contents of any non-volatile register it uses. Non-volatile registers are typically preserved on the stack. You will learn more about this in the next section.

Table 12-1. *GNU C++ calling convention requirements for AArch64 general-purpose registers*

Register	Type	Usage
X0	Volatile	First integer argument, return value, scratch register
X1	Volatile	Second integer argument, scratch register
X2	Volatile	Third integer argument, scratch register
X3	Volatile	Fourth integer argument, scratch register
X4	Volatile	Fifth integer argument, scratch register
X5	Volatile	Sixth integer argument, scratch register
X6	Volatile	Seventh integer argument, scratch register
X7	Volatile	Eighth integer argument, scratch register
X8	Volatile	Return by value address (structures), scratch register
X9–X15	Volatile	Scratch registers
X16–X17	Volatile	Intra-procedure-call registers, scratch registers
X18	Varies	Platform register
X19–X28	Non-volatile	Scratch registers
X29	Non-volatile	Frame pointer
X30	Non-volatile	Link register

A function that returns a structure by value must save this result to the memory location pointed to by X8. Otherwise, X8 can be used as a scratch register. Registers X16 and X17 are used to support veneers. A veneer is a small code patch that allows a branch instruction to access the full 64-bit address space of the AArch64 execution state. Register X18 is a platform-specific register. Arm advises against using this register in portable hand-coded assembly language functions since managing X18 as an ordinary non-volatile register might not work on all platforms. Keep in mind that the GNU C++ calling convention register requirements outlined in Table 12-1 might be different for other C++ compilers and host platforms. You should always consult the appropriate documentation to verify the calling convention requirements for the target C++ compiler and host platform.

Stack Arguments with Local Variables

Listing 12-2 shows the source code for example Ch12_02. This example illustrates the use of local variables on the stack. It also demonstrates how to preserve non-volatile registers on the stack and accessing C++ global variables from an assembly language function.

Listing 12-2. Example Ch12_02

```
//---------------------------------------------------
//                  Ch12_02.cpp
//---------------------------------------------------

#include <iostream>
#include <iomanip>
#include <cstdint>

using namespace std;

int32_t g_Val1 = 10;
int64_t g_Val2 = -20;

extern "C" void LocalVars_(int32_t a, int32_t b, int32_t c, int32_t d,
  int64_t e, int64_t f, int64_t g, int64_t h, int32_t* x, int64_t* y);

void LocalVars(int32_t a, int32_t b, int32_t c, int32_t d,
  int64_t e, int64_t f, int64_t g, int64_t h, int32_t* x, int64_t* y)
{
    int32_t temp0 = a + b + c;
    int32_t temp1 = d - g_Val1;
    int64_t temp2 = e + f + g;
    int64_t temp3 = h - g_Val2;

    *x = temp0 * temp1;
    *y = temp2 * temp3;
}

void PrintResult(const char* msg, int32_t a, int32_t b, int32_t c, int32_t d,
    int64_t e, int64_t f, int64_t g, int64_t h, int32_t x1, int64_t y1,
    int32_t x2, int64_t y2)
{
    const char nl = '\n';
```

```cpp
    const char* sep = " | ";
    const size_t w = 8;

    cout << nl << msg << nl;
    cout << "a = " << setw(w) << a << sep;
    cout << "b = " << setw(w) << b << sep;
    cout << "c = " << setw(w) << c << sep;
    cout << "d = " << setw(w) << d << nl;
    cout << "e = " << setw(w) << e << sep;
    cout << "f = " << setw(w) << f << sep;
    cout << "g = " << setw(w) << g << sep;
    cout << "h = " << setw(w) << h << nl;
    cout << "x1 = " << setw(w) << x1 << nl;
    cout << "x2 = " << setw(w) << x2 << nl;
    cout << "y1 = " << setw(w) << y1 << nl;
    cout << "y2 = " << setw(w) << y2 << nl;

    if (x1 != x2 || y1 != y2)
        cout << "Compare error!" << nl;
}

int main(int argc, char** argv)
{
    int32_t a, b, c, d, x1, x2;
    int64_t e, f, g, h, y1, y2;

    a = 10; b = -20; c = 30; d = -40;
    e = 50; f = -60; g = 70; h = -80;
    LocalVars(a, b, c, d, e, f, g, h, &x1, &y1);
    LocalVars_(a, b, c, d, e, f, g, h, &x2, &y2);
    PrintResult("LocalVarsA - Test Case #1", a, b, c, d, e, f, g, h, x1, y1, x2, y2);

    a = 100; b = -200; c = 300; d = -400;
    e = 500; f = -600; g = 700; h = -800;
    LocalVars(a, b, c, d, e, f, g, h, &x1, &y1);
    LocalVars_(a, b, c, d, e, f, g, h, &x2, &y2);
    PrintResult("LocalVarsA - Test Case #2", a, b, c, d, e, f, g, h, x1, y1, x2, y2);
}

//----------------------------------------------------
//                  Ch12_02_.s
//----------------------------------------------------

// extern "C" void LocalVars_(int32_t a, int32_t b int32_t c, int32_t d,
//   int64_t e, int64_t f, int64_t g, int64_t h, int32_t* x, int64_t* y);

        .equ ARG_X,48              // sp offset for x
        .equ ARG_Y,56              // sp offset for y
        .equ TEMP0,0               // sp offset for temp0
        .equ TEMP1,4               // sp offset for temp1
        .equ TEMP2,8               // sp offset for temp2
        .equ TEMP3,16              // sp offset for temp3
```

```
            .equ LOCAL_VAR_SIZE,32              // size of local var space

            .text
            .global LocalVars_
LocalVars_:

// Prologue
            stp x19,x20,[sp,-16]!               // push x19 and x20
            sub sp,sp,LOCAL_VAR_SIZE            // allocate local var space

// Calculate temp0
            add w8,w0,w1                        // w8 = a + b
            add w8,w8,w2                        // w8 = a + b + c
            str w8,[sp,TEMP0]                   // save temp0

// Calculate temp1
            ldr x19,=g_Val1                     // x19 points to g_Val1
            ldr w19,[x19]                       // w19 = g_Val1
            sub w8,w3,w19                        // w8 = d - g_Val1
            str w8,[sp,TEMP1]                   // save temp1

// Calculate temp2
            add x8,x4,x5                        // x8 = e + f
            add x8,x8,x6                        // x8 = e + f + g
            str x8,[sp,TEMP2]                   // save temp2

// Calculate temp3
            ldr x20,=g_Val2                     // x20 points to g_Val2
            ldr x20,[x20]                       // x20 = g_Val2
            sub x8,x7,x20                        // x8 = h - g_Val2
            str x8,[sp,TEMP3]                   // save temp3

// Calculate x
            ldr w0,[sp,TEMP0]                   // w0 = temp0
            ldr w1,[sp,TEMP1]                   // w1 = temp1
            mul w2,w0,w1                        // w2 = temp0 * temp1
            ldr x3,[sp,ARG_X]                   // x3 = x
            str w2,[x3]                         // save x

// Calculate y
            ldr x0,[sp,TEMP2]                   // x0 = temp2
            ldr x1,[sp,TEMP3]                   // x1 = temp3
            mul x2,x0,x1                        // x2 = temp2 * temp3
            ldr x3,[sp,ARG_Y]                   // x3 = y
            str x2,[x3]                         // save y

// Epilogue
            add sp,sp,LOCAL_VAR_SIZE            // release local storage
            ldp x19,x20,[sp],16                 // pop x19 and x20
            ret
```

The C++ code in Listing 12-2 begins with the definition of global variables g_Val1 and g_Val2. This is followed by a declaration statement for the assembly language function LocalVars_. Note that this function requires a mixture of int32_t and int64_t argument values. The C++ function LocalVars contains code that duplicates the calculations performed by LocalVars_. The remaining C++ code carries out test case initialization and displays results.

The assembly language code in Listing 12-2 begins with a series of equate statements that define stack offsets for argument values x and y. It also includes equate statements for local variables temp1, temp2, temp3, and temp4. The final equate statement, .equ LOCAL_VAR_SIZE,32, defines the amount of stack space that is used for local variables.

The first instruction of LocalVars_, stp x19,x20,[sp,-16]! (store pair of registers), saves non-volatile registers X19 and X20 on the stack. Unlike the A32 instruction set, the A64 instruction set does not include an explicit stack push instruction or equivalent alias instruction. Functions can use the stp and ldp (load pair of registers) to carry out stack push and pop operations. A function should avoid using the str instruction to push a single X register on the stack (e.g., str x0,[sp,-8]!) since this would result in an improperly aligned SP register. Most Armv8-64 platforms require quadword (16-byte) alignment of the SP register and will generate an exception if an instruction attempts to access the stack using an improperly aligned SP register. The next instruction, sub sp,sp,LOCAL_VAR_SIZE, allocates space on the stack for the local variables. Note that LOCAL_VAR_SIZE is 8 bytes larger than necessary to keep SP aligned on a quadword boundary. Figure 12-2 illustrates stack organization and register contents following execution of the prologue instructions in LocalVars_.

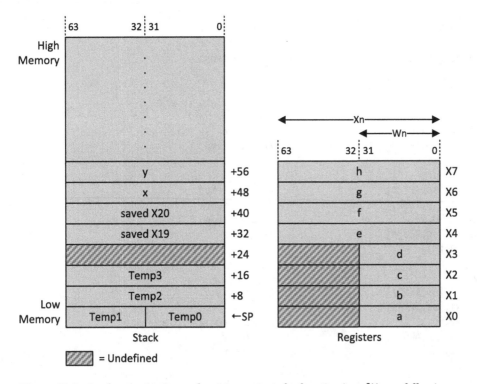

Figure 12-2. Stack organization and register contents for function LocalVars_ following execution of its prologue instructions

Following its prologue, function LocalVars_ calculates temp0, temp1, temp2, and temp3. Note that after each calculation, a str instruction saves the temporary result on the stack. The next two code blocks calculate and save values x and y. These code blocks use the ldr instruction to retrieve the previously calculated temporary values from the stack. The epilogue in function LocalVars_ uses an add sp,sp,LOCAL_VAR_SIZE instruction to release the local variable stack space that was allocated in the prologue. This is followed by a ldp x19,x20,[sp],16 instruction that restores the previously preserved non-volatile registers X19 and X20 from the stack. Here are the results for source code example Ch12_02:

```
LocalVarsA - Test Case #1
a =        10 | b =        -20 | c =        30 | d =       -40
e =        50 | f =        -60 | g =        70 | h =       -80
x1 =    -1000
x2 =    -1000
y1 =    -3600
y2 =    -3600


LocalVarsA - Test Case #2
a =       100 | b =       -200 | c =       300 | d =      -400
e =       500 | f =       -600 | g =       700 | h =      -800
x1 =   -82000
x2 =   -82000
y1 =  -468000
y2 =  -468000
```

Using Condition Flags

The source code examples in this section describe instructions that set the PSTATE condition flags N (negative), Z (zero), C (carry), and V (overflow). The first source code example explains compare operations and conditional branches. The second source code example highlights basic for-loops. This example also illustrates how to call Armv8-64 assembly language functions in accordance with the GNU C++ calling convention.

Compare Instructions

Listing 12-3 shows the source code for example Ch12_03. This example, which is a modified version of source code example Ch03_05, demonstrates the use of the cmp (compare) instruction. It also highlights the use of the PSTATE.NZCV condition flags and conditional branching.

Listing 12-3. Example Ch12_03

```
//----------------------------------------------------
//              Ch12_03.cpp
//----------------------------------------------------

#include <iostream>
#include <cstdint>
```

```cpp
using namespace std;

extern "C" bool CompareSumA_(int32_t a, int32_t b, int32_t c, int32_t* sum);
extern "C" bool CompareSumB_(int64_t a, int64_t b, int64_t c, int64_t* sum);
extern "C" bool CompareSumC_(int32_t a, int32_t b, int32_t c, int32_t* sum);

template <typename T>
void PrintResult(const char* msg, T a, T b, T c, T sum, bool result)
{
    const char nl = '\n';
    const char* sep = " | ";

    cout << msg << nl;
    cout << "a = " << a << sep;
    cout << "b = " << b << sep;
    cout << "c = " << c << sep;
    cout << "sum = " << sum << sep;
    cout << "result = " << boolalpha << result << nl;
    cout << nl;
}

void CompareSumA(void)
{
    bool result;
    int32_t a, b, c, sum;

    a = 10; b = 20; c = 30;
    result = CompareSumA_(a, b, c, &sum);
    PrintResult("CompareSumA_ (sum >= 100) - Test #1", a, b, c, sum, result);

    a = 100; b = -200; c = 400;
    result = CompareSumA_(a, b, c, &sum);
    PrintResult("CompareSumA_ (sum >= 100) - Test #2", a, b, c, sum, result);
}

void CompareSumB(void)
{
    bool result;
    int64_t a, b, c, sum;

    a = 10; b = 20; c = 30;
    result = CompareSumB_(a, b, c, &sum);
    PrintResult("CompareSumB_ (sum > 0) - Test #1", a, b, c, sum, result);

    a = 100; b = -200; c = 50;
    result = CompareSumB_(a, b, c, &sum);
    PrintResult("CompareSumB_ (sum > 0) - Test #2", a, b, c, sum, result);
}
```

```c
void CompareSumC(void)
{
    bool result;
    int32_t a, b, c, sum;

    a = 0x7ffffff0; b = 5; c = 10;
    result = CompareSumC_(a, b, c, &sum);
    PrintResult("CompareSumC_ (overflow?) - Test #1", a, b, c, sum, result);

    a = 0x7ffffff0; b = 5; c = 11;
    result = CompareSumC_(a, b, c, &sum);
    PrintResult("CompareSumC_ (overflow?) - Test #2", a, b, c, sum, result);

    a = 0x7ffffff0; b = 100; c = 200;
    result = CompareSumC_(a, b, c, &sum);
    PrintResult("CompareSumC_ (overflow?) - Test #3", a, b, c, sum, result);

    a = 0x8000000f; b = -5; c = -10;
    result = CompareSumC_(a, b, c, &sum);
    PrintResult("CompareSumC_ (overflow?) - Test #4", a, b, c, sum, result);
}

int main(int argc, char** argv)
{
    CompareSumA();
    CompareSumB();
    CompareSumC();
}
```

```asm
//---------------------------------------------------
//                 Ch12_03_.s
//---------------------------------------------------

// extern "C" bool CompareSumA_(int32_t a, int32_t b, int32_t c, int32_t* sum);

            .text
            .global CompareSumA_
CompareSumA_:

// Calculate a + b + c and save sum
            add w0,w0,w1                        // w0 = a + b
            add w0,w0,w2                        // w0 = a + b + c
            str w0,[x3]                         // save sum

// Is sum >= 100?
            cmp w0,100                          // Compare sum and 100
            b.ge SumGE100                       // jump if sum >= 100

            mov w0,#0                           // set return code to false
            ret
```

```
SumGE100:    mov w0,#1                            // set return code to true
             ret


// extern "C" bool CompareSumB_(int64_t a, int64_t b, int64_t c, int64_t* sum);

             .global CompareSumB_
CompareSumB_:

// Calculate a + b + c and save sum
             add x0,x0,x1                          // x0 = a + b
             adds x0,x0,x2                         // x0 = a + b + c
             str x0,[x3]                           // save sum

             b.gt SumGT0                           // jump if sum > 0

             mov w0,#0                             // set return code to false
             ret

SumGT0:      mov w0,#1                             // set return code to true
             ret


// extern "C" bool CompareSumC_(int32_t a, int32_t b, int32_t c, int32_t* sum);

             .global CompareSumC_
CompareSumC_:
             adds w4,w0,w1                         // w4 = a + b
             cset w5,vs                            // w5 = 1 on overflow

             adds w4,w4,w2                         // w4 = a + b + c
             cset w6,vs                            // w6 = 1 on overflow
             orr w0,w5,w6                          // w0 = 1 on overflow

             str w4,[x3]                           // save sum
             ret
```

Near the top of Listing 12-3 are the declarations for the assembly language functions that carry out various compare operations. The C++ functions CompareSumA, CompareSumB, and CompareSumC contain code that perform test case initialization. These functions also use the template function PrintResult to stream results to cout.

The assembly language function CompareSumA_ calculates the sum of three 32-bit wide signed integers and returns a bool value that indicates if the sum is greater than or equal to 100. The first two instructions of this function, add w0,w0,w1 and add w0,w0,w2, calculate a + b + c. The ensuing str w0,[x3] saves this result to the memory location pointed to by sum. The next instruction, cmp w0,100, compares the contents of W0 to the constant 100. The cmp instruction, which is an alias of the subs instruction, subtracts 100 from register W0 and updates the PSTATE.NZCV condition flags based on the result. The actual result of this subtraction is not saved. The ensuing b.ge SumGE100 (branch conditionally) instruction transfers control to the label SumGE100 if a + b + c >= 100 is true. The A64 conditional branch instruction uses the same mnemonic extensions as its A32 counterpart (see Chapter 3, Table 3-1). Note that in the A64 instruction form, a dot is employed to isolate the mnemonic extension from the primary instruction mnemonic, which improves readability.

Function CompareSumB_ sums three 64-bit wide signed integers and returns a bool value that indicates if the sum is greater than or equal to zero. Execution of CompareSumB_ begins with an add x0,x0,x1 instruction that calculates a + b. This is followed by an adds x0,x0,x2 (add, setting flags) instruction that calculates a + b + c and updates the PSTATE.NZCV flags based on the result. Like the A32 instruction set, the A64 instruction set also includes "s" variants of many arithmetic and bitwise logical instructions. Following the str x0,[x3] instruction is a b.gt SumGT0 instruction that transfers program control to the label SumGT0 if a + b + c > 0 is true. Note that in this function, a separate cmp instruction is not needed since the adds instruction has already set the PSTATE.NZCV condition flags.

The final compare function, CompareSumC_, returns a bool value that signifies the occurrence of an overflow during the summing of argument values a, b, and c. The first instruction of CompareSumC_, adds w4,w0,w1, calculates a + b. This is followed by a cset w5,vs (conditional set) instruction. This instruction sets W4 to 1 if the specified condition (PSTATE.V == 1) is true; otherwise, W4 is set to 0. The cset instruction can use any of the mnemonic extensions that are shown in Chapter 3, Table 3-1. The next two instructions, adds w4,w4,w2 and cset w6,vs, calculate a + b + c and set W6 to 1 if an overflow occurs. The ensuing orr w0,w5,w6 instruction combines the two intermediate cset results into a final result. Note that CompareSumC_ completed its overflow testing sans any branch instructions. Here is the output for source code example Ch12_03:

```
CompareSumA_ (sum >= 100) - Test #1
a = 10 | b = 20 | c = 30 | sum = 60 | result = false

CompareSumA_ (sum >= 100) - Test #2
a = 100 | b = -200 | c = 400 | sum = 300 | result = true

CompareSumB_ (sum > 0) - Test #1
a = 10 | b = 20 | c = 30 | sum = 60 | result = true

CompareSumB_ (sum > 0) - Test #2
a = 100 | b = -200 | c = 50 | sum = -50 | result = false

CompareSumC_ (overflow?) - Test #1
a = 2147483632 | b = 5 | c = 10 | sum = 2147483647 | result = false

CompareSumC_ (overflow?) - Test #2
a = 2147483632 | b = 5 | c = 11 | sum = -2147483648 | result = true

CompareSumC_ (overflow?) - Test #3
a = 2147483632 | b = 100 | c = 200 | sum = -2147483364 | result = true

CompareSumC_ (overflow?) - Test #4
a = -2147483633 | b = -5 | c = -10 | sum = -2147483648 | result = false
```

It should be noted that unlike the A32 instruction set, a mnemonic extension cannot be appended to an A64 instruction mnemonic to carry out conditional instruction execution (e.g., orrvs w0,w5,w6 is invalid). Instead, the cset, csel (conditional select), and b.cond instructions must be used to achieve the same outcome.

Looping

Listing 12-4 shows the source code for example Ch12_04. This example, which is an A64 implementation of source code example Ch03_06, demonstrates the basics of assembly language for-loops. It also illustrates assembly language function calling.

Listing 12-4. Example Ch12_04

```cpp
//----------------------------------------------------
//                  Ch12_04.cpp
//----------------------------------------------------

#include <iostream>
#include <cstdint>

using namespace std;

const int64_t g_ArgnMin = 1;
const int64_t g_ArgnMax = 1023;

extern "C" void SumSquares_(int64_t n, int64_t* sum_a, int64_t* sum_b);

int64_t SumSquaresA(int64_t n)
{
    int64_t sum = 0;

    for (int i = 1; i <= n; i++)
        sum += i * i;

    return sum;
}

int64_t SumSquaresB(int64_t n)
{
    int64_t sum = (n * (n + 1) * (2 * n + 1)) / 6;

    return sum;
}

void SumSquares(int64_t n, int64_t* sum_a, int64_t* sum_b)
{
    *sum_a = *sum_b = 0;

    if (n < g_ArgnMin || n > g_ArgnMax)
        return;

    *sum_a = SumSquaresA(n);
    *sum_b = SumSquaresB(n);
}
```

```cpp
void PrintResult(const char* msg, int64_t n, int64_t sum_a1, int64_t sum_a2, int64_t sum_b1,
int64_t sum_b2)
{
    const char nl = '\n';
    const char* sep = " | ";

    cout << nl << msg << nl;
    cout << "n = " << n << nl;
    cout << "sum_a1 = " << sum_a1 << sep << "sum_a2 = " << sum_a2 << nl;
    cout << "sum_b1 = " << sum_b1 << sep << "sum_b2 = " << sum_b2 << nl;

    if (sum_a1 != sum_a2 || sum_a1 != sum_b1 || sum_a1 != sum_b2)
        cout << "Compare error!\n";
}

int main(int argc, char** argv)
{
    int64_t n, sum_a1, sum_a2, sum_b1, sum_b2;

    n = 3;
    SumSquares(n, &sum_a1, &sum_b1);
    SumSquares_(n, &sum_a2, &sum_b2);
    PrintResult("SumSquares - Test #1", n, sum_a1, sum_a2, sum_b1, sum_b2);

    n = 42;
    SumSquares(n, &sum_a1, &sum_b1);
    SumSquares_(n, &sum_a2, &sum_b2);
    PrintResult("SumSquares - Test #2", n, sum_a1, sum_a2, sum_b1, sum_b2);

    n = 1023;
    SumSquares(n, &sum_a1, &sum_b1);
    SumSquares_(n, &sum_a2, &sum_b2);
    PrintResult("SumSquares - Test #3", n, sum_a1, sum_a2, sum_b1, sum_b2);

    return 0;
}

//-----------------------------------------------------
//                  Ch12_04_.s
//-----------------------------------------------------

// static int SumSquaresA_(int64_t n);

            .text
SumSquaresA_:

// Calculate sum of squares using for-loop
            mov x1,1                        // i = 1
            mov x2,0                        // sum = 0

Loop1:      madd x2,x1,x1,x2                // sum += i * i
```

```
            add x1,x1,1                    // i += 1
            cmp x1,x0
            b.le Loop1                     // jump if i <= n

            mov x0,x2                      // x0 = final sum
            ret

// static int SumSquaresB_(int64_t n);

SumSquaresB_:

// Calculate sum = (n * (n + 1) * (2 * n + 1)) / 6
            add x1,x0,1                    // x1 = n + 1
            mul x2,x0,x1                   // x2 = n * (n + 1)

            lsl x3,x0,1                    // r3 = 2 * n
            add x3,x3,1                    // r3 = 2 * n + 1
            mul x3,x3,x2                   // r3 = dividend

            mov x1,6                       // r1 = divisor
            sdiv x0,x3,x1                  // r0 = final sum
            ret

// extern "C" void SumSquares_(int64_t n, int64_t* sum_a, int64_t* sum_b);

            .equ SAVE_N,0                  // offset for save of n
            .equ SAVE_SUM_A,8              // offset for save of sum_a
            .equ SAVE_SUM_B,16             // offset for save of sum_b
            .equ SAVE_LR,24                // offset for save of lr

            .equ ARG_N_MIN,1               // argument n minimum value
            .equ ARG_N_MAX,1023            // argument n maximum value

            .equ LOCAL_VAR_SPACE,32        // local variable space

            .global SumSquares_
SumSquares_:
// Function prologue
            sub sp,sp,LOCAL_VAR_SPACE      // allocate local var space

// Save arguments to stack
            str x0,[sp,SAVE_N]             // save arg n
            str x1,[sp,SAVE_SUM_A]         // save arg sum_a
            str x2,[sp,SAVE_SUM_B]         // save arg sum_b
            str lr,[sp,SAVE_LR]            // save link register

// Set sum_a and sum_b to zero
            mov x3,0
            str x3,[x1]                    // sum_a = 0
            str x3,[x2]                    // sum_b = 0
```

```
// Verify n >= ARG_N_MIN && n <= ARG_N_MAX
          cmp x0,ARG_N_MIN
          b.lt Done                         // jump if n < ARG_N_MIN
          cmp x0,ARG_N_MAX
          b.gt Done                         // jump if n > ARG_N_MAX

// Calculate sum_a
          bl SumSquaresA_                   // call SumSquaresA_
          ldr x1,[sp,SAVE_SUM_A]
          str x0,[x1]                       // save sum_a

// Calculate sum_b
          ldr x0,[sp,SAVE_N]                // reload arg value n
          bl SumSquaresB_                   // call SumSquaresB_
          ldr x1,[sp,SAVE_SUM_B]
          str x0,[x1]                       // save sum_b

// Restore LR register
          ldr lr,[sp,SAVE_LR]               // restore link register

// Function epilogue
Done:     add sp,sp,LOCAL_VAR_SPACE         // release local var space
          ret
```

The C++ and assembly language code in Listing 12-4 includes functions that calculate sum of squares using the following equations:

$$sum_a = \sum_{i=1}^{n} i^2$$

$$sum_b = \frac{n(n+1)(2n+1)}{6}$$

The C++ code defines two functions, SumSquaresA and SumSquaresB, that calculate sum_a and sum_b, respectively. The function SumSquares performs some basic error checking and calls SumSquaresA and SumSquaresB. As you will soon see, the assembly language code follows the same design pattern as the C++ code. The remaining C++ code performs test case initialization and prints results.

The assembly language code in Listing 12-4 begins with the definition of function SumSquaresA_. This function calculates sum_a using a simple for-loop. It begins with a mov x1,1 instruction that sets i = 1. The next instruction, mov x2,0, initializes sum to zero. Each iteration of Loop1 begins with a madd x2,x1,x1,x2 instruction that calculates sum += i * i. The next instruction, add x1,x1,1, updates index variable i. The ensuing cmp x1,x0 and b.le Loop1 instructions ensure that Loop1 repeats while i <= n is true. The final instruction of SumSquaresA_, mov x0,x2, copies the final sum into X0 so that it can be returned to the calling function. The assembly language function SumSquaresB_ calculates sum_b using basic integer arithmetic.

The assembly language function SumSquares_ resembles its C++ counterpart. This function begins its execution with a sub sp,sp,LOCAL_VAR_SPACE instruction that allocates local variable space on the stack. The next code block contains a series of str instructions that save argument values n, sum_a, and sum_b on the stack. These values are saved since they are in volatile registers and SumSquares_ calls other functions. Register LR (X30) is also saved since this register contains the return address that SumSquares_ must use to return program control back to its calling function. Figure 12-3 illustrates organization of the stack and register contents following execution of the str lr,[sp,SAVE_LR] instruction.

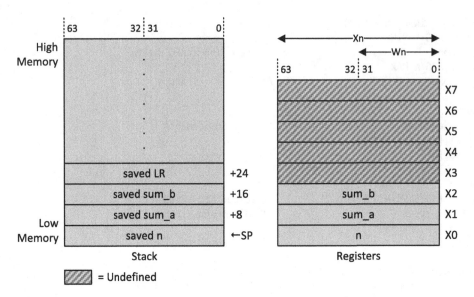

Figure 12-3. Stack organization and register contents for SumSquares_ following execution of the str lr,[sp,SAVE_LR] *instruction*

After the stack save operations, SumSquares_ sets sum_a and sum_b equal to zero. The next two instructions, cmp x0,ARG_N_MIN and b.lt Done, verify that n is not less than ARG_N_MIN. This is followed by the instruction pair cmp x0,ARG_N_MAX and b.gt Done that verifies n is not greater than ARG_N_MAX.

The bl SumSquaresA_ (branch with link) instruction calls function SumSquaresA_. Note that execution of this instruction also copies the address of the next instruction (i.e., the instruction located at PC + 4) into LR. The ensuing ldr x1,[sp,SAVE_SUM_A] and str x0,[x1] instructions save the calculated value to sum_a. Function SumSquaresB_ is called next. Note that a ldr x0,[sp,SAVE_N] instruction, which reloads X0 with n, precedes the bl SumSquaresB_ instruction. The result returned by SumSquaresB_ is saved to sum_b using the instruction pair ldr x1,[sp,SAVE_SUM_B] and ldr x1,[sp,SAVE_SUM_B].

Following execution of function SumSquaresB_, a ldr lr,[sp,SAVE_LR] instruction restores the LR register from the stack. This is followed by an add sp,sp,LOCAL_VAR_SPACE instruction that releases the previously allocated local stack space. Here are the results for source code example Ch12_04:

```
SumSquares - Test #1
n = 3
sum_a1 = 14 | sum_a2 = 14
sum_b1 = 14 | sum_b2 = 14

SumSquares - Test #2
n = 42
sum_a1 = 25585 | sum_a2 = 25585
sum_b1 = 25585 | sum_b2 = 25585

SumSquares - Test #3
n = 1023
sum_a1 = 357389824 | sum_a2 = 357389824
sum_b1 = 357389824 | sum_b2 = 357389824
```

Integer Arrays and Matrices

In Chapter 4, you learned how to use the A32 instruction set to code functions that accessed the elements of an array or matrix. In this chapter, you will learn how to perform the same operations using the A64 instruction set. The first source code example highlights simple arithmetic using the elements of an integer array. The second source code example explains how to sum the rows and columns of an integer matrix.

Integer Arrays

Listing 12-5 shows the source code for example Ch12_05. This example, which is an A64 implementation of example Ch04_01, illustrates how to access the elements of an integer array and simple integer arithmetic.

Listing 12-5. Example Ch12_05

```
//----------------------------------------------------
//                Ch12_05.cpp
//----------------------------------------------------

#include <iostream>
#include <iomanip>
#include <cstdint>

using namespace std;

extern "C" int CalcArraySumA_(const int* x, int n);
extern "C" uint64_t CalcArraySumB_(const uint64_t* x, uint32_t n);

int CalcArraySumA(const int* x, int n)
{
    int sum = 0;

    for (int i = 0; i < n; i++)
        sum += *x++;

    return sum;
}

uint64_t CalcArraySumB(const uint64_t* x, uint32_t n)
{
    uint64_t sum = 0;

    for (uint32_t i = 0; i < n; i++)
        sum += x[i];

    return sum;
}
```

```
void ArraySumA(void)
{
    const char nl = '\n';
    int x[] {3, 17, -13, 25, -2, 9, -6, 12, 88, -19, 9, 35};
    int n = sizeof(x) / sizeof(int);

    cout << "Results for ArraySumA" << nl;

    for (int i = 0; i < n; i++)
        cout << "x[" << i << "] = " << x[i] << nl;

    int sum1 = CalcArraySumA(x, n);
    int sum2 = CalcArraySumA_(x, n);

    cout << "sum1 = " << sum1 << " | sum2 = " << sum2 << nl << nl;
}

void ArraySumB(void)
{
    const char nl = '\n';
    uint64_t x[] = {0x10000000, 0x20000000, 0x30000000, 0x40000000,
                    0x50000000, 0x60000000, 0x70000000, 0x80000000,
                    0x90000000, 0xA0000000, 0xB0000000, 0xC0000000,
                    0xD0000000, 0xE0000000, 0xF0000000};
    uint32_t n = sizeof(x) / sizeof(uint64_t);

    cout << "Results for ArraySumB" << nl;

    for (uint32_t i = 0; i < n; i++)
        cout << "x[" << i << "] = " << x[i] << nl;

    uint64_t sum1 = CalcArraySumB(x, n);
    uint64_t sum2 = CalcArraySumB_(x, n);

    cout << "sum1 = " << sum1 << " | sum2 = " << sum2 << nl << nl;
}

int main()
{
    ArraySumA();
    ArraySumB();
    return 0;
}

//----------------------------------------------------
//                   Ch12_05_.s
//----------------------------------------------------

// extern "C" int CalcArraySumA_(const int* x, int n);
```

```
            .text
            .global CalcArraySumA_
CalcArraySumA_:

            mov w2,0                        // sum = 0
            cmp w1,w0                       // is n <= 0?
            b.le DoneA                      // jump if n <= 0

LoopA:      ldr w3,[x0],4                   // w3 = x[i]
            add w2,w2,w3                    // sum += x[i]

            subs w1,w1,1                    // n -= 1
            b.ne LoopA                      // jump if more data

DoneA:      mov w0,w2                       // w0 = final sum
            ret


// extern "C" uint64_t CalcArraySumB_(const uint64_t* x, uint32_t n);

            .global CalcArraySumB_
CalcArraySumB_:

            mov x2,0                        // sum = 0
            cmp w1,0                        // is n == 0?
            b.eq DoneB                      // jump if n == 0

            mov w3,0                        // i = 0

LoopB:      ldr x4,[x0,w3,uxtw 3]           // r5 = x[i]
            add x2,x2,x4                    // sum += x[i]

            add w3,w3,1                     // i += 1
            cmp w3,w1                       // is i == n?
            b.ne LoopB                      // jump if more data

DoneB:      mov x0,x2
            ret
```

Toward the top of listing 12-5 are the declarations for the assembly language functions CalcArraySumA_ and CalcArraySumB_. Note that CalcSumArrayB_ requires an input array of type uint64_t and an element count of type uint32_t. The C++ code includes functions CalcSumArrayA and CalcSumArrayB. These functions sum the elements of an integer array. The remaining C++ code performs test case initialization and displays results.

The first instruction of function CalcArraySumA_, mov w2,0, sets sum = 0. This is followed by the instruction pair cmp w1,w0 and b.le DoneA, which verifies that argument value n is greater than zero. The for-loop LoopA commences each iteration with a ldr w3,[x0],4 instruction that loads the value pointed to by X0 (i.e., the next element in array x) into register W3. The ensuing add w2,w2,w3 instruction adds the current element from array x to sum. This load-add instruction pair sequence repeats until all of the elements in array x have been processed.

Function CalcArraySumB_ employs a 32-bit wide index register to access elements in an array of 64-bit unsigned integers. Upon entry to this function, argument value n is tested to make sure it is greater than zero.

The mov w3,0 instruction sets i = 0. Each iteration of for-loop LoopB begins with a ldr x4,[x0,w3,uxtw 3] instruction that loads x[i] into X4. This instruction, which uses extended register addressing (see Chapter 10, Table 10-4), zero-extends index variable i in W3 to 64 bits. It then left shifts the zero-extend index value 3-bit positions and sums the shifted value with X0 to obtain the final memory address. The ensuing add x2,x2,x4 instruction calculates sum += x[i]. For-loop LoopB repeats until i is equal to n. Here are the results for source code example Ch12_05:

```
Results for ArraySumA
x[0] = 3
x[1] = 17
x[2] = -13
x[3] = 25
x[4] = -2
x[5] = 9
x[6] = -6
x[7] = 12
x[8] = 88
x[9] = -19
x[10] = 9
x[11] = 35
sum1 = 158 | sum2 = 158

Results for ArraySumB
x[0] = 268435456
x[1] = 536870912
x[2] = 805306368
x[3] = 1073741824
x[4] = 1342177280
x[5] = 1610612736
x[6] = 1879048192
x[7] = 2147483648
x[8] = 2415919104
x[9] = 2684354560
x[10] = 2952790016
x[11] = 3221225472
x[12] = 3489660928
x[13] = 3758096384
x[14] = 4026531840
sum1 = 32212254720 | sum2 = 32212254720
```

Integer Matrices

Listing 12-6 shows the source code for example Ch12_06, which demonstrates how to sum the rows and columns of an integer matrix. This example is an A64 implementation of source code example Ch04_04.

Listing 12-6. Example Ch12_06

```
//-----------------------------------------------------
//                    Ch12_06.cpp
//-----------------------------------------------------

#include <iostream>
#include <iomanip>
#include <cstdint>
#include <random>

using namespace std;

extern "C" bool CalcMatrixRowColSums_(int64_t* row_sums, int64_t* col_sums, const
int64_t* x, int nrows, int ncols);

void Init(int64_t* x, int nrows, int ncols)
{
    unsigned int seed = 13;
    uniform_int_distribution<> d {1, 200};
    mt19937 rng {seed};

    for (int i = 0; i < nrows * ncols; i++)
        x[i] = d(rng);
}

void PrintResult(const char* msg, const int64_t* row_sums, const int64_t* col_sums,
const int64_t* x, int nrows, int ncols)
{
    const int w = 6;
    const char nl = '\n';

    cout << msg;
    cout << "----------------------------------------\n";

    for (int i = 0; i < nrows; i++)
    {
        for (int j = 0; j < ncols; j++)
            cout << setw(w) << x[i* ncols + j];
        cout << "   " << setw(w) << row_sums[i] << nl;
    }

    cout << nl;

    for (int i = 0; i < ncols; i++)
        cout << setw(w) << col_sums[i];
    cout << nl;
}
```

```c
bool CalcMatrixRowColSums(int64_t* row_sums, int64_t* col_sums, const int64_t* x, int nrows,
int ncols)
{
    bool rc = false;

    if (nrows > 0 && ncols > 0)
    {
        for (int j = 0; j < ncols; j++)
            col_sums[j] = 0;

        for (int i = 0; i < nrows; i++)
        {
            row_sums[i] = 0;
            int k = i * ncols;

            for (int j = 0; j < ncols; j++)
            {
                int64_t temp = x[k + j];
                row_sums[i] += temp;
                col_sums[j] += temp;
            }
        }

        rc = true;
    }

    return rc;
}

int main()
{
    const int nrows = 7;
    const int ncols = 5;
    int64_t x[nrows][ncols];
    int64_t* px = &x[0][0];

    Init(px, nrows, ncols);

    int64_t row_sums1[nrows], col_sums1[ncols];
    int64_t row_sums2[nrows], col_sums2[ncols];

    const char* msg1 = "\nResults using CalcMatrixRowColSums\n";
    const char* msg2 = "\nResults using CalcMatrixRowColSums_\n";

    bool rc1, rc2;
    rc1 = CalcMatrixRowColSums(row_sums1, col_sums1, px, nrows, ncols);
    rc2 = CalcMatrixRowColSums_(row_sums2, col_sums2, px, nrows, ncols);
```

270

```
    if (!rc1)
        cout << "CalcMatrixRowSums failed\n";
    else
        PrintResult(msg1, row_sums1, col_sums1, px, nrows, ncols);

    if (!rc2)
        cout << "CalcMatrixRowSums_ failed\n";
    else
        PrintResult(msg2, row_sums2, col_sums2, px, nrows, ncols);

    return 0;
}
```

```
//---------------------------------------------------
//               Ch12_06_.s
//---------------------------------------------------

// extern "C" bool CalcMatrixRowColSums_(int64_t* row_sums, int64_t* col_sums,
//    const int64_t* x, int nrows, int ncols);

            .text
            .global CalcMatrixRowColSums_

CalcMatrixRowColSums_:
            cmp w3,0
            b.le Error                          // jump if nrows <= 0
            cmp w4,0
            b.le Error                          // jump if ncols <= 0

// Set col_sums to zero
            mov x5,x1                           // x5 = col_sums
            mov w6,w4                           // w6 = ncols
            mov x7,0
Loop0:      str x7,[x5],8                       // col_sums[j] = 0
            subs w6,w6,1
            b.ne Loop0

// Main processing loops
            mov w5,0                            // i = 0

Loop1:      mov w6,0                            // j = 0
            str x6,[x0,w5,sxtw 3]               // row_sums[i] = 0

            mul w7,w5,w4                        // w7 = i * ncols

Loop2:      add w8,w7,w6                        // w8 = i * ncols + j
            ldr x9,[x2,w8,sxtw 3]               // x9 = x[i][j]
```

```
// Update row_sums and col_sums using current x[i][j]
            add x10,x0,w5,sxtw 3        // x10 = ptr to row_sums[i]
            ldr x11,[x10]               // x11 = row_sums[i]
            add x11,x11,x9              // row_sums[i] += x[i][j]
            str x11,[x10]              // save updated row_sums[i]

            add x10,x1,w6,sxtw 3        // x10 = ptr to col_sums[j]
            ldr x11,[x10]               // x11 = col_sums[j]
            add x11,x11,x9              // col_sums[j] += x[i][j]
            str x11,[x10]              // save updated col_sums[j]

            add w6,w6,1                 // j += 1
            cmp w6,w4
            b.lt Loop2                  // jump if j < ncols

            add w5,w5,1                 // i += 1
            cmp w5,w3
            b.lt Loop1                  // jump if i < nrows

            mov w0,1                    // set success return code
            ret

Error:      mov w0,0                    // set error return code
            ret
```

Near the top of Listing 12-6 is a function named Init that initializes a test matrix with random values. The C++ function CalcMatrixRowColSums calculates row and column sums for matrix x. This function sweeps through matrix x using two nested for-loops. During each inner loop iteration, CalcMatrixRowColsSums adds matrix element x[i][j] to the appropriate entries in arrays col_sums and row_sums.

The assembly language function CalcMatrixRowSums_ mimics the nested for-loop and matrix element address calculations used in the C++ function CalcMatrixRowSums. It begins with a validation check of nrows and ncols to confirm that these argument values are greater than zero. This is followed by for-loop Loop0 that sets each element in col_sums to zero. Note that the first instruction in Loop0, str x7,[x5],8, uses a value of 8 for the post-indexed addressing constant since each element of col_sums is a 64-bit wide signed integer. Following execution of Loop0, the mov w5,0 instruction sets i = 0.

The outer for-loop Loop1 begins each iteration with a mov w6,0 instruction that sets j = 0. This is followed by a str x6,[x0,w5,sxtw 3] instruction that sets row_sums[i] = 0. The sxtw operator is used in this instruction since i, j, nrows, and ncols are 32-bit signed integers. (The uxtw operator would also work here since in this example, the previously mentioned variables are always greater than or equal to zero.) The ensuing mul w7,w5,w4 instruction calculates i * ncols.

The first instruction of for-loop Loop2, add w8,w7,w6, calculates i * ncols + j. The next instruction, ldr x9,[x2,w8,sxtw 3], loads x[i][j] into register X9. The next code block updates row_sums[i]. It begins with an add x10,x0,w5,sxtw 3 instruction that calculates the address of row_sums[i]. The next three instructions, ldr x11,[x10], add x11,x11,x9, and str x11,[x10], add x[i][j] to row_sums[i]. Following the updating of row_sums[i], the next code block calculates col_sums[j] += x[i][j] using a similar series of instructions. Loop2 continues to repeat so long as j < ncols is true. After Loop2 completes its execution, index variable i is updated and Loop1 repeats while i < nrows is true. Here is the output for source code example Ch12_06:

```
Results using CalcMatrixRowColSums
-------------------------------------------
    156    122     48    172    165    663
    179    194     36    195    152    756
     91    151    122    122    156    642
    159    129     78    145     69    580
      8    133     60    182     12    395
    145    172     95     75    100    587
    136     90     52    107     70    455

    874    991    491    998    724

Results using CalcMatrixRowColSums_
-------------------------------------------
    156    122     48    172    165    663
    179    194     36    195    152    756
     91    151    122    122    156    642
    159    129     78    145     69    580
      8    133     60    182     12    395
    145    172     95     75    100    587
    136     90     52    107     70    455

    874    991    491    998    724
```

Summary

Here are the key learning points for Chapter 12:

- A function can use the cmp instruction to set the PSTATE.NZCV condition flags. The "s" variant forms of some arithmetic and bitwise logical instructions (e.g., adds, ands, orrs, subs, etc.) also update the PSTATE.NZCV condition flags.

- The cset instruction sets its destination operand to 1 if the specified condition is true; otherwise, it is set to 0.

- The b.cond conditional branch instruction can be used to make logical decisions based on the state of the PSTATE condition flags.

- The madd instruction performs multiply-add operations using signed or unsigned integer operands.

- A function can use extended register addressing to load elements from an array or matrix using a 32-bit wide index variable.

- Argument values passed in a register or via the stack are not size-extended to 64 bits. A function must use an appropriate size-extend instruction (sxtb, sxth, sxtw, uxtb, uxth) or an ldr instruction form (ldrb, ldrh, ldrsb, ldrsh, ldrsw) to zero- or sign-extend a value to 32 or 64 bits.

- The GNU C++ calling convention uses register X0–X7 (or W0–W7) for the first eight integer (or pointer) argument values. Any remaining arguments are passed via the stack.

- The GNU C++ calling convention designates registers X0–X17 as volatile. It also designates X19–X30 as non-volatile. X18 is a platform-specific register.

CHAPTER 13

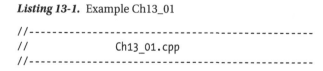

Armv8-64 Floating-Point Programming

In Chapter 6, you learned how to use the A32 instruction set to perform floating-point arithmetic using single-precision and double-precision values. You also learned how to use a variety of floating-point comparison and conversion instructions. In this chapter, you will learn about A64 floating-point instructions and assembly language programming. The chapter begins with a section that describes essential floating-point arithmetic. It continues with a second section that explains floating-point comparisons and conversions. The next section covers floating-point arithmetic using arrays and matrices. In the final section, you will learn how to call C++ floating-point library functions from an assembly language function.

Most of the Armv8-64 source code examples in this chapter are direct ports of the Armv8-32 source code examples that you saw in Chapter 6. As you work through the examples in this chapter, you will notice that there are many similarities between the Armv8-64 and Armv8-32 floating-point environments despite the disparate register architectures and different instruction mnemonics.

Floating-Point Arithmetic

This section contains source code examples that explain how to perform scalar floating-point arithmetic using the A64 instruction set. The source code examples demonstrate fundamental operations using both single-precision and double-precision values. The source code examples also elucidate the passing of floating-point argument and return values between a C++ and an Armv8-64 assembly language function.

Single-Precision Arithmetic

Source code example Ch13_01, shown in Listing 13-1, contains functions that perform conversions between Fahrenheit and Celsius temperature values. The C++ code begins with the declarations of functions ConvertFtoC_ and ConvertCtoF_. Note that these functions require a single argument value of type float and return a value of type float. The remaining C++ code exercises the two temperature conversion functions using several test values and displays the results.

Listing 13-1. Example Ch13_01

```
//--------------------------------------------------
//           Ch13_01.cpp
//--------------------------------------------------
```

© Daniel Kusswurm 2020
D. Kusswurm, *Modern Arm Assembly Language Programming*,
https://doi.org/10.1007/978-1-4842-6267-2_13

```cpp
#include <iostream>
#include <iomanip>

using namespace std;

extern "C" float ConvertFtoC_(float deg_f);
extern "C" float ConvertCtoF_(float deg_c);

int main()
{
    const int w = 10;
    float deg_fvals[] = {-459.67f, -40.0f, 0.0f, 32.0f, 72.0f, 98.6f, 212.0f};
    size_t nf = sizeof(deg_fvals) / sizeof(float);

    cout << setprecision(6);

    cout << "\n-------- ConvertFtoC Results --------\n";

    for (size_t i = 0; i < nf; i++)
    {
        float deg_c = ConvertFtoC_(deg_fvals[i]);

        cout << "  i: " << i << "  ";
        cout << "f: " << setw(w) << deg_fvals[i] << "  ";
        cout << "c: " << setw(w) << deg_c << '\n';
    }

    cout << "\n-------- ConvertCtoF Results --------\n";

    float deg_cvals[] = {-273.15f, -40.0f, -17.777778f, 0.0f, 25.0f, 37.0f, 100.0f};
    size_t nc = sizeof(deg_cvals) / sizeof(float);

    for (size_t i = 0; i < nc; i++)
    {
        float deg_f = ConvertCtoF_(deg_cvals[i]);

        cout << "  i: " << i << "  ";
        cout << "c: " << setw(w) << deg_cvals[i] << "  ";
        cout << "f: " << setw(w) << deg_f << '\n';
    }

    return 0;
}

//--------------------------------------------------
//                 Ch13_01_.s
//--------------------------------------------------
```

```
// Constants for temperature conversion functions
            .text
r4_ScaleFtoC:   .single 0.55555556          // 5 / 9
r4_ScaleCtoF:   .single 1.8                 // 9 / 5
r4_32p0:        .single 32.0

// extern "C" float ConvertFtoC_(float deg_f);

          .global ConvertFtoC_
ConvertFtoC_:

// Convert deg_f to Celsius
          ldr s1,r4_32p0              // s1 = 32
          ldr s2,r4_ScaleFtoC         // s2 = 5 / 9
          fsub s3,s0,s1               // s3 = deg_f - 32
          fmul s0,s3,s2               // s0 = (deg_f - 32) * 5 / 9
          ret

// extern "C" float ConvertCtoF_(float deg_c);

          .global ConvertCtoF_
ConvertCtoF_:

// Convert deg_c to Fahrenheit
          ldr s1,r4_32p0              // s1 = 32
          ldr s2,r4_ScaleCtoF         // s2 = 9 / 5
          fmul s3,s0,s2               // s3 = deg_c * 9 / 5
          fadd s0,s3,s1               // s3 = deg_c * 9 / 5 + 32
          ret
```

Functions ConvertFtoC_ and ConvertCtoF_ use the same equations that were used in source code example Ch06_01 to convert temperature values between Fahrenheit and Celsius. The assembly language source code in Listing 13-1 begins with a series of .single directives that define the floating-point constants needed to convert a temperature value from Fahrenheit to Celsius and vice versa. Note that these constants are defined in the same .text section as the assembly language functions ConvertFtoC_ and ConvertCtoF_, which means that they are read-only values.

The first instruction of ConvertFtoC_, ldr s1,r4_32p0, loads the single-precision floating-point value that is specified by the label r4_32p0 into register S1. Execution of this instruction loads 32.0 into S1. The form of the ldr instruction that is used here requires the source operand r4_32p0 to be located within ±1 megabyte of the PC register. This explains why the conversion constants were placed in the same .text section as the assembly language functions. The next instruction, ldr s2,r4_ScaleFtoC, loads the Fahrenheit to Celsius scale factor 0.55555556 into register S2.

Before examining the remaining assembly language code, a few words about the GNU C++ calling convention and floating-point values are necessary. According to the calling convention, the first eight floating-point argument values are passed to a function using registers S0–S7 (single-precision) or registers D0–D7 (double-precision). Any remaining floating-point arguments are passed via the stack. A function must use register S0 or D0 to return a single-precision or double-precision floating-point value to its caller.

Recall from the discussions in Chapter 10 that each floating-point S and D register occupies the low-order 32 and 64 bits of its corresponding V register (see Chapter 10, Figure 10-2). The GNU C++ calling convention designates all SIMD/FP V registers as volatile, except for the low-order 64 bits of registers V8–V15 (i.e., registers D8–D15). Like the general-purpose registers, a function must preserve the contents of any non-volatile SIMD/FP register it uses. Table 13-1 summaries the GNU C++ calling convention for the SIMD/FP registers. You will learn additional details about the GNU C++ calling convention and SIMD/FP register use later in this chapter.

Table 13-1. *SIMD/FP register use for GNU C++ calling convention*

Register	Type	Description
V0	Volatile	First floating-point argument, return value, scratch register
V1	Volatile	Second floating-point argument, scratch register
V2	Volatile	Third floating-point argument, scratch register
V3	Volatile	Fourth floating-point argument, scratch register
V4	Volatile	Fifth floating-point argument, scratch register
V5	Volatile	Sixth floating-point argument, scratch register
V6	Volatile	Seventh floating-point argument, scratch register
V7	Volatile	Eighth floating-point argument, scratch register
V8–V15	Non-volatile (only D8–D15)	Scratch registers
V16–V31	Volatile	Scratch registers

Following the two ldr instructions, ConvertFtoC_ uses a fsub s3,s0,s1 (floating-point subtract) instruction that calculates deg_f - 32.0. Note that argument value deg_f was passed to ConvertFtoC_ in register S0 per the GNU C++ calling convention. The next instruction, fmul s0,s3,s2 (floating-point multiply), calculates (deg_f - 32) * 5 / 9. No additional instructions are necessary since the required result is already in register S0.

Assembly language function ConvertCtoF_ uses similar A64 instructions to perform a Celsius to Fahrenheit conversion. The ldr s1,r4_32p0 and ldr s2,r4_ScaleCtoF instructions load the requisite conversion constants into registers S1 and S2. The ensuing fmul s3,s0,s2 instruction calculates deg_c * 9 / 5. This is followed by a fadd s0,s3,s1 (floating-point add) instruction that computes the final Fahrenheit temperature value. Here are the results for source code example Ch13_01:

```
-------- ConvertFtoC Results --------
  i: 0  f:   -459.67  c:   -273.15
  i: 1  f:       -40  c:       -40
  i: 2  f:         0  c:  -17.7778
  i: 3  f:        32  c:         0
  i: 4  f:        72  c:   22.2222
  i: 5  f:      98.6  c:        37
  i: 6  f:       212  c:       100

-------- ConvertCtoF Results --------
  i: 0  c:   -273.15  f:   -459.67
  i: 1  c:       -40  f:       -40
  i: 2  c:  -17.7778  f:         0
  i: 3  c:         0  f:        32
  i: 4  c:        25  f:        77
  i: 5  c:        37  f:      98.6
  i: 6  c:       100  f:       212
```

Double-Precision Arithmetic

Listing 13-2 shows the source code for example Ch13_02. In this example, the assembly language code calculates the surface area and volume of a sphere. Note that the declaration of function CalcSphereAreaVolume_ includes an argument value of type double for the radius and two pointers of type double* for the computed surface area and volume.

Listing 13-2. Example Ch13_02

```
//----------------------------------------------------
//                   Ch13_02.cpp
//----------------------------------------------------

#include <iostream>
#include <iomanip>

using namespace std;

extern "C" void CalcSphereAreaVolume_(double r, double* sa, double* vol);

int main(int argc, char** argv)
{
    double r[] = { 0.0, 1.0, 2.0, 3.0, 5.0, 10.0, 20.0, 32.0 };
    size_t num_r = sizeof(r) / sizeof(double);

    cout << setprecision(8);
    cout << "\n--------- Results for CalcSphereAreaVolume -----------\n";

    for (size_t i = 0; i < num_r; i++)
    {
        double sa = -1, vol = -1;

        CalcSphereAreaVolume_(r[i], &sa, &vol);

        cout << "i: " << i << "   ";
        cout << "r: " << setw(6) << r[i] << "   ";
        cout << "sa: " << setw(11) << sa << "   ";
        cout << "vol: " << setw(11) << vol << '\n';
    }

    return 0;
}

//----------------------------------------------------
//                   Ch13_02_.s
//----------------------------------------------------

// extern "C" void CalcSphereAreaVolume_(double r, double* sa, double* vol);

        .text
        .global CalcSphereAreaVolume_
CalcSphereAreaVolume_:
```

```
// Calculate surface area and volume
                ldr d5,r8_PI            // d5 = PI
                fmov d6,4.0            // d6 = 4.0
                fmov d7,3.0            // d7 = 3.0

                fmul d1,d0,d0          // d1 = r * r
                fmul d1,d1,d5          // d1 = r * r * PI
                fmul d1,d1,d6          // d1 = r * r * PI * 4
                str d1,[x0]           // save surface area

                fmul d2,d1,d0          // d2 = sa * r
                fdiv d3,d2,d7          // d3 = sa * r / 3
                str d3,[x1]           // save volume
                ret

r8_PI:      .double 3.14159265358979323846
```

Function CalcSphereAreaVolume_ uses the same equations that were employed in source code example Ch06_02 to calculate the surface area and volume of a sphere. The first instruction in CalcSphereAreaVolume_, ldr d5,r8_PI, loads π into register D5. In this instruction, the label r8_PI defines the memory location for the constant π, which is located immediately after the ret instruction. The next two instructions, fmov d6,4.0 (floating-point move) and fmov d7,3.0, load constants 4.0 and 3.0 into registers D6 and D7, respectively. A function can use the fmov instruction to a load single-precision or double-precision floating-point modified immediate constant. Table 6-2 (see Chapter 6) contains a list of valid floating-point modified immediate constants. The GNU assembler will generate an "invalid floating-point constant" error message if the fmov instruction is used with an invalid floating-point modified immediate constant. In these cases, the ldr instruction can be employed to load the required constant.

The next three instructions, fmul d1,d0,d0, fmul d1,d1,d5, and fmul d1,d1,d6, calculate the surface area. The ensuing str d1,[x0] instruction saves this value to the memory location specified by argument value sa. Following calculation of the surface area, the instruction pair, fmul d2,d1,d0 and fdiv d3,d2,d7 (floating-point divide), calculates the sphere's volume. The str d3,[x1] instruction saves this value to the memory location specified by argument value vol. Note that in this example, pointer arguments sa and vol were passed in registers X0 and X1, respectively. Here are the results for source code example Ch13_02:

```
--------- Results for CalcSphereAreaVolume -----------
i: 0  r:     0  sa:        0  vol:         0
i: 1  r:     1  sa:  12.566371  vol:  4.1887902
i: 2  r:     2  sa:  50.265482  vol:  33.510322
i: 3  r:     3  sa:  113.09734  vol:  113.09734
i: 4  r:     5  sa:  314.15927  vol:  523.59878
i: 5  r:    10  sa:  1256.6371  vol:  4188.7902
i: 6  r:    20  sa:  5026.5482  vol:  33510.322
i: 7  r:    32  sa:  12867.964  vol:  137258.28
```

Source code example Ch13_03 is an A64 implementation of source code example Ch06_03, which calculates the Euclidean distance between two points in 3D space. Function CalcDist_ requires six double-precision floating-point argument values. These values are passed in registers D0–D5.

Listing 13-3. Example Ch13_03

```cpp
//----------------------------------------------------
//                    Ch13_03.cpp
//----------------------------------------------------

#include <iostream>
#include <iomanip>
#include <random>
#include <cmath>

using namespace std;

extern "C" double CalcDist_(double x1, double y1, double z1, double x2, double y2, double z2);

void Init(double* x, double* y, double* z, size_t n, unsigned int seed)
{
    uniform_int_distribution<> ui_dist {1, 100};
    mt19937 rng {seed};

    for (size_t i = 0; i < n; i++)
    {
        x[i] = ui_dist(rng);
        y[i] = ui_dist(rng);
        z[i] = ui_dist(rng);
    }
}

double CalcDist(double x1, double y1, double z1, double x2, double y2, double z2)
{
    double tx = (x2 - x1) * (x2 - x1);
    double ty = (y2 - y1) * (y2 - y1);
    double tz = (z2 - z1) * (z2 - z1);
    double dist = sqrt(tx + ty + tz);

    return dist;
}

int main()
{
    const size_t n = 20;
    double x1[n], y1[n], z1[n];
    double x2[n], y2[n], z2[n];
    double dist1[n];
    double dist2[n];

    Init(x1, y1, z1, n, 29);
    Init(x2, y2, z2, n, 37);
```

```
    for (size_t i = 0; i < n; i++)
    {
        dist1[i] = CalcDist(x1[i], y1[i], z1[i], x2[i], y2[i], z2[i]);
        dist2[i] = CalcDist_(x1[i], y1[i], z1[i], x2[i], y2[i], z2[i]);
    }

    cout << fixed;

    for (size_t i = 0; i < n; i++)
    {
        cout << "i: " << setw(2) << i << "  ";

        cout << setprecision(0);

        cout << "p1(";
        cout << setw(3) << x1[i] << ",";
        cout << setw(3) << y1[i] << ",";
        cout << setw(3) << z1[i] << ") | ";

        cout << "p2(";
        cout << setw(3) << x2[i] << ",";
        cout << setw(3) << y2[i] << ",";
        cout << setw(3) << z2[i] << ") | ";

        cout << setprecision(4);
        cout << "dist1: " << setw(8) << dist1[i] << " | ";
        cout << "dist2: " << setw(8) << dist2[i] << '\n';
    }

    return 0;
}

//----------------------------------------------------
//               Ch13_03_.s
//----------------------------------------------------

// extern "C" double CalcDist_(double x1, double y1, double z1, double x2, double y2, double
z2);

        .text
        .global CalcDist_
CalcDist_:

// Calculate distance
        fsub d0,d3,d0                       // d0 = x2 - x1
        fmul d0,d0,d0                       // d0 = (x2 - x1) ** 2

        fsub d1,d4,d1                       // d1 = y2 - y1
        fmadd d0,d1,d1,d0                   // d0 += (y2 - y1) ** 2
```

```
        fsub d2,d5,d2                    // d2 = z2 - z1
        fmadd d0,d2,d2,d0                // d0 += (z2 - z1) ** 2

        fsqrt d0,d0                      // d0 = final distance
        ret
```

The first two instructions of CalcDist_, fsub d0,d3,d0 and fmul d0,d0,d0, calculate (x2 - x1) ** 2. The next instruction, fsub d1,d4,d1, calculates (y2 - y1). This is followed by a fmadd d0,d1,d1,d0 (floating-point fused multiply-add) instruction that computes (y2 - y1) ** 2 and adds this value to the intermediate sum in register D0. The ensuing instruction pair, fsub d2,d5,d2 and fmadd d0,d2,d2,d0, carries out the same operation for (z2 - z1) ** 2. Function CalcDist_ uses a fsqrt d0,d0 (floating-point square root) to calculate the final distance. Here are the results for source code example Ch13_03:

```
i:  0  p1( 87, 81, 29) | p2( 95, 14, 47) | dist1:  69.8355 | dist2:  69.8355
i:  1  p1( 35,  8, 98) | p2( 53, 20, 76) | dist1:  30.8545 | dist2:  30.8545
i:  2  p1( 77, 50, 46) | p2( 59, 31, 63) | dist1:  31.2090 | dist2:  31.2090
i:  3  p1( 34, 55, 34) | p2( 86, 69,  7) | dist1:  60.2412 | dist2:  60.2412
i:  4  p1( 73, 86, 85) | p2( 11, 63, 75) | dist1:  66.8805 | dist2:  66.8805
i:  5  p1( 84, 77, 68) | p2( 63, 29, 13) | dist1:  75.9605 | dist2:  75.9605
i:  6  p1( 74, 85, 25) | p2( 76, 31, 80) | dist1:  77.1038 | dist2:  77.1038
i:  7  p1( 14, 73, 18) | p2( 58, 63, 58) | dist1:  60.2993 | dist2:  60.2993
i:  8  p1(  6, 36, 41) | p2( 45,  1, 97) | dist1:  76.6942 | dist2:  76.6942
i:  9  p1( 51, 62, 15) | p2( 61, 90, 71) | dist1:  63.4035 | dist2:  63.4035
i: 10  p1( 26,  3, 29) | p2( 20, 41, 60) | dist1:  49.4065 | dist2:  49.4065
i: 11  p1(  7, 69,100) | p2( 10, 58, 92) | dist1:  13.9284 | dist2:  13.9284
i: 12  p1( 85, 32, 81) | p2( 71, 68, 93) | dist1:  40.4475 | dist2:  40.4475
i: 13  p1( 65,  1, 26) | p2( 83,  6, 24) | dist1:  18.7883 | dist2:  18.7883
i: 14  p1( 93, 48, 81) | p2( 14, 86, 12) | dist1: 111.5616 | dist2: 111.5616
i: 15  p1( 78, 96, 40) | p2( 21, 37, 73) | dist1:  88.4251 | dist2:  88.4251
i: 16  p1( 49, 73, 67) | p2( 81, 37, 98) | dist1:  57.2800 | dist2:  57.2800
i: 17  p1( 40, 74, 38) | p2( 61, 34, 61) | dist1:  50.6952 | dist2:  50.6952
i: 18  p1( 47, 68, 81) | p2( 48, 54, 18) | dist1:  64.5446 | dist2:  64.5446
i: 19  p1( 25, 44,  2) | p2( 66, 91, 47) | dist1:  76.9090 | dist2:  76.9090
```

Floating-Point Comparisons and Conversions

Many functions that carry out basic floating-point arithmetic are also likely to perform floating-point comparisons and conversions. The source code examples in this section explain A64 scalar floating-point comparison and conversion instructions. It begins with a source code example that demonstrates how to compare two floating-point values and make a logical decision based on the result. This is followed by an example that elucidates floating-point conversions using different numerical data types.

Floating-Point Comparisons

Listing 13-4 shows the source code for example Ch13_04. This example demonstrates floating-point comparisons using single-precision floating-point values. The C++ code in Listing 13-4 performs test case setup and exercises the assembly language function CompareF32_. Note that one of the test values in array b is a QNaN.

Listing 13-4. Example Ch13_04

```cpp
//----------------------------------------------------
//                  Ch13_04.cpp
//----------------------------------------------------

#include <iostream>
#include <iomanip>
#include <string>
#include <limits>

using namespace std;

extern "C" void CompareF32_(bool* results, float a, float b);

const char* c_OpStrings[] = {"UO", "LT", "LE", "EQ", "NE", "GT", "GE"};
const size_t c_NumOpStrings = sizeof(c_OpStrings) / sizeof(char*);

const string c_Dashes(72, '-');

template <typename T> void PrintResults(const bool* cmp_results, T a, T b)
{
    cout << "a = " << a << ", ";
    cout << "b = " << b << '\n';

    for (size_t i = 0; i < c_NumOpStrings; i++)
    {
        cout << c_OpStrings[i] << '=';
        cout << boolalpha << left << setw(6) << cmp_results[i] << ' ';
    }

    cout << "\n\n";
}

void CompareF32(void)
{
    const size_t n = 6;
    float a[n] {120.0, 250.0, 300.0, -18.0, -81.0, 42.0};
    float b[n] {130.0, 240.0, 300.0, 32.0, -100.0, 0.0};

    // Set NAN test value
    b[n - 1] = numeric_limits<float>::quiet_NaN();

    cout << "\nResults for CompareF32\n";
    cout << c_Dashes << '\n';

    for (size_t i = 0; i < n; i++)
    {
        bool cmp_results[c_NumOpStrings];
```

```
        CompareF32_(cmp_results, a[i], b[i]);
        PrintResults(cmp_results, a[i], b[i]);
    }
}

int main()
{
    CompareF32();
    return 0;
}

//----------------------------------------------------
//                  Ch13_04_.s
//----------------------------------------------------

// extern "C" void CompareF32_(bool* results, float a, float b);
            .text
            .global CompareF32_
CompareF32_:

            fcmpe s0,s1                     // compare a and b, update NZCV

            cset w1,vs                      // w1 = 1 if unordered
            strb w1,[x0,0]                  // save result

            cset w1,mi                      // w1 = 1 if a < b
            strb w1,[x0,1]                  // save result

            cset w1,ls                      // w1 = 1 if a <= b
            strb w1,[x0,2]                  // save result

            cset w1,eq                      // w1 = 1 if a == b
            strb w1,[x0,3]                  // save result

            cset w1,ne                      // w1 = 1 if a != b
            strb w1,[x0,4]                  // save result

            cset w1,gt                      // w1 = 1 if a > b
            strb w1,[x0,5]                  // save result

            cset w1,ge                      // w1 = 1 if a >= b
            strb w1,[x0,6]                  // save result
            ret
```

Recall from the discussions in Chapter 6 that a floating-point compare can have one of four outcomes: less than, equal, greater than, or unordered. The unordered outcome occurs if one or both operands are NaNs. The A64 instruction set includes two instructions that perform scalar floating-point compares: fcmp (floating-point quiet compare) and fcmpe (floating-point signaling compare). These instructions report their results using PSTATE.NZCV condition flags. The primary difference between the fcmp and fcmpe instructions is that the former generates an invalid operation (IXE) exception only when a SNaN operand is used; the latter generates an IXE exception for any NaN type. If the IXE exception is disabled, both instructions will set the IXC status bit in the FPSR.

The first instruction in CompareF32_, fcmpe s0,s1, compares the values in registers S0 (argument value a) and S1 (argument value b). As mentioned in the previous paragraph, the fcmp and fcmpe instructions update the PSTATE.NZCV flags directly. This means that unlike Armv8-32 code, it is not necessary to use a separate instruction to retrieve the condition flags from the FPSR. Following a fcmp or fcmpe instruction, a function can use any of the condition code mnemonic extensions shown in Chapter 6, Table 6-1, to make logical decisions based on the result of the compare operation.

Following the fcmpe s0,s1 instruction is a cset w1,vs instruction. This instruction sets register W1 to 1 if the compare result is unordered; otherwise, W1 is set to 0. The ensuing strb w1,[x0,0] instruction saves this value to results[0]. The subsequent cset/strb instruction pairs in CompareF32_ carry out similar operations for the remaining compare results. The fcmp and fcmpe instructions can also be used with double-precision floating-point values. Here are the results for source code example Ch13_04:

```
Results for CompareF32
----------------------------------------------------------------------
a = 120, b = 130
UO=false  LT=true   LE=true   EQ=false  NE=true   GT=false  GE=false

a = 250, b = 240
UO=false  LT=false  LE=false  EQ=false  NE=true   GT=true   GE=true

a = 300, b = 300
UO=false  LT=false  LE=true   EQ=true   NE=false  GT=false  GE=true

a = -18, b = 32
UO=false  LT=true   LE=true   EQ=false  NE=true   GT=false  GE=false

a = -81, b = -100
UO=false  LT=false  LE=false  EQ=false  NE=true   GT=true   GE=true

a = 42, b = nan
UO=true   LT=false  LE=false  EQ=false  NE=true   GT=false  GE=false
```

Floating-Point Conversions

Listing 13-5 shows the source code for example Ch13_05. This example explains how to perform conversions between integer and floating-point values. It also illustrates the use of additional GNU assembler directives.

Listing 13-5. Example Ch13_05

```cpp
//----------------------------------------------------
//              Ch13_05.cpp
//----------------------------------------------------

#include <iostream>
#include <iomanip>
#include <cmath>

using namespace std;
```

```
extern "C" double ConvertA_(float a, int b, unsigned int c, long long d, unsigned long
long e);
extern "C" int ConvertB_(int* x, const char** msg_strings, double a);

void ConvertA(void)
{
    const char nl = '\n';
    float a = 10.125f;
    int b = -20;
    unsigned int c = 30;
    long long d = -40;
    unsigned long long e = 50;

    double x = ConvertA_(a, b, c, d, e);

    cout << fixed << setprecision(6);
    cout << "\n----------Results for TestConvertA ----------\n";
    cout << "a: " << a << nl;
    cout << "b: " << b << nl;
    cout << "c: " << c << nl;
    cout << "d: " << d << nl;
    cout << "e: " << e << nl;
    cout << "x: " << x << nl;
}

void ConvertB(void)
{
    const char nl = '\n';
    const size_t n = 4;
    double a[n] = {M_PI, M_SQRT2 + 0.5, -M_E, -M_SQRT2};

    cout << fixed << setprecision(8);
    cout << "\n----------Results for TestConvertB ----------\n";

    for (size_t i = 0; i < n; i++)
    {
        const size_t m = 4;
        int x[m];
        const char* msg_strings[m];

        cout << "Test case #" << i << " using value " << a[i] << nl;
        ConvertB_(x, msg_strings, a[i]);

        for (size_t j = 0; j < m; j++)
            cout << "   " << setw(4) << x[j] << " - " << msg_strings[j] << nl;
        cout << nl;
    }
}
```

```
int main(void)
{
    ConvertA();
    ConvertB();
    return 0;
}
```

```
//----------------------------------------------------
//                  Ch013_05_.s
//----------------------------------------------------

// String table - used in ConvertB_
            .text
Str0:       .asciz "fcvtns - round to nearest"
Str1:       .asciz "fcvtps - round to plus infinity"
Str2:       .asciz "fcvtms - round to minus infinity"
Str3:       .asciz "fcvtzs - round to zero"
            .balign 4
```

```
// extern "C" double ConvertA_(float a, int b, unsigned int c, long long d, unsigned long
long e);

            .global ConvertA_
ConvertA_:  fcvt d0,s0                      // d0 = a as F64

            scvtf d1,w0                     // d1 = b as F64
            ucvtf d2,w1                     // d2 = c as F64

            scvtf d3,x2                     // d3 = d as F64
            ucvtf d4,x3                     // d4 = e as F64

            fadd d5,d0,d1                   // d5 = a + b
            fadd d6,d2,d3                   // d6 = c + d
            fadd d7,d5,d4                   // d7 = a + b + e
            fadd d0,d6,d7                   // d0 = final sum
            ret
```

```
// extern "C" int ConvertB_(int* x, const char** msg_strings, double a);

            .global ConvertB_
ConvertB_:

// Convert a to signed integer using different rounding modes
            fcvtns w2,d0                    // rm = to nearest (even)
            str w2,[x0,0]                   // save result
            adr x2,Str0                     // x2 = address of Str0
            str x2,[x1]                     // save ptr to string S0

            fcvtps w2,d0                    // rm = to plus infinity
            str w2,[x0,4]                   // save result
            adr x2,Str1                     // x2 = address of Str1
            str x2,[x1,8]                   // save ptr to string S1
```

```
      fcvtms w2,d0                    // rm = to minus infinity
      str w2,[x0,8]                   // save result
      adr x2,Str2                     // x2 = address of Str2
      str x2,[x1,16]                  // save ptr to string S2

      fcvtzs w2,d0                    // rm = to zero
      str w2,[x0,12]                  // save result
      adr x2,Str3                     // x2 = address of Str3
      str x2,[x1,24]                  // save ptr to string S3
      ret
```

The C++ code in Listing 13-5 includes a function named ConvertA. This function performs test case initialization for the assembly language function ConvertA_, which carries out a variety of conversion operations. Similarly, the C++ function ConvertB performs test case initialization for ConvertB_. This function contains code that executes double-precision floating-point to signed integer conversions using different rounding modes.

Immediately after the .text directive in Listing 13-5 is a series of text strings that have been defined using the GNU assembler directive .asciz. The .asciz directive allocates storage space for an ASCII text string. It also appends a null (0x00) terminating byte to the text string. Note that the ASCII text strings Str0-Str3 are read-only since they are defined in a .text section. Following the text string declarations is a .balign 4 directive. The .balign directive adjusts the value of the location counter upward so that it is aligned on a boundary that is an integral multiple of its argument value. In the current example, this guarantees that the first instruction of ConvertA_ will be properly aligned on a word boundary. If you comment out this directive and try executing the code, the program will crash since the first instruction of ConvertA_ will not be aligned on a word boundary (recall from the discussions in Chapter 10 that all A64 instructions must be aligned on a word boundary).

Function ConvertA_ begins its execution with a fcvt d0,s0 (floating-point convert) instruction that converts the single-precision value in S0 (argument value a) to double-precision and saves the result in register D0. The fcvt instruction can also be used to perform conversions between other floating-point formats (e.g., double-precision to single-precision, single-precision to half-precision, etc.). The next instruction, scvtf d1,w0 (signed integer convert), converts the signed integer in register W1 (argument value b) to double-precision and saves the result in D1. This is followed by a ucvtf d2,w1 (unsigned integer convert) that converts the unsigned integer in W1 (argument value c) to double-precision floating point. The final two conversion instructions in ConvertA_, scvtf d3,x2 and ucvtf d4,x3, convert 64-bit wide integer argument values d and e to double-precision. Each conversion instruction used in ConvertA_ carried out its operation using the rounding mode specified by the RMode field in the FPCR register. Following the conversion operations, function ConvertA_ uses a series of fadd instructions to calculate a + b + c + d + e.

Function ConvertB_ illustrates the use of instructions that carry out double-precision floating-point to 32-bit signed integer conversions using different rounding modes. The first instruction, fcvtns w2,d0 (convert floating-point to signed integer, round-to-nearest), converts the value in D0 (argument value a) to a 32-bit signed integer using round-to-nearest rounding. The ensuing str w2,[x0,0] instructions saves this result to x[0]. The next instruction, adr x2,Str0, loads the address of Str0 into register X1. This is followed by a str x2,[x1] instruction that saves the address of Str0 in msg_strings[0]. Defining text strings in an assembly language file and passing back pointers to the calling function is sometimes employed to reduce coupling between software modules.

The next three code blocks in ConvertB_ illustrate the use of the fcvtps (convert floating-point to signed integer, round to plus infinity), fcvtms (convert floating-point to signed integer, round to minus infinity), and fcvtzs (convert floating-point to signed integer, round-to-zero) instructions. The A64 instruction set also includes instructions that perform floating-point to unsigned integer conversions. The mnemonics for these instructions use a "u" suffix instead of an "s" suffix character (e.g., fcvtnu, fcvtpu, fcvtmu, and fcvtzu). The conversion instructions used in ConvertB_ can also be used with single-precision floating-point source operands and 64-bit integer destination operands. Here are the results for source code example Ch13_05:

```
----------Results for TestConvertA ----------
a: 10.125000
b: -20
c: 30
d: -40
e: 50
x: 30.125000

----------Results for TestConvertB ----------
Test case #0 using value 3.14159265
      3 - fcvtns - round to nearest
      4 - fcvtps - round to plus infinity
      3 - fcvtms - round to minus infinity
      3 - fcvtzs - round to zero

Test case #1 using value 1.91421356
      2 - fcvtns - round to nearest
      2 - fcvtps - round to plus infinity
      1 - fcvtms - round to minus infinity
      1 - fcvtzs - round to zero

Test case #2 using value -2.71828183
     -3 - fcvtns - round to nearest
     -2 - fcvtps - round to plus infinity
     -3 - fcvtms - round to minus infinity
     -2 - fcvtzs - round to zero

Test case #3 using value -1.41421356
     -1 - fcvtns - round to nearest
     -1 - fcvtps - round to plus infinity
     -2 - fcvtms - round to minus infinity
     -1 - fcvtzs - round to zero
```

Floating-Point Arrays and Matrices

In Chapter 12, you learned how to use the A64 instruction set to access individual elements and carry out calculations using integer arrays and matrices. In this section, you will learn how to perform similar operations using A64 instruction set with floating-point array and matrices. As you will soon see, the same assembly language coding techniques are often used for both integer and floating-point arrays and matrices.

Floating-Point Arrays

Listing 13-6 shows the source code for example Ch13_06. This example, which is an A64 implementation of source code example Ch06_06, calculates the sample mean and sample standard deviation of an array of double-precision floating-point values.

Listing 13-6. Example Ch13_06

```
//----------------------------------------------------
//                 Ch13_06.cpp
//----------------------------------------------------

#include <iostream>
#include <iomanip>
#include <cmath>

using namespace std;

extern "C" bool CalcMeanStdev_(double* mean, double* stdev, const double* x, int n);

bool CalcMeanStdev(double* mean, double* stdev, const double* x, int n)
{
    if (n < 2)
        return false;

    double sum = 0.0;
    double sum2 = 0.0;

    for (int i = 0; i < n; i++)
        sum += x[i];

    *mean = sum / n;

    for (int i = 0; i < n; i++)
    {
        double temp = x[i] - *mean;
        sum2 += temp * temp;
    }

    *stdev = sqrt(sum2 / (n - 1));
    return true;
}

int main()
{
    const char nl = '\n';
    double x[] = { 10, 2, 33, 19, 41, 24, 75, 37, 18, 97, 14, 71, 88, 92, 7};
    const int n = sizeof(x) / sizeof(double);

    double mean1 = 0.0, stdev1 = 0.0;
    double mean2 = 0.0, stdev2 = 0.0;
```

```
    bool rc1 = CalcMeanStdev(&mean1, &stdev1, x, n);
    bool rc2 = CalcMeanStdev_(&mean2, &stdev2, x, n);

    cout << fixed << setprecision(2);

    for (int i = 0; i < n; i++)
    {
        cout << "x[" << setw(2) << i << "] = ";
        cout << setw(6) << x[i] << nl;
    }

    cout << setprecision(6);

    cout << nl;
    cout << "rc1 = " << boolalpha << rc1;
    cout << "  mean1 = " << mean1 << "  stdev1 = " << stdev1 << nl;
    cout << "rc2 = " << boolalpha << rc2;
    cout << "  mean2 = " << mean2 << "  stdev2 = " << stdev2 << nl;
}

//----------------------------------------------------
//                  Ch13_06_.s
//----------------------------------------------------

// extern "C" bool CalcMeanStdev_(double* mean, double* stdev, const double* x, int n);

            .text
            .global CalcMeanStdev_
CalcMeanStdev_:
            cmp w3,2                        // is n < 2?
            b.lt InvalidArg                 // jump if n < 2

// Calculate mean
            movi d0,0                       // sum1 = 0.0
            movi d4,0                       // sum2 = 0.0
            mov w4,0                        // i = 0
            mov x5,x2                       // x5 = ptr to x

Loop1:      ldr d1,[x5],8                   // d1 = x[i]
            fadd d0,d0,d1                   // sum1 += x[i]
            add w4,w4,1                     // i += 1
            cmp w4,w3
            b.lt Loop1                      // jump if i < n

            scvtf d1,w3                     // d1 = n as double
            fdiv d2,d0,d1                   // d2 = sum1 / n (mean)
            str d2,[x0]                     // save mean
```

```
// Calculate standard deviation
            mov  w4,0                     // i = 0
            mov  x5,x2                    // x5 = ptr to x

Loop2:      ldr  d1,[x5],8                // d1 = x[i]
            fsub d3,d1,d2                 // d3 = x[i] - mean
            fmadd d4,d3,d3,d4             // sum2 += (x[i] - mean)**2

            add  w4,w4,1                  // i += 1
            cmp  w4,w3
            b.lt Loop2                    // jump if i < n

            sub  w3,w3,1                  // w3 = n - 1
            scvtf d1,w3                   // d1 = n - 1 as double

            fdiv d2,d4,d1                 // d2 = sum2 / (n - 1)
            fsqrt d3,d2                   // d3 = stdev

            str  d3,[x1]                  // save stdev
            mov  w0,1                     // set success return code
            ret

InvalidArg: mov  w0,0                     // set error return code
            ret
```

The C++ code in Listing 13-6 matches the C++ code of source code example Ch06_06. The assembly language function CalcMeanStdev_ begins its execution with the instruction pair cmp w3,2 and b.lt InvalidArg. This instruction pair verifies that argument value n is not less than two. Following validation of argument value n, the instructions movi d0,0 and movi d4,0 initialize sum1 (D0) and sum2 (D4). The movi (move immediate vector) instruction is an A64 SIMD instruction that loads an immediate value into each element of a vector register. The scalar variant is employed here to set both sum1 and sum2 equal to 0.0. The ensuing mov w4,0 instruction sets array element index i equal to zero. Each iteration of for-loop Loop1 begins with a ldr d1,[x5],8 instruction that loads x[i] into register D1. The next instruction, fadd d0,d0,d1, calculates sum1 += x[i]. For-loop Loop1 repeats until all of the elements in array x have been summed. Following calculation of sum1, CalcMeanStdev_ uses two instructions, scvtf d1,w3 and fdiv d2,d0,d1, to calculate the arithmetic mean.

For-loop Loop2 calculates the standard deviation. Each iteration of Loop2 also begins with a ldr d1,[x5],8 instruction that loads x[i] into register D1. Note that prior to the first iteration, registers W4 (i) and X5 (pointer to array x) were reinitialized. Following the ldr instruction, the fsub d3,d1,d2 and fmadd d4,d3,d3,d4 instructions calculate sum2 += (x[i] - mean) ** 2. Subsequent to the completion of Loop2, the instruction pair, sub w3,w3,1 and scvtf d1,w3, converts n - 1 to a double-precision floating-point value. This is followed by another instruction pair, fdiv d2,d4,d1 and fsqrt d3,d2, that calculates the standard deviation. Here are the results for source code example Ch13_06:

```
x[ 0] =  10.00
x[ 1] =   2.00
x[ 2] =  33.00
x[ 3] =  19.00
x[ 4] =  41.00
x[ 5] =  24.00
x[ 6] =  75.00
x[ 7] =  37.00
x[ 8] =  18.00
x[ 9] =  97.00
x[10] =  14.00
x[11] =  71.00
x[12] =  88.00
x[13] =  92.00
x[14] =   7.00

rc1 = true  mean1 = 41.866667  stdev1 = 33.530086
rc2 = true  mean2 = 41.866667  stdev2 = 33.530086
```

Floating-Point Matrices

Source code example Ch13_07 illustrates how to calculate the trace of a square matrix. This source code example is an A64 implementation of source code example Ch06_07.

Listing 13-7. Example Ch13_07

```cpp
//--------------------------------------------------
//               Ch13_07.cpp
//--------------------------------------------------

#include <iostream>
#include <iomanip>
#include <string>
#include <random>

using namespace std;

extern "C" bool CalcTrace_(double* trace, const double* x, int nrows, int ncols);

void Init(double* x, int nrows, int ncols)
{
    unsigned int seed = 47;
    uniform_int_distribution<> d {1, 1000};
    mt19937 rng {seed};
```

```cpp
    for (int i = 0; i < nrows; i++)
    {
        for (int j = 0; j < ncols; j++)
            x[i * ncols + j] = (double)d(rng);
    }
}

bool CalcTrace(double* trace, const double* x, int nrows, int ncols)
{
    if (nrows != ncols || nrows <= 0)
        return false;

    double sum = 0.0;

    for (int i = 0; i < nrows; i++)
        sum += x[i * ncols + i];

    *trace = sum;
    return true;
}

int main()
{
    const char nl = '\n';
    const int nrows = 10;
    const int ncols = 10;
    double x[nrows][ncols];
    double trace1, trace2;
    string dashes(72, '-');

    Init(&x[0][0], nrows, ncols);

    CalcTrace(&trace1, &x[0][0], nrows, ncols);
    CalcTrace_(&trace2, &x[0][0], nrows, ncols);

    cout << "\nTest Matrix\n";
    cout << dashes << nl;

    for (int i = 0; i < nrows; i++)
    {
        for (int j = 0; j < ncols; j++)
            cout << setw(6) << x[i][j] << ' ';

        cout << nl;
    }

    cout << "\ntrace1 = " << trace1 << nl;
    cout << "trace2 = " << trace2 << nl;

    return 0;
}
```

```
//------------------------------------------------------------
//                     Ch13_07_.s
//------------------------------------------------------------

// extern "C" bool CalcTrace_(double* trace, const double* x, int nrows, int ncols);

            .text
            .global CalcTrace_
CalcTrace_:
            cmp w2,w3
            b.ne InvalidArg                 // jump if nrows != ncols
            cmp w2,0
            b.le InvalidArg                 // jump if nrows <= 0

// Calculate matrix trace
            movi d0,0                       // sum = 0.0
            mov w4,0                        // i = 0

Loop1:      mul w5,w4,w3                    // w5 = i * ncols
            add w5,w5,w4                    // w5 = i * ncols + i

            ldr d1,[x1,w5,sxtw 3]           // d1 = x[i][i]
            fadd d0,d0,d1                   // sum += x[i][i]

            add w4,w4,1                     // i += 1
            cmp w4,w2
            b.lt Loop1                      // jump if not done

            str d0,[x0]                     // save trace value
            mov w0,1                        // set success return code
            ret

InvalidArg: mov w0,0                        // set error return code
            ret
```

The assembly language code in Listing 13-7 includes a function named CalcTrace_, which calculates the trace of a square matrix. Recall from the discussions in Chapter 6 that the trace of a square matrix is simply the sum of its main diagonal elements. Function CalcTrace_ begins it execution by verifying that argument values nrows (W2) and ncols (W3) are valid. Prior to the start of for-loop Loop1, the movi d0,0 instruction sets sum equal to zero. This is followed by a mov w4,0 instruction that sets index variable i equal to zero.

Each iteration of for-loop Loop1 begins with a mul w5,w4,w3 instruction that calculates i * ncols. The next instruction, add w5,w5,w4, computes i * ncols + i. The function CalcTrace_ then uses a ldr d1,[x1,w5,sxtw 3] instruction to load x[i][i] into register D1. The ensuing fadd d0,d0,d1 instruction calculates sum += x[i][i]. Execution of Loop1 continues until the diagonal element summing operation is complete. Here are the results for source code example Ch13_07:

```
Test Matrix
---------------------------------------------------------------------
  114    852    975    910    729    824    352    373    708    979
  800    934    646    396    415    307    707    231    247    635
  256    515     25    400     99    355    301    763    641     52
  323    734    186    770    918    289    271    697    274    510
  955    806    128    924    748    366      6    514    857    760
  696    129    554    548    936    878    513    482    178    910
  537    906    294     29     11    453    884    347    657    827
  943    844    745    351    268    928    362    310    527    532
  547    294    259    187    175    755    361    229    141    152
  390    108    472     79    969    434    146    348    515    369

trace1 = 5173
trace2 = 5173
```

Using C++ Floating-Point Library Functions

The final example of Chapter 13, Ch13_08, demonstrates how to call C++ library functions from an assembly language function. Listing 13-8 shows the source code for this example.

Listing 13-8. Example Ch13_08

```cpp
//---------------------------------------------------
//              Ch13_08.cpp
//---------------------------------------------------

#include <iostream>
#include <iomanip>
#include <cmath>

using namespace std;

extern "C" void CalcBSA_(double bsa[3], double ht, double wt);

void CalcBSA(double bsa[3], double ht, double wt)
{
    bsa[0] = 0.007184 * pow(ht, 0.725) * pow(wt, 0.425);
    bsa[1] = 0.0235 * pow(ht, 0.42246) * pow(wt, 0.51456);
    bsa[2] = sqrt(ht * wt / 3600.0);
}

int main()
{
    const int n = 6;
    const double ht[n] = { 150, 160, 170, 180, 190, 200 };
    const double wt[n] = { 50.0, 60.0, 70.0, 80.0, 90.0, 100.0 };
```

```
    cout << "---------- Body Surface Area Results ----------\n";
    cout << fixed;

    for (int i = 0; i < n; i++)
    {
        cout << setprecision(1);
        cout << "height: " << setw(6) << ht[i] << " cm\n";
        cout << "weight: " << setw(6) << wt[i] << " kg\n";

        double bsa1[3], bsa2[3];

        CalcBSA(bsa1, ht[i], wt[i]);
        CalcBSA_(bsa2, ht[i], wt[i]);

        for (int j = 0; j < 3; j++)
        {
            cout << setprecision(6);
            cout << "bsa1[" << j << "]: " << setw(10) << bsa1[j];
            cout << " | ";
            cout << "bsa2[" << j << "]: " << setw(10) << bsa2[j];
            cout << " (sq. m)\n";
        }

        cout << '\n';
    }

    return 0;
}

//-------------------------------------------------
//              Ch13_08_.s
//-------------------------------------------------

// extern "C" void CalcBSA_(double bsa[3], double ht, double wt);

            .text
            .global CalcBSA_
CalcBSA_:   stp lr,x19,[sp,-16]!            // push lr, x19
            stp d12,d13,[sp,-16]!           // push d12, d13
            stp d14,d15,[sp,-16]!           // push d14, d15

            mov x19,x0                      // x19 = bsa array ptr
            fmov d12,d0                     // d12 = height
            fmov d13,d1                     // d13 = weight

// Calculate bsa[0] = 0.007184 * pow(ht, 0.725) * pow(wt, 0.425)
            ldr d1,r8_0p725
            bl pow                          // calc pow(ht,0.725)
            fmov d14,d0                     // save result
            fmov d0,d13                     // d0 = weight
            ldr d1,r8_0p425
```

```
            bl pow                              // calc pow(wt,0.425)
            ldr d1,r8_0p007184
            fmul d2,d1,d14                      // 0.007184 * pow(ht,0.725)
            fmul d2,d2,d0                       // d2 *= pow(wt,0.425)
            str d2,[x19]                        // save bsa[0]


// Calculate bsa[1] = 0.0235 * pow(ht, 0.42246) * pow(wt, 0.51456)
            fmov d0,d12                         // d0 = height
            ldr d1,r8_0p42246
            bl pow                              // calc pow(ht,0.42246)
            fmov d14,d0                         // save result
            fmov d0,d13                         // d0 = weight
            ldr d1,r8_0p51456
            bl pow                              // calc pow(wt,0.51456)
            ldr d1,r8_0p0235
            fmul d2,d1,d14                      // 0.0235 * pow(ht,0.42246)
            fmul d2,d2,d0                       // d2 *= pow(wt,0.51456)
            str d2,[x19,8]                      // save bsa[1]


// Calculate bsa[2] = sqrt(ht * wt / 3600.0)
            fmul d0,d12,d13                     // d0 = ht * wt
            ldr d1,r8_3600p0
            fdiv d2,d0,d1                       // d2 = ht * wt / 3600
            fsqrt d2,d2                         // sqrt(ht * wt / 3600)
            str d2,[x19,16]                     // save bsa[2]


// Restore non-volatile registers & return
            ldp d14,d15,[sp],16                 // pop d14, d15
            ldp d12,d13,[sp],16                 // pop d12, d13
            ldp lr,x19,[sp],16                  // pop lr, x19
            ret


// Constants
            .balign 8
r8_0p007184:    .double 0.007184
r8_0p725:       .double 0.725
r8_0p425:       .double 0.425
r8_0p0235:      .double 0.0235
r8_0p42246:     .double 0.42246
r8_0p51456:     .double 0.51456
r8_3600p0:      .double 3600.0
```

The C++ and assembly language functions in Listing 13-8 contain code that calculate body surface area (BSA). BSA calculations are frequently employed to establish chemotherapy dosages for cancer patients. Table 13-2 lists three well-known BSA equations. In this table, each equation uses the symbol H for patient height (centimeters), W for patient weight (kilograms), and BSA for patient body surface area (square meters).

Table 13-2. *Body surface area equations*

Method	Equation
DuBois and DuBois	$BSA = 0.007184 \times H^{0.725} \times W^{0.425}$
Gehan and George	$BSA = 0.0235 \times H^{0.42246} \times W^{0.51456}$
Mosteller	$BSA = \sqrt{H \times W / 3600}$

The C++ code in Listing 13-8 includes a function named CalcBSA. This function calculates the three BSA values using the formulas in Table 13-2. The function main contains code that exercises CalcBSA and its assembly language counterpart CalcBSA_. It also streams results to cout.

Function CalcBSA_ begins its execution with a stp lr,x19,[sp,-16]! instruction that pushes registers LR and X19 on the stack. This is followed by two more stp instructions: stp d12,d13,[sp,-16]! and stp d14,d15,[sp,-16]!. These instructions save registers D12–D15 on the stack. Note that function CalcBSA_ does not use register D15, but it is included in the second stp instruction to keep the SP register aligned on a quadword boundary. The ensuing instruction triplet, mov x19,x0, fmov d12,d0, and fmov d13,d1, copies argument values bsa, ht, and wt into non-volatile registers. These argument values are preserved in non-volatile registers since CalcBSA_ calls other functions. Another option would be to preserve these values on the stack.

The next code block in CalcBSA_ starts with a ldr d1,r8_0p725 instruction that loads 0.725 into register D1. The ensuing bl pow instruction calls the C++ library function pow to calculate ht ** 0.725. This is followed by a fmov d14,d0 instruction that saves the return value from pow. Function CalcBSA_ calls pow again to calculate wt ** 0.425. Note that prior to this second use of pow, the instruction fmov d0,d13 loaded argument value wt into register D0 and the ldr d1,r8_0p425 instruction loaded 0.425 into register D1. Execution of the instruction pair, fmul d2,d1,d14 and fmul d2,d2,d0, completes the calculation of bsa[0].

Function CalcBSA_ uses a similar sequence of instructions to calculate bsa[1]. Note that prior to each pow call, the required values are loaded into registers D0 (argument value ht) and D1 (0.42246). The final BSA value, bsa[2], is calculated using straightforward double-precision floating-point arithmetic. Following calculation of the BSA values, the instruction triplet, ldp d14,d15,[sp],16, ldp d12,d13,[sp],16, and ldp lr,x19,[sp],16, pops registers D12–D15, LR, and X19 from the stack. Immediately after the ret instruction is a .balign 8 directive that aligns the location counter on a doubleword boundary. This is done to ensure doubleword alignment of the double-precision floating-point constants that follow the .balign directive. Here are the results for source code example Ch13_08:

```
---------- Body Surface Area Results ----------
height:   150.0 cm
weight:    50.0 kg
bsa1[0]:    1.432500 | bsa2[0]:    1.432500 (sq. m)
bsa1[1]:    1.460836 | bsa2[1]:    1.460836 (sq. m)
bsa1[2]:    1.443376 | bsa2[2]:    1.443376 (sq. m)

height:   160.0 cm
weight:    60.0 kg
bsa1[0]:    1.622063 | bsa2[0]:    1.622063 (sq. m)
bsa1[1]:    1.648868 | bsa2[1]:    1.648868 (sq. m)
bsa1[2]:    1.632993 | bsa2[2]:    1.632993 (sq. m)
```

```
height:   170.0 cm
weight:    70.0 kg
bsa1[0]:    1.809708 | bsa2[0]:    1.809708 (sq. m)
bsa1[1]:    1.831289 | bsa2[1]:    1.831289 (sq. m)
bsa1[2]:    1.818119 | bsa2[2]:    1.818119 (sq. m)

height:   180.0 cm
weight:    80.0 kg
bsa1[0]:    1.996421 | bsa2[0]:    1.996421 (sq. m)
bsa1[1]:    2.009483 | bsa2[1]:    2.009483 (sq. m)
bsa1[2]:    2.000000 | bsa2[2]:    2.000000 (sq. m)

height:   190.0 cm
weight:    90.0 kg
bsa1[0]:    2.182809 | bsa2[0]:    2.182809 (sq. m)
bsa1[1]:    2.184365 | bsa2[1]:    2.184365 (sq. m)
bsa1[2]:    2.179449 | bsa2[2]:    2.179449 (sq. m)

height:   200.0 cm
weight:   100.0 kg
bsa1[0]:    2.369262 | bsa2[0]:    2.369262 (sq. m)
bsa1[1]:    2.356574 | bsa2[1]:    2.356574 (sq. m)
bsa1[2]:    2.357023 | bsa2[2]:    2.357023 (sq. m)
```

Summary

Here are the key learning points for Chapter 13:

- The fadd, fsub, fmul, and fdiv instructions carry out floating-point addition, subtraction, multiplication, and division using either single-precision or double-precision operands.

- The fsqrt instruction calculates the square root of its source operand, which can be either a single-precision or double-precision value.

- The fcvt instruction performs conversions between different floating-point types (e.g., single-precision to double-precision, double-precision to single-precision, single-precision to half-precision, etc.).

- The scvtf and ucvtf instructions convert signed or unsigned integers to floating-point.

- The fcvtn[s|u], fcvtp[s|u], fcvtm[s|u], and fcvtz[s|u] instructions convert floating-point values to signed or unsigned integers using round-to-nearest, plus infinity, minus infinity, and zero, respectively.

- Per the GNU C++ calling convention, the first eight floating-point argument values are passed to a function using registers D0–D7 (S0–S7). Any remaining arguments are passed via the stack. A function must use register D0 (S0) to return a double-precision (single-precision) floating-point value to its caller.

- The GNU C++ calling convention designates registers D8–D15 as non-volatile. A function must preserve the value in any non-volatile register it uses. All other floating-point (and SIMD) registers are classified as volatile.

- The `.asciz` directive is used to define null-terminated text strings in assembly language code.

- The `.balign` directive adjusts the location counter upward to an integral multiple of its argument value.

CHAPTER 14

■ ■ ■

Armv8-64 SIMD Integer Programming

This chapter covers Armv8-64 SIMD programming using packed integer operands. The content is partitioned into two major sections. The first section focuses on basic packed arithmetic including addition, subtraction, multiplication, and shift operations. The purpose of this section is to illustrate essential Armv8-64 SIMD instruction usage. The second section presents Armv8-64 SIMD functions that are useful for image-processing applications. This section also explains how to use advanced macros and macro arguments.

The discussions in this and the next two chapters assume that you have a basic understanding of SIMD programming concepts. They also assume that you are familiar with the with Armv8-64 SIMD architecture, especially its register set. If your understanding of these topics is lacking, you may want to review the material presented in Chapters 7 and 10 before proceeding.

Packed Integer Arithmetic

In this section, you will learn how to use Armv8-64 SIMD instructions to perform basic arithmetic using packed integer operands. The first source code example describes packed integer addition and subtraction using both wraparound and saturated arithmetic. The second source code illustrates packed shift operations. The third and final source code example highlights packed integer multiplication.

Addition and Subtraction

Listing 14-1 shows the source code for example Ch14_01. This example elucidates packed integer arithmetic using signed and unsigned halfword (16-bit) integers. Source code example Ch14_01 also explains how to employ various Armv8-64 SIMD vector load and store instructions.

Listing 14-1. Example Ch14_01

```
//-------------------------------------------------
//              Vec128.h
//-------------------------------------------------

#pragma once
#include <string>
#include <cstdint>
#include <sstream>
#include <iomanip>
```

© Daniel Kusswurm 2020
D. Kusswurm, *Modern Arm Assembly Language Programming*,
https://doi.org/10.1007/978-1-4842-6267-2_14

```
struct alignas(16) Vec128
{
public:
    union
    {
        int8_t m_I8[16];
        int16_t m_I16[8];
        int32_t m_I32[4];
        int64_t m_I64[2];
        uint8_t m_U8[16];
        uint16_t m_U16[8];
        uint32_t m_U32[4];
        uint64_t m_U64[2];
        float m_F32[4];
        double m_F64[2];
    };
```

```
//---------------------------------------------------
//                  Ch14_01.cpp
//---------------------------------------------------

#include <iostream>
#include <string>
#include "Vec128.h"

using namespace std;

extern "C" void PackedAddI16_(Vec128 x[2], const Vec128& a, const Vec128& b);
extern "C" void PackedSubI16_(Vec128 x[2], const Vec128& a, const Vec128& b);
extern "C" void PackedAddU16_(Vec128 x[2], const Vec128& a, const Vec128& b);
extern "C" void PackedSubU16_(Vec128 x[2], const Vec128& a, const Vec128& b);

// Signed packed addition and subtraction
void PackedAddI16(void)
{
    Vec128 x[2], a, b;
    const char nl = '\n';

    a.m_I16[0] = 10;            b.m_I16[0] = 100;
    a.m_I16[1] = 200;           b.m_I16[1] = -200;
    a.m_I16[2] = 30;            b.m_I16[2] = 32760;
    a.m_I16[3] = -32766;        b.m_I16[3] = -400;
    a.m_I16[4] = 50;            b.m_I16[4] = 500;
    a.m_I16[5] = 60;            b.m_I16[5] = -600;
    a.m_I16[6] = 32000;         b.m_I16[6] = 1200;
    a.m_I16[7] = -32000;        b.m_I16[7] = -950;

    PackedAddI16_(x, a, b);
```

```
        cout << "\nResults for PackedAddI16 - Wraparound Addition\n";
        cout << "a:      " << a.ToStringI16() << nl;
        cout << "b:      " << b.ToStringI16() << nl;
        cout << "x[0]:   " << x[0].ToStringI16() << nl;
        cout << "\nResults for PackedAddI16 - Saturated Addition\n";
        cout << "a:      " << a.ToStringI16() << nl;
        cout << "b:      " << b.ToStringI16() << nl;
        cout << "x[1]:   " << x[1].ToStringI16() << nl;
}

void PackedSubI16(void)
{
        Vec128 x[2], a, b;
        const char nl = '\n';

        a.m_I16[0] = 10;           b.m_I16[0] = 100;
        a.m_I16[1] = 200;          b.m_I16[1] = -200;
        a.m_I16[2] = -30;          b.m_I16[2] = 32760;
        a.m_I16[3] = -32766;       b.m_I16[3] = 400;
        a.m_I16[4] = 50;           b.m_I16[4] = 500;
        a.m_I16[5] = 60;           b.m_I16[5] = -600;
        a.m_I16[6] = 32000;        b.m_I16[6] = 1200;
        a.m_I16[7] = -32000;       b.m_I16[7] = 950;

        PackedSubI16_(x, a, b);

        cout << "\nResults for PackedSubI16 - Wraparound Subtraction\n";
        cout << "a:      " << a.ToStringI16() << nl;
        cout << "b:      " << b.ToStringI16() << nl;
        cout << "x[0]:   " << x[0].ToStringI16() << nl;
        cout << "\nResults for PackedSubI16 - Saturated Subtraction\n";
        cout << "a:      " << a.ToStringI16() << nl;
        cout << "b:      " << b.ToStringI16() << nl;
        cout << "x[1]:   " << x[1].ToStringI16() << nl;
}

// Unsigned packed addition and subtraction
void PackedAddU16(void)
{
        Vec128 x[2], a, b;
        const char nl = '\n';

        a.m_U16[0] = 10;           b.m_U16[0] = 100;
        a.m_U16[1] = 200;          b.m_U16[1] = 200;
        a.m_U16[2] = 300;          b.m_U16[2] = 65530;
        a.m_U16[3] = 32766;        b.m_U16[3] = 40000;
        a.m_U16[4] = 50;           b.m_U16[4] = 500;
        a.m_U16[5] = 20000;        b.m_U16[5] = 25000;
        a.m_U16[6] = 32000;        b.m_U16[6] = 1200;
        a.m_U16[7] = 32000;        b.m_U16[7] = 50000;
```

```
    PackedAddU16_(x, a, b);

    cout << "\nResults for PackedAddU16 - Wraparound Addition\n";
    cout << "a:     " << a.ToStringU16() << nl;
    cout << "b:     " << b.ToStringU16() << nl;
    cout << "x[0]:  " << x[0].ToStringU16() << nl;
    cout << "\nResults for PackedAddU16 - Saturated Addition\n";
    cout << "a:     " << a.ToStringU16() << nl;
    cout << "b:     " << b.ToStringU16() << nl;
    cout << "x[1]:  " << x[1].ToStringU16() << nl;
}

void PackedSubU16(void)
{
    Vec128 x[2], a, b;
    const char nl = '\n';

    a.m_U16[0] = 10;          b.m_U16[0] = 100;
    a.m_U16[1] = 200;         b.m_U16[1] = 200;
    a.m_U16[2] = 30;          b.m_U16[2] = 7;
    a.m_U16[3] = 65000;       b.m_U16[3] = 5000;
    a.m_U16[4] = 60;          b.m_U16[4] = 500;
    a.m_U16[5] = 25000;       b.m_U16[5] = 28000;
    a.m_U16[6] = 32000;       b.m_U16[6] = 1200;
    a.m_U16[7] = 1200;        b.m_U16[7] = 950;

    PackedSubU16_(x, a, b);

    cout << "\nResults for PackedSubU16 - Wraparound Subtraction\n";
    cout << "a:     " << a.ToStringU16() << nl;
    cout << "b:     " << b.ToStringU16() << nl;
    cout << "x[0]:  " << x[0].ToStringU16() << nl;
    cout << "\nResults for PackedSubI16 - Saturated Subtraction\n";
    cout << "a:     " << a.ToStringU16() << nl;
    cout << "b:     " << b.ToStringU16() << nl;
    cout << "x[1]:  " << x[1].ToStringU16() << nl;
}

int main()
{
    string sep(75, '-');
    const char nl = '\n';

    PackedAddI16();
    PackedSubI16();
    cout << nl << sep << nl;
    PackedAddU16();
    PackedSubU16();
    return 0;
}
```

```
//-----------------------------------------------------
//                    Ch14_01_.s
//-----------------------------------------------------

// extern "C" void PackedAddI16_(Vec128 x[2], const Vec128& a, const Vec128& b);

            .text
            .global PackedAddI16_
PackedAddI16_:
            ldr q0,[x1]                     // q0 = a
            ldr q1,[x2]                     // q1 = b

            add v2.8h,v0.8h,v1.8h           // v2 = a + b (wraparound)
            str q2,[x0]                     // save result to x[0]

            sqadd v3.8h,v0.8h,v1.8h         // v3 = a + b (saturated)
            str q2,[x0,16]                  // save result to x[1]
            ret

// extern "C" void PackedSubI16_(Vec128 x[2], const Vec128& b, const Vec128& c);

            .global PackedSubI16_
PackedSubI16_:
            ldr q0,[x1]                     // q0 = a
            ldr q1,[x2]                     // q1 = b

            sub v2.8h,v0.8h,v1.8h           // v2 = a - b (wraparound)
            str q2,[x0]                     // save result to x[0]

            sqsub v3.8h,v0.8h,v1.8h         // v3 = a - b (saturated)
            str q2,[x0,16]                  // save result to x[1]
            ret

// extern "C" void PackedAddU16_(Vec128 x[2], const Vec128& a, const Vec128& b);

            .global PackedAddU16_
PackedAddU16_:
            ld1 {v0.8h},[x1]                // v0 = a
            ld1 {v1.8h},[x2]                // v1 = b

            add v2.8h,v0.8h,v1.8h           // v2 = a + b (wraparound)
            uqadd v3.8h,v0.8h,v1.8h         // v3 = a + b (saturated)

            st1 {v2.8h,v3.8h},[x0]          // save results to x
            ret

// extern "C" void PackedSubU16_(Vec128 x[2], const Vec128& a, const Vec128& b);

            .global PackedSubU16_
PackedSubU16_:
            ld1 {v0.8h},[x1]                // v0 = a
            ld1 {v1.8h},[x2]                // v1 = b
```

```
        sub v2.8h,v0.8h,v1.8h            // q2 = a - b (wraparound)
        uqsub v3.8h,v0.8h,v1.8h          // q3 = a - b (saturated)

        st1 {v2.8h,v3.8h},[x0]           // save results to x
        ret
```

Listing 14-1 begins with the declaration of a C++ structure named Vec128. This structure, which is the same one that you saw in Chapter 8, contains an anonymous C++ union that facilitates packed operand data exchange between functions written in C++ and assembly language. The alignas(16) specifier instructs the C++ compiler to align each instance of Vec128 on a 16-byte boundary. Structure Vec128 also includes member functions that format and display the contents of a Vec128 instance. Listing 14-1 does not show the source code for these member functions, but they are included in the downloadable software package.

Following the definition of Vec128 are the declarations for functions PackedAddI16_, PackedSubI16_, PackedAddU16_, and PackedSubU16_. Note that these functions require argument values of type Vec128. The C++ functions PackedAddI16, PackedSubI16, PackedAddU16, and PackedSubU16 contain code that perform test case initialization. These functions also display results of the calculations carried out by the assembly language functions.

Function PackedAddI16_ begins its execution with a ldr q0,[x1] instruction. This variant of the ldr instruction loads the 128-bit wide operand pointed to by register X1 (argument value a) into SIMD register Q0, which is an alias for SIMD register V0 (see Chapter 10, Figure 10-2). The ldr instruction cannot be used with V register operands but other Armv8-64 SIMD load instructions can as you will soon see. The next instruction, ldr q1,[x2], loads argument value b into register Q1 (V1). The ensuing add v2.8h,v0.8h,v1.8h (add vector) instruction performs packed integer addition using eight halfword (16-bit) integers. The .8h suffix that is appended to each V register operand is called an arrangement specifier. An arrangement specifier designates the element type that an Armv8-64 SIMD instruction uses when carrying out its calculations. Table 14-1 lists valid arrangement specifiers. You will see additional examples of arrangement specifier usage throughout this chapter and in Chapters 15 and 16.

Table 14-1. *Arrangement specifiers for Armv8-64 SIMD instructions*

Specifier	Vector Size	Data Type	Typical Use
.8b	64 bits	Packed bytes	8-bit integers
.16b	128 bits	Packed bytes	8-bit integers
.4h	64 bits	Packed halfwords	16-bit integers, half-precision floating-point
.8h	128 bits	Packed halfwords	16-bit integers, half-precision floating-point
.2s	64 bits	Packed words	32-bit integers, single-precision floating-point
.4s	128 bits	Packed words	32-bit integers, single-precision floating-point
.2d	128 bits	Packed doublewords	64-bit integers, double-precision floating-point

Following the add instruction, PackedAddI16_ uses a str q2,[x0] instruction that stores the packed addition result in x[0]. Like the ldr instruction, the str instruction cannot be used with a V register operand. The ensuing sqadd v3.8h,v0.8h,v1.8h (signed saturating add) instruction sums the elements of argument values a and b using saturated instead of wraparound arithmetic. This is followed by a str q2,[x0,16] instruction that saves the result to x[1]. Function PackedSubI16_ illustrates packed signed integer subtraction. This function is identical to PackedAddI16_ except for the use of the sub and sqsub (signed saturating subtract) instructions.

Functions PackedAddU16_ and PackedSubU16_ demonstrate packed integer addition and subtraction using unsigned 16-bit integer elements. The first instruction of PackedAddU16_, ld1 {v0.8h},[x1] (load multiple single-element structures), loads argument value a into register V0. Besides using V register operands, the ld1 instruction differs from the ldr instruction in that the former supports loading up to four consecutively numbered V registers. You will see examples of this in Chapters 15 and 16. The next instruction, ld1 {v1.8h},[x2], loads argument value b into register V1. This is followed by an add v2.8h,v0.8h,v1.8h instruction that performs packed addition using halfword elements. The ensuing uqadd v3.8h,v0.8h,v1.8h (unsigned saturating add) instruction also performs packed halfword addition using saturating arithmetic.

Following its additions, PackedAddU16_ uses a st1 {v2.8h,v3.8h},[x0] (store multiple single-element structures) to save the results. This instruction, which is the store counterpart of the ld1 instruction, saves the contents of registers V2 and V3 to x[0] and x[1], respectively. Function PackedSubU16_ performs packed unsigned halfword integer subtraction using the sub and uqsub v3.8h,v0.8h,v1.8h (unsigned saturating subtract) instructions. Here are the results for source code example Ch14_01:

```
Results for PackedAddI16 - Wraparound Addition
a:          10     200      30  -32766  |      50      60   32000  -32000
b:         100    -200   32760    -400  |     500    -600    1200    -950
x[0]:      110       0  -32746   32370  |     550    -540  -32336   32586

Results for PackedAddI16 - Saturated Addition
a:          10     200      30  -32766  |      50      60   32000  -32000
b:         100    -200   32760    -400  |     500    -600    1200    -950
x[1]:      110       0  -32746   32370  |     550    -540  -32336   32586

Results for PackedSubI16 - Wraparound Subtraction
a:          10     200     -30  -32766  |      50      60   32000  -32000
b:         100    -200   32760     400  |     500    -600    1200     950
x[0]:      -90     400   32746   32370  |    -450     660   30800   32586

Results for PackedSubI16 - Saturated Subtraction
a:          10     200     -30  -32766  |      50      60   32000  -32000
b:         100    -200   32760     400  |     500    -600    1200     950
x[1]:      -90     400   32746   32370  |    -450     660   30800   32586


------------------------------------------------------------------------


Results for PackedAddU16 - Wraparound Addition
a:          10     200     300   32766  |      50   20000   32000   32000
b:         100     200   65530   40000  |     500   25000    1200   50000
x[0]:      110     400     294    7230  |     550   45000   33200   16464

Results for PackedAddU16 - Saturated Addition
a:          10     200     300   32766  |      50   20000   32000   32000
b:         100     200   65530   40000  |     500   25000    1200   50000
x[1]:      110     400   65535   65535  |     550   45000   33200   65535

Results for PackedSubU16 - Wraparound Subtraction
a:          10     200      30   65000  |      60   25000   32000    1200
b:         100     200       7    5000  |     500   28000    1200     950
x[0]:    65446       0      23   60000  |   65096   62536   30800     250
```

Results for PackedSubI16 - Saturated Subtraction

a:	10	200	30	65000		60	25000	32000	1200
b:	100	200	7	5000		500	28000	1200	950
x[1]:	0	0	23	60000		0	0	30800	250

Shift Operations

Listing 14-2 shows the source code for example Ch14_02. This example demonstrates packed shift operations using halfword elements.

Listing 14-2. Example Ch14_02

```
//----------------------------------------------------
//                  Ch14_02.cpp
//----------------------------------------------------

#include <iostream>
#include "Vec128.h"

using namespace std;

extern "C" bool PackedShiftA_(Vec128* x, const Vec128& a);
extern "C" bool PackedShiftB_(Vec128* x, const Vec128& a, const Vec128& b);
extern "C" bool PackedShiftC_(Vec128* x, const Vec128& a);

void PackedShiftA(void)
{
    Vec128 x[3], a;
    const char nl = '\n';

    a.m_U16[0] = 0x1234;
    a.m_U16[1] = 0xFF9B;
    a.m_U16[2] = 0x00CC;
    a.m_U16[3] = 0xBD98;
    a.m_U16[4] = 0x00FF;
    a.m_U16[5] = 0xAAAA;
    a.m_U16[6] = 0x0F0F;
    a.m_U16[7] = 0x0065;

    PackedShiftA_(x, a);
    cout << "\nPackedShiftA_ (shl 4, sshr 2, ushr 3)\n";
    cout << "a:   " << a.ToStringX16() << nl;
    cout << "x[0]: " << x[0].ToStringX16() << nl;
    cout << "x[1]: " << x[1].ToStringX16() << nl;
    cout << "x[2]: " << x[2].ToStringX16() << nl;
}
```

```
void PackedShiftB(void)
{
    Vec128 x[2], a, b;
    const char nl = '\n';

    a.m_U16[0] = 0x1234;     b.m_I16[0] = 3;
    a.m_U16[1] = 0xFF9B;     b.m_I16[1] = -4;
    a.m_U16[2] = 0x00CC;     b.m_I16[2] = 2;
    a.m_U16[3] = 0xBD98;     b.m_I16[3] = -6;
    a.m_U16[4] = 0x00FF;     b.m_I16[4] = 7;
    a.m_U16[5] = 0xAAAA;     b.m_I16[5] = 1;
    a.m_U16[6] = 0x0F0F;     b.m_I16[6] = -2;
    a.m_U16[7] = 0x0065;     b.m_I16[7] = 5;

    PackedShiftB_(x, a, b);
    cout << "\nPackedShiftB_ (sshl, ushl)\n";
    cout << "a:    " << a.ToStringX16() << nl;
    cout << "b:    " << b.ToStringI16() << nl;
    cout << "x[0]: " << x[0].ToStringX16() << nl;
    cout << "x[1]: " << x[1].ToStringX16() << nl;
}

void PackedShiftC(void)
{
    Vec128 x[4], a;
    const char nl = '\n';

    a.m_U16[0] = 0x1234;
    a.m_U16[1] = 0xFF9B;
    a.m_U16[2] = 0x00CC;
    a.m_U16[3] = 0xEA98;
    a.m_U16[4] = 0x00FF;
    a.m_U16[5] = 0xAAAA;
    a.m_U16[6] = 0x0F0F;
    a.m_U16[7] = 0x0065;

    PackedShiftC_(x, a);
    cout << "\nPackedShiftC_ (sshll 4, sshll2 4, ushll 4, ushll2 4)\n";
    cout << "a:    " << a.ToStringX16() << nl;
    cout << "x[0]: " << x[0].ToStringX32() << nl;
    cout << "x[1]: " << x[1].ToStringX32() << nl;
    cout << "x[2]: " << x[2].ToStringX32() << nl;
    cout << "x[3]: " << x[3].ToStringX32() << nl;
}

int main(void)
{
    string sep(75, '-');
```

```
    PackedShiftA();
    cout << '\n' << sep << '\n';
    PackedShiftB();
    cout << '\n' << sep << '\n';
    PackedShiftC();
    return 0;
}


//----------------------------------------------------
//                  Ch14_02_.s
//----------------------------------------------------

// extern "C" bool PackedShiftA_(Vec128* x, const Vec128& a);

            .text
            .global PackedShiftA_
PackedShiftA_:
            ld1 {v0.8h},[x1]            // v0 = a

            shl v1.8h,v0.8h,4           // left shift
            sshr v2.8h,v0.8h,2          // signed right shift
            ushr v3.8h,v0.8h,3          // unsigned right shift

            st1 {v1.8h,v2.8h,v3.8h},[x0]    // save results to x
            ret

// extern "C" bool PackedShiftB_(Vec128* x, const Vec128& a, const Vec128& b);

            .global PackedShiftB_
PackedShiftB_:
            ld1 {v0.8h},[x1]            // v0 = a
            ld1 {v1.8h},[x2]            // v1 = b (shift counts)

            sshl v2.8h,v0.8h,v1.8h      // signed shift
            ushl v3.8h,v0.8h,v1.8h      // unsigned shift

            st1 {v2.8h,v3.8h},[x0]      // save results to x
            ret

// extern "C" bool PackedShiftC_(Vec128* x, const Vec128& a);

            .global PackedShiftC_
PackedShiftC_:
            ld1 {v0.8h},[x1]            // v0 = a

            sshll v1.4s,v0.4h,4         // signed left shift (low half)
            sshll2 v2.4s,v0.8h,4        // signed left shift (top half)
            ushll v3.4s,v0.4h,4         // unsigned left shift (low half)
            ushll2 v4.4s,v0.8h,4        // unsigned left shift (top half)

            st1 {v1.4s,v2.4s,v3.4s,v4.4s},[x0]  // save results to x
            ret
```

The C++ code in Listing 14-2 includes three functions named PackedShiftA, PackedShiftB, and PackedShiftC. Like the previous example, these functions perform test case initialization and display results.

The first instruction of assembly language function PackedShiftA_, ld1 {v0.8h},[x1], loads argument value a into register V0. This is followed by a shl v1.8h,v0.8h,4 (shift left) instruction that left shifts each halfword element in register V0 by four bits and saves the result to register V1. The next instruction, sshr v2.8h,v0.8h,2 (signed shift right) performs a 2-bit arithmetic right shift of each halfword element in V0. The ensuing ushr v3.8h,v0.8h,3 instruction (unsigned shift right) carries out a 3-bit logical right shift of each halfword element in V0. Function PackedShiftA_ then uses a st1 {v1.8h,v2.8h,v3.8h},[x0] instruction to save its shift results to array elements x[0], x[1], and x[2].

Function PackedShiftB_ demonstrates packed halfword shift operations using variable bit counts. This function employs the instruction pair ld1 {v0.8h},[x1] and ld1 {v1.8h},[x2] to load argument values a and b into register V0 and V1, respectively. The next instruction, sshl v2.8h,v0.8h,v1.8h (signed left shift register), shifts each halfword element in register V0 using the bit count specified by the low-order byte of the corresponding element in register V1. If the element shift count in V1 is positive, the sshl instruction performs a left shift; otherwise, it performs an arithmetic right shift. The ensuing ushl v3.8h,v0.8h,v1.8h (unsigned shift left register) instruction is the unsigned counterpart of the sshl instruction. Like the sshl instruction, the ushl instruction also requires signed shift bit count elements in its second source operand. Following the packed variable shift operations, function PackedShiftB_ uses a st1 {v2.8h,v3.8h},[x0] to save the results to array x.

Function PackedShiftC_ begins its execution with a ld1 {v0.8h},[x1] instruction that loads argument value a into register V0. The next instruction, sshll v1.4s,v0.4h,4 (signed shift left long immediate), sign-extends the four low-order halfwords in register V0 to 32 bits and then shifts each of these values left by 4 bits. The result is then saved in register V1. The ensuing sshll2 v2.4s,v0.8h,4 performs the same operation using the four high-order halfwords in register V0. Note that in this instruction, register V0 uses an arrangement specifier of .8h instead of .4h. Figure 14-1 illustrates execution of the sshll and sshll2 instructions.

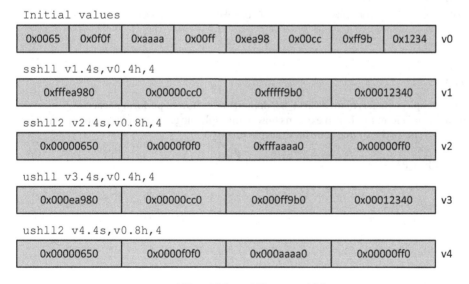

Figure 14-1. *Execution of the sshll, sshll2, ushll, and ushll2 instructions using halfword integers*

Function PackedShiftC_ then uses the instructions ushll v3.4s,v0.4h,4 (unsigned shift left long immediate) and ushll2 v4.4s,v0.8h,4, which are the unsigned counterparts of sshll and sshll2. Execution of these instructions is also shown in Figure 14-1. A st1 {v1.4s,v2.4s,v3.4s,v4.4s},[x0] instruction saves all of the calculated shift results to array x. Here are the results for source code example Ch14_02:

```
PackedShiftA_ (shl 4, sshr 2, ushr 3)
a:       1234    FF9B    00CC    BD98  |   00FF    AAAA    0F0F    0065
x[0]:    2340    F9B0    0CC0    D980  |   0FF0    AAA0    F0F0    0650
x[1]:    048D    FFE6    0033    EF66  |   003F    EAAA    03C3    0019
x[2]:    0246    1FF3    0019    17B3  |   001F    1555    01E1    000C


---------------------------------------------------------------------

PackedShiftB_ (sshl, ushl)
a:       1234    FF9B    00CC    BD98  |   00FF    AAAA    0F0F    0065
b:          3      -4       2      -6  |      7       1      -2       5
x[0]:    91A0    FFF9    0330    FEF6  |   7F80    5554    03C3    0CA0
x[1]:    91A0    0FF9    0330    02F6  |   7F80    5554    03C3    0CA0


---------------------------------------------------------------------

PackedShiftC_ (sshll 4, sshll2 4, ushll 4, ushll2 4)
a:       1234    FF9B    00CC    EA98  |   00FF    AAAA    0F0F    0065
x[0]:       00012340        FFFFF9B0  |       00000CC0        FFFEA980
x[1]:       00000FF0        FFFAAAA0  |       0000F0F0        00000650
x[2]:       00012340        000FF9B0  |       00000CC0        000EA980
x[3]:       00000FF0        000AAAA0  |       0000F0F0        00000650
```

Multiplication

The next source code example, which is named Ch14_03, demonstrates how to perform packed multiplication using halfword elements. It also explains how to multiply the elements of a vector operand by a scalar value. Listing 14-3 shows the source code for example Ch14_03.

Listing 14-3. Example Ch14_03

```cpp
//----------------------------------------------------
//              Ch14_03.cpp
//----------------------------------------------------

#include <iostream>
#include <string>
#include "Vec128.h"

using namespace std;

extern "C" bool PackedMulA_(Vec128* x, const Vec128& a, const Vec128& b, int16_t c);
```

```
void PackedMulA(void)
{
    Vec128 x[4], a, b;
    const int16_t c = 5;
    const char nl = '\n';
    string sep(75, '-');

    a.m_I16[0] = 10;        b.m_I16[0] = 6;
    a.m_I16[1] = 7;         b.m_I16[1] = 13;
    a.m_I16[2] = -23;       b.m_I16[2] = -75;
    a.m_I16[3] = 41;        b.m_I16[3] = 9;
    a.m_I16[4] = 6;         b.m_I16[4] = 37;
    a.m_I16[5] = -33;       b.m_I16[5] = 28;
    a.m_I16[6] = 19;        b.m_I16[6] = 56;
    a.m_I16[7] = 16;        b.m_I16[7] = -18;

    PackedMulA_(x, a, b, c);

    cout << "\nPackedMulA_\n";
    cout << sep << nl;

    cout << "a:    " << a.ToStringI16() << nl;
    cout << "b:    " << b.ToStringI16() << nl << nl;
    cout << "x[0]: " << x[0].ToStringI16() << nl << nl;
    cout << "x[1]: " << x[1].ToStringI16() << nl << nl;
    cout << "x[2]: " << x[2].ToStringI32() << nl;
    cout << "x[3]: " << x[3].ToStringI32() << nl;
}

int main(void)
{
    PackedMulA();
    return 0;
}

//--------------------------------------------------
//                 Ch14_03_.s
//--------------------------------------------------

// extern "C" bool PackedMulA_(Vec128 x[4], const Vec128& a, const Vec128& b, int16_t c);

            .text
            .global PackedMulA_
PackedMulA_:
            ld1 {v0.8h},[x1]            // v0 = a
            ld1 {v1.8h},[x2]            // v1 = b

            mul v2.8h,v0.8h,v1.8h       // a * b (vector 16-bit)
            st1 {v2.8h},[x0],16         // save result x[0]
```

```
mov v3.8h[0],w3                    // load c into low 16 bits
mul v2.8h,v0.8h,v3.8h[0]           // mul elements in a by c
st1 {v2.8h},[x0],16                // save result to x[1]

smull v2.4s,v0.4h,v1.4h            // signed mul long
smull2 v3.4s,v0.8h,v1.8h
st1 {v2.4s,v3.4s},[x0]             // results to x[2], x[3]
ret
```

The C++ code in Listing 14-3 begins with the declaration of function PackedMulA_. Note that this function requires three arguments of type Vec128 along with a scalar value of type int16_t. The C++ function PackedMulA performs test case initialization and exercises PackedMulA_. It also streams results to cout.

Function PackedMulA_ begins its execution with the instruction pair ld1 {v0.8h},[x1] and ld1 {v1.8h},[x2]. These instructions load argument values a and b into registers V0 and V1, respectively. The ensuing mul v2.8h,v0.8h,v1.8h (multiply vector) instruction multiplies the corresponding halfword elements of its two source operands and saves the low-order 16 bits of each product in V2. The st1 {v2.8h},[x0],16 instruction then saves this result to x[0].

The next instruction, mov v3.8h[0],w3 (move general-purpose register to vector element), copies the low-order 16 bits of register W3 (argument value c) into the low-order 16 bits of register V3. Note that this instruction does not alter any other bits in register V3. The ensuing mul v2.8h,v0.8h,v3.8h[0] (multiply vector by element) instruction multiplies each halfword element in register V0 by the low-order halfword element of register V3. The st1 {v2.8h},[x0],16 that follows saves this result to x[1].

The final code block in PackedMulA_ illustrates the use of the smull (signed multiply long vector) and smull2 instructions. These instructions carry out signed SIMD multiplication. The first instruction of this block, smull v2.4s,v0.4h,v1.4h, multiples the four low-order halfword elements of V0 and V1. It then saves the full 32-bit element products in register V2. Then, the next instruction, smull2 v3.4s,v0.8h,v1.8h, calculates products using the four high-order halfword elements of source operands V0 and V1. Note that these registers use an arrangement specifier of .8h instead of .4h. The penultimate instruction of PackedMulA_, st1 {v2.4s,v3.4s},[x0], saves the results to x[2] and x[3]. The A64 instruction set also includes the instructions umull (unsigned multiply long vector) and umull2 that perform unsigned integer multiplication. Here are the results for source code example Ch14_03.

```
PackedMulA_
----------------------------------------------------------------------------
a:        10      7     -23      41   |      6     -33      19      16
b:         6     13     -75       9   |     37      28      56     -18

x[0]:     60     91    1725     369   |    222    -924    1064    -288

x[1]:     50     35    -115     205   |     30    -165      95      80

x[2]:            60             91    |           1725             369
x[3]:           222           -924    |           1064            -288
----------------------------------------------------------------------------
```

The A64 SIMD instructions used in this section's source code examples all employed halfword elements. Most of these instructions can also be used with byte, word, or doubleword elements by simply changing the arrangement specifier. You will see examples of this in the next section and in Chapters 15 and 16.

Packed Integer Image Processing

In Chapter 8, you learned how to code SIMD functions to carry out common image-processing operations. In this section, you will learn how to code similar function using the A64 SIMD instruction set. The first example contains code that determines the minimum and maximum values in an array of unsigned 8-bit integers. The second example illustrates pixel clipping. The final source code explains how to calculate basic statistics for a grayscale image.

Pixel Minimum and Maximum

Listing 14-4 shows the source code for example Ch14_04. This example, which is an A64 implementation of source code example Ch08_04, determines the minimum and maximum values in an array of unsigned 8-bit integers.

Listing 14-4. Example Ch14_04

```
//--------------------------------------------------
//                Ch14_04.h
//--------------------------------------------------

#pragma once
#include <cstdint>

// Ch08_04.cpp
extern void Init(uint8_t* x, uint64_t n, unsigned int seed);
extern bool CalcMinMaxU8(uint8_t* x_min, uint8_t* x_max, const uint8_t* x, uint64_t n);

// Ch08_04_BM.cpp
extern void MinMaxU8_BM(void);

// Ch08_04_.s
extern "C" bool CalcMinMaxU8_(uint8_t* x_min, uint8_t* x_max, const uint8_t* x, uint64_t n);

// Common constants
const uint64_t c_NumElements = 16 * 1024 * 1024 + 7;
const unsigned int c_RngSeedVal = 23;


//--------------------------------------------------
//                Ch14_04.cpp
//--------------------------------------------------

#include <iostream>
#include <cstdint>
#include <random>
#include "Ch14_04.h"
#include "AlignedMem.h"

using namespace std;
```

```
void Init(uint8_t* x, uint64_t n, unsigned int seed)
{
    uniform_int_distribution<> ui_dist {5, 250};
    mt19937 rng {seed};

    for (uint64_t i = 0; i < n; i++)
        x[i] = (uint8_t)ui_dist(rng);

    // Use known values for min & max (for test purposes)
    x[(n / 4) * 3 + 1] = 2;
    x[n / 4 + 11] = 3;
    x[n / 2] = 252;
    x[n / 2 + 13] = 253;
    x[n / 8 + 5] = 4;
    x[n / 8 + 7] = 254;
}

bool CalcMinMaxU8(uint8_t* x_min, uint8_t* x_max, const uint8_t* x, uint64_t n)
{
    if (n == 0)
        return false;

    if (!AlignedMem::IsAligned(x, 16))
        return false;

    uint8_t x_min_temp = 255;
    uint8_t x_max_temp = 0;

    for (uint64_t i = 0; i < n; i++)
    {
        uint8_t val = *x++;

        if (val < x_min_temp)
            x_min_temp = val;
        else if (val > x_max_temp)
            x_max_temp = val;
    }

    *x_min = x_min_temp;
    *x_max = x_max_temp;
    return true;
}

void MinMaxU8()
{
    uint64_t n = c_NumElements;
    AlignedArray<uint8_t> x_aa(n, 16);
    uint8_t* x = x_aa.Data();

    Init(x, n, c_RngSeedVal);
```

```
    uint8_t x_min1 = 0, x_max1 = 0;
    uint8_t x_min2 = 0, x_max2 = 0;
    bool rc1 = CalcMinMaxU8(&x_min1, &x_max1, x, n);
    bool rc2 = CalcMinMaxU8_(&x_min2, &x_max2, x, n);

    cout << "\nMinMaxU8\n";
    cout << "rc1: " << rc1 << "   x_min1: " << (int)x_min1;
    cout << "   x_max1: " << (int)x_max1 << '\n';
    cout << "rc2: " << rc2 << "   x_min2: " << (int)x_min2;
    cout << "   x_max2: " << (int)x_max2 << '\n';
}

int main()
{
    MinMaxU8();
    MinMaxU8_BM();
    return 0;
}


//-----------------------------------------------------
//                    Ch14_04_.s
//-----------------------------------------------------

// extern "C" bool CalcMinMaxU8_(uint8_t* x_min, uint8_t* x_max, const uint8_t* x, uint64_t n);

            .text
            .global CalcMinMaxU8_
CalcMinMaxU8_:

// Validate arguments
            cmp x3,0
            b.eq InvalidArg                  // jump if n == 0
            tst x2,0x0f
            b.ne InvalidArg                  // jump if x not 16b aligned

// Initialize
            mov w4,255
            dup v2.16b,w4
            mov v3.16b,v2.16b                // v2:v3 = packed min (32)
            eor v4.16b,v4.16b,v4.16b
            eor v5.16b,v5.16b,v5.16b         // v4:v5 = packed max (32)

            cmp x3,32
            b.lo SkipLoop1                   // jump if n < 32

// Main processing loop
Loop1:      ld1 {v0.16b,v1.16b},[x2],32      // load block of 32 pixels

            umin v2.16b,v2.16b,v0.16b
            umin v3.16b,v3.16b,v1.16b        // update pixel minimums
            umax v4.16b,v4.16b,v0.16b
            umax v5.16b,v5.16b,v1.16b        // update pixel maximums
```

```
            sub x3,x3,32                    // n -= 32
            cmp x3,32
            b.cs Loop1                      // jump if n >= 32

// Reduce packed minimums and maximums to scalar values
SkipLoop1:  umin v0.16b,v2.16b,v3.16b
            uminv b1,v0.16b
            umov w4,v1.b[0]                 // w4 = pixel min value

            umax v0.16b,v4.16b,v5.16b
            umaxv b1,v0.16b
            umov w5,v1.b[0]                 // w5 = pixel max value

            cmp x3,0
            b.eq SaveMinMax                 // jump if n == 0

// Process final pixels
Loop2:      ldrb w6,[x2],1                  // w6 = pixel value
            cmp w6,w4
            csel w4,w6,w4,lo                // update pixel min value
            cmp w6,w5
            csel w5,w6,w5,hi                // update pixel max value

            subs x3,x3,1                    // n -= 1
            b.ne Loop2                      // repeat until done

// Save results
SaveMinMax: strb w4,[x0]                    // save minimum to x_min
            strb w5,[x1]                    // save maximum to x_max
            mov w0,1                        // set success return code
            ret

InvalidArg: mov w0,0                        // set error return code
            ret
```

The C++ code in Listing 14-4 includes a function named Init that initializes an array of type uint8_t using random values. The next function, CalcMinMaxU8, is a C++ implementation of the min-max algorithm. The C++ function MinMaxU8 performs test case initialization. It also exercises the min-max calculating functions CalcMinMaxU8 and CalcMinMaxU8_. The AlignedArray<uint8_t> x_aa(n, 16) instance at the beginning of MinMaxU8 is a template class that dynamically allocates an aligned array of type uint8_t. Chapter 8 contains additional information about this class. The uint8_t* x = x_aa.Data() statement that follows obtains a pointer to the array data for use in functions CalcMinMaxU8 and CalcMinMaxU8_.

Function CalcMinMaxU8_ begins its execution with the instruction pair cmp x3,0 and b.eq InvalidArg. These instructions confirm that argument value n is not equal to zero. The next two instructions, tst x2,0x0f and b.ne InvalidArg, verify that argument value x is aligned on a 16-byte boundary. The tst (test bits) instruction performs a bitwise AND of its two source operands and updates the PSTATE.NZCV condition flags based on the result. The actual result of the bitwise AND operation is discarded.

The next code block in CalcMinMaxU8_ carries out initialization tasks for the min-max algorithm. It begins with a mov w4,255 instruction that loads 255 into register W4. This is followed by a dup v2.16b,w4 (duplicate general-purpose register to vector) instruction that copies the low-order byte in W4 to each byte element of register V2. Execution of the ensuing mov v3.16b,v2.16b instruction completes the initialization of register pair V2:V3 as a packed pixel minimum. The next two instructions, eor v4.16b,v4.16b,v4.16b and eor v5.16b,v5.16b,v5.16b, initialize register pair V4:V5 as a packed maximum.

The main processing loop is next. Note that just before the start of for-loop Loop1 is the instruction pair cmp x3,32 and b.lo SkipLoop1. This instruction pair tests argument value n to see if it is less than 32. If it is, the branch instruction skips over Loop1. The reason for this test is that Loop1 processes 32 pixels during each iteration; execution of this for-loop with less than 32 available pixels would generate an invalid result.

Each iteration of Loop1 begins with a ld1 {v0.16b,v1.16b},[x2],32 instruction that loads 32 pixel values into register pair V0:V1. This instruction also adds 32 to the array x pointer in register X2 so that it points to the next block of 32 pixels. The next two instructions, umin v2.16b,v2.16b,v0.16b and umin v3.16b,v3.16b,v1.16b, update the pixel minimums that are maintained in V2:V3. The umin (unsigned minimum) instruction compares corresponding elements in its two source operands and saves the smaller value to the corresponding element of the destination operand. The pixel maximum values in registers V4:V5 updated next using the instruction sequence umax v4.16b,v4.16b,v0.16b and umax v5.16b,v5.16b,v1.16b (unsigned maximum). The ensuing sub x3,x3,32 calculates n -= 32 and Loop1 repeats until the number of remaining pixels is less than 32.

Following execution of Loop1, the packed pixel minimums and maximums in register pairs V2:V3 and V4:V5 are reduced to a single scalar value. The umin v0.16b,v2.16b,v3.16b instruction reduces the number of pixel minimum values from 32 to 16. This is followed by a uminv b1,v0.16b (unsigned minimum across vector) instruction that copies the smallest byte element in register V0 to B1. The ensuing umov w4,v1.b[0] moves this value into register W4. The next code block, umax v0.16b,v4.16b,v5.16b, umaxv b1,v0.16b (unsigned maximum across vector), and umov w5,v1.b[0], yields the largest byte element in register W5.

For-loop Loop2 processes the final few pixels in the array using scalar instructions and the general-purpose registers. Note that Loop2 is skipped if n (X3) is equal to zero. The csel (conditional select) instructions in Loop2 copy the first source operand to the destination operand if the specified condition is true; otherwise, the second source operand is copied to the destination operand. CalcMinMaxU8_ saves the final pixel minimum and maximum values using the instructions strb r4,[x0] and strb r5,[x1]. Here are the results for source code example Ch14_04:

```
MinMaxU8
rc1: 1  x_min1: 2  x_max1: 254
rc2: 1  x_min2: 2  x_max2: 254

Running benchmark function MinMaxU8_BM - please wait
Benchmark times save to file Ch14_04_MinMaxU8_BM_RpiOmega.csv
```

Table 14-2 contains benchmark timing measurements for the functions CalcMinMaxU8 and CalcMinMaxU8_. These measurements were made using the hardware and software configurations described in Appendix A. Chapter 8 also contains additional details about the benchmark timing measurements used in this book.

Table 14-2. *Mean execution times (microseconds) for pixel min-max functions (16777223 elements)*

C++ (CalcMinMaxU8)	Assembly Language (CalcMinMaxU8_)
34805	4353

Pixel Clipping

Pixel clipping is an image-processing technique that bounds the intensity values of each pixel in an image between two threshold limits. This technique is often used to reduce the dynamic range of an image by eliminating its extremely dark and light pixels. Source code example Ch14_05, shown in Listing 14-5, illustrates how to use the A64 SIMD instruction set to clip the pixels of an 8-bit grayscale image.

Listing 14-5. Example Ch14_05

```
//--------------------------------------------------
//                  Ch14_05.h
//--------------------------------------------------

#pragma once
#include <cstdint>

struct ClipData
{
    uint8_t* m_Des;                 // destination buffer pointer
    uint8_t* m_Src;                 // source buffer pointer
    uint64_t m_NumPixels;           // number of pixels
    uint64_t m_NumClippedPixels;    // number of clipped pixels
    uint8_t m_ThreshLo;             // low threshold
    uint8_t m_ThreshHi;             // high threshold
};

// Ch14_05.cpp
extern void Init(uint8_t* x, uint64_t n, unsigned int seed);
extern bool ClipPixelsCpp(ClipData* cd);

// Ch14_05a_.s
extern "C" bool ClipPixelsA_(ClipData* cd);

// Ch14_05b_.s
extern "C" bool ClipPixelsB_(ClipData* cd);

// Ch14_05_BM.cpp
extern void ClipPixels_BM(void);

// Ch14_05_Misc.cpp
extern void PrintClipDataStructOffsets(void);

// Algorithm constants
const uint8_t c_ThreshLo = 10;
const uint8_t c_ThreshHi = 245;
const uint64_t c_NumPixels = 8 * 1024 * 1024;
const unsigned int c_Seed = 157;

//--------------------------------------------------
//                  Ch14_05.cpp
//--------------------------------------------------
```

```cpp
#include <iostream>
#include <random>
#include <memory.h>
#include "Ch14_05.h"
#include "AlignedMem.h"

using namespace std;

void Init(uint8_t* x, uint64_t n, unsigned int seed)
{
    uniform_int_distribution<> ui_dist {0, 255};
    default_random_engine rng {seed};

    for (size_t i = 0; i < n; i++)
        x[i] = (uint8_t)ui_dist(rng);
}

bool ClipPixelsCpp(ClipData* cd)
{
    uint8_t* src = cd->m_Src;
    uint8_t* des = cd->m_Des;
    uint64_t num_pixels = cd->m_NumPixels;

    if (num_pixels == 0 || (num_pixels % 64) != 0)
        return false;

    if (!AlignedMem::IsAligned(src, 16))
        return false;
    if (!AlignedMem::IsAligned(des, 16))
        return false;

    uint64_t num_clipped_pixels = 0;
    uint8_t thresh_lo = cd->m_ThreshLo;
    uint8_t thresh_hi = cd->m_ThreshHi;

    for (uint64_t i = 0; i < num_pixels; i++)
    {
        uint8_t pixel = src[i];

        if (pixel < thresh_lo)
        {
            des[i] = thresh_lo;
            num_clipped_pixels++;
        }
        else if (pixel > thresh_hi)
        {
            des[i] = thresh_hi;
            num_clipped_pixels++;
        }
        else
            des[i] = src[i];
    }
```

```
        cd->m_NumClippedPixels = num_clipped_pixels;
        return true;
}

void ClipPixels(void)
{
        const char nl = '\n';

        AlignedArray<uint8_t> src(c_NumPixels, 16);
        AlignedArray<uint8_t> des1(c_NumPixels, 16);
        AlignedArray<uint8_t> des2(c_NumPixels, 16);
        AlignedArray<uint8_t> des3(c_NumPixels, 16);

        Init(src.Data(), c_NumPixels, c_Seed);

        ClipData cd1;
        cd1.m_Src = src.Data();
        cd1.m_Des = des1.Data();
        cd1.m_NumPixels = c_NumPixels;
        cd1.m_NumClippedPixels = c_NumPixels + 1;
        cd1.m_ThreshLo = c_ThreshLo;
        cd1.m_ThreshHi = c_ThreshHi;

        ClipData cd2;
        cd2.m_Src = src.Data();
        cd2.m_Des = des2.Data();
        cd2.m_NumPixels = c_NumPixels;
        cd2.m_NumClippedPixels = c_NumPixels + 1;
        cd2.m_ThreshLo = c_ThreshLo;
        cd2.m_ThreshHi = c_ThreshHi;

        ClipData cd3;
        cd3.m_Src = src.Data();
        cd3.m_Des = des3.Data();
        cd3.m_NumPixels = c_NumPixels;
        cd3.m_NumClippedPixels = c_NumPixels + 1;
        cd3.m_ThreshLo = c_ThreshLo;
        cd3.m_ThreshHi = c_ThreshHi;

        bool rc1 = ClipPixelsCpp(&cd1);
        bool rc2 = ClipPixelsA_(&cd2);
        bool rc3 = ClipPixelsB_(&cd3);

        cout << "\nResults for ClipPixels\n";
        cout << "  rc1:                      " << boolalpha << rc1 << nl;
        cout << "  rc2:                      " << boolalpha << rc2 << nl;
        cout << "  rc3:                      " << boolalpha << rc3 << nl;
        cout << "  cd1.m_NumPixels1:         " << cd1.m_NumPixels << nl;
        cout << "  cd2.m_NumPixels2:         " << cd2.m_NumPixels << nl;
        cout << "  cd3.m_NumPixels3:         " << cd3.m_NumPixels << nl;
        cout << "  cd1.m_NumClippedPixels1:  " << cd1.m_NumClippedPixels << nl;
```

```
        cout << "  cd2.m_NumClippedPixels2: " << cd2.m_NumClippedPixels << nl;
        cout << "  cd3.m_NumClippedPixels3: " << cd3.m_NumClippedPixels << nl;

        if (cd1.m_NumClippedPixels != cd2.m_NumClippedPixels)
            cout << "  NumClippedPixels compare error\n";
        if (cd1.m_NumClippedPixels != cd2.m_NumClippedPixels)
            cout << "  NumClippedPixels compare error\n";

        if (memcmp(des1.Data(), des2.Data(), c_NumPixels) != 0)
            cout << "  Pixel buffer memory compare error\n";
        if (memcmp(des1.Data(), des3.Data(), c_NumPixels) != 0)
            cout << "  Pixel buffer memory compare error\n";
}

int main(void)
{
//    PrintClipDataStructOffsets();
    ClipPixels();
    ClipPixels_BM();
    return 0;
}

//----------------------------------------------------
//                 Ch14_05_Macros_.inc
//----------------------------------------------------

// Macro ClipPix
//
// Input:           Vreg - original source pixels
//
// Output:          Vreg - clipped pixels
//
// Data registers:  v16 - packed m_ThreshLo
//                  v17 - packed m_ThreshHi
//                  v18 - packed 0x01
//                  x8 - num_clipped_pixels
//
// Temp registers:  v0, v1, v2, v3, x9

            .macro ClipPix Vreg
            umax v0.16b,\Vreg\().16b,v16.16b      // clip to thresh_lo
            umin v1.16b,v0.16b,v17.16b            // clip to thresh_hi

            cmeq v2.16b,v1.16b,\Vreg\().16b       // compare clipped to original
            not v2.16b,v2.16b
            and v3.16b,v2.16b,v18.16b             // clipped if lane = 0x01
            addv b3,v3.16b                        // b3 = num clipped pixels

            umov w9,v3.b[0]
            add x8,x8,x9                          // num_clipped_pixels += x9
            mov \Vreg\().16b,v1.16b               // save clipped pixels
            .endm
```

```
//----------------------------------------------------
//                  Ch14_05a_.s
//----------------------------------------------------

            .include "Ch14_05_Macros_.inc"

// extern "C" bool ClipPixels_(ClipData* cd);

            .equ m_Des,0
            .equ m_Src,8
            .equ m_NumPixels,16
            .equ m_NumClippedPixels,24
            .equ m_ThreshLo,32
            .equ m_ThreshHi,33

            .equ NPPI,64                    // num pixels per iteration

            .text
            .global ClipPixelsA_
ClipPixelsA_:
// Load elements from structure
            mov x7,x0                       // x7 = cd
            ldr x0,[x7,m_Des]
            ldr x1,[x7,m_Src]
            ldr x2,[x7,m_NumPixels]
            ldrb w3,[x7,m_ThreshLo]
            ldrb w4,[x7,m_ThreshHi]

// Validate structure values
            cmp x2,0
            b.eq InvalidArg                 // m_NumPixels == 0
            tst x2,0x3f
            b.ne InvalidArg                 // m_NumPixels % 64 != 0

            tst x0,0x0f
            b.ne InvalidArg                 // m_Des not 16b aligned
            tst x1,0x0f
            b.ne InvalidArg                 // m_Src not 16b aligned

// Initialize
            dup v16.16b,w3                  // v16 = packed m_ThreshLo
            dup v17.16b,w4                  // v17 = packed m_ThreshHi
            movi v18.16b,0x01               // v18 = packed 0x01
            mov x8,0                        // num_clipped_pixels = 0

// Main processing loop
Loop1:      ld1 {v4.16b-v7.16b},[x1],NPPI   // load pixel block

            ClipPix v4                      // clip pixels in v4
            ClipPix v5                      // clip pixels in v5
            ClipPix v6                      // clip pixels in v6
            ClipPix v7                      // clip pixels in v7
```

```
        st1 {v4.16b-v7.16b},[x0],NPPI        // save clipped pix

        subs x2,x2,NPPI                      // num_pixels -= NPPI
        b.ne Loop1

        str x8,[x7,m_NumClippedPixels]       // save m_NumClippedPixels
        mov w0,1                             // set success return code
        ret

        mov w0,1
        ret

InvalidArg: mov w0,0                         // set error return code
        ret
```

The C++ code in Listing 14-5 begins with declaration of a structure named ClipData. This structure maintains the data that is used by the pixel-clipping algorithm. The first C++ function in Listing 14-5 is named Init. This function initializes the elements of a uint8_t array using random values, which simulates the pixel values of a grayscale image. The function ClipPixelsCpp is a C++ implementation of the pixel-clipping algorithm. This function starts by validating num_pixels for correct size and divisibility by 64. As mentioned in Chapter 8, restricting the algorithm to images that contain an even multiple of 64 pixels is not as inflexible as it might appear since most digital camera images are sized using this multiple pixel due to the processing requirements of the JPEG compression algorithms. Following validation of num_pixels, the source and destination pixel buffers are checked for proper alignment.

The procedure used in ClipPixelsCpp to perform pixel clipping is straightforward. A simple for-loop examines each pixel element in the source image buffer. If a source image pixel buffer intensity value is found to be below thresh_lo or above thresh_hi, the corresponding threshold limit is saved in the destination buffer. Source image pixels whose intensity values lie between the two threshold limits are copied to the destination pixel buffer unaltered. The for-loop in ClipPixelsCpp also counts the number of clipped pixels (num_clipped_pixels) for comparison purposes with the assembly language version of the algorithm.

Function ClipPixels employs the C++ template class AlignedArray to allocate and manage the required image pixel buffers. Following source image pixel buffer initialization, ClipPixels primes three instances of ClipData (cd1, cd2, and cd3) for use by the pixel-clipping functions ClipPixelsCpp, ClipPixelsA_, and ClipPixelsB_. It then invokes these functions and compares the results for any discrepancies.

The assembly language code in Listing 14-5 begins with the definition of a macro named ClipPix. Note that this macro is defined in a separate assembler include file named Ch14_05_Macros_.inc. Macro ClipPix contains instructions that perform pixel clipping on a block of 16 pixels. Prior to using this macro, a function must load m_ThreshLo, m_ThreshHi, and 0x01 into the byte elements of registers V16, V17, and V18, respectively.

The .macro directive statement for ClipPix includes a single argument named Vreg. This argument represents an Armv8-64 SIMD V register that contains a block of 16 pixels. The first instruction in ClipPix, umax v0.16b,\Vreg\().16b,v16.16b, clips the pixels in Vreg to thresh_lo. In this statement, the assembler substitutes the user-supplied register name for the symbol \Vreg\(). Note that the macro argument name Vreg includes the prefix string "\" and the suffix string "\()". To use a macro argument name inside a macro definition, it must be prefixed with a backslash ("\") character. It is also sometimes necessary to append the suffix string "\()" to a macro argument name. This helps the GNU assembler distinguish the macro argument name string from the ensuing text. In the umax instruction, the "\()" suffix string prevents the assembler from parsing the .16b arrangement specifier as a macro directive (recall that all GNU assembler directives begin with a "." character).

Following the umax instruction is a umin v1.16b,v0.16b,v17.16b instruction that clips the pixels in Vreg to thresh_hi. The next instruction, cmeq v2.16b,v1.16b,\Vreg\().16b (compare bitwise equal), compares the byte elements in Vreg (original pixels) and V1 (clipped pixels). It sets the corresponding byte element in V2 to 0xFF if the source element operands are equal; otherwise, the byte element in V2 is set to 0x00. The ensuing instruction triplet, not v2.16b,v2.16b, and v3.16b,v2.16b,v18.16b, and addv b3,v3.16b, calculates the number of clipped pixels in the current block and saves this result in register B3. Recall from the discussions in Chapter 10 that register B3 is the low-order byte of register V3 (see Chapter 10, Figure 10-2). Figure 14-2 illustrates the pixel-clipping operation used by macro ClipPix in greater detail. After counting the number of clipped pixels in the current pixel block, ClipPix uses the instructions umov w9,v3.b[0] and add x8,x8,x9 to update num_clipped_pixels, which is maintained in register X8.

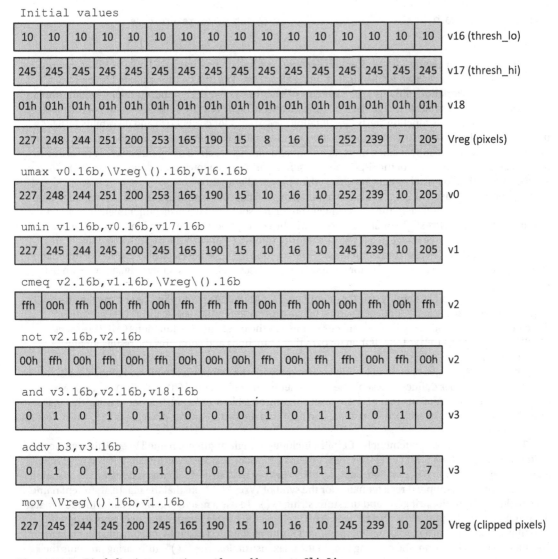

Figure 14-2. *Pixel-clipping operation performed by macro ClipPix*

Just before the definition of function ClipPixelsA_ in Listing 14-5 is the statement .include "Ch14_05_Macros_.inc". This assembly language directive is equivalent to the C++ preprocessor #include directive. The quotes that surround the .include directive filename are required. Following the .include directive is a series of .equ directives that define offsets for members of the ClipData structure. The .equ NPPI,64 directive that follows defines the number of pixels that for-loop Loop1 will process during each iteration. Function ClipPixelsA_ begins its execution with a series of load instructions that copy values from the supplied ClipData structure into registers. This is followed by a code block that validates m_NumPixels for size. The next code block verifies that both m_Des and m_Src are aligned on a 16-byte boundary.

Prior to the start of for-loop Loop1, the dup v16.16b,w3 and dup v17.16b,w4 instructions load m_ThreshLo and m_ThreshHi into each byte element of register V16 and V17, respectively. The next instruction, movi v18.16b,0x01 (move immediate vector), loads 0x01 into each byte element of V18. This is followed by a mov x8,0 instruction that sets num_clipped_pixels equal to zero.

Each iteration of Loop1 begins with a ld1 {v4.16b-v7.16b},[x1],NPPI instruction that loads NPPI pixels into registers V4-V7. The pixel values in each V register are then clipped using the macro ClipPix. Note that each use of ClipPix employs a different register argument. The ensuing st1 {v4.16b-v7.16b},[x0],NPPI instruction saves the clipped pixels to the destination pixel buffer. Following execution of for-loop Loop1, the str x8,[x7,m_NumClippedPixels] instruction saves the final number of clipped pixels.

Example Ch14_05 also includes an assembly language function named ClipPixelsB_. This function, which is included for benchmarking purposes, differs from ClipPixelsA_ in that it processes 16 pixels per iteration of Loop1 instead of 64. The source code for ClipPixelsB_ is not shown in Listing 14-5 but is included in the downloadable software package. Here are the results for source code example Ch14_05:

```
Results for ClipPixels
  rc1:                     true
  rc2:                     true
  rc3:                     true
  cd1.m_NumPixels1:        8388608
  cd2.m_NumPixels2:        8388608
  cd3.m_NumPixels3:        8388608
  cd1.m_NumClippedPixels1: 654518
  cd2.m_NumClippedPixels2: 654518
  cd3.m_NumClippedPixels3: 654518

Running benchmark function ClipPixels_BM - please wait
Benchmark times save to file Ch14_05_ClipPixels_BM_RpiOmega.csv
```

Table 14-3 contains benchmark timing measurements for the functions ClipPixelsCpp, ClipPixelsA_, and ClipPixelsB_. Note that there is a nontrivial performance difference between assembly language functions ClipPixelsA_ and ClipPixelsB_. Recall that these functions processed 64 and 16 pixels per iteration of for-loop Loop1, respectively. The processing of multiple elements per for-loop iteration reduces the number of branch and counter update instructions that are executed. The former is especially important since program branches can disrupt the processor's front-end and execution pipelines, which affects overall performance. The reduction or elimination of for-loop branching and counter update operations is an optimization technique known as loop unrolling (or loop unwinding).

Table 14-3. *Mean execution times (microseconds) for pixel-clipping functions (8388608 pixels)*

C++ (ClipPixelsCpp)	Assembly Language (ClipPixelsA_)	Assembly Language (ClipPixelsB_)
30458	3942	4341

Image Statistics

Listing 14-6 shows the source code for example Ch14_06. This example calculates the mean and standard deviation of grayscale image using its pixel intensity values.

Listing 14-6. Example Ch14_06

```
//--------------------------------------------------
//              Ch14_06.h
//--------------------------------------------------

#pragma once
#include <cstdint>

struct ImageStats
{
    uint8_t* m_PixelBuffer;
    uint64_t m_NumPixels;
    uint64_t m_PixelSum;
    uint64_t m_PixelSumSquares;
    double m_PixelMean;
    double m_PixelSd;
};

// Ch14_06.cpp
extern bool CalcImageStatsCpp(ImageStats& im_stats);

// Ch14_06_.asm
extern "C" bool CalcImageStats_(ImageStats& im_stats);

// Ch04_06_BM.cpp
extern void CalcImageStats_BM(void);

//--------------------------------------------------
//              Ch14_06.cpp
//--------------------------------------------------

#include <iostream>
#include <iomanip>
#include <cstdint>
#include <stdexcept>
#include <cmath>
#include "Ch14_06.h"
#include "AlignedMem.h"
#include "ImageMatrix.h"
```

```cpp
using namespace std;

bool CalcImageStatsCpp(ImageStats& im_stats)
{
    uint64_t num_pixels = im_stats.m_NumPixels;
    const uint8_t* pb = im_stats.m_PixelBuffer;

    // Perform validation checks
    if (!AlignedMem::IsAligned(pb, 16))
        return false;
    if (num_pixels == 0)
        return false;
    if (num_pixels % 64 != 0)
        return false;

    // Calculate intermediate sums
    uint64_t pixel_sum = 0;
    uint64_t pixel_sum_squares = 0;

    for (size_t i = 0; i < num_pixels; i++)
    {
        uint32_t pval = pb[i];

        pixel_sum += pval;
        pixel_sum_squares += pval * pval;
    }

    im_stats.m_PixelSum = pixel_sum;
    im_stats.m_PixelSumSquares = pixel_sum_squares;

    // Calculate mean and standard deviation
    im_stats.m_PixelMean = (double)im_stats.m_PixelSum / im_stats.m_NumPixels;

    double temp0 = (double)im_stats.m_NumPixels * im_stats.m_PixelSumSquares;
    double temp1 = (double)im_stats.m_PixelSum * im_stats.m_PixelSum;
    double var_num = temp0 - temp1;
    double var_den = (double)im_stats.m_NumPixels * (im_stats.m_NumPixels - 1);

    im_stats.m_PixelSd = sqrt(var_num / var_den);
    return true;
}

void CalcImageStats()
{
    const char nl = '\n';
    const char* image_fn = "../../Data/ImageB.png";

    ImageMatrix im(image_fn, PixelType::Gray8, Channel::R);
    uint64_t num_pixels = im.GetNumPixels();
    uint8_t* pb = im.GetPixelBuffer<uint8_t>();
```

```
    if (num_pixels % 64 != 0)
    {
        cout << "Error: number of pixels in image " << image_fn << nl;
        cout << "must be an integral multiple of 64.\n";
        return;
    }

    ImageStats is1;
    is1.m_PixelBuffer = pb;
    is1.m_NumPixels = num_pixels;

    ImageStats is2;
    is2.m_PixelBuffer = pb;
    is2.m_NumPixels = num_pixels;

    bool rc1 = CalcImageStatsCpp(is1);
    bool rc2 = CalcImageStats_(is2);

    // Display results
    const char* s = " | ";
    const unsigned int w1 = 22;
    const unsigned int w2 = 12;
    cout << fixed << setprecision(5) << left;
    cout << "\nResults for CalcImageStats - image_fn = " << image_fn << nl;

    if (!rc1 || !rc2)
    {
        cout << "Bad return code\n";
        cout << "  rc1 = " << rc1 << nl;
        cout << "  rc2 = " << rc2 << nl;
        return;
    }

    cout << setw(w1) << "m_NumPixels:";
    cout << setw(w2) << is1.m_NumPixels << s;
    cout << setw(w2) << is2.m_NumPixels << nl;

    cout << setw(w1) << "m_PixelSum:";
    cout << setw(w2) << is1.m_PixelSum << s;
    cout << setw(w2) << is2.m_PixelSum << nl;

    cout << setw(w1) << "m_PixelSumOfSquares:";
    cout << setw(w2) << is1.m_PixelSumSquares << s;
    cout << setw(w2) << is2.m_PixelSumSquares << nl;

    cout << setw(w1) << "m_PixelMean:";
    cout << setw(w2) << is1.m_PixelMean << s;
    cout << setw(w2) << is2.m_PixelMean << nl;
```

```
        cout << setw(w1) << "m_PixelSd:";
        cout << setw(w2) << is1.m_PixelSd << s;
        cout << setw(w2) << is2.m_PixelSd << nl;
}

int main()
{
    try
    {
        CalcImageStats();
        CalcImageStats_BM();
    }

    catch (exception& ex)
    {
        cout << "exception has occurred - " << ex.what() << '\n';
    }

    return 0;
}

//----------------------------------------------------
//                  Ch14_06_Macros_.inc
//----------------------------------------------------

// Macro UpdateSums
//
// Input:          Vreg - image pixel block
//
// Data registers: v16 - loop_packed pixel_sum
//                 v17 - loop_packed pixel_sum_squares
//
// Temp registers: v4, v5, v6, v7
//

            .macro UpdateSums Vreg
// Update loop_pixel_sum
            uxtl v4.8h,\Vreg\().8b                  // zero-extend pixel
            uxtl2 v5.8h,\Vreg\().16b                // values to halfwords
            add v4.8h,v4.8h,v5.8h                   // temp pixel_sum

            uxtl v5.4s,v4.4h                        // zero-extend loop
            uxtl2 v6.4s,v4.8h                       // pixel_sum to words
            add v7.4s,v5.4s,v6.4s                   // update
            add v16.4s,v16.4s,v7.4s                 // loop_pixel_sum

// Update loop_pixel_sum_squares
            umull v4.8h,\Vreg\().8b,\Vreg\().8b     // temp pixel_sum_squares (lo)
            uxtl v5.4s,v4.4h                        // zero-extend to words
            uxtl2 v6.4s,v4.8h
            add v7.4s,v5.4s,v6.4s                   // update loop
            add v17.4s,v17.4s,v7.4s                 // loop_pixel_sum_squares
```

333

```
            umull2 v4.8h,\Vreg\().16b,\Vreg\().16b  // temp pixel_sum_squares (hi)
            uxtl v5.4s,v4.4h                         // zero-extend to words
            uxtl2 v6.4s,v4.8h
            add v7.4s,v5.4s,v6.4s                    // update
            add v17.4s,v17.4s,v7.4s                  // loop_pixel_sum_squares
            .endm


//---------------------------------------------------
//              Ch14_06_.s
//---------------------------------------------------

            .include "Ch14_06_Macros_.inc"

// extern "C" bool CalcImageStats_(ImageStats& im_stats);

            .equ m_PixelBuffer,0
            .equ m_NumPixels,8
            .equ m_PixelSum,16
            .equ m_PixelSumSquares,24
            .equ m_PixelMean,32
            .equ m_PixelSd,40

            .text
            .global CalcImageStats_
CalcImageStats_:

// Load and validate values in im_stats struct
            mov x7,x0
            ldr x0,[x7,m_PixelBuffer]
            tst x0,0x0f                              // jump if m_PixelBuffer
            b.ne InvalidArg                          // not 16b aligned

            ldr x1,[x7,m_NumPixels]                  // x1 = m_NumPixels
            cbz x1,InvalidArg                        // jump if m_NumPixels == 0

            tst x1,0x3f                              // jump if
            b.ne InvalidArg                          // m_NumPixels% 64 != 0

// Initialize
            eor v18.16b,v18.16b,v18.16b              // pixel_sum
            eor v19.16b,v19.16b,v19.16b              // pixel_sum_squares
            mov x2,x1                                // num_pixels = m_NumPixels

// Main processing loop
Loop1:      eor v16.16b,v16.16b,v16.16b              // loop_pixel_sum
            eor v17.16b,v17.16b,v17.16b              // loop_pixel_sum_squares

            ld1 {v0.16b-v3.16b},[x0],64              // load next pixel block
```

```
        UpdateSums v0
        UpdateSums v1
        UpdateSums v2
        UpdateSums v3

        uxtl v4.2d,v16.2s              // extend
        uxtl2 v5.2d,v16.4s             // loop_pixel_sum

        add v18.2d,v18.2d,v4.2d        // update pixel_sum
        add v18.2d,v18.2d,v5.2d

        uxtl v4.2d,v17.2s              // extend
        uxtl2 v5.2d,v17.4s             // loop_pixel_sum_squares

        add v19.2d,v19.2d,v4.2d        // update pixel_sum_squares
        add v19.2d,v19.2d,v5.2d

        subs x2,x2,64                  // num_pixels -= 64
        b.ne Loop1

// Reduce packed m_PixelSum and m_PixelSumSquares to scalar values
        addp v0.2d,v18.2d,v18.2d
        mov x4,v0.d[0]
        str x4,[x7,m_PixelSum]

        addp v1.2d,v19.2d,v19.2d
        mov x5,v1.d[0]
        str x5,[x7,m_PixelSumSquares]

// Calculate mean and standard deviation
        ucvtf d0,x1                    // d0 = n
        sub x1,x1,1
        ucvtf d1,x1                    // d1 = n - 1
        ucvtf d2,x4                    // d2 = m_PixelSum
        ucvtf d3,x5                    // d3 = m_PixelSumSquares

        fdiv d4,d2,d0                  // d4 = m_PixelMean
        str d4,[x7,m_PixelMean]        // save m_PixelMean

        fmul d4,d0,d3                  // d4 = n * m_PixelSumSquares
        fmul d5,d2,d2                  // d5 = m_PixelSum ** 2
        fsub d6,d4,d5                  // d6 = variance numerator
        fmul d7,d0,d1                  // d7 = variance denominator
        fdiv d0,d6,d7                  // d0 = variance
        fsqrt d1,d0                    // d1 = m_PixelSd
        str d1,[x7,m_PixelSd]          // save m_PixelSd

        mov w0,1                       // set success return code
        ret

InvalidArg: mov w0,0                   // set error return code
        ret
```

335

The mean and standard deviation of the pixels in a grayscale image can be calculated using the following equations:

$$\bar{x} = \frac{1}{n} \sum_i x_i$$

$$s = \sqrt{\frac{n \sum_i x_i^2 - \left(\sum_i x_i\right)^2}{n(n-1)}}$$

In the mean and standard deviation equations, the symbol x_i represents an image buffer pixel and n denotes the number of pixels. If you study these equations carefully, you will notice that two intermediate sums must be calculated: the sum of all pixels and the sum of all pixel values squared. Once these quantities are known, the mean and standard deviation can be determined using simple floating-point arithmetic. The standard deviation equation that is detailed here is simple to calculate using SIMD arithmetic and suitable for this source code example. For other use cases, however, this same equation is often unsuitable for standard deviation calculations especially those that involve floating-point values. You may want to consult the references listed in Appendix B before using this equation in one of your own programs.

Listing 14-6 begins with the C++ header file Ch14_06.h. This file includes the declaration of a structure named ImageStats, which contains the data that is used by the C++ and assembly language statistical calculating functions. The C++ function CalcImageStatsCpp is the principal C++ calculating function. This function requires a pointer to an ImageStats structure as its sole argument. Following argument validation, CalcImageStatsCpp initializes the ImageStats intermediate sums m_PixelSum, m_PixelSumOfSquares, and m_NumPixelsInRange to zero. A simple for-loop follows, which calculates m_PixelSum and m_PixelSumOfSquares. Following computation of the intermediate sums, CalcImageStatsCpp calculates the final mean and standard deviation. The remaining code in Listing 14-6 performs test case initialization, invokes the calculating functions, and streams results to cout.

The assembly language code in Listing 14-6 begins with the definition of a macro named UpdateSums whose instructions will be described shortly. Function CalcImageStats_ begins its execution with a code block that verifies m_PixelBuffer is aligned on a 16-byte boundary. This is followed by a validation check of m_NumPixels. Note the use of the cbz x1,InvalidArg (compare branch on zero) instruction. This instruction branches to label InvalidArg if m_NumPixels (X1) is zero. Following argument validation, CalcImageStats_ uses the instruction pair eor v18.16b,v18.16b,v18.16b and eor v19.16b,v19.16b,v19.16b to initialize packed doubleword versions of pixel_sum and pixel_sum_squares to zero. Function CalcImageStats_ uses doubleword sums to facilitate the processing of high-resolution 8-bit grayscale images without explicit checks for arithmetic overflows. The ensuing mov x2,x1 instruction initializes the loop counter num_pixels.

For-loop Loop1 begins each iteration with the instructions eor v16.16b,v16.16b,v16.16b and eor v17.16b,v17.16b,v17.16b that initialize loop_packed_sum and loop_packed_sum_squares to zero. Registers V16 and V17 maintain packed word sums for a single iteration of Loop1. The next instruction, ld1 {v0.16b-v3.16b},[x0],64, loads a block of 64 pixels into registers V0–V3. This is followed by four applications of the macro UpdateSums, which updates loop_pixel_sum and loop_pixel_sum_squares using the pixel values in registers V0–V3.

The first two instructions of macro UpdateSums, uxtl v4.8h,\Vreg\().8b (unsigned extend long) and uxtl2 v5.8h,\Vreg\().16b, zero-extend the pixel byte values in Vreg to halfwords. The ensuing add v4.8h,v4.8h,v5.8h instruction sums the zero-extended halfword values. The next two instructions, uxtl v5.4s,v5.4h and uxtl2 v6.4s,v4.8h, zero-extend the halfword intermediate sums in register V4 to word values. This is followed by two add instructions that sum these word values with loop_pixel_sum (V16). Figure 14-3 illustrates this operation in greater detail.

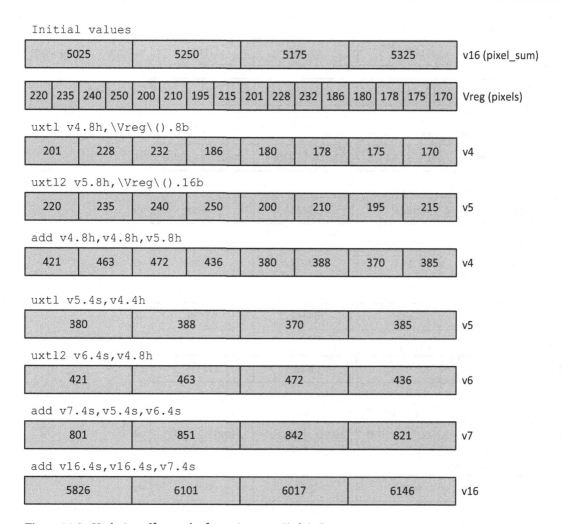

Figure 14-3. Updating of loop_pixel_sum *in macro* UpdateSums

The next two code blocks in macro UpdateSums update loop_pixel_sum_squares. The first code block begins with a umull v4.8h,\Vreg\().8b,\Vreg\().8b (unsigned multiply long vector) instruction that squares the eight low-order pixel values in register Vreg. This instruction saves its halfword products in register V4. The ensuing uxtl v5.4s,v4.4h and uxtl2 v6.4s,v4.8h instructions zero-extend these halfwords to words. This is followed by the instruction pair add v7.4s,v5.4s,v6.4s and add v17.4s,v17.4s,v7.4s, which updates loop_pixel_sum_squares (V17). Following this operation is a second code block that processes the eight high-order pixel values in register Vreg. Note that this code block uses a umull2 instruction to calculate the halfword squares instead of umull. Figure 14-4 illustrates the updating of loop_pixel_sum_squares in greater detail.

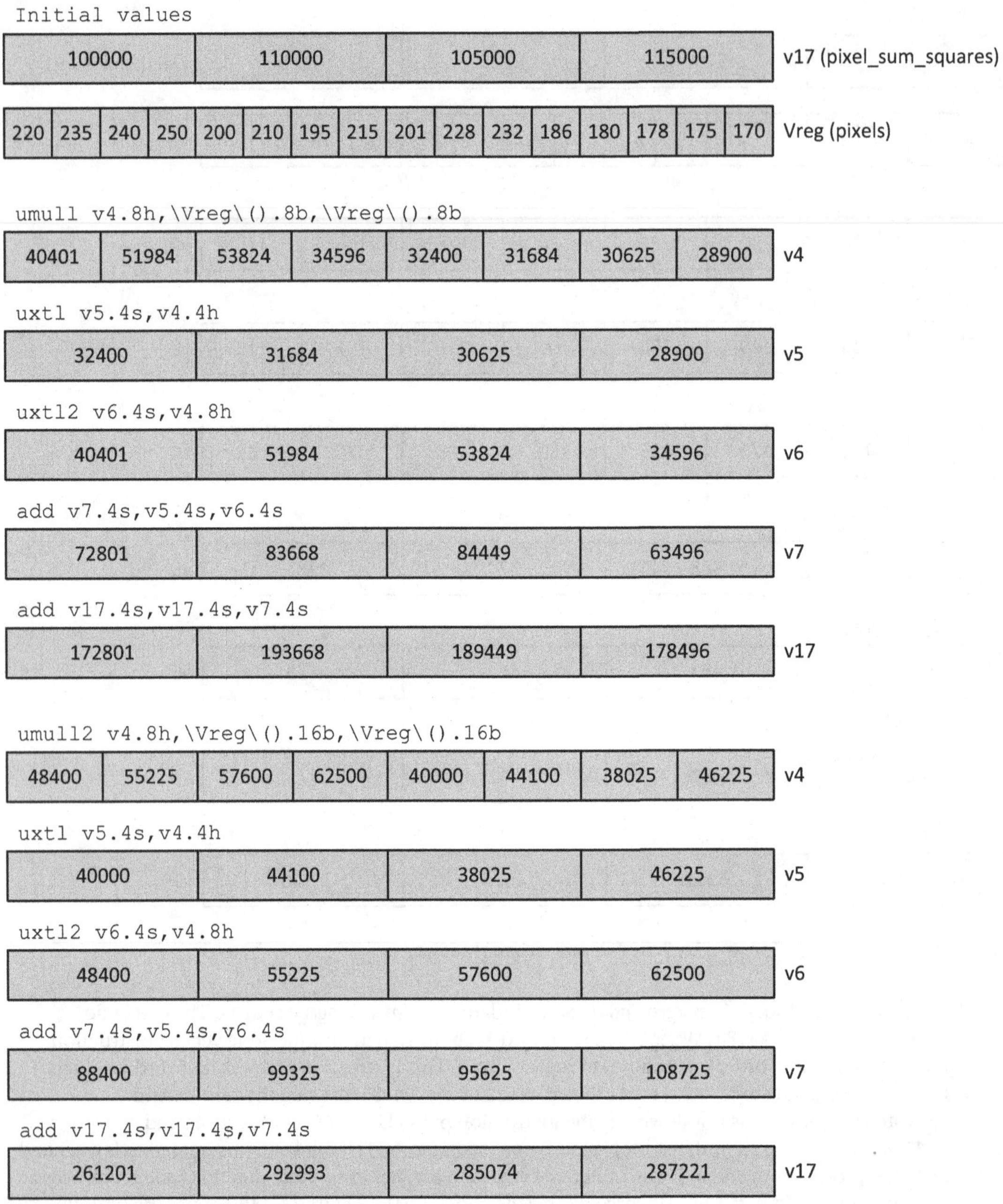

Initial values

| 100000 | 110000 | 105000 | 115000 | v17 (pixel_sum_squares) |

| 220 | 235 | 240 | 250 | 200 | 210 | 195 | 215 | 201 | 228 | 232 | 186 | 180 | 178 | 175 | 170 | Vreg (pixels) |

umull v4.8h,\Vreg\().8b,\Vreg\().8b

| 40401 | 51984 | 53824 | 34596 | 32400 | 31684 | 30625 | 28900 | v4 |

uxtl v5.4s,v4.4h

| 32400 | 31684 | 30625 | 28900 | v5 |

uxtl2 v6.4s,v4.8h

| 40401 | 51984 | 53824 | 34596 | v6 |

add v7.4s,v5.4s,v6.4s

| 72801 | 83668 | 84449 | 63496 | v7 |

add v17.4s,v17.4s,v7.4s

| 172801 | 193668 | 189449 | 178496 | v17 |

umull2 v4.8h,\Vreg\().16b,\Vreg\().16b

| 48400 | 55225 | 57600 | 62500 | 40000 | 44100 | 38025 | 46225 | v4 |

uxtl v5.4s,v4.4h

| 40000 | 44100 | 38025 | 46225 | v5 |

uxtl2 v6.4s,v4.8h

| 48400 | 55225 | 57600 | 62500 | v6 |

add v7.4s,v5.4s,v6.4s

| 88400 | 99325 | 95625 | 108725 | v7 |

add v17.4s,v17.4s,v7.4s

| 261201 | 292993 | 285074 | 287221 | v17 |

Figure 14-4. *Updating of loop_pixel_sum_squares in macro UpdateSums*

Immediately after its use of macro UpdateSums, CalcImageStat_ uses a series of uxtl, uxtl2, and add instructions to update the quadword pixel_sum and pixel_sum_squares values that are maintained in registers V18 and V19. Following completion of for-loop Loop1, the addp v0.2d,v18.2d,v18.2d (add pair vector) instruction calculates m_PixelSum. The ensuing instruction pair mov x4,v0.d[0] and str x4,[x7, m_PixelSum] saves this result in the ImageStats structure. Function CalcImageStats_ uses a similar series of instruction to calculate and save m_PixelSumSquares. The final code section of CalcImageStats_ calculates the image mean and standard deviation using scalar floating-point arithmetic. Here are the results for source code example Ch14_06:

```
Results for CalcImageStats - image_fn = ../../Data/ImageB.png
m_NumPixels:         2457600     | 2457600
m_PixelSum:          286011802   | 286011802
m_PixelSumOfSquares: 44075675366 | 44075675366
m_PixelMean:         116.37850   | 116.37850
m_PixelSd:           66.26073    | 66.26073

Running benchmark function CalcImageStats_BM - please wait
Benchmark times save to file Ch14_06_CalcImageStats_BM_RpiOmega.csv
```

Table 14-4 contains benchmark timing measurements for the functions CalcImageStatsCpp and CalcImageStats_.

Table 14-4. *Mean execution times (microseconds) for image statistic functions using test image ImageB.png*

C++ (CalcImageStatsCpp)	Assembly Language (CalcImageStats_)
2844	1740

Summary

Here are the key learning points for Chapter 14:

- A function can use the ldr and str instructions to load and store 64- and 128-bit wide vector values. These instructions must use Q register operands when loading/storing 128-bit wide operands.

- The ld1 and st1 instructions can be used to load and store multiple (1–4) Armv8-64 SIMD V registers.

- Most A64 SIMD instructions require arrangement specifiers, which specify the element sizes that an instruction will use.

- The add and sub instructions are used to carry out packed integer addition and subtraction using signed and unsinged operands.

- The sqadd/sqsub and uqadd/uqsub instructions perform signed and unsigned packed integer addition/subtraction using saturated arithmetic.

- The shl instruction shifts each element in a vector using an immediate bit count. The instructions sshr and ushr perform signed and unsigned right shifts using an immediate bit count. The instructions sshl and ushl perform variable left or right shifts using bit counts that are specified in a SIMD register.

- Functions can use the mul instruction to perform packed multiplication. The smull/smull2 and umull/umull2 instructions carry out packed long multiplication using signed and unsigned integers.

- The uxtl and uxtl2 instructions zero-extend packed unsigned integer values. Functions can also use the sxtl and sxtl2 instructions to sign-extend packed signed integer values.

- Functions can use the dup instruction to copy a value from a general-purpose register into each element of a SIMD register.

- The smin/smax and umin/umax instructions carry out signed and unsigned minimum/maximum operations using corresponding elements of two vector operands. The sminv/smaxv and uminv/umaxv instructions calculate a single signed or unsigned minimum/maximum value across a single vector operand.

- Assembly language files can use the .include directive to incorporate macros or other assembly language statements.

CHAPTER 15

■ ■ ■

Armv8-64 SIMD Floating-Point Programming

In the previous chapter, you learned basic Armv8-64 SIMD assembly language programming using packed integer operands. In this chapter, you will learn how to carry out SIMD operations using packed single-precision and double-precision floating-point operands. The first section includes three source code examples that demonstrate common packed floating-point operations including basic arithmetic, data comparisons, and data conversions. The second section contains source code examples that illustrate Armv8-64 SIMD computations using floating-point arrays. The final section explains how to perform common operations using 4 × 4 matrices.

Packed Floating-Point Arithmetic

This section contains source code examples that explicate fundamental SIMD arithmetic using packed single-precision and double-precision floating-point operands. The first source code example illustrates packed floating-point arithmetic including addition, subtraction, multiplication, and division. The second source code example explains how to perform packed floating-point comparisons. The third and final source code example covers packed floating-point conversions. The source code examples in this section demonstrate important concepts related to floating-point SIMD instruction usage. You will learn how to code floating-point SIMD calculating functions later in this chapter.

Basic Arithmetic

Listing 15-1 shows the source code for example Ch15_01. This example demonstrates common arithmetic operations using packed single-precision and double-precision floating-point operands.

Listing 15-1. Example Ch15_01

```
//-------------------------------------------------
//              Ch15_01.cpp
//-------------------------------------------------

#include <iostream>
#include <cmath>
#include "Vec128.h"

using namespace std;
```

© Daniel Kusswurm 2020
D. Kusswurm, *Modern Arm Assembly Language Programming*,
https://doi.org/10.1007/978-1-4842-6267-2_15

```
extern "C" void PackedMathF32_(Vec128 x[9], const Vec128& a, const Vec128& b);
extern "C" void PackedMathF64_(Vec128 x[9], const Vec128& a, const Vec128& b);

void PackedMathF32(void)
{
    const char nl = '\n';
    Vec128 x[9], a, b;

    a.m_F32[0] = 36.0f;              b.m_F32[0] = -1.0f / 9.0f;
    a.m_F32[1] = 1.0f / 32.0f;       b.m_F32[1] = 64.0f;
    a.m_F32[2] = 2.0f;               b.m_F32[2] = -0.0625f;
    a.m_F32[3] = 42.0f;              b.m_F32[3] = 8.666667f;

    PackedMathF32_(x, a, b);

    cout << ("\nResults for PackedMathF32_\n");
    cout << "a:          " << a.ToStringF32() << nl;
    cout << "b:          " << b.ToStringF32() << nl;
    cout << nl;
    cout << "fadd:       " << x[0].ToStringF32() << nl;
    cout << "fsub:       " << x[1].ToStringF32() << nl;
    cout << "fmul:       " << x[2].ToStringF32() << nl;
    cout << "fdiv:       " << x[3].ToStringF32() << nl;
    cout << "fabs(a):    " << x[4].ToStringF32() << nl;
    cout << "fneg(b):    " << x[5].ToStringF32() << nl;
    cout << "fminnm:     " << x[6].ToStringF32() << nl;
    cout << "fmaxnm:     " << x[7].ToStringF32() << nl;
    cout << "fsqrt(a):   " << x[8].ToStringF32() << nl;
}

void PackedMathF64(void)
{
    const char nl = '\n';
    Vec128 x[9], a, b;

    a.m_F64[0] = 36.0;               b.m_F64[0] = -M_SQRT2;
    a.m_F64[1] = M_PI;               b.m_F64[1] = 2.0;

    PackedMathF64_(x, a, b);

    cout << ("\nResults for PackedMathF64_\n");
    cout << "a:          " << a.ToStringF64() << nl;
    cout << "b:          " << b.ToStringF64() << nl;
    cout << nl;
    cout << "fadd:       " << x[0].ToStringF64() << nl;
    cout << "fsub:       " << x[1].ToStringF64() << nl;
    cout << "fmul:       " << x[2].ToStringF64() << nl;
    cout << "fdiv:       " << x[3].ToStringF64() << nl;
    cout << "fabs(a):    " << x[4].ToStringF64() << nl;
    cout << "fneg(b):    " << x[5].ToStringF64() << nl;
    cout << "fminnm:     " << x[6].ToStringF64() << nl;
```

```
        cout << "fmaxnm:   " << x[7].ToStringF64() << nl;
        cout << "fsqrt(a): " << x[8].ToStringF64() << nl;
}

int main()
{
    PackedMathF32();
    PackedMathF64();
    return 0;
}

//-------------------------------------------------
//                  Ch15_01_.s
//-------------------------------------------------

// extern "C" void PackedMathF32_(Vec128 x[9], const Vec128& a, const Vec128& b);

            .text
            .global PackedMathF32_
PackedMathF32_:
            ld1 {v0.4s},[x1]            // v0 = a
            ld1 {v1.4s},[x2]            // v1 = b

            fadd v2.4s,v0.4s,v1.4s      // v2 = a + b
            st1 {v2.4s},[x0],16         // save result to x[0]

            fsub v2.4s,v0.4s,v1.4s      // v2 = a - b
            st1 {v2.4s},[x0],16         // save result to x[1]

            fmul v2.4s,v0.4s,v1.4s      // v2 = a * b
            st1 {v2.4s},[x0],16         // save result to x[2]

            fdiv v2.4s,v0.4s,v1.4s      // v2 = a / b
            st1 {v2.4s},[x0],16         // save result to x[3]

            fabs v2.4s,v0.4s            // v2 = abs(a)
            st1 {v2.4s},[x0],16         // save result to x[4]

            fneg v2.4s,v1.4s            // v2 = -b
            st1 {v2.4s},[x0],16         // save result to x[5]

            fminnm v2.4s,v0.4s,v1.4s    // v2 = min(a, b)
            st1 {v2.4s},[x0],16         // save result to x[6]

            fmaxnm v2.4s,v0.4s,v1.4s    // v2 = max(a, b)
            st1 {v2.4s},[x0],16         // save result to x[7]

            fsqrt v2.4s,v0.4s           // v2 = sqrt(a)
            st1 {v2.4s},[x0],16         // save result to x[8]
            ret
```

```
// extern "C" void PackedMathF64_(Vec128 x[9], const Vec128& a, const Vec128& b);

            .global PackedMathF64_
PackedMathF64_:
            ld1 {v0.2d},[x1]                   // v0 = a
            ld1 {v1.2d},[x2]                   // v1 = b

            fadd v2.2d,v0.2d,v1.2d             // v2 = a + b
            st1 {v2.2d},[x0],16               // save result to x[0]

            fsub v2.2d,v0.2d,v1.2d             // v2 = a - b
            st1 {v2.2d},[x0],16               // save result to x[1]

            fmul v2.2d,v0.2d,v1.2d             // v2 = a * b
            st1 {v2.2d},[x0],16               // save result to x[2]

            fdiv v2.2d,v0.2d,v1.2d             // v2 = a / b
            st1 {v2.2d},[x0],16               // save result to x[3]

            fabs v2.2d,v0.2d                   // v2 = abs(a)
            st1 {v2.2d},[x0],16               // save result to x[4]

            fneg v2.2d,v1.2d                   // v2 = -b
            st1 {v2.2d},[x0],16               // save result to x[5]

            fminnm v2.2d,v0.2d,v1.2d           // v2 = min(a, b)
            st1 {v2.2d},[x0],16               // save result to x[6]

            fmaxnm v2.2d,v0.2d,v1.2d           // v2 = max(a, b)
            st1 {v2.2d},[x0],16               // save result to x[7]

            fsqrt v2.2d,v0.2d                  // v2 = sqrt(a)
            st1 {v2.2d},[x0],16               // save result to x[8]
            ret
```

The C++ code in Listing 15-1 contains two functions named PackedMathF32 and PackedMathF64. These functions initialize test cases for the assembly language functions PackedMathF32_ and PackedMathF64_, respectively. They also stream their results to cout. Note that this example includes code that performs SIMD operations using both single-precision and double-precision floating-point operands. Unlike Armv8-32, Armv8-64 fully supports SIMD operations using packed double-precision floating-point operands.

The assembly language function PackedMathF32_ begins its execution with a ld1 {v0.4s},[x1] that loads argument value a into register V0. This is followed by a ld1 {v1.4s},[x2] instruction that loads argument value b into register V1. The ensuing fadd v2.4s,v0.4s,v1.4s (floating-point add) instruction adds corresponding elements in registers V0 and V1. The results are then saved to the corresponding elements in register V2. Note that the fadd instruction employs the arrangement specifier .4s, which denotes the use of single-precision floating-point elements (see Chapter 14, Table 14-1, for a list of valid arrangement specifiers). The st1 {v2.4s},[x0],16 that follows saves the computed packed sums to x[0]. Function PackedMathF32_ then employs the fsub (floating-point subtract), fmul (floating-point multiply), and fdiv (floating-point divide) to carry out packed single-precision floating-point subtraction, multiplication, and division. A series of st1 instructions is then used to save the calculated results to x[1], x[2], and x[3].

The ensuing instruction pairs in PackedMathF32_ carry out other common floating-point SIMD operations. The fabs v2.4s,v0.4s instruction calculates packed absolute values. This is followed by a fneg v2.4s,v1.4s instruction that performs packed floating-point negation. The fminnm v2.4s,v0.4s,v1.4s and fmaxnm v2.4s,v0.4s,v1.4s instructions calculate minimum and maximum values using the corresponding elements of their source operands. These instructions handle NaN operands in accordance with the IEEE 754-2008 standard. The final SIMD calculating instruction in PackedMathF32_, fsqrt v2.4s,v0.4s, calculates packed square roots.

The function PackedMathF64_ is the double-precision counterpart of PackedMathF32_. Note that the SIMD instructions in this function employ the arrangement specifier .2d, which signifies the use of double-precision floating-point elements. Here are the results for source code example Ch15_01:

```
Results for PackedMathF32_
a:              36.000000        0.031250   |      2.000000       42.000000
b:              -0.111111       64.000000   |     -0.062500        8.666667

fadd:           35.888889       64.031250   |      1.937500       50.666668
fsub:           36.111111      -63.968750   |      2.062500       33.333332
fmul:           -4.000000        2.000000   |     -0.125000      364.000000
fdiv:         -324.000000        0.000488   |    -32.000000        4.846154
fabs(a):        36.000000        0.031250   |      2.000000       42.000000
fneg(b):         0.111111      -64.000000   |      0.062500       -8.666667
fminnm:         -0.111111        0.031250   |     -0.062500        8.666667
fmaxnm:         36.000000       64.000000   |      2.000000       42.000000
fsqrt(a):        6.000000        0.176777   |      1.414214        6.480741

Results for PackedMathF64_
a:                      36.000000000000   |          3.141592653590
b:                      -1.414213562373   |          2.000000000000

fadd:                   34.585786437627   |          5.141592653590
fsub:                   37.414213562373   |          1.141592653590
fmul:                  -50.911688245431   |          6.283185307180
fdiv:                  -25.455844122716   |          1.570796326795
fabs(a):                36.000000000000   |          3.141592653590
fneg(b):                 1.414213562373   |         -2.000000000000
fminnm:                 -1.414213562373   |          2.000000000000
fmaxnm:                 36.000000000000   |          3.141592653590
fsqrt(a):                6.000000000000   |          1.772453850906
```

Comparisons

The next source code example, Ch15_02, highlights packed comparisons using single-precision and double-precision floating-point operands. Listing 15-2 shows the source code for this example. Like the previous example, the C++ code in Listing 15-2 performs test case initialization. It also exercises the assembly language functions PackedCompareF32_ and PackedCompareF64_ and displays the results.

Listing 15-2. Example Ch15_02

```cpp
//----------------------------------------------------
//                  Ch15_02.cpp
//----------------------------------------------------

#include <iostream>
#include <iomanip>
#include <cmath>
#include "Vec128.h"

using namespace std;

extern "C" void PackedCompareF32_(Vec128 x[8], const Vec128& a, const Vec128& b);
extern "C" void PackedCompareF64_(Vec128 x[8], const Vec128& a, const Vec128& b);

const char* c_CmpStr[8] =
{
    "EQ", "NE", "GT", "GE", "LT", "LE", "a LTO", "b GTO"
};

void PackedCompareF32(void)
{
    const char nl = '\n';
    Vec128 x[8], a, b;

    a.m_F32[0] = 2.0;           b.m_F32[0] = -4.0;
    a.m_F32[1] = 17.0;          b.m_F32[1] = 12.0;
    a.m_F32[2] = -6.0;          b.m_F32[2] = -6.0;
    a.m_F32[3] = 3.0;           b.m_F32[3] = 8.0;

    PackedCompareF32_(x, a, b);

    cout << "\nResults for PackedCompareF32_\n";
    cout << setw(11) << 'a' << ':' << a.ToStringF32() << nl;
    cout << setw(11) << 'b' << ':' << b.ToStringF32() << nl;
    cout << nl;

    for (int j = 0; j < 8; j++)
        cout << setw(11) << c_CmpStr[j] << ':' << x[j].ToStringX32() << nl;
}

void PackedCompareF64(void)
{
    const char nl = '\n';
    Vec128 x[8], a, b;

    a.m_F64[0] = -2.0;          b.m_F64[0] = -4.0;
    a.m_F64[1] = M_SQRT2;       b.m_F64[1] = M_PI;

    PackedCompareF64_(x, a, b);
```

```cpp
    cout << "\nResults for PackedCompareF64_\n";
    cout << setw(11) << 'a' << ':' << a.ToStringF64() << nl;
    cout << setw(11) << 'b' << ':' << b.ToStringF64() << nl;
    cout << nl;

    for (int j = 0; j < 8; j++)
        cout << setw(11) << c_CmpStr[j] << ':' << x[j].ToStringX64() << nl;
}

int main()
{
    PackedCompareF32();
    PackedCompareF64();
    return 0;
}

//--------------------------------------------------
//                  Ch15_02_.s
//--------------------------------------------------

// extern "C" void PackedCompareF32_(Vec128 x[8], const Vec128& a, const Vec128& b);

            .text
            .global PackedCompareF32_
PackedCompareF32_:
            ld1 {v0.4s},[x1]                // v0 = a
            ld1 {v1.4s},[x2]                // v1 = b

            fcmeq v2.4s,v0.4s,v1.4s         // packed a == b
            st1 {v2.4s},[x0],16             // save result to x[0]

            not v2.16b,v2.16b               // packed a != b
            st1 {v2.4s},[x0],16             // save result to x[1]

            fcmgt v2.4s,v0.4s,v1.4s         // packed a > b
            st1 {v2.4s},[x0],16             // save result to x[2]

            fcmge v2.4s,v0.4s,v1.4s         // packed a >= b
            st1 {v2.4s},[x0],16             // save result to x[3]

            fcmgt v2.4s,v1.4s,v0.4s         // packed a < b
            st1 {v2.4s},[x0],16             // save result to x[4]

            fcmge v2.4s,v1.4s,v0.4s         // packed a <= b
            st1 {v2.4s},[x0],16             // save result to x[5]

            fcmlt v2.4s,v0.4s,0.0           // packed a < 0
            st1 {v2.4s},[x0],16             // save result to x[6]

            fcmgt v2.4s,v1.4s,0.0           // packed b > 0
            st1 {v2.4s},[x0],16             // save result to x[7]
            ret
```

```
// extern "C" void PackedCompareF64_(Vec128 x[8], const Vec128& a, const Vec128& b);

        .global PackedCompareF64_
PackedCompareF64_:
        ld1 {v0.2d},[x1]                // v0 = a
        ld1 {v1.2d},[x2]                // v1 = b

        fcmeq v2.2d,v0.2d,v1.2d         // packed a == b
        st1 {v2.2d},[x0],16             // save result to x[0]

        not v2.16b,v2.16b               // packed a != b
        st1 {v2.2d},[x0],16             // save result to x[1]

        fcmgt v2.2d,v0.2d,v1.2d         // packed a > b
        st1 {v2.2d},[x0],16             // save result to x[2]

        fcmge v2.2d,v0.2d,v1.2d         // packed a >= b
        st1 {v2.2d},[x0],16             // save result to x[3]

        fcmgt v2.2d,v1.2d,v0.2d         // packed a < b
        st1 {v2.2d},[x0],16             // save result to x[4]

        fcmge v2.2d,v1.2d,v0.2d         // packed a <= b
        st1 {v2.2d},[x0],16             // save result to x[5]

        fcmlt v2.2d,v0.2d,0.0           // packed a < 0
        st1 {v2.2d},[x0],16             // save result to x[6]

        fcmgt v2.2d,v1.2d,0.0           // packed b > 0
        st1 {v2.2d},[x0],16             // save result to x[7]
        ret
```

The assembly language function PackedCompareF32_ begins its execution with the instruction pair ld1 {v0.4s},[x1] and ld1 {v1.4s},[x2]. These instructions load argument values a and b into registers V0 and V1, respectively. The next instruction, fcmeq v2.4s,v0.4s,v1.4s (floating-point compare equal), compares corresponding single-precision elements in source operands V0 and V1. If the elements are equal, the corresponding element in V2 is set to 0xFFFFFFFF; otherwise, it is set to 0x00000000. The ensuing st1 {v2.4s},[x0],16 instruction saves this result to x[0]. The A64 SIMD instruction set does not include a fcmne instruction. To perform a packed not equal comparison, a function must negate the results of a fcmeq instruction. In function PackedCompareF32_, the not v2.16b,v2.16b instruction calculates this result. Note the use of the .16b alignment specifier. This arrangement specifier is employed here since the not instruction cannot be used with a .4s alignment specifier (the result would be the same with a .4s alignment specifier since the not instruction just negates individual bits). The st1 {v2.4s},[x0],16 instruction saves this result to x[1].

The next two packed floating-point compare instructions, fcmgt v2.4s,v0.4s,v1.4s (floating-point compare greater than) and fcmge v2.4s,v0.4s,v1.4s (floating-point compare greater than or equal), compare corresponding elements in V0 and V1 for greater than and greater than or equal, respectively. Function PackedCompareF32_ uses two st1 instructions to save these results to x[2] and x[3]. The A64 instructions fcmlt and fcmle cannot be used with SIMD register operands. To perform packed less than or less than or equal comparisons with register operands, a function must use the fcmgt and fcmge instructions with reversed operands. In function PackedCompareF32_, the fcmgt v2.4s,v1.4s,v0.4s and fcmge v2.4s,v1.4s,v0.4s instructions perform packed a < b and a <= b comparisons.

The final two comparisons in function PackedCompareF32_, fcmlt v2.4s,v0.4s,0.0 and fcmgt v2.4s,v1.4s,0.0, compare elements in V0 (argument value a) for less than zero and V1 (argument value b) for greater than zero. The A64 floating-point packed compare instructions (e.g., fcmeq, fcmgt, fcmge, fcmlt, and fcmle) cannot be used with immediate constants other than zero. Function PackedCompareF64_ uses the same packed floating-point compare instructions as PackedCompareF32_, but with packed double-precision operands. Here are the results for source code example Ch15_02:

```
Results for PackedCompareF32_
        a:       2.000000    17.000000   |    -6.000000     3.000000
        b:      -4.000000    12.000000   |    -6.000000     8.000000

       EQ:      00000000    00000000    |    FFFFFFFF    00000000
       NE:      FFFFFFFF    FFFFFFFF    |    00000000    FFFFFFFF
       GT:      FFFFFFFF    FFFFFFFF    |    00000000    00000000
       GE:      FFFFFFFF    FFFFFFFF    |    FFFFFFFF    00000000
       LT:      00000000    00000000    |    00000000    FFFFFFFF
       LE:      00000000    00000000    |    FFFFFFFF    FFFFFFFF
   a LTO:      00000000    00000000    |    FFFFFFFF    00000000
   b GTO:      00000000    FFFFFFFF    |    00000000    FFFFFFFF

Results for PackedCompareF64_
        a:              -2.000000000000   |            1.414213562373
        b:              -4.000000000000   |            3.141592653590

       EQ:      0000000000000000   |    0000000000000000
       NE:      FFFFFFFFFFFFFFFF   |    FFFFFFFFFFFFFFFF
       GT:      FFFFFFFFFFFFFFFF   |    0000000000000000
       GE:      FFFFFFFFFFFFFFFF   |    0000000000000000
       LT:      0000000000000000   |    FFFFFFFFFFFFFFFF
       LE:      0000000000000000   |    FFFFFFFFFFFFFFFF
   a LTO:      FFFFFFFFFFFFFFFF   |    0000000000000000
   b GTO:      0000000000000000   |    FFFFFFFFFFFFFFFF
```

Conversions

Listing 15-3 shows the source code for example Ch15_03. This example explains how to perform conversions between packed integer and floating-point operands. It also demonstrates the use of an A64 assembly language jump table.

Listing 15-3. Example Ch15_03

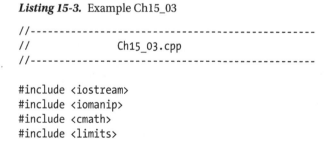

```cpp
//--------------------------------------------------
//              Ch15_03.cpp
//--------------------------------------------------

#include <iostream>
#include <iomanip>
#include <cmath>
#include <limits>
```

```cpp
#include "Vec128.h"

using namespace std;

// The order of values in the following enum must match the jump table
// that's defined in Ch15_03_.s.
enum CvtOp : unsigned int
{
    F32_I32, I32_F32,
    F64_I64, I64_F64,
    F32_U32, U32_F32,
    F64_U64, U64_F64,
    F32_F64, F64_F32
};

extern "C" bool PackedConvert_(Vec128 x[2], const Vec128& a, CvtOp cvt_op, const Vec128*
b = nullptr);

void PackedConvertA(void)
{
    const char nl = '\n';
    Vec128 x[2], a;

    // F32_I32
    a.m_I32[0] = 10;
    a.m_I32[1] = -500;
    a.m_I32[2] = 600;
    a.m_I32[3] = -1024;
    PackedConvert_(x, a, CvtOp::F32_I32);
    cout << "\nResults for CvtOp::F32_I32\n";
    cout << "a:    " << a.ToStringI32() << nl;
    cout << "x[0]: " << x[0].ToStringF32() << nl;

    // I32_F32
    a.m_F32[0] = -1.25f;
    a.m_F32[1] = 100.875f;
    a.m_F32[2] = -200.0f;
    a.m_F32[3] = (float)M_PI;
    PackedConvert_(x, a, CvtOp::I32_F32);
    cout << "\nResults for CvtOp::I32_F32\n";
    cout << "a:    " << a.ToStringF32() << nl;
    cout << "x[0]: " << x[0].ToStringI32() << nl;

    // F64_I64
    a.m_I64[0] = 1000;
    a.m_I64[1] = -500000000000;
    PackedConvert_(x, a, CvtOp::F64_I64);
    cout << "\nResults for CvtOp::F64_I64\n";
    cout << "a:    " << a.ToStringI64() << nl;
    cout << "x[0]: " << x[0].ToStringF64() << nl;
```

```
    // I64_F64
    a.m_F64[0] = -122.66666667;
    a.m_F64[1] = 1234567890123.75;
    PackedConvert_(x, a, CvtOp::I64_F64);
    cout << "\nResults for CvtOp::I64_F64\n";
    cout << "a:    " << a.ToStringF64() << nl;
    cout << "x[0]: " << x[0].ToStringI64() << nl;
}

void PackedConvertB(void)
{
    const char nl = '\n';
    Vec128 x[2], a;

    // F32_U32
    a.m_U32[0] = 10;
    a.m_U32[1] = 500;
    a.m_U32[2] = 600;
    a.m_U32[3] = 1024;
    PackedConvert_(x, a, CvtOp::F32_U32);
    cout << "\nResults for CvtOp::F32_U32\n";
    cout << "a:    " << a.ToStringU32() << nl;
    cout << "x[0]: " << x[0].ToStringF32() << nl;

    // U32_F32
    a.m_F32[0] = 1.25f;
    a.m_F32[1] = 100.875f;
    a.m_F32[2] = 200.0f;
    a.m_F32[3] = (float)M_PI;
    PackedConvert_(x, a, CvtOp::U32_F32);
    cout << "\nResults for CvtOp::U32_F32\n";
    cout << "a:    " << a.ToStringF32() << nl;
    cout << "x[0]: " << x[0].ToStringU32() << nl;

    // F64_U64
    a.m_I64[0] = 1000;
    a.m_I64[1] = 420000000000;
    PackedConvert_(x, a, CvtOp::F64_U64);
    cout << "\nResults for CvtOp::F64_U64\n";
    cout << "a:    " << a.ToStringU64() << nl;
    cout << "x[0]: " << x[0].ToStringF64() << nl;

    // U64_F64
    a.m_F64[0] = 698.40;
    a.m_F64[1] = 1234567890123.75;
    PackedConvert_(x, a, CvtOp::U64_F64);
    cout << "\nResults for CvtOp::U64_F64\n";
    cout << "a:    " << a.ToStringF64() << nl;
    cout << "x[0]: " << x[0].ToStringU64() << nl;
}
```

```
void PackedConvertC(void)
{
    const char nl = '\n';
    Vec128 x[2], a, b;

    // F32_F64
    a.m_F64[0] = M_PI;
    a.m_F64[1] = M_LOG10E;
    b.m_F64[0] = -M_E;
    b.m_F64[1] = M_LN2;
    PackedConvert_(x, a, CvtOp::F32_F64, &b);
    cout << "\nResults for CvtOp::F32_F64\n";
    cout << "a:    " << a.ToStringF64() << nl;
    cout << "b:    " << b.ToStringF64() << nl;
    cout << "x[0]: " << x[0].ToStringF32() << nl;

    // F64_F32
    a.m_F32[0] = 1.0f / 9.0f;
    a.m_F32[1] = 100.875f;
    a.m_F32[2] = 200.0f;
    a.m_F32[3] = (float)M_SQRT2;
    PackedConvert_(x, a, CvtOp::F64_F32);
    cout << "\nResults for CvtOp::F64_F32\n";
    cout << "a:    " << a.ToStringF32() << nl;
    cout << "x[0]: " << x[0].ToStringF64() << nl;
    cout << "x[1]: " << x[1].ToStringF64() << nl;
}

int main()
{
    PackedConvertA();
    PackedConvertB();
    PackedConvertC();
    return 0;
}

//----------------------------------------------------
//                    Ch15_03_.s
//----------------------------------------------------

// The order of values in the following jump table must match the enum
// that's defined in Ch15_03.cpp.
            .text
            .balign 8
CvtTab:     .quad F32_I32, I32_F32
            .quad F64_I64, I64_F64
            .quad F32_U32, U32_F32
            .quad F64_U64, U64_F64
            .quad F32_F64, F64_F32
```

```
            .equ NumCvtTab,(. - CvtTab) / 8      // Number of entries in CvtTab

// extern "C" bool PackedConvert_(Vec128& x, const Vec128& a, CvtOp cvt_op, const Vec128*
b);

            .global PackedConvert_
PackedConvert_:
            cmp x2,NumCvtTab
            b.hs InvalidArg

            adr x4,CvtTab                         // x4 = points to CvtTab
            add x4,x4,x2,lsl 3                     // x4 = points to table entry
            ldr x4,[x4]                            // x4 = target jump address

            mov x2,x0                              // x2 = ptr to x
            mov w0,1                               // valid cvt_op return code
            br x4                                  // jump to target

// ----- Signed conversions -----

// Convert packed F32 <--- I32
F32_I32:    ld1 {v0.4s},[x1]
            scvtf v1.4s,v0.4s                     // signed integer to SPFP
            st1 {v1.4s},[x2]
            ret

// Convert packed I32 <--- F32
I32_F32:    ld1 {v0.4s},[x1]
            fcvtns v1.4s,v0.4s                    // SPFP to signed integer
            st1 {v1.4s},[x2]
            ret

// Convert packed F64 <--- I64
F64_I64:    ld1 {v0.2d},[x1]
            scvtf v1.2d,v0.2d                     // signed integer to DPFP
            st1 {v1.2d},[x2]
            ret

// Convert packed I64 <--- F64
I64_F64:    ld1 {v0.2d},[x1]
            fcvtns v1.2d,v0.2d                    // DPFP to signed integer
            st1 {v1.2d},[x2]
            ret

// ----- Unsigned conversions -----

// Convert packed F32 <--- U32
F32_U32:    ld1 {v0.4s},[x1]
            ucvtf v1.4s,v0.4s                     // unsigned integer to SPFP
            st1 {v1.4s},[x2]
            ret
```

```
// Convert packed U32 <--- F32
U32_F32:    ld1 {v0.4s},[x1]
            fcvtnu v1.4s,v0.4s                // SPFP to unsigned integer
            st1 {v1.4s},[x2]
            ret


// Convert packed F64 <--- U64
F64_U64:    ld1 {v0.2d},[x1]
            ucvtf v1.2d,v0.2d                 // unsigned integer to DPFP
            st1 {v1.2d},[x2]
            ret


// Convert packed U64 <--- F64
U64_F64:    ld1 {v0.2d},[x1]
            fcvtnu v1.2d,v0.2d                // DPFP to unsigned integer
            st1 {v1.2d},[x2]
            ret


// ----- FP conversions -----

// Convert packed F32 <--- F64
F32_F64:    ld1 {v0.2d},[x1]
            ld1 {v2.2d},[x3]
            fcvtn v1.2s,v0.2d                 // low-order F64 values
            fcvtn2 v1.4s,v2.2d                // high-order F64 values
            st1 {v1.4s},[x2]
            ret


// Convert packed F64 <--- F32
F64_F32:    ld1 {v0.4s},[x1]
            fcvtl v1.2d,v0.2s                 // low-order F32 values
            fcvtl2 v2.2d,v0.4s                // high-order F32 values
            st1 {v1.2d,v2.2d},[x2]
            ret


InvalidArg: mov w0,0                          // invalid cvt_op return code
            ret
```

The C++ code in Listing 15-3 begins with the declaration of assembly language function PackedConvert_. This function performs various conversions between packed integer and floating-point operands. PackedConvert_ requires an argument of type CvtOp, which specifies the type of conversion to perform. The C++ functions PackedConvertA, PackedConvertB, and PackedConvertC contain code that perform test case initialization for signed integer to floating-point, unsigned integer to floating-point, and floating-point to floating-point conversions. These functions also contain code that stream results to cout.

The assembly language code in Listing 15-3 begins with the definition of a jump table named CvtTab. This table is basically a 64-bit implementation of the jump table that you saw in source code example Ch09_03. The entries in CvtTab are labels located inside the function PackedConvert_. The target of each label is a short code block that performs a specific packed conversion. The .quad directive is employed for each CvtTab table entry since these values represent 64-bit addresses. Note that a .balign 8 directive is used just before the start of CvtTab to ensure that the table is aligned on a doubleword boundary. The .equ NumCvtTab,(. - CvtTab) / 8 directive that follows sets NumCvtTab equal to the number of entries in

CvtTab. Within the parenthetical expression of this directive, the dot symbol represents the current value of the location counter. Subtracting CvtTab from this value and dividing by eight yields the number of table entries. Note that CvtTab is defined in a .text section, which means that it contains read-only values.

Function PackedConvert_ begins its execution with the instruction pair cmp x2,NumCvtTab and b.hs InvalidArg, which validates argument value cvt_op. The next instruction, adr x4,CvtTab, loads the address of CvtTab into register X4. The ensuing add x4,x4,x2,lsl 3 instruction calculates the address of the correct entry in CvtTab. This is followed by a ldr x4,[x4] instruction that loads the specified CvtTab entry into register X4. The mov x2,x0 instruction copies argument value x into register X2, and the mov w0,1 instruction sets the return code to true. Execution of the br x4 (branch to register) instruction transfers program control to the specified target label. Each labeled code block in PackedConvert_ performs a specific packed conversion. Note that the conversion instructions in these code blocks used different arrangement specifiers. Table 15-1 summarizes the packed conversion instructions that are used in PackedConvert_. This table also includes other frequently used A64 SIMD conversion instructions.

Table 15-1. *Frequently used A64 SIMD conversion instructions*

Mnemonic	Description
fcvtl, fcvtl2	Floating-point to floating-point (higher precision)
fcvtn, fcvtn2	Floating-point to floating-point (lower precision)
fcvtms, fcvtmu	Floating-point to signed/unsigned integer (round to minus infinity)
fcvtns, fcvtnu	Floating-point to signed/unsigned integer (round to nearest)
fcvtps, fcvtpu	Floating-point to signed/unsigned integer (round to plus infinity)
fcvtzs, fcvtzu	Floating-point to signed/unsigned integer (round to zero)
scvtf, ucvtf	Signed/unsigned integer to floating-point

The floating-point conversions performed in the code blocks designated by the labels F32_F64 and F64_F32 are slightly different than the integer to floating-point conversions. In code block F32_F64, the fcvtn v1.2s,v0.2d and fcvtn2 v1.4s,v2.2d (floating-point convert to lower precision) instructions carry out packed double-precision to single-precision conversions using the current FPCR rounding mode. Note that execution of the fcvtn2 instruction does not modify the low-order 64 bits of register V1. In code block F64_F32, the instruction pair fcvtl v1.2d,v0.2s and fcvtl2 v2.2d,v0.4s (floating-point convert to higher precision) performs a packed single-precision to double-precision conversion. Here are the results for source code example Ch15_03:

```
Results for CvtOp::F32_I32
a:              10            -500  |           600           -1024
x[0]:    10.000000     -500.000000  |    600.000000    -1024.000000

Results for CvtOp::I32_F32
a:       -1.250000      100.875000  |   -200.000000        3.141593
x[0]:           -1             101  |          -200               3

Results for CvtOp::F64_I64
a:                          1000  |                  -500000000000
x[0]:        1000.000000000000  |  -500000000000.000000000000
```

```
Results for CvtOp::I64_F64
a:              -122.666666670000  |      1234567890123.750000000000
x[0]:                        -123  |               1234567890124

Results for CvtOp::F32_U32
a:                 10         500  |           600           1024
x[0]:       10.000000  500.000000  |    600.000000    1024.000000

Results for CvtOp::U32_F32
a:           1.250000  100.875000  |    200.000000       3.141593
x[0]:               1         101  |           200              3

Results for CvtOp::F64_U64
a:                           1000  |                420000000000
x[0]:          1000.000000000000  |   420000000000.000000000000

Results for CvtOp::U64_F64
a:              698.400000000000  |      1234567890123.750000000000
x[0]:                        698  |               1234567890124

Results for CvtOp::F32_F64
a:             3.141592653590  |            0.434294481903
b:            -2.718281828459  |            0.693147180560
x[0]:       3.141593    0.434294  |    -2.718282       0.693147

Results for CvtOp::F64_F32
a:           0.111111  100.875000  |    200.000000       1.414214
x[0]:           0.111111111939  |        100.875000000000
x[1]:           200.000000000000  |          1.414213538170
```

Packed Floating-Point Arrays

The source code examples of this section implement floating-point array calculating functions using the A64 SIMD instruction set. The first example uses SIMD arithmetic to calculate a correlation coefficient for a set of data points. The second example demonstrates RGB to grayscale image conversion.

Correlation Coefficient

Listing 15-4 shows the source code for example Ch15_04. This source code example illustrates how to calculate a correlation coefficient using packed single-precision floating-point arithmetic. This example also demonstrates how to perform commonly used auxiliary operations using packed floating-point operands.

Listing 15-4. Example Ch15_04

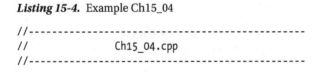

```
//------------------------------------------------
//              Ch15_04.cpp
//------------------------------------------------
```

```cpp
#include <iostream>
#include <iomanip>
#include <string>
#include <random>
#include "AlignedMem.h"

using namespace std;

extern "C" bool CalcCorrCoef_(float* rho, float sums[5], const float* x, const float* y,
size_t n, float epsilon);

const size_t c_Alignment = 16;

void Init(float* x, float* y, size_t n, unsigned int seed)
{
    uniform_real_distribution<float> dist1 {0.0, 50.0};
    normal_distribution<float> dist2 {25.0, 7.0};
    mt19937 rng {seed};

    for (size_t i = 0; i < n; i++)
    {
        x[i] = round(dist1(rng));
        y[i] = x[i] + round(dist2(rng));
//      cout << setw(10) << x[i] << ", " << setw(10) << y[i] << endl;
    }
}

bool CalcCorrCoef(float* rho, float sums[5], const float* x, const float* y, size_t n, float
epsilon)
{
    // Make sure n is valid
    if (n == 0)
        return false;

    // Make sure x and y are properly aligned
    if (!AlignedMem::IsAligned(x, c_Alignment))
        return false;
    if (!AlignedMem::IsAligned(y, c_Alignment))
        return false;

    // Calculate and save sum variables
    float sum_x = 0, sum_y = 0, sum_xx = 0, sum_yy = 0, sum_xy = 0;

    for (size_t i = 0; i < n; i++)
    {
        sum_x += x[i];
        sum_y += y[i];
        sum_xx += x[i] * x[i];
        sum_yy += y[i] * y[i];
        sum_xy += x[i] * y[i];
    }
```

```
    sums[0] = sum_x;
    sums[1] = sum_y;
    sums[2] = sum_xx;
    sums[3] = sum_yy;
    sums[4] = sum_xy;

    // Calculate rho
    float rho_num = n * sum_xy - sum_x * sum_y;
    float rho_den = sqrt(n * sum_xx - sum_x * sum_x) * sqrt(n * sum_yy - sum_y * sum_y);

    if (rho_den >= epsilon)
    {
        *rho = rho_num / rho_den;
        return true;
    }
    else
    {
        *rho = 0;
        return false;
    }
}

int main()
{
    const char nl = '\n';
    const size_t n = 103;
    AlignedArray<float> x_aa(n, c_Alignment);
    AlignedArray<float> y_aa(n, c_Alignment);
    float sums1[5], sums2[5];
    float rho1, rho2;
    float epsilon = 1.0e-9;
    float* x = x_aa.Data();
    float* y = y_aa.Data();

    Init(x, y, n, 71);

    bool rc1 = CalcCorrCoef(&rho1, sums1, x, y, n, epsilon);
    bool rc2 = CalcCorrCoef_(&rho2, sums2, x, y, n, epsilon);

    cout << "Results for CalcCorrCoef\n\n";

    if (!rc1 || !rc2)
    {
        cout << "Invalid return code ";
        cout << "rc1 = " << boolalpha << rc1 << ", ";
        cout << "rc2 = " << boolalpha << rc2 << nl;
        return 1;
    }

    int w = 14;
    string sep(w * 3, '-');
```

```
    cout << fixed << setprecision(6);
    cout << "Value     " << setw(w) << "C++" << " " << setw(w) << "A64 SIMD" << nl;
    cout << sep << nl;

    cout << setprecision(2);
    cout << "sum_x:    " << setw(w) << sums1[0] << " " << setw(w) << sums2[0] << nl;
    cout << "sum_y:    " << setw(w) << sums1[1] << " " << setw(w) << sums2[1] << nl;
    cout << "sum_xx:   " << setw(w) << sums1[2] << " " << setw(w) << sums2[2] << nl;
    cout << "sum_yy:   " << setw(w) << sums1[3] << " " << setw(w) << sums2[3] << nl;
    cout << "sum_xy:   " << setw(w) << sums1[4] << " " << setw(w) << sums2[4] << nl;
    cout << "rho:      " << setw(w) << rho1 << " " << setw(w) << rho2 << nl;
    return 0;
}


//------------------------------------------------
//                Ch15_04_.s
//------------------------------------------------


// Macro UpdateSums
//
// Arguments:    VregX    x values register
//               VregY    y values register
//
// Registers:    V16.4s   sum_x
//               v17.4s   sum_y
//               v18.4s   sum_xx
//               v19.4s   sum_yy
//               v20.4s   sum_xy

            .macro UpdateSums VregX,VregY
            fadd v16.4s,v16.4s,\VregX\().4s          // update sum_x
            fadd v17.4s,v17.4s,\VregY\().4s          // update sum_y
            fmla v18.4s,\VregX\().4s,\VregX\().4s    // update sum_xx
            fmla v19.4s,\VregY\().4s,\VregY\().4s    // update sum_yy
            fmla v20.4s,\VregX\().4s,\VregY\().4s    // update sum_xy
            .endm

// extern "C" bool CalcCorrCoef_(float* rho, float sums[5], const float* x, const float* y,
// size_t n, float epsilon);

            .text
            .global CalcCorrCoef_
CalcCorrCoef_:

// Validate arguments
            cbz x4,InvalidArg                // jump if n == 0
            tst x2,0x0f
            b.ne InvalidArg                  // jump if x not 16 aligned
            tst x3,0x0f
            b.ne InvalidArg                  // jump if y not 16 aligned
            mov x5,x4                        // save n for later
```

```
// Initialize
            eor v16.16b,v16.16b,v16.16b        // sum_x = 0
            eor v17.16b,v17.16b,v17.16b        // sum_y = 0
            eor v18.16b,v18.16b,v18.16b        // sum_xx = 0
            eor v19.16b,v19.16b,v19.16b        // sum_yy = 0
            eor v20.16b,v20.16b,v20.16b        // sum_xy = 0

            cmp x4,16
            b.lo SkipLoop1                     // jump if n < 16

// Main processing loop
Loop1:      ld1 {v0.4s,v1.4s,v2.4s,v3.4s},[x2],64   // load 16 x values
            ld1 {v4.4s,v5.4s,v6.4s,v7.4s},[x3],64   // load 16 y values

            UpdateSums v0,v4
            UpdateSums v1,v5
            UpdateSums v2,v6
            UpdateSums v3,v7

            sub x4,x4,16                       // n -= 16
            cmp x4,16
            b.hs Loop1                         // repeat if n >= 16

// Reduce packed sums to scalar values
SkipLoop1:  faddp v16.4s,v16.4s,v16.4s
            faddp v16.4s,v16.4s,v16.4s         // s16 = sum_x

            faddp v17.4s,v17.4s,v17.4s
            faddp v17.4s,v17.4s,v17.4s         // s17 = sum_y

            faddp v18.4s,v18.4s,v18.4s
            faddp v18.4s,v18.4s,v18.4s         // s18 = sum_xx

            faddp v19.4s,v19.4s,v19.4s
            faddp v19.4s,v19.4s,v19.4s         // s19 = sum_yy

            faddp v20.4s,v20.4s,v20.4s
            faddp v20.4s,v20.4s,v20.4s         // s20 = sum_xy

// Update sums with final elements
            cbz x4,SkipLoop2                   // jump if n == 0
Loop2:      ldr s1,[x2],4                      // s0 = x value
            ldr s2,[x3],4                      // s1 = y value

            fadd s16,s16,s1                    // update sum_x
            fadd s17,s17,s2                    // update sum_y
            fmla s18,s1,v1.4s[0]               // update sum_xx
            fmla s19,s2,v2.4s[0]               // update sum_yy
            fmla s20,s1,v2.4s[0]               // update sum_xy
```

```
            subs x4,x4,1                    // n -= 1
            b.ne Loop2

// Save sum values to sums[] array
SkipLoop2:  stp s16,s17,[x1],8              // save sum_x, sum_y
            stp s18,s19,[x1],8              // save sum_xx, sum_yy
            str s20,[x1]                    // save sum_xy

// Calculate rho numerator
            scvtf s21,x5                    // s21 = n
            fmul s1,s21,s20                 // n * sum_xy
            fmls s1,s16,v17.4s[0]           // n * sum_xy - sum_x * sum_y

// Calculate rho denominator
            fmul s2,s21,s18                 // n * sum_xx
            fmsub s2,s16,s16,s2             // n * sum_xx - sum_x * sum_x
            fsqrt s2,s2
            fmul s3,s21,v19.4s[0]           // n * sum_yy
            fmsub s3,s17,s17,s3             // n * sum_yy - sum_y * sum_y
            fsqrt s3,s3
            fmul s4,s2,s3                   // s4 = rho_den

            fcmp s4,s0                      // is rho_den < epsilon?
            b.lo BadRhoDen                  // jump if yes
            fdiv s5,s1,s4                   // s5 = rho
            str s5,[x0]                     // save rho
            mov w0,1                        // set success return code
            ret

BadRhoDen:  eor v5.16b,v5.16b,v5.16b        // set rho to zero
            str s5,[x0]                     // save rho
            mov w0,0                        // set error return code
            ret

InvalidArg: mov w0,0                        // set error return code
            ret
```

A correlation coefficient measures the strength of association between two variables. Correlation coefficients can range in value from -1.0 to +1.0, signifying a perfect negative or positive relationship between the two variables. Real-world correlation coefficients are rarely equal to these theoretical limits. A correlation coefficient of 0.0 indicates that no association exists between the two variables. The C++ and assembly language functions in source code example Ch15_04 calculate the well-known Pearson correlation coefficient using the following equation:

$$\rho = \frac{n \sum_i x_i y_i - \sum_i x_i \sum_i y_i}{\sqrt{n \sum_i x_i^2 - \left(\sum_i x_i\right)^2} \sqrt{n \sum_i y_i^2 - \left(\sum_i y_i\right)^2}}$$

To calculate a Pearson correlation coefficient, a function must compute the following five sum variables:

$$sum_x = \sum_i x_i$$

$$sum_y = \sum_i y_i$$

$$sum_{xx} = \sum_i x_i^2$$

$$sum_{yy} = \sum_i y_i^2$$

$$sum_{xy} = \sum_i x_i y_i$$

In Listing 15-4, the C++ function CalcCorrCoef demonstrates how to calculate a correlation coefficient. This function begins its execution by validating argument value n for a value greater than zero. It also validates array pointers x and y for alignment on a 16-byte boundary. Function CalcCorrCoef then calculates the previously defined sum variables using a simple for-loop. Following execution of this for-loop, CalcCorreCoef saves the final values of the sum variables for comparison and display purposes. It then computes the intermediate values rho_num and rho_den. Before computing the final correlation coefficient rho, CalcCorrCoef verifies that rho_den is greater than or equal to epsilon.

The assembly language source code in Listing 15-4 begins with the definition of a macro named UpdateSums. The function CalcCorreCoef_ uses this macro to calculate the five sum variables needed for the correlation coefficient equation. Macro UpdateSums requires two arguments: VregX and VregY. These arguments represent the registers that contain packed single-precision floating-point x and y values. Macro UpdateSums also uses registers V16–V20 for packed versions of sum_x, sum_y, sum_xx, sum_yy, and sum_xy, respectively. Note that UpdateSums uses the fmla (floating-point fused multiply-add) instructions to update variables sum_xx, sum_yy, and sum_xy. This instruction performs packed multiplication using the elements of its two source operands. It then adds the intermediate product elements to the elements in the destination operand. Like its scalar counterpart, the fmla instruction carries out its calculations using only a single rounding operation for each SIMD element.

Function CalcCorrCoef_ begins its execution with a validation check of argument value n for size. It then verifies that array pointers x and y are aligned on a 16-byte boundary. Following argument validation is a series of eor instructions that initialize packed versions of the five sum variables to zero. The next instruction pair, cmp x4,16 and b.lo SkipLoop1, branches around for-loop Loop1 if the number of data points is less than 16. The reason for this check is that Loop1 processes 16 data points per iteration.

The first instruction of Loop1, ld1 {v0.4s,v1.4s,v2.4s,v3.4s},[x2],64, loads 16 data points from array x into registers V0–V3. The ensuing ld1 {v4.4s,v5.4s,v6.4s,v7.4s},[x3],64 instruction loads 16 data points from array y into registers V4–V7. This is followed by four applications of the macro UpdateSums. Note that each use of macro UpdateSums employs a different set of register arguments. The first UpdateSums register argument contains the x values and the second register holds the y values. For-loop Loop1 repeats until the number of remaining elements is less than 16.

Following execution of Loop1, CalcCorrCoef uses a series of faddp (floating-point add pairwise) to reduce the packed sum variables to scalar values. The faddp instruction concatenates the vector elements in two source operands; it then performs pairwise add options using adjacent elements. Using two consecutive faddp instructions with the same source register yields a single scalar value in the low-order 32 bits of destination register.

After the packed sum reductions, for-loop Loop2 employs scalar arithmetic to update the five sum variables using the final few data points if any remain. The next three instructions, stp s16,s17,[x1],8, stp s18,s19,[x1],8, and str s20,[x1], save all five sum variables to array specified by argument value sums. The final code block in CalcCorrCoef calculates rho using straightforward scalar floating-point arithmetic. Note that this code block employs the fmsub (floating-point fused multiply-subtract scalar) instruction. The fmsub instruction multiplies the first two source operands, subtracts this product from the third source operand, and saves the result in the destination operand. Here are the results for source code example Ch15_04:

```
Results for CalcCorrCoef

Value              C++          A64 SIMD
-------------------------------------------
sum_x:          2567.00          2567.00
sum_y:          5158.00          5158.00
sum_xx:        88805.00         88805.00
sum_yy:       289566.00        289566.00
sum_xy:       154182.00        154182.00
rho:               0.92             0.92
```

Image Conversion – RGB to Grayscale

The next source code example, which is named Ch15_05, explains how to perform an RGB to grayscale image conversion using SIMD arithmetic. This example also demonstrates the use of additional A64 SIMD load instructions. Listing 15-5 shows the source code for example Ch15_05.

Listing 15-5. Example Ch15_05

```
//-----------------------------------------------------
//              ImageMisc.h
//-----------------------------------------------------

#pragma once

struct RGB32
{
    // Do not change order of elements below
    uint8_t m_R;
    uint8_t m_G;
    uint8_t m_B;
    uint8_t m_A;
};

//-----------------------------------------------------
//              Ch15_05.h
//-----------------------------------------------------
```

```
#pragma once
#include <cstdint>
#include "ImageMatrix.h"

// Ch15_05.cpp
extern float g_Coef[];
extern bool ConvertRgbToGsCpp(uint8_t* pb_gs, const RGB32* pb_rgb, size_t num_pixels, const
float* coef);

// Ch15_05_.s
extern "C" bool ConvertRgbToGs_(uint8_t* pb_gs, const RGB32* pb_rgb, size_t num_pixels,
const float* coef);

// Ch15_05_BM.cpp
extern void ConvertRgbToGs_BM(void);

//-------------------------------------------------
//                  Ch15_05.cpp
//-------------------------------------------------

#include <iostream>
#include <stdexcept>
#include "Ch15_05.h"
#include "AlignedMem.h"
#include "ImageMatrix.h"

using namespace std;

// Image size limits
size_t g_NumPixelsMin = 16;
size_t g_NumPixelsMax = 256 * 1024 * 1024;

// RGB to grayscale conversion coefficients
float g_Coef[] {0.2126f, 0.7152f, 0.0722f};

bool CompareGsImages(const uint8_t* pb_gs1,const uint8_t* pb_gs2, size_t num_pixels)
{
    for (size_t i = 0; i < num_pixels; i++)
    {
        if (abs((int)pb_gs1[i] - (int)pb_gs2[i]) > 1)
            return false;
    }

    return true;
}

bool ConvertRgbToGsCpp(uint8_t* pb_gs, const RGB32* pb_rgb, size_t num_pixels, const float*
coef)
{
    if (num_pixels < g_NumPixelsMin || num_pixels > g_NumPixelsMax)
        return false;
```

```
    if (num_pixels % 16 != 0)
        return false;

    if (!AlignedMem::IsAligned(pb_gs, 16))
        return false;
    if (!AlignedMem::IsAligned(pb_rgb, 16))
        return false;

    for (size_t i = 0; i < num_pixels; i++)
    {
        uint8_t r = pb_rgb[i].m_R;
        uint8_t g = pb_rgb[i].m_G;
        uint8_t b = pb_rgb[i].m_B;

        float gs_temp = r * coef[0] + g * coef[1] + b * coef[2] + 0.5f;

        if (gs_temp < 0.0f)
            gs_temp = 0.0f;
        else if (gs_temp > 255.0f)
            gs_temp = 255.0f;

        pb_gs[i] = (uint8_t)gs_temp;
    }

    return true;
}

void ConvertRgbToGs(void)
{
    const char nl = '\n';
    const char* fn_rgb = "../../Data/ImageC.png";
    const char* fn_gs1 = "Ch15_05_ConvertRgbToGs_ImageC_GS1.png";
    const char* fn_gs2 = "Ch15_05_ConvertRgbToGs_ImageC_GS2.png";

    ImageMatrix im_rgb(fn_rgb, PixelType::Rgb32);
    int im_h = im_rgb.GetHeight();
    int im_w = im_rgb.GetWidth();
    size_t num_pixels = im_h * im_w;
    ImageMatrix im_gs1(im_h, im_w, PixelType::Gray8);
    ImageMatrix im_gs2(im_h, im_w, PixelType::Gray8);
    RGB32* pb_rgb = im_rgb.GetPixelBuffer<RGB32>();
    uint8_t* pb_gs1 = im_gs1.GetPixelBuffer<uint8_t>();
    uint8_t* pb_gs2 = im_gs2.GetPixelBuffer<uint8_t>();

    cout << "Results for ConvertRgbToGs\n";
    cout << "Converting RGB image " << fn_rgb << nl;
    cout << "    im_h = " << im_h << " pixels\n";
    cout << "    im_w = " << im_w << " pixels\n";
```

```
    // Exercise conversion functions
    bool rc1 = ConvertRgbToGsCpp(pb_gs1, pb_rgb, num_pixels, g_Coef);
    bool rc2 = ConvertRgbToGs_(pb_gs2, pb_rgb, num_pixels, g_Coef);

    if (rc1 && rc2)
    {
        cout << "Saving grayscale image #1 - " << fn_gs1 << nl;
        im_gs1.SaveToPngFile(fn_gs1);

        cout << "Saving grayscale image #2 - " << fn_gs2 << nl;
        im_gs2.SaveToPngFile(fn_gs2);

        if (CompareGsImages(pb_gs1, pb_gs2, num_pixels))
            cout << "Grayscale image compare OK\n";
        else
            cout << "Grayscale image compare failed\n";
    }
    else
        cout << "Invalid return code\n";
}

int main()
{
    try
    {
        ConvertRgbToGs();
        ConvertRgbToGs_BM();
    }

    catch (exception& ex)
    {
        cout << "exception has occurred - " << ex.what() << '\n';
    }

    catch (...)
    {
        cout << "Unexpected exception has occurred\n";
    }

    return 0;
}

//---------------------------------------------------
//                Ch15_05_Macros_.inc
//---------------------------------------------------

// Macro U8toF32 (uses v3 and v7 as temp registers)
        .macro U8toF32 Vd0,Vd1,Vd2,Vd3,Vs
        uxtl  v3.8h, \Vs\().8b              // promote to U16
        uxtl2 v7.8h, \Vs\().16b
```

```
            uxtl   \Vd0\().4s, v3.4h          // promote to U32
            uxtl2  \Vd1\().4s, v3.8h
            ucvtf  \Vd0\().4s, \Vd0\().4s      // convert to F32
            ucvtf  \Vd1\().4s, \Vd1\().4s

            uxtl   \Vd2\().4s, v7.4h          // promote to U32
            uxtl2  \Vd3\().4s, v7.8h
            ucvtf  \Vd2\().4s, \Vd2\().4s      // convert to F32
            ucvtf  \Vd3\().4s, \Vd3\().4s
            .endm

// Macro F32toU8
            .macro F32toU8 Vd,Vs0,Vs1,Vs2,Vs3
            fcvtnu \Vs0\().4s, \Vs0\().4s      // convert F32 to U32
            fcvtnu \Vs1\().4s, \Vs1\().4s
            uqxtn  v0.4h, \Vs0\().4s           // convert to U16
            uqxtn2 v0.8h, \Vs1\().4s

            fcvtnu \Vs2\().4s, \Vs2\().4s      // convert F32 to U32
            fcvtnu \Vs3\().4s, \Vs3\().4s
            uqxtn  v1.4h, \Vs2\().4s           // convert to U16
            uqxtn2 v1.8h, \Vs3\().4s

            uqxtn  \Vd\().8b, v0.8h            // convert to U8
            uqxtn2 \Vd\().16b, v1.8h
            .endm

// Macro MulCoef
            .macro MulCoef Vs0,Vs1,Vs2,Vs3,Vcoef
            fmul   \Vs0\().4s, \Vs0\().4s, \Vcoef\().4s
            fmul   \Vs1\().4s, \Vs1\().4s, \Vcoef\().4s
            fmul   \Vs2\().4s, \Vs2\().4s, \Vcoef\().4s
            fmul   \Vs3\().4s, \Vs3\().4s, \Vcoef\().4s
            .endm

// Macro SumRGB (uses v7 as temp register)
            .macro SumRGB Vr, Vg, Vb, Vc
            fadd   \Vr\().4s, \Vr\().4s, \Vg\().4s
            fadd   v7.4s, \Vb\().4s, \Vc\().4s
            fadd   \Vr\().4s, \Vr\().4s, V7.4s
            .endm

//---------------------------------------------------
//              Ch15_05_.s
//---------------------------------------------------

            .include "Ch15_05_Macros_.inc"

// extern "C" bool ConvertRgbToGs_(uint8_t* pb_gs, const RGB32* pb_rgb, size_t num_pixels,
const float* coef);
```

```
            .text
            .global ConvertRgbToGs_
ConvertRgbToGs_:

// Validate arguments
            ldr x4,=g_NumPixelsMin        // make sure num_pixels
            ldr x4,[x4]                   // is >= g_NumPixelsMin
            cmp x2,x4
            b.lo InvalidArg

            ldr x4,=g_NumPixelsMax        // make sure num_pixels
            ldr x4,[x4]                   // is <= g_NumPixelsMax
            cmp x2,x4
            b.hi InvalidArg

            tst x2,0x0f                   // num_pixels must be even
            b.ne InvalidArg               // multiple of 16

            tst x0,0x0f                   // make sure both
            b.ne InvalidArg               // pixel buffers are
            tst x1,0x0f                   // aligned to a 16-byte
            b.ne InvalidArg               // boundary

// Initialize constants - all registers contain packed SPFP elements
// v4 = coef[0] v5 = coef[1], v6 = coef[2], v29 = 0.5

            ld3r {v4.4s,v5.4s,v6.4s},[x3] // load packed coefficients
            fmov v29.4s,0.5               // load packed 0.5

// Main processing loop
Loop1:      ld4 {v0.16b,v1.16b,v2.16b,v3.16b},[x1],64    // load 16 RGB32

            U8toF32 v16,v17,v18,v19,v0    // convert red pixels
            U8toF32 v20,v21,v22,v23,v1    // convert green pixels
            U8toF32 v24,v25,v26,v27,v2    // convert blue pixels

            MulCoef v16,v17,v18,v19,v4    // red pixels * coef[0]
            MulCoef v20,v21,v22,v23,v5    // green pixels * coef[1]
            MulCoef v24,v25,v26,v27,v6    // blue pixels * coef[2]

            SumRGB v16,v20,v24,v29        // sum r, g, b channels
            SumRGB v17,v21,v25,v29        // registers v16:19
            SumRGB v18,v22,v26,v29        // contain grayscale
            SumRGB v19,v23,v27,v29        // pixel values as F32

            F32toU8 v2,v16,v17,v18,v19    // convert back to U8
            st1 {v2.16b},[x0],16          // save 16 GS pixels

            subs x2,x2,16                 // n -= 16
            b.ne Loop1
```

```
        mov w0,1                              // set success return code
        ret

InvalidArg: mov w0,0                          // set error return code
        ret
```

A variety of algorithms exist to convert an RGB image into a grayscale image. One frequently used technique calculates grayscale pixel values using a weighted sum of the RGB color components. In this source code example, RGB pixels are converted to grayscale pixels using the following equation:

$$GS(x,y) = R(x,y)W_r + G(x,y)W_g + B(x,y)W_b$$

Each RGB color component weight (or coefficient) is a floating-point number between 0.0 and 1.0. The sum of all three coefficients normally equals 1.0. The exact values used for the color component coefficients are usually based on published standards that reflect a multitude of visual factors including properties of the target color space, display device characteristics, and perceived image quality. Appendix B contains some references that you can consult if you are interested in learning more about RGB to grayscale image conversion.

The source code in Listing 15-5 opens with declaration of a structure named RGB32. This structure is declared in the header file ImageMisc.h and specifies the color component ordering scheme of each RGB pixel. The function ConvertRgbToGsCpp contains a C++ implementation of the RGB to grayscale conversion algorithm. This function uses an ordinary for-loop that sweeps through the RGB32 image pixel buffer pb_rgb and computes grayscale pixel values using the previously defined conversion equation. Note that in this example, RGB32 element m_A (pixel alpha channel) is not used in any of the calculations. Each calculated grayscale pixel value is adjusted by a rounding factor and clipped to [0.0, 255.0] before it is saved to the grayscale image pixel buffer pointed to by pb_gs.

The assembly language code in Listing 15-5 begins with a series of macro definitions. The function ConvertRgbToGs_ uses these macros and they will be explained shortly. Function ConvertRgbToGs_ begins its execution with a series of code blocks that validate argument value num_pixels. It then checks the source and destination pixel buffer pointers for alignment on a 16-byte boundary. Following argument validation, the ld3r {v4.4s,v5.4s,v6.4s},[x3] (load single three-element structure and replicate) instruction loads the red, green, and blue color conversion coefficients. Following execution of this instruction, each single-precision floating-point element in register V4 contains coef[0] (red coefficient), each element in register V5 contains coef[1] (green coefficient), and each element in register V6 contains coef[2] (blue coefficient) as shown in Figure 15-1. The A64 SIMD instruction set also includes the instructions ld1r, ld2r, and ld4r, which replicate elements in one, two, or four registers. The next instruction, fmov v29.4s,0.5, loads the constant 0.5 into each element of register V29.

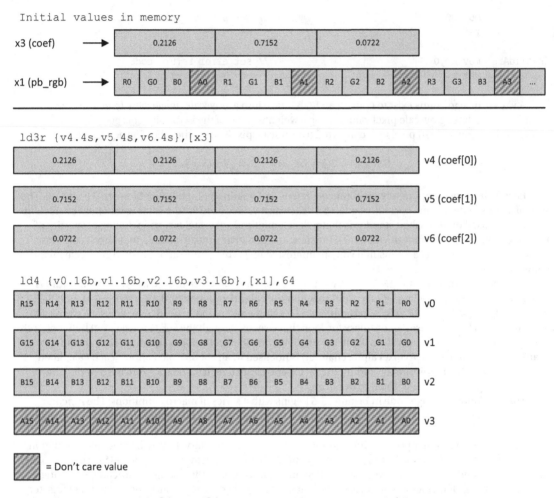

Figure 15-1. *Execution of the* `ld3r` *and* `ld4` *instructions in function* `ConvertRgbToGs_`

Each iteration of for-loop `Loop1` begins with a `ld4 {v0.16b,v1.16b,v2.16b,v3.16b},[x1],64` (load multiple four-element structures with de-interleaving) instruction that loads 16 red, green, blue, and alpha channel pixel values into registers V0, V1, V2, and V3 as shown in Figure 15-1. Note that function `ConvertRgbToGs_` ignores the alpha channel pixel values in register V3 since these values are not required for RGB to grayscale conversions.

The next code block in `ConvertRgbToGs_` employs macro `U8toF32` to convert the RGB pixel values from unsigned 8-bit integers to single-precision floating-point. This macro uses the instruction pair `uxtl v3.8h,\` `Vs\().8b` and `uxtl2 v7.8h,\Vs\().16b` to promote the unsigned 8-bit pixel values to unsigned 16-bit integers. It then uses the instruction quartet `uxtl \Vd0\().4s, v3.4h`, `uxtl2 \Vd1\().4s,v3.8h`, `ucvtf \` `Vd0\().4s,\Vd0\().4s`, and `ucvtf \Vd1\().4s,\Vd1\().4s` to convert eight unsigned 16-bit integers to single-precision floating-point. The instruction quartet that follows converts the remaining eight pixels to single-precision floating-point.

Following conversion of the pixel values to floating-point, `ConvertRgbGs_` uses the macro `MulCoef` to multiply each packed set of color channel pixels by the corresponding color coefficient. Macro `MulCoef` uses the `fmul` instruction to carry out its calculations. The code block that follows employs the `SumRGB` macro to carry out the color conversion equation's summing operation.

After each block of 16 pixels is converted from RGB to grayscale, ConvertRgbGs_ uses macro F32toU8 to convert the single-precision floating-point values to unsigned 8-bit integers. Note that this macro makes use of the uqxtn and uqxtn2 (unsigned saturating extract narrow) instructions, which perform unsigned integer size reductions using saturated arithmetic. The use of saturated arithmetic by these instructions eliminates the need to perform an explicit pixel-clipping operation similar to what was carried out in the C++ function ConvertRgbGsCpp. Following the use of the F32toU8 macro, ConvertRgbGs_ uses a st1 {v2.16b},[x0],16 instruction to save the converted grayscale pixels to the pixel buffer pointed to by argument value pb_gs. The subs x2,x2,16 instruction calculates n -= 16 and for-loop Loop1 repeats until all pixel have been processed. Here are the results for source code example Ch15_05:

```
Results for ConvertRgbToGs
Converting RGB image ../../Data/ImageC.png
  im_h = 960 pixels
  im_w = 640 pixels
Saving grayscale image #1 - Ch15_05_ConvertRgbToGs_ImageC_GS1.png
Saving grayscale image #2 - Ch15_05_ConvertRgbToGs_ImageC_GS2.png
Grayscale image compare OK

Running benchmark function ConvertRgbToGs_BM - please wait
Benchmark times save to file Ch15_05_ConvertRgbToGs_BM_RpiOmega.csv
```

Table 15-2 shows the benchmark timing measurements for the C++ and assembly language versions of the RGB to grayscale color conversion functions.

Table 15-2. *Benchmark timing measurements (microseconds) for RGB to grayscale image conversion functions using image file ImageC.png*

C++ (**ConvertRgbGsCpp**)	Assembly Language (**ConvertRgbGs_**)
2136	1745

Packed Floating-Point Matrices

In this section, you will learn how to use the A64 SIMD instruction set to code functions that perform common operations using 4 × 4 matrices. The first subsection demonstrates 4 × 4 matrix multiplication using both single-precision and double-precision floating-point values. The second subsection explains how to code macros that perform 4 × 4 matrix trace calculations and transpose operations.

Matrix Multiplication

Listing 15-6 shows the source code for example Ch15_06. This example is an Armv8-64 implementation of source code example Ch09_07 that demonstrates how to multiply two 4 × 4 matrices using SIMD arithmetic. Before proceeding, you might want to review the matrix multiplication equations presented in Chapter 9 since these equations also apply to source code example Ch15_06.

Listing 15-6. Example Ch15_06

```
//---------------------------------------------------
//                  Ch15_06.h
//---------------------------------------------------

// Ch15_06.cpp
extern void Mat4x4MulF32(float* m_des, const float* m_src1, const float* m_src2);
extern void Mat4x4MulF64(double* m_des, const double* m_src1, const double* m_src2);

// Ch15_06_.s
extern "C" void Mat4x4MulF32_(float* m_des, const float* m_src1, const float* m_src2);
extern "C" void Mat4x4MulF64_(double* m_des, const double* m_src1, const double* m_src2);

// Ch15_06_BM.cpp
extern void Mat4x4MulF32_BM(void);
extern void Mat4x4MulF64_BM(void);


//---------------------------------------------------
//                  Ch15_06.cpp
//---------------------------------------------------

#include <iostream>
#include <iomanip>
#include "Ch15_06.h"
#include "MatrixF32.h"
#include "MatrixF64.h"

using namespace std;

void Mat4x4MulF32(MatrixF32& m_src1, MatrixF32& m_src2)
{
    const size_t nr = m_src1.GetNumRows();
    const size_t nc = m_src2.GetNumCols();
    MatrixF32 m_des1(nr ,nc);
    MatrixF32 m_des2(nr ,nc);

    MatrixF32::Mul4x4(m_des1, m_src1, m_src2);
    Mat4x4MulF32_(m_des2.Data(), m_src1.Data(), m_src2.Data());

    cout << fixed << setprecision(1);

    m_src1.SetOstream(12, "  ");
    m_src2.SetOstream(12, "  ");
    m_des1.SetOstream(12, "  ");
    m_des2.SetOstream(12, "  ");

    cout << "\nResults for Mat4x4MulF32\n";
    cout << "Matrix m_src1\n" << m_src1 << '\n';
    cout << "Matrix m_src2\n" << m_src2 << '\n';
    cout << "Matrix m_des1\n" << m_des1 << '\n';
    cout << "Matrix m_des2\n" << m_des2 << '\n';
```

```
    if (m_des1 != m_des2)
        cout << "\nMatrix compare failed - Mat4x4MulF32\n";
}

void Mat4x4MulF64(MatrixF64& m_src1, MatrixF64& m_src2)
{
    const size_t nr = m_src1.GetNumRows();
    const size_t nc = m_src2.GetNumCols();
    MatrixF64 m_des1(nr ,nc);
    MatrixF64 m_des2(nr ,nc);

    MatrixF64::Mul4x4(m_des1, m_src1, m_src2);
    Mat4x4MulF64_(m_des2.Data(), m_src1.Data(), m_src2.Data());

    cout << fixed << setprecision(1);

    m_src1.SetOstream(12, "  ");
    m_src2.SetOstream(12, "  ");
    m_des1.SetOstream(12, "  ");
    m_des2.SetOstream(12, "  ");

    cout << "\nResults for Mat4x4MulF64\n";
    cout << "Matrix m_src1\n" << m_src1 << '\n';
    cout << "Matrix m_src2\n" << m_src2 << '\n';
    cout << "Matrix m_des1\n" << m_des1 << '\n';
    cout << "Matrix m_des2\n" << m_des2 << '\n';

    if (m_des1 != m_des2)
        cout << "\nMatrix compare failed - Mat4x4MulF64\n";
}

void Mat4x4MulF32Test(void)
{
    const size_t nr = 4;
    const size_t nc = 4;
    MatrixF32 m_src1(nr ,nc);
    MatrixF32 m_src2(nr ,nc);

    const float src1_row0[] = { 10, 11, 12, 13 };
    const float src1_row1[] = { 20, 21, 22, 23 };
    const float src1_row2[] = { 30, 31, 32, 33 };
    const float src1_row3[] = { 40, 41, 42, 43 };

    const float src2_row0[] = { 100, 101, 102, 103 };
    const float src2_row1[] = { 200, 201, 202, 203 };
    const float src2_row2[] = { 300, 301, 302, 303 };
    const float src2_row3[] = { 400, 401, 402, 403 };

    m_src1.SetRow(0, src1_row0);
    m_src1.SetRow(1, src1_row1);
    m_src1.SetRow(2, src1_row2);
    m_src1.SetRow(3, src1_row3);
```

```
    m_src2.SetRow(0, src2_row0);
    m_src2.SetRow(1, src2_row1);
    m_src2.SetRow(2, src2_row2);
    m_src2.SetRow(3, src2_row3);

    Mat4x4MulF32(m_src1, m_src2);
}

void Mat4x4MulF64Test(void)
{
    const size_t nr = 4;
    const size_t nc = 4;
    MatrixF64 m_src1(nr ,nc);
    MatrixF64 m_src2(nr ,nc);

    const double src1_row0[] = { -10, 11, 12, 13 };
    const double src1_row1[] = { 20, -21, 22, 23 };
    const double src1_row2[] = { 30, 31, -32, 33 };
    const double src1_row3[] = { 40, 41, 42, -43 };

    const double src2_row0[] = { -100, 101, 102, 103 };
    const double src2_row1[] = { 200, -201, 202, 203 };
    const double src2_row2[] = { 300, 301, -302, 303 };
    const double src2_row3[] = { 400, 401, 402, -403 };

    m_src1.SetRow(0, src1_row0);
    m_src1.SetRow(1, src1_row1);
    m_src1.SetRow(2, src1_row2);
    m_src1.SetRow(3, src1_row3);

    m_src2.SetRow(0, src2_row0);
    m_src2.SetRow(1, src2_row1);
    m_src2.SetRow(2, src2_row2);
    m_src2.SetRow(3, src2_row3);

    Mat4x4MulF64(m_src1, m_src2);
}

int main()
{
    Mat4x4MulF32Test();
    Mat4x4MulF64Test();
    Mat4x4MulF32_BM();
    Mat4x4MulF64_BM();
    return 0;
}

//-------------------------------------------------
//                 Ch15_06_.s
//-------------------------------------------------
```

```
// extern "C" void Mat4x4MulF32_(float* m_des, const float* m_src1, const float* m_src2);

            .text
            .global Mat4x4MulF32_
Mat4x4MulF32_:

// Load m_src1 into v0:v3
            ld1 {v0.4s-v3.4s},[x1]

// Load m_src2 into v4:v7
            ld1 {v4.4s-v7.4s},[x2]

// Row 0
            fmul v16.4s,v4.4s,v0.s[0]
            fmla v16.4s,v5.4s,v0.s[1]
            fmla v16.4s,v6.4s,v0.s[2]
            fmla v16.4s,v7.4s,v0.s[3]
            st1 {v16.4s},[x0],16

// Row 1
            fmul v17.4s,v4.4s,v1.s[0]
            fmla v17.4s,v5.4s,v1.s[1]
            fmla v17.4s,v6.4s,v1.s[2]
            fmla v17.4s,v7.4s,v1.s[3]
            st1 {v17.4s},[x0],16

// Row 2
            fmul v18.4s,v4.4s,v2.s[0]
            fmla v18.4s,v5.4s,v2.s[1]
            fmla v18.4s,v6.4s,v2.s[2]
            fmla v18.4s,v7.4s,v2.s[3]
            st1 {v18.4s},[x0],16

// Row 3
            fmul v19.4s,v4.4s,v3.s[0]
            fmla v19.4s,v5.4s,v3.s[1]
            fmla v19.4s,v6.4s,v3.s[2]
            fmla v19.4s,v7.4s,v3.s[3]
            st1 {v19.4s},[x0]
            ret

// extern "C" void Mat4x4MulF64_(double* m_des, const double* m_src1, const double* m_src2);

            .global Mat4x4MulF64_
Mat4x4MulF64_:

// Load m_src1 into v0:v7
            ld1 {v0.4s-v3.4s},[x1],64
            ld1 {v4.4s-v7.4s},[x1]
```

```
// Load m_src2 into v16:v23
        ld1 {v16.4s-v19.4s},[x2],64
        ld1 {v20.4s-v23.4s},[x2]

// Row 0
        fmul v24.2d,v16.2d,v0.d[0]          // cols 0 & 1
        fmla v24.2d,v18.2d,v0.d[1]
        fmla v24.2d,v20.2d,v1.d[0]
        fmla v24.2d,v22.2d,v1.d[1]

        fmul v25.2d,v17.2d,v0.d[0]          // cols 2 & 3
        fmla v25.2d,v19.2d,v0.d[1]
        fmla v25.2d,v21.2d,v1.d[0]
        fmla v25.2d,v23.2d,v1.d[1]
        st1 {v24.2d,v25.2d},[x0],32

// Row 1
        fmul v24.2d,v16.2d,v2.d[0]          // cols 0 & 1
        fmla v24.2d,v18.2d,v2.d[1]
        fmla v24.2d,v20.2d,v3.d[0]
        fmla v24.2d,v22.2d,v3.d[1]

        fmul v25.2d,v17.2d,v2.d[0]          // cols 2 & 3
        fmla v25.2d,v19.2d,v2.d[1]
        fmla v25.2d,v21.2d,v3.d[0]
        fmla v25.2d,v23.2d,v3.d[1]
        st1 {v24.2d,v25.2d},[x0],32

// Row 2
        fmul v24.2d,v16.2d,v4.d[0]          // cols 0 & 1
        fmla v24.2d,v18.2d,v4.d[1]
        fmla v24.2d,v20.2d,v5.d[0]
        fmla v24.2d,v22.2d,v5.d[1]

        fmul v25.2d,v17.2d,v4.d[0]          // cols 2 & 3
        fmla v25.2d,v19.2d,v4.d[1]
        fmla v25.2d,v21.2d,v5.d[0]
        fmla v25.2d,v23.2d,v5.d[1]
        st1 {v24.2d,v25.2d},[x0],32

// Row 3
        fmul v24.2d,v16.2d,v6.d[0]          // cols 0 & 1
        fmla v24.2d,v18.2d,v6.d[1]
        fmla v24.2d,v20.2d,v7.d[0]
        fmla v24.2d,v22.2d,v7.d[1]

        fmul v25.2d,v17.2d,v6.d[0]          // cols 2 & 3
        fmla v25.2d,v19.2d,v6.d[1]
        fmla v25.2d,v21.2d,v7.d[0]
        fmla v25.2d,v23.2d,v7.d[1]
        st1 {v24.2d,v25.2d},[x0]
        ret
```

The C++ code in Listing 15-6 includes two functions named Mat4x4MulF32 and Mat4x4MulF64. These functions exercise the C++ and assembly language matrix multiplication routines using single-precision and double-precision floating-point values, respectively. The C++ classes MatrixF32 and MatrixF64 are simple wrapper classes for single-precision and double-precision floating-point matrices, respectively. The source code for these classes is not shown in Listing 15-6 but is included with the source code download package. The remaining C++ code performs test case initialization and streams results to cout.

Function Mat4x4MulF32_ begins its execution with a ld1 {v0.4s, v1.4s, v2.4s, v3.4s},[x1] instruction that loads matrix m_src1 into registers V0–V3. This is followed by a ld1 {v4.4s, v5.4s, v6.4s, v7.4s},[x2] instruction that loads matrix m_src2 into registers V4–V7. The ensuing code block uses a series of fmul and fmla instructions to calculate the first row (row 0) of matrix m_des. This code block computes row 0 using the equations that are shown in Chapter 9. Note that the second source operand of each fmul/fmla instruction is a scalar value. These instructions multiply each element of the first source operand by the scalar element that is designated by the subscript operator in the second source code operand. Following calculation of row 0, a st1 {v16.4s},[x0],16 instruction saves the result to m_des. Rows 1, 2, and 3 of matrix m_des are then calculated using similar sequences of fmul/fmla instructions.

Function Mat4x4MulF64_ uses the same basic algorithm as Mat4x4MulF32_ to calculate the product of two double-precision floating-point 4 × 4 matrices. The first instruction pair of Mat4x4MulF64_, ld1 {v0.4s-v3.4s},[x1],64 and ld1 {v4.4s-v7.4s},[x1], loads matrix m_src1 into registers V0–V7. The ensuing instruction pair, ld1 {v16.4s-v19.4s},[x2],64 and ld1 {v20.4s-v23.4s},[x2], loads matrix m_src2 into registers V16–V23. Function Mat4x4MulF64_ uses two distinct fmul/fmla code blocks to calculate each row result. The reason for this is that a 128-bit wide Armv8-64 SIMD register can hold only two double-precision floating-point values. Following the calculation of each destination matrix row, a st1 instruction saves the result to m_des.

It should be noted that both Mat4x4MulF32_ and Mat4x4MulF64_ are coded for standard C++ row-major ordered matrices. These functions cannot be used with column-major ordered matrices without modifications. Here are the results for source code example Ch15_06:

```
Results for Mat4x4MulF32
Matrix m_src1
          10.0        11.0        12.0        13.0
          20.0        21.0        22.0        23.0
          30.0        31.0        32.0        33.0
          40.0        41.0        42.0        43.0

Matrix m_src2
         100.0       101.0       102.0       103.0
         200.0       201.0       202.0       203.0
         300.0       301.0       302.0       303.0
         400.0       401.0       402.0       403.0

Matrix m_des1
       12000.0     12046.0     12092.0     12138.0
       22000.0     22086.0     22172.0     22258.0
       32000.0     32126.0     32252.0     32378.0
       42000.0     42166.0     42332.0     42498.0

Matrix m_des2
       12000.0     12046.0     12092.0     12138.0
       22000.0     22086.0     22172.0     22258.0
       32000.0     32126.0     32252.0     32378.0
       42000.0     42166.0     42332.0     42498.0
```

```
Results for Mat4x4MulF64
Matrix m_src1
        -10.0           11.0           12.0           13.0
         20.0          -21.0           22.0           23.0
         30.0           31.0          -32.0           33.0
         40.0           41.0           42.0          -43.0

Matrix m_src2
       -100.0          101.0          102.0          103.0
        200.0         -201.0          202.0          203.0
        300.0          301.0         -302.0          303.0
        400.0          401.0          402.0         -403.0

Matrix m_des1
      12000.0         5604.0         2804.0         -400.0
       9600.0        22086.0          400.0        -4806.0
       6800.0          400.0        32252.0       -13612.0
       -400.0        -8802.0       -17608.0        42498.0

Matrix m_des2
      12000.0         5604.0         2804.0         -400.0
       9600.0        22086.0          400.0        -4806.0
       6800.0          400.0        32252.0       -13612.0
       -400.0        -8802.0       -17608.0        42498.0

Running benchmark function Mat4x4MulF32_BM - please wait
Benchmark times save to file Ch15_06_Mat4x4MulF32_BM_RpiOmega.csv

Running benchmark function Mat4x4MulF64_BM - please wait
Benchmark times save to file Ch15_06_Mat4x4MulF64_BM_RpiOmega.csv
```

Table 15-3 shows the benchmark timing measurements for the C++ and assembly language versions of the matrix multiplication functions.

Table 15-3. *Benchmark timing measurements (microseconds) for C++ and assembly language 4 × 4 matrix multiplication functions*

MatrixF32::Mul4x4	Mat4x4MulF32_	MatrixF64::Mul4x4	Max4x4MulF64_
10292	3756	16727	7233

Matrix Trace and Transposition

The trace of a square matrix is the sum of its main diagonal elements. In source code example Ch13_07, you learned how to calculate the trace of a square matrix of double-precision floating-point values using scalar arithmetic. In source code example Ch15_07, you will learn how to code macros that calculate trace values using 4 × 4 matrices of single-precision and double-precision values. You will also learn how write macro code that transposes 4 × 4 matrices. Using macros for common 4 × 4 matrix operations such as trace and transposition often results in better performance since there is no function call overhead. Listing 15-7 shows the source code for example Ch15_07.

Listing 15-7. Example Ch15_07

```cpp
//----------------------------------------------------
//                  Ch15_07.cpp
//----------------------------------------------------

#include <iostream>
#include <iomanip>
#include "MatrixF32.h"
#include "MatrixF64.h"

using namespace std;

extern "C" float Mat4x4TraceF32_(const float* m_src1);
extern "C" double Mat4x4TraceF64_(const double* m_src1);
extern "C" void Mat4x4TransposeF32_(float* m_des, const float* m_src1);
extern "C" void Mat4x4TransposeF64_(double* m_des, const double* m_src1);

void Mat4x4TestF32(MatrixF32& m_src1)
{
    const char nl = '\n';
    const size_t nr = m_src1.GetNumCols();
    const size_t nc = m_src1.GetNumRows();
    MatrixF32 m_des1(nr, nc);
    MatrixF32 m_des2(nr, nc);

    MatrixF32::Transpose(m_des1, m_src1);
    Mat4x4TransposeF32_(m_des2.Data(), m_src1.Data());

    cout << fixed << setprecision(1);

    m_src1.SetOstream(12, "  ");
    m_des1.SetOstream(12, "  ");
    m_des2.SetOstream(12, "  ");

    cout << "\nResults for Mat4x4TestF32\n";
    cout << "Matrix m_src1\n" << m_src1 << nl;
    cout << "Matrix m_des1 (transpose of m_src1)\n" << m_des1 << nl;
    cout << "Matrix m_des2 (transpose of m_src1)\n" << m_des2 << nl;

    if (m_des1 != m_des2)
        cout << "\nMatrix transpose compare failed\n";

    float m_trace1 = m_src1.Trace();
    float m_trace2 = Mat4x4TraceF32_(m_src1.Data());
    cout << "m_trace1 = " << m_trace1 << nl;
    cout << "m_trace2 = " << m_trace2 << nl;

    if (m_trace1 != m_trace2)
        cout << "\nMatrix trace compare failed\n";
}
```

```
void Mat4x4TestF64(MatrixF64& m_src1)
{
    const char nl = '\n';
    const size_t nr = m_src1.GetNumCols();
    const size_t nc = m_src1.GetNumRows();
    MatrixF64 m_des1(nr, nc);
    MatrixF64 m_des2(nr, nc);

    MatrixF64::Transpose(m_des1, m_src1);
    Mat4x4TransposeF64_(m_des2.Data(), m_src1.Data());

    cout << fixed << setprecision(1);

    m_src1.SetOstream(12, "   ");
    m_des1.SetOstream(12, "   ");
    m_des2.SetOstream(12, "   ");

    cout << "\nResults for Mat4x4TestF64\n";
    cout << "Matrix m_src1\n" << m_src1 << nl;
    cout << "Matrix m_des1 (transpose of m_src1)\n" << m_des1 << nl;
    cout << "Matrix m_des2 (transpose of m_src1)\n" << m_des2 << nl;

    if (m_des1 != m_des2)
        cout << "\nMatrix transpose compare failed\n";

    float m_trace1 = m_src1.Trace();
    float m_trace2 = Mat4x4TraceF64_(m_src1.Data());
    cout << "m_trace1 = " << m_trace1 << nl;
    cout << "m_trace2 = " << m_trace2 << nl;

    if (m_trace1 != m_trace2)
        cout << "\nMatrix trace compare failed\n";
}

void Mat4x4TestF32(void)
{
    const size_t nr = 4;
    const size_t nc = 4;
    MatrixF32 m_src1(nr ,nc);

    const float src1_row0[] = { 10, 11, 12, 13 };
    const float src1_row1[] = { 20, 21, 22, 23 };
    const float src1_row2[] = { 30, 31, 32, 33 };
    const float src1_row3[] = { 40, 41, 42, 43 };

    m_src1.SetRow(0, src1_row0);
    m_src1.SetRow(1, src1_row1);
    m_src1.SetRow(2, src1_row2);
    m_src1.SetRow(3, src1_row3);
```

```
    Mat4x4TestF32(m_src1);
}

void Mat4x4TestF64(void)
{
    const size_t nr = 4;
    const size_t nc = 4;
    MatrixF64 m_src1(nr ,nc);

    const double src1_row0[] = { 100, 110, 120, 130 };
    const double src1_row1[] = { 200, 210, 220, 230 };
    const double src1_row2[] = { 300, 310, 320, 330 };
    const double src1_row3[] = { 400, 410, 420, 430 };

    m_src1.SetRow(0, src1_row0);
    m_src1.SetRow(1, src1_row1);
    m_src1.SetRow(2, src1_row2);
    m_src1.SetRow(3, src1_row3);

    Mat4x4TestF64(m_src1);
}

int main()
{
    Mat4x4TestF32();
    Mat4x4TestF64();
    return 0;
}

//----------------------------------------------------
//                  Ch15_07_.s
//----------------------------------------------------

// Macro Mat4x4TraceF32
//
// Input Registers          Other Registers
// ----------------------------------------------------
// v0   a3 a2 a1 a0          s4  matrix trace value
// v1   b3 b2 b1 b0          s5  temp register
// v2   c3 c2 c1 c0
// v3   d3 d2 d1 d0

            .macro Mat4x4TraceF32
            mov s4,v0.4s[0]                 // s4 = m[0][0]
            mov s5,v1.4s[1]                 // s5 = m[1][1]
            fadd s4,s4,s5                   // s4 = m[0][0] + m[1][1]

            mov s5,v2.4s[2]                 // s5 = m[2][2]
            fadd s4,s4,s5                   // s4 += m[2][2]
```

```
            mov s5,v3.4s[3]                    // s5 = m[3][3]
            fadd s4,s4,s5                       // s5 = += m[3][3]
            .endm
```

```
// Macro Mat4x4TraceF64
//
// Input Registers          Other Registers
// ------------------------------------------------
// v1:v0     a3 a2 a1 a0     d16 matrix trace value
// v3:v2     b3 b2 b1 b0     d17 temp register
// v5:v4     c3 c2 c1 c0
// v7:v6     d3 d2 d1 d0

            .macro Mat4x4TraceF64
            mov d16,v0.2d[0]                    // d16 = m[0][0]
            mov d17,v2.2d[1]                    // d17 = m[1][1]
            fadd d16,d16,d17                    // d16 = m[0][0] + m[1][1]

            mov d17,v5.2d[0]                    // d17 = m[2][2]
            fadd d16,d16,d17                    // d16 = m[0][0] + m[1][1]

            mov d17,v7.2d[1]                    // d16 = m[3][3]
            fadd d16,d16,d17                    // d17 = m[0][0] + m[1][1]
            .endm
```

```
// Mat4x4TransposeF32
//
// Input Registers       Output Registers      Temp Registers
// -----------------------------------------------------------
// v0     a3 a2 a1 a0     v0    d0 c0 b0 a0     v4
// v1     b3 b2 b1 b0     v1    d1 c1 b1 a1     v5
// v2     c3 c2 c1 c0     v2    d2 c2 b2 a2     v6
// v3     d3 d2 d1 d0     v3    d3 c3 b3 a3     v7

            .macro Mat4x4TransposeF32
            trn1 v4.4s,v0.4s,v1.4s              // b2 a2 b0 a0
            trn2 v5.4s,v0.4s,v1.4s              // b3 a3 b1 a1
            trn1 v6.4s,v2.4s,v3.4s              // d2 c2 d0 c0
            trn2 v7.4s,v2.4s,v3.4s              // d3 c3 d1 c1

            trn1 v0.2d,v4.2d,v6.2d              // d0 c0 b0 a0
            trn1 v1.2d,v5.2d,v7.2d              // d1 c1 b1 a1
            trn2 v2.2d,v4.2d,v6.2d              // d2 c2 b2 a2
            trn2 v3.2d,v5.2d,v7.2d              // d3 c3 b3 a3
            .endm
```

```
// Mat4x4TransposeF64
//
// Input Registers          Output Registers
// ------------------------------------------------
// v1:v0    a3 a2 a1 a0      v17:v16   d0 c0 b0 a0
// v3:v2    b3 b2 b1 b0      v19:v18   d1 c1 b1 a1
// v5:v4    c3 c2 c1 c0      v21:v20   d2 c2 b2 a2
// v7:v6    d3 d2 d1 d0      v23:v22   d3 c3 b3 a3

          .macro Mat4x4TransposeF64
          trn1 v16.2d,v0.2d,v2.2d          // b0 a0
          trn1 v17.2d,v4.2d,v6.2d          // d0 c0
          trn2 v18.2d,v0.2d,v2.2d          // b1 a1
          trn2 v19.2d,v4.2d,v6.2d          // d1 c1

          trn1 v20.2d,v1.2d,v3.2d          // b2 a2
          trn1 v21.2d,v5.2d,v7.2d          // d2 c2
          trn2 v22.2d,v1.2d,v3.2d          // b3 a3
          trn2 v23.2d,v5.2d,v7.2d          // d3 c3
          .endm

// extern float Mat4x4TraceF32_(const float* m_src1);

          .global Mat4x4TraceF32_
Mat4x4TraceF32_:
          ld1 {v0.4s-v3.4s},[x0]           // v0:v3 = m_src1

          Mat4x4TraceF32                   // calculate trace

          fmov s0,s4
          ret

// extern double Mat4x4TraceF64_(const double* m_src1);

          .global Mat4x4TraceF64_
Mat4x4TraceF64_:
          ld1 {v0.2d-v3.2d},[x0],64        // load m_src1 into
          ld1 {v4.2d-v7.2d},[x0]           // v0:v7

          Mat4x4TraceF64                   // calculate trace

          fmov d0,d16
          ret

// extern void Mat4x4TransposeF32_(float* m_des, const float* m_src1);

          .global Mat4x4TransposeF32_
Mat4x4TransposeF32_:
          ld1 {v0.4s-v3.4s},[x1]           // v0:v3 = m_src1

          Mat4x4TransposeF32               // transpose m_src1
```

383

```
            st1 {v0.4s-v3.4s},[x0]               // save result to m_des
            ret

// extern void Mat4x4TransposeF64_(float* m_des, const float* m_src1);

            .global Mat4x4TransposeF64_
Mat4x4TransposeF64_:
            ld1 {v0.2d-v3.2d},[x1],64             // v0:v3 = rows 0 and 1
            ld1 {v4.2d-v7.2d},[x1]                // v4:v7 = rows 2 and 3

            Mat4x4TransposeF64                    // transpose m_src1

            st1 {v16.2d-v19.2d},[x0],64           // save rows 0 and 1
            st1 {v20.2d-v23.2d},[x0]              // save rows 2 and 3
            ret
```

The organization of the C++ code in Listing 15-7 is akin to the previous example. It includes two functions named Mat4x4TestF32 and Mat4x4TestF64. These functions exercise the C++ and assembly language matrix trace and transposition functions using single-precision and double-precision floating-point values, respectively. The remaining C++ code performs test case initialization and displays results.

The assembly language code in Listing 15-7 begins with the definition of a macro named Mat4x4TraceF32. This macro generates code that calculates the trace of a 4 × 4 matrix of single-precision floating-point values. Macro Mat4x4TraceF32 requires the source matrix to be loaded in registers V0–V3. The first instruction of this macro, mov s4,v0.4s[0] (move vector element to scalar), loads matrix element m[0][0] into register S4. The ensuing mov s5,v1.4s[1] instruction loads matrix element m[1][1] into register S5. This is followed by an fadd s4,s4,s5 instruction that calculates m[0][0] + m[1][1]. The next instruction pair, mov s5,v2.4s[2] and fadd s4,s4,s5, adds m[2][2] to the intermediate sum in register S4. The final two instructions of Mat4x4TraceF32, mov s5,v3.4s[3] and fadd s4,s4,s5, complete trace calculation with the addition of m[3][3]. Macro Mat4x4TraceF64 uses a similar sequence of instructions to calculate the trace of a 4 × 4 matrix of double-precision floating-point values. Note that the mov and fadd instructions in this macro use the .2d arrangement specifier for double-precision floating-point elements.

Macro Mat4x4TransposeF32 generates code that transposes a 4 × 4 matrix of single-precision floating-point values. This macro uses the trn1 (transpose vectors primary) and trn2 (transpose vectors secondary) instructions. The trn1 instruction places even-numbered elements from the two source operands into consecutive elements of the destination operand. The trn2 instruction is similar to the trn1 instruction except that it uses odd-numbered instead of even-numbered elements.

Macro Mat4x4TransposeF32 requires the source matrix to be loaded in registers V0–V3. Figure 15-2 illustrates the sequence of trn1 and trn2 instructions that macro Max4x4TransposeF32 uses to transpose a 4 × 4 matrix of single-precision floating-point values. Note that in the second code block, the trn1 and trn2 instructions use an arrangement specifier of .2d instead of .4s. Using the .2d arrangement specifier with single-precision floating-point elements transposes pairs of elements as shown in Figure 15-2.

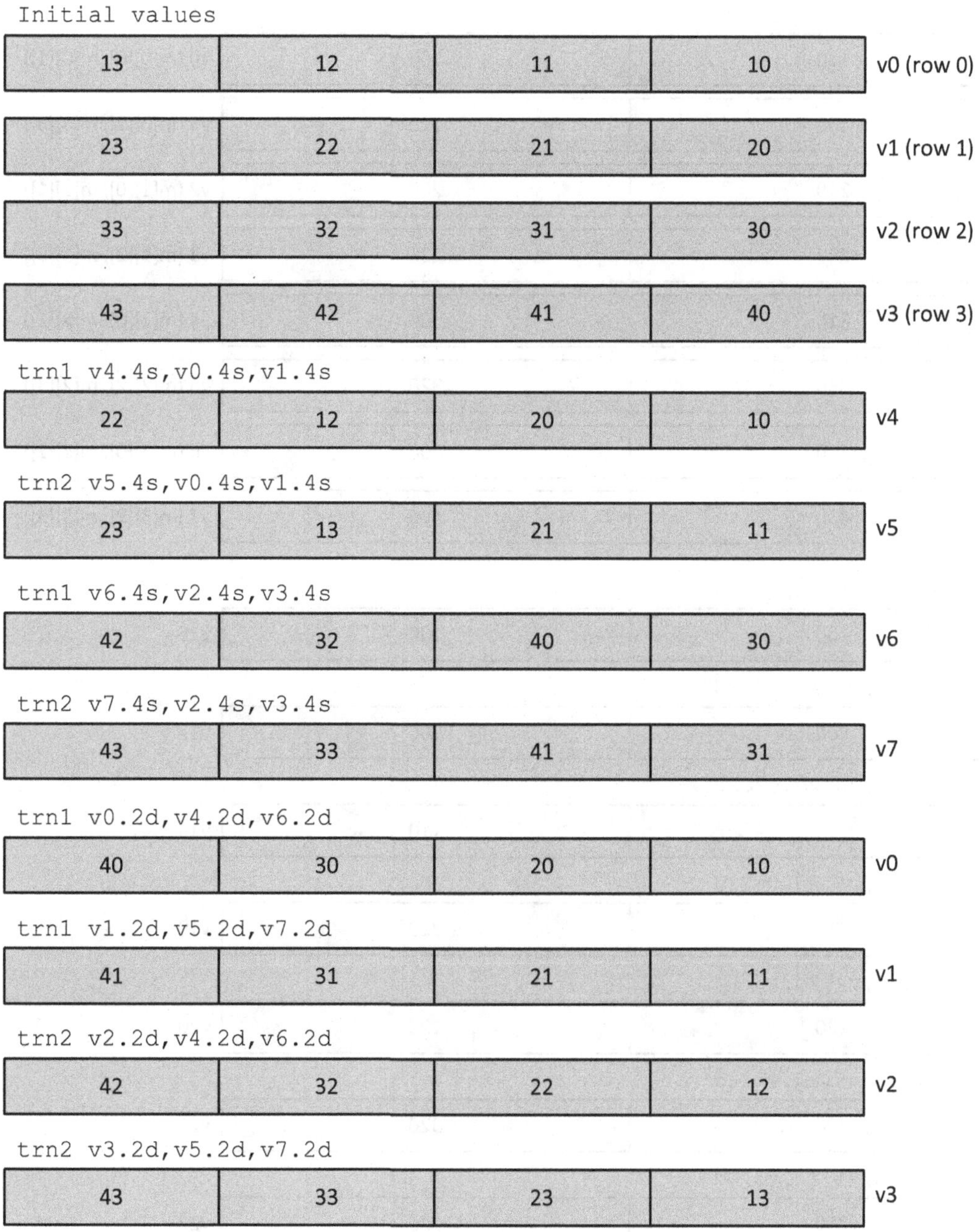

Initial values

13	12	11	10	v0 (row 0)

23	22	21	20	v1 (row 1)

33	32	31	30	v2 (row 2)

43	42	41	40	v3 (row 3)

trn1 v4.4s,v0.4s,v1.4s

22	12	20	10	v4

trn2 v5.4s,v0.4s,v1.4s

23	13	21	11	v5

trn1 v6.4s,v2.4s,v3.4s

42	32	40	30	v6

trn2 v7.4s,v2.4s,v3.4s

43	33	41	31	v7

trn1 v0.2d,v4.2d,v6.2d

40	30	20	10	v0

trn1 v1.2d,v5.2d,v7.2d

41	31	21	11	v1

trn2 v2.2d,v4.2d,v6.2d

42	32	22	12	v2

trn2 v3.2d,v5.2d,v7.2d

43	33	23	13	v3

Figure 15-2. *Transposition of a 4 × 4 matrix of single-precision floating-point values matrix using* trn1 *and* trn2

Macro Mat4x4TransposeF64 is the double-precision floating-point counterpart of macro Mat4x4TransposeF32. This macro requires the source matrix to be loaded in registers V0-V7. Figure 15-3 illustrates the sequence of trn1 and trn2 instructions that Max4x4TransposeF64 uses to transpose a 4 × 4 matrix of double-precision floating-point values.

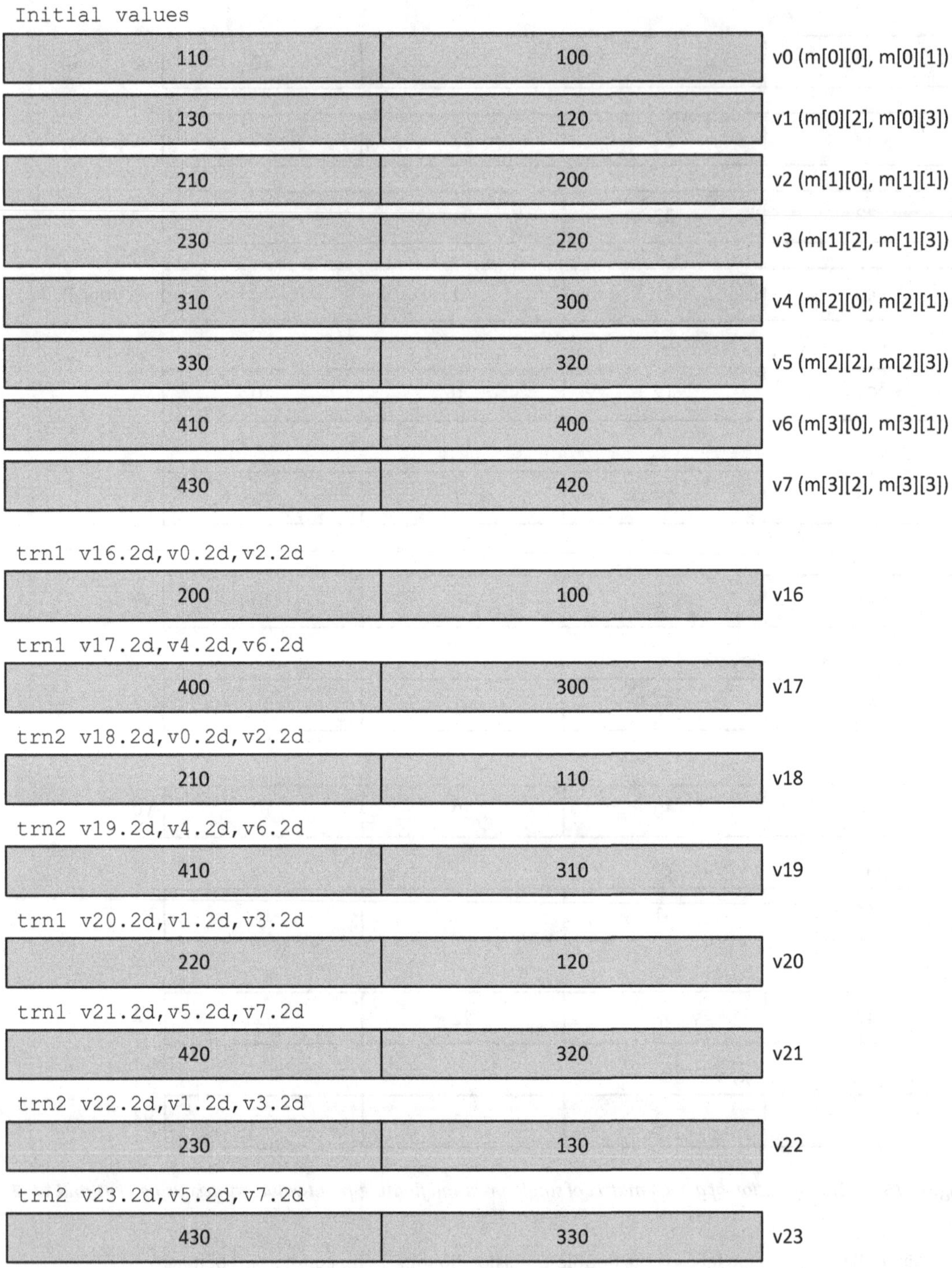

Initial values

110	100	v0 (m[0][0], m[0][1])
130	120	v1 (m[0][2], m[0][3])
210	200	v2 (m[1][0], m[1][1])
230	220	v3 (m[1][2], m[1][3])
310	300	v4 (m[2][0], m[2][1])
330	320	v5 (m[2][2], m[2][3])
410	400	v6 (m[3][0], m[3][1])
430	420	v7 (m[3][2], m[3][3])

trn1 v16.2d,v0.2d,v2.2d

200	100	v16

trn1 v17.2d,v4.2d,v6.2d

400	300	v17

trn2 v18.2d,v0.2d,v2.2d

210	110	v18

trn2 v19.2d,v4.2d,v6.2d

410	310	v19

trn1 v20.2d,v1.2d,v3.2d

220	120	v20

trn1 v21.2d,v5.2d,v7.2d

420	320	v21

trn2 v22.2d,v1.2d,v3.2d

230	130	v22

trn2 v23.2d,v5.2d,v7.2d

430	330	v23

Figure 15-3. Transposition of a 4 × 4 matrix of double-precision floating-point values matrix using trn1 and trn2

The functions Mat4x4TraceF32_ and Mat4x4TraceF64_ employ the previously expounded trace macros to calculate their respective values. Similarly, functions Mat4x4TransposeF32_ and Max4x4TransposeF64_ use the transpose macros to carry out their respective transpose operations. It should be noted that the ld4 instruction can also be employed to transpose a 4 × 4 matrix that resides in memory. You will learn how to do this in Chapter 16. Here are the results for source code example Ch15_07:

```
Results for Mat4x4TestF32
Matrix m_src1
        10.0            11.0            12.0            13.0
        20.0            21.0            22.0            23.0
        30.0            31.0            32.0            33.0
        40.0            41.0            42.0            43.0

Matrix m_des1 (transpose of m_src1)
        10.0            20.0            30.0            40.0
        11.0            21.0            31.0            41.0
        12.0            22.0            32.0            42.0
        13.0            23.0            33.0            43.0

Matrix m_des2 (transpose of m_src1)
        10.0            20.0            30.0            40.0
        11.0            21.0            31.0            41.0
        12.0            22.0            32.0            42.0
        13.0            23.0            33.0            43.0

m_trace1 = 106.0
m_trace2 = 106.0


Results for Mat4x4TestF64
Matrix m_src1
        100.0           110.0           120.0           130.0
        200.0           210.0           220.0           230.0
        300.0           310.0           320.0           330.0
        400.0           410.0           420.0           430.0

Matrix m_des1 (transpose of m_src1)
        100.0           200.0           300.0           400.0
        110.0           210.0           310.0           410.0
        120.0           220.0           320.0           420.0
        130.0           230.0           330.0           430.0

Matrix m_des2 (transpose of m_src1)
        100.0           200.0           300.0           400.0
        110.0           210.0           310.0           410.0
        120.0           220.0           320.0           420.0
        130.0           230.0           330.0           430.0

m_trace1 = 1060.0
m_trace2 = 1060.0
```

Summary

Here are the key learning points for Chapter 15:

- All A64 floating-point SIMD instructions must be used with arrangement specifiers, which designate the element sizes (e.g., .4s for single-precision, .2d for double-precision) that the instructions will use.

- Functions can use the fadd, fsub, fmul, and fdiv instructions to perform packed floating-point addition, subtraction, multiplication, and division.

- Functions can use the fminnm and fmaxnm instructions to carry out packed floating-point minimum and maximum operations.

- The fabs and fsqrt instructions calculate packed floating-point absolute values and square roots.

- Functions can use the fcmeq, fcmgt, and fcmge instructions to perform packed floating-point equal, greater than, or greater than or equal comparisons. Other comparisons (not equal, less than, less than or equal) can be achieved using one of these instructions with packed negation or switched operands.

- The A64 SIMD instruction set includes a variety of instructions that perform floating-point conversions. Table 15-1 summarizes commonly used conversion instructions.

- Functions can use the fmla and fmls instructions to perform fused multiply-add and fused multiply-subtract operations, respectively.

- The trn1 and trn2 instructions perform packed element transpositions.

- The ld1r, ld2r, ld3r, and ld4r instructions load one-, two-, three-, and four-element structures to all elements of one, two, three, and four registers, respectively.

- The ld4 instruction loads and de-interleaves multiple four-element structures into four registers. Functions can also use the ld2 and ld3 instructions to load and de-interleave multiple two- and three-element structures into two or three registers, respectively.

■ ■ ■

Armv8-64 Advanced SIMD Programming

Chapter 16 examines source code examples that carry out Advanced SIMD calculations. The first source code example demonstrates how to code convolution functions using A64 fused multiply-add (FMA) instructions. This is followed by a source example that illustrates vector cross product calculations. The final two source code examples highlight SIMD calculations using 4 × 4 matrices of single-precision floating-point values.

The assembly language functions presented in this chapter are somewhat longer than the ones you saw in previous chapters. However, you have already seen most of the A64 instructions that are used in these functions. The assembly language functions in this chapter also make extensive use of macros, which improves source code comprehension and facilitates code reuse.

Signal Processing

In previous chapters, you studied source code examples that employed various A64 FMA instructions (e.g., fmadd and fmla). Recall that a FMA operation performs a floating-point multiplication followed by a floating-point addition using only a single rounding operation. FMA operations are used extensively in signal processing functions. In this section, you will learn how to use FMA instructions to implement a discrete convolution function. It begins with a brief overview of essential convolution mathematics. The purpose of this overview is to explain just enough theory to understand the source code example. This is followed by a source code example that implements a practical discrete convolution function using A64 SIMD FMA instructions.

Convolution Essentials

Convolution is a mathematical operation that blends an input signal with a response signal to produce an output signal. Formally, the convolution of input signal f and response signal g is defined as follows:

$$h(t) = \int_{-\infty}^{+\infty} f(t-\tau) g(\tau) d\tau$$

where h represents the output signal. The notation $f * g$ is commonly used to denote the convolution of signals f and g.

© Daniel Kusswurm 2020

D. Kusswurm, *Modern Arm Assembly Language Programming*,
https://doi.org/10.1007/978-1-4842-6267-2_16

Convolutions are used extensively in a wide variety of scientific and engineering applications. Many signal processing and image-processing techniques are based on convolution theory. In these domains, discrete arrays of sampled data points are typically used to represent the input, response, and output signals. A discrete convolution can be calculated using the following equation:

$$h[i] = \sum_{k=-M}^{M} f[i-k]g[k]$$

where $i = 0, 1, ..., N-1$ and $M = \lfloor N_g/2 \rfloor$. In the preceding equation, N denotes the number of elements in both the input and output signal arrays and N_g symbolizes the size of the response signal array. The explanations and source code examples in this chapter assume that N_g is an odd integer greater than or equal to three. If you examine the discrete convolution equation carefully, you will notice that each element in output signal array h is computed using a relatively uncomplicated sum-of-products calculation that encompasses the elements of input signal array f and response signal array g. These types of calculations are easy to implement using A64 SIMD FMA instructions.

In digital signal processing, many applications use smoothing operators to reduce the amount of noise that is present in a raw signal. For example, the top plot in Figure 16-1 shows a raw data signal that contains a fair amount of noise. The bottom plot in Figure 16-1 shows the same signal following the application of a smoothing operator. In this example, the smoothing operator is a convolution of the original raw signal and a set of discrete coefficients that approximate a Gaussian (or low-pass) filter. These coefficients correspond to the response signal array g that is incorporated in the discrete convolution equation. The response signal array is often called a convolution kernel or convolution mask.

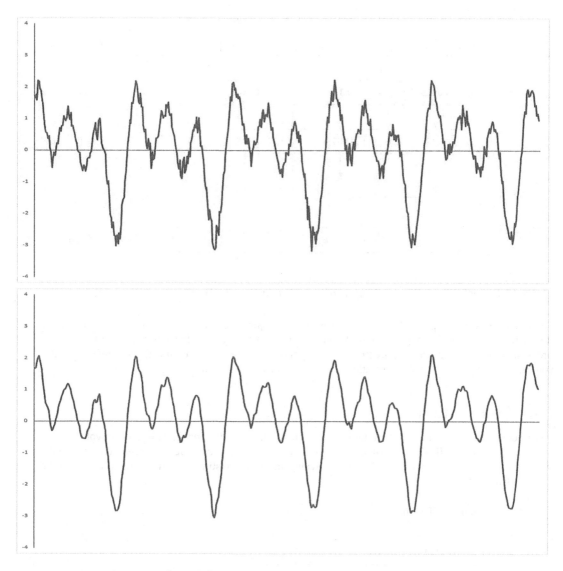

Figure 16-1. *Raw data signal (top plot) and its smoothed counterpart (bottom plot)*

The discrete convolution equation can be implemented in source code using a couple of nested for-loops. During each outer for-loop iteration, the convolution kernel center point g[0] is superimposed over the current input signal array element f[i]. The inner for-loop calculates the intermediate products as shown in Figure 16-2. These intermediate products are then summed and saved to output signal array element h[i], which is also shown in Figure 16-2. The source code example presented in the next section implements a SIMD convolution function using the techniques described in this paragraph.

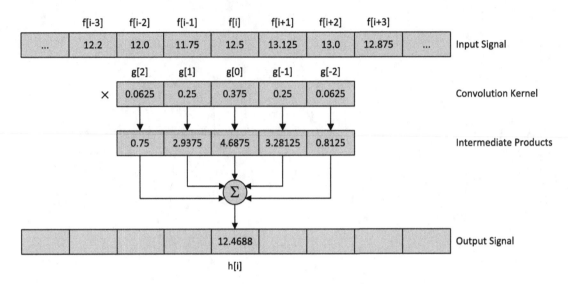

Figure 16-2. Application of a smoothing operator with an input signal element

The purpose of the preceding overview was to provide just enough background math to understand the source code examples. Numerous books have been published that explain convolution and signal processing theory in significantly greater detail. Appendix B contains a list of introductory references that you can consult for additional information about signal processing theory and convolutions.

FMA Convolution

Source code example Ch16_01 illustrates how to implement a one-dimensional discrete convolution function using A64 SIMD FMA instructions. It also elucidates the performance benefits of convolution functions that use fixed-size vs. variable-size convolution kernels. Listing 16-1 shows the source code for example Ch16_01.

Listing 16-1. Example Ch16_01

```
//--------------------------------------------------
//              Ch16_01.h
//--------------------------------------------------

#pragma once

// Ch16_01_Misc.cpp
extern void CreateSignal(float* x, int n, int kernel_size, unsigned int seed);
extern void PadSignal(float* x2, int n2, const float* x1, int n1, int ks2);

// Ch16_01.cpp
extern unsigned int g_RngSeedVal;
extern bool ConvolveKsN(float* y, const float* x, int num_pts, const float* kernel, int
kernel_size);
extern bool ConvolveKs5(float* y, const float* x, int num_pts, const float* kernel, int
kernel_size);
```

```
// Ch16_01_.s
extern "C" bool ConvolveKsN_(float* y, const float* x, int num_pts, const float* kernel, int
kernel_size);
extern "C" bool ConvolveKs5_(float* y, const float* x, int num_pts, const float* kernel, int
kernel_size);

// Ch16_01_BM.cpp
extern void Convolve_BM(void);

//-------------------------------------------------
//                  Ch16_01_Misc.cpp
//-------------------------------------------------

#include <iostream>
#include <random>
#include <cmath>
#include "Ch16_01.h"

using namespace std;

void CreateSignal(float* x, int n, int kernel_size, unsigned int seed)
{
    const float degtorad = (float)(M_PI / 180.0);
    const float t_start = 0;
    const float t_step = 0.002f;
    const int m = 3;
    const float amp[m] {1.0f, 0.80f, 1.20f};
    const float freq[m] {5.0f, 10.0f, 15.0f};
    const float phase[m] {0.0f, 45.0f, 90.0f};

    uniform_int_distribution<> ui_dist {0, 500};
    default_random_engine rng {seed};
    float t = t_start;

    for (int i = 0; i < n; i++, t += t_step)
    {
        float x_val = 0;

        for (int j = 0; j < m; j++)
        {
            float omega = 2.0f * (float)M_PI * freq[j];
            float x_temp1 = amp[j] * sin(omega * t + phase[j] * degtorad);
            int rand_val = ui_dist(rng);
            float noise = (float)((rand_val) - 250) / 10.0f;
            float x_temp2 = x_temp1 + x_temp1 * noise / 100.0f;

            x_val += x_temp2;
        }

        x[i] = x_val;
    }
}
```

```cpp
//-------------------------------------------------
//                  Ch16_01.cpp
//-------------------------------------------------

#include <iostream>
#include <iomanip>
#include <memory>
#include <fstream>
#include <stdexcept>
#include "Ch16_01.h"
#include "AlignedMem.h"

using namespace std;

// Signal and kernel size limits
int g_NumPtsMin = 16;
int g_NumPtsMax = 16 * 1024 * 1024;
int g_KernelSizeMin = 3;
int g_KernelSizeMax = 15;
unsigned int g_RngSeedVal = 97;

void Convolve(void)
{
    const char nl = '\n';
    const int n1 = 512;
    const float kernel[] { 0.0625f, 0.25f, 0.375f, 0.25f, 0.0625f };
    const int ks = sizeof(kernel) / sizeof(float);
    const int ks2 = ks / 2;
    const int n2 = n1 + ks2 * 2;
    const unsigned int alignment = 16;

    // Create signal array
    AlignedArray<float> x1_aa(n1, alignment);
    AlignedArray<float> x2_aa(n2, alignment);

    float* x1 = x1_aa.Data();
    float* x2 = x2_aa.Data();

    CreateSignal(x1, n1, ks, g_RngSeedVal);
    PadSignal(x2, n2, x1, n1, ks2);

    // Perform convolutions
    AlignedArray<float> y1_aa(n1, alignment);
    AlignedArray<float> y2_aa(n1, alignment);
    AlignedArray<float> y3_aa(n1, alignment);
    AlignedArray<float> y4_aa(n1, alignment);

    float* y1 = y1_aa.Data();
    float* y2 = y2_aa.Data();
    float* y3 = y3_aa.Data();
    float* y4 = y4_aa.Data();
```

394

```
    bool rc1 = ConvolveKsN(y1, x2, n1, kernel, ks);
    bool rc2 = ConvolveKsN_(y2, x2, n1, kernel, ks);
    bool rc3 = ConvolveKs5(y3, x2, n1, kernel, ks);
    bool rc4 = ConvolveKs5_(y4, x2, n1, kernel, ks);

    cout << "Results for Convolve\n";
    cout << "  rc1 = " << boolalpha << rc1 << nl;
    cout << "  rc2 = " << boolalpha << rc2 << nl;
    cout << "  rc3 = " << boolalpha << rc3 << nl;
    cout << "  rc4 = " << boolalpha << rc4 << nl;

    if (!rc1 || !rc2 || !rc3 || !rc4)
        return;

    // Save data
    const char* fn = "Ch16_01_ConvolveResults.csv";
    ofstream ofs(fn);

    if (ofs.bad())
        cout << "File create error - " << fn << nl;
    else
    {
        const char* delim = ", ";

        ofs << fixed << setprecision(7);
        ofs << "i, x1, y1, y2, y3, y4\n";

        for (int i = 0; i < n1; i++)
        {
            ofs << setw(5) << i << delim;
            ofs << setw(10) << x1[i] << delim;
            ofs << setw(10) << y1[i] << delim;
            ofs << setw(10) << y2[i] << delim;
            ofs << setw(10) << y3[i] << delim;
            ofs << setw(10) << y4[i] << nl;
        }

        ofs.close();
        cout << "\nConvolution results saved to file " << fn << nl;
    }
}

bool ConvolveKsN(float* y, const float* x, int num_pts, const float* kernel, int kernel_size)
{
    int ks2 = kernel_size / 2;

    if ((kernel_size & 1) == 0)
        return false;

    if (kernel_size < g_KernelSizeMin || kernel_size > g_KernelSizeMax)
        return false;
```

```
    if (num_pts < g_NumPtsMin || num_pts > g_NumPtsMax)
        return false;

    if (num_pts % 16 != 0)
        return false;

    x += ks2;    // x points to first signal point

    for (int i = 0; i < num_pts; i++)
    {
        float sum = 0;

        for (int k = -ks2; k <= ks2; k++)
        {
            float x_val = x[i - k];
            float kernel_val = kernel[k + ks2];

            sum += kernel_val * x_val;
        }

        y[i] = sum;
    }

    return true;
}

bool ConvolveKs5(float* y, const float* x, int num_pts, const float* kernel, int kernel_size)
{
    int ks2 = kernel_size / 2;

    if (kernel_size != 5)
        return false;

    if (num_pts < g_NumPtsMin || num_pts > g_NumPtsMax)
        return false;

    if (num_pts % 16 != 0)
        return false;

    x += ks2;    // x points to first signal point

    for (int i = 0; i < num_pts; i++)
    {
        float sum = 0;
        int j = i + ks2;

        sum += x[j] * kernel[0];
        sum += x[j - 1] * kernel[1];
        sum += x[j - 2] * kernel[2];
        sum += x[j - 3] * kernel[3];
        sum += x[j - 4] * kernel[4];
```

```
            y[i] = sum;
        }

    return true;
}

int main()
{
    try
    {
        Convolve();
        Convolve_BM();
    }

    catch (exception& ex)
    {
        cout << "exception has occurred - " << ex.what() << '\n';
    }

    return 0;
}
```

```
//---------------------------------------------------
//                  Ch16_01_.s
//---------------------------------------------------

// extern "C" bool ConvolveKsN_(float* y, const float* x, int num_pts, const float* kernel,
int kernel_size);

            .text
            .global ConvolveKsN_
ConvolveKsN_:

// Validate arguments
            tst w4,0x01
            b.eq InvalidArg1                    // jump if kernel_size is even

            ldr x5,=g_KernelSizeMin
            ldr w5,[x5]
            cmp w4,w5
            b.lt InvalidArg1                    // jump if kernel_size too small

            ldr x5,=g_KernelSizeMax
            ldr w5,[x5]
            cmp w4,w5
            b.gt InvalidArg1                    // jump if kernel_size too big

            ldr x5,=g_NumPtsMin
            ldr w5,[x5]
            cmp w2,w5
            b.lt InvalidArg1                    // jump if num_pts too small
```

```
            ldr   x5,=g_NumPtsMax
            ldr   w5,[x5]
            cmp   w2,w5
            b.gt  InvalidArg1                      // jump if num_pts too big

            tst   w2,0x0f
            b.ne  InvalidArg1                      // jump if num_pts % 16 != 0

// Initialize
            sxtw  x2,w2                            // sign-extend num_pts
            sxtw  x4,w4                            // sign-extend kernel_size

            lsr   x5,x4,1                          // ks2 = kernel_size / 2
            add   x1,x1,x5,lsl 2                   // x += ks2 (first data point)
            mov   x6,0                             // i = 0

// Processing loops
Loop1a:     movi  v0.4s,0                          // packed loop sums = 0.0
            neg   x7,x5                            // k = -ks2

Loop2a:     sub   x8,x6,x7                         // x8 = i - k
            add   x9,x1,x8,lsl 2                   // x9 = ptr to x[i-k]
            ld1   {v1.4s},[x9]                     // v1 = x[i-k:i-k+3]

            add   x10,x7,x5                        // x10 = k + ks2
            add   x11,x3,x10,lsl 2                 // x11 = ptr to kernel[k+ks2]
            ld1r  {v2.4s},[x11]                    // v2 = packed kernel[k+ks2]

            add   x7,x7,1                          // k += 1
            cmp   x7,x5                            // is k > ks2?

            fmla  v0.4s,v1.4s,v2.4s                // x[i-k:i-k+3] * kernel[k+ks2]

            b.le  Loop2a                           // jump if k <= ks2

            st1   {v0.4s},[x0],16                  // save y[i:i+3]

            add   x6,x6,4                           // i += 4
            cmp   x6,x2
            b.lt  Loop1a                           // jump if i < num_pts

            mov   w0,1                             // set success return code
            ret

InvalidArg1:
            mov   w0,0                             // set error return code
            ret

// extern "C" bool ConvolveKs5_(float* y, const float* x, int num_pts, const float* kernel,
// int kernel_size);
```

```
            .global ConvolveKs5_
ConvolveKs5_:

// Validate arguments
            cmp w4,5
            b.ne InvalidArg2                    // jump if kernel_size != 5

            ldr x5,=g_NumPtsMin
            ldr w5,[x5]
            cmp w2,w5
            b.lt InvalidArg2                    // jump if num_pts too small

            ldr x5,=g_NumPtsMax
            ldr w5,[x5]
            cmp w2,w5
            b.gt InvalidArg2                    // jump if num_pts too big

            tst w2,0x0f
            b.ne InvalidArg2                    // jump if num_pts % 16 != 0

// Initialize
            sxtw x2,w2                          // sign-extend num_pts
            sxtw x4,w4                          // sign-extend kernel_size

            ld1r {v0.4s},[x3],4                 // v0 = packed kernel[0]
            ld1r {v1.4s},[x3],4                 // v1 = packed kernel[1]
            ld1r {v2.4s},[x3],4                 // v2 = packed kernel[2]
            ld1r {v3.4s},[x3],4                 // v3 = packed kernel[3]
            ld1r {v4.4s},[x3]                   // v4 = packed kernel[4]

            add x1,x1,8                         // x1 ptr first x[] data point
            mov x5,0                            // i = 0
            mov x6,-4                           // offset to next x[]

// Processing loop
Loop1b:     add x7,x5,2                         // j = i + ks2
            add x8,x1,x7,lsl 2                  // x8 = ptr to x[j]
            add x5,x5,4                          // i += 4
            cmp x5,x2                           // is i >= num_pts?

            ld1 {v16.4s},[x8],x6               // v16 = x[j:j+3]
            fmul v5.4s,v16.4s,v0.4s            // x[j:j+3] * kernel[0]

            ld1 {v17.4s},[x8],x6               // v17 = x[j-1:j+2]
            fmla v5.4s,v17.4s,v1.4s            // x[j-1:j+2] * kernel[1]

            ld1 {v18.4s},[x8],x6               // v18 = x[j-2:j+1]
            fmla v5.4s,v18.4s,v2.4s            // x[j-2:j+1] * kernel[2]

            ld1 {v19.4s},[x8],x6               // v19 = x[j-3:j]
            fmla v5.4s,v19.4s,v3.4s            // x[j-3:j] * kernel[3]
```

```
        ld1 {v20.4s},[x8],x6              // v19 = x[j-4:j-1]
        fmla v5.4s,v20.4s,v4.4s           // x[j-4:j-1] * kernel[4]

        st1 {v5.4s},[x0],16               // save y[i:i+3]
        b.lt Loop1b                       // jump if i >= num_pts

        mov w0,1                          // set success return code
        ret

InvalidArg2:
        mov w0,0                          // set error return code
        ret
```

The C++ code in Listing 16-1 begins with the header file Ch16_01.h, which contains the requisite function declarations for this example. The source code for function CreateSignal is next. This function constructs a synthetic input signal for test purposes. The synthetic input signal consists of three separate sinusoidal waveforms that are summed together. Each waveform includes a small amount of random noise. The input signal generated by CreateSignal is the same signal that is shown in the top plot of Figure 16-1.

When performing convolutions, it is often necessary to pad the input signal array with extra elements to avoid invalid memory accesses when the center point of the convolution kernel is superimposed over input signal array elements located near the beginning and end of the array. The function PadSignal creates a padded copy of input signal array x1 by reflecting the edge elements of x1 and saving these elements along with the original input signal array elements in array x2. Figure 16-3 shows an example of a padded input signal array that is compatible with a five-element convolution kernel. Note that n2, the size of the padded buffer, must equal n1 + ks2 * 2, where n1 represents the number of input signal array elements in x1 and ks2 corresponds to floor(kernel_size / 2).

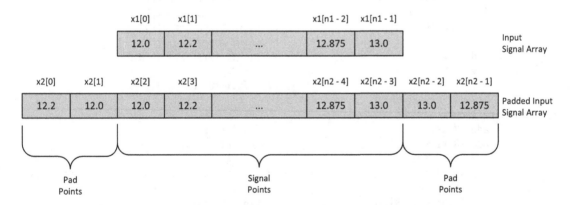

Figure 16-3. *Padded input signal array following execution of* PadSignal *using a five-element convolution kernel*

The convolution functions in source code example Ch16_01 use single-precision floating-point signal arrays and convolution kernels. Recall that a 128-bit wide Armv8-64 SIMD register can hold four single-precision floating-point values, which means that a SIMD implementation of the convolution algorithm can carry out FMA calculations using four signal points simultaneously. Figure 16-4 contains two graphics that illustrate a five-element convolution kernel along with an arbitrary segment of an input signal array. Below the graphics are the equations that convolve the four input signal points f[i:i+3] with a five-element convolution kernel. These equations are a straightforward expansion of the discrete convolution equation that was discussed in the previous section. Note that each column of the SIMD convolution equation set includes a single kernel value and four consecutive elements from the input signal array. This means that a convolution function can be easily implemented using SIMD FMA instructions as you will soon see.

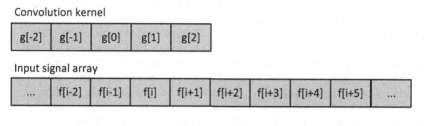

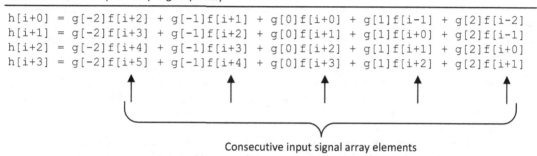

Consecutive input signal array elements

Figure 16-4. *SIMD convolution equations for a five-element convolution kernel*

The C++ function Convolve contains code that exercises several different implementations of the discrete convolution algorithm. Near the top of this function is a single-precision floating-point array named kernel, which contains the convolution kernel coefficients. The coefficients in kernel represent a discrete approximation of a Gaussian filter. When convolved with an input signal array, these coefficients reduce the amount of noise that is present in a signal as shown in the bottom plot of Figure 16-1. The padded input signal array x2 is created next using the previously described functions CreateSignal and PadSignal.

Following generation of the input signal array x2, function Convolve allocates storage space for four output signal arrays using the C++ template class AlignedArray. The functions that implement different variations of the convolution algorithms are then exercised. The first two functions, ConvolveKsN and ConvolveKsN_, contain C++ and assembly language code that carry out their convolutions using the nested for-loop technique that was described in the previous section. The functions ConvolveKs5 and ConvolveKs5_ are optimized for convolution kernels containing five elements. Real-world signal processing software frequently employs convolution functions that are optimized for specific kernel sizes since they are often significantly faster as you will soon see.

The function ConvolveKsN begins its execution by validating argument values kernel_size and num_pts. The next statement, x += ks2, adjusts the input signal array pointer x so that it points to the first true input signal array element. Recall that the input signal array x is padded with extra values to ensure correct processing when the convolution kernel is superimposed over the first two and last two input signal elements. Following the adjustment of pointer x is the code that performs the convolution. The nested for-loops implement the discrete convolution equation that was described earlier in this chapter. Note that the index value used for kernel is offset by ks2 to account for the negative indices of the inner for-loop. Following function ConvolveKsN is the function ConvolveKs5. This function differs from ConvolveKsN in that it eliminates the inner for-loop and uses explicit C++ statements to calculate the convolution's sum-of-products.

The function ConvolveKsN_ is the assembly language counterpart of ConvolveKsN. This function begins its execution by validating argument values kernel_size and num_pts. Following argument validation, ConvolveKsN_ uses the instruction pair sxtw x2,w2 and sxtw x4,w4 to sign-extend num_pts and kernel_size to 64 bits. The next instruction, lsr x5,x4,1, calculates ks2 = floor(kernel_size / 2). This is followed by an add x1,x1,x5,lsl 2 instruction that initializes register X1 as a pointer to the first data point in array x. The final initialization code block instruction mov x6,0 sets i = 0.

The first instruction of for-loop Loop1a, movi v0.4s,0, initializes the packed FMA sums to zero. This is followed by a neg x7,x5 (negate) instruction that sets index variable k = -ks2. Each iteration of for-loop Loop2a begins with the instruction triplet sub x8,x6,x7, add x9,x1,x8,lsl 2, and ld1 {v1.4s},[x9] that loads elements x[i-k:i-k+3] into register V1. This is followed by another instruction triplet, add x10,x7,x5, add x11,x3,x10,lsl 2, and ld1r {v2.4s},[x11], that loads kernel[k+ks2] into each element of register V2. The fmla v0.4s,v1.4s,v2.4s instruction multiplies signal point elements x[i-k:i-k+3] by kernel element kernel[k+ks2]; it then sums these products with the elements in register V0. Following completion of Loop2a, the st1 {v0.4s},[x0],16 instruction saves four output signal points to y[i:i+3].

Listing 16-1 also includes the function ConvolveKs5_, which is the assembly language counterpart of ConvolveKs5. Execution of function ConvolveKs5_ starts with the validation of argument values kernel_size and num_pts. Following argument validation, the instructions sxtw x2,w2 and sxtw x4,w4 sign-extend num_pts and kernel_size to 64 bits. The ensuing ld1r {v0.4s},[x3],4 instruction loads kernel[0] into each element of register V0. This is followed by four more ld1r instructions that load kernel[1]-kernel[4] into each element of registers V1-V4, respectively. The final initialization code block sets register X1 as a pointer to the first input signal data point in array x and index variable i (X5) to zero. This code block also includes a mov x6,-4 instruction, which loads -4 into register X6 for use as a post-indexed offset when loading elements from input signal array x.

Each iteration of for-loop Loop1b begins with an add x7,x5,2 instruction that calculates j = i + ks2. The ensuing add x8,x1,x7,lsl 2 instruction loads register X8 with the address of input signal array element x[j]. The add x5,x5,4 instruction that follows calculates i += 4. This is followed by a cmp x5,x2 instruction that checks for i >= num_pts. Note that the associated b.lt Loop1b instruction is placed after the SIMD calculating instructions. This branch instruction is still valid since none of the SIMD instructions alter the PSTATE.NZCV condition flags.

Following the cmp instruction is a ld1 {v16.4s},[x8],x6 instruction that loads input signal elements x[j:j+3] into register V16. The ld1 instruction also updates the input signal array pointer in X8 so that it points to element x[j-1]. This is followed by a fmul v5.4s,v16.4s,v0.4s instruction that multiplies each element in V16 by kernel[0]. Following the fmul instruction is a ld1 {v17.4s},[x8],x6 instruction that loads input signal elements x[j-1:j+2] into register V17. The fmla v5.4s,v17.4s,v1.4s that follows multiplies elements x[j-1:j+2] by kernel[1] and adds the resultant element products to the sums in register V5. Function ConvolveKs5_ then employs three additional ld1/fmla instruction pairs to complete the convolution for the current set of four input signal points. This is followed by a st1 {v5.4s},[x0],16 instruction that saves these results to y[i:i+3]. Here are the results for source code example Ch16_01:

```
Results for Convolve
  rc1 = true
  rc2 = true
  rc3 = true
  rc4 = true

Convolution results saved to file Ch16_01_ConvolveResults.csv

Running benchmark function Convolve_BM - please wait
Benchmark times save to file Ch16_01_Convolve_BM_RpiOmega.csv
```

Table 16-1 shows the benchmark timing measurements for the convolution functions. As alluded to earlier in this section, the size-optimized convolution functions Convolve1Ks5 and Convolve1Ks5_ are considerably faster than their nonsize-optimized counterparts.

Table 16-1. *Mean execution times (microseconds) for convolution functions using five-element convolution kernel (2,000,000 signal points)*

ConvolveKsN	ConvolveKsN_	ConvolveKs5	ConvolveKs5_
21714	8156	4652	3899

Vector and Matrix Operations

In this section, you will learn how to calculate vector cross products using SIMD arithmetic. You will also learn how to code SIMD functions that perform matrix-vector multiplication and matrix inversion using 4 × 4 matrices.

Vector Cross Products

The next source code example, Ch16_02, demonstrates vector cross product calculations using arrays of three-dimensional vectors. Listing 16-2 shows the source code for example Ch16_02.

Listing 16-2. Example Ch16_02

```
//--------------------------------------------------
//              Ch16_02.h
//--------------------------------------------------

#pragma once

// Simple vector structure
typedef struct
{
    float X;        // X component
    float Y;        // Y component
    float Z;        // Z component
} Vector;

// Vector structure of arrays
typedef struct
{
    float* X;       // X components
    float* Y;       // Y components
    float* Z;       // Z components
} VectorSoA;

const size_t c_Align = 16;
```

```cpp
// Ch16_02.cpp
void CrossProdAOS(Vector* c, const Vector* a, const Vector* b, size_t n);
void CrossProdSOA(VectorSoA& c, const VectorSoA& a, const VectorSoA& b, size_t n);

// Ch16_02_.asm
extern "C" void CrossProdAOS_(Vector* c, const Vector* a, const Vector* b, size_t n);
extern "C" void CrossProdSOA_(VectorSoA& c, const VectorSoA& a, const VectorSoA& b,
    size_t n);

// Ch16_02_BM.cpp
extern void CrossProd_BM(void);

// Ch16_02_Misc.cpp
void InitVec(Vector* a_aos, Vector* b_aos, VectorSoA& a_soa, VectorSoA& b_soa, size_t n);
bool CompareCP(Vector* c1_aos, Vector* c2_aos, VectorSoA& c1_soa, VectorSoA& c2_soa,
    size_t n);

//--------------------------------------------------
//                   Ch16_02.cpp
//--------------------------------------------------

#include <iostream>
#include <iomanip>
#include <memory>
#include "Ch16_02.h"
#include "AlignedMem.h"

using namespace std;

void CrossProdAOS(Vector* c, const Vector* a, const Vector* b, size_t n)
{
    for (size_t i = 0; i < n; i++)
    {
        c[i].X = a[i].Y * b[i].Z - a[i].Z * b[i].Y;
        c[i].Y = a[i].Z * b[i].X - a[i].X * b[i].Z;
        c[i].Z = a[i].X * b[i].Y - a[i].Y * b[i].X;
    }
}

void CrossProdSOA(VectorSoA& c, const VectorSoA& a, const VectorSoA& b, size_t n)
{
    for (size_t i = 0; i < n; i++)
    {
        c.X[i] = a.Y[i] * b.Z[i] - a.Z[i] * b.Y[i];
        c.Y[i] = a.Z[i] * b.X[i] - a.X[i] * b.Z[i];
        c.Z[i] = a.X[i] * b.Y[i] - a.Y[i] * b.X[i];
    }
}
```

```
void CrossProd(void)
{
    const char nl = '\n';
    const char* sep = " | ";

    const size_t align = c_Align;
    const size_t num_vec = 18;

    unique_ptr<Vector> a_aos_up {new Vector[num_vec] };
    unique_ptr<Vector> b_aos_up {new Vector[num_vec] };
    unique_ptr<Vector> c1_aos_up {new Vector[num_vec] };
    unique_ptr<Vector> c2_aos_up {new Vector[num_vec] };
    Vector* a_aos = a_aos_up.get();
    Vector* b_aos = b_aos_up.get();
    Vector* c1_aos = c1_aos_up.get();
    Vector* c2_aos = c2_aos_up.get();

    AlignedArray<float> a_soa_x_aa(num_vec, align);
    AlignedArray<float> a_soa_y_aa(num_vec, align);
    AlignedArray<float> a_soa_z_aa(num_vec, align);
    AlignedArray<float> b_soa_x_aa(num_vec, align);
    AlignedArray<float> b_soa_y_aa(num_vec, align);
    AlignedArray<float> b_soa_z_aa(num_vec, align);
    AlignedArray<float> c1_soa_x_aa(num_vec, align);
    AlignedArray<float> c1_soa_y_aa(num_vec, align);
    AlignedArray<float> c1_soa_z_aa(num_vec, align);
    AlignedArray<float> c2_soa_x_aa(num_vec, align);
    AlignedArray<float> c2_soa_y_aa(num_vec, align);
    AlignedArray<float> c2_soa_z_aa(num_vec, align);

    VectorSoA a_soa, b_soa, c1_soa, c2_soa;
    a_soa.X = a_soa_x_aa.Data();
    a_soa.Y = a_soa_y_aa.Data();
    a_soa.Z = a_soa_z_aa.Data();
    b_soa.X = b_soa_x_aa.Data();
    b_soa.Y = b_soa_y_aa.Data();
    b_soa.Z = b_soa_z_aa.Data();
    c1_soa.X = c1_soa_x_aa.Data();
    c1_soa.Y = c1_soa_y_aa.Data();
    c1_soa.Z = c1_soa_z_aa.Data();
    c2_soa.X = c2_soa_x_aa.Data();
    c2_soa.Y = c2_soa_y_aa.Data();
    c2_soa.Z = c2_soa_z_aa.Data();

    InitVec(a_aos, b_aos, a_soa, b_soa, num_vec);

    CrossProdAOS(c1_aos, a_aos, b_aos, num_vec);
    CrossProdAOS_(c2_aos, a_aos, b_aos, num_vec);
    CrossProdSOA(c1_soa, a_soa, b_soa, num_vec);
    CrossProdSOA_(c2_soa, a_soa, b_soa, num_vec);
```

```cpp
    bool compare_cp = CompareCP(c1_aos, c2_aos, c1_soa, c2_soa, num_vec);

    cout << "Results for CrossProd\n";
    cout << fixed << setprecision(1);

    for (size_t i = 0; i < num_vec; i++)
    {
        const unsigned int w = 7;
        cout << "Vector cross product #" << i << nl;

        cout << "  a:      ";
        cout << setw(w) << a_aos[i].X << sep;
        cout << setw(w) << a_aos[i].Y << sep;
        cout << setw(w) << a_aos[i].Z << "   ";

        cout << "  b: ";
        cout << setw(w) << b_aos[i].X << sep;
        cout << setw(w) << b_aos[i].Y << sep;
        cout << setw(w) << b_aos[i].Z << nl;

        if (compare_cp)
            cout << "  c:      ";
        else
            cout << "  c1_aos: ";

        cout << setw(w) << c1_aos[i].X << sep;
        cout << setw(w) << c1_aos[i].Y << sep;
        cout << setw(w) << c1_aos[i].Z << nl;

        if (!compare_cp)
        {
            cout << "  c2_aos: ";
            cout << setw(w) << c2_aos[i].X << sep;
            cout << setw(w) << c2_aos[i].Y << sep;
            cout << setw(w) << c2_aos[i].Z << nl;

            cout << "  c1_soa: ";
            cout << setw(w) << c1_soa.X[i] << sep;
            cout << setw(w) << c1_soa.Y[i] << sep;
            cout << setw(w) << c1_soa.Z[i] << nl;

            cout << "  c2_soa: ";
            cout << setw(w) << c2_soa.X[i] << sep;
            cout << setw(w) << c2_soa.Y[i] << sep;
            cout << setw(w) << c2_soa.Z[i] << nl;
        }
    }
}
```

```
int main()
{
    CrossProd();
    CrossProd_BM();
    return 0;
}


//--------------------------------------------------
//                  Ch16_02_.s
//--------------------------------------------------

// Macro VecCp
//
// Input:   s0 = a.x, s1 = a.y, s2 = a.z
//          s3 = b.x, s4 = b.y, s5 = b.z
//
// Output:  s19 = c.x, s20 = c.y, s21 = c.z

            .macro VecCp
            fmul s16,s1,s5                  // c.X = a.Y * b.Z - a.Z * b.Y
            fmsub s19,s2,s4,s16

            fmul s17,s2,s3                  // c.Y = a.Z * b.X - a.X * b.Z
            fmsub s20,s0,s5,s17

            fmul s18,s0,s4                  // c.Z = a.X * b.Y - a.Y * b.X
            fmsub s21,s1,s3,s18
            .endm

// Macro VecCp4
//
// Input:   v0 = a.x, v1 = a.y, v2 = a.z
//          v3 = b.x, v4 = b.y, v5 = b.z
//
// Output:  v19 = c.x, v20 = c.y, v21 = c.z

            .macro VecCp4
            fmul v19.4s,v1.4s,v5.4s         // c.X = a.Y * b.Z - a.Z * b.Y
            fmls v19.4s,v2.4s,v4.4s

            fmul v20.4s,v2.4s,v3.4s         // c.Y = a.Z * b.X - a.X * b.Z
            fmls v20.4s,v0.4s,v5.4s

            fmul v21.4s,v0.4s,v4.4s         // c.Z = a.X * b.Y - a.Y * b.X
            fmls v21.4s,v1.4s,v3.4s
            .endm

// Macro VecCp4AOS
//
// Input:   x1 = Vector* a, x2 = Vector* b, x0 = Vector* c
```

```
            .macro VecCp4AOS
            ld3 {v0.4s,v1.4s,v2.4s},[x1],48      // load vectors (a)
            ld3 {v3.4s,v4.4s,v5.4s},[x2],48      // load vectors (b)
            VecCp4                                // calc cross products
            st3 {v19.4s,v20.4s,v21.4s},[x0],48   // save vectors (c)
            .endm

// Macro VecCp4SOA
//
// Input:   x7 = float* a.X, x8 = float* a.Y, x9 = float* a.Z
//          x10 = float* b.X, x11 = float* b.Y, x12 = float* b.Z
//          x13 = float* c.X, x14 = float* c.Y, x15 = float* c.Z

            .macro VecCp4SOA
            ld1 {v0.4s},[x7],16                  // load a.X components
            ld1 {v1.4s},[x8],16                  // load a.Y components
            ld1 {v2.4s},[x9],16                  // load a.Z components

            ld1 {v3.4s},[x10],16                 // load b.X components
            ld1 {v4.4s},[x11],16                 // load b.Y components
            ld1 {v5.4s},[x12],16                 // load b.Z components

            VecCp4                                // calc cross products

            st1 {v19.4s},[x13],16                // save c.X components
            st1 {v20.4s},[x14],16                // save c.Y components
            st1 {v21.4s},[x15],16                // save c.Z components
            .endm

// extern "C" void CrossProdAOS_(Vector* c, const Vector* a, const Vector* b, size_t n);

            .text
            .global CrossProdAOS_
CrossProdAOS_:
            cmp x3,16
            b.lo SkipLoop1A                       // skip loop if n < 16

// Main processing loop
Loop1A:     VecCp4AOS
            VecCp4AOS
            VecCp4AOS
            VecCp4AOS

            sub x3,x3,16                          // n -= 16
            cmp x3,16                             // is n >= 16?
            b.hs Loop1A                           // jump if n >= 16

SkipLoop1A: cbz x3,DoneA                          // jump if no more vectors
```

```
Loop2A:      ldp s0,s1,[x1],8             // s0,s1,s2 = a.X,a.Y,a.Z
             ldr s2,[x1],4

             ldp s3,s4,[x2],8             // s3,s4,s5 = b.X,b.Y,b.Z
             ldr s5,[x2],4

             VecCp                        // calc cross product

             stp s19,s20,[x0],8           // save vector c
             str s21,[x0],4

             subs x3,x3,1                 // n -= 1
             b.ne Loop2A
DoneA:       ret
```

```
// extern "C" void CrossProdSOA_(VectorSoA& c, const VectorSoA& a, const VectorSoA& b,
size_t n);

             .global CrossProdSOA_
CrossProdSOA_:
             ldp x7,x8,[x1],16            // x7,x8,x9 =
             ldr x9,[x1]                  // a.X,a.Y,a.Z

             ldp x10,x11,[x2],16          // x10,x11,x12 =
             ldr x12,[x2]                 // b.X,b.Y,b.Z

             ldp x13,x14,[x0],16          // x13,x14,x15 =
             ldr x15,[x0]                 // c.X,c.Y,c.Z

             cmp x3,16
             b.lo SkipLoop1B              // skip loop if n < 16

// Main processing loop
Loop1B:      VecCp4SOA
             VecCp4SOA
             VecCp4SOA
             VecCp4SOA

             sub x3,x3,16                 // n -= 16
             cmp x3,16                    // is n >= 16?
             b.hs Loop1B                  // jump if n >= 16

SkipLoop1B: cbz x3,DoneB

Loop2B:      ldr s0,[x7],4                // s0 = a.X
             ldr s1,[x8],4                // s1 = a.Y
             ldr s2,[x9],4                // s2 = a.Z

             ldr s3,[x10],4               // s3 = a.X
             ldr s4,[x11],4               // s4 = a.Y
             ldr s5,[x12],4               // s5 = a.Z
```

```
        VecCp                          // calc cross product

        str s19,[x13],4                // save c.X
        str s20,[x14],4                // save c.Y
        str s21,[x15],4                // save c.Z

        subs x3,x3,1                   // n -= 1
        b.ne Loop2B
DoneB:  ret
```

The cross product of two three-dimensional linearly independent vectors **a** and **b** is a third vector **c** that is perpendicular to both **a** and **b**. The x, y, and z components of **c** can be calculated using the following three equations:

$$c_x = a_y b_z - a_z b_y$$

$$c_y = a_z b_x - a_x b_z$$

$$c_z = a_x b_y - a_y b_x$$

The C++ header file that is shown in Listing 16-2 includes the structure definitions Vector and VectorSoA. The structure Vector contains three single-precision floating-point values X, Y, and Z that represent the components of a three-dimensional vector. The structure VectorSoA incorporates three pointers to single-precision floating-point arrays. Each array contains the values for a single vector component. Source code example Ch16_02 uses these structures to compare the performance of two different vector cross product calculating algorithms. The first algorithm performs its calculations using an array of structures (AOS), while the second algorithm exploits a structure of arrays (SOA). The C++ vector cross product calculating functions are named CrossProdAOS and CrossProdSOA. Both functions use simple for-loops to carry out their calculations. Note that function CrossProdAOS requires arguments of type Vector, while CrossProdSOA uses arguments of type VectorSOA.

The C++ function CrossProd performs test case initialization and exercises the vector cross product calculating functions. This function uses the C++ template class unique_ptr<Vector> to allocate storage for three vector AOSs. Each unique_ptr<Vector> AOS instance represents how this type of data construct is commonly employed in many real-world programs. Function CrossProd also uses the C++ template class AlignedArray<float> to allocate properly aligned storage space for the vector SOAs. Following data structure allocation, the function InitVec initializes vector sets a_aos, b_aos, a_soa, and b_soa using random values. It then exercises both the C++ and assembly language vector cross product calculating functions.

The assembly language code in Listing 16-2 commences with the definitions of four macros. The first macro is named VecCp. This macro includes instructions that calculate a single vector cross product using scalar single-precision floating-point arithmetic. Prior to using macro VecCp, the x, y, and z components for source vectors a and b must be loaded into registers S0–S2 and S3–S5, respectively. Macro VecCp saves the components of the calculated cross product vector c in registers S19–S21. Following macro VecCp is another macro named VecCp4. This macro emits code that calculates four vector cross products using SIMD arithmetic. Note that the x, y, and z components for SIMD vectors a and b must be loaded in registers V0–V2 and V3–V5, respectively. Macro VecCp4 saves the resultant vector c cross product components in registers V19–V21.

Macro VecCp4 is used in the next macro definition, which is named VecCp4AOS. This macro uses the ld3 instruction to load and de-interleave the x, y, and z components of AOS vectors a and b as illustrated in Figure 16-5. Following the loading of these source vectors, VecCp4AOS uses the VecCp4 macro to calculate the required cross products. It then saves the results using a st3 (store multiple three-element structures) instruction as shown in Figure 16-6. Note that the st3 instruction interleaves the x, y, and z components of the three vectors in registers V19–V21.

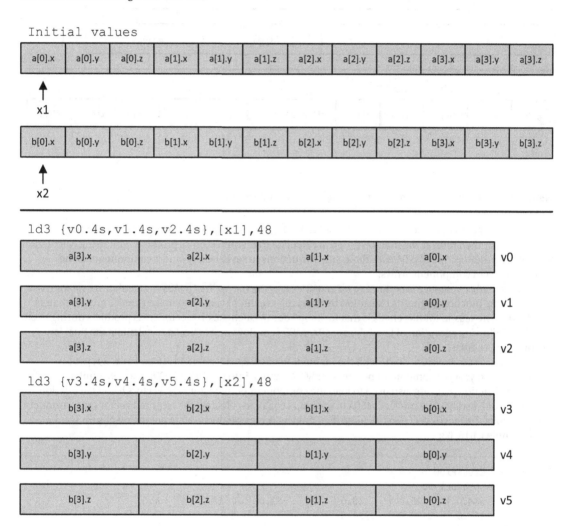

Figure 16-5. *AOS vector component load using two ld3 instructions*

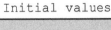

Initial values

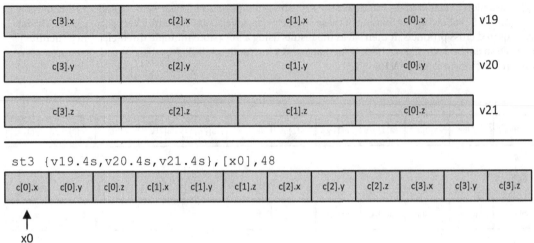

Figure 16-6. AOS vector component store using the st3 instruction

The final macro definition, VecCp4SOA, loads its SOA vector components using six separate ld1 instructions. It then utilizes the macro VecCp4 to calculate the required cross products. Following calculation of the cross products, VecCp4SOA uses three st1 instructions to save the x, y, and z components to the appropriate SOA component arrays.

The assembly language function CrossProdAOS_ uses the macro VecCp4AOS to calculate its vector cross products. This function begins its execution by checking argument value n to make sure it's greater than or equal to 16. The reason for this check is that for-loop Loop1A calculates 16 vector cross products during each iteration. Following execution of Loop1A, CrossProdAOS_ employs macro VecCp to calculate the final few vector cross products.

Function CrossProdSOA_ starts with the instruction pair ldp x7,x8,[x1],16 and ldr x9,[x1] that loads the x, y, and z component pointers for SOA vector a into registers X7, X8, and X9. Similar ldp/ldr instruction pairs are also used to load the component pointers for SOA vectors b and c. Function CrossProdSOA_ uses the macro VecCp4SOA in for-loop Loop1B to calculate the required vector cross products. It also exploits the macro VecCp to calculate the final few vector products. Here are the results for source code example Ch16_02:

```
Results for CrossProd
Vector cross product #0
    a:       44.0 |    26.0 |     18.0    b:    81.0 |    18.0 |     6.0
    c:     -168.0 |  1194.0 |  -1314.0
Vector cross product #1
    a:       83.0 |    90.0 |     59.0    b:    49.0 |    46.0 |     9.0
    c:    -1904.0 |  2144.0 |   -592.0
Vector cross product #2
    a:       83.0 |     9.0 |     83.0    b:    89.0 |    31.0 |    38.0
    c:    -2231.0 |  4233.0 |   1772.0
Vector cross product #3
    a:       21.0 |    69.0 |     41.0    b:    36.0 |    95.0 |    59.0
    c:      176.0 |   237.0 |   -489.0
```

```
Vector cross product #4
  a:        68.0 |       8.0 |      61.0   b:     89.0 |     68.0 |     66.0
  c:     -3620.0 |     941.0 |    3912.0
Vector cross product #5
  a:         1.0 |      93.0 |      34.0   b:     29.0 |     36.0 |     98.0
  c:      7890.0 |     888.0 |   -2661.0
Vector cross product #6
  a:        49.0 |      19.0 |      88.0   b:     76.0 |     76.0 |     27.0
  c:     -6175.0 |    5365.0 |    2280.0
Vector cross product #7
  a:        64.0 |      42.0 |      38.0   b:     96.0 |     60.0 |     37.0
  c:      -726.0 |    1280.0 |    -192.0
Vector cross product #8
  a:        74.0 |      79.0 |      60.0   b:     28.0 |     10.0 |     16.0
  c:       664.0 |     496.0 |   -1472.0
Vector cross product #9
  a:        41.0 |       5.0 |      59.0   b:     22.0 |     12.0 |     95.0
  c:      -233.0 |   -2597.0 |     382.0
Vector cross product #10
  a:        39.0 |      24.0 |       6.0   b:      1.0 |     59.0 |     55.0
  c:       966.0 |   -2139.0 |    2277.0
Vector cross product #11
  a:        17.0 |       4.0 |      35.0   b:     29.0 |     43.0 |     16.0
  c:     -1441.0 |     743.0 |     615.0
Vector cross product #12
  a:        25.0 |      98.0 |      77.0   b:     77.0 |     56.0 |     56.0
  c:      1176.0 |    4529.0 |   -6146.0
Vector cross product #13
  a:         3.0 |      96.0 |      78.0   b:     33.0 |     10.0 |     89.0
  c:      7764.0 |    2307.0 |   -3138.0
Vector cross product #14
  a:        71.0 |      67.0 |      58.0   b:     34.0 |     60.0 |     69.0
  c:      1143.0 |   -2927.0 |    1982.0
Vector cross product #15
  a:        86.0 |      89.0 |      56.0   b:     73.0 |      9.0 |     91.0
  c:      7595.0 |   -3738.0 |   -5723.0
Vector cross product #16
  a:        74.0 |      40.0 |      54.0   b:     78.0 |     35.0 |     55.0
  c:       310.0 |     142.0 |    -530.0
Vector cross product #17
  a:        48.0 |      85.0 |      23.0   b:      8.0 |     18.0 |      4.0
  c:       -74.0 |      -8.0 |     184.0

Running benchmark function CrossProd_BM - please wait
Benchmark times save to file Ch16_02_CrossProd_BM_RpiOmega.csv
```

Table 16-2 shows the benchmark timing measurements for the cross product calculating functions. In this example, the AOS technique is appreciably faster than the SOA method.

Table 16-2. *Benchmark timing measurements (microseconds) for vector cross product calculating functions (1,000,000 cross products)*

CrossProdAOS	CrossProdAOS_	CrossProdSOA	CrossProdSOA_
8803	8668	17456	11347

Matrix-Vector Multiplication

Many computer graphics and image-processing algorithms perform matrix-vector multiplications using 4×4 matrices and 4×1 vectors. In 3D computer graphics software, these types of calculations are universally employed to perform affine transformations (e.g., translation, rotation, and scaling) using homogeneous coordinates. Figure 16-7 shows the equations that can be used to multiply a 4×4 matrix by a 4×1 vector. Note that the components of vector **b** are a simple sum-of-products calculation of the matrix's columns and the individual components of vector **a**. Figure 16-7 also shows a sample matrix-vector multiplication calculation using real numbers.

$$\begin{bmatrix} b_w \\ b_x \\ b_y \\ b_z \end{bmatrix} = \begin{bmatrix} m_{00} & m_{01} & m_{02} & m_{03} \\ m_{10} & m_{11} & m_{12} & m_{13} \\ m_{20} & m_{21} & m_{22} & m_{23} \\ m_{30} & m_{31} & m_{32} & m_{33} \end{bmatrix} \begin{bmatrix} a_w \\ a_x \\ a_y \\ a_z \end{bmatrix} \qquad \begin{bmatrix} 304 \\ 564 \\ 824 \\ 1084 \end{bmatrix} = \begin{bmatrix} 10 & 11 & 12 & 13 \\ 20 & 21 & 22 & 23 \\ 30 & 31 & 32 & 33 \\ 40 & 41 & 42 & 43 \end{bmatrix} \begin{bmatrix} 5 \\ 6 \\ 7 \\ 8 \end{bmatrix}$$

$$b_w = m_{00}a_w + m_{01}a_x + m_{02}a_y + m_{03}a_z \qquad 304 = 10(5) + 11(6) + 12(7) + 13(8)$$

$$b_x = m_{10}a_w + m_{11}a_x + m_{12}a_y + m_{13}a_z \qquad 564 = 20(5) + 21(6) + 22(7) + 23(8)$$

$$b_y = m_{20}a_w + m_{21}a_x + m_{22}a_y + m_{23}a_z \qquad 824 = 30(5) + 31(6) + 32(7) + 33(8)$$

$$b_z = m_{30}a_w + m_{31}a_x + m_{32}a_y + m_{33}a_z \qquad 1084 = 40(5) + 41(6) + 42(7) + 43(8)$$

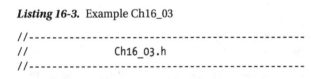

col0 col1 col2 col3

Figure 16-7. *Equations for matrix-vector multiplication along with a calculation example*

Listing 16-3 shows the source code for example Ch16_03. This example demonstrates how to multiply a single 4×4 matrix with a set of 4×1 vectors that are stored in an array.

Listing 16-3. Example Ch16_03

```
//-------------------------------------------------
//              Ch16_03.h
//-------------------------------------------------

#pragma once
```

```
// Simple 4x1 vector structure
struct Vec4x1F32
{
    float W, X, Y, Z;
};

// Ch16_03.cpp
extern void InitVecArray(Vec4x1F32* a, size_t n);
extern bool MatVecMulF32Cpp(Vec4x1F32* b, float m[4][4], Vec4x1F32* a, size_t n);

// Ch16_03_.asm
extern "C" bool MatVecMulF32_(Vec4x1F32* b, float m[4][4], Vec4x1F32* a, size_t n);

// Ch16_03_BM.cpp
extern void MatVecMulF32_BM(void);

// Constants
const size_t c_Align = 16;

//-------------------------------------------------
//                  Ch16_03.cpp
//-------------------------------------------------

#include <iostream>
#include <iomanip>
#include <random>
#include <cmath>
#include "Ch16_03.h"
#include "AlignedMem.h"

using namespace std;

bool VecCompare(const Vec4x1F32* v1, const Vec4x1F32* v2)
{
    static const float eps = 1.0e-12f;

    bool b0 = (fabs(v1->W - v2->W) <= eps);
    bool b1 = (fabs(v1->X - v2->X) <= eps);
    bool b2 = (fabs(v1->Y - v2->Y) <= eps);
    bool b3 = (fabs(v1->Z - v2->Z) <= eps);

    return b0 && b1 && b2 && b3;
}

void InitVecArray(Vec4x1F32* a, size_t n)
{
    uniform_int_distribution<> ui_dist {1, 500};
    mt19937 rng {187};
```

```
    for (size_t i = 0; i < n; i++)
    {
        a[i].W = (float)ui_dist(rng);
        a[i].X = (float)ui_dist(rng);
        a[i].Y = (float)ui_dist(rng);
        a[i].Z = (float)ui_dist(rng);
    }

    if (n >= 4)
    {
        // Known values for test purposes
        a[0].W =  5; a[0].X =  6; a[0].Y =  7; a[0].Z =  8;
        a[1].W = 15; a[1].X = 16; a[1].Y = 17; a[1].Z = 18;
        a[2].W = 25; a[2].X = 26; a[2].Y = 27; a[2].Z = 28;
        a[3].W = 35; a[3].X = 36; a[3].Y = 37; a[3].Z = 38;
    }
}

bool MatVecMulF32Cpp(Vec4x1F32* b, float m[4][4], Vec4x1F32* a, size_t n)
{
    if (n == 0 || (n % 4) != 0)
        return false;

    if (!AlignedMem::IsAligned(a, c_Align) || !AlignedMem::IsAligned(b, c_Align))
        return false;

    for (size_t i = 0; i < n; i++)
    {
        b[i].W =  m[0][0] * a[i].W + m[0][1] * a[i].X;
        b[i].W += m[0][2] * a[i].Y + m[0][3] * a[i].Z;

        b[i].X =  m[1][0] * a[i].W + m[1][1] * a[i].X;
        b[i].X += m[1][2] * a[i].Y + m[1][3] * a[i].Z;

        b[i].Y =  m[2][0] * a[i].W + m[2][1] * a[i].X;
        b[i].Y += m[2][2] * a[i].Y + m[2][3] * a[i].Z;

        b[i].Z =  m[3][0] * a[i].W + m[3][1] * a[i].X;
        b[i].Z += m[3][2] * a[i].Y + m[3][3] * a[i].Z;
    }

    return true;
}

void MatVecMulF32(void)
{
    const char nl = '\n';
    const size_t num_vec = 8;
```

```cpp
alignas(c_Align) float m[4][4]
{
    10.0, 11.0, 12.0, 13.0,
    20.0, 21.0, 22.0, 23.0,
    30.0, 31.0, 32.0, 33.0,
    40.0, 41.0, 42.0, 43.0
};

AlignedArray<Vec4x1F32> a_aa(num_vec, c_Align);
AlignedArray<Vec4x1F32> b1_aa(num_vec, c_Align);
AlignedArray<Vec4x1F32> b2_aa(num_vec, c_Align);

Vec4x1F32* a = a_aa.Data();
Vec4x1F32* b1 = b1_aa.Data();
Vec4x1F32* b2 = b2_aa.Data();

InitVecArray(a, num_vec);

bool rc1 = MatVecMulF32Cpp(b1, m, a, num_vec);
bool rc2 = MatVecMulF32_(b2, m, a, num_vec);

cout << "Results for MatVecMulF32\n";

if (!rc1 || !rc2)
{
    cout << "Invalid return code\n";
    cout << "  rc1 = " << boolalpha << rc1 << nl;
    cout << "  rc2 = " << boolalpha << rc2 << nl;
    return;
}

const unsigned int w = 8;
cout << fixed << setprecision(1);

for (size_t i = 0; i < num_vec; i++)
{
    cout << "Test case #" << i << '\n';

    cout << "b1: ";
    cout << "   " << setw(w) << b1[i].W << ' ';
    cout << "   " << setw(w) << b1[i].X << ' ';
    cout << "   " << setw(w) << b1[i].Y << ' ';
    cout << "   " << setw(w) << b1[i].Z << nl;

    cout << "b2: ";
    cout << "   " << setw(w) << b2[i].W << ' ';
    cout << "   " << setw(w) << b2[i].X << ' ';
    cout << "   " << setw(w) << b2[i].Y << ' ';
    cout << "   " << setw(w) << b2[i].Z << nl;
```

```
        if (!VecCompare(&b1[i], &b2[i]))
        {
            cout << "Error - vector compare failed\n";
            return;
        }
    }
}

int main()
{
    MatVecMulF32();
    MatVecMulF32_BM();
    return 0;
}
```

```
//---------------------------------------------------
//                  Ch16_03_.s
//---------------------------------------------------

// Macro Mat4x4MulVec
//
// Input:   v0 = matrix m column 0
//          v1 = matrix m column 1
//          v2 = matrix m column 2
//          v3 = matrix m column 3
//          x0 = pointer to vector b
//          x2 = pointer to vector a
//
// Temp registers: v4, v5

            .macro Mat4x4MulVec
            ld1 {v4.4s},[x2],16              // load vector a[i]

            fmul v5.4s,v0.4s,v4.s[0]         // col[0] * a[i].W
            fmla v5.4s,v1.4s,v4.s[1]         // col[1] * a[i].X
            fmla v5.4s,v2.4s,v4.s[2]         // col[2] * a[i].Y
            fmla v5.4s,v3.4s,v4.s[3]         // col[3] * a[i].Z

            st1 {v5.4s},[x0],16              // save vector b[i]
            .endm

// extern "C" bool MatVecMulF32_(Vec4x1F32* b, float m[4][4], Vec4x1F32* a, size_t n);

            .text
            .global MatVecMulF32_
MatVecMulF32_:

// Validate arguments and perform required initializations
            cbz x3,InvalidArg               // jump if n == 0
            tst x3,0x03
            b.ne InvalidArg                 // jump if n % 4 != 0
```

```
            tst x0,0x0f
            b.ne InvalidArg                 // jump if b not aligned
            tst x2,0x0f
            b.ne InvalidArg                 // jump if a not aligned

            ld4 {v0.4s-v3.4s},[x1]          // load transpose of m

// Main processing loop
Loop1:      Mat4x4MulVec
            Mat4x4MulVec
            Mat4x4MulVec
            Mat4x4MulVec

            subs x3,x3,4                    // n -= 4
            b.ne Loop1                      // repeat until done

            mov w0,1                        // set success return code
            ret

InvalidArg: mov w0,0                        // set error return code
            ret
```

The C++ code in Listing 16-3 begins with the header file Ch16_03.h that contains the requisite function declarations. This file also includes a structure named Vec4x1F32, which incorporates the four components of a 4 × 1 column vector. The source code file Ch16_03.cpp contains the function MatVecMulF32Cpp. This function implements the matrix-vector multiplication equations that are shown in Figure 16-7. The remaining C++ code in Listing 16-3 performs test case initializations, invokes the calculating functions, and displays the results.

Near the top of the assembly language code in Listing 16-3 is a macro definition named Mat4x4MulVec. This macro generates code that calculates the product of a 4 × 4 matrix and 4 × 1 vector. Note that prior to using this macro, the columns of the 4 × 4 matrix must be loaded into registers V0–V3. Also note that registers X0 and X2 must point to Vec4x1F32 arrays b and a, respectively. Macro Mat4x4MulVec uses a four-instruction sequence of fmul and fmla instructions to calculate the required matrix-vector product.

Function MatVecMulF32_ begins its execution with code block that validates argument value n. It then checks Vec4x1F32 array pointers a and b for alignment on a 16-byte boundary. The ensuing ld4 {v0.4s-v3.4s},[x1] loads matrix m into registers V0–V3 with de-interleaving. Following execution of this instruction, registers V0, V1, V2, and V3 contain matrix m columns 0, 1, 2, and 3, respectively. For-loop Loop1 employs macro Mat4x4MulVec to calculate four matrix-vector products during each iteration. Here are the results for source code example Ch16_03:

```
Results for MatVecMulF32
Test case #0
b1:     304.0       564.0       824.0       1084.0
b2:     304.0       564.0       824.0       1084.0
Test case #1
b1:     764.0       1424.0      2084.0      2744.0
b2:     764.0       1424.0      2084.0      2744.0
```

```
Test case #2
b1:     1224.0     2284.0     3344.0     4404.0
b2:     1224.0     2284.0     3344.0     4404.0
Test case #3
b1:     1684.0     3144.0     4604.0     6064.0
b2:     1684.0     3144.0     4604.0     6064.0
Test case #4
b1:    13353.0    24713.0    36073.0    47433.0
b2:    13353.0    24713.0    36073.0    47433.0
Test case #5
b1:    11943.0    22193.0    32443.0    42693.0
b2:    11943.0    22193.0    32443.0    42693.0
Test case #6
b1:    11925.0    21725.0    31525.0    41325.0
b2:    11925.0    21725.0    31525.0    41325.0
Test case #7
b1:    12315.0    23055.0    33795.0    44535.0
b2:    12315.0    23055.0    33795.0    44535.0

Running benchmark function MatVecMulF32_BM - please wait
Benchmark times save to file Ch16_03_MatVecMulF32_BM_RpiOmega.csv
```

Table 16-3 shows the benchmark timing measurements for the matrix-vector multiplication functions.

Table 16-3. *Benchmark timing measurements (microseconds) for matrix-vector multiplication functions (1,000,000 vectors)*

MatVecMulF32Cpp	MatVecMulF32_
10670	7677

Matrix Inversion

Matrix inversion is another common operation that is often applied to 4 × 4 matrices. In this section, you will examine a program that calculates the inverse of a 4 × 4 matrix of single-precision floating-point values. Listing 16-4 shows the source code for example Ch16_04.

Listing 16-4. Example Ch16_04

```
//--------------------------------------------------
//                 Ch16_04.h
//--------------------------------------------------

#pragma once

#include "MatrixF32.h"

const float c_Epsilon = 1.0e-5;

// Ch16_04.cpp
```

```
extern bool Mat4x4InvF32(MatrixF32& m_inv, const MatrixF32& m, float epsilon);

// Ch16_04_Test.cpp
extern bool TestMat4x4F32(const MatrixF32& m1, const MatrixF32& m2);

// Ch16_04_.s
extern "C" bool Mat4x4InvF32_(float* m_inv, const float* m, float epsilon);

// Ch16_04_Test.s
extern "C" void Mat4x4AddF32_(float* m_des, const float* m_src1, const float* m_src2);
extern "C" void Mat4x4MulF32_(float* m_des, const float* m_src1, const float* m_src2);
extern "C" void Mat4x4MulScalarF32_(float* m_des, const float* m_src1, float sv);
extern "C" float Mat4x4TraceF32_(const float* m_src1);

// Ch16_04_BM.cpp
extern void Mat4x4InvF32_BM(const MatrixF32& m);

//------------------------------------------------
//              Ch16_04.cpp
//------------------------------------------------

#include <iostream>
#include <cmath>
#include "Ch16_04.h"
#include "MatrixF32.h"

using namespace std;

bool Mat4x4InvF32(MatrixF32& m_inv, const MatrixF32& m, float epsilon)
{
    // The intermediate matrices below are declared static for benchmarking purposes.
    static const size_t nrows = 4;
    static const size_t ncols = 4;
    static MatrixF32 m2(nrows, ncols);
    static MatrixF32 m3(nrows, ncols);
    static MatrixF32 m4(nrows, ncols);
    static MatrixF32 I(nrows, ncols, true);
    static MatrixF32 tempA(nrows, ncols);
    static MatrixF32 tempB(nrows, ncols);
    static MatrixF32 tempC(nrows, ncols);
    static MatrixF32 tempD(nrows, ncols);

    MatrixF32::Mul4x4(m2, m, m);
    MatrixF32::Mul4x4(m3, m2, m);
    MatrixF32::Mul4x4(m4, m3, m);

    float t1 = m.Trace4x4();
    float t2 = m2.Trace4x4();
    float t3 = m3.Trace4x4();
```

421

```
    float t4 = m4.Trace4x4();

    float c1 = -t1;
    float c2 = -1.0 / 2.0 * (c1 * t1 + t2);
    float c3 = -1.0 / 3.0 * (c2 * t1 + c1 * t2 + t3);
    float c4 = -1.0 / 4.0 * (c3 * t1 + c2 * t2 + c1 * t3 + t4);

    // Make sure matrix is not singular.
    bool is_singular = (fabs(c4) < epsilon);

    if (!is_singular)
    {
        // Calculate = -1.0 / c4 * (m3 + c1 * m2 + c2 * m + c3 * I)
        MatrixF32::MulScalar(tempA, I, c3);
        MatrixF32::MulScalar(tempB, m, c2);
        MatrixF32::MulScalar(tempC, m2, c1);
        MatrixF32::Add(tempD, tempA, tempB);
        MatrixF32::Add(tempD, tempD, tempC);
        MatrixF32::Add(tempD, tempD, m3);
        MatrixF32::MulScalar(m_inv, tempD, -1.0 / c4);
    }

    return is_singular;
}

void RunMat4x4InvF32(const MatrixF32& m, const char* msg)
{
    const char nl = '\n';
    cout << "---------- " << msg << " ----------- \n";
    cout << "\nTest Matrix\n";
    cout << m << nl;

    const float epsilon = c_Epsilon;
    const size_t nrows = m.GetNumRows();
    const size_t ncols = m.GetNumCols();
    MatrixF32 m_inv_a(nrows, ncols);
    MatrixF32 m_ver_a(nrows, ncols);
    MatrixF32 m_inv_b(nrows, ncols);
    MatrixF32 m_ver_b(nrows, ncols);

    for (int i = 0; i <= 1; i++)
    {
        string fn;
        bool is_singular;
        MatrixF32 m_inv(nrows, ncols);
        MatrixF32 m_ver(nrows, ncols);

        if (i == 0)
        {
            fn = "Mat4x4InvF32";
```

```
                is_singular = Mat4x4InvF32(m_inv, m, epsilon);

                if (!is_singular)
                    MatrixF32::Mul(m_ver, m_inv, m);
        }
        else
        {
            fn = "Mat4x4InvF32_";
            is_singular = Mat4x4InvF32_(m_inv.Data(), m.Data(), epsilon);

            if (!is_singular)
                MatrixF32::Mul(m_ver, m_inv, m);
        }

        if (is_singular)
            cout << fn << " - Test matrix is singular\n";
        else
        {
            cout << fn << " - Inverse Matrix\n";
            cout << m_inv << nl;

            // RoundToI() used for display purposes, can be removed.
            cout << fn << " - Verify Matrix\n";
            m_ver.RoundToI(epsilon);
            cout << m_ver << nl;
        }
    }
}

int main()
{
    // Test Matrix #1 - Non-Singular
    MatrixF32 m1(4, 4);
    const float m1_row0[] = { 2, 7, 3, 4 };
    const float m1_row1[] = { 5, 9, 6, 4.75 };
    const float m1_row2[] = { 6.5, 3, 4, 10 };
    const float m1_row3[] = { 7, 5.25, 8.125, 6 };
    m1.SetRow(0, m1_row0);
    m1.SetRow(1, m1_row1);
    m1.SetRow(2, m1_row2);
    m1.SetRow(3, m1_row3);

    // Test Matrix #2 - Non-Singular
    MatrixF32 m2(4, 4);
    const float m2_row0[] = { 0.5, 12, 17.25, 4 };
    const float m2_row1[] = { 5, 2, 6.75, 8 };
    const float m2_row2[] = { 13.125, 1, 3, 9.75 };
    const float m2_row3[] = { 16, 1.625, 7, 0.25 };
    m2.SetRow(0, m2_row0);
    m2.SetRow(1, m2_row1);
    m2.SetRow(2, m2_row2);
```

```
    m2.SetRow(3, m2_row3);

    // Test Matrix #3 - Singular
    MatrixF32 m3(4, 4);
    const float m3_row0[] = { 2, 0, 0, 1 };
    const float m3_row1[] = { 0, 4, 5, 0 };
    const float m3_row2[] = { 0, 0, 0, 7 };
    const float m3_row3[] = { 0, 0, 0, 6 };
    m3.SetRow(0, m3_row0);
    m3.SetRow(1, m3_row1);
    m3.SetRow(2, m3_row2);
    m3.SetRow(3, m3_row3);

    RunMat4x4InvF32(m1, "Test Case #1");
    RunMat4x4InvF32(m2, "Test Case #2");
    RunMat4x4InvF32(m3, "Test Case #3");

    Mat4x4InvF32_BM(m1);
    return 0;
}


//---------------------------------------------------
//                  Ch16_04_Macros_.inc
//---------------------------------------------------


// Macro Mat4x4AddF32
//
// Input Registers                   Input Registers
// -----------------------------------------------------------
// A0    a3 a2 a1 a0                  B0    w3 w2 w1 w0
// A1    b3 b2 b1 b0                  B1    x3 x2 x1 x0
// A2    c3 c2 c1 c0                  B2    y3 y2 y1 y0
// A3    d3 d2 d1 d0                  B3    z3 z2 z1 z0
//
// Output Registers
// -----------------------------------------------------------
// C0    a3+w3 a2+w2 a1+w1 a0+w0
// C1    b3+x3 b2+x2 b1+x1 b0+x0
// C2    c3+y3 c2+y2 c1+y1 c0+y0
// C3    d3+z3 d2+z2 d1+z1 d0+z0

            .macro Mat4x4AddF32 C0,C1,C2,C3, A0,A1,A2,A3, B0,B1,B2,B3

            fadd \C0\().4s, \B0\().4s, \A0\().4s    // row 0
            fadd \C1\().4s, \B1\().4s, \A1\().4s    // row 1
            fadd \C2\().4s, \B2\().4s, \A2\().4s    // row 2
            fadd \C3\().4s, \B3\().4s, \A3\().4s    // row 3
```

```
        .endm

// Macro Mat4x4MulF32
//
// Input Registers              Input Registers
// -----------------------------------------------------------
// A0   a3 a2 a1 a0             B0   w3 w2 w1 w0
// A1   b3 b2 b1 b0             B1   x3 x2 x1 x0
// A2   c3 c2 c1 c0             B2   y3 y2 y1 y0
// A3   d3 d2 d1 d0             B3   z3 z2 z1 z0
//
// Output Registers
// -----------------------------------------------------------
// C0   row 0 of A * B
// C1   row 1 of A * B
// C2   row 2 of A * B
// C3   row 3 of A * B

        .macro Mat4x4MulF32 C0,C1,C2,C3, A0,A1,A2,A3, B0,B1,B2,B3

        fmul \C0\().4s, \B0\().4s, \A0\().s[0]      // row 0
        fmla \C0\().4s, \B1\().4s, \A0\().s[1]
        fmla \C0\().4s, \B2\().4s, \A0\().s[2]
        fmla \C0\().4s, \B3\().4s, \A0\().s[3]

        fmul \C1\().4s, \B0\().4s, \A1\().s[0]      // row 1
        fmla \C1\().4s, \B1\().4s, \A1\().s[1]
        fmla \C1\().4s, \B2\().4s, \A1\().s[2]
        fmla \C1\().4s, \B3\().4s, \A1\().s[3]

        fmul \C2\().4s, \B0\().4s, \A2\().s[0]      // row 2
        fmla \C2\().4s, \B1\().4s, \A2\().s[1]
        fmla \C2\().4s, \B2\().4s, \A2\().s[2]
        fmla \C2\().4s, \B3\().4s, \A2\().s[3]

        fmul \C3\().4s, \B0\().4s, \A3\().s[0]      // row 3
        fmla \C3\().4s, \B1\().4s, \A3\().s[1]
        fmla \C3\().4s, \B2\().4s, \A3\().s[2]
        fmla \C3\().4s, \B3\().4s, \A3\().s[3]
        .endm

// Macro Mat4x4MulScalarF32
//
// Input Registers              Output Registers
// -----------------------------------------------------------
// A0   a3 a2 a1 a0             B0   a3*VS a2*VS a1*VS a0*VS
// A1   b3 b2 b1 b0             B1   b3*VS b2*VS b1*VS b0*VS
// A2   c3 c2 c1 c0             B2   c3*VS c2*VS c1*VS c0*VS
// A3   d3 d2 d1 d0             B3   d3*VS d2*VS d1*VS d0*VS
//
// Other Registers
```

```
// ------------------------------------------------------------
// VS   scalar multiplier

          .macro Mat4x4MulScalarF32 B0,B1,B2,B3, A0,A1,A2,A3, VS

          fmul \B0\().4s, \A0\().4s, \VS\().s[0]   // row 0
          fmul \B1\().4s, \A1\().4s, \VS\().s[0]   // row 1
          fmul \B2\().4s, \A2\().4s, \VS\().s[0]   // row 2
          fmul \B3\().4s, \A3\().4s, \VS\().s[0]   // row 3
          .endm


// Macro Mat4x4TraceF32
//
// Input Registers               Other Registers
// ------------------------------------------------------------
// VA    a3 a2 a1 a0              SA   matrix trace
// VB    b3 b2 b1 b0              SB   temp register
// VC    c3 c2 c1 c0
// VD    d3 d2 d1 d0

          .macro Mat4x4TraceF32 SA, VA, VB, VC, VD, SB

          mov \SA, \VA\().4s[0]              // SA = M[0][0]
          mov \SB, \VB\().4s[1]              // SA = M[1][1]
          fadd \SA, \SA, \SB                 // SA += SB
          mov \SB, \VC\().4s[2]              // SB = M[2][2]
          fadd \SA, \SA, \SB                 // SA += SB
          mov \SB, \VD\().4s[3]              // SB = M[3][3]
          fadd \SA, \SA, \SB                 // SA += SB
          .endm


//----------------------------------------------------
//              Ch16_04_.s
//----------------------------------------------------

          .include "Ch16_04_Macros_.inc"

// Algorithm constants
          .text
r4_n0p333: .single -0.333333333
          .balign 16
r4_4x4I:  .single 1.0, 0.0, 0.0, 0.0
          .single 0.0, 1.0, 0.0, 0.0
          .single 0.0, 0.0, 1.0, 0.0
          .single 0.0, 0.0, 0.0, 1.0

// extern "C" bool Mat4x4InvF32_(float* m_inv, const float* m, float epsilon);

          .global Mat4x4InvF32_
Mat4x4InvF32_:

// Prologue
```

426

```
        stp d8,d9,[sp,-16]!            // push d8, d9
        stp d10,d11,[sp,-16]!          // push d10, d11
        sub sp,sp,16                   // allocate local space

        str s0,[sp]                    // save epsilon for later

// load m into v0:v3
        ld1 {v0.4s-v3.4s},[x1]         // load  m

// Calculate t1 = trace(m)
        Mat4x4TraceF32 s28, v0,v1,v2,v3, s27       // s28 = t1

// Calculate m2 = m * m and t2 = trace(m2)
        Mat4x4MulF32 v4,v5,v6,v7, v0,v1,v2,v3, v0,v1,v2,v3

        Mat4x4TraceF32 s29, v4,v5,v6,v7, s27       // s29 = t2

// Calculate m3 = m * m * m and t3 = trace(m3)
        Mat4x4MulF32 v16,v17,v18,v19, v4,v5,v6,v7, v0,v1,v2,v3

        Mat4x4TraceF32 s30, v16,v17,v18,v19, s27   // s30 = t3

// Calculate m4 = m * m * m * m and t4 = trace(m4)
        Mat4x4MulF32 v20,v21,v22,v23, v16,v17,v18,v19, v0,v1,v2,v3

        Mat4x4TraceF32 s31, v20,v21,v22,v23, s27   // s31 = t4

// Calculate c1 = -t1
        fneg s8,s28                    // s8 = c1

// Calculate c2 = -1.0 / 2.0 * (c1 * t1 + t2)
        fmul s24,s8,s28                // c1 * t1
        fadd s24,s24,s29               // c1 * t1 + t2
        fmov s25,-0.5
        fmul s9,s25,s24                // c2

// Calculate c3 = -1.0 / 3.0 * (c2 * t1 + c1 * t2 + t3)
        fmul s24,s9,s28                // c2 * t1
        fmul s25,s8,s29                // c1 * t2
        fadd s25,s25,s30               // c1 * t2 + t3
        fadd s25,s25,s24               // sum of above expressions
        ldr s26,r4_n0p333
        fmul s10,s26,s25               // c3

// Calculate c4 = -1.0 / 4.0 * (c3 * t1 + c2 * t2 + c1 * t3 + t4)
        fmul s24,s10,s28               // c3 * t1
        fmul s25,s9,s29                // c2 * t2
        fmul s26,s8,s30                // c1 * t3
        fadd s26,s26,s31               // c1 * t3 + t4
        fadd s27,s24,s25
```

```
            fadd s11,s27,s26              // sum of above expressions
            fmov s25,-0.25
            fmul s11,s25,s11             // c4

// Test fabs(c4) < epsilon for singular matrix
            fabs s28,s11                 // s28 = fabs(c4)
            ldr s29,[sp]                 // s29 = epsilon
            fcmp s28,s29                 // is matrix singular?
            cset w3,lo                   // w3 = 1 if singular, else 0
            b.lo Done                    // jump if singular

// Register content summary
//   v0-v3       m              s8   c1
//   v4-v7       m2             s9   c2
//   v16-v19     m3             s10  c3
//   v20-v23     m4             s11  c4

// Calculate = -1.0 / c4 * (m3 + c1 * m2 + c2 * m + c3 * I)
    adr x4,r4_4x4I
    ld1 {v24.4s-v27.4s},[x4]                               // load I

    Mat4x4MulScalarF32 v24,v25,v26,v27, v24,v25,v26,v27, v10   // c3 * I

    Mat4x4MulScalarF32 v0,v1,v2,v3, v0,v1,v2,v3, v9           // c2 * m

    Mat4x4MulScalarF32 v4,v5,v6,v7, v4,v5,v6,v7, v8           // c1 * m2

    Mat4x4AddF32 v28,v29,v30,v31, v24,v25,v26,v27, v0,v1,v2,v3 // c3 * I + c2 * m

    Mat4x4AddF32 v28,v29,v30,v31, v28,v29,v30,v31, v4,v5,v6,v7 // += c1 * m2

    Mat4x4AddF32 v28,v29,v30,v31, v28,v29,v30,v31, v16,v17,v18,v19  // += m3

    fmov s4,-1.0
    fdiv s4,s4,s11                                          // -1.0 / c4
    Mat4x4MulScalarF32 v0,v1,v2,v3, v28,v29,v30,v31, v4     // inverse
    st1 {v0.4s-v3.4s},[x0]                                  // save m_inv

// Epilogue
Done:       mov w0,w3                     // set return code
            add sp,sp,16                  // release local space
            ldp d10,d11,[sp],16           // pop d10, d11
            ldp d8,d9,[sp],16             // pop d8,d9
            ret
```

The multiplicative inverse of a matrix is defined as follows: Let $\mathbf{A}$ and $\mathbf{X}$ represent $n \times n$ matrices. Matrix $\mathbf{X}$ is an inverse of $\mathbf{A}$ if $\mathbf{AX} = \mathbf{XA} = \mathbf{I}$, where $\mathbf{I}$ denotes an $n \times n$ identity matrix (i.e., a matrix of all zeros except for the main diagonal elements aii, which are equal to one). Figure 16-8 shows an example of an inverse matrix. It is important to note that inverses do not exist for all $n \times n$ matrices. A matrix without an inverse is called a singular matrix.

$$A = \begin{bmatrix} 6 & 2 & 2 \\ 2 & -2 & 2 \\ 0 & 4 & 2 \end{bmatrix} \quad X = \begin{bmatrix} 0.1875 & -0.0625 & -0.125 \\ 0.0625 & -0.1875 & 0.125 \\ -0.125 & 0.375 & 0.25 \end{bmatrix} \quad AX = XA = I = \begin{bmatrix} 1 & 0 & 0 \\ 0 & 1 & 0 \\ 0 & 0 & 1 \end{bmatrix}$$

Figure 16-8. *Matrix A and its multiplicative inverse Matrix X.*

The inverse of a 4 × 4 matrix can be calculated using a variety of mathematical techniques. Source code example Ch16_04 uses a computational method that is based on the Cayley-Hamilton theorem, which employs common matrix operations that are straightforward to implement using SIMD arithmetic. Here are the required equations:

$$\mathbf{A}^1 = \mathbf{A}; \mathbf{A}^2 = \mathbf{AA}; \mathbf{A}^3 = \mathbf{AAA}; \mathbf{A}^4 = \mathbf{AAAA}$$

$$trace(\mathbf{A}) = \sum_i a_{ii}$$

$$t_n = trace(\mathbf{A}^n)$$

$$c_1 = -t_1$$

$$c_2 = -\frac{1}{2}(c_1 t_1 + t_2)$$

$$c_3 = -\frac{1}{3}(c_2 t_1 + c_1 t_2 + t_3)$$

$$c_4 = -\frac{1}{4}(c_3 t_1 + c_2 t_2 + c_1 t_3 + t_4)$$

$$\mathbf{A}^{-1} = -\frac{1}{c_4}(\mathbf{A}^3 + c_1\mathbf{A}^2 + c_2\mathbf{A}^3 + c_3\mathbf{I})$$

Toward the top of the C++ code is a function named Mat4x4InvF32. This function calculates the inverse of a 4 × 4 matrix of single-precision floating-point values using the previously defined equations. Function Mat4x4InvF32 uses the C++ class MatrixF32 to perform many of the required intermediate computations including matrix addition, multiplication, and trace. The source code for class MatrixF32 is not shown in Listing 16-4 but is included with the source code download package. Note that the intermediate matrices in function Mat4x4InvF32 are declared using the static qualifier to avoid constructor overhead when performing benchmark timing measurements. The drawback of using the static qualifier here means that function Mat4x4InvF32 is not thread-safe (a thread-safe function can be used simultaneously by multiple threads). Following calculation of trace values t1–t4, Mat4x4InvF32 computes c1–c4 using simple scalar floating-point arithmetic. It then checks to make sure the source matrix m is not singular by comparing c4 against epsilon. If matrix m is not singular, the final inverse is calculated. The remaining C++ code performs test case initialization and exercises both the C++ and assembly language matrix inversion functions.

The assembly language code in Listing 16-4 begins with a series of macros that generate code for the elementary operations that are needed to calculate the inverse of a 4 × 4 matrix. The first macro, Mat4x4AddF32, emits code that adds two 4 × 4 matrices. Note that this macro requires 12 argument registers: A0–A3 for source matrix A, B0–B3 for source matrix B, and C0–C3 for destination matrix C. Macro Mat4x4AddF32 uses four fadd instructions to calculate C = A + B. The next macro is named Mat4x4MulF32. This macro

429

generates code that calculates the product of two 4 × 4 matrices. The register arguments for this macro are the same as macro Mat4x4AddF32. Macro Mat4x4MulF32 uses sequences of fmul and fmla instructions to calculate the matrix product C = A * B.

The next macro in Listing 16-4 is named Mat4x4MulScalarF32. This macro generates code that multiplies each element of a 4 × 4 matrix by a scalar value. Note that macro Mat4x4MulScalarF32 uses the multiply element variant of the fmul instruction. The final macro, Mat4x4TraceF32, generates code that calculates the trace of a 4 × 4 matrix. This macro uses the scalar single-precision floating-point mov and fadd instructions to calculate the required trace value.

The assembly language function Mat4x4InvF32_ employs the same series of operations as its C++ counterpart to calculate the inverse of a 4 × 4 matrix of single-precision values. The prologue of this function uses the instruction pair stp d8,d9,[sp,-16]! and stp d10,d11,[sp,-16]! to save non-volatile registers D8–D11 on the stack. This is followed by a sub sp,sp,16 that allocates 16 bytes of stack space for local storage. Function Mat4x4InvF32_ uses only four bytes of this space, but 16 bytes are allocated so that the SP register remains aligned on a quadword boundary. The next instruction, str s0,[sp], saves epsilon on the stack for later use.

Following its prologue, Mat4x4InvF32_ uses a ld1 {v0.4s-v3.4s},[x1] instruction to load matrix m into registers V0–V3. It then exploits the macros Mat4x4TraceF32 and Mat4x4MulF32 to calculate t1, t2, t3, and t4. Following calculation of these values, Mat4x4InvF32_ uses simple scalar floating-point arithmetic to calculate c1, c2, c3, and c4. It then compares c4 against epsilon. If fabs(c4) < epsilon is true, matrix m is singular and function Mat4x4InvF32_ skips the final set of calculations. If matrix m is not singular, function Mat4x4InvF32_ uses sequences of macros Mat4x4MulScalarF32 and Mat4x4AddF32 to calculate the required inverse. It then employs a st1 {v0.4s-v3.4s},[x0] to save m_inv. The epilogue of function Mat4x4AddF32 includes the instruction pair ldp d10,d11,[sp],16 and ldp d8,d9,[sp],16, which restores non-volatile registers D8–D11. Here are the results for source code example Ch16_04:

```
---------- Test Case #1 -----------

Test Matrix
        2            7            3            4
        5            9            6         4.75
      6.5            3            4           10
        7         5.25        8.125            6

Mat4x4InvF32 - Inverse Matrix
 -0.943926      0.91657     0.197547    -0.425579
-0.0568818     0.251148   0.00302831    -0.165952
  0.545399    -0.647656    -0.213597     0.505123
  0.412456    -0.412053    0.0561248     0.124363

Mat4x4InvF32 - Verify Matrix
        1            0            0            0
        0            1            0            0
        0            0            1            0
        0            0            0            1

Mat4x4InvF32_ - Inverse Matrix
 -0.94392     0.916564     0.197546    -0.425576
-0.0568815     0.251147    0.0030283    -0.165951
  0.545396    -0.647651    -0.213596      0.50512
  0.412454     -0.41205    0.0561244     0.124362
```

```
Mat4x4InvF32_ - Verify Matrix
          1            0            0            0
          0            1            0            0
          0            0            1            0
          0            0            0            1

---------- Test Case #2 -----------

Test Matrix
        0.5           12        17.25            4
          5            2         6.75            8
     13.125            1            3         9.75
         16        1.625            7         0.25

Mat4x4InvF32 - Inverse Matrix
0.00165165   -0.0690239    0.0549591    0.0389348
  0.135369    -0.359846     0.242038   -0.0903252
-0.0350097     0.239298    -0.183964    0.0772214
-0.0053352     0.056194    0.0603606   -0.0669085

Mat4x4InvF32 - Verify Matrix
          1            0            0            0
          0            1            0            0
          0            0            1            0
          0            0            0            1

Mat4x4InvF32_ - Inverse Matrix
0.00165165   -0.0690239     0.054959    0.0389347
  0.135369    -0.359845     0.242038   -0.0903252
-0.0350097     0.239297    -0.183964    0.0772213
-0.0053352     0.056194    0.0603606   -0.0669084

Mat4x4InvF32_ - Verify Matrix
          1            0            0            0
          0            1            0            0
          0            0            1            0
          0            0            0            1

---------- Test Case #3 -----------

Test Matrix
          2            0            0            1
          0            4            5            0
          0            0            0            7
          0            0            0            6

Mat4x4InvF32 - Test matrix is singular
Mat4x4InvF32_ - Test matrix is singular

Running benchmark function Mat4x4InvF32_BM - please wait
Benchmark times save to file Ch16_04_Mat4x4InvF32_BM_RpiOmega.csv
```

431

Table 16-4 shows the benchmark timing measurements for the matrix-vector multiplication functions.

Table 16-4. *Benchmark timing measurements (microseconds) for matrix inversion functions (100,000 inversions)*

Mat4x4InvF32	Mat4x4InvF32_
38973	8123

Summary

Here are the key learning points for Chapter 16:

- A function can use FMA instructions (e.g., `fmadd` and `fmla`) to implement numerically oriented algorithms such as discrete convolutions, which are used extensively in a wide variety of problem domains including signal processing and image processing.

- Like high-level languages, the performance of an assembly language function or algorithm can vary depending on the data structures that are used (e.g., array of structures vs. structure of arrays).

- Assembly language macros are often used to improve code comprehension and facilitate reuse. They also improve performance by eliminating the overhead of a function call.

- The `ld4` instruction can be used to load the transpose of a 4 × 4 matrix of single-precision values.

CHAPTER 17

■ ■ ■

Optimization Strategies and Techniques

In the preceding chapters, you learned about the fundamentals of Armv8 assembly language programming. You also learned how to exploit the SIMD capabilities of the Armv8 platform to accelerate the performance of computationally intensive algorithms. To maximize the performance of your Armv8 assembly language code, it is often necessary to understand specific aspects regarding the inner workings of an Armv8 processor. In this chapter, you will explore the internal hardware components of a modern Armv8 multicore processor and its underlying microarchitecture. You will also learn how to apply specific coding strategies and techniques to boost the performance of your Armv8 assembly language code.

The content of this should be regarded as an introductory tutorial of its topics. A comprehensive examination of Armv8 microarchitectures and assembly language optimization techniques would minimally require several lengthy chapters, or conceivably an entire book. The primary sources for this chapter's material are the Arm Cortex processor software optimization reference guides, which can be downloaded from the websites listed in Appendix B. You are strongly encouraged to consult these important reference guides for additional information regarding Armv8 microarchitectures and assembly language optimization techniques.

Armv8 Microarchitecture

The performance capabilities of an Armv8 processor are principally determined by its underlying microarchitecture. A processor's microarchitecture is characterized by the organization and operation of its hardware components, which includes instruction fetch pipelines, instruction decoders, execution pipelines, and memory caches. Software developers who understand the basics of a processor's microarchitecture can often glean constructive insights that enable them to develop more efficient code.

The remainder of this section explains Armv8 microarchitecture concepts using the Arm Cortex-A72 and Cortex-A77 processors as illustrative examples. The high-level organization and operation of other recent Arm Cortex processors (e.g., Cortex-A73, Cortex-A75, Cortex-A76, and Cortex-A78) are comparable to the Cortex-A72 and Cortex-A77. Higher-numbered processors in the Cortex family generally provide enhanced performance as you will soon see.

Cortex Microarchitecture

The architectural details of a processor based on the Arm Cortex microarchitecture are best examined using the framework of a modern multicore processor. Figure 17-1 shows a simplified block diagram of a Cortex-A72 quad-core processor. Note that each processor core includes a first-level (L1) instruction and

© Daniel Kusswurm 2020
D. Kusswurm, *Modern Arm Assembly Language Programming*,
https://doi.org/10.1007/978-1-4842-6267-2_17

first-level data cache, which are labeled I-Cache and D-Cache. As implied by their names, these on-chip memory caches contain instructions and data that a processor core can access rapidly. The four Cortex-A72 processors cores also share a second-level (L2) unified cache, which holds both instructions and data. Besides enhanced performance, the L1 and L2 caches bolster the execution of independent instruction streams in parallel without having to constantly access main memory.

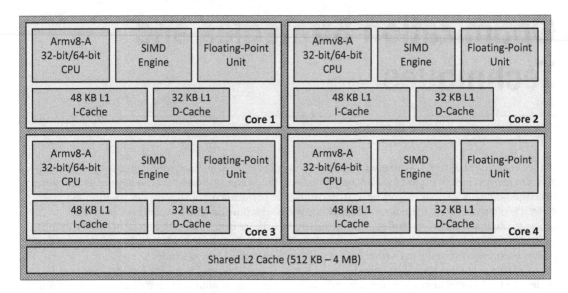

Figure 17-1. *Arm Cortex-A72 block diagram*

Figure 17-2 shows a block diagram of a Cortex-A77 quad-core processor. Unlike the Cortex-A72, each Cortex-A77 core contains its own private L2 cache. The four Cortex-A77 cores also share a common L3 cache. The use of private L2 caches in conjunction with a separate L3 cache helps to enhance the performance of a Cortex-A77 processor compared to a Cortex-A72. Note that in both Figures 17-1 and 17-2, the L2 and L3 cache sizes are variable. Cortex series processors can be fabricated using smaller caches to reduce power consumption or larger caches to boost performance.

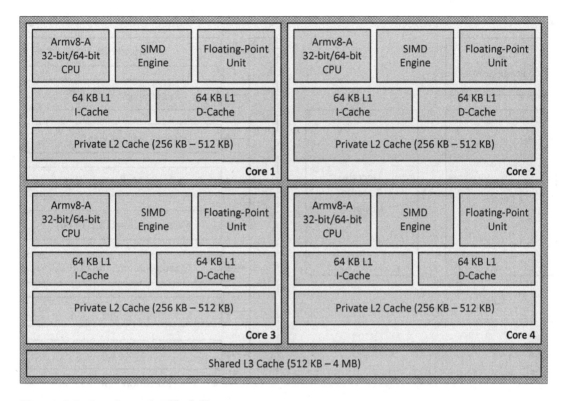

Figure 17-2. *Arm Cortex-A77 block diagram*

A processor core can fetch instructions from or access data in an L1 cache faster than an L2 cache. Similarly, fetching instructions or accessing data in an L2 cache is faster than an L3 cache. A cache miss occurs when a processor core requires an instruction or data item that is not present in its cache hierarchy and must be loaded from main memory. If an executing function's memory access pattern results in an excessive number of cache misses, performance will be adversely affected since accessing data in main memory takes significantly longer compared the processor's cache hierarchy.

Cortex Front-End Pipeline

During program execution, an Arm Cortex processor core performs five elementary instructional operations: fetch, decode, dispatch, execute, and retire. The particulars of these operations are determined by the functionality of the microarchitecture's pipelines. Figure 17-3 shows a streamlined block diagram of pipeline functionality in a Cortex-A72 processor. In the paragraphs that follow, the operations performed by these pipelines are examined in greater detail.

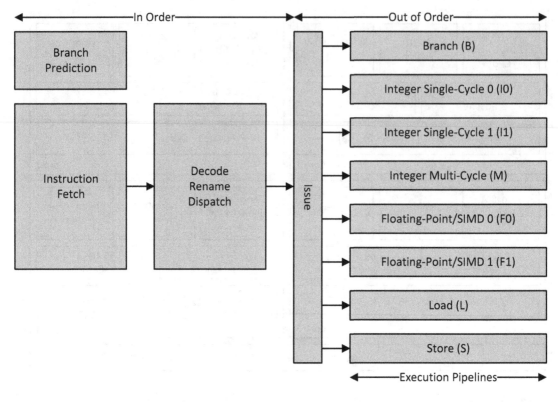

Figure 17-3. *Cortex-A72 microarchitecture pipeline*

The instruction fetch unit grabs Armv8 assembly language instructions and prepares them for execution. This unit can load instructions from either the L1 I-Cache, L2 Cache, L3 Cache (if present), or main memory.

The instruction decode unit translates Armv8 assembly language instructions into micro-ops. A micro-op is a self-contained low-level instruction that is ultimately executed by one of the processor's execution pipelines, which are discussed in the next section. The number of micro-ops generated by the decoder for an Armv8 instruction varies depending on its complexity. Simple register-register instructions such as add r2,r1,r0 or sub x2,x1,x0 are translated into a single micro-op. Instructions that perform more complex operations are translated into multiple micro-ops. The translation of Armv8 instructions into micro-ops facilitates several architectural and performance benefits including instruction-level parallelism (i.e., the simultaneous execution of multiple instructions) and out-of-order executions.

The rename unit maps a processor's architectural registers (both general-purpose and FP/SIMD) to internal private registers. This helps eliminate false dependencies between repetitive uses of the same register. Listing 17-1 contains an example of a false dependency. In this example, the first two code blocks load register X0 with a value from memory, perform a simple addition, and save the result back to memory. The actions perform by these two code blocks are independent despite their common use of register X0. With register renaming, the processor maps register X0 to an internal private register. This facilitates simultaneous execution of both code blocks. Following execution of code block 2 (which can occur before the completion of code block 1), the internal private register is "renamed" to X0 so that it contains the correct value for the mul x1,x0,x0 instruction in code block 3.

Listing 17-1. False dependency example

```
// code block 1
ldr x0,[x1]
add x0,x0,1
str x0,[x1]

// code block 2
ldr x0,[sp]
add x0,x0,4
str x0,[sp]

// code block 3
mul x1,x0,x0
```

The dispatch unit forwards micro-ops to the issue unit for execution. The issue unit holds each micro-op in a queue until its operands are available. It then distributes the micro-op to the appropriate execution pipeline. The issue unit can simultaneously distribute one micro-op to each execution pipeline during a cycle. Micro-ops are frequently distributed to the execution pipelines out of order compared to the original sequence of assembly language instructions. Following micro-op execution, the processor accumulates and reorders the micro-op results so that from the perspective of an executing function, all assembly language instructions appear to execute sequentially.

The branch prediction unit helps the instruction fetch unit select the next set of instructions to fetch by predicting the branch targets that are most likely to execute based on recent code execution patterns. A branch target is simply the destination operand of a branch or return instruction. The branch prediction unit also facilitates speculative executions of assembly language instructions before the outcome of a branch decision is known.

Figure 17-4 shows a simplified block diagram of pipeline functionality for a Cortex-A77 processor. The in order pipeline units (instruction fetch, decode, rename, dispatch, and branch prediction) of a Cortex-A77 processor perform the same basic functions as a Cortex-A72 processor, but have been optimized for significantly better performance and reduced power consumption. The Cortex-A77 also encompasses additional execution pipelines, which boosts performance.

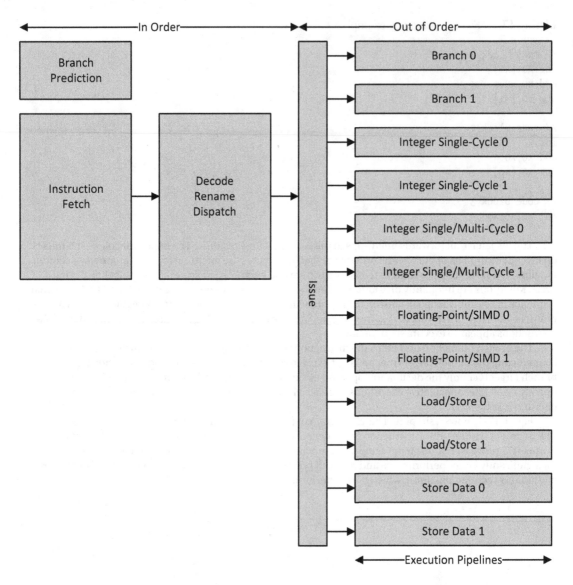

Figure 17-4. *Cortex-A77 microarchitecture pipeline*

Cortex Execution Pipelines

The Cortex execution pipelines, shown on the right in Figures 17-3 and 17-4, execute micro-ops distributed by issue unit queues. Each execution pipeline incorporates hardware that performs micro-op calculations or operations. For example, the Integer Single-Cycle execution pipeline executes micro-ops that carry out basic integer addition, subtraction, and compare operations. They also carry out elementary bitwise logical (e.g., AND, OR, and exclusive OR) operations. The floating-point/SIMD execution pipelines execute scalar floating-point arithmetic micro-ops. These pipelines also execute both integer and floating-point SIMD micro-ops.

Both the Cortex-A72 and Cortex-A77 contain multiple instances of select execution pipelines. This facilitates simultaneously execution of specific micro-ops. For example, the Cortex-A72 and Cortex-A77 can perform two independent scalar floating-point additions in parallel since they contain two floating-point/SIMD execution pipelines. As mentioned earlier, the Cortex-A77 includes additional execution pipelines compared to the Cortex-A72. Like the Cortex-A77's larger caches, these extra execution pipelines contribute to its better performance.

Table 17-1 contains a list of common A64 instructions and their utilized execution pipelines on a Cortex A-72 processor. The same execution pipelines are used for the corresponding A32 instructions. In this table, a slash in execution pipeline column signifies that an instruction's micro-ops can be executed on either pipeline (see Figure 17-3 for the execution pipeline name abbreviations). A comma signifies that multiple execution pipelines are required to execute an instruction's micro-ops. The Arm Cortex processor software optimization guides, which can be downloaded from the websites shown in Appendix B, contain comprehensive execution pipeline information for all A32 and A64 instructions.

Table 17-1. *Execution pipelines for common A64 instructions*

Class	A64 Instruction	Execution Pipeline(s)
Integer arithmetic	add, adc, sub	I0/I1
	and, orr, eor	I0/I1
	mul, smull, umull	M
	sdiv, udiv	M
Load and store	ldr (register, unsigned immediate offset)	L
	ldr (register, immediate post-indexed offset)	L, I0/I1
	ldr (register, immediate pre-indexed offset)	L, I0/I1
	str (register, unsigned immediate offset)	S
	str (register, immediate post-indexed offset)	S, I0/I1
	str (register, immediate pre-indexed offset)	S, I0/I1
Branch	b, ret	B
	bl, blr	I0/I1, B
Scalar floating-point	fabs, fadd, fsub, fmul	F0/F1
	fdiv	F0
	fsqrt, fcmp	F1
Integer SIMD	add, sub, addp	F0/F1
	mul, mla	F0
	shl	F1
Floating-point SIMD	fadd, fsub	F0/F1
	fmul, fmla	F0/F1
	fdiv	F0

Optimizing Armv8 Assembly Language Code

This section discusses optimization strategies and techniques that you can use to improve the performance of your Armv8 assembly language code. These techniques are recommended for use in code that targets recent Arm Cortex microarchitectures. The optimization strategies and techniques are organized into five general categories:

- Basic techniques

- Floating-point arithmetic

- Program branches

- Data alignment

- SIMD techniques

    It is important to keep in mind that the optimization techniques discussed in this section must be applied in a prudent manner. For example, it makes little sense to add extra instructions to a function just to use a recommended technique or instruction form only once. None of the optimization strategies and techniques described in this section will remedy an inappropriate or poorly designed algorithm. The Arm Cortex processor software optimization reference guides contain additional information about the optimization strategies and techniques discussed in this section. The optimization guides also include instruction execution latency and throughput measurements. These measurements are useful when evaluating which assembly language instructions (or sequence of instructions) to use in a function.

Basic Techniques

The following coding strategies and techniques are frequently employed to improve the performance of Armv8 assembly language code.

- Minimize use of the ldr pseudo instruction (e.g., ldr r0,=Val1 or ldr x0,=Val1), especially in for-loops. Use the mov/movw/movt (A32) or mov/movz/movk (A64) instructions (or uninterrupted sequences of these instructions) to load an address or constant value into register.

- Always use the non-condition-flag setting instruction forms (e.g., add r2,r1,r0 or add x2,x1,x0 instead of adds r2,r1,r0 or adds x2,x1,x0) except when condition flag results are explicitly required for program branches or subsequent conditional instruction execution.

- Consider placing simple read-only constants (e.g., .byte, .short, .word, .quad, .single, and .double) in a code (.text) section before the start of a function or after its final executable instruction. Also consider placing small read-only tables (both lookup and jump), arrays, text strings, and other data structures in a code section.

- Place large read-only tables, arrays, text strings, and data structures in a data (.data) section to preclude flushing (i.e., removal) of assembly language instructions from the L1 instruction cache.

- Use the literal form of the ldr instruction (e.g., ldr r0,label, ldr x0,label, ldr s0,label, ldr d0,label, etc.) to load constants that are located within ±4095 bytes (A32) or ±1 megabyte (A64) of the ldr instruction.

- Use registers to hold frequently used constants and intermediate values. This includes integers, floating-point, and SIMD values.

- Organize register use to minimize data dependencies and register spills. A register spill occurs when a function must temporarily save the contents of a register to memory to free the register for other calculations.

- If a general-purpose register spill is necessary, consider using a volatile SIMD register for temporary storage when coding functions that target Cortex-A76 or higher-numbered processors. On these processors, transfers between the general-purpose and SIMD registers have lower latency than accesses to the cache hierarchy.

- Process arrays and matrices using small groups of consecutive elements to maximize reuse of resident cache hierarchy data.

- Consider implementing multiple versions of performance-critical algorithms using different data structures or instruction sequences and compare benchmark timing measurements.

Floating-Point Arithmetic

The following coding strategies and techniques can be employed to improve the performance of Armv8 assembly language code that performs floating-point operations. These guidelines apply to both scalar and SIMD floating-point calculations.

- Use single-precision instead of double-precision floating-point values whenever possible.

- Arrange floating-point instruction sequences to minimize register dependencies. Exploit multiple destination register operands to save intermediate results if necessary.

- Partially or completely unroll for-loops that contain floating-point calculations, especially loops that contain sequences of floating-point addition, multiplication, or fused multiply-add operations.

- Do not use denormalized floating-point constants.

- Exploit formulas and algorithms that are immune to floating-point arithmetic underflows and denormalized values.

- Consider enabling flush-to-zero mode if an excessive number of denormalized values are expected to occur when performing floating-point arithmetic.

Branch Instructions

Conditional branch instructions are potentially time-consuming operations to perform since they can affect the contents of the processor's front-end pipelines and internal caches. These instructions are also a performance concern given their frequency of use. The following optimization techniques can be employed to minimize the adverse performance effects of branch instructions and improve the accuracy of the branch prediction unit:

- Organize code to minimize the number of executed branch instructions.

- Partially or completely unroll short processing loops to reduce the number of executed conditional branch instructions. However, avoid excessive loop unrolling since this may result in slower executing code.

- In A32 code, minimize or eliminate data-dependent branches using conditional instruction forms (e.g., addeq, subne, etc.). Limit the use of conditional instruction forms to low-latency integer instructions (e.g., add, sub, and, orr, eor, etc.), load instructions, and store instructions.

- In A64 code, favor use of the csel, cset, and fcsel instructions instead of a conditional branch instruction where possible.

- Align frequently called functions and branch targets inside performance-critical for-loops on a 16-byte boundary.

- Avoid using more than two branches within the same 16-byte aligned quadword of code memory.

- Move code that is unlikely to execute (e.g., error-handling code) to another program section or different memory page.

Data Alignment

Armv8 processors do not require proper alignment of multibyte values in memory unless specifically enabled by the operating system. However, functions that manipulate improperly aligned data can trigger the processor into performing additional memory cycles. To avoid these situations, the following data alignment practices should be observed:

- Align multibyte integer and floating-point values to their natural boundaries.

- Align 64- and 128-bit wide packed integer and floating-point values to their natural boundaries.

- Avoid use of store instructions with memory operands that span a 16-byte boundary.

- Avoid use of quadword load instructions with memory operands that are not aligned on a 4-byte boundary.

- Avoid use of load instructions with memory operands that span a cache-line boundary. The Cortex A-7X processor family uses 64-byte wide cache lines.

- Pad data structures to ensure proper alignment of each structure member.

- Align small arrays and short text strings in a data structure to prevent cache-line splits. A cache-line split occurs when the bytes of a multibyte data item are split across a cache-line boundary.

- Benchmark the performance of different data structures (e.g., structure of arrays vs. array of structures).

SIMD Techniques

The following techniques should be observed by any function that performs SIMD computations using A32 or A64 instructions.

- Partially or completely unroll for-loops that contain packed integer or floating-point calculations.

- Minimize register dependencies to exploit multiple execution pipelines.

- Load and keep frequently used memory operands and packed constants in a SIMD register.

- Process arrays and matrices using small blocks of consecutive elements to maximize reuse of resident cache hierarchy data.

Summary

Here are the key learning points for Chapter 17:

- The performance of many assembly language functions can be improved by implementing the optimization strategies and techniques outlined in this chapter.

- The recommended optimization techniques must be judiciously applied. It is not uncommon to encounter coding situations where a recommend strategy or technique is not the best approach.

- To achieve optimal performance for a specific algorithm or function, it may be necessary to code multiple versions and compare benchmark timing measurements.

- Do not spend an excessive amount of time trying to maximize performance of an assembly language function, especially when the code will execute on a variety of Armv8 processors. Focus on performance gains that are relatively easy to attain (e.g., implementing an algorithm or function using SIMD instead of scalar arithmetic).

- None of the optimization strategies and techniques discussed in this chapter will ameliorate an inappropriate or poorly designed algorithm.

APPENDIX A

■ ■ ■

Development Tools and Source Code

Appendix A discusses the development tools and computer systems that were used to create the source code examples published in this book. It begins with a section that defines the requirements for a host computer that is compatible with this book's source code. This is followed by a section that explains how to download, install, build, and execute the source code examples. The final section includes additional details regarding the benchmark timing measurements published in this book.

Host Computer

This section details the requirements for a host computer that can be used to execute the source code examples published in this book. It includes the following subsections:

- Hardware Requirements

- Software Requirements

- Initial Setup

- Additional Configuration – Required

- Additional Configuration – Optional

Hardware Requirements

The source code examples that accompany this book were developed using a Raspberry Pi 4 Model B with 4 GB of RAM and a 64 GB micro SD card. Figure A-1 shows a Raspberry Pi 4 Model B mounted in an acrylic case. The Raspberry Pi 4 Model B is the recommended host computer for this book's source code due to its low cost, global availability, and acceptable performance. However, the 32-bit source code examples can be built and executed on any Raspberry Pi Model 3 or Model 4 with at least 1 GB of RAM. These models can also be used to build and execute the 64-bit source code examples.

© Daniel Kusswurm 2020
D. Kusswurm, *Modern Arm Assembly Language Programming*,
https://doi.org/10.1007/978-1-4842-6267-2

Figure A-1 Raspberry Pi 4 Model B

The Raspberry Pi 4 Model B includes a Broadcom BCM2711 SoC (system on a chip), which incorporates a quad-core Arm Cortex-A72 processor. The Raspberry Pi 3 contains a Broadcom BCM2837 SoC. This device incorporates a quad-core Arm Cortex-A53 processor. You can also build and execute the source code examples using any single-board computer (SBC) that meets the following requirements:

- Armv8-compliant processor or SoC
- Minimum 1 GB RAM
- Mainline Linux support
- GNU toolchain compatibility

Software Requirements

The official operating system for Raspberry Pi SBCs is Raspberry Pi OS (formerly called Raspbian). This operating system is a ported version of Debian Linux that has been optimized for use with Raspberry Pi SBCs. Raspberry Pi OS is available in both 32-bit and 64-bit versions. As I write this, the 64-bit version is a beta release.

The book's source code examples were developed using Raspberry Pi OS, both 32-bit and 64-bit versions, as the host operating system. The source code examples can be built using the GNU C++ compiler (g++), GNU assembler (as), and GNU Make (make). These development tools are included with Raspberry Pi OS. The 64-bit source code examples were also tested on a Raspberry Pi 4 Model B running Ubuntu 20.04 LTS 64-bit server.

Initial Setup

To install Raspberry Pi OS, you will need a Raspberry Pi Model 3 or 4 SBC with at least 1 GB of RAM and the following accessories:

- Micro SD card (recommended size 32 GB or larger)

- USB micro SD card reader

- Power supply with a USB micro (Pi 3) or USB-C (Pi 4) connector

- USB keyboard and USB mouse

- HDMI monitor

- HDMI cable, HDMI to HDMI (Pi 3), or micro HDMI to HDMI (Pi 4)

- Heatsinks

- Case (optional)

For more information regarding Raspberry Pi SBCs and required accessories, visit the official Raspberry Pi website at `www.raspberrypi.org`.

▨ **Note** Many USB power supplies are not compatible with the Raspberry Pi. You must use a USB power supply that is specifically designed to work with a Raspberry Pi 3 or Pi 4 SBC.

Numerous online retailers sell Raspberry Pi starter kits that contain a complete set of accessories. Most of these kits also include a micro SD card with Raspberry Pi OS (32-bit) already installed. To get your Raspberry Pi system up and running, follow the instructions included with your kit.

To install (or reinstall) Raspberry Pi OS (32-bit) on a micro SD card for use with a Raspberry Pi Model 3 or 4, you can use the Raspberry Pi Imager as follows:

1. Download the Raspberry Pi Imager from `www.raspberrypi.org/downloads/`. Note that there are different versions of the Imager for Windows, Mac OS X, and Ubuntu.

2. Install the Imager.

3. Insert a micro SD card into a USB micro SD card reader. Then insert the card reader into a USB port.

4. Start the Imager program. Click **CHOOSE OS**.

5. Choose one of the following Raspberry Pi OS (32-bit) options:

    a. Select **Raspberry Pi OS (32-bit)** to install the Raspberry Pi Desktop.

    b. Select **Raspberry Pi OS Full (32-bit)** to install the Raspberry Pi Desktop and recommended applications, which includes additional programming tools for Python and Java, educational software, and LibreOffice. This option is available under **Raspberry Pi OS (other)** in the **Operating System** selection box.

6. Click **CHOOSE SD CARD**. Select the correct micro SD card. Note that the Imager will delete any existing files on this card.

7. Click **WRITE** to install the OS image on the micro SD card.

8. Following completion of the installation, insert the micro SD card into the Raspberry Pi's micro SD card slot. Power up the SBC and follow the onscreen instructions to configure your Raspberry Pi.

As mentioned earlier, Raspberry Pi OS (64-bit) is currently available as a beta release. To install this operating system on a micro SD card for use with a Raspberry Pi Model 3 or 4, you can use the Raspberry Pi Imager as follows:

1. Download the Raspberry Pi Imager from `www.raspberrypi.org/downloads/`. Note that there are different versions of the Imager for Windows, Mac OS X, and Ubuntu.

2. Download the Raspberry Pi OS (64-bit) image file from `www.raspberrypi.org/forums/viewtopic.php?f=117&t=275370`.

3. Install the Imager.

4. Insert a micro SD card into a USB micro SD card reader. Then insert the card reader into a USB port.

5. Start the Imager program. Click **CHOOSE OS**, and then click **Use custom**.

6. In the **Select Image** dialog box, navigate to and select the Raspberry Pi OS (64-bit) image file that you previously downloaded.

7. Click **CHOOSE SD CARD**. Select the correct micro SD card. Note that the Imager will delete any existing files on this card.

8. Click **WRITE** to install the OS image on the micro SD card.

9. Following completion of the installation, insert the micro SD card into the Raspberry Pi's micro SD card slot. Power up the system and follow the onscreen instructions to configure your Raspberry Pi.

For more information about installing Raspberry Pi OS, both 32-bit and 64-bit, see `www.raspberrypi.org/documentation/installation/installing-images/README.md`.

You can also install Ubuntu 20.04 LTS 64-bit server on a Raspberry Pi Model 3 or 4. For more information, see the instructions at `https://ubuntu.com/download/raspberry-pi`.

Additional Configuration – Required

A few of the source code examples require libpng, which is a freely available library for processing PNG image files (`www.libpng.org/pub/png/`). Perform the following steps to install this library:

1. Open a terminal window.

2. Type `sudo apt install libpng-dev` and press enter.

3. Select yes to install the PNG image library if it is not already installed.

To install the latest updates for Raspberry Pi OS (32-bit or 64-bit) or Ubuntu 20.04 LTS 64-bit server, perform the following steps:

1. Open a terminal window.

2. Type `sudo apt update` and press enter.

3. Type `sudo apt full-upgrade` and press enter.

You should periodically run these commands to install the latest operating system updates and security patches. For more information about updating Raspberry Pi OS, see `www.raspberrypi.org/documentation/raspbian/updating.md`.

Additional Configuration – Optional

The following optional programs are extremely useful add-ons when using a Raspberry Pi SBC as a software development system:

- To access files on a Raspberry Pi from a Windows PC or Mac OS X, you can install a Samba Server. See `https://pimylifeup.com/raspberry-pi-samba/` for more information.

- To access a Windows shared folder from a Raspberry Pi or other Linux system, see `www.techrepublic.com/article/how-to-permanently-mount-a-windows-share-on-linux/` for more information.

You can overclock the CPU and GPU on a Raspberry Pi 4 Model B to improve its performance. For more information about overclocking a Raspberry Pi 4 Model B and the associated risks, see `www.tomshardware.com/reviews/raspberry-pi-4-b-overclocking,6188.html`.

■ **Caution**   Do not attempt to overclock a Raspberry Pi 4 Model B without an adequate cooling system that includes a fan and heatsinks for the Broadcom BCM2711 SoC, SDRAM memory module, and USB controller chip.

Source Code

In this section you will learn how to download and install the source code examples. You will also learn how to build and execute a source code example.

Download and Install

Use the following steps to download and install the book's source code on a Raspberry Pi 3 or 4:

1. Open the Raspberry Pi File Manager. In your home directory, create a directory named ModArmAsm.

2. Start Chromium (or any other web browser) and open the following website: `www.github.com/apress/modern-arm-assembly-language-programming`. Save a ZIP file of the source code in the directory ModArmAsm.

3. Using the Raspberry Pi File Manager, open a window that shows the directory ModArmAsm.

4. Right-click the source code ZIP file and select **Extract Here**.

Following ZIP file extraction, you should see a directory for each chapter that includes source code examples as shown in Figure A-2. You should also see two directories named Data and Include. These directories contain test image files and shared C++ include files, respectively. The Sh directory contains ancillary shell scripts for building the complete set of source code examples. The files for each source code example reside in separate subdirectories (e.g., ~/ModArmAsm/Chapter02/Ch02_01, ~/ModArmAsm/Chapter02/Ch02_02, etc.).

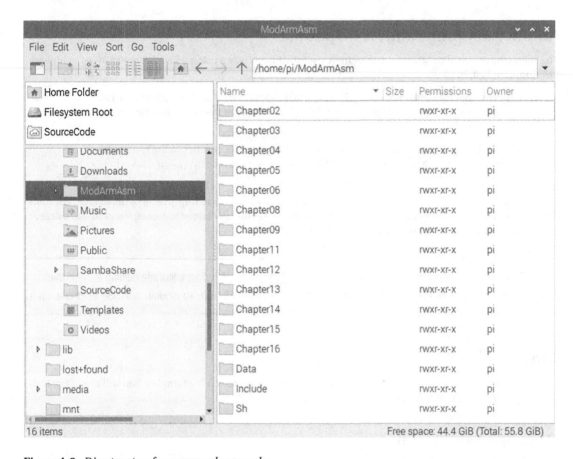

Figure A-2. *Directory tree for source code examples*

Build and Execute

Each source code example subdirectory includes a makefile that can be used to build an executable file. You will learn more about makefiles in the next section. To build and execute a source code example on Raspberry Pi OS (32-bit), perform the following steps:

1. Open a terminal window in your home folder.

2. Using the cd command, change the current working directory to a source code example directory. For example, to build and execute source code example Ch02_01, type cd ModArmAsm/Chapter02/Ch02_01 and press enter.

3. To build source code example Ch02_01, type make and press enter.

4. To run source code example Ch02_01, type ./Ch02_01 and press enter.

To build and execute a source code example on Raspberry Pi OS (64-bit) or Ubuntu 20.04 LTS 64-bit server, you can perform the same steps using a 64-bit source code example (e.g., use Ch11_01 instead of Ch02_01). Note that each 32- and 64-bit source code example must be built on a host computer running a 32- or 64-bit version of Raspberry Pi OS (or other compatible version of Linux), respectively.

Make Utility

GNU Make ("Make") is a software development utility that facilitates automated program builds. It is typically installed on computers that run Linux. Make uses dependency rules to specify the source code (e.g., C++ and header files) and intermediate (e.g., object module files) needed to build a target. A target can be any type of file but is usually an executable file. Dependency rules are defined in a special file called a makefile. Each dependency rule includes one or more shell commands that instruct Make how to build a target or intermediate file.

The biggest advantage of using Make is its ability to selectively execute commands based on changes that occur to a target's dependencies. For example, Make will recompile only the source code files that have changed since it was last run. It uses the last modified datetime stamp of each dependent file to accomplish this.

The remainder of this section briefly discusses the makefiles that were created for this book's source code examples. It is important to note that the subsequent paragraphs are not intended to be a tutorial on Make or how to create makefiles. Comprehensive usage information for Make and makefile dependency rule creation is available online at www.gnu.org/software/make/manual/.

Listing A-1 shows the makefile for source code example Ch02_01. Most of the other source code examples use a makefile that is identical to the one discussed in this section except for the target name.

Listing A-1. Source code example Ch02_01 makefile

```
# Target, include, and object directories
TARGET = Ch02_01
INCDIR1 = .
INCDIR2 = ../../Include
OBJDIR = obj

# include files
CPPINCFILES1 = $(wildcard $(INCDIR1)/*.h)
CPPINCFILES2 = $(wildcard $(INCDIR2)/*.h)
ASMINCFILES1 = $(wildcard $(INCDIR1)/*.inc)
ASMINCFILES2 = $(wildcard $(INCDIR2)/*.inc)

# .cpp files in current directory
CPPFILES = $(wildcard *.cpp)
CPPOBJFILES_ = $(CPPFILES:.cpp=.o)
CPPOBJFILES = $(patsubst %, $(OBJDIR)/%, $(CPPOBJFILES_))

# .s files in current directory
ASMFILES = $(wildcard *.s)
ASMOBJFILES_ = $(ASMFILES:.s=.o)
ASMOBJFILES = $(patsubst %, $(OBJDIR)/%, $(ASMOBJFILES_))

# Target object files
OBJFILES = $(CPPOBJFILES) $(ASMOBJFILES)
```

```
# g++ and assembler options - required
GPPOPT = -march=armv8-a+simd -O3 -std=c++14 -Wall
ASMOPT = -march=armv8-a+simd

# g++ and assembler options - optional (uncomment to enable)
DEBUG = -g
LISTFILE_CPP = -Wa,-aghl=$(OBJDIR)/$(basename $<).lst -save-temps=$(OBJDIR)
LISTFILE_ASM = -aghlms=$(OBJDIR)/$(basename $<).lst

# Create directory for object and temp files
MKOBJDIR := $(shell mkdir -p $(OBJDIR))

# Build rules
$(TARGET): $(OBJFILES)
        g++ $(OBJFILES) -o $(TARGET)

# Note: full recompiles/assembles on any include file changes
$(OBJDIR)/%.o: %.cpp $(CPPINCFILES1) $(CPPINCFILES2)
        g++ $(DEBUG) $(LISTFILE_CPP) $(GPPOPT) -I$(INCDIR1) -I$(INCDIR2) -c $< -o $@

$(OBJDIR)/%.o: %.s $(ASMINCFILES1) $(ASMINCFILES2)
        as  $(DEBUG) $(LISTFILE_ASM) $(ASMOPT) -I$(INCDIR1) -I$(INCDIR2) $< -o $@

.PHONY:   clean

clean:
        rm -f $(TARGET)
        rm -rf $(OBJDIR)
```

The first line in Listing A-1, TARGET = Ch02_01, sets the makefile variable TARGET equal to the text string Ch02_01. Like most programming languages, a makefile can use variables (which are sometimes called macros) to streamline rule creation and eliminate duplication. The next three statements assign text strings to the variables INCDIR1, INCDIR2, and OBJDIR. The variables INCDIR1 and INCDIR2 define the directories that contain include files, while OBJDIR defines the directory that is used to store object module files and other temporary files.

The next statement, CPPINCFILES1 = $(wildcard $(INCDIR1)/*.h), builds a list of all .h files located in the directory INCDIR1 and assigns this list to the variable CPPINCFILES1. This statement uses the variable INCDIR1 that was defined in the previous group of statements. Note that the variable name INCDIR1 is surrounded by parenthesis and includes a leading $ symbol. This syntax is required when using a previously defined variable. The text wildcard is a Make function that performs file searches using a search pattern. In the current statement, wildcard searches INCDIR1 for all *.h files. The remaining statements in this block initialize variables CPPINCFILES2, ASMINCFILES1, and ASMINCFILES2 using the same technique.

The first statement of the next group, CPPFILES = $(wildcard *.cpp), builds a list of all .cpp files in the current directory and assigns this list to the variable CPPFILES. The next two statements build a list of .o (object module) files that correspond to the .cpp files in the current directory and assign this list to the variable CPPOBJFILES. The ensuing statement group uses the same technique to build a list of object modules that correspond to the .s (assembly language) files in the current directory and assigns this list to ASMOBJFILES. This is followed by the statement OBJFILES = $(CPPOBJFILES) $(ASMOBJFILES), which sets OBJFILES equal to a list of all object modules files that are needed to build the executable file TARGET.

The next two makefile variables, GPPOPT and ASMOPT, contain option switches for the GNU C++ compiler and GNU assembler. These switches are required and should not be changed. The -march=armv8-a+simd option switch directs the GNU C++ compiler to generate Armv8-compatible code and to emit

SIMD instructions when appropriate. This switch also notifies the GNU assembler that assembly language source code files contain Armv8 instructions and Armv8 SIMD instructions. The -O3 option instructs the C++ compiler to generate the fastest possible code. The drawback of using this option is somewhat slower compile times. The -std=c++14 switch enables compilation of the C++ source code using the ANSI C++ 2014 standard. The -Wall option enables nearly all GNU C++ compiler warning messages.

The next variable group controls optional features. The DEBUG variable instructs the GNU C++ compiler and assembler to generate debugging information for use with the GNU debugger (gdb). The variables LISTFILE_CPP and LISTFILE_ASM include switches that enable the generation of listing files. Note that the compiler and assembler listing files are saved in the OBJDIR directory.

Following the definition of LISTFILE_ASM is the statement MKOBJDIR := $(shell mkdir -p $(OBJDIR)). This statement instructs Make to create the subdirectory OBJDIR. Recall that this directory contains the target's object module files, temporary files, and listing files.

The build statement group begins with a $(TARGET): $(OBJFILES) dependency rule. This rule informs Make that TARGET depends on the object module files defined by the variable OBJFILES. The ensuing statement, g++ $(OBJFILES) -o $(TARGET), is the shell command that Make runs to build the executable file TARGET. More specifically, this command links the object modules defined by OBJFILES into a single executable file. Note that this makefile statement is indented with a tab character, which is required.

The next dependency rule, $(OBJDIR)/%.o: %.cpp $(CPPINCFILES1) $(CPPINCFILES2), notifies Make that each .o file in OBJDIR depends on a corresponding .cpp file in the current directory. Each .o file also depends on the include files defined by the variables CPPINCFILES1 and CPPINCFILES2. Make uses the ensuing shell command g++ $(DEBUG) $(LISTFILE_CPP) $(GPPOPT) -I$(INCDIR1) -I$(INCDIR2) -c $< -o $@ to compile a C++ source code file. In this statement, Make replaces the automatic variable $< with the name of the C++ file. It also replaces the automatic variable $@ with the name of the object module file. The -c switch instructs the g++ to skip the link step, while the -o switch directs g++ to save the output object module to a file named $@. A similar dependency rule and shell command pair are also used for the assembly language files.

The statement .PHONY: clean defines a phony (or nonfile) target named clean. Typing make clean in a terminal window instructs Make to execute the shell commands rm -f $(TARGET) and rm -rf $(OBJDIR). These commands delete the file TARGET and remove the subdirectory OBJDIR. The make clean command is often used to force a complete rebuild of a target executable.

Benchmark Timing Measurements

All benchmark timing measurements presented in this book were made using executable files compiled with g++ version 8.3.0, gas version 2.31.1, and the previously described code generation options. The timing measurements were performed on a Raspberry Pi 4 Model B with 4 GB of RAM, a 64 GB micro SD card, and Raspberry Pi OS (32-bit or 64-bit beta release). The Raspberry Pi 4 Model B was overclocked using the following settings:

- over_voltage=4

- arm_freq=1800

- gpu_freq=600

The arm_freq (CPU) and gpu_freq (GPU) frequency settings are in MHz and 20% higher than the standard clock frequencies. For more information about these settings and the risks associated with overclocking a Raspberry Pi 4 Model B, see www.tomshardware.com/reviews/raspberry-pi-4-b-overclocking,6188.html.

■ ■ ■

References and Additional Resources

This appendix contains lists of the references that were consulted during preparation of this book. It also includes additional references and resources that readers of this book will find useful. The references are grouped into the following categories:

- Arm programming
- Arm architecture
- Algorithm references
- Software development tools
- C++ references

Arm Programming

The following list includes indispensable Armv8 programming reference manuals and other Armv8-related documents published by Arm Limited:

> *Armv8-A Instruction Set Architecture,* https://developer.arm.com/architectures/learn-the-architecture/armv8-a-instruction-set-architecture
>
> *Arm Architecture Reference Manual (Armv8, for Armv8-A architecture profile),* https://developer.arm.com/docs/ddi0487/fb/arm-architecture-reference-manual-armv8-for-armv8-a-architecture-profile
>
> *ARM Cortex-A Series Programmer's Guide for ARMv8-A Documentation,* https://developer.arm.com/docs/den0024/latest
>
> *Cortex-A72 Software Optimization Guide,* https://developer.arm.com/documentation/uan0016/a/
>
> *Arm Cortex-A75 Software Optimization Guide,* https://developer.arm.com/documentation/101398/0200/
>
> *Arm Cortex-A76 Software Optimization Guide,* https://developer.arm.com/documentation/swog307215/a
>
> *Arm Cortex-A77 Software Optimization Guide,* https://developer.arm.com/documentation/swog011050/c/

Arm Developer Glossary, https://developer.arm.com/support/arm-glossary

Understanding the Armv8.x extensions, https://developer.arm.com/
architectures/learn-the-architecture/understanding-the-armv8-x-
extensions

Armv8-A Memory Model, https://developer.arm.com/architectures/learn-
the-architecture/armv8-a-memory-model

M-Profile Architectures, https://developer.arm.com/architectures/cpu-
architecture/m-profile

R-Profile Architectures, https://developer.arm.com/architectures/cpu-
architecture/r-profile

NEON Programmer's Guide Version: 1.0, https://developer.arm.com/
architectures/cpu-architecture/m-profile/docs/den0018/latest/neon-
programmers-guide-version-10

Procedure Call Standard for the Arm Architecture, https://developer.arm.com/
docs/ihi0042/latest

*Procedure Call Standard for the ARM 64-bit Architecture (AArch64) with SVE
support,* https://developer.arm.com/docs/100986/0000

Shore, Chris, *Porting to 64-bit Arm - White Paper,* https://community.arm.com/
developer/ip-products/processors/b/processors-ip-blog/posts/porting-
to-arm-64-bit

Arm Architecture

The following resources contain useful information about Arm Cortex processors and microarchitectures:

Frumusanu, Andrei, *ARM Reveals Cortex-A72 Architecture Details,*
www.anandtech.com/show/9184/arm-reveals-cortex-a72-architecture-
details

Frumusanu, Andrei, *The ARM Cortex A73 – Artemis Unveiled,* www.anandtech.
com/print/10347/arm-cortex-a73-artemis-unveiled

Frumusanu, Andrei, *Arm's Cortex-A76 CPU Unveiled: Taking Aim at the Top for
7nm,* www.anandtech.com/print/12785/arm-cortex-a76-cpu-unveiled-7nm-
powerhouse

Frumusanu, Andrei, *Arm's New Cortex-A77 CPU Micro-architecture: Evolving
Performance,* www.anandtech.com/print/14384/arm-announces-cortexa77-cpu-ip

Frumusanu, Andrei, *Arm's New Cortex-A78 and Cortex-X1 Microarchitectures: An
Efficiency and Performance Divergence,* www.anandtech.com/print/15813/arm-
cortex-a78-cortex-x1-cpu-ip-diverging

Humrick, Matt, *Exploring DynamIQ and ARM's New CPUs: Cortex-A75,
Cortex-A55,* www.anandtech.com/print/11441/dynamiq-and-arms-new-cpus-
cortex-a75-a55

BCM2711, Raspberry Pi Foundation, www.raspberrypi.org/documentation/
hardware/raspberrypi/bcm2711/README.md

Algorithm References

The following resources were consulted to develop some of the source code algorithms presented in this book:

Forman S. Acton, *REAL Computing Made REAL – Preventing Errors in Scientific and Engineering Calculations*, ISBN 978-0486442211, Dover Publications, 2005

Tony Chan, Gene Golub, Randall LeVeque, *Algorithms for Computing the Sample Variance: Analysis and Recommendations*, The American Statistician, Volume 37 Number 3 (1983), p. 242–247

David Goldberg, *What Every Computer Scientist Should Know About Floating-Point Arithmetic*, ACM Computing Surveys, Volume 23 Issue 1 (March 1991), p. 5–48

Rafael C. Gonzalez and Richard E. Woods, *Digital Image Processing, Fourth Edition*, ISBN 978-0-133-35672-4, 2018

Anthony Pettofrezzo, *Matrices and Transformations*, ISBN 0-486-63634-8, Dover Publications, 1978

Hans Schneider and George Barker, *Matrices and Linear Algebra*, ISBN 0-486-66014-1, Dover Publications, 1989

Eric W. Weisstein, *Convolution*, Mathworld, `http://mathworld.wolfram.com/Convolution.html`

Eric W. Weisstein, *Correlation Coefficient*, Mathworld, `http://mathworld.wolfram.com/CorrelationCoefficient.html`

Eric W. Weisstein, *Cross Product*, Mathworld, `http://mathworld.wolfram.com/CrossProduct.html`

Eric W. Weisstein, *Least Squares Fitting*, Mathworld, `http://mathworld.wolfram.com/LeastSquaresFitting.html`

Eric W. Weisstein, *Matrix Multiplication*, Mathworld, `http://mathworld.wolfram.com/MatrixMultiplication.html`

David M. Young and Robert Todd Gregory, *A Survey of Numerical Mathematics, Volume 1*, ISBN 0-486-65691-8, Dover Publications, 1988

Algorithms for calculating variance, Wikipedia, `https://en.wikipedia.org/wiki/Algorithms_for_calculating_variance`

Body surface area, Wikipedia, `https://en.wikipedia.org/wiki/Body_surface_area`

Grayscale, Wikipedia, `https://en.wikipedia.org/wiki/Grayscale`

Software Development Tools

The following list includes references for the software development tools that were used to develop this book's source code examples:

GNU Binutils, www.gnu.org/software/binutils/

GNU Compiler Collection, www.gnu.org/software/gcc/

GNU Make, www.gnu.org/software/make/

Portable Network Graphics, www.libpng.org/pub/png/

C++ References

The following resources contain practical information about C++ programming and the C++ Standard Template Library:

Ivor Horton, *Using the C++ Standard Template Libraries*, Apress, ISBN 978-1-4842-0005-6, 2015

Nicolai M. Josuttis, *The C++ Standard Library – A Tutorial and Reference, Second Edition*, Addison Wesley, ISBN 978-0-321-62321-8, 2012

Bjarne Stroustrup, *The C++ Programming Language, Fourth Edition*, Addison Wesley, ISBN 978-0-321-56384-2, 2013

cplusplus.com, www.cplusplus.com

Index

© Daniel Kusswurm 2020
D. Kusswurm, *Modern Arm Assembly Language Programming*,
https://doi.org/10.1007/978-1-4842-6267-2

▓ B

■ C, D

■ E

■ F